CRIME IN THE STREETS AND CRIME IN THE SUITES

CRIME IN THE STREETS AND CRIME IN THE SUITES

Perspectives on Crime and Criminal Justice

Doug A. Timmer
North Central College

D. Stanley Eitzen
Colorado State University

Allyn and Bacon
Boston London Sydney Toronto

Copyright © 1989 by Allyn and Bacon
A Division of Simon & Schuster
160 Gould Street
Needham Heights, MA 02194

Series Editor: Karen Hanson
Cover Administrator: Linda K. Dickinson
Manufacturing Buyer: Tamara McCracken
Editorial-Production Service: Kathy Smith

Library of Congress Cataloging-in Publication Data

Timmer, Doug A.
  Crime in the streets and crime in the
suites.

  1. Crime and criminals—United States.
2. Criminal justice, Administration of—
United States.   3. Right and left (Political
science) I. Eitzen, D. Stanley. II. Title.
HV6777.T56   1989   364′.973   88-33304
ISBN 0-205-11977-8

Printed in the United States of America

10   9   8   7   6   5   4   3   2   1   94   93   92   91   90   89

Contents

v

Preface

This book is a collection of articles on crimes and their control. The focus is on a host of controversial issues related to crime and criminal justice. We have selected twenty-one key issues for which there is considerable public and scholarly debate. The issues are divided into four categories: (1) what is crime?; (2) types of crimes; (3) criminal law and policing; and (4) courts and corrections. Some of the issues involve long-standing debates; these include gun control, capital punishment, and whether lower-class persons are prone to criminal behavior. Other debates are more contemporary and deal with the issues of black-on-black crime, sentencing reform, private policing, and private prisons.

We have provided a general introduction to each of the categories of issues. For each specific issue, we have chosen two readings that highlight the wide divergence of political approaches to it. One represents the "conservative" approach, while the other typifies a "progressive" analysis. Under the "conservative" rubric are positions that focus on the individual or the immediate social milieu, that accept the existing social order as essentially fair and just, and that propose solutions to crime problems which emphasize individual adaptation and limited social reform. There are two basic assumptions of the "progressive" argument. First, the sources of crime and its selective control are found in the political economy rather than in individuals. Second, effective crime control from this perspective requires fundamental changes in the structure of American social and economic institutions.

The organization of this book—contrasting polar positions on issues—is deliberate. Each article selected represents a strong point of view which is measured against a fundamentally different point of view. Michael Harrington, in his book *Taking Sides*, has argued that the presentation of opposing positions is both fruitful and inevitable.

> Truths about society can be discovered only if one takes sides. . . . You must stand somewhere in order to see social reality, and where you stand will determine much of what you see and how you see it. The data of society are, for all practical purposes, infinite. You need criteria that will provisionally permit you to bring some order into that chaos of data and to distinguish between relevant and irrelevant factors or, for that matter, to establish that there are facts in the

first place. These criteria cannot be based upon the data for they are the precondition of the data. They represent—and the connotations of the phrase should be savored—a "point of view." That involves intuitive choices, a value-laden sense of what is meaningful and what is not. . . . I am . . . a deeply biased man, a taker of sides; but that is not really distinctive at all. Everyone else is as biased as I am, including the most "objective" social scientist. The difference between us is that I am frank about my values while many other analysts fool both themselves and their audiences with the illusion that they have found an intellectual perch that is free of Earth's social field of gravity. (Michael Harrington, *Taking Sides* [New York: Holt, Rinehart and Winston, 1985], pp. 1–2)

The examination of "conservative" and "progressive" arguments and analyses on each issue should, we hope: (1) illustrate the lack of consensus among observers of crime and its control; (2) demonstrate the positive and negative consequences of various crime control policies; and (3) inform and enliven debate on these important problems.

Acknowledgments

We want to thank the authors whose works appear in this volume. In addition, Doug Timmer thanks Kathryn Talley for making both his thinking and writing more legible, and Janan Wagner for her clerical assistance and attention to detail.

D. A. T.
D. S. E.

CRIME IN THE STREETS
AND CRIME IN THE SUITES

Part 1
WHAT IS CRIME?

Most Americans believe they know what crime is. In fact, for many, the question "What is crime?" is probably never given any thought or discussion because the answer is taken-for-granted; it is self-evident. However, progressive analysis of the fundamental definition or nature of crime is significantly different than more traditional conservative and liberal perspectives.

Distinct assumptions about *what crime is* are important because they are linked directly to questions concerning the *causes of crime*. Questions concerning the *causes of crime* are necessarily tied to the issue of *controlling* crime. In other words, we will not be able to initiate social policies and practices that do away with crime unless we know what causes it, and we will not know what causes it unless we know what it is.

We have organized the debate surrounding the question "What is crime?" around four issues. First, we focus on the problem of the relationship between law and crime. Which gives rise to which? Second, we turn to the measurement of crime in society. What do crime rates really tell us? Third, we target the question of the causes of crime, the issue of criminogenesis. Is crime a property of persons or societies? Is crime the product of the traits and characteristics of individual offenders or is it generated by the way social institutions are organized and operate? And fourth, we conclude the argument between conservative and progressive efforts to define crime by taking up the issue of who in society is a criminal. Is crime essentially the activity of lower-class persons, or is it apparent in all social classes?

LAW AND CRIME

Conservative and liberal perspectives generally assume that law is what criminalizes particular behaviors that most persons and groups in a community or society disapprove of. From this angle, law is simply a way of sanctioning those behaviors and persons who have already been identified as violating the overall interest of the community. In this sense, crime precedes law. Law is a protective reaction against behavior and persons who are found to be morally and politically unacceptable in a community. And, law tends to be protective of the interests of the entire community. Conservative and liberal analyses of crime and criminal justice usually take for granted that theft, vagrancy, and drug laws, for example, are attempts to control behavior and persons by sanctioning activities found threatening to the whole community; therefore, these laws represent protection for the whole community. The bottom line, from this perspective, is that crime is what gives rise to criminal law, and those who violate the law are violating the decent and respectable part of the community and should be punished.

In American society, the conservative and liberal perspective on the relationship between law and crime seems self-evident and commonsensical to many. It is a popular view. It has not, however, escaped the challenge of a radical or progressive view.

Radical and progressive analysis of the historical relationship between law and crime suggests that conservative and liberal conclusions need to be turned on their heads: this analysis posits that crime is produced by and through the law, and thus, law precedes crime. This alternative analysis also maintains that, rather than serving and protecting the interests of the entire community, criminal law serves and protects particular groups, organizations, classes, races, and sexes in society at the expense of other groups, organizations, classes, races, and sexes. Powerful interests in society serve and protect their own interests by using the law to criminalize the previously non-criminal behavior of powerless elements in society. Behavior and persons not considered bad, wrong, or harmful may become criminal as the powerful create and enforce the criminal law. The powerful are careful, however, not to criminalize their own behavior—even if it is undeniably bad, wrong, or harmful.

In an excerpt in this section ("Crime and the State"), Drew Humphries points out that historically, crime only appears as a violation of law after certain conditions have evolved in society. According to Humphries, crime develops only with the advent of a dominant economic class, a marginal economic class, and a state. Under these conditions, the dominant economic class will influence the state to use the law to criminalize certain behaviors and persons in the marginal economic class, thus serving and protecting the dominant class interest. From this perspective, theft, vagrancy, and drug laws in Europe and the U.S. do not function to protect equally the entire community. Theft laws protect disproportionately the wealth and income-producing property of dominant economic classes; vagrancy laws help to assure a steady supply of cheap labor to this same class; and both vagrancy and anti-drug laws provide a means of controlling the surplus labor of a marginal economic class that is at least a potential threat to dominant interests.

From this radical or progressive point of view, crime is what results from the dominant interests' use of the state and the law as they attempt to maintain and service their position in society vis-a-vis more marginal interests.

MEASURING CRIME

In their attempts to answer the question "What is crime?", conservative and some liberal commentators have tended to accept official crime statistics at face value. In other words, crime is what is reflected in and measured by official crime statistics. An excerpt from the 1986 *FBI Uniform Crime Report* is included in this section as an example of official crime statistics.

Those taking this perspective contend that the roughly 12½ million crimes reported to the police and included in the FBI's official report in 1986 are a fairly accurate estimate of the amount of crime in American society. Although these conservative or liberal analysts may accept the criticism that these rates are not completely accurate, they do believe them to be at least highly correlated with the actual incidence of crime in society.

This approach is based on the assumption that official crime statistics indicate both the amount of crime and the kinds of people who willfully violate society's laws. Since these official statistics are compiled primarily for conventional street crimes like burglary, theft, robbery, assault, rape, and murder, they lead to the conclusion that crime is concentrated in a lower class where individuals have a weaker commitment to society and where these kinds of crimes tend to predominate. From this perspective, the solution to the "crime problem" normally involves efforts to socialize and punish lower-class offenders so that they will have a greater respect for, and adherence to, the rules and laws of society. And, since official crime statistics clearly show that crime in American society is concentrated in the lower class, members of this class require more external control of their behavior and therefore, it is only natural that the police should concentrate their efforts in lower-class neighborhoods, i.e., where most crime occurs.

From a progressive point of view, however, crime is not defined simply by the use of official crime rates. Crime is not sufficiently measured by the FBI's official crime statistics. Self-reported crime and surveys of criminal victimization, for example, indicate that there is probably three to four times more crime in American society than is reported in official statistics.

But the progressive objection to using official crime rates to define crime does not stop here. From the progressive perspective, official crime rates are not a measure of how much crime there is, but a measure of how a society reacts, or fails to react, to crime. The progressive position is that official crime statistics indicate how society responds only to certain kinds of offenses and disproportionately labels as criminal the poor and minorities. In addition, progressives believe there is a self-fulfilling prophecy at work as certain crimes are identified by FBI crime reports as the most threatening and troublesome. This directs the attention of the police to these crimes and thus excludes other potentially harmful behavior from extensive police activity. Beyond this, progressives also point out that official agencies may deliberately increase or decrease crime rates for bureaucratic and political reasons. Police departments, for example, may manipulate crime rates through the processes of "unfounding" (declaring that unsolved crimes never occurred) and "defounding" (lowering serious felony crimes to less serious misdemeanor crimes) to appear more efficient and effective in their battle against crime.

Perhaps the most important criticism of official crime statistics from a progressive perspective is that they only measure one kind of crime in American society—the street crimes of the poor and the working-class. As our selection contends here, official crime rates do not adequately define crime because they do not measure the criminal activities of affluent and powerful individuals, groups, organizations, corporations, and governments. What about "crimes that do not count" in official crime rates? What about white-collar, organized, corporate, and political crimes? Since official crime statistics and rates do not recognize or measure these types of crimes, they divert attention away from the crimes of the powerful (or what some radical criminologists call the "crimes of capital") and toward the crimes of the powerless. This turns out to be a diversionary tactic, which helps maintain the current imbalance of power in American society. The powerless underclass can be seen as the enemy, the source of society's problems, and efforts at keeping them in line are more easily justified.

CRIMINOGENESIS

Another part of the different answers that conservative and progressive perspectives provide to the question of "What is crime?" has to do with what causes crime. The issue here is, what is it that generates crime? What is it that makes someone or something criminal? Who or what is ultimately the source of crime? Who or what is it that ultimately has criminal properties?

The conservative position here is that crime is a property of an individual. The individual offender is the primary source of crime, and crime is caused by the individual criminal. Different conservative versions of this approach variously identify the specific source of criminal behavior as the physiology, chemistry, psychology, personality, or morality of the individual. Armed robbers have antisocial personalities; violent rapists suffer chemical imbalances in the brain; physicians who engage in Medicare abuse are "type A" and greedy; and ruthless Watergate criminals were amoral pathological persons. It is important to note that there is a crime control or criminal justice policy and practice inherent in this conservative view of crime. To make crime go away, the individual offender must be changed, since crime is caused by, or is a property of, this offender. To control crime, the individual must be adjusted to the social order—through punishment, medical and psychiatric treatment, counseling, or other discipline and training.

The progressive approach is much different. From this perspective, crime is a property of social institutions. Crime is caused by the way in which societies and their institutions are organized and operate. When economic institutions are organized and operate to generate high levels of inequality in society, high levels of both property and violent crime occur on the street among those experiencing the worst of the inequality. When economic institutions are organized and operate to generate high levels of profit in society, high levels of white-collar and corporate crime occur in the suites among those charged with maintaining high profit margins. From this perspective, fee-for-service mechanisms are more responsible for Medicare abuse than are greedy physicians. Electoral processes and governments left open to the influence of big money are more of a source of political crime and corruption than are amoral politicians. Illegal toxic waste dumps are more the result of an economy driven by the profit motive than they are the result of conservative corporate boards of directors who lack social conscience.

The progressive view also implies a particular crime control or criminal justice policy and practice. If crime is caused by the way in which society and its institutions are organized and operate, then it is precisely the organization and operation of society and its institutions, not individual offenders, that must be changed if crime is to subside or disappear. Here, social reform becomes synonymous with crime control and criminal justice.

CLASS AND CRIME

As has been made clear earlier, conservative and even many liberal analysts of crime define it primarily as those harmful behaviors—those street crimes (thefts and assaults)—perpetuated by the members of lower social classes. In its most conservative expressions, this view finds the causes of this criminal behavior in the biological and psychological traits and characteristics of lower-class individuals. In its liberal expression—represented by the excerpt from Walter Miller provided in this section—the causes of crime are located in the social, economic, and cultural conditions of lower-class life.

All of this is strongly objected to in progressive analyses of crime. Crime cannot be defined adequately by an accounting of the harmful behaviors of the lower class. Crime is present throughout the American class structure. All classes—ruling, middle, working, the poor—perpetuate harmful acts. All classes are equally criminal, both in terms of the frequency and the severity of their harmful activities. It is true that many of the approximately 20,000 homicides in the U.S. last year occurred in the context of the lower class, but consider 30,000 deaths resulting from unnecessary surgeries and drug prescriptions by upper-middle class physicians. Add to this the 15,000 worker deaths associated with American corporations' failure to adhere to occupational health and safety regulations and laws. There is surely lower-class property crime, but we must also recognize the far more costly monopoly price-fixing and gouging, stock and securities fraud, and military procurement abuses that go on all the time. It is obvious, from a progressive point of view, that what we know about the range of harmful and victimizing behavior in American society points to "the myth of lower-class criminality."

Progressives go on to explain that the middle and ruling classes are capable of separating crime and harm in society. Through their extraordinary ability to influence the political and legal apparatus to create and enforce laws that criminalize the harmful behaviors of the poor and working class and avoid laws and enforcement practices that criminalize their own harmful activities, much of society—even some of the poor and working class—fails to regard any ruling and middle-class behavior and persons as criminal, no matter how harmful they are. Therefore, even though from a progressive perspective crime is not class specific, studies continue to show that the fear of crime is. People tend to fear the crimes of the lower classes much more than being victimized in an equally or even more serious way by the acts of the upper or ruling classes. But just because these acts by the ruling and middle classes are not defined or perceived as crimes, they are no less harmful. Although the mugger's victimization may be more immediate and visible than the surgeon's fraud, the corporation's price-fixing, or the government's violation of privacy, the latter are victimizations nonetheless. They are, from a progressive point of view, serious victimizations that should be criminalized, policed and punished.

Crime and Punishment

Warren E. Burger

Today, for the 12th time, you allow me this opportunity to lay before you problems concerning the administration of justice as I see them from my chair. For this, Mr. President and fellow members of the American Bar Association, I thank you.

On previous occasions I have discussed with you a range of needs of our system. Your responses, beginning in 1969, were a major factor in bringing into being the Institute for Court Management, the National Center for State Courts, the provision for court administrators in the federal system, and many other changes. In light of my subject today, I should also mention the important contributions made beginning in 1970 by your Commission on Correctional Facilities and Services. The value of these improvements is beyond precise calculation. But the value is great. We do not always agree, but our differences are few indeed. All I ask for is equal time.

The new president who has just taken office is confronted with a host of great problems, domestic and world-wide: inflation, unemployment, energy, and overblown government, a breakdown of our educational system, a weakening of family ties, and a vast increase in crime. As he looks beyond our shores, he sees grave, long-range problems, which begin 90 miles off the shores of Florida and extend around the globe.

Today I will focus on a single subject, although one of large content. Crime and the fear of crime have permeated the fabric of American life, damaging the poor and minorities even more than the affluent. A recent survey indicates 46 per cent of women and 48 per cent of blacks are "significantly frightened" by pervasive crime in America.

Seventy-five years ago, Roscoe Pound shook this Association with his speech on "The Causes of Popular Dissatisfaction with the Administration of Justice." In the 1976 Pound Conference, we reviewed his great critique but also examined criminal justice. My distinguished colleague, Judge Leon Higginbotham, carefully noted the imperative need for balance in criminal justice between the legitimate rights of the accused and the rights of all others, including the victims. And, of course, we are all victims of every crime.

Source: Warren E. Burger, "Annual Report to the American Bar Association by the Chief Justice of the United States," *American Bar Association Journal* 67 (March 1981):290–293. Reprinted with permission from the *ABA Journal,* The Lawyer's Magazine.

When I speak of "crime and punishment" I embrace the entire spectrum beginning with an individual's first contact with police authority through the stages of arrest, investigation, adjudication, and corrective confinement. At every stage the system cries out for change, and I do not exclude the adjudicatory stage. At each step in this process the primary goal, for both the individual and society, is protection and security. This theme runs throughout all history.

When our distant ancestors came out of caves and rude tree dwellings thousands of years ago to form bands and tribes and later towns, villages, and cities, they did so to satisfy certain fundamental human needs: mutual protection, human companionship, and later for trade and commerce. But the basic need was *security*—security of the person, the family, the home, and of property. Taken together, this is the meaning of a civilized society.

Today the proud American boast that we are the most civilized, most prosperous, most peace-loving people leaves a bitter aftertaste. We have prospered. We are, and have been, peace-loving in our relations with other nations. But, like it or not, today here at home we are approaching the status of an impotent society—whose capability of maintaining elementary security on the streets, in schools, and for the homes of our people is in doubt.

I thought of this recently in a visit to the medieval city of Bologna, Italy. There, still standing, are walled enclaves of a thousand years ago with a high corner tower where watch was kept for roving, hostile street gangs. When the householder left his barricaded enclave, he had a company of spearmen and others with crossbows and battle axes as guards.

Possibly some of our problem of behavior stems from the fact that we have virtually eliminated from public schools and higher education any effort to teach values of integrity, truth, personal accountability, and respect for others' rights. This was recently commented on by a distinguished world statesman, Charles Malik, former president of the U.N. General Assembly. Speaking to a conference on education, he said: "I search in vain for any reference to the fact that character, personal integrity, spiritual depth, the highest moral standards, the wonderful living values of the great tradition, have anything to do with the business of the university or with the world of learning."

Perhaps what Dr. Malik said is not irrelevant to what gives most Americans such deep concern in terms of behavior in America today.

I pondered long before deciding to concentrate today on this sensitive subject of crime, and I begin by reminding ourselves that under our enlightened Constitution and Bill of Rights, whose bicentennials we will soon celebrate, we have established a system of criminal justice that provides more protection, more safeguards, more guarantees for those accused of crime than any other nation in all history. The protective armor we give to each individual when the state brings a charge is great indeed. This protection was instituted—and it has expanded steadily since the turn of the century—because of our profound fear of the power of kings and states developed by an elite class to protect the status quo—their status above all else—and it was done at the expense of the great masses of ordinary people.

Two hundred years ago we changed that. Indeed, in the past 30 or 40 years, we have changed it so much that some now question whether the changes have produced a dangerous imbalance.

I put to you this question: Is a society redeemed if it provides massive safeguards for accused persons, including pretrial freedom for most crimes, defense lawyers at public expense, trials and appeals, retrials and more appeals—almost without end—and yet fails to provide elementary protection for its law-abiding citizens? I ask you to ponder this question as you hear me out.

Time does not allow, nor does my case require me to burden you with masses of detailed statistics. I assure you the statistics are not merely grim; they are frightening. Let me begin near home: Washington, D.C., the capital of our enlightened country, in 1980 had more criminal homicides than Sweden and Denmark combined with an aggregate population of more than 12 million as against 650,000 for Washington, D.C. And Washington is not unique. From New York City, to Los Angeles, to Miami the story on increase in violent crime from 1979 to 1980 is much the same. New York City, with about the same population as Sweden, has 20 times as many homicides. The United States has 100 times the rate of burglary of Japan. Overall, violent crime in the U.S. sharply increased from 1979 to 1980, continuing a double-digit rate. More than one quarter of all the households in this country are victimized by some kind of criminal activity at least once each year.

The *New York Times* recently reported that one documented study estimated that the chances of any person arrested for a felony in New York City of being punished in any way—apart from the arrest record—were 108 to 1! And it is clear that thousands of felonies go unreported in that city, as in all others.

For at least ten years many of our national leaders and those of other countries have spoken of international terrorism, but our rate of routine, day-by-day terrorism in almost any large city exceeds the casualties of all the reported "international terrorists" in any given year.

Why do we show such indignation over alien terrorists and such tolerance for the domestic variety?

Must we be hostages within the borders of our own self-styled, enlightened, civilized country? Accurate figures on the cost of home burglar alarms, of three locks on each door—and sadly, of handgun sales for householders—are not available, but they run into hundreds of millions of dollars.

What the American people want is that crime and criminals be brought under control so that we can be safe on the streets and in our homes and for our children to be safe in schools and at play. Today that safety is fragile.

It needs no more recital of the frightening facts and statistics to focus attention on the problem—a problem easier to define than to correct. We talk of having criminals make restitution or having the state compensate the victims. The first is largely unrealistic; the second is unlikely. Neither meets the central problem. Nothing will bring about swift changes in the terror that stalks our streets and endangers our homes, but I will make a few suggestions.

To do this I must go back over some history which may help explain our dilemma.

For a quarter of a century I regularly spent my vacations visiting courts and prisons in other countries, chiefly Western Europe. My mentors in this educational process were two of the outstanding penologists of our time: The late James V. Bennett, director of the United States Bureau of Prisons, and the late Torsten Ericksson, his counterpart in Sweden, where crime rates were once low, poverty was nonexistent, correctional systems enlightened and humane. Each was a vigorous advocate of using prisons for educational and vocational training.

I shared and still share with them the belief that poverty and unemployment are reflected in crime rates, chiefly crimes against property. But if poverty were the principal cause of crimes, as was the easy explanation given for so many years, crime would have been almost nonexistent in affluent Sweden and very high in Spain and Portugal. But the hard facts simply did not and do not support the easy claims that poverty is the controlling factor; it is just one factor. America's crime rate today exceeds our crime rate during the Great Depression.

We must not be misled by clichés and slogans that if we but abolish poverty, crime will also disappear. There is more to it than that. A far greater factor is the deterrent effect of swift and certain consequences: swift arrest, prompt trial, certain penalty, and—at some point—finality of judgment.

To speak of crime in America and not mention drugs and drug-related crime would be an oversight of large dimension. The destruction of lives by drugs is more frightening than all the homicides we suffer. The victims are not just the young who become addicts. Their families and, in turn, their victims and all of society suffer over a lifetime. I am not wise enough to venture a solution. Until we effectively seal our many thousands of miles of borders, which would require five or ten times the present border guard personnel and vastly enlarge the internal drug enforcement staffs, there is little else we can do. Our Fourth and Fifth amendments and statutes give the same broad protection to drug pushers as they give to you and me, and judges are oath-bound to apply those commands.

It is clear that there is a startling amount of crime committed by persons on release awaiting trial, on parole, and on probation release. It is not uncommon for an accused finally to be brought to trial with two, three, or more charges pending. Overburdened prosecutors and courts tend to drop other pending charges when one conviction is obtained.[1] Should we be surprised if the word gets around in the "criminal community" that you can commit two or three crimes for the price of only one and that there is not much risk in committing crimes while awaiting trial?

Deterrence is the primary core of any effective response to the reign of terror in American cities. Deterrence means speedy action by society, but that process runs

---

[1]The official D.C. reports show that in the last quarter of 1975, *i.e.*, October, November, and December, 1975, 569 of all the persons arrested for serious crimes were, *at the time of their arrest*, awaiting trial on one or more prior indictments. In that same period *402* persons who were arrested were, at the time of arrest, at large either on parole from a penal institution, on probation after a judgment of conviction, or on a conditional release other than the traditional parole. Remarks of Warren E. Burger at the A.L.I. opening session, May 18, 1976.

up against the reality that many large cities have either reduced their police forces or failed to keep them in balance with double-digit crime inflation.

A first step to achieve deterrence is to have larger forces of better trained officers. Thanks to the F.B.I. Academy, we have the pattern for such training.

A second step is to re-examine statutes on pretrial release at every level. This requires that there be a sufficient number of investigators, prosecutors, and defenders—and judges—to bring defendants to trial swiftly. Any study of the statistics will reveal that "bail crime" reflects a great hole in the fabric of our protection against internal terrorism.

To change this melancholy picture will call for spending more money than we have ever before devoted to law enforcement, and even this will be for naught if we do not re-examine our judicial process and philosophy with respect to finality of judgments. The search for "perfect" justice has led us on a course found nowhere else in the world. A true miscarriage of justice, whether 20, 30, or 40 years old, should always be open to review, but the judicial process becomes a mockery of justice if it is forever open to appeals and retrials for errors in the arrest, the search, or the trial.

Traditional appellate review is the cure for errors. But we have forgotten that simple truth. Our search for true justice must not be twisted into an endless quest for technical errors unrelated to guilt or innocence. The system has gone so far that Judge Henry Friendly, in proposing to curb abuses of collateral attack, entitled his article, "Is Innocence Irrelevant?" And Justice Jackson once reminded us that the Constitution should not be read as a "suicide pact."

Each of these men, of course, echoed what another great jurist, Justice Benjamin Cardozo, wrote more than 50 years ago in his essays, *The Nature of the Judicial Process*.

I am not advocating a new idea but merely restating an old one that we have ignored. At this point judicial discretion and judicial restraint require me to stop and simply to repeat that governments were instituted and exist chiefly to protect people. If governments fail in this basic duty they are not excused or redeemed by showing that they have established the most perfect systems to protect the claims of defendants in criminal cases. A government that fails to protect both the rights of accused persons and also all other people has failed in its mission. I leave it to you whether the balance has been fairly struck.

Let me now try to place this in perspective: first, the bail reform statutes of recent years, especially as to nonviolent crimes, were desirable and overdue; second, the provisions for a lawyer for every defendant were desirable and overdue; third, statutes to ensure speedy trials are desirable, but only if the same legislation provides the means to accomplish the objective.

Many enlightened countries succeed in holding criminal trials within four to eight weeks after arrest. First nonviolent offenders are generally placed on probation, free to return to a gainful occupation under close supervision. But I hardly need remind this audience that our criminal process often goes on two, three, four, or more years before the accused runs out of all the options. Even after sentence and confinement, the warfare continues with endless streams of petitions for writs, suits against parole boards, wardens, and judges.

So we see a paradox. Even while we struggle toward correction, education, and rehabilitation of the offender, our system encourages prisoners to continue warfare with society. The result is that whatever may have been the defendant's hostility toward the police, the witnesses, the prosecutor, the judge and jurors—and the public defender who failed to win his case—those hostilities are kept alive. How much chance do you think there is of changing or rehabilitating a person who is encouraged to keep up years of constant warfare with society?

The dismal failure of our system to stem the flood of crime repeaters is reflected in part in the massive number of those who go in and out of prisons. In a nation that has been thought to be the world leader in so many areas of human activity, our system of justice, not simply the prisons, produces the world's highest rate of "recall" for those who are processed through it. How long can we tolerate this rate of recall and the devastation it produces?

What I suggest now—and this Association with its hundreds of state and local affiliates can be a powerful force—is a "damage control program." It will be long; it will be controversial; it will be costly, but less costly than the billions in dollars and thousands of blighted lives now hostage to crime.

To do this is as much a part of our national defense as the Pentagon budget.

Sometimes we speak glibly of a "war on crime." A war is indeed being waged, but it is a war by a small segment of society against the whole of society. Now a word of caution: That "war" will not be won simply by harsher sentences; not by harsh mandatory minimum sentence statutes; not by abandoning the historic guarantees of the Bill of Rights. And perhaps, above all, it will not be accomplished by self-appointed armed citizen police patrols. At age 200, this country has outgrown the idea of private law and vigilantes. Volunteer community watchman services are quite another matter.

Now let me present the ultimate paradox. After society has spent years and often a modest fortune to put just one person behind bars, we become bored. The media lose interest, and the individual is forgotten. Our humanitarian concern evaporates. In all but a minority of the states we confine the person in an overcrowded, understaffed institution with little or no library facilities, little if any educational program or vocational training. I have visited American prisons built more than 100 years ago for 800 prisoners, but with 2,000 crowded today inside their ancient walls.

Should you look at the records you will find that the 300,000 persons now confined in penal institutions are heavily weighted with offenders under age 30. A majority of them cannot meet minimum standards of reading, writing, and arithmetic. Plainly this goes back to our school systems. A sample of this was reflected in a study of pupils in a large city where almost one half of the third graders failed reading. This should not surprise us, for today we find some high school graduates who cannot read or write well enough to hold simple jobs.

Here are a few steps which ought to be considered:

(1) Restore to all pretrial release laws the crucial element of dangerousness to the community, based on a combination of the evidence then available and the defendant's past record, to deter crime while on bail;

(2) Provide for trial within weeks of arrest for most cases, except for extraordinary cause shown;

(3) Priority for review on appeal within eight weeks of a judgment of guilt;

(4) Following exhaustion of appellate review, confine all subsequent judicial review to claims of miscarriage of justice.

And finally:

A. We must accept the reality that to confine offenders behind walls without trying to change them is an expensive folly with short-term benefits—a "winning of battles while losing the war";

B. Provide for generous use of probation for first nonviolent offenders, with intensive supervision and counseling and swift revocation if probation terms are violated;

C. A broad-scale program of physical rehabilitation of the penal institutions to provide a decent setting for expanded educational and vocational training;

D. Make all vocational and educational programs mandatory with credit against the sentence for educational progress—literally a program to "learn the way out of prison," so that no prisoner leaves without at least being able to read, write, do basic arithmetic, and have a marketable skill;

E. Generous family visitation in decent surroundings to maintain family ties, with rigid security to exclude drugs or weapons;

F. Counseling services after release paralleling the "after-care" services in Sweden, Holland, Denmark, and Finland.

All this should be aimed at developing the prisoner's respect for self, respect for others, accountability for conduct, and appreciation of the value of work, of thrift, and of family.

G. Encourage religious groups to give counsel on ethical behavior and occupational adjustment during and after confinement.

The two men I spoke of as my mentors beginning 25 years ago—James V. Bennett and Torsten Eriksson of Sweden—were sadly disappointed at the end of their careers on their great hopes for rehabilitation of offenders. A good many responsible, qualified observers are reaching the stage that we must now accept the harsh truth that there may be some incorrigible human beings who cannot be changed except by God's own mercy to that one person. But we cannot yet be certain, and in our own interest—in the interest of billions in dollars lost to crime and blighted if not destroyed lives, we must try to deter and try to cure.

This will be costly in the short run, and the short run will not be brief. This illness our society suffers has been generations in developing, but we should begin at once to divert the next generation from the dismal paths of the past to inculcate a sense of personal accountability in each school child, to the end that our homes, schools, and streets will be safe for all.

LAW AND CRIME 2

Crime and the State

Drew Humphries

Crime is pervasive in American society. It is a political issue, a news item, a popular subject for the entertainment and media industries, a personal fear, and a reality for many. Criminologists and sociologists are frequently called upon to study the behavior of criminals or to make recommendations about how to deal with the crime problem. Each of the main paradigms in sociology has a different approach for studying crime. The conservative tradition understands crime as the failure of the individual to conform to the norms of society. This comes about because of conflicts or inconsistencies in the norms or because of weakness in the socialization process whereby individuals are taught how to behave. Conservative studies of crime focus on inadequate socializing agents such as the single-parent family where divorce, desertion, or death are identified as the causes of incomplete socialization and consequent wrongdoing on the part of children and teenagers. The conservative tradition emphasizes structurally repressive remedies for these weaknesses. One strategy is to bolster socializing agencies—like the family, the school, and the church—by integrating them with policing agencies. The Police Athletic League, for example, illustrates the conservative response because police sponsorship of and participation in recreation activities with youths from low-income families are intended to compensate for the socialization received in the home which is assumed to be inadequate. Overall, the conservative tradition seeks to reintegrate society by reinforcing the value consensus upon which it is assumed to rest.

The liberal tradition in criminology reveals more diversity in the study of crime than does the conservative approach. Liberal criminologists are also concerned with values but attribute criminal behavior to value distortions, suggesting, for example, that the overemphasis on material rewards in American society together with discrimination contribute to high rates of deviance and crime. Liberals also attribute crime to conflicts within society. Liberals define society as a system of competing groups each pursuing specific interests. This conception is called "pluralism" and accounts for crime by holding that an interest group which succeeds in enacting criminal legislation has the power to impose criminal and/or deviant

Source: Drew Humphries, "Crime and the State" (pp. 224–239). From *Sociology: Class, Consciousness, and Contradiction* by Albert J. Szymanski and Ted George Goertzel. Copyright © 1979 by Litton Educational Publishing, Inc. Reproduced by permission of Wadsworth, Inc.

labels on less powerful groups. This generalization is referred to as "labeling theory" and has opened up a new line of inquiry for liberal criminologists: the contribution of the criminal justice system itself to the generation of crime. The argument is not complex: creation of deviant labels is the product of political conflict and the application of these labels sustains deviant behavior by informing an audience how to react to the labeled individual.

The shortcomings of both conservative and liberal criminology have been noted by radicals. The focus on agencies of social control fails to raise moral and social questions about the nature of society. Conservatives assume that consensus over cultural values integrates and holds society together. Liberals assume that interest group conflict defines society. Neither tradition questions these assumptions. Consequently, each holds that it is possible to create a well-regulated and fair system of justice under the present economic and political conditions.

Marxist criminology offers a different analysis of crime. Radicals see crime as a legal category created by the state and used by the economically dominant social class for its own purposes. . . . The radical analysis of the state argues that its chief function is to defend the interests of the ruling class against the exploited class in society. Much of the information we have about crime confirms this analysis. For example, self-reported studies of crime show that most people have committed an act for which they could be criminally prosecuted at some time during their lives. This is true for all social classes, all races, and all ethnic groups. However, when we examine statistics to see who is arrested, prosecuted, and convicted by the state for crimes, we find that it is primarily young, black, men living in urban low-income areas. Thus, our criminal justice system does not enforce the norms of society equally against everyone. It enforces them selectively against groups on the bottom of society. Unlike conservative and liberal traditions, the radical approach to crime questions not only the agencies of social control but the society in which they function. Moral and political questions are at the heart of Marxist criminology and lead us to an understanding of crime that is historical and structural in the broadest sense. . . . This chapter explores these questions. We will trace the origins of crime and its historical relation to the state in class societies. We will examine in particular the role of criminal justice in contemporary society. We will look at crime as a business and at crime as it is committed by the poorest and most marginalized classes in American society. We will consider the relationship between the destruction of productive life and the application of the penal sanction. And, finally, we will consider the question of the reform of the criminal justice system in America.

History of Crime and the State

Any analysis begins with a definition and the study of crime is no exception. Liberal and conservative criminologists define crime as a legal category and also incorporate the values underlying the law as part of their analyses. If the law condemns certain behavior and if law-enforcement officials pursue its suppression, then often the work of liberal and conservative criminologists contains the same moral bias. Marxists begin with the same legal definition of crime but analyze it critically, that is, they do not accept its moral bias. Crime is taken as nothing more than an instrument through which the state uses violence and coercion to impose legitimately the conditions of order. It spells out a set of procedures that compel the state to move against those who violate the law and require punishment upon conviction. It also lists the acts and omissions to act that the state deems sufficiently damaging to necessitate punishment. Marxists begin with the legal definition of crime in order to examine the conditions under which activity comes to be defined as socially injurious and therefore properly subject to the criminal sanction within the moral framework of the state. Here, the moral bias of law is an object of sociological investigation. In a very general sense, we can identify three conditions under which an activity becomes a crime: (1) a state exercising jurisdiction over a given territory, (2) a dominant social class affecting the development of criminal law, and (3) a pool of uprooted individuals bearing no legal relation to the means of production. Historically, these conditions came into being at different times and we turn now to an examination of these developments.

While people have had disputes throughout human history, and people have violated norms held by others in all types of societies, crime as a legally defined set of behaviors prohibited by the state is a relatively recent event. In primitive societies, disputes were settled between family or clan groups. There might have been a leader or clan head to whom complaints could be referred but there was no state to define behavior as criminal. Often disputes were settled informally without the mediation of leaders. In Oriental despotic society, people could be punished at the discretion of the rulers. There was often no code of laws defining what was criminal and what was not. It was only with the development of feudalism in the thirteenth century that crime came to be formally defined in English law.

Anglo-Saxon law remained weak prior to the Norman invasion in 1066 because the kings possessed no means to compel litigants to appear before the court. The customary blood feud, a form of private vengeance, settled most disputes under these circumstances. Personal injury and cattle theft provoked private war between the kindred of a wrongdoer and the kindred of the person wronged. The feud, however, could be forestalled by compensation: the amount was fixed by custom and was used to determine the value of a man's life and the measure of his fine. Those who refused to provide compensation denied justice and were considered to be outlaws. In prefeudal England, society was agrarian and composed of a large portion of freemen each residing in homesteads and answerable for his own "fense."

Norman law identified crime for the first time and defined it as a legal instrumentality of the feudal state. William the Conqueror exacted an oath of fealty from all freemen and lords, made criminal law turn on the violation of the king's peace, and did away with the compensation system. Henry II (twelfth century) centralized English law by instituting a permanent court of professional judges as well as by sending itinerant judges throughout the land and by introducing the inquest and the writ as normal parts of the justice system. Jurist Ranulf de Glanville (twelfth century) distinguished civil wrongs from crimes and defined treason (the slaying of the king or betrayal of his person, realm, or army), concealment of treasure, breach of the king's peace, homicide, arson, robbery, rape, and forgery as crimes. By the end of Henry III's reign (thirteenth century) the Magna Carta brought the sovereign under the rule of the law and completed the main outlines of the modern state. Historically, then, crime emerged as a set of institutions properly imposing punishment and corresponded to the consolidation of the state.

Such a development rarely occurs, however, without a clash between the rights and obligations defined by custom and those newly identified in central law. Many of the behaviors that were considered criminal by the feudal state of the time were things the peasants had done for generations and that they always considered to be appropriate and morally correct. The criminal code was used to enforce the will of the feudal nobility against the peasants. Norman law defined the parties to a dispute not as equal clan members as under Anglo-Saxon law but as propertied individuals. Norman law criminalized the Anglo-Saxon system of compensation and the right to private war. The clash between customary and central law produces a special type of criminal, the social bandit, who like Robin Hood, followed custom and became an outlaw in relation to the Norman crown. The social bandit, however, provided some inspiration for the peasantry being forced to conform to the Norman law through the sheriffs, the itinerant judges, and the local lords. Thus, the criminal justice system originated as part of the structure of class domination in feudal society. And, as society changed, the nature of the criminal code and the criminal justice system had to change to reflect the needs of the changing class structure.

Historically, the economically dominant social class has used the penal sanction to its advantage. By the fifteenth century, English wealth was no longer measured simply in land but increasingly by the goods produced in one nation for exchange in another. The mercantilists, the producers of movable and exchangeable products, represented a social class that prospered from the increase in commerce but that suffered from the restrictions still imposed by feudal law. One restriction was the feudal law of theft, which held that no servant could steal property from his master on the grounds that the servant belonged to the master. When a master turned over property to a servant, the master transferred custody and not possession, since both the property and the servant remained in the possession of the master. As the mercantile relation between buyer and seller replaced the feudal relation between master and servant, the law of theft inhibited buying and selling to a degree that made commercial transactions dependent on feudal bonds of loyalty. This contradiction was resolved by the Carrier Case, which revolutionized the law of theft in the fifteenth century. The facts of the case are straightforward: an Italian merchant hired an English carrier to transport merchandise to South

Hampton for shipment to Italy. The carrier took the bales of cotton, broke them open in transit, and apparently disposed of the contents to his own advantage. After much deliberation the judges held that the carrier in breaking open the bales illegally converted his legitimate custody to possession and was therefore guilty of larceny. What this decision did was encourage trade by exonerating merchants from the feudal responsibility of watching over the transporters of goods. The judges were influenced in this decision by the mercantile interests of the king himself, by the credit arrangements that obligated the English crown to Italian mercantilists, and by the rising importance of the mercantile class. The favorable decision represents the role played by an economically dominant social class in the exercise of state power and in particular in the formulation of criminal law, that is, in defining the circumstances under which the monopoly over the use of coercion would be imposed in commercial life.

Marginalization

Crime as an instrument of the state is shaped by underlying processes of marginalization. Marginalization refers to the destruction of a class or class fragment's relation to the means of sustaining and reproducing social life. As we know, an economic class is defined in relation to the means of production. All persons who live by tilling the land and by consuming its produce are peasants. All persons who live by selling their labor to another in exchange for a wage are proletarians. In this context, the relation to the means of production identifies the way in which an entire class acquires the resources to live from day to day and from generation to generation. Under certain conditions, this vital link can be broken and when it is the social class in question is left without the materials to create a livelihood.

This process of marginalization occurs for many different reasons. Historically, European peasants were subjected to marginalization when the enclosure laws defined commonly held lands to be the private property of the nobility and when the state forcibly expelled the peasantry from the land. The enclosure laws assisted in the expropriation of common lands by the nobility, that is, in the theft of peasant lands. In addition, the state and factory owners assisted in the deployment of marginalized peasants by imprisonment and transportation to penal colonies, as well as by offering wage labor as a substitute livelihood. The relation between crime and marginalization is complex and is best illustrated by historical example.

In the eighteenth century the administration of justice reflected social class inequities based on title and tenure to land. English peasants and prosperous freemen claimed pasture rights to common lands, while local lords exercised land tenure including title to game and vegetation. The chase was a symbol of wealth and privilege, for the crime of poaching restricted the hunt to those lords earning substantial incomes from their estates. Less affluent lords, merchants, miners, and free as well as peasant farmers risked fine, imprisonment, and transportation for poaching and they justified it by customary claim to the game as well as by hatred for the gamekeepers and lords. That poaching was already a crime signifies that this customary right had already been appropriated and taken over by the lords as a private privilege. In addition, the crime of poaching was used to appropriate one of the last customary rights: the claim to common pasturage on the landed estates. Local lords closed off the common pasture lands for use in producing game animals for the commercial meat market. The enclosure was contested by merchants and free farmers who pursued the matter through the courts and organized destruction of the game animals in order to clear the common lands for pasturing their own herds. Poaching became a tactic in the fight to impose expropriation: those who resisted the enclosure by killing game animals were charged with poaching. The King's court upheld the lords' action and the penal institutions absorbed marginalized producers.

The struggle to retain material resources in the face of impending factory work can be seen by examining the situation in Germany in the 1840s. The theft of wood in the Rhineland represented an effort to maintain and increase the ability of agricultural producers to survive independently of the wage. On the one hand, the price of timber appreciated over the 1800s and corresponded to the Prussian state's move to preserve forest acres for private and state profit. On the other hand, the parceling of land in agricultural districts reduced the resources available to small farmers and peasants, making them dependent on the smallest rises in prices. Price increases threw peasants into the situation where exercising customary rights to forest products was their only means of survival. The expropriation of forest lands by the state was part of the destruction of communal norms that had begun in the sixteenth century. By the 1840s, however, this movement jeopardized the livelihood of an entire class in the Rhineland. Peasant usage of forest products—fodder for cattle, wood for building and fuel—was made punishable by fine and imprisonment. The peasant movement to continue use of forest products represented a struggle against the legal expropriation of forest products and against the conditions that otherwise would have forced the peasantry into factory work. The state intervened in this process and thereby underwrote the deployment of workers into the factory by criminalizing customary relation to forest products: wood gathering became a crime.

This brief historical overview has shown that crime is not only a legal instrumentality dependent on the creation of the state and a ruling class but also that application of the criminal law is tied to the existence of marginalized classes. Revision of the English law of theft advanced mercantile interests by removing feudal obligations from commercial relations. The poaching laws signal the penetration of capital into agriculture and the resulting pressures to utilize even common lands for the purpose of commercial trade. The wood theft laws of Germany outlawed a means of subsistence and forced marginalized peasants onto the wage and into factory work. In the course of further developments, crime and criminals take on more modern features as wage labor and capital define the major class divisions in society.

Crime in America

In capitalist society, the capitalist owns or controls the means of production and the workers sell their labor in exchange for a wage. The wage-labor exchange is the source of antagonism between the capitalist and the working class: workers receive a wage in exchange for the value they produce for the capitalist; the wage is determined by the amount of time it takes to produce a commodity; and its value is determined by the creativity and energy of the worker. The difference between the value conferred on a commodity by labor and the amount of wage received by the worker is the source of profits in a capitalist society. Part of the value created by the working class is legally appropriated—taken over—in the form of profits by the capitalist class. Crime as a legal instrument sustains this relationship by imposing the conditions of wage labor and by mediating the resulting class contradictions. The state invokes the penal sanction against those who would jeopardize order based upon fundamental class differences by challenging the wage-labor exchange itself and/or by reproducing the conditions of life outside the limits set by wage labor. This, however, is only one side of the coin. The penal sanction ignores much of the wrongdoing of the capitalist class. Socially injurious behavior traceable to the capitalist class is often not proscribed by the criminal code. Starvation stems not from the difficulties of agricultural production but from the production and distribution of foodstuffs for profits: if production is unprofitable, then the resulting food shortages are not criminal; they are simply good business. Moreover, when the capitalist class is subject to legal action, it faces civil litigation involving *negotiations* to determine if a wrong did occur, and if damage is demonstrated the remedy is fine and/or compensation. Only in cases where wrongdoing is blatant is the capitalist class subject to the penal sanctions, as in Watergate or in the Patty Hearst trial where failure to prosecute would substantiate charges of class bias.

Under these conditions, the state confronts the problem of mediating class antagonisms, that is, the problem of persuasively securing broad-based consent for its capitalist conception of order. The judicial system mediates by formally guaranteeing the norm of equality under the law. The police, the courts, and prisons do protect the life and property of all individuals by apprehending, prosecuting, and convicting some portion—albeit a class-biased portion—of those who commit crime. All classes and races are protected formally, even though the equal treatment standard is routinely violated in applying the penal sanction. In addition, the mass media serve to mediate class antagonisms. Prime-time television, for instance, glorifies policing and fans the relentless war on criminals. Criminals are frequently portrayed as vicious, dangerous, and psychologically deranged. The media obscures the relation between marginalization and crime by emphasizing only the tie between emotional disturbance expressed as violence and the ability of the police to suppress it.

The most important way that the state mediates class antagonisms is by responding to the real increase in crime. In America all measures show that crime is on the increase. The Federal Bureau of Investigation measures crime by the number of offenses known to the police and by the number of arrests made annually. These measures are based on data for the seven index offenses of homicide, forcible rape, aggravated assault, robbery, grand larceny, and auto theft. The Uniform Crime Report publishes the annual crime rate based on the index offenses and it shows a steady increase in crime over the last several decades and a sharper increase since 1970. This relation holds true when the crime measures are reported as a rate per 100,000 population: the seven index offenses increased by about a third from 1970 to 1975. This increase holds true for property crimes and personally violent crimes. It is highlighted by findings from victimization surveys sponsored by the U.S. Department of Justice: when citizens are questioned directly about the type and frequency of criminal victimization the resulting estimate of crime far exceeds the rate reported by the Uniform Crime Report. When the state responds to crime with prevention and/or control programs, it addresses the real issue of victimization for which there is deep concern.

Crime in America is even more complex an issue than this, however. As a legitimate instrument of coercion, it imposes the conditions of capitalist wage labor. As a feature of ideology, it organizes broad support for the state's programs. In addition, the process of marginalization operates to sever class connections to the means of production, while the penal sanction anticipates that some potential for resistance—organized or not—exists amid the forces making up society. We will take a closer look at syndicated crime and street crime, which illustrate the complex reality of the crime problem in America, by grouping together legally defined crimes in two recognizable patterns. These crimes were selected over others because they tie together upper-class and lower-class crime within the same framework.

Syndicated Crime

Syndicated crime illustrates how some crime is tolerated when it is useful to the capitalist class. Syndicated crime refers to (1) the monopolization of vice together with its black-market organization and (2) to both industrial and labor racketeering. Crime syndicates organize in the illegal marketplace supplying illicit commodities and services to fulfill consumer demand. They also provide management with the means of preventing unionization and controlling labor. In many countries of the world, the relation between the black market and the syndicate's suppression of labor is quite obvious. In France, after World War II, Marseilles gangsters monopolized prostitution and gambling under municipal protection, and in return brutally suppressed Communist strikes in the city. In Saigon, during the later part of the Vietnamese war, high-ranking government officials organized the heroin trade as a means of financing urban counterinsurgency programs that required constant payoffs for the citywide network of informers and agents. In the United States, the relationships between the black markets and labor, between syndicated crime and governmental authority, resemble the situation in other countries.

The conditions that make black markets and racketeering possible in this country are *structural* and are only related to special ethnic groups insofar as each has occupied such positions. The Irish, Jews, and Italians, as well as native Protestants, have all organized prostitution, drugs, alcohol, and gambling, and also been involved in racketeering. Such organization requires the existence of four conditions: (1) a market ethic supporting an exploitable demand for illegal services and commodities, (2) a political system hostile to the emergence of a left-wing labor movement, (3) decentralized government vulnerable to local graft and corruption, and (4) a ruling class that is not threatened by organized crime and that benefits from its continued existence. Syndicated crime's ability to suppress labor is consistent with the attempts on the part of the ruling class state personnel to mediate fundamental class antagonisms. Syndicates purchase municipal protection for vice by providing extralegal policing power for the state. The ruling class and the state purchase class harmony in exchange for illegally franchising vice.

Syndicated crime figures have typically specialized in one of the vices: Al Capone organized beer-running in Chicago during Prohibition, Lucky Luciano enlarged the scale on which prostitution had been organized previously and introduced heroin into the trade. These monopolies existed by virtue of the political influence wielded by the syndicated crime leaders. This influence, however, has both political and economic qualifications. It stems from the more conservative tendencies within an ethnic working-class community and historically has been used to oppose the militancy of immigrant workers from these same communities. In 1926, for example, when Mussolini's goodwill ambassador landed on Lake Michigan, Al Capone was on the welcoming committee to quell the potential for Italian working-class antifascist riots. Capone himself claimed repeatedly that he was not a radical and that he wanted to preserve the American system.

The amount of political influence wielded by syndicated crime depends on the kind of resources it possesses. Resources available to organized crime through the vice rackets and services are substantially less than the resources available to the ruling class with its access to manufacturing and construction profits. In addition to vice revenues, syndicated crime derives financial support from racketeering in the competitive service sector. Here racketeering has been known to stabilize the market by guaranteeing predictable labor relations and an absence of competition in services like car towing, garbage hauling, and bakery products. Nonetheless, these resources are small in relation to those of large-scale manufacturing. In this sense, the influence of the syndicate is limited by the monopoly capitalist class. The downfall of Al Capone illustrates this relationship. When prominent Chicago Republicans began to see that racketeering was no longer in their interests, they secured President Hoover's intervention, thereby bringing federal proceedings against Capone. Within three years, Capone was serving a ten-year sentence for income tax evasion. There was no doubt as to who controlled Chicago.

Syndicated crime is not only politically conservative and subservient to the ruling class, it is one instrument through which the ruling class has attacked the labor movement. Prior to the 1935 Wagner Act, which recognized unions and collective bargaining, gangsters had been used to stop unionization. With legitimate unions, gangsters shifted grounds and worked to suppress wages and to control the labor movement. Syndicated crime was able to suppress wages by forming paper locals (locals with no rank and file control) and then negotiating "sweetheart" contracts with management in the service sector. In transportation and manufacturing, gangsters suppressed militant tendencies in various unions by murder, intimidations, and terrorism, and thereby assisted in creating an essentially conservative labor movement in the United States, that is, a labor movement whose concern was with the improvement of wage conditions and not the capitalist system itself. The no-strike agreement during World War II and the McCarthy period completed the suppression of militant tendencies in the labor movement and assured capital of a stable and predictable labor force.

Street Crime

Street crime illustrates how the criminal justice system is used to maintain control over people who are victims of the marginalization process. Street crime refers to the personally violent offenses including homicide, aggravated assault, robbery, and forcible rape, as well as that portion of property crime organized around street life. Personally violent street crimes involve intraclass patterns of victimization, where both the assailant and victim are poor or working class. These are crimes of spontaneous violence committed by recently marginalized populations that in turn have been concentrated in American ghettos. Southern blacks and poor whites were pushed off the land by drought, forced land sales, and Jim Crow laws, and were then redeployed to the industrial North by the demand for labor and high wages during the first and second world wars. When the demand for surplus labor collapsed after World War II, black and other minority workers lost the wage and suffered chronic unemployment and underemployment. These events reveal that capitalism cannot sustain the conditions of full employment in an expanding labor market. They also demonstrate the impact of a racially segmented labor market on the process of marginalization. Black and other minority workers are most vulnerable because of placement in unstable, low-paying jobs. Marginalization concentrated those who no longer possessed a relation to productive life in the ghetto and the state legitimated this concentration by the provision of welfare, income maintenance, and other programs.

The ghetto and its street life mark the destruction of an entire class's relation to productive life. The brutalization and the exploitation of the street result from the absolute deterioration of social life and the destruction of the essentially social character of consciousness. Such deterioration occurs when the productive foundations underpinning social life are destroyed; it is revealed by the spontaneous pattern of violence and intraclass victimization associated with street crime. Homicides often begin as aggravated assaults and frequently start as spontaneous quarrels between people who know each other, such as drinking partners, neighbors, and family members. Quarrels occur in the home about as frequently as they occur in downtown bars and on inner-city streets where marginalized groups are concentrated.

Young black males are overrepresented both as assailants and as victims in murders and in aggravated assault cases. Aggravated assault victims are most frequently young males from nonwhite low-income groups; the assailants are predominantly black or Latin. The typical assault involves black males and this situation is only slightly more frequent than black males assaulting black women. Recent evidence suggests that male-female assaults are substantially underreported for all races and social classes and that they are more likely to surface in hospital emergency rooms as accidents than in arrest reports. Closely associated with male-female assaults is rape. Rape is not the result of provocation or enticement on the part of the victim; nor is it related to the victim's character or reputation. Rape is an act of sexual aggression in which the primary goal is the conquest and degradation of the victim. Surveys indicate that rape is both an intraclass and intrarace crime: the most frequent rape situation involves a black man and a black woman coming from low-income areas. This suggests how patriarchy affects already high rates of victimization in low-income areas.

Heroin addiction also contributes to the deterioration of life in the ghetto by intensifying intraclass and intrarace patterns of victimization. Studies of addicts undergoing methadone treatment suggest that most addicts have been arrested for property crime prior to the onset of addiction. Its effect is to increase the frequency of arrests and of victimization. Again, most robberies and burglaries victimize low-income, nonwhite communities. This pattern links marginals with syndicated crime at two levels. First, heroin syndicates are reluctant to enter into the retail distribution of the drug: black and Latin narcotics entrepreneurs drawn from marginal populations now distribute heroin at the street level. Second, heroin syndicates are dependent on an active consumer demand and consequently on the exploitation of social deterioration in the ghetto. Both levels provide justification for increased police surveillance programs, including undercover teams and networks of police informers, thereby increasing the level of police repression in the ghetto.

Social Justice

Anticrime programs have failed to reduce the inordinately high rates of victimization that characterize American cities. Intensified police patrols do not affect the incidence of crime. Pretrial diversion programs and plea bargaining only circumvent the right to trial and redirect the defendants to minimal security programs. The effect of longer sentences and even the effect of the death penalty are largely undetermined in relation to the incidence of crime. Rehabilitation programs produce only minor effects in preventing future crimes because far too many ex-inmates continue to commit crimes and to be returned to prison. The criminal justice system has failed to reduce crime. Recognition of this failure has produced several different reactions among criminologists and criminal justice practitioners.

The New Realism

On many issues conservatives and liberals tend to agree with what has been called the New Realism. The New Realism is a reform strategy designed to reconcile class antagonisms by imposing harsher measures on offenders and by upholding the formal standard of equality under the law. The logic of the position is clear: if the state is granted the necessary authority to suppress marginalized classes, then the state can fulfill its obligation to protect all citizens from victimization. In policing, the New Realism includes several developments. Police discretion has been increased by recent Supreme Court decisions; civilian auxiliary units accountable to police precincts now patrol urban neighborhoods; the image of the police has been improved by the more balanced race and sex composition of the force. This new image of police-community integration overlays the real change: the increased freedom with which the police patrols now deal with the problem of containing marginal groups and the increased organized support the police have for carrying out this activity. In corrections, advocates of the New Realism have modified sentencing law in several states. The new sentences are longer and fixed by statute so that judges cannot alter the length of imprisonment. In addition, state and federal prison construction programs have resumed, indicating that the state is prepared to allocate scarce resources to control institutions even in times of economic crisis. Consequently, those convicted are to face longer sentences, the expected increase in the prison population is to be absorbed into the newly constructed prisons, and if resistance to the conditions of incarceration arises, the death penalty exists to guarantee order.

The problem with the New Realism stems from its most basic assumption, namely that it is possible to reconcile the class antagonisms at the heart of crime through the increased use of coercion. Repression will not noticeably affect the victimization rate because it fails to recognize the underlying causes of crime. The New Realism simply relies on the organization of support among the criminally victimized to legitimate repressive measures against those who victimize. It provides no remedy for those who are marginalized because these programs ignore the role of productive life in creating constructive social life. And it discourages community democracy because citizen participation is limited to police programming instead of extended to autonomous community organizations where practical equality defines the goal.

Meaning of Crime

Anticrime programs must be developed with the recognition that the causes of community destruction are rooted in capitalism and that the fight to reduce crime must represent a struggle against the destruction of productive and social life that must also foster democratic social relations within and between communities. Some Marxist criminologists have outlined specific measures for reducing crime. For the immediate situation, there are reforms recommended by the state's agencies of social control which might reduce crime without pitting the working class against itself—better street lighting, escort services for the elderly, victim compensation programs. These reforms provide some protection for the victim without intensifying and legitimating the process of marginalization. In addition, community crime control programs must be explored. These programs must remain independent of the criminal justice system and involve community members in social defense efforts at the same time that they explore how race and sex divide the working class. Women have organized against rape, for instance, and black political groups have organized against police harassment and brutality; such examples suggest that the fight against crime is only part of a much larger contest. At a minimum this contest is for the achievement of full economic rights in the United States, including the right to work, the right to health, the right to housing, and the right to recreative activity. This is a fight against the conditions imposed by the wage, the process of marginalization, and the effects of a racially segmented labor market.

This larger fight has been won in countries where socialist revolutions have taken place and one result of revolution has been a drastic change in the meaning of crime and the methods for dealing with it. In Cuba, for example, crimes are defined as activities that endanger the goal of the revolution. The power of the state to impose punishment is used to foster socialist and democratic relations. It is a crime, for example, for a husband to rape his wife on the grounds that in socialist societies equality in the family is a primary goal of the revolution. It should be noted that in the United States forcible intercourse between marriage partners is not a crime. While the incidence and distribution of crime in Cuba is not known, the method for dealing with it is. Popular tribunals organized on a neighborhood basis and peopled by nonprofessional community members represent one important institution of justice in Cuba. Those in a community define the terms of their own justice system by direct participation. The people decide whether a crime has been committed and what to do about it. Underlying this participation, however, is a network of mass organizations where community members discuss and study the principles of socialism. These mass organizations furnish the guidelines and generate the skills necessary to participate effectively and responsibly in the popular tribunals. Thus, these tribunals are not examples of vigilante justice where personal interest or private passion determine the outcome. The popular tribunals grow out of and remain democratic to the extent that they are related to Cuba's mass organizations.

The organization of society, then, determines whether the fight against crime can be waged democratically as in Cuba or whether it is waged repressively as in the United States. As we have pointed out, the New Realism is a philosophy that would criminalize marginals to the extent that the state personnel and criminal justice experts can secure the necessary popular consent. This philosophy does not address the underlying antagonisms of social class; nor can it do so. These antagonisms, as we have noted, were based on the wage-labor exchange that characterizes capitalism. In this exchange, proletarian advantage would jeopardize the economic dominance of the capitalist class. Capitalist dominance, however, means an organization of society that continually subjects workers to marginalization simply because the economy cannot sustain the conditions of full employment when the labor pool is expanding. In this respect, the wage-labor exchange is also the condition for the process of marginalization and the penal sanction not only imposes the conditions of wage labor but also punishes attempts to exist outside the wage. Thus, labor militancy as well as other forms of militancy are suppressed to the same extent that street violence is. Criminal syndicates together with their exploitative effects in the ghetto are permitted to operate as long as their criminal activities contribute to suppression of militancy. These relations account for the face of crime in America. Modern crime, it must be recalled, is the product of previous historical developments, including the creation of a wage-labor class by process of marginalization, the development of the modern state complete with specialized justice institutions, and, finally, the division of society into economically defined classes.

Summary

A definition of crime represents the legal conditions under which the state, as an instrument of an economically dominant class, exercises its power to punish. The body of criminal law presupposes a class-based state with a territorial jurisdiction. This condition occurred only toward the end of the thirteenth century in England. Historically, the English criminal law paralleled the transformation of the feudal mode to the capitalist mode of production, where, for example, the expansion of commerce redefined the law of larceny and the enclosure laws forced the peasantry off the land and eventually into the factory as wage-labor. Crime under contemporary American capitalism also represents the coercive power of the state and further indicates marginalization of workers, that is, the expulsion of older workers from and the inability to employ new workers in the productive world. Under these conditions, organized crime illustrates how marginal as well as productive workers are implicated in the criminal underworld. Vice and labor racketeering can be seen as protected but illegal monopolies where the capitalist class purchases labor peace at the expense of marginalized workers. Workers, marginalized from productive labor, congregated in northern ghettos where the quality of social life, especially its violence, followed collapse of the job market for national minorities. The illegal markets created by vice racketeering contributed to the absolute deterioration of social life by introducing heroin and reorganizing prostitution and generally transforming marginals into consumers of illegal and debilitating commodities. The prevalence of crime need not contribute to such deterioration, and this is evidenced in socialist countries where crime as the coercive power of the state is used to further the aims of the revolution. Here, punishment is imposed on practices and activities that violate principles of equality, whether racial, sexual, or class, and is the outcome of popular tribunals as in Cuba, where nonprofessional citizens participate in the creation of justice on a collective basis.

Crime in the United States:
Uniform Crime Reports, 1986

Crime in the United States contains statistical documentation of criminal activity that has taken place in our country during the past year. Its various tables and graphs provide a measurement of crime that has been proven through five decades to be a valuable aid to the law enforcement community. The data represent much more; they depict a national problem shared jointly by every aspect of American society.

The real impact of crime cannot be demonstrated in statistical terms. These pages do not depict, for example, the anger, fear, and frustration suffered by the victims of crime. We cannot see the pain and heartache endured by the families of murder victims, including 78 law enforcement officers feloniously killed in the line of duty. The vast economic burden resulting from criminality, direct losses as well as enormous costs for maintaining a criminal justice apparatus to prevent, detect, and punish those responsible, is not portrayed. From these pages, we cannot discern the long hours, the arduous efforts, and the sacrifices made by our dedicated law enforcement agencies to thwart crime and apprehend lawbreakers.

Crime figures represent a full range of detrimental effects upon our society. Thus, decreases in crime rates are indeed welcomed news. From 1982 to 1984, we experienced such declines. In 1985, however, a reversal of that trend took place. The overall Crime Index increased by 5 percent, and violent crime alone rose by 4 percent. There are few social statements more tragic than these.

Plausible explanations for crime fluctuations are frequently offered, but their accuracy is often questionable and certainly controversial. Law enforcement remains diligent; our citizenry has increasingly taken an active role in the fight against lawlessness. Yet, we see crime rising.

Whatever the reasons for the crime increase last year, the course we must take is clear. It is up to all of law enforcement, the criminal justice community, and of course, each and every citizen to do more. We must take full advantage of every resource available to fight crime; to enact laws that protect the public while ensur-

Source: *Crime in the United States: Uniform Crime Reports*, Federal Bureau of Investigation, U.S. Justice Department, Washington, D.C., 1986, pp. iii, 1–3, 40–42. Reprinted with permission from FBI Uniform Crime Reports.

ing that lawbreakers are brought to justice; to direct our research, our strategies, our funding, our training, and our manpower to their most effective ends, not only to solve crime but also to prevent it. . . . (William H. Webster, FBI Director)

. . . Summary of the Uniform Crime Reporting Program

The Uniform Crime Reporting (UCR) Program is a nationwide cooperative venture of nearly 16,000 city, county, and state law enforcement agencies which voluntarily report data on crimes brought to their attention. Serving as a national clearinghouse, the FBI has tabulated the data produced by the Program for over 5 decades, and throughout the years, has issued periodic assessments of the nature and type of crime in the Nation. Although its primary objective is to generate a reliable set of criminal statistics for use in law enforcement administration, operation, and management, the Program's data have become one of the leading social indicators in the country. The American public looks to UCR for information on fluctuations in the level of crime, while criminologists, sociologists, legislators, municipal planners, the press, and other students of criminal justice use the statistics for varied research and planning purposes.

Historical Background

In the 1920s, the International Association of Chiefs of Police (IACP) recognized a need for national crime statistics and formed the Committee on Uniform Crime Records to develop a system of uniform police statistics. After studying state criminal codes and making an evaluation of the recordkeeping practices in use, the Committee in 1929 completed a plan for crime reporting which became the foundation of the UCR Program.

Since offenses known to law enforcement were the most readily available crime information, the Committee elected to survey local agencies to obtain data on crimes brought to their attention. Realizing that not all crimes are reported, the Committee evaluated various offenses on the basis of their seriousness, frequency of occurrence, pervasiveness in all geographic areas of the country, and likelihood of being reported to law enforcement. Using those criteria, seven offenses were chosen to serve as an Index for gauging fluctuations in the overall volume and rate of crime. Known jointly as the Crime Index, these offenses included the violent crimes of murder and nonnegligent manslaughter, forcible rape, robbery, and aggravated assault and the property crimes of burglary, larceny-theft, and motor vehicle theft. By congressional mandate, arson was added as the eighth Index offense in 1979.

During the early planning of the Program, it was recognized that the differences among criminal codes precluded a mere aggregation of state statistics to arrive at a national total. Further, because of the variances in punishment for the same offenses in different state codes, no distinction between felony and misdemeanor crimes was possible. To avoid these problems and provide nationwide uniformity in crime reporting, standardized offense definitions were formulated. Today, as at the Program's outset, law enforcement agencies submit data in accordance with the UCR standard definitions without regard for local statutes. The definitions used by the Program are set forth in Appendix II of this publication.

In January 1930, 400 cities representing 20 million inhabitants in 43 states began participating in the UCR Program. In that same year, Congress enacted legislation under Title 28, Section 534, of the United States Code authorizing the Attorney General to gather crime information. The Attorney General, in turn, designated the FBI to serve as the national clearinghouse for the data collected. Since that time, data based on uniform classifications and procedures for reporting have been obtained from the Nation's law enforcement agencies.

Throughout its more than 50 years of operation, the Program has remained virtually unchanged in terms of the data collected and disseminated. As time progressed, evaluations of the Program were suggested, and one study was conducted in 1958. By the 1980s, a broad utility had evolved for UCR, and law enforcement had expanded its capabilities to supply information related to crime. When a thorough evaluative study of UCR was again proposed, an immediate review of the Program seemed appropriate.

The Bureau of Justice Statistics (BJS), recognizing its role in the wide spectrum of national criminal justice statistics, agreed to underwrite a comprehensive UCR Program study and redesign effort comprised of three phases. To be conducted by an independent contractor, the first two phases were structured to determine what, if any, changes should be made to the current Program. The third phase would involve implementation of the changes identified. Abt Associates Inc. of Cambridge, Massachusetts, overseen by the FBI, BJS, and a Steering Committee comprised of prestigious individuals representing a myriad of disciplines, commenced the first of the three phases in 1982.

During the first phase, the historical evolution of the Program was examined. All aspects of the Program, including the objectives and intended user audience, data items, reporting mechanisms, quality control, publications and user services, and relationships with other criminal justice data systems, were studied.

Early in 1984, a conference on the future of UCR was held in Elkridge, Maryland. This meeting launched the second phase of the study, which would examine alternative potential futures for UCR and conclude with a set of recommended changes. Attendees at this conference reviewed work conducted during the first phase and discussed the potential changes that should be considered during phase two.

Findings from the evaluation's first phase and input on the alternatives for the future being developed in phase two were also major topics of discussion at the seventh National UCR Conference in July, 1984. Overlapping these two phases was a survey of law enforcement agencies.

Phase two ended in early 1985 with the production of a draft "Blueprint for the Future of the Uniform Crime Reporting Program." The study's Steering Committee reviewed the draft report at a March, 1985, meeting and made various recommendations for revision. The Committee members, however, endorsed the report's concepts.

In April, 1985, the phase two recommendations were presented at the eighth National UCR Conference. While various considerations for the final report were set forth, the overall concept for the revised Program was unanimously approved. The joint IACP/National Sheriffs' Association (NSA) Committee on UCR also issued a resolution endorsing the Blueprint.

The final report, the "Blueprint for the Future of the Uniform Crime Reporting Program," was released in the summer of 1985. It specifically outlines recommendations for an expanded, improved UCR Program to meet informational needs into the next century. With the first two phases now complete, the third and final phase will consist of implementing the adopted improvements. As implementation progresses, the amount of information available will greatly increase, and UCR can better serve its large and varied audience.

Advisory Groups

Providing vital links between local law enforcement and the FBI in the conduct of the UCR Program are the IACP and the NSA. The IACP's Committee on Uniform Crime Records, as it has since the Program began, represents the thousands of police departments nationwide. The NSA's Committee on Uniform Crime Reporting, established in June, 1966, encourages sheriffs throughout the country to fully participate in the Program. Both committees serve in advisory capacities concerning the UCR Program's operation.

The Association of State Uniform Crime Reporting Programs and committees on UCR within individual state law enforcement associations are also active in promoting interest in the UCR Program. These organizations foster widespread and more intelligent use of uniform crime statistics and lend assistance to contributors when the need arises.

Methods of Data Collection

The information compiled by UCR contributors is forwarded to the FBI either directly from the local law enforcement agency or through a state-level UCR Program. Agencies submitting directly to the FBI are provided continuing guidance and support on an individual basis.

State-level UCR Programs are very effective intermediaries between the FBI and its local contributors. Many of the 41 state Programs have mandatory reporting requirements and collect data beyond the national UCR scope to address crime problems germane to their particular locales. In most cases, these agencies are also able to provide more direct and frequent service to participating law enforcement agencies, to make information more readily available for use at the state level, and to contribute to more streamlined operations at the national level.

With the development of a state UCR Program, the FBI ceases direct collection of data from individual law enforcement agencies within the state. Instead, information from local agencies is forwarded to the national Program through the state data collection agency.

The conditions under which these systems are developed ensure consistency and comparability in the data submitted to the national Program, as well as provide for regular and timely reporting of national crime data. These conditions are: (1) The state Program must conform to national Uniform Crime Reports' standards, definitions, and information requirements. The states are not, of course, prohibited from collecting other statistical data beyond the national requirements. (2) The state criminal justice agency must have a proven, effective, statewide Program and have instituted acceptable quality control procedures. (3) Coverage within the state by a state agency must be, at least, equal to that attained by the national Uniform Crime Reports. (4) The state agency must have adequate field staff assigned to conduct audits and to assist contributing agencies in record practices and crime reporting procedures. (5) The state agency must furnish to the FBI all of the detailed data regularly collected by the FBI in the form of duplicate returns, computer printouts, and/or magnetic tapes. (6) The state agency must have the proven capability (tested over a period of time) to supply all the statistical data required in time to meet national Uniform Crime Reports' publication deadlines.

To fulfill its responsibilities in connection with the UCR Program, the FBI continues to edit and review individual agency reports for both completeness and quality; has direct contact with individual contributors within the state when necessary in connection with crime reporting matters, coordinating such contact with the state agency; and upon request, conducts training programs within the state on law enforcement records and crime reporting procedures. Should circumstances develop whereby the state agency does not comply with the aforementioned requirements, the national Program may reinstitute a direct collection of Uniform Crime Reports from law enforcement agencies within the state.

Reporting Procedures

Based on records of all reports of crime received from victims, officers who discover infractions, or other sources, law enforcement agencies across the country tabulate the number of Crime Index or Part I offenses brought to their attention during each month. Specifically, the crimes reported to the FBI are murder and nonnegligent manslaughter, forcible rape, robbery, aggravated assault, burglary, larceny-theft, motor vehicle theft, and arson.

Whenever complaints of crime are determined through investigation to be unfounded or false, they are eliminated from an agency's count. The number of "actual offenses known" is reported to the FBI regardless of whether anyone is arrested for the crime, stolen property is recovered, or prosecution is undertaken.

Another integral part of the monthly submission is the total number of actual Crime Index offenses cleared. Crimes are "cleared" in one of two ways: (1) at least one person is arrested, charged, and turned over to the court for prosecution; or (2) by exceptional means when some element beyond police control precludes the arrest of an offender. Law enforcement agencies also report the number of Index crime clearances which involve only offenders under the age of 18; the value of property stolen and recovered in connection with the offenses; and detailed information pertaining to criminal homicide and arson.

In addition to its primary collection on Crime Index (Part I) offenses, the UCR Program solicits monthly data on persons arrested for all crimes except traffic violations. The age, sex, race, and ethnic origin of arrestees are reported by crime category, both Part I and Part II. Part II offenses include all crimes not classified as Part I.

Various data on law enforcement officers killed or assaulted are collected on a monthly basis. The number of full-time sworn and civilian personnel are reported annually, as of October 31 . . . .

. . . Crime Index Tabulations

This Section's tabular portions present data on crime in the United States as a whole; geographic divisions; individual states; Metropolitan Statistical Areas; cities, towns, and counties; and college and university campuses. Also furnished in the following tables are national averages for the value of property stolen in connection with Crime Index offenses; further breakdowns by type for the robbery, burglary, larceny-theft, and arson classifications; and data on the type and value of property stolen and recovered.

Information on those offenses reported to law enforcement gives a reliable indication of criminal activity. In reviewing the tables in this report, it must be remembered, however, that many factors can cause the volume and type of crime to vary from place to place. Population, one of these factors, is used in computing crime rates; however, all communities are affected to some degree by seasonal or transient populations. Since counts of current, permanent population are used in their construction, crime rates do not account for short-term population variability. . . .

National data can serve as a guide for the law enforcement administrator in analyzing the local crime count, as well as the performance of the jurisdiction's law enforcement agency. The analysis, however, should not end with a comparison based on data presented in this publication. It is only through an appraisal of local conditions that a clear picture of the community crime problem or the effectiveness of the law enforcement operation is possible.

Note

The collection of statistics on arson as a Crime Index offense began in 1979. However, 1985 annual figures are not available for inclusion in tables presenting statistics for the total United States.

Crime Index Total

Following 3 consecutive years of decline, the Crime Index total rose 5 percent to 12.4 million offenses in 1985. Five- and 10-year percent changes showed the 1985 total was 7 percent below the 1981 level but 10 percent higher than in 1976.

All offenses comprising the Index increased in number from 1984 to 1985. Overall violent crime was up 4 percent with murder rising 2 percent; forcible rape, 4 percent; robbery, 3 percent; and aggravated assault, 6 percent.

The number of property crimes increased 5 percent for the 2-year period. Burglary increased 3 percent; larceny-theft, 5 percent; and motor vehicle theft, 7 percent.

Considering 5- and 10-year time frames, the 1985 violent and property crime totals each showed declines from the 1981 figures, 3 and 8 percent, respectively. Both categories, however, registered increases as compared to 1976. Violent crime was up 32 percent and property crime, 7 percent. National estimates of volume and rate per 100,000 inhabitants for all Crime Index offenses covering the past decade are set forth in the following table. Crime rates relate the incidence of reported crime to population. [See Table 1.]

Table 2, "Index of Crime, United States, 1985," shows current year estimates for MSAs, rural counties, and cities and towns outside metropolitan areas (other cities).

Provided in Table 3, "Index of Crime, Regional Offense and Population Distribution, 1985," are data showing the geographical distribution of estimated Index crimes and population. When utilizing figures presented on a regional basis in this publication, the reader is cautioned to consider each region's proportion of the total United States population. For example, while the Southern States accounted for the largest volume of Crime Index offenses in 1985, they also represented the greatest regional population.

Table 1 Index of Crime, United States, 1976–1985

	Population[1]	Crime Index total[2]	Modified Crime Index total[1]	Violent crime[4]	Property crime[4]	Murder and non-negligent man-slaughter	Forcible rape	Robbery	Aggra-vated assault	Burglary	Larceny-theft	Motor vehicle theft	Arson[3]
Number of offenses:													
1976	214,659,000	11,349,700		1,004,210	10,345,500	18,780	57,080	427,810	500,530	3,108,700	6,270,800	966,000	
1977	216,332,000	10,984,500		1,029,580	9,955,000	19,120	63,500	412,610	534,350	3,071,500	5,905,700	977,700	
1978	218,059,000	11,209,000		1,085,550	10,123,400	19,560	67,610	426,930	571,460	3,128,300	5,991,000	1,004,100	
1979	220,099,000	12,249,500		1,208,030	11,041,500	21,460	76,390	480,700	629,480	3,327,700	6,601,000	1,112,800	
1980	225,349,264	13,408,300		1,344,520	12,063,700	23,040	82,990	565,840	672,650	3,795,200	7,136,900	1,131,700	
1981	229,146,000	13,423,800		1,361,820	12,061,900	22,520	82,500	592,910	663,900	3,779,700	7,194,400	1,087,800	
1982	231,534,000	12,974,400		1,322,390	11,652,000	21,010	78,770	553,130	669,480	3,447,100	7,142,500	1,062,400	
1983	233,981,000	12,108,600		1,258,090	10,850,500	19,310	78,920	506,570	653,290	3,129,900	6,712,800	1,007,900	
1984	236,158,000	11,881,800		1,273,280	10,608,500	18,690	84,230	485,010	685,350	2,984,400	6,591,900	1,032,200	
1985	238,740,000	12,430,000		1,327,440	11,102,600	18,980	87,340	497,870	723,250	3,073,300	6,926,400	1,102,900	
Percent change; number of offenses:													
1985/1984		+4.6		+4.3	+4.7	+1.6	+3.7	+2.7	+5.5	+3.0	+5.1	+6.8	
1985/1981		−7.4		−2.5	−8.0	−15.7	+5.9	−16.0	+8.9	−18.7	−3.7	+1.4	
1985/1976		+9.5		+32.2	+7.3	+1.1	+53.0	+16.4	+44.5	−1.1	+10.5	+14.2	
Rate per 100,000 inhabitants:													
1976		5,287.3		467.8	4,819.5	8.8	26.6	199.3	233.2	1,448.2	2,921.3	450.0	
1977		5,077.6		475.9	4,601.7	8.8	29.4	190.7	247.0	1,419.8	2,729.9	451.9	
1978		5,140.3		497.8	4,642.5	9.0	31.0	195.8	262.1	1,434.6	2,747.4	460.5	
1979		5,565.5		548.9	5,016.6	9.7	34.7	218.4	286.0	1,511.9	2,999.1	505.6	
1980		5,950.0		596.6	5,353.3	10.2	36.8	251.1	298.5	1,684.1	3,167.0	502.2	
1981		5,858.2		594.3	5,263.9	9.8	36.0	258.7	289.7	1,649.5	3,139.7	474.7	
1982		5,603.6		571.1	5,032.5	9.1	36.0	238.9	289.2	1,488.8	3,084.8	458.8	
1983		5,175.0		537.7	4,637.4	8.3	33.7	216.5	279.2	1,337.7	2,868.9	430.8	
1984		5,031.3		539.2	4,492.1	7.9	35.7	205.4	290.2	1,263.7	2,791.3	437.1	
1985		5,206.5		556.0	4,650.5	7.9	36.6	208.5	302.9	1,287.3	2,901.2	462.0	
Percent change; rate per 100,000 inhabitants:													
1985/1984		+3.5		+3.1	+3.5		+2.5	+1.5	+4.4	+1.9	+3.9	+5.7	
1985/1981		−11.1		−6.4	−11.7	−19.4	+1.7	−19.4	+4.6	−22.0	−7.6	−2.7	
1985/1976		−1.5		+18.9	−3.5	−10.2	+37.6	+4.6	+29.9	−11.1	−.7	+2.7	

[1]Populations are Bureau of the Census provisional estimates as of July 1, except April 1, 1980, preliminary census counts, and are subject to change.
[2]Because of rounding, the offenses may not add to totals.
[3]Although arson data are included in the trend and clearance tables, sufficient data are not available to estimate totals for this offense.
[4]Violent crimes are offenses of murder, forcible rape, robbery, and aggravated assault. Property crimes are offenses of burglary, larceny-theft, and motor vehicle theft. Data are not included for the property crime of arson.
All rates were calculated on the offenses before rounding.

Table 2 Index of Crime, United States, 1985

Area	Population[1]	Crime Index total	Modified Crime Index total[2]	Violent crime[3]	Property crime[3]	Murder and non-negligent man-slaughter	Forcible rape	Robbery	Aggra-vated assault	Burglary	Larceny-theft	Motor vehicle theft	Arson[2]
United States Total	**238,740,000**	**12,430,026**		**1,327,436**	**11,102,590**	**18,976**	**87,340**	**497,874**	**723,246**	**3,073,348**	**6,926,380**	**1,102,862**	
Rate per 100,000 inhabitants		5,206.5		556.0	4,650.5	7.9	36.6	208.5	302.9	1,287.3	2,901.2	462.0	
Metropolitan Statistical Area	181,840,905												
Area actually reporting[4]	98.3%	10,655,250		1,189,462	9,465,788	15,851	75,701	481,106	616,804	2,604,382	5,848,582	1,012,824	
Estimated totals	100.0%	10,766,536		1,197,320	9,569,216	15,945	76,316	482,892	622,167	2,631,603	5,914,952	1,022,661	
Rate per 100,000 inhabitants		5,920.9		658.4	5,262.4	8.8	42.0	265.6	342.1	1,447.2	3,252.8	562.4	
Other Cities	22,954,873												
Area actually reporting[4]	94.4%	991,330		68,658	922,672	1,044	4,580	9,320	53,714	216,037	664,398	42,237	
Estimated totals	100.0%	1,051,366		73,125	978,241	1,125	4,872	9,989	57,139	229,432	704,069	44,740	
Rate per 100,000 inhabitants		4,580.1		318.6	4,261.6	4.9	21.2	43.5	248.9	999.5	3,067.2	194.9	
Rural Area	33,943,222												
Area actually reporting[4]	90.1%	562,918		51,847	511,071	1,694	5,594	4,461	40,098	195,393	283,311	32,367	
Estimated totals	100.0%	612,124		56,991	555,133	1,906	6,152	4,993	43,940	212,313	307,359	35,461	
Rate per 100,000 inhabitants		1,803.4		167.9	1,635.5	5.6	18.1	14.7	129.5	625.5	905.5	104.5	

[1]Populations are Bureau of the Census provisional estimates as of July 1, 1985, and are subject to change.

[2]Although arson data are included in the trend and clearance tables, sufficient data are not available to estimate totals for this offense.

[3]Violent crimes are offenses of murder, forcible rape, robbery, and aggravated assault. Property crimes are offenses of burglary, larceny-theft, and motor vehicle theft. Data are not included for the property crime of arson.

[4]The percentage representing area actually reporting will not coincide with the ratio between reported and estimated crime totals, since these data represent the sum of the calculations for individual states which have varying populations, portions reporting, and crime rates.

Table 3 Index of Crime, Regional Offense and Population Distribution, 1985

Region	Population	Crime Index total	Modified Crime Index total[1]	Murder and non-negligent man-slaughter	Forcible rape	Robbery	Aggra-vated assault	Burglary	Larceny-theft	Motor vehicle theft	Arson[1]
United States Total[2]	**100.0**	**100.0**		**100.0**	**100.0**	**100.0**	**100.0**	**100.0**	**100.0**	**100.0**	
Northeastern States	20.8	18.6		16.1	16.3	29.2	18.6	17.0	17.5	24.6	
Midwestern States	24.8	22.2		19.5	22.8	19.6	20.8	20.5	23.1	22.9	
Southern States	34.3	34.6		43.0	37.1	28.5	38.0	36.7	34.5	29.8	
Western States	20.0	24.6		21.4	23.8	22.8	22.5	25.7	24.8	22.7	

[1]Although arson data are included in the trend and clearance tables, sufficient data are not available to estimate totals for this offense.
[2]Because of rounding, percentages may not add to totals.

The Politics of Crime Rates

D. Stanley Eitzen and Doug A. Timmer

Crimes Omitted from Traditional Sources of Criminal Statistics

A fundamental problem with the official crime statistics is that they direct attention toward certain crimes and away from others. In doing so, they inform us as to what crimes are the most important. But are these officially recognized crimes (the FBI index crimes) the most important? Are they the most violent? Are they the most expensive in terms of property loss? Let's look at four areas of considerable criminal activity that are all but overlooked by official crime counters and crime stoppers: tax evasion, business fraud, corporate crimes, and political crimes.

Tax Evasion

There is an irregular economy in the United States where millions of individuals and companies evade billions of dollars in taxes. Involved are thousands of small businesses—bars, restaurants, retail stores, repair shops, and other legal enterprises as well as illegal activities such as gambling, drug sales, prostitution, and the sale of stolen property—that deal with cash customers. Because there are no official records, businesses can skim off a portion of the cash receipts, thus reporting a lower-than-actual amount of income. Employees can be paid in cash thereby helping the employer to evade Social Security payments, the cost of unemployment insurance, worker's compensation, and medical insurance. The employee, in turn, need not report this income because there is no record. Employees who receive cash from customers for services (e.g., waiters, cab drivers, music teachers) often do not report all or a part of their income to the government, thereby avoiding taxes they should legally pay. The amount involved in this underground economy is not trivial. One estimate in 1981 was $275 billion annually or 10 percent of the Gross National Product (Gersten, 1981). The number of people involved in this vast underground has been estimated at 20 million (*U.S. News & World Report*,

Source: Reprinted with permission of Macmillan Publishing Company from *Criminology: Crime and Criminal Justice* by D. Stanley Eitzen and Doug A. Timmer. (New York: Macmillan 1985). (pp. 99–104, 108–109)

1979). The amount of money these persons failed to pay in taxes involved, at minimum, $50 billion (Schultz, 1980). It is important to note that most of the activities
involved here occur in legitimate business activities. The Internal Revenue Service
has estimated that only 25 percent of the underground economy involves illegal
activities (reported in Tuky, 1981).

In addition to the failure to report income, there are other forms of tax cheating.
In 1979 the IRS estimated that some $18 billion was overdeclared in deductions
on income tax returns. The IRS conducted a nationwide study of 5000 households
and found that 27 to 32 percent of those interviewed admitted to being "less than
absolutely honest" in completing their 1979 tax returns. Moreover, the study
found that about half considered understating income or overstating expenses or
charitable deductions as acceptable behaviors (reported in Rankin, 1980).

The amounts of money lost in government revenues by these various means of
tax evasion clearly surpasses the amount of property stolen and reflected in the
FBI official statistics. Yet, because income tax evasion is not included in the Crime
Index, the public is unaware of the magnitude of this type of criminality. Also, once
again their ire is directed away from the criminal activities of the middle and upper
classes and toward those of the less affluent.

Fraud

Another area of criminal activity that often goes undetected, unreported, and/or
unpunished is fraud. Some criminologists have argued that fraud—the use of
deceit, lies, or misrepresentation in the marketplace—is "the most prevalent
crime in America" (Sutherland and Cressey, 1974, p. 42). Some examples of recent
fraudulent schemes are (see Simon and Eitzen, 1982, pp. 89–91):

- A 1979 government study found that motorists were overcharged an average
  of $150 per car per year for repairs.
- Medicaid abuses (overcharges to the government and underservice to
  patients) by doctors, hospitals, nursing homes, and druggists was estimated in
  1979 to total $8 billion annually.
- Stock in the Equity Funding Corporation rose from $6 a share to $80 a share
  from 1967 to 1972. This phenomenal growth was the result of faked reports
  about assets, sales, and earnings including the issuing of 64,000 phony life
  insurance policies. The company actually had *never* earned any money since
  1967 and when this became known, shareholders lost between $2 and 3 billion
  (Dirks and Gross, 1974; Blumdell in Moffett, 1976, pp. 42–89).

The important point concerning the crime of fraud is that the economic costs to
the victims and the public (higher prices for goods, increased taxes for government
activities) are huge when compared with the relatively small economic costs of
street crimes.

Corporate Crimes

The crimes of corporate America are much more costly and violent to Americans than are street crimes, yet they are not included in the official statistics on crime. Let's look briefly at the economic magnitude of some of these illegal activities first.

Price fixing by companies supposedly in competition costs consumers billions. In 1980, for example, the Federal Trade Commission, after an eight-year study, released data showing that consumers were overcharged by 15 percent for ready-to-eat cereals over a 15-year period. These overcharges in the cereal industry, it was alleged, were the direct result of the monopoly held by Kellogg, General Mills, and General Foods. Their parallel pricing and control of the market resulted in consumers paying $100 million more annually than they would if there were true competition (Associated Press, October 3, 1980). One review of cases of proven price fixing between 1963 and 1972 revealed that the practice occurred among companies producing and marketing the following: steel wheels, pipe, bed springs, metal shelving, steel casings, refuse collection, swimsuits, structural steel, baking flour, fertilizer, acoustical ceiling materials, beer, gasoline, asphalt, book matches, linen, school construction, plumbing fixtures, dairy products, auto repair, athletic equipment, ready-mix concrete, shoes, and wholesale meat (Hay and Kelley, 1974). What the extra cost is to consumers of these illegal practices in these industries (and the list is a partial one) is unknown but surely runs into the several billions of dollars.

Corporate crimes also do violence to human life (see Simon and Eitzen, 1982, pp. 97–130). Corporate violence occurs from the production and sale of unsafe products (e.g., the Corvair and the Pinto), to the sale of adulterated foods (the meat-packing industry, among others, has a history of this), and the refusal to eliminate or improve dangerous working conditions (e.g., in the mines, the production of asbestos and vinyl chloride, and in the textile industry). Corporations also place people in jeopardy by the indiscriminate waste of resources and the pollution of the environment.

Political Crimes

There are a number of crimes committed by government officials that do harm to people. They involve the illegal use of power for political purposes by those in positions of legitimate authority. Sykes has listed the following misuses of power as political crimes:

> The dismissal of persons from their jobs for revealing governmental corruption; discriminatory prosecution on the basis of political opinions; the manufacturing of evidence, including the use of perjured testimony; unlawful sentencing; the premeditated and unlawful repression of legal dissent; entrapment; illegal wiretapping; illegal search and seizure; unlawful arrests; illegal treatment of prisoners; illegal denial of the right to vote; illegal awards of state

and federal contracts; bribery to influence the political process; unlawful use of force by the police; and military war crimes. (Sykes, 1978, p. 221)

When the public relies on government data for crime rates there is the problem that the government does not report its own wrongdoings. The FBI, whose index informs us of the extent of crimes annually, is, in fact, itself guilty of numerous crimes listed above by Sykes (Simon and Eitzen, 1982, pp. 204–211; Sykes, 1980, pp. 55–58).

Political crimes point to two problems: who monitors the monitors? and the facts of political deviance are generally hidden from us because we are dependent on the government for data, that if revealed, would damn them.

The crucial question raised by examining crimes outside the FBI index is: Why do some crimes "count" while others do not? There are several possible answers. Among them:

1. Acts of violence are universally abhorred in American society.
2. In a capitalist society the laws and law enforcement exist to protect private property.
3. Focusing on street crimes reinforces the commonly held belief that the poor and minorities are threats to stability and must be controlled.
4. Street crimes are easier to identify and control than other types.
5. Crimes are defined by the powerful, therefore, the actions of the powerless are monitored whereas those of the powerful are not.
6. Law enforcement agencies are more secure if they control the powerless rather than challenge the powerful.

The Radical Perspective: The Politics of Crime Rates

Official crime statistics reveal to the public that street crimes against persons and property are on the rise. The radical perspective argues that such a view is naive. A prominent sociologist of this persuasion, Richard Quinney, has argued that we must understand the political context of crime rates:

> Crime rates . . . have to be understood for their political construction and the political uses they serve. It is for political purposes that criminal statistics are gathered and for political needs that criminal statistics are recorded and interpreted. For that reason, American crime rates are subject to great manipulation, from their inception to their use. It is impossible to know from any statistic the "true" rate of crime. Whether crime is increasing or decreasing in the United States is a question that can never be answered objectively without considering the politics of the times. (Quinney, 1979, p. 65)

There are several political uses of crime rates. As we noted in the previous section, the police need high crime rates to justify their existence. They need appropriations from various political units for higher salaries, better equipment, and more personnel. They cannot let crime get out of hand, however, or the public will call for a purge of the old policies and personnel. Thus, "the police have a [political] interest in maintaining both a high and a low rate of crime" (Quinney, 1979, p. 65).

The crimes stressed by the FBI Crime Index are aimed at certain categories of people and divert attention away from the criminal activities of others. The focus is on the criminal acts of the underclass. Blacks, for example, are disproportionately arrested (between three and four times the rates for whites) and imprisoned (about 1 in every 20 black men between the ages of 25 and 35 is either in jail or prison on any day, compared with 1 of every 163 white men in the same age group) (Quinney, 1979, p. 344). As Quinney has stated:

> To overrepresent the amount of crime by blacks is to make a political statement: that blacks are inferior (at least socially) and that they must be further controlled. *Racism is thereby maintained by the legal system in the recording and reporting of crime rates.* (Quinney, 1979, p. 66) (Emphasis added.)

The singling out of other members of the underclass means that the legal system, through its institutionalized selectivity regarding crime rates, reinforces and maintains the system of inequality.

By focusing on street crimes, the message is that these are the most serious of crimes. As we have noted, however, by far the most serious crimes in both property loss and violence to human life are corporate and political crimes, not street crimes. To reemphasize that point: in 1977 the Joint Economic Committee of Congress estimated that the total cost in 1976 of crimes against property (robbery, larceny, burglary, and auto theft), the crimes we are most worried about, totalled $4 billion. Yet, we tend to ignore those property crimes of the affluent—fraudulent bankruptcy, bribery, kickbacks, embezzlement, consumer fraud, and computer crime—which in 1976 totalled $44 billion, 11 times the amount for street crimes (cited in Doleschal, 1979, p. 5). The adherents of the radical perspective interpret the official emphasis on street crimes as a deliberate means to protect the interests of the wealthy and powerful. It is important to the advantaged to have society's social problems viewed by the populace as centered among the underclass. As long as this happens, the system that advantages some and disadvantages others goes unchallenged, and the efforts at crime control are directed at the "enemy" criminal class in our society. In the view of radical criminologists, then, crime is not a behavior found unusually among the lower classes, although street crime is. Street crime is a lower-class phenomenon because of restricted opportunities in society. From this view, both the street criminals and their victims are victims. The problem, then, is the structure of society that perpetuates inequality. The greatest danger to the social order is not crime by the underclass, but the crimes by the powerful (Dod, Platt, Schwendinger, Shank, and Takagi, 1976, p. 1).

The emphasis on street crimes and solutions aimed at changing criminals, and stricter penalties to punish them, also deflect attention away from the social conditions that promote criminality. Although we know that there are social and political factors that artificially inflate the rates of street crimes by members of the underclass, the fact remains that they are most likely to engage in these types of crimes. . . . Although President Reagan, in his war on crime, attacks the moral deterioration of America's families and schools, he ignores the structural reasons that account for the prevalence of street crimes by the underclass: slums, over-crowding, economic exploitation, unemployment, subordination, and institutional discrimination, all of which offer members of certain segments of society no reason for hope and no stake in the system. Advocates of the radical perspective argue that capitalism and the organization of the economy is the problem rather than the solution. As Jerome Skolnick has put it:

> For people who are fearful of crime (and which of us isn't?), the hard line rhetoric sounds appealing. It might even cut crime by a few percentage points, or it might not, depending upon how well the economy does in the next few years. The steadfast refusal of the Administration, however, to even consider the causes of crime may be politically safe, but it is hard to see how it will make our streets and homes significantly safer. (Skolnick, 1981, p. 3)

References

Associated Press (1980) (October 3).

Blumdell, W. E. (1976) "Equity Funding: I Did It for the Jollies." In D. Moffett (ed.), *Swindled.* New York: Dow-Jones Books, pp. 42–89.

Dirks, R. L., and L. Gross (1974) *The Great Wall Street Scandal.* New York: McGraw-Hill.

Dod, S., T. Platt, H. Schwendinger, G. Shank, and P. Takagi (1976) "The Politics of Street Crime," *Crime and Social Justice* 5 (Spring/Summer):1–4.

Doleschal, E. (1979) "Crime—Some Popular Beliefs," *Crime and Delinquency* 25 (January):1–8.

Gersten, A. (1981) "Underground Economy's Tunnels Spread," *Rocky Mountain News* (February 8):82, 85.

Hay, G. A., and D. Kelley (1974) "An Empirical Survey of Price Fixing Conspiracies," *The Journal of Law and Economics* 17 (April):13–38.

Quinney, R. (1979) *Criminology,* 2nd ed. Boston: Little, Brown.

Rankin, D. (1980) "Cheating Found on the Rise," *The New York Times* (April 22):D2.

Schultz, T. (1980) "How Millions Cheat (and Beat) the IRS," *Dallas Times Herald* (March 30):M1–M6.

Simon, D. R., and D. S. Eitzen (1982) *Elite Deviance.* Boston: Allyn & Bacon.

Skolnick, J. (1981) "The Attorney General's Crime Report Has a Familiar Sound," *Los Angeles Times* (August 23): Part IV, 3.

Sutherland, E. H., and D. R. Cressey (1974) *Criminology,* 9th ed. Philadelphia: Lippincott.

Sykes, G. M. (1978) *Criminology.* New York: Harcourt, Brace and Jovanovich.

Sykes, G. M. (1980) *The Future of Crime.* Washington, D.C.: U.S. Government Printing Office.

Tuky, C. (1981) "What the Underground Economy Costs You," *Money* 10 (April):74–77.

U.S. News & World Report (1979) "The Underground Economy," *U.S. News & World Report* (October 22):49–56.

CRIMINOGENESIS 1

The Criminal Personality

Stanton E. Samenow

Sixteen years ago, at age fifty-five, Dr. Samuel Yochelson gave up his psychiatric practice in Buffalo to move to Washington, D.C., where he began a second career in psychiatry. Saint Elizabeth's Hospital, a federal psychiatric facility, was designated as the site of the Program for the Investigation of Criminal Behavior, where Dr. Yochelson served as the project director. The National Institute of Mental Health is the parent organization of Saint Elizabeth's Hospital.

When Dr. Yochelson began the study, he had four objectives: (1) to understand the personality makeup of the criminal, (2) to develop techniques to alter the personality disorders productive of crime, (3) to shed light on aspects of legal responsibility, and (4) to develop techniques for preventing criminal behavior. Our intensive study has a broad base in that its two hundred fifty-five participants come from a variety of backgrounds. Half of the criminals were patients in the forensic psychiatry division at Saint Elizabeth's, and the rest came to us from the courts and community agencies. Blacks and whites, grade school dropouts and college graduates, criminals from affluent families and those from impoverished families, from the suburbs and from the inner city, from intact homes and from broken homes, were included in the study. In this study of hardcore criminals, almost every category of criminal offense is represented. We have studied the families of many of the criminals at length and have interviewed their friends and employers.

Our early focus was a search for psychological and sociological factors that we thought were causative of criminal behavior. In addition, such physical studies as electro-encephalograms, blood chemistry, steroid chemistry, and chromosomes were undertaken but yielded inconclusive results. Dr. Yochelson began taking histories, spending thirty hours with each criminal. In addition to studying patients at Saint Elizabeth's, he also provided them with group and individual therapy under conditions of privileged communication.

Dr. Yochelson approached the work using the concepts and techniques drawn primarily from psychoanalysis; however, although Dr. Yochelson's orientation in his thinking about human behavior was psychoanalytic, he was actually eclectic in the procedures that he used in his early work with criminals. Dr. Yochelson

Source: Stanton E. Samenow, "The Criminal Personality: New Concepts and New Procedures for Change." This article first appeared in *The Humanist* issue of September/October 1978 (pp. 16–19) and is reprinted by permission.

believed that if he could get to the roots of what causes criminal behavior, he could provide the criminal with insights that would help him to change. He found that early childhood fears, wishes, and conflicts, which were often difficult to obtain from neurotic patients, were easily recalled by the criminals. To his consternation, he found that after several years of intensive treatment, in which they gained many insights, his criminal patients were still committing crimes. However, the crimes were now more sophisticated, and the insights they had gained were being used to excuse what they did. Insight became "incite." In following the lead of the therapist, the criminal discovered even more people against whom he was incited. The criminal became skillful in seizing upon any adversity in his life and blaming it for his criminality. Traditional therapy became just one more criminal enterprise. The efforts to help him were exploited by the criminal to make himself look good and to substantiate his view of himself and of the outside world.

As Dr. Yochelson discovered that the criminal used psychological and sociological explanations to his own advantage, he became more sophisticated in his questioning techniques. Rather than accept the criminal's self-serving stories, he began to question the criminal's role in creating those adversities of which he complained. Hundreds of hours of probing and treatment revealed no factor or set of factors in the criminal's background as causative of crime.

It became evident that as early as the age of four, the criminal, as a child, was a different type of person. In most cases, his parents' way of life was totally different from his own. Furthermore, no matter what kind of community he lived in, his siblings and most of the other children lived within the expectations and rules of society. The criminal was an early social dropout and shunned most of the conventional activities and interests of his peers. He wanted a different kind of life. To make his mark on this world he had to do the forbidden. So he sought out and associated with other children like himself. His family was never sure where he was or whether he was telling the truth. Lying, fighting, and stealing began early in his life. He virtually compelled new attitudes and behavior on the part of others whose lives he regularly touched. The criminal as a child rejected his parents, responsible peers, and school—before he was ever rejected by them. These patterns remained consistent regardless of the environment in which the criminal was raised or the opportunities that he was offered. To live within the restraints of the responsible world was "sissy," "lame," or "weak." As a young child, the criminal made a series of choices, and criminal patterns were operative by age ten. By that time, he was adept at identifying and exploiting the weaknesses of others for his own purposes.

We had believed that the patients in Saint Elizabeth's Hospital's forensic psychiatry division were mentally ill. This was another misconception. Not one participant in our study was mentally ill, unless one wants to torture the definition of mental illness. However, approximately 5 percent experienced transient psychotic episodes in confinement. But during the psychosis, they had no desire to commit crimes. The content of their thinking was anti-crime. They believed that they were in touch with God and were appointed to wage the battle of good and evil, or there was some other highly religious or spiritual content to the psychosis. Each criminal was in contact with reality and totally in control of himself. To avoid a long period of imprisonment, each had sought admission to the hospital by malingering insanity. Once admitted to the hospital, the criminal tried to convince the staff that he was recovering so he could be released as quickly as possible. No differences existed in personality patterns between forensic psychiatry patients and those criminals whom we studied who had never been in Saint Elizabeth's.

The first five years' experience was sobering. It was difficult to give up our theories and therapeutic techniques. Yet, it became increasingly obvious that we had to do so if we were to have a chance of achieving our objective—changing the criminal. Procedures that were useful in the past when we helped responsible people with their problems in living were not effective with criminals.

Once we stopped asking why and ceased searching for causes, new vistas opened. We began to ask who the criminal was. The result was a new profile of the hard-core criminal, based on our analysis of his thinking as we studied and worked with him for thousands of hours. Ever since he or his family could remember, the career criminal lived a life different from responsible people. The criminal pursues power and control for his own sake, injuring others in the process. To be an ordinary, responsible citizen is, for him, to be a nonentity, a "nothing" in this world. Criminal excitement sustains his life. He commits thousands of arrestable crimes, although he is rarely, if ever, apprehended. (If apprehended, he more often than not avoids conviction and confinement.) Although tough and daring, the criminal has his sentimental side. He is tender with babies, gives money to charity, observes religious practices, writes poetry, composes music, and does good deeds for others. Occasionally, he becomes fed up with his way of life and genuinely wants to change. But eventually overriding all good intentions is the desire for excitement and a disdain for the boredom of a responsible life. The sentimental side of the criminal constitutes an important part of his self-concept. Every criminal, no matter how many thousands of crimes he has committed, believes that he is basically decent. To satisfy others, he acknowledges that he broke the law (he does know right from wrong), but within himself he believes that he is a good person, not a criminal.

We have identified a total of fifty-two thinking patterns that are present in all the criminals in our study. At the outset, we surmised that we would discover different profiles for criminals who had committed different kinds of crimes—property, sex, and assault. This turned out not to be the case. Criminals do differ in the types of crimes they commit and in their *modi operandi*. The man who uses stealth and cunning may avoid fights for fear of physical injury, but, more significantly, he looks down on the criminal who uses force, seeing him as crude. The criminal who uses "muscle" regards the conman as "weak" or "sissy." However, if one examines how criminals live their lives, how they regard themselves and the outside world, the similarities far outweigh the differences. Furthermore, we found that the criminal charged with a sexual offense has committed other types of crimes. The same is true of the others, although their police records do not reveal this. Both the white-collar criminal and the street criminal conduct their lives in the same way, even though their styles in crime suggest that they are different types of people. All criminals are habitual liars. They fail to put themselves in the place of others (unless it is to scheme a crime). They do not know what responsible decision making is, because they have prejudged most situations and find no need to ascertain facts and consider alternative courses of action. They believe that the world is their oyster and that people are pawns, while they have no obligation to anyone. In short, they share all fifty-two thinking patterns that we describe in our writings. Criminality goes far beyond mere arrestability. It pertains to the way in which a person thinks and lives his life.

The thinking patterns that we identify are not restricted to the hard-core criminal. They are present to a degree in all of us. For example, the basically responsible person occasionally gets angry. The consequences may be the alienation of others, a decrement in performance, and a lack of logic in thinking. However, for the criminal, anger is a way of life. Whenever the world does not accord him the status he thinks he deserves, he becomes angry. The criminal's reaction of anger may not be observable at the time (it is often to his advantage to conceal it), but it is expressed later when he exploits and injures another person during a crime. Anger in the responsible person and anger in the criminal result in different consequences.

There may well be larceny in every soul and lust in every heart, but most of us have mental processes to deter behavior that injures others. The criminal also has these processes to a degree. He knows that one day he may well get caught. He also has a conscience. However, he has the capacity to eliminate deterrent considerations from his thinking with almost surgical precision. His evaluation of himself depends on a never-ending series of thrusts for power and attempts to control other people. Considerations of getting caught or of conscience are overlooked in his pursuit of his immediate, self-aggrandizing objectives.

Our objective has been to do more than just describe the criminal. Efforts to combat crime have been rooted in the ideas concerned with what causes criminal behavior. Those who have believed that the environment is largely responsible have recommended both remedial and preventive measures to promote changes in the environment. Those who have hoped to alter the psychological makeup of the criminal have approached criminality using many of the techniques that they have found successful in treating other maladaptive behavior. Most important is to help him learn to live a responsible life.

The task of change is much greater than we had ever imagined. Changing the environment does not change the inner man. Slums are cleared, job opportunities are offered, schooling is provided, but crime remains. More of our criminals had jobs than were unemployed. But providing a criminal with job skills and then a job results in a criminal with a job rather than a criminal without a job. He remains a criminal. He may utilize his job for his own gain, commit crimes on the job, or use his job as a mantle of respectability, which leaves him free to live a secret life of crime outside his work. Conventional psychological approaches have failed. After sixteen years of conducting our studies, we do not know what causes crime. However, many conditions are treated without knowing what the causes are, including childhood autism, schizophrenia, some forms of depression, and a variety of physical illnesses. We have found that it is possible to help career criminals become responsible citizens without knowing what causes crime. What is required is to change the thinking patterns of a lifetime. The criminal must abandon his lifelong patterns of thought and action and learn about a way of life that he has heretofore spurned. He must be *habilitated*, not rehabilitated.

In the process of change, we function more as educators than as psychotherapists. As agents of change, we teach the criminal the thinking patterns that are necessary in order to live responsibly. Responsibility is a word that either has too concrete a meaning or is used so vaguely that it has no operational meaning. We teach the criminal specific corrective concepts that are mandatory if one is to live constructively and with integrity. The thinking patterns for responsible living are learned by most people early in life, but they are brand new to the criminal.

The criminal has feelings, but these are not the currency of our transactions, because he can justify anything by talking about feelings. Thinking remains the focus. Feelings change after thinking changes.

We assume a moralistic stance in our work; the criminal has the capacity to choose. Indeed, he has made choices all his life. He is not a victim. If he chooses to enter our program, he has to pay a price—he has to endure the absence of criminal excitement and the difficulties inherent in resolving a new set of problems. Instead of relieving fear and guilt, we teach the criminal that fear is a necessary guide to responsible living. We teach him that he must become more guilty rather than less guilty. From the time of our initial meeting, which lasts three hours, we hold up a mirror to him and, in a calm, persistent manner, try to capitalize on and intensify whatever self-disgust is present. We approach him initially at a time when he has failed, even as a criminal. He has been arrested and is about to be confined or is already in confinement. We then present his options—suicide, more crime and its consequences, or change.

This program is successful with a minority of hard-core criminals. Nevertheless, if one believes that society should help those who will avail themselves of it, this program offers a path. To change one hard-core criminal means saving society from incalculable injury. The criminal's "reward" from this program comes only as he puts what he learns into practice and has experiences that are totally new. We do not attempt to raise his self-esteem by expressing our approval when he makes some changes. Rather, as he becomes increasingly self-critical and implements the correctives that he is taught, he develops self-respect based on achievement in the responsible world. We have succeeded in changing some hard-core criminals and have followed them for years after they have been in the daily intensive part of this yearlong program.

How well any new study is received depends in part on scientific criteria of evaluation. However, in the area of a social problem where controversy is heated, the pendulum of public opinion is often a determinant in response to new findings. In the 1960s, an era of upheaval and change, it was widely thought that crime was a product of adverse social conditions, whether it was a specific feature of life, such as unemployment, or a general condition, such as a "sick society." The 1967 report by the President's Commission on Law Enforcement and Administration of Justice stated:

> In a sense, social and economic conditions "cause" crime. Crime flourishes, and always has flourished, in city slums, those neighborhoods where overcrowding, economic deprivation, social disruption, and racial discrimination are endemic.

The suburban life was also viewed as a contributor to the breeding of emotional poverty and neglect, because of the value placed on materialism and the competition for status. Unemployment, the quality of education, racial discrimination, and violence in the media were among other environmental factors seen as causing crime. Ramsey Clark, the attorney general during part of the 1960s, maintained that America's "national character and condition . . . create capabilities for crime."

In the 1960s many hoped that crime could be reduced through changing the environment.

> And so it is probable that crime will continue to increase during this period, unless there are drastic changes in general social and economic conditions and in the effectiveness of the criminal justice system (President's Commission, 1967, p. 5).

Programs were launched to provide people with better living conditions and greater opportunities. These programs had a variety of objectives—a major one was the reduction of crime. But by the beginning of the next decade, the disillusionment became apparent. Despite the expenditure of vast sums of money, crime continued to be as major a national problem as ever, and a wave of terrorism in the form of skyjackings, kidnapings, and taking hostages was mounting.

People from many walks of life looked to professionals in the mental health field to treat criminals. Community programs, forensic psychiatry services, and counseling in penal institutions were prolific during the 1960s. Techniques that had been successful with noncriminals were applied to criminals. There was disillusionment with psychological approaches comparable to the sociological remedies. In appraising psychotherapeutic efforts with criminals, psychologist Robert Hare observed in 1970:

> With few exceptions, the traditional forms of psychotherapy, including psychoanalysis, group therapy, client-centered therapy, and psychodrama, have proved ineffective in the treatment of psychopathy. Nor have the biological therapies, including psychosurgery, electroshock therapy, and the use of various drugs, fared much better.

A major obstacle to formulating effective programs and policies has been the fact that program planners have had to function in an atmosphere of crisis. They have needed a great deal more information than they have had available to them. In 1967, J. Edgar Hoover stated in his introduction to the *Uniform Crime Reports* for 1966: "One vital need remains clearly apparent; namely, meaningful information for sound decision making." Programs designed to change the environment did not alter what a criminal wanted out of life or how he functioned in life. Traditional psychological programs designed to reach the inner man were of limited value. Society became, in a sense, more conservative in its approach to criminals. By the mid-1970s, rehabilitation as an objective was dying. People did not know how to reform criminals and were becoming increasingly willing to admit it. There was a loud call for more stringent law enforcement and for stricter penalties; however, what policymakers, lawyers, and those who worked with criminals have lacked is a detailed knowledge of who the criminal is. Our profile of the criminal personality has been of interest because no other study that we are aware of has reported the results of tens of thousands of hours spent studying the criminal's pattern of thinking. The information we provide is being regarded by some as a resource for the formulation of social policy on how society should deal with individual criminals.

At this time our program has not been replicated by others. Clearly, it is not a comprehensive solution to the crime problem, but it does present another alternative and a new set of considerations. The findings are at odds with the current thinking about crime and criminals, and we are not among the modern-day "conservative criminologists" who simply urge that criminals should be punished. We are critical of the conventional awareness and the procedures growing out of them.

The Poverty of Criminals and the Crime of Poverty
Jeffrey Reiman

Criminal justice is a very visible part of the American scene. As fact and fiction, countless images of crime and the struggle against it assail our senses daily, even hourly. In every newspaper, in every TV or radio newscast, there is at least one criminal justice story and often more. It is as if we live in an embattled city, besieged by the forces of crime and bravely defended by the forces of the law, and as we go about our daily tasks, we are always conscious of the war raging not very far away; newspapers bring us daily and newscasts bring us hourly reports from the "front." Between reports, we are vividly reminded of the stakes and the desperateness of the battle by fictionalized portrayals of the struggle between the forces of the law and the breakers of the law. There is scarcely an hour on television without some dramatization of the struggle against crime (In the *TV Guide* for the week of February 19 through February 25, 1983, I counted *125* hours of programming in which the struggle against crime is featured. Keep in mind that there are only 168 hours in a week, and TV stations do not broadcast all around the clock. Also I counted only the regular channels serving the metropolitan Washington, D.C. area and did not include cable or other limited access channels. Remember, too, that 98 percent of American homes have televisions, and it is estimated that they are on an average of six hours a day!)[1] If we add to this the news accounts, the panel discussions, and the political speeches about crime, there can be no doubt that as fact or fantasy or both, criminal justice is vividly present in the imaginations of most Americans.

This is no accident. Everyone can relate to criminal justice in personal and emotional terms. Everyone has some fear of crime, and . . . just about everyone has committed some. And everyone knows the primitive satisfaction of seeing justice done and the evildoers served up their just desserts. Furthermore, in reality or in fiction, criminal justice is naturally dramatic. It contains the acts of courage and cunning, the high risks and high stakes, and the life-and-death struggle between good and evil that are missing from the routine lives so many of us lead. To identify with the struggle against crime is to expand one's experience vicariously to include the danger, the suspense, the triumphs, the meaningfulness—in a word, the

Source: Jeffrey Reiman, "The Poverty of Criminals and the Crime of Poverty" (pp. 116–128). Reprinted with permission of Macmillan Publishing Company from *The Rich Get Richer and the Poor Get Prison* by Jeffrey Reiman. (New York: Macmillan 1984).

drama—often missing in ordinary life. How else can we explain the seemingly bottomless appetite Americans have for the endless repetition, in only slightly altered form, of the same theme: the struggle of the forces of law against the forces of crime? Criminal justice has a firm grip on the imaginations of Americans and is thus in a unique position to convey a message to Americans and to convey it with drama and with conviction.

Let us now look at this message in detail. Our task falls naturally into two parts. There is an ideological message, a message supportive of the status quo, built into any criminal justice system by its very nature. Even if the criminal justice system were not failing, even if it were not biased against the poor, it would still—by its very nature—broadcast a message supportive of established institutions. This is *the implicit ideology of criminal justice.* Beyond this, there is an additional ideological message conveyed by the *failure* of the system and by its *biased* concentration on the poor. I call this the *bonus of bias.*

The Implicit Ideology of Criminal Justice

Any criminal justice system like ours conveys a subtle, yet powerful message in support of established institutions. It does this for two interconnected reasons: first, because it concentrates on *individual* wrongdoers. This means that *it diverts our attention away from our institutions, away from consideration of whether our institutions themselves are wrong or unjust or indeed "criminal."*

Second, the criminal law is put forth as the *minimum neutral ground rules* for any social living. We are taught that no society can exist without rules against theft and violence, and thus the criminal law is put forth as politically neutral, as the minimum requirements for *any* society, as the minimum obligations that any individual owes his fellows to make social life of any decent sort possible. Thus, it not only diverts our attention away from the possible injustice of our social institutions, but *the criminal law bestows upon those institutions the mantle of its own neutrality.* Since the criminal law protects the established institutions (e.g., the prevailing economic arrangements are protected by laws against theft, etc.), attacks on those established institutions become equivalent to violations of the minimum requirements for any social life at all. In effect, the criminal law enshrines the established institutions as equivalent to the minimum requirements for *any* decent social existence—and it brands the individual who attacks those institutions as one who has declared war on *all* organized society and who must therefore be met with the weapons of war.

This is the powerful magic of criminal justice. By virtue of its focus on *individual* criminals, it diverts us from the evils of the *social* order. By virtue of its presumed neutrality, it transforms the established social (and economic) order from being merely *one* form of society open to critical comparison with others into *the* conditions of *any* social order and thus immune from criticism. Let us look more closely at this process.

What is the effect of focusing on individual guilt? Not only does this divert our attention from the possible evils in our institutions, but it puts forth half the problem of justice as if it were the *whole* problem. To focus on individual guilt is to ask whether or not the individual citizen has fulfilled his obligations to his fellow citizens. *It is to look away from the issue of whether his fellow citizens have fulfilled their obligations to him.* To look only at individual responsibility is to look away from social responsibility. To look only at individual criminality is to close one's eyes to social injustice and to close one's ears to the question of whether our social institutions have exploited or violated the individual. *Justice is a two-way street—but criminal justice is a one-way street.* Individuals owe obligations to their fellow citizens because their fellow citizens owe obligations to them. Criminal justice focuses on the first and looks away from the second. *Thus, by focusing on individual responsibility for crime, the criminal justice system literally acquits the existing social order of any charge of injustice!*

This is an extremely important bit of ideological alchemy. It stems from the fact that the same act can be criminal or not, unjust or just, depending on the conditions in which it takes place. Killing someone is ordinarily a crime. But if it is in self-defense or to stop a deadly crime, it is not. Taking property by force is usually a crime. But if the taking is just retrieving what has been stolen, then no crime has been committed. Acts of violence are ordinarily crimes. But if the violence is provoked by the threat of violence or by oppressive conditions, then, like the Boston Tea Party, what might ordinarily be called criminal is celebrated as just. This means that when we call an act a crime *we are also making an implicit judgment about the conditions in response to which it takes place.* When we call an act a crime, we are saying that the conditions in which it occurs are not themselves criminal or deadly or oppressive or so unjust as to make an extreme response reasonable or justified, that is, to make such a response noncriminal. This means that when the system holds an individual responsible for a crime, *it implicitly conveys the message that the social conditions in which the crime occurred are not responsible for the crime*, that they are not so unjust as to make a violent response to them excusable.

Judges are prone to hold that an individual's responsibility for a violent crime is diminished if it was provoked by something that might lead a "reasonable man" to respond violently and that criminal responsibility is eliminated if the act was in response to conditions so intolerable that any "reasonable man" would have been likely to respond in the same way. In this vein, the law acquits those who kill or injure in self-defense and treats lightly those who commit a crime when confronted with extreme provocation. The law treats leniently the man who kills his wife's lover and the woman who kills her brutal husband, even when neither has acted directly in self-defense. By this logic, when we hold an individual completely responsible for a crime, we are saying that the conditions in which it occurred are such that a "reasonable man" should find them tolerable. In other words, by focusing on individual responsibility for crimes, *the criminal justice system broadcasts the message that the social order itself is reasonable and not intolerably unjust.*

Thus the criminal justice system focuses moral condemnation on individuals and deflects it away from the social order that may have either violated the individual's rights or dignity or literally pushed him or her to the brink of crime. This not only serves to carry the message that our social institutions are not in need of fundamental questioning, but it further suggests that the justice of our institutions is obvious, not to be doubted. Indeed, since it is deviations from these institutions that are crimes, the established institutions become the implicit standard of justice from which criminal deviations are measured.

This leads to the second way in which a criminal justice system always conveys an implicit ideology. It arises from the presumption that the criminal law is nothing but the politically neutral minimum requirements of any decent social life. What is the consequence of this?

Obviously, as already suggested, this presumption transforms the prevailing social order into justice incarnate and all violations of the prevailing order into injustice incarnate. This process is so obvious that it may be easily missed.

Consider, for example, the law against theft. It does indeed seem to be one of the minimum requirements of social living. As long as there is scarcity, any society— capitalist or socialist—will need rules preventing individuals from taking what does not belong to them. But the law against theft is more: It is a law against stealing what individuals *presently* own. *Such a law has the effect of making present property relations a part of the criminal law.*

Since stealing is a violation of law, this means that present property relations become the implicit standard of justice against which criminal deviations are measured. Since criminal law is thought of as the minimum requirements of any social life, this means that present property relations become equivalent to the minimum requirements of *any* social life. And the criminal who would alter the present property relations becomes nothing less than someone who is declaring war on all organized society. The question of whether this "war" is provoked by the injustice or brutality of the society is swept aside. Indeed, this suggests yet another way in which the criminal justice system conveys an ideological message in support of the established society.

Not only does the criminal justice system acquit the social order of any charge of injustice, it specifically cloaks the society's own crime-producing tendencies. I have already observed that by blaming the individual for a crime, the society is acquitted of the charge of injustice. I would like to go further now and argue that by blaming the individual for a crime, the society is acquitted of the charge of *complicity* in that crime. This is a point worth developing, since many observers have maintained that modern competitive societies such as our own have structural features that tend to generate crime. Thus, holding the individual responsible for his or her crime serves the function of taking the rest of society off the hook for their role in sustaining and benefiting from social arrangements that produce crime. Let us take a brief detour to look more closely at this process.

Cloward and Ohlin argue in their book *Delinquency and Opportunity*[2] that much crime is the result of the discrepancy between social goals and the legitimate opportunities available for achieving them. Simply put, in our society everyone is encouraged to be a success, but the avenues to success are open only to some. The conventional wisdom of our free enterprise democracy is that anyone can be a success if he or she has the talent and the ambition. Thus, if one is not a success, it is because of one's own shortcomings: laziness or lack of ability or both. On the other hand, opportunities to achieve success are not equally open to all. Access to the best schools and the best jobs is effectively closed to all but a few of the poor and becomes more available only as one goes up the economic ladder. The result is that many are called but few are chosen. And many who have taken the bait and accepted the belief in the importance of success and the belief that achieving success is a result of individual ability must cope with the feelings of frustration and failure that result when they find the avenues to success closed. Cloward and Ohlin argue that one method of coping with these stresses is to develop alternative avenues to success. Crime is such an alternative avenue. Crime is a means by which people who believe in the American dream pursue it when they find the traditional routes barred. Indeed, it is plain to see that the goals pursued by most criminals are as American as apple pie. I suspect that one of the reasons that American movie-goers enjoy gangster films—movies in which gangsters such as Al Capone, Bonnie and Clyde, or Butch Cassidy and the Sundance Kid are the heroes, as distinct from police and detective films whose heroes are defenders of the law—is that even where they deplore the hero's methods, they identify with his or her notion of success, since it is theirs as well, and respect the courage and cunning displayed in achieving that success.

It is important to note that the discrepancy between success goals and legitimate opportunities in America is not an aberration. It is a structural feature of modern competitive industrialized society, a feature from which many benefits flow. Cloward and Ohlin write that

> a crucial problem in the industrial world . . . is to locate and train the most talented persons in every generation, irrespective of the vicissitudes of birth, to occupy technical work roles. . . . Since we cannot know in advance who can best fulfill the requirements of the various occupational roles, the matter is presumably settled through the process of competition. But how can men throughout the social order be motivated to participate in this competition? . . .
>
> One of the ways in which the industrial society attempts to solve this problem is by defining success-goals as potentially accessible to all, regardless of race, creed, or socioeconomic position.[3]

But since these universal goals are urged to encourage a competition to weed out the best, there are necessarily fewer openings than seekers. And since those who achieve success are in a particularly good position to exploit their success to make access for their own children easier, the competition is rigged to work in favor of the middle and upper classes. As a result, "many lower-class persons . . . are the victims of a contradiction between the goals toward which they have been led to orient themselves and socially structured means of striving for these goals."[4]

[The poor] experience desperation born of the certainty that their position in the economic structure is relatively fixed and immutable—a desperation made all the more poignant by their exposure to a cultural ideology in which failure to orient oneself upward is regarded as a moral defect and failure to become mobile as proof of it.[5]

The outcome is predictable. "Under these conditions, there is an acute pressure to depart from institutional norms and to adopt illegitimate alternatives."[6]

In brief, this means that the very way in which our society is structured to draw out the talents and energies that go into producing our high standard of living has a costly side effect: It produces crime. But by holding individuals responsible for this crime, those who enjoy that high standard of living can have their cake and eat it. They can reap the benefits of the competition for success and escape the responsibility of paying for the costs of that competition. By holding the poor crook legally and morally guilty, the rest of society not only passes the costs of competition on to the poor, but they effectively deny that they (the affluent) are the beneficiaries of an economic system that exacts such a high toll in frustration and suffering.

Willem Bonger, the Dutch Marxist criminologist, maintained that competitive capitalism produces egotistic motives and undermines compassion for the misfortunes of others and thus makes human beings literally *more capable of crime*—more capable of preying on their fellows without moral inhibition or remorse—than earlier cultures that emphasized cooperation rather than competition.[7] Here again, the criminal justice system relieves those who benefit from the American economic system of the costs of that system. By holding criminals morally and individually responsible for their crimes, we can forget that the motives that lead to crime—the drive for success at any cost, linked with the beliefs that success means outdoing others and that violence is an acceptable way of achieving one's goals—are the *same motives* that powered the drive across the American continent and that continue to fuel the engine of America's prosperity.

David Gordon, a contemporary political economist, maintains "that nearly all crimes in capitalist societies represent perfectly *rational* responses to the structure of institutions upon which capitalist societies are based."[8] That is, like Bonger, Gordon believes that capitalism tends to provoke crime in all economic strata. This is so because most crime is motivated by a desire for property or money and is an understandable way of coping with the pressures of inequality, competition, and insecurity, all of which are essential ingredients of capitalism. Capitalism depends, Gordon writes,

on basically competitive forms of social and economic interaction and upon substantial inequalities in the allocation of social resources. Without inequalities, it would be much more difficult to induce workers to work in alienating environments. Without competition and a competitive ideology, workers might not be inclined to struggle to improve their relative income and status in society by working harder. Finally, although rights of property are protected, capitalist societies do not guarantee economic security to most of their individual members. Individuals must fend for themselves, finding the best available opportunities to provide for themselves and their families. . . . Driven by the fear of economic insecurity and by a competitive desire to gain some of the goods unequally distributed throughout the society, many individuals will eventually become "criminals."[9]

To the extent that a society makes crime a reasonable alternative for a large number of its members from all classes, that society is itself not very reasonably or humanely organized and bears some degree of responsibility for the crime it encourages. Since the criminal law is put forth as the minimum requirements that can be expected of any "reasonable man," its enforcement amounts to a denial of the real nature of the social order to which Gordon and the others point. Here again, by blaming the individual criminal, the criminal justice system serves implicitly but dramatically to acquit the society of its criminality.

The Bonus of Bias

We now consider the additional ideological bonus that is derived from the criminal justice system's bias against the poor. This bonus is a product of the association of crime and poverty in the popular mind. This association, the merging of the "criminal classes" and the "lower classes" into the "dangerous classes," was not invented in America. The word "villain" is derived from the Latin *villanus,* which means a farm servant. And the term "villein" was used in feudal England to refer to a serf who farmed the land of a great lord and who was literally owned by that lord.[10] In this respect, our present criminal justice system is heir to a long tradition.

The value of this association was already seen when we explored the "average citizen's" concept of the Typical Criminal and the Typical Crime. It is quite obvious that throughout the great mass of middle America, far more fear and hostility are directed toward the predatory acts of the poor than the rich. Compare the fate of politicians in recent history who call for tax reform, income redistribution, prosecution of corporate crime, and any sort of regulation of business that would make it better serve American social goals with that of politicians who erect their platform on a call for "law and order," more police, less limits on police power, and stiffer prison sentences for criminals—and consider this in light of what we have already seen about the real dangers posed by corporate crime and "business-as-usual."

It seems clear that Americans have been systematically deceived as to what are the greatest dangers to their lives, limbs and possessions. The very persistence with which the system functions to apprehend and punish poor crooks and ignore or slap on the wrist equally or more dangerous individuals is testimony to the sticking power of this deception. That Americans continue to tolerate the gentle treatment meted out to white-collar criminals, corporate price fixers, industrial polluters, and political-influence peddlers while voting in droves to lock up more poor people faster and longer indicates the degree to which they harbor illusions as to who most threatens them. It is perhaps also part of the explanation for the continued dismal failure of class-based politics in America. American workers rarely seem able to forget their differences and unite to defend their shared interests against the rich whose wealth they produce. Ethnic divisions serve this divisive function well, but undoubtedly the vivid portrayal of the poor—and, of course, the blacks—as hovering birds of prey waiting for the opportunity to snatch away the workers' meager gains serves also to deflect opposition away from the upper classes. A politician who promises to keep working class communities free of blacks and their prisons full of them can get their votes even if the major portion of his or her policies amount to continuation of favored treatment of the rich at their expense.

The most important "bonus" derived from the identification of crime and poverty is that it paints the picture that the threat to decent middle Americans comes from those below them on the economic ladder, not those above. For this to happen the system must not only identify crime and poverty, but *it must also fail to reduce crime so that it remains a real threat*. By doing this, it deflects the fear and discontent of middle Americans, and their possible opposition, away from the wealthy. The two politicians who most clearly gave voice to the discontent of middle Americans in the post-World War II period were George Wallace and Spiro Agnew. Is it any accident that their politics was extremely conservative and their anger reserved for the poor (the welfare chiselers) and the criminal (the targets of law and order)?

There are other bonuses as well. For instance, if the criminal justice system functions to send out a message that bestows legitimacy on present property relations, the dramatic impact is greatly enhanced if the violator of the present arrangements is without property. In other words, the crimes of the well-to-do "redistribute" property among the haves. In that sense, they do not pose a symbolic challenge to the larger system in which some have much and many have little or nothing. If the criminal threat can be portrayed as coming from the poor, then the punishment of the poor criminal becomes a morality play in which the sanctity and legitimacy of the system in which some have plenty and others have little or nothing is dramatically affirmed. It matters little who the poor criminals really victimize. What counts is that middle Americans come to fear that those poor criminals are out to steal what they own.

There is yet another bonus for the powerful in America, produced by the identification of crime and poverty. It might be thought that the identification of crime and poverty would produce sympathy for the criminals. My suspicion is that it produces or at least reinforces the reverse: *hostility toward the poor.*

Indeed, there is little evidence that Americans are very sympathetic to poor criminals. Very few Americans believe poverty to be a cause of crime (6 percent of those questioned in a 1981 survey, although 21 percent thought unemployment was a cause).[11] Other surveys find that most Americans believe that the police should be tougher than they are now in dealing with crime (83 percent of those

questioned in a 1972 survey); that courts do not deal harshly enough with criminals (83 percent of those questioned in a 1980 survey)[12]; that a majority of Americans would like to see the death penalty for convicted murderers (67 percent of
those questioned in 1980)[13]; and that most would be more likely to vote for a candidate who advocated tougher sentences for lawbreakers (83 percent of those questioned in a 1972 survey).[14] Indeed, the experience of Watergate seems to suggest
that sympathy for criminals begins to flower only when we approach the higher
reaches of the ladder of wealth and power. For some poor ghetto youth who robs a
liquor store, five years in the slammer is our idea of tempering justice with mercy.
When a handful of public officials try to walk off with the U.S. Constitution, a few
months in a minimum security prison will suffice. If the public official is high
enough, resignation from office and public disgrace tempered with a $60,000-a-
year pension is punishment enough.

My view is that since the criminal justice system, in fact and fiction, deals with
individual legal and *moral guilt,* the association of crime with poverty does not
mitigate the image of individual moral responsibility for crime, the image that
crime is the result of an individual's poor character. My suspicion is that it does the
reverse: It generates the association of poverty and individual moral failing and
thus *the belief that poverty itself is a sign of poor or weak character.* The clearest evidence that Americans hold this belief is to be found in the fact that attempts to aid
the poor are regarded as acts of charity rather than as acts of justice. Our welfare
system has all the demeaning attributes of an institution designed to give handouts
to the undeserving and none of the dignity of an institution designed to make good
on our responsibilities to our fellow human beings. If we acknowledged the degree
to which our economic and social institutions themselves breed poverty, we would
have to recognize our own responsibilities toward the poor. If we can convince ourselves that the poor are poor because of their own shortcomings, particularly moral
shortcomings like incontinence and indolence, then we need acknowledge no such
responsibility to the poor. Indeed, we can go further and pat ourselves on the back
for our generosity in handing out the little that we do, and of course, we can make
our recipients go through all the indignities that mark them as the undeserving
objects of our benevolence. By and large, this has been the way in which Americans
have dealt with their poor.[15] It is a way that enables us to avoid asking the question
of why the richest nation in the world continues to produce massive poverty. It is
my view that this conception of the poor is subtly conveyed by the way our criminal
justice system functions.

Obviously, no ideological message could be more supportive of the present
social and economic order than this. It suggests that poverty is a sign of individual
failing, not a symptom of social or economic injustice. It tells us loud and clear that
massive poverty in the midst of abundance is not a sign pointing toward the need
for fundamental changes in our social and economic institutions. It suggests that
the poor are poor because they deserve to be poor, or at least because they lack the
strength of character to overcome poverty. When the poor are seen to be poor in
character, then economic poverty coincides with moral poverty and the economic

order coincides with the moral order. As if a divine hand guided its workings, capitalism leads to everyone getting what they morally deserve!

If this association takes root, then when the poor individual is found guilty of a crime, the criminal justice system acquits the society of its responsibility not only for crime *but for poverty as well.*

With this, the ideological message of criminal justice is complete. The poor rather than the rich are seen as the enemies of the majority of decent middle Americans. Our social and economic institutions are held to be responsible for neither crime nor poverty and thus are in need of no fundamental questioning or reform. The poor are poor because they are poor of character. The economic order and the moral order are one. And to the extent that this message sinks in, the wealthy can rest easily—even if they cannot sleep the sleep of the just.

Thus, we can understand why the criminal justice system creates the image of crime as the work of the poor and fails to reduce it so that the threat of crime remains real and credible. The result is ideological alchemy of the highest order. The poor are seen as the real threat to decent society. The ultimate sanctions of criminal justice dramatically sanctify the present social and economic order, and *the poverty of criminals makes poverty itself an individual moral crime!*

Such are the ideological fruits of a losing war against crime whose distorted image is reflected in the criminal justice carnival mirror and widely broadcast to reach the minds and imaginations of America.

Notes

1. A report to the Federal Communications Commission estimates that by the time the average American child reaches age 14, he or she has seen 13,000 human beings killed by violence on television. Although a few of these are probably killed by science fiction monsters, the figure still suggests that the extent of the impact of the televised portrayal of crime and the struggle against it, on the imaginations of Americans, is nothing short of astounding. See Eve Merriam, "We're Teaching Our Children that Violence is Fun," in *Violence: An Element of American Life*, eds., K. Taylor and F. Soady, Jr. (Boston: Holbrook Press, 1972), p. 155. For a list of the 20 police programs (which does not include detective programs and other shows in which the fight against crime is the theme) aired on ABC, CBS, and NBC, the three major networks, see Center for Research on Criminal Justice, *The Iron Fist*

and the Velvet Glove: An Analysis of the U.S. Police, pp. 194–195.

2. Richard A. Cloward and Lloyd E. Ohlin, *Delinquency and Opportunity: A Theory of Delinquent Gangs* (New York: The Free Press, 1960), esp. pp. 77–107.

3. Ibid., p. 81.

4. Ibid., p. 105.

5. Ibid., p. 107.

6. Ibid., p. 105.

7. Willem Bonger, *Criminality and Economic Conditions*, abridged and with an introduction by Austin T. Turk (Bloomington, Ind.: Indiana University Press, 1969), pp. 7–12, 40–47. Willem Adriaan Bonger was born in Holland in 1876 and died by his own hand in 1940 rather than submit to the Nazis. His *Criminalité et conditions économiques* first appeared in 1905. It was translated into English and published in the United States in 1916. Ibid., pp. 3–4.

8. David M. Gordon, "Capitalism, Class and Crime in America," *Crime and Delinquency* (April 1973), p. 174.

9. Ibid., p. 174.

10. William and Mary Morris, *Dictionary of Word and Phrase Origins*, II (New York: Harper and Row, 1967), p. 282.

11. *Sourcebook-1981*, p. 192.

12. Ibid., p. 205.

13. Ibid., pp. 210–211.

14. *Sourcebook-1974*, pp. 203, 204, 223, 207; see also p. 177.

15. Historical documentation of this can be found in David J. Rothman, *The Discovery of the Asylum: Social Order and Disorder in the New Republic* (Boston: Little, Brown, 1971); and in Frances Fox Piven and Richard A. Cloward, *Regulating the Poor: The Functions of Public Welfare* (New York: Pantheon, 1971), which carries the analysis up to the present.

Lower Class Culture as a Generating Milieu of Gang Delinquency

Walter Miller

The etiology of delinquency has long been a controversial issue, and is particularly so at present. As new frames of reference for explaining human behavior have been added to traditional theories, some authors have adopted the practice of citing the major postulates of each school of thought as they pertain to delinquency, and going on to state that causality must be conceived in terms of the dynamic interaction of a complex combination of variables on many levels. The major sets of etiological factors currently adduced to explain delinquency are, in simplified terms, the physiological (delinquency results from organic pathology), the psychodynamic (delinquency is a "behavioral disorder" resulting primarily from emotional disturbance generated by a defective mother-child relationship), and the environmental (delinquency is the product of disruptive forces, "disorganization," in the actor's physical or social environment).

This paper selects one particular kind of "delinquency"[1] —law-violating acts committed by members of adolescent street corner groups in lower class communities—and attempts to show that the dominant component of motivation underlying these acts consists in a directed attempt by the actor to adhere to forms of behavior, and to achieve standards of value as they are defined within that community. It takes as a premise that the motivation of behavior in this situation can be approached most productively by attempting to understand the nature of cultural forces impinging on the acting individual as they are perceived *by the actor himself*—although by no means only that segment of these forces of which the actor is consciously aware—rather than as they are perceived and evaluated from the reference position of another cultural system. In the case of "gang" delin-

---

[1]The complex issues involved in deriving a definition of "delinquency" cannot be discussed here. The term "delinquent" is used in this paper to characterize behavior or acts committed by individuals within specified age limits which if known to official authorities could result in legal action. The concept of a "delinquent" individual has little or no utility in the approach used here; rather, specified types of *acts* which may be committed rarely or frequently by few or many individuals are characterized as "delinquent."

Source: Walter Miller, "Lower Class Culture as a Generating Milieu of Gang Delinquency," *Journal of Social Issues* 14 (1958):5–19. Copyright © 1958 by The Society for the Psychological Study of Social Issues. Reprinted with permission.

quency, the cultural system which exerts the most direct influence on behavior is that of the lower class community itself—a long-established, distinctively patterned tradition with an integrity of its own—rather than a so-called "delinquent subculture" which has arisen through conflict with middle class culture and is oriented to the deliberate violation of middle class norms.

The bulk of the substantive data on which the following material is based was collected in connection with a service-research project in the control of gang delinquency. During the service aspect of the project, which lasted for three years, seven trained social workers maintained contact with twenty-one corner group units in a "slum" district of a large eastern city for periods of time ranging from ten to thirty months. Groups were Negro and white, male and female, and in early, middle, and late adolescence. Over eight thousand pages of direct observational data on behavior patterns of group members and other community residents were collected; almost daily contact was maintained for a total time period of about thirteen worker years. Data include workers' contact reports, participant observation reports by the writer—a cultural anthropologist—and direct tape recordings of group activities and discussions.[2]

Focal Concerns of Lower Class Culture

There is a substantial segment of present-day American society whose way of life, values, and characteristic patterns of behavior are the product of a distinctive cultural system which may be termed "lower class." Evidence indicates that this cultural system is becoming increasingly distinctive, and that the size of the group which shares this tradition is increasing.[3] The lower class way of life, in common with that of all distinctive cultural groups, is characterized by a set of focal concerns—areas or issues which command widespread and persistent attention and a high degree of emotional involvement. The specific concerns cited here, while by no means confined to the American lower classes, constitute a distinctive *patterning* of concerns which differs significantly, both in rank order and weight-

---

[2]A three year research project is being financed under National Institutes of Health Grant M–1414, and administered through the Boston University School of Social Work. The primary research effort has subjected all collected material to a uniform data-coding process. All information bearing on some seventy areas of behavior (behavior in reference to school, police, theft, assault, sex, collective athletics, etc.) is extracted from the records, recorded on coded data cards, and filed under relevant categories. Analysis of these data aims to ascertain the actual nature of customary behavior in these areas, and the extent to which the social work effort was able to effect behavioral changes.

[3]Between 40 and 60 per cent of all Americans are directly influenced by lower class culture, with about 15 per cent, or twenty-five million, comprising the "hard core" lower class group—defined primarily by its use of the "female-based" household as the basic form of child-rearing unit and of the "serial monogamy" mating pattern as the primary form of marriage. The term "lower class culture" as used here refers most specifically to the way of life of the "hard core" group; systematic research in this area would probably reveal at least four to six major subtypes of lower class culture, for some of which the "concerns" presented here would be differently weighted, especially for those subtypes in which "law-abiding" behavior has a high overt valuation. It is impossible within the compass of this short paper to make the finer intracultural distinctions which a more accurate presentation would require.

ing from that of American middle class culture. The following chart presents a highly schematic and simplified listing of six of the major concerns of lower class culture. Each is conceived as a "dimension" within which a fairly wide and varied range of alternative behavior patterns may be followed by different individuals under different situations. They are listed roughly in order of the degree of *explicit* attention accorded each, and, in this sense represent a weighted ranking of concerns. The "perceived alternatives" represent polar positions which define certain parameters within each dimension. As will be explained in more detail, it is necessary in relating the influence of these "concerns" to the motivation of delinquent behavior to specify *which* of its aspects is oriented to, whether orientation is *overt* or *covert*, *positive* (conforming to or seeking the aspect), or *negative* (rejecting or seeking to avoid the aspect).

The concept "focal concern" is used here in preference to the concept "value" for several interrelated reasons: (1) It is more readily derivable from direct field observation. (2) It is descriptively neutral—permitting independent consideration of positive and negative valences as varying under different conditions, whereas "value" carries a built-in positive valence. (3) It makes possible more refined analysis of subcultural differences, since it reflects actual behavior, whereas "value" tends to wash out intracultural differences since it is colored by notions of the "official" ideal.

Chart 1   Focal Concerns of Lower Class Culture

Area	Perceived Alternatives (state, quality, condition)	
1. *Trouble:*	law-abiding behavior	law-violating behavior
2. *Toughness:*	physical prowess, skill; "masculinity"; fearlessness, bravery, daring	weakness, ineptitude; effeminacy; timidity, cowardice, caution
3. *Smartness:*	ability to outsmart, dupe, "con"; gaining money by "wits"; shrewdness, adroitness in repartee	gullibility, "con-ability"; gaining money by hard work; slowness, dull-wittedness, verbal maladroitness
4. *Excitement:*	thrill; risk, danger; change, activity	boredom; "deadness," safeness; sameness, passivity
5. *Fate:*	favored by fortune, being "lucky"	ill-omened, being "unlucky"
6. *Autonomy:*	freedom from external constraint; freedom from superordinate authority; independence	presence of external constraint; presence of strong authority; dependency, being "cared for"

Trouble: Concern over "trouble" is a dominant feature of lower class culture. The concept has various shades of meaning; "trouble" in one of its aspects represents a situation or a kind of behavior which results in unwelcome or complicating involvement with official authorities or agencies of middle class society. "Getting into trouble" and "staying out of trouble" represent major issues for male and female, adults and children. For men, "trouble" frequently involves fighting or sexual adventures while drinking; for women, sexual involvement with disadvantageous consequences. Expressed desire to avoid behavior which violates moral or legal norms is often based less on an explicit commitment to "official" moral or legal standards than on a desire to avoid "getting into trouble," e.g., the complicating consequences of the action.

The dominant concern over "trouble" involves a distinction of critical importance for the lower class community—that between "law-abiding" and "non-law-abiding" behavior. There is a high degree of sensitivity as to where each person stands in relation to these two classes of activity. Whereas in the middle class community a major dimension for evaluating a person's status is "achievement" and its external symbols, in the lower class, personal status is very frequently gauged along the law-abiding-non-law-abiding dimension. A mother will evaluate the suitability of her daughter's boyfriend less on the basis of his achievement potential than on the basis of his innate "trouble" potential. This sensitive awareness of the opposition of "trouble-producing" and "non-trouble-producing" behavior represents both a major basis for deriving status distinctions, and an internalized conflict potential for the individual.

As in the case of other focal concerns, which of two perceived alternatives—"law-abiding" or "non-law-abiding"—is valued varies according to the individual and the circumstances; in many instances there is an overt commitment to the "law-abiding" alternative, but a covert commitment to the "non-law-abiding." In certain situations, "getting into trouble" is overtly recognized as prestige-conferring; for example, membership in certain adult and adolescent primary groupings ("gangs") is contingent on having demonstrated an explicit commitment to the law-violating alternative. It is most important to note that the choice between "law-abiding" and "non-law-abiding" behavior is still a choice *within* lower class culture; the distinction between the policeman and the criminal, the outlaw and the sheriff, involves primarily this one dimension; in other respects they have a high community of interests. Not infrequently brothers raised in an identical cultural milieu will become police and criminals respectively.

For a substantial segment of the lower class population "getting into trouble" is not in itself overtly defined as prestige-conferring, but is implicitly recognized as a means to other valued ends, e.g., the covertly valued desire to be "cared for" and subject to external constraint, or the overtly valued state of excitement or risk. Very frequently "getting into trouble" is multi-functional, and achieves several sets of valued ends.

Toughness: The concept of "toughness" in lower class culture represents a compound combination of qualities or states. Among its most important components are physical prowess, evidenced both by demonstrated possession of strength and endurance and athletic skill; "masculinity," symbolized by a distinctive complex of acts and avoidances (bodily tatooing; absence of sentimentality; non-concern with "art," "literature," conceptualization of women as conquest objects, etc.); and bravery in the face of physical threat. The model for the "tough guy"—hard, fearless, undemonstrative, skilled in physical combat—is represented by the movie gangster of the thirties, the "private eye," and the movie cowboy.

The genesis of the intense concern over "toughness" in lower class culture is probably related to the fact that a significant proportion of lower class males are reared in a predominantly female household, and lack a consistently present male figure with whom to identify and from whom to learn essential components of a "male" role. Since women serve as a primary object of identification during pre-adolescent years, the almost obsessive lower class concern with "masculinity" probably resembles a type of compulsive reaction-formation. A concern over homosexuality runs like a persistent thread through lower class culture. This is manifested by the institutionalized practice of baiting "queers," often accompanied by violent physical attacks, an expressed contempt for "softness" or frills, and the use of the local term for "homosexual" as a generalized pejorative epithet (e.g., higher class individuals or upwardly mobile peers are frequently characterized as "fags" or "queers"). The distinction between "overt" and "covert" orientation to aspects of an area of concern is especially important in regard to "toughness." A positive overt evaluation of behavior defined as "effeminate" would be out of the question for a lower class male; however, built into lower class culture is a range of devices which permit men to adopt behaviors and concerns which in other cultural milieux fall within the province of women, and at the same time to be defined as "tough" and manly. For example, lower class men can be professional short-order cooks in a diner and still be regarded as "tough." The highly intimate circumstances of the street corner gang involve the recurrent expression of strongly affectionate feelings towards other men. Such expressions, however, are disguised as their opposite, taking the form of ostensibly aggressive verbal and physical interaction (kidding, "ranking," roughhousing, etc.).

Smartness: "Smartness," as conceptualized in lower class culture, involves the capacity to outsmart, outfox, outwit, dupe, "take," "con" another or others, and the concomitant capacity to avoid being outwitted, "taken," or duped oneself. In its essence, smartness involves the capacity to achieve a valued entity—material goods, personal status—through a maximum use of mental agility and a minimum use of physical effort. This capacity has an extremely long tradition in lower class culture, and is highly valued. Lower class culture can be characterized as "non-intellectual" only if intellectualism is defined specifically in terms of control over a particular body of formally learned knowledge involving "culture" (art, literature, "good" music, etc.), a generalized perspective on the past and present conditions of our own and other societies, and other areas of knowledge imparted by formal educational institutions. This particular type of mental attainment is, in general, overtly disvalued and frequently associated with effeminacy; "smartness" in the lower class sense, however, is highly valued.

The lower class child learns and practices the use of this skill in the street corner situation. Individuals continually practice duping and outwitting one another through recurrent card games and other forms of gambling, mutual exchanges of insults, and "testing" for mutual "con-ability." Those who demonstrate competence in this skill are accorded considerable prestige. Leadership roles in the corner group are frequently allocated according to demonstrated capacity in the two areas of "smartness" and "toughness"; the ideal leader combines both, but the "smart" leader is often accorded more prestige than the "tough" one—reflecting a general lower class respect for "brains" in the "smartness" sense.[4]

The model of the "smart" person is represented in popular media by the card shark, the professional gambler, the "con" artist, the promoter. A conceptual distinction is made between two kinds of people: "suckers," easy marks, "lushes," dupes, who work for their money and are legitimate targets of exploitation; and sharp operators, the "brainy" ones, who live by their wits and "getting" from the suckers by mental adroitness.

Involved in the syndrome of capacities related to "smartness" is a dominant emphasis in lower class culture on ingenious aggressive repartee. This skill, learned and practiced in the context of the corner group, ranges in form from the widely prevalent semi-ritualized teasing, kidding, razzing, "ranking," so characteristic of male peer group interaction, to the highly ritualized type of mutual insult interchange known as "the dirty dozens," "the dozens," "playing house," and other terms. This highly patterned cultural form is practiced on its most advanced level in adult male Negro society, but less polished variants are found throughout lower class culture—practiced, for example, by white children, male and female, as young as four or five. In essence, "doin' the dozens" involves two antagonists who vie with each other in the exchange of increasingly inflammatory insults, with incestuous and perverted sexual relations with the mother a dominant theme. In this form of insult interchange, as well as on other less ritualized occasions for joking, semi-serious, and serious mutual invective, a very high premium is placed on ingenuity, hair-trigger responsiveness, inventiveness, and the acute exercise of mental faculties.

Excitement: For many lower class individuals the rhythm of life fluctuates between periods of relatively routine or repetitive activity and sought situations of great emotional stimulation. Many of the most characteristic features of lower class life are related to the search for excitement or "thrill." Involved here are the highly prevalent use of alcohol by both sexes and the widespread use of gambling of all kinds—playing the numbers, betting on horse races, dice, cards. The quest for excitement finds what is perhaps its most vivid expression in the highly patterned

---

[4]The "brains-brawn" set of capacities are often paired in lower class folk lore or accounts of lower class life, e.g., "Brer Fox" and "Brer Bear" in the Uncle Remus stories, or George and Lennie in "Of Mice and Men."

practice of the recurrent "night on the town." This practice, designated by various terms in different areas ("honky-tonkin'"; "goin' out on the town"; "bar hoppin'"), involves a patterned set of activities in which alcohol, music, and sexual adventuring are major components. A group or individual sets out to "make the rounds" of various bars or night clubs. Drinking continues progressively throughout the evening. Men seek to "pick up" women, and women play the risky game of entertaining sexual advances. Fights between men involving women, gambling, and claims of physical prowess, in various combinations, are frequent consequences of a night of making the rounds. The explosive potential of this type of adventuring with sex and aggression, frequently leading to "trouble," is semi-explicitly sought by the individual. Since there is always a good likelihood that being out on the town will eventuate in fights, etc., the practice involves elements of sought risk and desired danger.

Counterbalancing the "flirting with danger" aspect of the "excitement" concern is the prevalence in lower class culture of other well established patterns of activity which involve long periods of relative inaction, or passivity. The term "hanging out" in lower class culture refers to extended periods of standing around, often with peer mates, doing what is defined as "nothing," "shooting the breeze," etc. A definite periodicity exists in the pattern of activity relating to the two aspects of the "excitement" dimension. For many lower class individuals the venture into the high risk world of alcohol, sex, and fighting occurs regularly once a week, with interim periods devoted to accommodating to possible consequences of these periods, along with recurrent resolves not to become so involved again.

Fate: Related to the quest for excitement is the concern with fate, fortune, or luck. Here also a distinction is made between two states—being "lucky" or "in luck," and being unlucky or jinxed. Many lower class individuals feel that their lives are subject to a set of forces over which they have relatively little control. These are not directly equated with the supernatural forces of formally organized religion, but relate more to a concept of "destiny," or man as a pawn of magical powers. Not infrequently this often implicit world view is associated with a conception of the ultimate futility of directed effort towards a goal: if the cards are right, or the dice good to you, or if your lucky number comes up, things will go your way; if luck is against you, it's not worth trying. The concept of performing semi-magical rituals so that one's "luck will change" is prevalent; one hopes that as a result he will move from the state of being "unlucky" to that of being "lucky." The element of fantasy plays an important part in this area. Related to and complementing the notion that "only suckers work" (Smartness) is the idea that once things start going your way, relatively independent of your own effort, all good things will come to you. Achieving great material rewards (big cars, big houses, a roll of cash to flash in a fancy night club), valued in lower class as well as in other parts of American culture, is a recurrent theme in lower class fantasy and folk lore; the cocaine dreams of Willie the Weeper or Minnie the Moocher present the components of this fantasy in vivid detail.

The prevalence in the lower class community of many forms of gambling, mentioned in connection with the "excitement" dimension, is also relevant here. Through cards and pool which involve skill, and thus both "toughness" and "smartness"; or through race horse betting, involving "smartness"; or through playing the numbers, involving predominantly "luck," one may make a big killing with a minimum of directed and persistent effort within conventional occupational channels. Gambling in its many forms illustrates the fact that many of the persistent features of lower class culture are multi-functional—serving a range of desired ends at the same time. Describing some of the incentives behind gambling has involved mention of all of the focal concerns cited so far—Toughness, Smartness, and Excitement, in addition to Fate.

Autonomy: The extent and nature of control over the behavior of the individual—an important concern in most cultures—has a special significance and is distinctively patterned in lower class culture. The discrepancy between what is overtly valued and what is covertly sought is particularly striking in this area. On the overt level there is a strong and frequently expressed resentment of the idea of external controls, restrictions on behavior, and unjust or coercive authority. "No one's gonna push *me* around," or "I'm gonna tell him he can take the job and shove it. . . ." are commonly expressed sentiments. Similar explicit attitudes are maintained to systems of behavior-restricting rules, insofar as these are perceived as representing the injunctions, and bearing the sanctions of superordinate authority. In addition, in lower class culture a close conceptual connection is made between "authority" and "nurturance." To be restrictively or firmly controlled is to be cared for. Thus the overtly negative evaluation of superordinate authority frequently extends as well to nurturance, care, or protection. The desire for personal independence is often expressed in such terms as "I don't need *nobody* to take care of me. I can take care of myself!" Actual patterns of behavior, however, reveal a marked discrepancy between expressed sentiment and what is covertly valued. Many lower class people appear to seek out highly restrictive social environments wherein stringent external controls are maintained over their behavior. Such institutions as the armed forces, the mental hospital, the disciplinary school, the prison or correctional institution, provide environments which incorporate a strict and detailed set of rules defining and limiting behavior, and enforced by an authority system which controls and applies coercive sanctions for deviance from these rules. While under the jurisdiction of such systems, the lower class person generally expresses to his peers continual resentment of the coercive, unjust, and arbitrary exercise of authority. Having been released, or having escaped from these milieux, however, he will often act in such a way as to insure recommitment, or choose recommitment voluntarily after a temporary period of "freedom."

Lower class patients in mental hospitals will exercise considerable ingenuity to insure continued commitment while voicing the desire to get out; delinquent boys will frequently "run" from a correctional institution to activate efforts to return them; to be caught and returned means that one is cared for. Since "being controlled" is equated with "being cared for," attempts are frequently made to "test" the severity or strictness of superordinate authority to see if it remains firm. If intended or executed rebellion produces swift and firm punitive sanctions, the individual is reassured, at the same time that he is complaining bitterly at the injustice of being caught and punished. Some environmental milieux, having been tested in this fashion for the "firmness" of their coercive sanctions, are rejected, ostensibly for being too strict, actually for not being strict enough. This is frequently so in the case of "problematic" behavior by lower class youngsters in the public schools, which generally cannot command the coercive controls implicitly sought by the individual.

A similar discrepancy between what is overtly and covertly desired is found in the area of dependence-independence. The pose of tough rebellious independence often assumed by the lower class person frequently conceals powerful dependency cravings. These are manifested primarily by obliquely expressed resentment when "care" is not forthcoming rather than by expressed satisfaction when it is. The concern over autonomy-dependency is related both to "trouble" and "fate." Insofar as the lower class individual feels that his behavior is controlled by forces which often propel him into "trouble" in the face of an explicit determination to avoid it, there is an implied appeal to "save me from myself." A solution appears to lie in arranging things so that his behavior will be coercively restricted by an externally imposed set of controls strong enough to forcibly restrain his inexplicable inclination to get in trouble. The periodicity observed in connection with the "excitement" dimension is also relevant here; after involvement in trouble-producing behavior (assault, sexual adventure, a "drunk"), the individual will actively seek a locus of imposed control (his wife, prison, a restrictive job); after a given period of subjection to this control, resentment against it mounts, leading to a "break away" and a search for involvement in further "trouble."

Focal Concerns of the Lower Class Adolescent Street Corner Group

The one-sex peer group is a highly prevalent and significant structural form in the lower class community. There is a strong probability that the prevalence and stability of this type of unit is directly related to the prevalence of a stabilized type of lower class child-rearing unit—the "female-based" household. This is a nuclear kin unit in which a male parent is either absent from the household, present only sporadically, or, when present, only minimally or inconsistently involved in the support and rearing of children. This unit usually consists of one or more females of child-bearing age and their offspring. The females are frequently related to one another by blood or marriage ties, and the unit often includes two or more generations of women, e.g., the mother and/or aunt of the principal child-bearing female.

The nature of social groupings in the lower class community may be clarified if we make the assumption that it is the *one-sex peer unit* rather than the two-parent family unit which represents the most significant relational unit for both sexes in lower class communities. Lower class society may be pictured as comprising a set of age-graded one-sex groups which constitute the major psychic focus and reference group for those over twelve or thirteen. Men and women of mating age leave these groups periodically to form temporary marital alliances, but these lack stability, and after varying periods of "trying out" the two-sex family arrangement, gravitate back to the more "comfortable" one-sex grouping, whose members exert strong pressure on the individual *not* to disrupt the group by adopting a two-sex household pattern of life.[5] Membership in a stable and solidary peer unit is vital to the lower class individual precisely to the extent to which a range of essential functions—psychological, educational, and others, are not provided by the "family" unit.

The adolescent street corner group represents the adolescent variant of this lower class structural form. What has been called the "delinquent gang" is one subtype of this form, defined on the basis of frequency of participation in law-violating activity; this subtype should not be considered a legitimate unit of study per se, but rather as one particular variant of the adolescent street corner group. The "hanging" peer group is a unit of particular importance for the adolescent male. In many cases it is the most stable and solidary primary group he has ever belonged to; for boys reared in female-based households the corner group provides the first real opportunity to learn essential aspects of the male role in the context of peers facing similar problems of sex-role identification.

The form and functions of the adolescent corner group operate as a selective mechanism in recruiting members. The activity patterns of the group require a high level of intra-group solidarity; individual members must possess a good capacity for subordinating individual desires to general group interests as well as the capacity for intimate and persisting interaction. Thus highly "disturbed" individuals, or those who cannot tolerate consistently imposed sanctions on "deviant" behavior cannot remain accepted members; the group itself will extrude those whose behavior exceeds limits defined as "normal." This selective process produces a type of group whose members possess to an unusually high degree both the *capacity* and *motivation* to conform to perceived cultural norms, so that the nature of the system of norms and values oriented to is a particularly influential component of motivation.

Focal concerns of the male adolescent corner group are those of the general cultural milieu in which it functions. As would be expected, the relative weighting and importance of these concerns pattern somewhat differently for adolescents than for adults. The nature of this patterning centers around two additional "concerns" of particular importance to this group—concern with "belonging," and with "status." These may be conceptualized as being on a higher level of abstraction than concerns previously cited, since "status" and "belonging" are achieved *via* cited concern areas of Toughness, etc.

---

[5]Further data on the female-based household unit (estimated as comprising about 15 per cent of all American "families") and the role of one-sex groupings in lower class culture are contained in Walter B. Miller, Implications of Urban Lower Class Culture for Social Work. *Social Service Review*, 1959, *33*, No. 3.

Belonging: Since the corner group fulfills essential functions for the individual, being a member in good standing of the group is of vital importance for its members. A continuing concern over who is "in" and who is not involves the citation and detailed discussion of highly refined criteria for "in-group" membership. The phrase "he hangs with us" means "he is accepted as a member in good standing by current consensus"; conversely, "he don't hang with us" means he is not so accepted. One achieves "belonging" primarily by demonstrating knowledge of and a determination to adhere to the system of standards and valued qualities defined by the group. One maintains membership by acting in conformity with valued aspects of Toughness, Smartness, Autonomy, etc. In those instances where conforming to norms of this reference group at the same time violates norms of other reference groups (e.g., middle class adults, institutional "officials"), immediate reference group norms are much more compelling since violation risks invoking the group's most powerful sanction: exclusion.

Status: In common with most adolescents in American society, the lower class corner group manifests a dominant concern with "status." What differentiates this type of group from others, however, is the particular set of criteria and weighting thereof by which "status" is defined. In general, status is achieved and maintained by demonstrated possession of the valued qualities of lower class culture—Toughness, Smartness, expressed resistance to authority, daring, etc. It is important to stress once more that the individual orients to these concerns *as they are defined within lower class society*; e.g., the status-conferring potential of "smartness" in the sense of scholastic achievement generally ranges from negligible to negative.

The concern with "status" is manifested in a variety of ways. Intragroup status is a continued concern, and is derived and tested constantly by means of a set of status-ranking activities; the intra-group "pecking order" is constantly at issue. One gains status within the group by demonstrated superiority in Toughness (physical prowess, bravery, skill in athletics and games such as pool and cards), Smartness (skill in repartee, capacity to "dupe" fellow group members), and the like. The term "ranking," used to refer to the pattern of intra-group aggressive repartee, indicates awareness of the fact that this is one device for establishing the intra-group status hierarchy.

The concern over status in the adolescent corner group involves in particular the component of "adultness," the intense desire to be seen as "grown up," and a corresponding aversion to "kid stuff." "Adult" status is defined less in terms of the assumption of "adult" responsibility than in terms of certain external symbols of adult status—a car, ready cash, and, in particular, a perceived "freedom" to drink, smoke, and gamble as one wishes and to come and go without external restrictions. The desire to be seen as "adult" is often a more significant component of much involvement in illegal drinking, gambling, and automobile driving than the explicit enjoyment of these acts as such.

The intensity of the corner group member's desire to be seen as "adult" is sufficiently great that he feels called upon to demonstrate qualities associated with adultness (Toughness, Smartness, Autonomy) to a much greater degree than a lower class adult. This means that he will seek out and utilize those avenues to these qualities which he perceives as available with greater intensity than an adult and less regard for their "legitimacy." In this sense the adolescent variant of lower class culture represents a maximization or an intensified manifestation of many of its most characteristic features.

Concern over status is also manifested in reference to other street corner groups. The term "rep" used in this regard is especially significant, and has broad connotations. In its most frequent and explicit connotation, "rep" refers to the "toughness" of the corner group as a whole relative to that of other groups; a "pecking order" also exists among the several corner groups in a given interactional area, and there is a common perception that the safety or security of the group and all its members depends on maintaining a solid "rep" for toughness vis-a-vis other groups. This motive is most frequently advanced as a reason for involvement in gang fights: "We *can't* chicken out on this fight; our rep would be shot!"; this implies that the group would be relegated to the bottom of the status ladder and become a helpless and recurrent target of external attack.

On the other hand, there is implicit in the concept of "rep" the recognition that "rep" has or may have a dual basis—corresponding to the two aspects of the "trouble" dimension. It is recognized that group as well as individual status can be based on both "law-abiding" and "law-violating" behavior. The situational resolution of the persisting conflict between the "law-abiding" and "law-violating" bases of status comprises a vital set of dynamics in determining whether a "delinquent" mode of behavior will be adopted by a group, under what circumstances, and how persistently. The determinants of this choice are evidently highly complex and fluid, and rest on a range of factors including the presence and perceptual immediacy of different community reference-group loci (e.g., professional criminals, police, clergy, teachers, settlement house workers), the personality structures and "needs" of group members, the presence in the community of social work, recreation, or educational programs which can facilitate utilization of the "law-abiding" basis of status, and so on.

What remains constant is the critical importance of "status" both for the members of the group as individuals and for the group as a whole insofar as members perceive their individual destinies as linked to the destiny of the group, and the fact that action geared to attain status is much more acutely oriented to the fact of status itself than to the legality or illegality, morality or immorality of the means used to achieve it.

Lower Class Culture and the Motivation of Delinquent Behavior

The customary set of activities of the adolescent street corner group includes activities which are in violation of laws and ordinances of the legal code. Most of these center around assault and theft of various types (the gang fight; auto theft; assault on an individual; petty pilfering and shoplifting; "mugging"; pocketbook theft). Members of street corner gangs are well aware of the law-violating nature of these acts; they are not psychopaths, nor physically or mentally "defective"; in fact, since the corner group supports and enforces a rigorous set of standards which demand a high degree of fitness and personal competence, it tends to recruit from the most "able" members of the community.

Why, then, is the commission of crimes a customary feature of gang activity? The most general answer is that the commission of crimes by members of adolescent street corner groups is motivated primarily by the attempt to achieve ends, states, or conditions which are valued, and to avoid those that are disvalued within their most meaningful cultural milieu, through those culturally available avenues which appear as the most feasible means of attaining those ends.

The operation of these influences is well illustrated by the gang fight—a prevalent and characteristic type of corner group delinquency. This type of activity comprises a highly stylized and culturally patterned set of sequences. Although details vary under different circumstances, the following events are generally included. A member or several members of group A "trespass" on the claimed territory of group B. While there they commit an act or acts which group B defines as a violation of its rightful privileges, an affront to their honor, or a challenge to their "rep." Frequently this act involves advances to a girl associated with group B; it may occur at a dance or party; sometimes the mere act of "trespass" is seen as deliberate provocation. Members of group B then assault members of group A, if they are caught while still in B's territory. Assaulted members of group A return to their "home" territory and recount to members of their group details of the incident, stressing the insufficient nature of the provocation ("I just *looked* at her! Hardly even said anything!"), and the unfair circumstances of the assault ("About *twenty* guys jumped just the *two* of us!"). The highly colored account is acutely inflammatory; group A, perceiving its honor violated and its "rep" threatened, feels obligated to retaliate in force. Sessions of detailed planning now occur; allies are recruited if the size of group A and its potential allies appears to necessitate larger numbers; strategy is plotted, and messengers dispatched. Since the prospect of a gang fight is frightening to even the "toughest" group members, a constant rehearsal of the provocative incident or incidents and the essentially evil nature of the opponents accompanies the planning process to bolster possibly weakening motivation to fight. The excursion into "enemy" territory sometimes results in a full scale fight; more often group B cannot be found, or the police appear and stop the fight, "tipped off" by an anonymous informant. When this occurs, group members express disgust and disappointment; secretly there is much relief; their honor has been avenged without incurring injury; often the anonymous tipster is a member of one of the involved groups.

The basic elements of this type of delinquency are sufficiently stabilized and recurrent as to constitute an essentially ritualized pattern, resembling both in structure and expressed motives for action classic forms such as the European "duel," the American Indian tribal war, and the Celtic clan feud. Although the arousing and "acting out" of individual aggressive emotions are inevitably involved in the gang fight, neither its form nor motivational dynamics can be adequately handled within a predominantly personality-focused frame of reference.

It would be possible to develop in considerable detail the processes by which the commission of a range of illegal acts is either explicitly supported by, implicitly demanded by, or not materially inhibited by factors relating to the focal concerns of lower class culture. In place of such a development, the following three statements condense in general terms the operation of these processes:

1. *Following cultural practices which comprise essential elements of the total life pattern of lower class culture automatically violates certain legal norms.*
2. *In instances where alternate avenues to similar objectives are available, the non-law-abiding avenue frequently provides a relatively greater and more immediate return for a relatively smaller investment of energy.*
3. *The "demanded" response to certain situations recurrently engendered within lower class culture involves the commission of illegal acts.*

The primary thesis of this paper is that the dominant component of the motivation of "delinquent" behavior engaged in by members of lower class corner groups involves a positive effort to achieve states, conditions, or qualities valued within the actor's most significant cultural milieu. If "conformity to immediate reference group values" is the major component of motivation of "delinquent" behavior by gang members, why is such behavior frequently referred to as negativistic, malicious, or rebellious? Albert Cohen, for example, in *Delinquent Boys* (Glencoe: Free Press, 1955) describes behavior which violates school rules as comprising elements of "active spite and malice, contempt and ridicule, challenge and defiance." He ascribes to the gang "keen delight in terrorizing 'good' children, and in general making themselves obnoxious to the virtuous." A recent national conference on social work with "hard-to-reach" groups characterized lower class corner groups as "youth groups in conflict with the culture of their (*sic*) communities." Such characterizations are obviously the result of taking the middle class community and its institutions as an implicit point of reference.

A large body of systematically interrelated attitudes, practices, behaviors, and values characteristic of lower class culture are designed to support and maintain the basic features of the lower class way of life. In areas where these differ from features of middle class culture, action oriented to the achievement and maintenance of the lower class system may violate norms of middle class culture and be perceived as deliberately non-conforming or malicious by an observer strongly cathected to middle class norms. This does not mean, however, that violation of the middle class norm is the dominant component of motivation; it is a by-product of action primarily oriented to the lower class system. The standards of lower class culture cannot be seen merely as a reverse function of middle class culture—as middle class standards "turned upside down"; lower class culture is a distinctive tradition many centuries old with an integrity of its own.

From the viewpoint of the acting individual, functioning within a field of well-structured cultural forces, the relative impact of "conforming" and "rejective" elements in the motivation of gang delinquency is weighted preponderantly on the conforming side. Rejective or rebellious elements are inevitably involved, but their influence during the actual commission of delinquent acts is relatively small compared to the influence of pressures to achieve what is valued by the actor's most immediate reference groups. Expressed awareness by the actor of the element of rebellion often represents only that aspect of motivation of which he is explicitly conscious; the deepest and most compelling components of motivation—adherence to highly meaningful group standards of Toughness, Smartness, Excitement, etc.—are often unconsciously patterned. No cultural pattern as well-established as the practice of illegal acts by members of lower class corner groups could persist if buttressed primarily by negative, hostile, or rejective motives; its principal motivational support, as in the case of any persisting cultural tradition, derives from a positive effort to achieve what is valued within that tradition, and to conform to its explicit and implicit norms.

CLASS AND CRIME 2

Crime Throughout the Class Structure
William Ryan

The trouble with the official crime picture is that it has the effect of grossly distorting the average citizen's image of what crime is all about. It minimizes and deflects attention from one kind of crime (the common kind that one's neighbors commit) and exaggerates and spotlights another, less common, kind (the code name is "crime-in-the-street" which is presumably committed by "criminals").

Out of the total spectrum of crime, very little is committed in the streets. Even crimes of violence—particularly rape, murder, and aggravated assault—are indoor events, and the participants are usually well acquainted and often related. Robbery, however, is more typically a street crime, and the crime-in-the-street crowd are usually talking about muggings and purse-snatchings. But this sort of thing is really relatively rare. The overall chances of any single individual being killed, assaulted, raped, or robbed on the street by a stranger in the course of any given year are much, much less than one in a thousand. For the one person in a thousand who is the victim, it is of course, a very serious, damaging, and frightening experience; but for the community as a whole, there are many more widespread social problems. Consider the probabilities of being the victim in other situations involving common social problems: the chances of being injured in an automobile accident in any given year are one in sixty—sixteen times greater than the probability of being a victim in the streets. One might reasonably expect hysteria about automotive safety to be sixteen times greater than the panic about street crime, and Ralph Nader to be more of a hero than J. Edgar Hoover. The chances of being divorced are five times greater, of being admitted to a mental hospital about three times greater; and the chances of a worker being unemployed for six months or more are about ten times greater. Yet, knowing these facts, can anyone seriously imagine a Presidential electoral campaign revolving around the issue of auto safety, or mental illness, or full employment, or family breakdown? It's inconceivable. Why does the American public respond so strongly to the issue of law and order?

There are at least two reasons. One is that the myopic view represented in the conventional wisdom about crime seems to provide at least some vague rationale

Source: William Ryan, "Crime Throughout the Class Structure" (pp. 205–212). From *Blaming the Victim* by William Ryan. Copyright © 1971, 1976 by William Ryan. Reproduced by permission of Pantheon Books, a Division of Random House, Inc.

for the tasks we set for our police; and it is comforting to keep the illusion that police are engaged in law enforcement. Another is that it permits us to keep believing that crime is fertilized by the slums and nurtured by low socio-economic status. We can then go on talking about some mythical separate group of criminals—most of whom, of course, are poor or black or both—dangerous and threatening to the life of the community. We do this through the device of defining as criminal only persons arrested by the police.

What are we to think if it can be demonstrated (as I will attempt to do a bit further on) that the chances of a poor black ghetto-dweller in the city being arrested are about three times greater than those of a thief being arrested (even though there is a slight but insubstantial overlap between these two groups)? For one thing, it means that when we draw up a composite picture of what the "criminal" is like, there will be an enormous component of poor blacks (though for most of them, their crimes are usually petty, often of a vague and undefined character, and, not infrequently, completely nonexistent), and only a small proportion of the picture will be contributed by the thief (and just a trace by the professional thief). The idea that we can know what criminals are like by studying the characteristics of convicted offenders rests on a shaky and completely insupportable assumption—that convicted criminals are a representative sample of all law violators. Nothing could be further from the truth. Consider ladies and gentlemen of the jury, a few more pieces of evidence.

Exhibit A: Of the seven major offenses that make up the FBI Crime Index—murder, rape, aggravated assault, robbery, burglary, larceny over $50, and car theft—there are about four million reported offenses annually. On the average, about one-fifth of these reported crimes are "cleared by arrest." (i.e., written off the books). These rates vary according to the type of crime: crimes of personal violence have high clearance rates, those against property have low clearance rates. When we add to this information the facts previously described—that the majority of such crimes are not reported by the victims, particularly the crimes of burglary and larceny—it is rather obvious that those arrested for serious felonies are a very small sample of those who commit felonies. Adding these two pieces of information together, we come out with the following picture: probably more than one-half of murderers and rapists are arrested, but fewer than one-fourth of those who commit robbery and only a tiny fraction—no more than five per cent—of thieves and burglars are arrested.

Exhibit B: In the police business, the felony arrest is the frosting on the cake—less than one-fifth of all arrests made. The wholesale business is pulling in drunks; this, along with other liquor offenses, accounts for about two out of five of all arrests made. Add gambling and the array of ambiguous crimes like vagrancy, disorderly conduct, and breach of the peace, and we account for about sixty per cent of all arrests.

It should not be surprising that policemen believe very firmly that criminals are lower class, marginal, unreliable, dangerous people, of whom a greatly disproportionate number are black. How could a policeman think otherwise? How could he function if he didn't believe that the group of persons he arrests and the group of persons who are criminals are essentially one and the same group? The police officer's definition of the criminal, based on his observation of the people he arrests, covers a rather narrow spectrum of law violators. On the one hand, the patrolman on the beat knows very little about the full-time thief, burglar, safe-cracker—persons who make their living from crime, and for whom crime is an occupation, indeed, a profession. At the other extreme, he knows little about the millions of criminals who are camouflaged within the general population: the embezzler, the tax-evader, the shoplifter, the employed middle class drunk, the wife-beater, the price-fixer, the briber, the grafter, the slum merchant who defrauds his customers. The group of law violators he knows (whose characteristics he uses to define the boundaries of the criminal class) are those who break the law openly, publicly, and very often, on the streets of our cities. He knows the homeless drunk who flops in doorways, but not the drunk who staggers home at eight o'clock from the corner tavern or the commuter train bar car and flops into bed in his own home. He knows, as a criminal, the young ghetto street-hustler who he picks up in a crap game in a vacant store front. He doesn't know *me* as a violator of gambling laws, though I play poker every other Thursday with a group of high class friends—doctors, Yale professors, psychologists; all of us are technically criminals just as much as the young fellow the police scoop up in the crap game. The average patrolman has no contact whatever with the bank teller who embezzles thousands of dollars from his employer or the suburban housewife who regularly steals a couple of dollars worth of groceries from the supermarket. And if he found a Cadillac or Continental belonging to someone like General Electric's former Vice-President William Ginn (one of those convicted in the "Great Conspiracy" to fix prices of electrical equipment at an artificially high level) parked in front of a fireplug, he would doubtless think two or three times before even tagging it.

Even if they tried very hard, then, to tell it like it is, the police could not do so accurately because they do not see it like it is. They recognize the black man as a criminal—or, generously, as a potential criminal—but haven't the vaguest idea what most thieves look like. This is the reason why black people are more in peril of arrest than thieves.

Let me try to demonstrate this with numbers. In a large city of, say, one million people, the police will make about 45,000 arrests in a single year. Of those arrested, about ten or twelve thousand will be poor and black. On the average, perhaps 60,000 residents of that city will be poor and black. If you are a poor black ghetto dweller, then, the odds are about one out of five or six that you will be arrested in the next twelve months. Suppose you commit larceny. According to the Ellis study, in this city there will be about 10,000 cases of larceny. As a result of police action, there will be only 700 arrests for larceny. Thus, in absolute numbers, about sixteen or eighteen black poor persons will be arrested for every thief arrested; and, in statistical terms, the poor black person is about three times more likely to be arrested than the thief. (The competent, well-trained professional thief, of course, is virtually immunized from arrest.)

As Melvin Adams tried to teach us, there are law violators and then there are law violators. The process continues as the arrested person moves from the precinct station to the court house. The court system that deals with those arrested has the function of refining the raw material, the crude oil, turned up by police operations. Theoretically, the court system is there to make a judgment about the validity of the police action—the arrested person, you will remember from eighth-grade civics class, is innocent until proved guilty. We have constructed an elaborate system of safeguards to protect the rights of those accused of crime: the preliminary hearing, the right to bail, the grand jury hearing, the right to counsel, the strict rules of trial by jury. A closer examination of the data, however, suggests that the judicial process does not seem to sort out the innocent from the guilty, so much as the well-to-do from the poor. There is a steady series of advantages accruing to the more affluent defendant.[1] He is considerably more likely to receive a preliminary hearing and, therefore, to have his case dismissed and not even brought to trial. Having money, he is more likely to be released on bail, which also has a substantial bearing on the outcome of his case. During all these procedures, he is much more likely to have his own lawyer working hard to take advantage of these many procedural protections and also working directly to influence the police and the prosecutor to drop the charges altogether.

But what about when the defendant gets into the courtroom itself? Here, certainly, it must be true that the great adversary system of pitting lawyer against lawyer in the cockpit of trial before a jury of the defendant's peers must work to finally achieve justice? Alas, it is not true. In the first place, about four out of five defendants actually brought to the point of trial plead guilty. If a trial is held, in most cases it is without a jury. Thus, despite all we have been taught—by Perry Mason, The Defenders, and other programs for educating the public—in the criminal judicial process, trial by jury is a very rare event, occurring in no more than five or ten per cent of felony cases brought to the courtroom. In the far more common cases of arrest for misdemeanors, the prevalence of trial by jury is minuscule. The likelihood of an arrested person being tried before a jury is remote indeed.

After conviction, the disadvantages of the poor continue: they are substantially less likely to receive a suspended sentence or probation, more likely to be sent to jail or prison.

The final, and most direct evidence is a set of studies that show there is no substantial relationship between social class and the commission of crimes, but that there is a very marked relationship between class and conviction for crime. Short and Nye[2] reported a specific comparison between two measures of criminalhood: one, reported behavior; the other, institutionalization. Five out of six boys in training schools for delinquents were drawn from the bottom half of the socio-economic ladder; but, judging by self-reports of behavior, there was an almost even distribution of delinquent acts among different socio-economic groups.

The lesson of all this is plain: the fact that half or more of persons arrested for crimes of personal violence, and that forty to fifty per cent of prisoners in jails and penitentiaries are black says nothing at all about the criminality of black people.

And that an even higher proportion of persons arrested are poor and imprisoned sheds no light whatever on the criminality of the poor. These facts only identify the objects of police and court activity. There are law violators and there are law violators; one kind gets arrested, the other kind is usually left alone.

Notes

1. S. S. Nagel, "The Tipped Scales of American Justice," *Trans-action*, III, No. 4 (May–June, 1966), pp. 3–9.
2. J. F. Short and F. I. Nye, "Reported Behavior as a Criterion of Deviant Behavior," *Social Problems*, V (1957), pp. 207–13.

Part 2
TYPES OF CRIMES

In Part 1 we observed that the official crime rates disseminated by the FBI direct public attention to traditional property and violent crimes (i.e., street crimes). To focus public attention selectively on these crimes limits the "crime problem" in society to the illicit activities of poor and of marginal citizens. But there are other types of crimes and criminals. There are crimes by individuals because of a violation of official morality (so-called victimless crimes); crimes by individuals occupying social positions such as employee, doctor, or government official (white-collar crimes); crimes by criminal organizations (organized crimes); crimes by otherwise legitimate organizations (corporate crimes); and crimes by individuals against governments and crimes of governments (political crimes). In short, crimes are not limited to the stealing, mugging, raping, and murdering committed predominantly by the lower classes; crimes are found throughout the social structure and are committed by both individuals and organizations.

The crime issues in this section center on five types of crime—conventional street crime, victimless crime, organized crime, corporate crime, and political crime.

STREET CRIME: OFFENSES AGAINST PERSONS AND PROPERTY

The crimes listed by the FBI in its index of crimes are traditionally known as *street crimes*. Public opinion surveys reveal consistently that these are the crimes Americans most fear. Offenders who commit the violent crimes of murder, rape, assault, and robbery are issued the strongest penalties. The most prevalent street crimes, however, are crimes against property—burglary, larceny, and motor vehicle theft.

The first four issues in this section are devoted to street crimes. The first issue is theoretical—what is the fundamental explanation for the prevalence of street crimes? Politicians' answers to this question direct public policy regarding street crime. The prevailing theoretical explanation is crucial; bad theory will lead to policies that will not work. A theory that meshes with reality, on the other hand, will lead to fruitful policies that will lessen the problem. The conservative position on this issue—that street crime is the consequence of *bad people*—is presented by two of its most visible proponents, Harvard professors James Q. Wilson and Richard J. Herrnstein. The opposing view, the perspective that street crime is mainly a consequence of social structure, is presented by Tony Platt.

The second issue examines the racial category disproportionately victimized by and punished for street crimes—blacks. The questions examined here involve the prevalence of black-on-black crime, the fundamental question of why blacks are disproportionately singled out as street criminals, and the question of social justice.

The violent personal act of rape highlights the overarching question regarding street crime: Is rape the consequence of individual pathology or is it fundamentally a manifestation of a sexist society?

The final street crime issue considered here investigates the alleged relationship between drugs and street crime. It is widely believed that much of street crime is the result of drug addicts engaging in predatory crimes to support their habits. However, this question remains: Is illegal drug use and addiction a source of other serious street crime only because American society has chosen to criminalize that drug use and addiction?

VICTIMLESS CRIMES

Crimes such as murder, robbery, kidnapping, and rape are almost universally considered evil acts in society. Other crimes that are less widely held as such, sex between consenting nonmarried adults, recreational drug use, and gambling, are violations of codified morality. These "crimes" by willing adults have been the subject of intense debate. Are they crimes? Are they victimless? The conservative answer, which prevails, is that they are crimes because they violate official morality and the law. The criminal justice system devotes an enormous amount of money, personnel, court time, and prison space to apprehending and processing the perpetrators of these crimes. The contrasting articles on this issue depart from our usual format. The first, rather than presenting the conservative view, offers the liberal position that victimless crimes should be decriminalized for the self-evident reason that there are no victims. This position is argued by Edwin Schur, the originator of the term *victimless crime*. The second article presents the progressive position, which, ironically, agrees in part with conservatives that these are not victimless activities. There is indeed a crime and a victim. But, unlike conservatives who focus on the violation of "morality" by "criminals," the progressive position focuses on the crimes' victims, the ones suffering the political and economic exploitation and criminal acts of both the state, through selective and class-biased law enforcement, and organized crime, through the provision of illegal goods and services.

ORGANIZED CRIME

Organized crime refers to business enterprises that are organized to make a profit through criminal activities. These enterprises profit from four types of activities: (1) providing illegal goods and services for which there is consumer demand (e.g., gambling, narcotics, loansharking, prostitution, and pornography); (2) illegal acts of extortion, control of labor unions, car theft rings, and hiring illegal immigrants to work in sweatshop-type factories; (3) illegal control and sponsorship of legitimate business such as resort hotels, real estate development, and banking; and (4) the massive corruption of political and law enforcement officials who provide protection for these illegal organizations and their operations.

The issue addressed here is a longstanding debate among criminologists: Is there a Mafia or not? The traditional approach is that organized crime in the United States is the product of the conspiratorial activities of about twenty-four families in the largest American cities. Membership is limited in ethnicity to Sicilian or Italian families. These families are tightly organized in a secret organization that controls all of organized crime's illegal activities. The progressives argue that the image of the Mafia that most Americans accept does not correspond with reality. There are several ethnic groups involved, and sometimes ethnicity is irrelevant. More important, there is a national network that involves institutionalized relations among legitimate business/financial people, union leaders, politicians, law-enforcement officials, and the agents of organized crime. All of these elements cooperate to coordinate the production and distribution of illegal goods and services.

CORPORATE CRIME

Broadly defined, corporate crime refers to the "illegal and/or socially harmful behaviors that result from deliberate decision making by corporate executives in accordance with the operative goals of their organizations" (R. C. Kramer, "Corporate Crime," in P. Wickman and T. Dailey, eds., *White Collar and Economic Crime* [Lexington Books, 1982], p. 75). This definition is significant because it focuses on the organization as the perpetrator, and not on a person. Moreover, this definition goes beyond the criminal law to include "socially harmful behaviors." This is the issue addressed here. The conservative position is that corporate crimes are those that violate federal and state statutes. The research on the illegal behaviors of 582 large corporations by Clinard and Yeager is based on this assumption. But this frees corporations to legally engage in profitable activities that willfully harm people. What about selling proven dangerous products (e.g., pesticides, drugs, or food) overseas, when it is illegal to do so within the United States? What about promoting an unsafely designed automobile such as the Ford Pinto? Or, what about being excessively slow to promote a safe work environment for workers? The critique of Clinard's research by T. R. Young raises the fundamental question: Are such legal, but harmful, activities by corporations crimes? If they are not, he argues, the concept has no meaning.

POLITICAL CRIME

The issue addressed here is basic: What is a political crime? Conservatives perceive such crimes as activities against the government, that is, acts of dissent and violence whose purpose is to challenge and change the existing political order. The fundamental assumption of conservatives is that the law and the state are neutral. Since these exist for the common good, any challenge to them should be suppressed. The progressive view of political crimes stems from an opposite assumption—that the law and the state are tools of the powerful. Thus, the political order itself may be criminal since it can be unjust. Moreover, government, just like a corporation, can follow policies that violate its own law. Examples of this include Irangate, CIA interventions in the domestic affairs of other nations, and a variety of war crimes.

Crime and Its Explanation

James Q. Wilson and Richard J. Herrnstein

Predatory street crimes are most commonly committed by young males. Violent crimes are more common in big cities than in small ones. High rates of criminality tend to run in families. The persons who frequently commit the most serious crimes typically begin their criminal careers at a quite young age. Persons who turn out to be criminals usually do not do very well in school. Young men who drive recklessly and have many accidents tend to be similar to those who commit crimes. Programs designed to rehabilitate high-rate offenders have not been shown to have much success, and those programs that do manage to reduce criminality among certain kinds of offenders often increase it among others.

These facts about crime—some well known, some not so well known—are not merely statements about traits that happen occasionally, or in some places but not others, to describe criminals. They are statements that, insofar as we can tell, are pretty much true everywhere. They are statements, in short, about human nature as much as about crime.

All serious political and moral philosophy, and thus any serious social inquiry, must begin with an understanding of human nature. Though society and its institutions shape man, man's nature sets limits on the kinds of societies we can have. Cicero said that the nature of law must be founded on the nature of man (*a natura hominis discenda est natura juris*). This [essay] is an effort to set forth an understanding of human nature by examining one common, if regrettable, manifestation of that nature—criminality. We could have chosen to understand human nature by studying work, or sexuality, or political activity; we chose instead to approach it through the study of crime, in part out of curiosity and in part because crime, more dramatically than other forms of behavior, exposes the connection between individual dispositions and the social order.

The problem of social order is fundamental: How can mankind live together in reasonable order? Every society has, by definition, solved that problem to some degree, but not all have done so with equal success or without paying a high cost in other things—such as liberty—that we also value. If we believe that man is natu-

---

rally good, we will expect that the problem of order can be rather easily managed; if we believe him to be naturally wicked, we will expect the provision of order to require extraordinary measures; if we believe his nature to be infinitely plastic, we will think the problem of order can be solved entirely by plan and that we may pick and choose freely among all possible plans. Since every known society has experienced crime, no society has ever entirely solved the problem of order. The fact that crime is universal may suggest that man's nature is not infinitely malleable, though some people never cease searching for an anvil and hammer sufficient to bend it to their will.

Some societies seem better able than others to sustain order without making unacceptable sacrifices in personal freedom, and in every society the level of order is greater at some times than at others. These systematic and oft-remarked differences in the level of crime across time and place suggest that there is something worth explaining. But to find that explanation, one cannot begin with the society as a whole or its historical context, for what needs explanation is not the behavior of "society" but the behavior of individuals making up a society. Our intention is to offer as comprehensive an explanation as we can manage of why some individuals are more likely than others to commit crimes.

The Problem of Explanation

That intention is not easily realized, for at least three reasons. First, crime is neither easily observed nor readily measured. As we shall see later in this chapter, there is no way of knowing the true crime rate of a society or even of a given individual. Any explanation of why individuals differ in their law-abidingness may well founder on measurement errors. If we show that Tom, who we think has committed a crime, differs in certain interesting ways from Dick, who we think has not, when in fact both Tom and Dick have committed a crime, then the "explanation" is meaningless.

Second, crime is very common, especially among males. Using interviews and questionnaires, scholars have discovered that the majority of all young males have broken the law at least once by a relatively early age. By examining the police records of boys of a given age living in one place, criminologists have learned that a surprisingly large fraction of all males will be arrested at least once in their lives for something more serious than a traffic infraction. Marvin Wolfgang found that 35 percent of all the males born in Philadelphia in 1945 and living there between the ages of ten and eighteen had been arrested at least once by their eighteenth birthday and 43 percent had been arrested before their thirtieth birthday.[1] Nor is this a peculiarly American phenomenon. Various surveys have found that the proportion of British males who had been convicted in court before their twenty-first birthdays ranged from 15 percent in the nation as a whole to 31 percent for a group of boys raised in London. David Farrington estimates that 44 percent of all the males in "law-abiding" Britain will be arrested sometime in their lives.[2] If committing a crime at least once is so commonplace, then it is quite likely that there will be few, if any, large differences between those who never break the law and those who break it at least once—even if we had certain knowledge of which was which. Chance events as much as or more than individual predispositions will determine who commits a crime.

Third, the word "crime" can be applied to such varied behavior that it is not clear that it is a meaningful category of analysis. Stealing a comic book, punching a friend, cheating on a tax return, murdering a wife, robbing a bank, bribing a politician, hijacking an airplane—these and countless other acts are all crimes. Crime is as broad a category as disease, and perhaps as useless. To explain why one person has ever committed a crime and another has not may be as pointless as explaining why one person has ever gotten sick and another has not. We are not convinced that "crime" is so broad a category as to be absolutely meaningless—surely it is not irrelevant that crime is that form of behavior that is against the law—but we do acknowledge that it is difficult to provide a true and interesting explanation for actions that differ so much in their legal and subjective meanings.

To deal with these three difficulties, we propose to confine ourselves, for the most part, to explaining why some persons commit serious crimes at a high rate and others do not. By looking mainly at serious crimes, we escape the problem of comparing persons who park by a fire hydrant to persons who rob banks. By focusing on high-rate offenders, we do not need to distinguish between those who never break the law and those who (for perhaps chance reasons) break it only once or twice. And if we assume (as we do) that our criminal statistics are usually good enough to identify persons who commit a lot of crimes even if these data are poor at identifying accurately those who commit only one or two, then we can be less concerned with measurement errors.

The Meaning of Crime

A crime is any act committed in violation of a law that prohibits it and authorizes punishment for its commission. If we propose to confine our attention chiefly to persons who commit serious crimes at high rates, then we must specify what we mean by "serious." The arguments we shall make and the evidence we shall cite . . . will chiefly refer to aggressive, violent, or larcenous behavior; they will be, for the most part, about persons who hit, rape, murder, steal, and threaten.

In part, this limited focus is an unfortunate accident: We report only what others have studied, and by and large they have studied the causes of what we call predatory street crime. We would like to draw on research into a wider variety of law-violating behavior—embezzlement, sexual deviance, bribery, extortion, fraud—but very little such research exists.

But there is an advantage to this emphasis on predatory crime. Such behavior, except when justified by particular, well-understood circumstances (such as war), is condemned, in all societies and in all historical periods, by ancient tradition, moral sentiments, and formal law. Graeme Newman . . . interviewed people in six nations (India, Indonesia, Iran, Italy, the United States, and Yugoslavia) about their attitudes toward a variety of behaviors and concluded that there is a high— indeed, virtually universal—agreement that certain of these behaviors were wrong and should be prohibited by law.[3] Robbery, stealing, incest, and factory pollution were condemned by overwhelming majorities in every society; by contrast, abortion and homosexuality, among other acts, were thought to be crimes in some places but not in others. Interestingly, the characteristics of the individual respondents in these countries—their age, sex, education, social class—did not make much difference in what they thought should be treated as crimes. Newman's finding merely reinforces a fact long understood by anthropologists: Certain acts are regarded as wrong by every society, preliterate as well as literate; that among these "universal crimes" are murder, theft, robbery, and incest.[4]

Moreover, people in different societies rate the seriousness of offenses, especially the universal crimes, in about the same way. Thorsten Sellin and Marvin E. Wolfgang developed a scale to measure the relative gravity of 141 separate offenses. This scale has been found to be remarkably stable, producing similar rankings among both American citizens and prison inmates[5] as well as among Canadians,[6] Puerto Ricans,[7] Taiwanese,[8] and Belgian Congolese.[9]

By drawing on empirical studies of behaviors that are universally regarded as wrong and similarly ranked as to gravity, we can be confident that we are in fact theorizing about *crime* and human nature and not about actions that people may or may not think are wrong. If the studies to which we refer were to include commercial price-fixing, political corruption, or industrial monopolization, we would have to deal with the fact that in many countries these actions are not regarded as criminal at all. If an American business executive were to bring all of the nation's chemical industries under his control, he would be indicted for having formed a monopoly; a British business executive who did the same thing might be elevated to the peerage for having created a valuable industrial empire. Similarly, by omitting studies of sexual deviance (except forcible rape), we avoid modifying our theory to take into account changing social standards as to the wrongness of these acts and the legal culpability of their perpetrators. In short, we seek . . . to explain why some persons are more likely than others to do things that all societies condemn and punish.

To state the same thing a bit differently, we will be concerned more with criminality than with crime. Travis Hirschi and Michael Gottfredson have explained this important distinction as follows. *Crimes* are short-term, circumscribed events that result from the (perhaps fortuitous) coming together of an individual having certain characteristics and an opportunity having certain (immediate and deferred) costs and benefits. Because the theory we offer . . . takes into account both these individual characteristics and situational features, we think it helps to explain why an individual will commit even one crime, but for reasons already explained, we recognize that the capacity of that theory to discriminate in an interesting and well-supported way between persons who do and do not commit a single offense is weak. *Criminality* refers to "stable differences across individuals in the propensity to commit criminal (or equivalent) acts."[10] The "equivalent" acts will be those that satisfy, perhaps in entirely legal ways, the same traits and predispositions that lead, in other circumstances, to crime. For example, a male who is very impulsive and so cannot resist temptation may, depending on circumstances, take toys from his playmates, money from his mother, billfolds from strangers, stamps from the office, liquor in the morning, extra chocolate cake at dinner time, and a nap whenever he feels like it. Some of these actions break the law, some do not.

The Categories of Explanation

Because we state that we intend to emphasize individual differences in behavior or predisposition, some readers may feel that we are shaping the argument in an improper manner. These critics believe that one can explain crime only by beginning with the society in which it is found. Emile Durkheim wrote: "We must, then, seek the explanation of social life in the nature of society itself."[11] Or, put another way, the whole is more than the sum of its parts. We do not deny that social arrangements and institutions, and the ancient customs that result from living and working together, affect behavior, often profoundly. But no explanation of social life explains anything until it explains individual behavior. Whatever significance we attach to ethnicity, social class, national character, the opinions of peers, or the messages of the mass media, the only test of their explanatory power is their ability to account for differences in how individuals, or groups of individuals, behave.

Explaining individual differences is an enterprise much resisted by some scholars. To them, this activity implies reducing everything to psychology, often referred to as "mere psychology." David J. Bordua, a sociologist, has pointed out the bias that can result from an excessive preference for social explanations over psychological ones.[12] Many criminologists, he comments, will observe a boy who becomes delinquent after being humiliated by his teacher or fired by his employer, and will conclude that his delinquency is explained by his "social class." But if the boy becomes delinquent after having been humiliated by his father or spurned by his girl friend, these scholars will deny that these events are explanations because they are "psychological." Teachers and employers are agents of the class structure, fathers and girl friends are not; therefore, the behavior of teachers and employers must be more important.

We believe that one can supply an explanation of criminality—and more important, of law-abidingness—that begins with the individual in, or even before, infancy and that takes into account the impact on him of subsequent experiences in the family, the school, the neighborhood, the labor market, the criminal justice system, and society at large. Yet even readers who accept this plan of inquiry as reasonable may still doubt its importance. To some, explaining crime is unnecessary because they think the explanation is already known; to others, it is impossible, since they think it unknowable.

Having taught a course on the causes of crime, and having spoken to many friends about our research, we have become acutely aware that there is scarcely any topic—except, perhaps, what is wrong with the Boston Red Sox or the Chicago Cubs—on which people have more confident opinions. Crime is caused, we are told, by the baby boom, permissive parents, brutal parents, incompetent schools, racial discrimination, lenient judges, the decline of organized religion, televised violence, drug addiction, ghetto unemployment, or the capitalist system. We note certain patterns in the proffered explanations. Our tough-minded friends blame crime on the failings of the criminal justice system; our tender-minded ones blame it on the failings of society.

We have no *a priori* quarrel with any of these explanations, but we wonder whether all can be true, or true to the same degree. The baby boom may help explain why crime rose in the 1960s and 1970s, but it cannot explain why some members of that boom became criminals and others did not. It is hard to imagine that both permissive and brutal parents produce the same kind of criminals, though it is conceivable that each may contribute to a different kind of criminality. Many children may attend bad schools, but only a small minority become serious criminals. And in any case, there is no agreement as to what constitutes an incompetent school. Is it an overly strict one that "labels" mischievous children as delinquents, or is it an overly lax one that allows normal mischief to degenerate into true delinquency? Does broadcast violence include a football or hockey game, or only a detective story in which somebody shoots somebody else? Economic conditions may affect crime, but since crime rates were lower in the Great Depression than during the prosperous years of the 1960s, the effect is, at best, not obvious or simple. The sentences given by judges may affect the crime rate, but we are struck by the fact that the most serious criminals begin offending at a very early age, long before they encounter, or probably even hear of, judges, whereas those who do not commit their first crime until they are adults (when, presumably, they have some knowledge of law and the courts) are the least likely to have a long or active criminal career. Racism and capitalism may contribute to crime, but the connection must be rather complicated, since crime has risen in the United States (and other nations) most rapidly during recent times, when we have surely become less racist and (given the growth of governmental controls on business) less capitalist. In any event, high crime rates can be found in socialist as well as capitalist nations, and some capitalist nations, such as Japan and Switzerland, have very little crime. In view of all this, some sorting out of these explanations might be useful.

But when we discuss our aims with scholars who study crime, we hear something quite different. There is no well-accepted theory of the causes of crime, we are told, and it is unlikely that one can be constructed. Many explanations have been advanced, but all have been criticized. What is most needed is more research, not better theories. Any theory specific enough to be testable will not explain very much, whereas any theory broad enough to explain a great deal will not be testable. It is only because they are friends that some of our colleagues refrain from muttering about fools rushing in where wise men, if not angels, fear to tread. . . .

But there is one version of the claim that explaining crime is impossible to which we wish to take immediate exception. That is the view, heard most frequently from those involved with criminals on a case-by-case basis (probation officers and therapists, for example), that the causes of crime are unique to the individual criminal. Thus, one cannot generalize about crime because each criminal is different. Now, in one sense that argument is true—no two offenders are exactly alike. But we are struck by the fact that there are certain obvious patterns to criminality, suggesting that something more than random individual differences is at work. We think these obvious patterns, if nothing else, can be explained.

Patterns in Criminality

Crime is an activity disproportionately carried out by young men living in large cities. There are old criminals, and female ones, and rural and small-town ones, but, to a much greater degree than would be expected by chance, criminals are young urban males. This is true, insofar as we can tell, in every society that keeps any reasonable criminal statistics.[13] These facts are obvious to all, but sometimes their significance is overlooked. Much time and effort may be expended in trying to discover whether children from broken homes are more likely to be criminals than those from intact ones, or whether children who watch television a lot are more likely to be aggressive than those who watch it less. These are interesting questions, and we shall have something to say about them, but even if they are answered satisfactorily, we will have explained rather little about the major differences in criminality. Most children raised in broken homes do not become serious offenders; roughly half of such children are girls, and . . . females are often only one-tenth as likely as males to commit crimes. Crime existed abundantly long before the advent of television and would continue long after any hint of violence was expunged from TV programs. Any worthwhile explanation of crime must account for the major, persistent differences in criminality.

The fact that these regularities exist suggests that it is not impossible, in principle, to provide a coherent explanation of crime. It is not like trying to explain why some people prefer vanilla ice cream and others chocolate. . . . There are other regularities in criminality beyond those associated with age, sex, and place. There is mounting evidence that, on the average, offenders differ from nonoffenders in physique, intelligence, and personality. Some of these differences may not themselves be a cause of crime but only a visible indicator of some other factor that does contribute to crime . . . for example, we shall suggest that a certain physique is related to criminality, not because it causes people to break the law, but because a particular body type is associated with temperamental traits that predispose people to offending. Other individual differences, such as in personality, may directly contribute to criminality.

There are two apparent patterns in criminality that we have yet to mention, though they are no doubt uppermost in the minds of many readers—class and

race. To many people, it is obvious that differences in social class, however defined, are strongly associated with lawbreaking. The poor, the unemployed, or the
"underclass" are more likely than the well-to-do, the employed, or the "respectable
poor" to commit certain kinds of crimes. We are reluctant, however, at least at the
outset, to use class as a major category of explanations of differences in criminality
for two reasons.

First, scholars who readily agree on the importance of age, sex, and place as factors related to crime disagree vigorously as to whether social class, however defined, is associated with crime. Their dispute may strike readers who have worked
hard to move out of slums and into middle-class suburbs as rather bizarre; can anyone seriously doubt that better-off neighborhoods are safer than poorer ones? As
John Braithwaite has remarked, "It is hardly plausible that one can totally explain
away the higher risks of being mugged and raped in lower class areas as a consequence of the activities of middle class people who come into the area to perpetrate
such acts."[14]

We have much sympathy with his view, but we must recognize that there are arguments against it. When Charles R. Tittle, Wayne J. Villemez, and Douglas A.
Smith reviewed thirty-five studies of the relationship between crime rates and social class, they found only a slight association between the two variables.[15] When
crime was measured using official (e.g., police) reports, the connection with social
class was stronger than when it was measured using self-reports (the crimes admitted to by individuals filling out a questionnaire or responding to an interview).
This conclusion has been challenged by other scholars who find, on the basis of
more extensive self-report data than any previously used, that crime, especially
serious crime, is much more prevalent among lower-class youth.[16] Michael J.
Hindelang, Travis Hirschi, and Joseph G. Weis have shown that self-report studies
tend to measure the prevalence of trivial offenses, including many things that
would not be considered a crime at all (e.g., skipping school, defying parents, or
having unmarried sex).[17] Even when true crimes are reported, they are often so
minor (e.g., shoplifting a pack of gum) that it is a mistake—but, alas, a frequently
made mistake—to lump such behavior together with burglary and robbery as measures of criminality. We agree with Hindelang et al., as well as with many others,[18]
who argue that when crime is properly measured, the relationship between it and
social class is strong—lower-class persons are much more likely to have committed
a serious "street" crime than upper-status ones. But we recognize that this argument continues to be controversial, and so it seems inappropriate to begin an explanation of criminality by assuming that it is based on class.

Our second reason for not starting with class as a major social factor is, to us,
more important. Unlike sex, age, and place, class is an ambiguous concept. A
"lower-class" person can be one who has a low income, but that definition lumps
together graduate students, old-age pensioners, welfare mothers, and unemployed
steelworkers—individuals who would appear to have, as far as crime is concerned,
little in common. Many self-report studies of crime use class categories so broad as
to obscure whatever connection may exist between class and criminality.[19] And

studies of delinquency typically describe a boy as belonging to the class of his father, even if the boy in his own right, in school or in the labor force, is doing much better or much worse than his father.[20] By lower class one could also mean having a low prestige occupation, but it is not clear to us why the prestige ranking of one's occupation should have any influence on one's criminality.

Class may, of course, be defined in terms of wealth or income, but using the concept in this way to explain crime, without further clarification, is ambiguous as to cause and effect. One's wealth, income, status, or relationship to the means of production could cause certain behavior (e.g., "poor people must steal to eat"), or they could themselves be caused by other factors (impulsive persons with low verbal skills tend to be poor and to steal). By contrast, one's criminality cannot be the cause of, say, one's age or sex. As we proceed through our analysis in the chapters that follow, we shall take up the various possible components of social class, such as schooling and labor-market experiences, to see what effect they may have on individual differences in criminality. But we shall not begin with the assumption that we know what class is and that it can be only the cause, and never the consequence, of criminality.

Race is also a controversial and ambiguous concept in criminological research. Every study of crime using official data shows that blacks are heavily overrepresented among persons arrested, convicted, and imprisoned.[21] Some people, however, suspect that official reports are contaminated by the racial bias of those who compile them. Self-report studies, by contrast, tend to show fewer racial differences in criminality, but these studies have the same defect with respect to race as they do with regard to class—they overcount trivial offenses, in which the races do not differ, and undercount the more serious offenses, in which they do differ.[22] Moreover, surveys of the victims of crimes reveal that of the offenders whose racial identity could be discerned by their victims, about half were black; for the most serious offenses, two-thirds were black.[23] Though there may well be some racial bias in arrests, prosecutions, and sentences, there is no evidence . . . that it is so great as to account for the disproportionate involvement of blacks in serious crime, as revealed by both police and victimization data and by interviews with prison inmates.[24]

Our reason for not regarding, at least at the outset, race as a source of individual differences in criminality is not that we doubt that blacks are overrepresented in crime. Rather, there are two other considerations. First, racial differences exist in some societies and not others, yet all societies have crime. Though racial factors may affect the crime rate, the fundamental explanation for individual differences in criminality ought to be based—indeed, must be based, if it is to be a general explanation—on factors that are common to all societies.

Second, we find the concept of race to be ambiguous, but in a different way from the ambiguity of class. There is no reason to believe that the genes determining one's skin pigmentation also affect criminality. At one time in this nation's history, persons of Irish descent were heavily overrepresented among those who had committed some crime, but it would have been foolish then to postulate a trait called

"Irishness" as an explanation. If racial or ethnic identity affects the likelihood of committing a crime, it must be because that identity co-varies with other characteristics and experiences that affect criminality. The proper line of inquiry, then, is first to examine those other characteristics and experiences to see how and to what extent they predispose an individual toward crime, and then to consider what, if anything, is left unexplained in the observed connection between crime and racial identity. After examining constitutional, familial, educational, economic, neighborhood, and historical factors, there may or may not be anything left to say on the subject of race.

Notes

1. M. Wolfgang, "Crime in a Birth Cohort," *Proceedings of the American Philosophical Society* 117 (1973):404–411.
2. D. P. Farrington, "Longitudinal Research on Crime and Delinquency," in N. Morris and M. Tonry (eds.), *Crime and Justice: An Annual Review of Research* 1 (Chicago: University of Chicago Press, 1979).
3. G. Newman, *Comparative Deviance* (New York: Elsevier, 1976).
4. E. A. Hoebel, *The Law of Primitive Man* (Cambridge, MA: Harvard University Press, 1954).
5. T. Sellin and M. Wolfgang, *The Measurement of Delinquency* (New York: John Wiley, 1964).
6. D. Akman and A. Normandeau, "Towards the Measurement of Criminality in Canada," *Acta Criminologica* 1 (1968):135–260.
7. A. Valez-Diaz and E. Megargee, "An Investigation of Differences in Value Judgments Between Youthful Offenders and Nonoffenders in Puerto Rico," *Journal of Criminal Law, Criminology, and Police Science* 61 (1971):549–556.
8. Hsu, cited in C. F. Wellford, "Labelling Theory and Criminology," *Social Problems* 22 (1975):332–345.
9. Deboeck and Houschou, cited in Wellford, op. cit.
10. T. Hirschi and M. Gottfredson, "The Dis-

tinction Between Crime and Criminality," unpublished paper, Department of Sociology, University of Arizona (April 1974).
11. E. Durkheim, The Rules of Sociological Method, S. A. Solovay and J. H. Mueller (trans.), G. E. G. Catlin (ed.), (New York: Free Press, 1964), p. 102.
12. D. J. Bordua, "Some Comments on Theories of Group Delinquency," *Sociological Inquiry* 32 (1962):245–260.
13. L. Radzinowicz and J. King, *The Growth of Crime* (New York: Basic Books, 1977).
14. J. Braithwaite, "The Myth of Social Class and Criminality Reconsidered," *American Sociological Review* 46 (1981):36–57.
15. C. R. Tittle, W. J. Villemez, and D. A. Smith, "The Myth of Social Class and Criminality," *American Sociological Review* 43 (1979):643–656.
16. D. S. Elliott and S. S. Ageton, "Reconciling Race and Class Differences in Self-Reported and Official Estimates of Delinquency," *American Sociological Review* 45 (1980):95–110.
17. M. J. Hindelang, T. Hirschi, and J. G. Weis, "Correlates of Delinquency," *American Sociological Review* 44 (1979):995–1014.
18. For example, G. Kleck, "On the Use of Self-Report Data to Determine the Class Distribution of Criminal and Delinquent Behavior," *American Sociological Review* 47 (1982):427–433.

19. R. E. Johnson, *Juvenile Delinquency and Its Origins* (Cambridge, England: Cambridge University Press, 1979).
20. Braithwaite, op. cit.
21. For example, M. Wolfgang, R. F. Figlio, and T. Sellin, *Delinquency in a Birth Cohort*, (Chicago: University of Chicago Press, 1972).
22. Hindelang, Hirschi, and Weis, op. cit.
23. Ibid., p. 1002.
24. A. Blumstein, "On the Racial Disproportionality of the United States' Prison Populations," *Journal of Criminal Law and Criminology* 73 (1982):1259–1281.

STREET CRIME: BAD GUYS OR MARGINALIZATION? 2

"Street" Crime—A View from the Left

Tony Platt

According to survey after survey, "street" crime ranks as one of the most serious problems in working class communities. In 1948, only 4% of the population felt that crime was their community's *worst* problem. By 1972, according to a Gallup Poll, 21% of the residents of metropolitan centers reported crime as their *major* concern.[1]

People not only *think* that they are threatened by crime; they are also taking action to defend themselves. Several years ago, Chicago citizens formed the South Shore Emergency Patrol, composed of some two hundred black and white residents, to patrol the streets at night and weekends; in Boston's Dorchester area, the community has begun crime patrols; in New York, Citizens Action for a Safer Harlem has organized block-watcher programs, street associations and escort services for the elderly, while an armed citizens' vigilance group patrols the streets of Brooklyn on the look-out for arson and burglaries; in San Francisco, a member of the Board of Supervisors recently urged the formation of citizen anti-crime patrols to curb muggings; and in the relative peace and quiet of a college town like Berkeley, the Committee Against Rape and several neighborhood associations are meeting to plan ways of stopping violent attacks against women.[2]

The phenomenon of "street" crime has been largely ignored by the U.S. left. On the one hand, it is treated moralistically and attributed to the parasitical elements in capitalist society, mechanically following Marx and Engels's famous statement in the *Communist Manifesto* that the "lumpenproletariat may, here and there, be swept into the movement by a proletarian revolution; its conditions of life, however, prepare it far more for the part of a bribed tool of reactionary intrigue."[3] On the other hand, "street" crime is either glossed over as an invention of the FBI to divert attention away from the crimes of the ruling class or romanticized as a form of primitive political rebellion. Whether it is a form of reactionary individualism, or a fiction promoted by the bourgeoisie to cause confusion and false consciousness, or another manifestation of class struggle, is not a matter of theoretical assertion and cannot be decided by dogmatic references to Marxist texts. What is first

Source: Tony Platt, " 'Street' Crime—A View from the Left," *Crime and Social Justice* 9 (Spring/Summer 1978), pp. 26–33. Reprinted by permission from *Crime and Social Justice*, P.O. Box 40601, San Francisco, CA 94140.

needed is a thorough investigation of the scope and nature of "street" crime, concrete information about its varieties and rates and an appreciation of its specific historical context. This essay sets out to summarize and analyze the available information, thus providing a realistic basis for developing political strategy.

Reporting Crime

In 1931, the International Association of Chiefs of Police developed the Uniform Crime Reports (UCR) system and selected seven felony offenses for index purposes, on the grounds that the victims, or someone representing them, would more likely report such crimes to the police. The seven offense groups include: homicide, robbery, aggravated assault, forcible rape, burglary, larceny (grand theft) and auto theft. These are the crime statistics from which trends in the incidence of criminality are regularly reported in the media. When these reported crimes are converted into rates per 100,000 population and comparisons are made across time, for example 1968 to 1973, each of the index crimes, with the exception of auto theft, increased 25% to 50%. In 1976, according to the UCR, nearly 11.5 million serious crimes were reported to the police, a 33% increase from 1972, and a 76% increase from 1967.[4]

Critics of the FBI's reporting system have pointed out that the dramatic increase in crime rates is exaggerated and misleading since it reflects higher rates of *reporting* crime, technological improvements in data processing, better record-keeping systems and political manipulation by the police, rather than a real increase in the level of crime. While there is no evidence to support sensational media announcements about *sudden crime waves*, crime is certainly not exaggerated by the FBI. On the contrary, it is grossly underestimated.

The most accurate information about the scope of "street" crime is to be found in the federal government's Victimization Surveys. The Surveys, part of a statistical program called the National Crime Panel created by the Law Enforcement Assistance Administration (LEAA) in 1973, are an attempt to assess the extent and character of criminal victimization by means of a representative probability sampling of households, businesses and persons over the age of 12. The Surveys, which do *not* include homicide, kidnapping, so-called "victimless" crimes (such as prostitution, pimping, sale of drugs, etc.) and business crimes (such as fraud, false advertising, tax evasion, etc.), are limited to personal (rape, assault and armed robbery) and property (theft, auto theft and burglary) crimes.

Most "street" crime is not reported to the police. The Census Bureau recently concluded that there were nearly four times as many crimes committed in 1975 and 1976 as reported to the police.[5] A 1973 victimization study found that fewer than one in five persons report larceny to the police.[6] Some experts estimate that only 10% of all rapes are reported; the reporting rate for wife-beating is even lower.[7] A "self-report" study estimates that about one out of every thirty delinquent acts comes to the attention of the police.[8]

The primary reason for not reporting crimes is the belief that the police are either incapable of solving crimes or are likely to aggravate the situation by brutalizing or intimidating the victims. This distrust of the police is realistically based on the extensive experiences of working class communities, especially racial and national minorities, with police brutality and ineffectiveness. According to a recent national public opinion survey, blacks think that the police are doing a poor job almost three times more than do whites.[9] (See Table 1.)

Table 1 Evaluation of police performance (percent responding "good") by family income and race of respondent, eight impact cities: aggregate

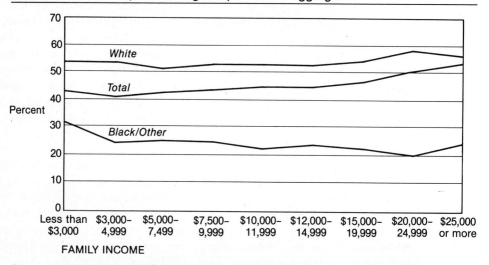

Source: James Garofolo, Public Opinion About Crime, U.S. Dept. of Justice, LEAA, 1977.

According to a recent study by Paul Takagi, black males are killed by the police at a rate 13 times higher than for white males.[10] But police killings are only a small part of the total level of state brutality directed at the civilian population. It is not an exaggeration to say that millions of Americans now alive have been beaten by the police. Data cited by James Q. Wilson, a political scientist at Harvard, show that 5% of all blacks (over one million people) and 2% of all whites (over four million people) report themselves unjustifiably beaten by the police. And sociologist Albert Reiss, in a LEAA-financed study, found that the police used unnecessary force in 3% of all police-citizen encounters, representing hundreds of thousands of cases of brutality per year. When these data are understood in the context of peer and family relationships, a very large proportion of the population on a day-to-day basis faces or fears the possibility of police violence.[11]

Additionally, the police have a very poor track record in solving and prosecuting serious "street" crime. A two-year Rand study, released in 1976, reported that substantially more than 50% of all serious crimes reported to the police receive no more than superficial investigation by detectives and investigators. Unless the patrolman on the scene makes an arrest or a patrol car accidentally stops a burglar for speeding, concludes Rand, there is little chance of a successful prosecution.[12]

The selective recruitment and militaristic training of the police, aggravated by institutionalized racism and sexism, encourage them to regard "high crime" areas as either a combat zone requiring the dispassionate objectivity of a professional soldier or a "subculture" of violence and depravity where victimization is culturally inevitable. Not surprisingly, policing the ghettos and barrios vacillates from extraordinary violence to cynical resignation.

This does not mean that all rank and file police operate in this way. There are many individual officers and a small number of progressive caucuses, such as the Afro-American Patrolmen's League in Chicago and Officers for Justice in San Francisco, who are genuinely concerned about protecting working class communities from crime. But their efforts are easily frustrated, partly because the roots of "street" crime are deeply embedded in social conditions over which they have no control, and partly because their efforts are continuously undermined and sabotaged by the political police and "red squads," who make it their business to destroy community and political organizations which are trying to combat drug pushing, pimping, rape and other forms of parasitical criminality.

Scope of Crime

According to a 1977 Gallup Poll and a survey of 70 countries, the U.S. has the highest crime rate of all capitalist and European countries. One of every five homes was victimized by crime; 15% of working class communities reported that they were afraid of being victimized by crime in their own homes, while 43% thought that crime had increased in their neighborhood.[13]

During 1974, according to the Victimization Surveys, over 39.5 million persons over the age of 12 were victimized by selected, serious crimes, an increase of 7.5% over 1973. In 1975, there was another 2% increase to nearly 40.5 million estimated incidents of victimization.[14] And the latest Census Bureau study reports over 41 million for 1976.[15] This is almost four times higher than the FBI's UCR Index. Moreover, it should be remembered that these estimates do *not* include homicide, "victimless" crimes (illegal drugs and prostitution, for example) or the "hidden" figures of "white-collar" crime—price-fixing, health and safety violations, tax fraud, embezzlement, false advertising, etc.—which cause immense suffering and untold deprivation in working class communities.

The Victimization Surveys have caused considerable embarrassment to the government, which had hoped to use them to demonstrate that LEAA's "war on crime" was winning some major battles. The Surveys, however, have instead demonstrated that the rate of "street" crime has gradually increased, despite the 55% increase in criminal justice expenditures from $11 billion in 1971 to $17 billion in 1975; despite the fact that the number of police almost doubled in the decade between 1965 and 1975; despite a flourishing criminal justice-industrial complex which has upgraded the technological capacity of the police and introduced computers, weapons systems, data retrieval devices and modern communications equipment to a hitherto "backward" bureaucracy; despite the advice and thousands of research studies conducted by the "best and brightest" scholars from the most privileged universities and corporate think tanks.

Not surprisingly, the federal government recently called a halt to the Victimization Surveys, even though they were widely regarded as one of the very few worthwhile and reliable projects initiated by LEAA. The reasons for this action are quite obvious. Not only did the Surveys expose the bankruptcy and incredible waste of the government's "war on crime." They also supported the conclusion that "street" crime is not simply a *byproduct* of the capitalist mode of production, a logistics problem to be solved by technocrats trained in "systems analysis." Rather, it is shown to be a phenomenon *endemic* to capitalism at its highest stage of development.

Victims of Street Crime

"Street" crime is primarily an *intra-class* and *intra-racial* phenomenon, media stereotypes to the contrary.[16] White women are most likely to be raped by white men; young black men are most likely to be robbed by other young black men; and working class families are most likely to have their homes vandalized or ripped off by strangers living only a few blocks away.

The victims of "street" crime are overwhelmingly poor people, particularly blacks and Chicanos living in metropolitan areas. LEAA's 1973 Victimization Surveys found that, with the exception of theft, families with annual incomes under $3,000 were the most likely to be victimized by serious crimes of violence and property loss.[17] Another study, using the same indices, reported that the unemployed were more likely to be victims of crime in rates two to three times higher than those employed.[18]

Racial and national minorities, especially blacks, have the highest rate of victimization. A 1975 LEAA study in the five largest cities found that:

Blacks and Chicanos in Philadelphia and Los Angeles are most likely to be victimized by assault and robbery.

Blacks in Philadelphia and Chicago are the most victimized by theft.

Black family households in all five cities suffer the highest rates of burglary and auto theft.

In Philadelphia, blacks are twice as likely as whites to be burglarized.

In Chicago, blacks are twice as likely as whites to be victimized by auto theft.[19]

Follow-up nationwide studies, released in 1976, similarly found that the highest incidence of violent and property crime is among the poor and unemployed, spe-

Table 2

Type of victimization	Race of victim	
	White	Black and other races
Base	143,217,000	19,019,000
Rape and attempted rape	90	158
Robbery	599	1,388
Robbery and attempted robbery with injury	207	473
Serious assault	108	294
Minor assault	99	179
Robbery without injury	213	589
Attempted robbery without injury	179	326
Assault	2,554	2,929
Aggravated assault	954	1,656
With injury	301	599
Attempted assault with weapon	653	1,057
Simple assault	1,600	1,272
With injury	399	289
Attempted assault without weapon	1,201	983
Personal larceny with contact	267	678
Purse snatching	57	126
Attempted purse snatching	44	47
Pocket picking	166	504
Personal larceny without contact	9,209	7,671

Source: Michael Hindelang et al., Sourcebook of Criminal Justice Statistics-1974, U.S. Dept. of Justice, LEAA, 1975.

cifically, the superexploited sectors of the working class, young men and single or separated women. Blacks have higher victimization rates than whites for rape, robbery and assault. Moreover, blacks over age 20 are robbed at two to three times the rate of their white counterparts.[20] (See Table 2.)

While crimes of violence account for less than 10% of "street" crimes, they are an important source of demoralization and victimization in working class communities. Rape, assault, child- and wife-beating and homicide not only cause great personal suffering to the victims and their relatives and close friends, but also undermine collective solidarity.

This is *not* a recent phenomenon. Family life under industrial capitalism, as Engels observed in *The Condition of the Working Class in England*, was "almost impossible for the worker." Impoverished living conditions, long hours of work and little time for recreation made family life a continuous round of problems and tensions. Wives and children, doubly exploited by economic dependency and male supremacist ideology, are regular targets of brutal assaults. "Yet the working man," noted Engels in 1845, "cannot escape from the family, must live in the family, and the consequence is a perpetual succession of family troubles, domestic quarrels, most demoralizing for parents and children alike."[21]

Under monopoly capitalism, social and family life is particularly difficult in the superexploited sectors of the working class, where economic hardship, a chaotic labor market, uprooted community life ("urban renewal") and deteriorating social services provide a fertile environment for individualism and demoralization. A recent study, prepared for the W.E.B. DuBois Conference on Black Health in 1976, reveals for example that about 95% of blacks victimized by homicide are killed by other blacks.

> In 1974, almost 11,000 of the 237,000 deaths of nonwhites in the United States, the overwhelming majority of whom were black, were from homicide. More than six percent of the black males who died during this year were victims of homicide as were over two percent of the black females. Among blacks *homicide* was the *fourth leading cause of death*, exceeded only by major cardiovascular diseases, malignant neoplasms, and accidents. All of the infectious diseases taken together took a lesser toll than did homicide.

White men are killed by homicide at a rate of 9.3 per 100,000 compared to a rate of 77.9 per 100,000 for black men of comparable age. To put it another way, "the difference in life expectation between white and black males is seven years. Almost a fifth of that is due to homicide. . . . More than twice as many blacks died from homicide in 1974 as from automobile accidents, and homicides accounted for about 40 percent as many deaths as cancer."[22]

While the Victimization Surveys and other studies show that minorities are responsible for a higher incidence of violent "street" crimes, such as rape, robbery, assault and homicide, than whites, this does not mean that crime is simply a *racial* phenomenon.[23] Historically, "street" crime has tended to be concentrated in the marginalized sectors of the labor force and in the demoralized layers of the working class, irrespective of skin color or ethnic origin.[24] Today, it is those families with annual incomes below the poverty line which fill the police stations, jails and hospital emergency rooms. Since blacks, Chicanos, Native Americans and Puerto Ricans are disproportionately concentrated in the superexploited sectors of the working class, they are also disproportionately represented in police records and as victims of crime.

The risk of victimization is closely tied to the material conditions of life. Black women suffer a higher rate of rape than white women because they are more exposed to the insecurities of public transportation and poorly policed streets; the elderly, living on fixed incomes in downtown rooming houses, are much more physically vulnerable than their counterparts in suburban "leisure" communities; families that cannot afford to install burglar alarms or remodel their homes into fortresses are easier prey for rip-offs and thefts; small businesses, unable to buy the protection of private security agencies, are more likely to be burglarized; apartment buildings, guarded by rent-a-cops, doormen and security fences have a lower rate of burglary than public housing projects and tenements; and working parents, hustling low-paying jobs with erratic hours in order to pay the daily bills, cannot hire tutors, counselors and psychiatrists or turn to private schools when their children become "delinquency" problems.

Crime and Class

The current high level of crime and victimization within the marginalized sectors of the working class can be partly understood in the context of the capitalist labor market. The "relative surplus population" is not an aberration or incidental by-product. Rather it is continuously reproduced as a necessary element of the capitalist mode of production and is, to quote Marx, the "*lever* of capitalist accumulation. . . . It forms a disposable industrial reserve army that belongs to capital quite as absolutely as if the latter had bred it at its own cost. Independently of the limits of the actual increase of population, it creates, for the changing needs of the self-expansion of capital, a mass of human material always ready for exploitation."[25]

For this population, the economic conditions of life are unusually desperate and degrading. The high level of property crime and petty hustles cannot be separated from the problems of survival. Commenting on the process of primitive accumulation in 15th and 16th century England, Marx observed that the rising bourgeoisie destroyed the pre-existing modes of production through the forcible expropriation of people's land and livelihood, thus creating a "free" proletariat which "could not possibly be absorbed by the nascent manufactures as fast as it was thrown upon the world." Thousands of peasants were "turned *en masse* into beggars, robbers, vagabonds . . . and 'voluntary' criminals. . . ."[26] For these victims of capitalism, crime was both a means of survival and an effort to resist the discipline and deadening routine of the workhouse and factory.[27]

But crime was not only a manifestation of early capitalism, with its unconcealed plunder, terrorism and unstable labor market. Crime was endemic to both the rural and urban poor in 18th century England.[28] And at the peak of industrial capitalism in the mid-19th century, Engels vividly described the prevalence of theft, prostitution and other types of widespread victimization in working class communities. "The British nation," he concluded, "has become the most criminal in the world."[29]

With at least 41 million persons annually victimized by serious "street" crimes in the United States, it is clear that monopoly capitalism has aggravated rather than reduced the incidence of crime. Recent studies, prepared for the United Nations report on *Economic Crises and Crime*, support the argument that the rate of criminal victimization is not only correlated with crises and "downturns" in the capitalist economy, but also with the "long-term effects of economic growth,"[30] thus giving support to Marx's "absolute law of capitalist accumulation—in proportion as capital accumulates, the lot of the laborer, be his payment high or low, must grow worse."[31] The economic underpinnings of "street" crime are underscored by the findings of the Victimization Surveys that over 90% of serious offenses are property-related (theft, burglary, robbery, etc.).[32] Not surprisingly, most "street" crime is disproportionately concentrated in the superexploited sectors of the working class where unemployment rates of 50% are not uncommon.

But "street" crime is not only related to economic conditions; nor is it solely restricted to working class neighborhoods. A series of national studies, conducted by Martin Gold and his colleagues, found little difference in rates of juvenile delinquency between blacks and whites or working class and petty bourgeois families.[33] Their latest study reports that "white girls are no more nor less frequently or seriously delinquent than black girls; and white boys, no more nor less *frequently* delinquent than black boys; but white boys are *less seriously* delinquent than black boys." (See Table 3.) Moreover, when delinquency is correlated with socioeconomic status, it is found that "higher status" boys (i.e., the sons of the petty bourgeoisie for the most part) are more likely than working class boys to commit thefts, steal cars and commit assaults.[34]

"Street" crime, like white chauvinism and male supremacy, is most brutal in (although by no means limited to) the superexploited sectors of the working class. Monopoly capitalism emiserates increasingly larger portions of the working class and proletarianizes the lower strata of the petty bourgeoisie, degrades workers' skills and competency in the quest for higher productivity, and organizes family and community life on the basis of its most effective exploitability. It consequently makes antagonism rather than reciprocity the norm of social relationships.[35]

Table 3   Frequency and Seriousness of Delinquent Behavior by Race and Sex

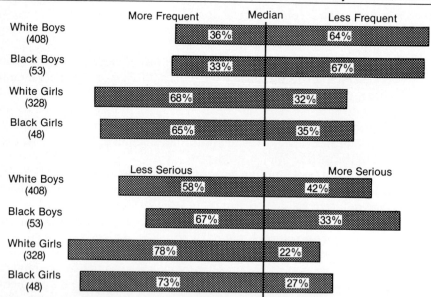

Source: Jay Williams and Martin Gold, "From Delinquent Behavior to Official Delinquency." © 1972 by the Society for the Study of Social Problems, Inc. Reprinted from *Social Problems*, Vol. 20, No. 2, Fall, 1972, p. 216 by permission.

Under monopoly capitalism, family and peer relationships become even more brutal and attenuated. The family as an economic unit is totally separated, except as a consumer, from the productive processes of society. Adolescents are denied access to the labor market and forced to depend on their parents, who bear the costs of their subsistence and education. As a result, millions of youth, including many of the children of the petty bourgeoisie, "become subject to an extraordinary variety of social problems that accompany the statuses of dependent able-bodied persons in our society."[36]

"It is only in its era of monopoly," writes Harry Braverman in *Labor and Monopoly Capital*, "that the capitalist mode of production takes over the totality of individual, family, and social needs and, in subordinating them to the market, also reshapes them to serve the needs of capital." While more and more of the population "is packed ever more closely together in the urban environment, the atomization of social life proceeds apace. . . . The social structure, built upon the market, is such that relations between individuals and social groups do not take place directly, as cooperative human encounters, but through the market as relations of purchase and sale."

As more family members are required to work and the pressures of urban life intensify, the family is required to "strip for action in order to survive and 'succeed' in the market society." Thus, urban life, governed by capital and the profit motive, "is both chaotic and profoundly hostile to all feelings of community." The "universal market," to use Braverman's appropriate term, not only destroys the material foundations of cooperative social relations, but also permeates even the most private domain of personal life, setting husband against wife, neighbor against neighbor.[37] "In short," as Engels observed over a century ago, "everyone sees in his neighbor an enemy to be got out of the way, or, at best, a tool to be used for his own advantage."[38]

Crime as Rebellion?

There is a tendency within the New Left to glorify crime as "primitive rebellion" and interpret it as a form of spontaneous anticapitalist revolt. There is definitely some support for this position when we examine previous historical eras.

According to Eric Hobsbawm's well-known study of criminality in precapitalist and agrarian societies, "social banditry" was a form of class struggle and often a precursor or accompaniment to peasant revolutions. "The point about social bandits," he writes, "is that they are peasant outlaws whom the lord and state regard as criminals, but who remain within peasant society, and are considered by their people as heroes, as champions, avengers, fighters for justice, perhaps even leaders of liberation, and in any case as men to be admired, helped and supported." This respect for "social bandits" was based on their defense of the oppressed and their selective theft of the oppressor's crops and property.[39]

"Social banditry" or its equivalent persisted throughout at least two hundred years of primitive accumulation, as displaced peasants asserted their traditional communal rights to subsistence through poaching, smuggling and ship-wrecking against bourgeois claims to the supremacy of capitalist private property.[40]

But not all criminality was a blow to class rule in agrarian and early capitalist societies. Peasant society was also victimized by "professional" criminals and "common robbers" who did not make any class distinctions between their victims; and the rural and urban poor in eighteenth century England were regularly demoralized by theft, robbery and other types of *intra-class* victimization.

Criminality as an effective, though limited, method of waging class warfare began to decline with the development of industrial capitalism. There were two important reasons for this. First, modernization reduced the means of protection and survival. The technology of communications and rapid forms of transportation, combined with economic development, public administration and the growth of the state, deprived banditry of the technical and social conditions under which it flourishes. Second, and more importantly, the organized working class developed collective, political associations which were far superior to individual criminality or even the organized self-help of banditry. As Engels observed:

> The earliest, crudest, and least fruitful form of rebellion was that of crime. . . . The workers soon realized that crime did not help matters. The criminal could protest against the existing order of society only singly, as one individual; the whole might of society was brought to bear upon each criminal, and crushed him with its immense superiority. Besides, theft was the most primitive form of protest, and for this reason, if no other, it never becomes the universal expression of the public opinion of the working-man, however much they might approve of it in silence.[41]

Under monopoly capitalism, "street" crime bears little resemblance to the social banditry of Sicilian peasants, of the pastoral nomads of Central Asia or even of the rural poor in mercantile England. Contemporary "bandits" are more likely to rip off their neighbor or rob the local mom and pop store than to hold up a bank or kidnap a corporate executive. And they are more likely to be regarded as pariahs in the community than to be welcomed as heroes. Nor can theft from supermarkets and chain stores (which is widespread) be considered a modern equivalent of banditry, because bourgeois rule is not weakened by such activity, and the cost of such theft is generally passed on to the consumer in the form of higher prices or inferior commodities. It is only among ultra-leftist sects, which have no base of support within working class communities, that such banditry is still practiced and glorified.

Conclusion

The political solution to "street" crime does not lie in *mystifying* its reality by reactionary allusions to "banditry," nor in *reducing* it to a manifestation of "lumpen" viciousness. The former is utopian and dangerous because it defends practices that undermine the safety and solidarity of the working class (and glorifies spontaneity and putschism); the latter objectively legitimates the bourgeoisie's attack on superexploited workers, especially black and brown workers.

While "street" crime is associated with the most demoralized sectors of the working class, we must be careful about making mechanical and ahistorical generalizations about the "lumpen" and "dangerous class." As Paul Hirst has correctly pointed out, Marx and Engels took a very harsh and uncompromising attitude to "street" crime, not from a moralistic perspective, but out of concern for building a disciplined and principled workers' movement. "Their standpoint," notes Hirst, "was uncompromisingly political and based on the proletarian class position. Marx and Engels ask of any social class or sociopolitical activity, what is its effectivity in the struggle of the proletariat for socialism, does it contribute to the political victory of the exploited and oppressed?"[42]

Marx and Engels based their evaluation on both a class analysis of criminality and a concrete investigation of the role of the "lumpenproletariat" in specific political struggles. Thus, they argued that the "lumpen" weakens the workers' movement by living off the workers' productive labor, for example by theft, as well as by serving the bourgeoisie as informers, spies, collaborators and adventurists.[43]

The contemporary workers' movement must take an equally uncompromising stand against organized, parasitical forms of victimization and against "criminals" and prisoners who become "snitches" and agents of the political police. Pimping, gambling rackets, illegal drug operations, etc., are just as damaging to working class communities as any "legal" business which profits from people's misery and desperation.

But we must be careful to distinguish organized criminality from "street" crime and the "lumpen" from the superexploited sectors of the working class. Most "street" crime is not organized and not very profitable. Most theft, for example, is committed by individuals, and each incidence of "street" theft amounts to much less than $100.[44] Moreover, there is typically no direct economic advantage associated with crimes of personal violence—rape, homicide, assault, etc.

The conditions of life in the superexploited sectors create both high levels of "street" crime *and* political militancy. The urban black community, for example, is hit the hardest by "street" crime, but it is also the locus of tremendous resistance and struggle—as witnessed by the civil rights movement, the ghetto revolts of the 1960s, and the antirepression struggles of today. Moreover, of the thousands of blacks who annually go to prison for serious crimes of victimization, many have become transformed by the collective experience of prison life and participate in numerous acts of solidarity, self-sacrifice and heroism—as witnessed by the conversion of Malcolm X, George Jackson and countless other anonymous militants in the strikes and uprisings at Soledad, San Quentin, Attica, etc.

While the link between "street" crime and economic conditions is clearly established, we must guard against economism. Crime is not simply a matter of poverty, as evidenced by the unparalleled criminality and terrorism of the ruling class. Nor is "street" crime explained by poverty, for petty bourgeois youth in the United States are probably just as delinquent as their working class counterparts, and there are many impoverished nations in the world that do not in any way approach the high level of criminality in this country. The problem of "street" crime should be approached not only as a product of the unequal distribution of wealth and chaotic labor market practices, but also as an important aspect of the demoralizing social relations and individualistic ideology that characterize the capitalist mode of production at its highest stage of development.

Footnotes

1. Center for Research on Criminal Justice, *The Iron Fist and the Velvet Glove*. San Francisco: Institute for the Study of Labor and Economic Crisis (1977):14.
2. *Christian Science Monitor* (November 13, 1973); *New York Times* (April 16, 1977; July 21, 1977); *San Francisco Chronicle* (January 25, 1978). According to the *Law Enforcement News* (January 3, 1978), the Law Enforcement Assistance Administration is now funding some 600 anticrime projects at a cost of $37 million.
3. Karl Marx and Frederick Engels, *The Communist Manifesto*. New York: Appleton-Century-Crofts (1955):20–21.
4. "The Politics of Street Crime," *Crime and Social Justice* 5(Spring-Summer, 1976): 1–4.
5. *San Francisco Chronicle* (February 20, 1978).
6. Michael Hindelang et al., *Sourcebook of Criminal Justice Statistics:1974*. Washington, D.C.: U.S. Government Printing Office (1975):233.
7. Center for Research on Criminal Justice: 14.
8. Jay Williams and Martin Gold, "From Delinquent Behavior to Official Delinquency," *Social Problems* 20,2 (Fall, 1972):209–29.
9. James Garofolo, *Public Opinion About Crime*. Washington, D.C.: U.S. Government Printing Office (1977):28.
10. "The Management of Police Killings," *Crime and Social Justice* 8 (Fall-Winter, 1977): 34–43.

11. "The Management of Police Killings":42.
12. *U.S. News and World Report* (October 10, 1977).
13. *San Francisco Chronicle* (December 22, 1977).
14. Law Enforcement Assistance Administration, *Criminal Victimization in the United States: A Comparison of 1973 and 1974 Findings*. Washington, D.C.: U.S. Government Printing Office (1976).
15. *San Francisco Chronicle* (February 20, 1978).
16. Law Enforcement Assistance Administration, *Criminal Victimization in the United States: 1973*. Washington, D.C.: U.S. Government Printing Office (1976).
17. See note 16 above.
18. John E. Conklin, *The Impact of Crime*. New York: Macmillan (1975):26.
19. Law Enforcement Assistance Administration, *Criminal Victimization Surveys in the Nation's Five Largest Cities*. Washington, D.C.: U.S. Government Printing Office (1975).
20. LEAA, *Criminal Victimization in the U.S.: 1973*.
21. Frederick Engels, *The Condition of the Working Class in England*. Moscow: Progress Publishers (1973):168.
22. Yongsock Shin, Davor Jedlicka and Everett Lee, "Homicide Among Blacks," *Phylon* 38,4 (December, 1977):398–407.
23. For data on the high homicide rate among Native Americans, see Charles Reasons,

"Crime and the Native American," in Reasons and Kuykendall, eds., *Race, Crime and Justice*. Pacific Palisades, Ca.: Goodyear (1972):79–95; for data on alcohol-related deaths among blacks in Georgia, see George Lowe and Eugene Hodges, "Race and the Treatment of Alcoholism in a Southern State," *Social Problems* 20,2 (Fall, 1972): 240–52; for a discussion of the high rates of rape, robbery and assault among blacks, albeit from a cultural and "racial" perspective, see Michael Hindelang, "Race and Involvement in Common Law Personal Crimes," *American Sociological Review* 43,1 (February, 1978):93–109.

24. See, for example, Edward Green, "Race, Social Status, and Criminal Arrest," in Reasons and Kuykendall: 103–23.
25. Karl Marx, *Capital*, Vol. 1. New York: International Publishers (1975):632.
26. Marx: 734.
27. Dario Melossi, "The Penal Question in *Capital.*" *Crime and Social Justice* 5(Spring-Summer, 1976):26–33.
28. See, for example, Douglas Hay et al., *Albion's Fatal Tree: Crime and Society in Eighteenth-Century England*. New York: Pantheon (1975).
29. Engels: 168.
30. United Nations Social Defense Research Institute. *Economic Crises and Crime*. Rome: UNSDRI (1976).
31. Marx: 645.
32. LEAA, *Criminal Victimization in the U.S.: 1973*.
33. Williams and Gold: 209–29; Martin Gold

and David Reimer, "Changing Patterns of Delinquent Behavior Among Americans 13 Through 16 Years Old: 1967–1972." *Crime and Delinquency Literature* 7,4 (December, 1975):483–517.

34. Williams and Gold: 215–18. These findings have been confirmed by Paul Takagi in a current (unpublished) study of delinquency among Chinese youth in San Francisco. For a methodological critique of the Gold studies, see Hindelang, "Race and Involvement In Common Law Personal Crimes": 103–04.
35. See, for example, David Harvey, *Social Justice and the City*. London: Johns Hopkins University Press (1973).
36. Herman Schwendinger and Julia Schwendinger, "Delinquency and the Collective Varieties of Youth," *Crime and Social Justice* 5(Spring–Summer, 1976):7–25.
37. Harry Braverman, *Labor and Monopoly Capital*. New York: Monthly Review Press (1974):271–83.
38. Engels:170–71.
39. Eric Hobsbawm, *Bandits*. New York: Delacorte (1969):13–23.
40. See, for example, Douglas Hay et al.
41. Engels:250–51.
42. Paul Hirst, "Marx and Engels on Law, Crime and Morality," in Taylor, Walton and Young, eds., *Critical Criminology*. London: Routledge and Kegan Paul (1975):203–32.
43. See note 42 above.
44. LEAA, *Criminal Victimization in the U.S.: 1973*.

BLACKS AS VICTIMS: BLACKS VS. BLACKS OR THE STRUCTURE VS. BLACKS? 1

When Brother Kills Brother: Black-on-Black Violence

Richard Stengel

Delfonic McCray, 13, was big for his age, 6 ft. tall. He liked basketball and girls, and kept love letters carefully folded in his Michael Jackson wallet. He and a friend were on their way to a Chicago Bulls basketball game and stopped at a housing project on the west side of Chicago to see a girlfriend. As they approached the back entrance of a graffiti-scarred tenement, a group of youths taunted them. Delfonic approached tentatively, then turned and ran. One of the youths casually drew a .22-cal. handgun and shot him. "We had a good kid coming along," said Delfonic's grandmother. Now that he was becoming a man, she had gone out and bought him a new suit. "I had no way of knowing he would be buried in it," she said.

Four-year-old Demont Beans was playing on his tricycle in front of his home in south-central Los Angeles. In the front yard of a neighboring house, James Barnett, 23, was arguing with his girlfriend and her brother. Police say Barnett drew a .22-cal. revolver. The bullet he fired struck Demont in the head. The boy was rushed to Martin Luther King Jr.–Drew Medical Center, where the average daily admissions to the trauma center include four gunshot wounds, three stabbings and three cases of "blunt assault" to the head. Demont died on the operating table. For Dr. Arthur W. Fleming, the chief of surgery, it was nothing new. "This is the closest thing to a combat hospital that you'll find in peace-time," he says.

Colin Fowles, 32, was once known as the fastest man in the North American Soccer League. He was a star player on the Fort Lauderdale Strikers from the team's founding in 1977 until its dissolution two years ago. Fowles kept in shape by playing in amateur leagues, as he was doing one night two weeks ago during a pickup game in Dade County's Bunche Park, outside Miami. As half time neared in the scoreless match, a noisy squabble several hundred feet from the game erupted in gunfire. The gunmen charged onto the playing field, firing wildly at witnesses to their fight and anyone else who got in the way. Fowles, who once outran a quarter horse for 80 yards, could not outrun the bullets flying at him. Said Charles Benedict, an eyewitness: "What happened to Colin was cold-blooded murder."

Every murder is different in its own way. Each has its own perverse logic, its own cast of mourners, its own sad finality. But a staggering number these days have something in common, something that has become part of a frighteningly familiar but largely unspoken national scourge: the epidemic of violence by young blacks against other young blacks.

The leading cause of death among black males ages 15 to 24 in the U.S. is not heart disease, not cancer, not any natural cause. It is murder by other blacks. More than 1 out of every 3 blacks who die in that age group is the victim of a homicide. Across America, particularly among the underclass in the nation's urban ghettos, brother is killing brother in a kind of racial fratricide. More than 40% of all the nation's murder victims are black, and 94% of those who commit these murders are black. The 6,000 or so Americans who lost their lives because of black-on-black violence in 1981 alone rivals the number of black servicemen killed during the twelve years of the Viet Nam conflict.

The statistics add up to a horrifying equation. In America today, a white female has 1 chance in 606 of becoming a murder victim. A white male has 1 chance in 186. A black female has 1 chance in 124. A black male has 1 chance in 29.

The problem is particularly acute in major cities where black gangs proliferate. In Chicago in 1983, 412 of the 729 homicides were blacks killing blacks. Between July and November last year in Detroit, more than 100 children—they cannot be called anything else, they were under 17—were shot. All but four were black. The Watts riots of 1965 caused 34 deaths. That figure is currently equaled every 38 days among blacks in Los Angeles.

"The uncomfortable fact," writes Charles Silberman, author of *Criminal Violence, Criminal Justice*, "is that black offenders account for a disproportionate number of the crimes that evoke the most fear." This fear is felt by all Americans, but the anxiety felt by blacks is more intense, more pervasive, more real, for they are the ones who suffer most from violence. The white fear of black violence, recently personified by Subway Vigilante Bernhard Goetz, does not reflect reality: only 5% of the nation's 11,300 one-on-one slayings in 1983 involved whites killed by blacks.

The issue of black-on-black violence is a disquieting and sensitive subject, one that is often left in silence by the growing number of blacks who have made it into the middle class and by traditional civil rights leaders who prefer to speak out on other issues. "Today we are faced with a new American dilemma, one that is especially difficult for black leaders and members of the black middle class," says Glenn Loury, a professor of public policy at Harvard. "The bottom stratum of the black community has compelling problems that can no longer be blamed solely on white racism, and which force us to confront fundamental failures in black society."

The violence of today seems divorced from rationale and motive. The murders are mindless, random, indiscriminate. Young black men seem to be murdering one another with a malign indifference, killing with the casual air of Bruce Lee dispatching men in a kung fu movie. For some, it seems as if murder has become a kind of noxious fashion or wanton recreation. "Members of the new generation kill, maim and injure without reason or remorse," writes Silberman.

The psychology that seems to underlie the epidemic is as numbing as the statistics. Many of these young killers display an absence of what psychiatrists call affect. They show no discernible emotional reaction to what they have done. Some seem incapable even of regarding their victims as human beings. The senseless nature of it all baffles Paul Maurice, a retired black homicide detective from New York. "It appears that they don't have any idea of the consequences of taking someone's life," he says. "When you get a guy to 'fess up as to why he did it, you get very shoddy answers: 'He took my coat.' 'He took my dollar.' 'He stepped on my girlfriend's foot.'"

The stories told by those who have emerged from this world have the ring of tales by escaped adventurers from a savage land. Danny Sanders of Brooklyn has spent 13 of his 35 years behind bars. Now he works for the Fortune Society, a group that helps ex-convicts. "When we were robbing people, the trick was to get the money without hurting anybody. Now the kids brag about hurting their victims." Danny claims that he has never backed down from a fight in his life, but he is skittish about this new generation. A group of teenagers recently demanded money from him while he waited for the subway. He forked it over. "I ain't scared," he says. "But I ain't crazy either."

Marvin Brinston, 19, was once a mean walker of Oakland's mean streets. One day, he experienced a sidewalk epiphany. "Two men were arguing," he recalls. "One just straight up and shot the other. It dawned on me how they got killed by just talking. And that scared me. I just had to get away from that." Now Brinston is doing landscaping and maintenance work for A.C. Transit, the East Bay bus system.

Gil Johnson, 24, of the Bronx, N.Y., is uneasy about the younger generation. "They don't take no talking. They just come out shooting." He had a friend who was killed after stepping on someone else's foot. "If he had said, 'I'm sorry' or 'Scuse me' or something like that, he'd be alive today."

What is the explanation for this murderousness? Why are blacks disproportionately represented as victims and victimizers, as predators and prey? One partial explanation, some experts contend, is the hopelessness that pervades the urban ghetto, which fosters a kind of street-corner nihilism, a feeling that nothing is worth anything. Says James M. Evans Jr., a social worker who organized a workshop last year in Washington on the subject of black-on-black violence: "They believe they have nothing to lose. Even if they should lose their own lives, they feel they will not have lost very much. Besides, why should they be good, they ask. There is no reward for good behavior." Paul Hubbard, vice president of an independent urban planning agency called New Detroit Inc., is struck by the sense of detachment and despair among violent young blacks. "They have a value system much different from ours, and they don't have a reason for adopting our value system because we haven't been able to show them why they should."

Dr. Mark L. Rosenberg of the Centers for Disease Control in Atlanta and Sociologist Evan Stark of Rutgers University have written that three broad themes emerge from the literature about violence: "The importance of unacceptable levels of poverty, racial discrimination and gender inequality; the cultural acceptance of violence as a way to manage dilemmas these and other situations pose; and the ready availability of lethal agents that can be used in violence against others or self." Social scientists see additional reasons: high unemployment, drugs, gangs, and the rise in female-headed households and births out of wedlock. The rate of black teenage unemployment in the nation's cities is more than 50% in some areas. The future is not cheering either. In those same cities, more than half the black children are born out of wedlock.

All of this breeds a shadow society where traditional values are scarce and violence is promiscuous. For young black men, violence can become a warped form of self-assertion, a kind of "I kill, therefore I am." Snuffing out another life perversely affirms their own. Almost 40 years ago, Ralph Ellison wrote in *Invisible Man* about violence as a way for black men to assert their existence to themselves: "You ache with the need to convince yourself that you do exist in the real world, that you're a part of all the sound and anguish."

But why are blacks killing other blacks? That is the one question on which there is almost universal agreement: proximity. "You pick on what's close," says Social Worker Evans. Harvard Psychiatry Professor Alvin Poussaint suggests in his book *Why Blacks Kill Blacks* that such violence is a manifestation of self-hatred and repressed rage, which he says are a legacy of racism. Killing someone who mirrors oneself is a reflection of hating oneself. "Violence can be a potent drug for the oppressed person." Poussaint says, "Reacting to the futility of his life, the individual derives an ultimate sense of power when he holds the fate of another human being in his hands." Poussaint goes so far as to suggest that ultimately the victims may bring their fate upon themselves, subconsciously provoking the murder and making it a kind of willed suicide. Poussaint notes, as do many others, that the easy availability of handguns gives power to the powerless. What the Colt six-shooter was to the Wild West is what the "Saturday-night special" is to the ghetto: the great equalizer.

Some suggest that for blacks in the ghetto, crime and a life of violence are an occupational choice, like becoming a doctor or lawyer is for a child from the suburbs. In the ghetto, suggests Benjamin Carmichael in an article in *Black Perspectives on Crime and the Criminal Justice System*, the successful criminal cuts a glamorous figure and projects an enviable life-style, becoming a role model for youngsters whose only glimpse of wealth is on *Dynasty* or *Dallas*. Says Joseph Lowery, president of the Southern Christian Leadership Conference (S.C.L.C.): "You cannot ignore the fact that a poor black guy has little chance of succeeding, except in the seedy world of crime."

One legacy of segregation is that blacks have long viewed the police and the criminal justice system as tools of oppression rather than remedies for it. Even today, some experts argue, the criminal justice system spurs black-on-black violence by practicing a double standard. R. Eugene Pincham, a black Illinois Appellate Court judge, lists the four tiers of crime: white on white, white on black, black on white, and black on black. "The punishment is most severe for black-on-white crime," he says, more severe than either white on white or white on black. The punishment is mildest for black on black. Notes Pincham: "It thereby gives tacit approval of black-on-black crime."

Examples of the double standard are not hard to find. In Georgia, a person is eleven times as likely to receive the death penalty for killing a white as for killing a black. About 70% of the black men on death row in the U.S. killed whites. Retired Detective Paul Maurice sees the issue from a more personal perspective: "A homicide detective gets no Brownie points for solving a black-on-black killing, and no extra help." A vicious circle ensues: blacks are less likely to report crimes against them because they do not expect the police to attempt to solve them.

Programs for dealing with black-on-black violence cannot begin to cope with the problem. A few imaginative efforts are being made at the local or community level. In Oakland, officials have persuaded some youths to exchange guns and knives for brooms and brushes. Four years ago, Robert J. Shamoon, the tough-talking assistant operations manager of the East Bay Area transit system, had had enough of local gangs who defaced his buses on the outside and turned them into anxious prisons on the inside. He announced that if there was a reduction in vandalism and graffiti, he would use the money saved to create jobs for those who had been doing the damage. The community responded. The transit system is saving about $500,000 a year, and has helped create 175 jobs, many of which are held by youths who once used the buses as a mobile drug supermarket. Vernon Lewis, 22, formerly defaced the buses he now works to keep clean. Says he: "The reason we were out there destroying buses is that we didn't have nothing to do. We were the problem."

In Atlanta, the police are looking to the citizens for help. George Napper, the city's black public safety commissioner, helped create Partnership Against Crime, a program in which citizens and police identify safety problems in communities and work out ways to deal with them. So far, that has involved shifting police patrol hours, setting up neighborhood-watch programs and business-watch groups.

This month in Savannah, which ranks fourth among U.S. cities in homicide rates, a 31-member, N.A.A.C.P.-sponsored citizens task force on black-vs.-black violence was created. Curtis Cooper, president of the Savannah N.A.A.C.P., noted that blacks are usually both perpetrator and victim in Chatham County. The task force, he says, was designed "to wake people up about the seriousness of this problem." Eugene H. Gadsden, a black superior court judge and a member of the task force, asserted that community involvement was essential. "We're the ones being affected most," said Gadsden, "and we ought to be able to do something about it."

In other cities, individuals, many of them wounded by violence, have tried to make a difference. Rita Smith is a Harlem legend. Her son David was shot in 1979, an act that moved her to mobilize her neighborhood to protest the violence that was undoing it. She and her neighbors lobbied for increased police protection of their area, set up neighborhood-watch groups and a special crime hot line.

In Chicago, Paul Hall started a boys' club that offers tutoring, karate courses and music lessons. He has also set up a hot line for gang members who need help. During its first three weeks, he received more than 300 calls. Two years ago, Edward G. Gardner, founder and board chairman of Soft Sheen Products Co. in Chicago, started a "Black-on-Black Love Campaign," which was designed to reduce crime in the black community by promoting discipline and self-esteem. With a budget of $200,000 and 140 volunteers, the campaign uses posters and bumper stickers, radio and newspaper spots to send out the message "Replace black-on-black crime with black love." The program is also being sponsored in six other cities by the American Health and Beauty Aids Institute, a consortium of minority-owned companies.

Many young blacks feel that the traditional black leadership has shied away from confronting the question of black-on-black violence. "They are not in tune or touch with the streets," says Willie Mathews as he leans against his convenience store in Miami's Coconut Grove section. "They have moved away. There's nothing wrong with that, it's just that they don't see what happens on the corners. The real leaders are people who live here and are trying to help these kids."

Black leaders fear, perhaps with good reason, that too much public discussion of the black crime problem would serve only to provide ammunition to bigots and undermine the support of the white community. "It's a dangerous area," says the S.C.L.C.'s Lowery, "and it's unfair to focus on crime so people think it is synonymous with the black community."

Yet some black leaders have begun to speak out, arguing that the reality can no longer be discussed only in whispers or totally ignored. "To admit these failures is likely to be personally costly for black leaders," says Harvard Professor Loury, "and may also play into the hands of lingering racist sentiments. Not to admit them, however, is to forestall their resolution and to allow the racial polarization of the country to worsen." Earl T. Shinhoster, 35, executive director of the Southeastern district of the N.A.A.C.P., is among a new generation of rising black activists. "Leaders have to put themselves on the line," he says. "Unless black people address the problem, it won't be addressed by the nation."

One emerging theme is that of the black victim. Blacks are beginning to shift their perspective, seeing themselves not just as victims of white oppression but as victims of crime. While some are still denouncing the police for abusing criminals, many are condemning police for not being more vigilant. Robert Farrell, a city councilman from the black south-central section of Los Angeles, says the No. 1 priority of his constituents is not jobs, housing or education but putting a stop to violent crime. "We want an integrated police force," says Farrell, "but when the time comes when we need the police, we don't care whether they're black, white, brown or yellow."

As black Author Stanley Crouch wrote in the *Village Voice* in the wake of the Goetz shootings, some black perceptions nourished by the civil rights movement are changing. In automatically defending the black teenage criminal, suggested Crouch, blacks were also hurting themselves. "Race was one thing, crime another. It was no longer second nature for black people to take the side of the impoverished colored teenager who created so many of their own problems." There is a realization, compelled by force of circumstance, that blacks must look at themselves first as victims of crime and only second as victims of racism. To understand the crime is not to condone the criminal, suggests Silberman. "To excuse violence because black offenders are the victims of poverty and discrimination is racism of the most virulent sort; it is to continue to treat black people as if they were children incapable of making moral decisions or of assuming responsibility for their own actions and choices."

At the funeral of Ben Wilson, a promising young basketball player who was gunned down for no apparent reason in Chicago last year, Jesse Jackson took up the issue of black-on-black violence. "All of the murders that we didn't react to set the stage for this one," said Jackson in his eulogy. "We are losing more lives in the streets of America than we lost in the jungles of Viet Nam. We must be as serious about ending the war at home as the war abroad." Yes, black-on-black violence is a black problem. But above all it is an American problem. Segregating it from the rest of American life, treating it as an ill-kept secret that can be either ignored or rationalized away, is as damaging and insidious as segregation itself. "Crime is the same for all of us," says the noted black playwright Charles Fuller, author of *A Soldier's Play*. "We cannot abrogate our role as participants in American life."

BLACKS AS VICTIMS: BLACKS VS. BLACKS OR THE STRUCTURE VS. BLACKS? 2

"Black on Black" Crime: The Myth and the Reality

Bernard D. Headley

> Until we have the courage to free ourselves of many of the myths we know to be patently false, there will never be any serious alteration of the patterns of crime in this country.
>
> *The Honorable John Conyers,*
> *United States House of Representatives*

Few domestic or local issues in the United States (and to some extent Great Britain) in recent years have gripped the public's attention and become a platform for exploitative politicians more than the problem of "street crime." While the dominant white media never fail to underscore incidents of so-called "black on white" crime (i.e., "street crimes" committed by blacks against whites), attention is increasingly being drawn to the fact that "street crime" is essentially committed by low-income blacks against other low-income blacks (so-called "black on black" crime). The prevailing notion being: the physical survival and well-being of the black community in America is threatened more by blacks killing or stealing from other blacks ("threats from within") than from external or systemic forces ("threats from without").

This notion is being articulated not only by the white capitalist media (who profit from stories about crime), but also increasingly by leading figures among the black petty bourgeoisie—politicians, academics, journalists, and law enforcement personnel—who, like their white counterparts, have a vested interest in promoting this belief. They benefit significantly from employment in an ever-expanding criminal justice industry.

The present discussion is an attempt to dispel the underlying myth that intra-race and intra-class directed "street crime" (i.e., "black on black" or "poor on poor" crime) represents the single most dangerous threat to the survival and well-

Source: Bernard D. Headley, " 'Black on Black' Crime: The Myth and the Reality," *Crime and Social Justice*, No. 20 (1983), pp. 50–61. Reprinted by permission from *Crime and Social Justice*, P. O. Box 40601, San Francisco, CA 94140.

being of black and poor Americans. Furthermore, I hope to show that the recurring presence of this myth tends to clutter a proper analysis of crime in black and working class communities and, more important, that the continued propagation of the notion of "black on black" crime (even among leading black intellectuals) indicates an unwitting internalization of one of white America's most cherished characterizations of black people, i.e., "Negroes are 'naturally' violent." At the same time it overlooks those crimes committed by white corporate America against black and working class Americans—crimes far more deadly and threatening to their survival than so-called "black on black" or "poor on poor" crimes.

Finally, I will argue that before discussions of "crime reduction" and "crime prevention" among black and working class Americans can take place, it is first necessary to view the phenomenon of "street crime" within the framework of a class analysis: the relation of dispossessed groups to the means of production.

Alarming Trends

The myth that crimes committed by blacks against other blacks pose the single most dangerous threat to the black community is one that the black community itself (including the black press) has helped promulgate. And while there is no disputing the alarming trends in which blacks in the United States have criminally victimized each other, I will argue that when this phenomenon is placed in perspective with other forms of class victimization, our priorities will appear to be essentially misplaced. But first a look at some of the "frightening statistics," and at the way the phenomenon of "black on black" crime has been treated in one leading black publication.

So "horrifying" has been the phenomenon of "black on black" crime that *Ebony* magazine, only a few years ago, devoted an entire issue to its most grotesque aspects, citing at will the grim statistics. For example, the editorial pointed out that more blacks were killed by other blacks in the United States in 1977 than were killed in the entire nine-year duration of the Vietnam War. According to this editorial, "Most of the 5,734 blacks killed on the battlefields of Black America in one year (1977) could have survived Vietnam since Blacks who died there (5,711) averaged only 634 per year" (*Ebony*, 1979: 37). Based on these and other statistics, the editorial concluded that homicide is the leading cause of death among inner-city black males 15 to 44 years old, outnumbering deaths due to heart disease, cancer, sickle cell anemia, and other natural causes.

To reinforce the seriousness of the issue, the federal Law Enforcement Assistance Administration (LEAA) reported that for 1973, 87% of all robberies, rapes, and assaults involving black victims were committed by other blacks (LEAA, 1976; see also LEAA, 1975; Platt, 1978).

Again, there is no disputing the fact that the victims of "street crimes" are overwhelmingly poor people, particularly blacks and Chicanos, living in urban metropolitan areas. There is no arguing here that racial and national minorities, especially blacks, do have the highest rate of "street crime" victimization, and that in the few instances where perpetrators have been apprehended, they have indeed come from among the same superexploited sectors as their victims.

Undeniably, these are frightening trends that cannot be easily dismissed. Why poor blacks victimize other poor blacks is a question I shall return to, but we must bear in mind that viewing crime as a problem peculiar to a disadvantaged racial group becomes just one other way of blaming the victim. It diverts attention from the real causes of crime. Crime is not the result of blackness (which is what the notion of "black on black" crime implies), but rather of a complex of social and economic conditions—a negative "situational matrix"—brought on by the capitalist mode of production, in which both the black victim and the black victimizer are inextricably locked in a deadly game of survival.

More Dangerous Threats

Let us look objectively, however, at the prevailing notion that "street crimes" committed by blacks against other blacks constitute the most serious threat to the survival and unity of the black community. I suggest that if we examine black criminal victimization on a par with some less noticeable forms of victimization in the United States—which are no less criminal—directed against black and working class Americans, it should cause us to raise some questions about the "threat" of "black on black" or "poor on poor" crime.

Police Victimization

One such form of external victimization, for example, is police brutality (what the police manuals blandly refer to as "deadly force"). Another recent *Ebony* magazine article cites that, nationwide, blacks constitute fully 45% of police homicides in the United States (see *Ebony*, 1981), a figure quite disproportionate to their representation in the total U.S. population of approximately 12%.

About 60% of all police homicides recorded between 1970 and 1972 in New York City were black citizens (see *New York Times*, 1973). Clark (1974) reports that three quarters of all victims of police shootings between 1970 and 1973 were members of minority groups; about half were black and one quarter were of Hispanic ethnicity.

Takagi (1974), in his review of civilian deaths resulting from police use of force in California, reported that the incidence rate of such deaths increased by two and one-half times between 1962 and 1969, and that these rates have remained constantly nine times higher for blacks than for whites over the past 18 years. Robin (1973) investigated civilian deaths resulting from police force in Philadelphia that occurred between 1960 and 1970, and found that nearly 90% of those killed were black—whereas the local black community during this time accounted for only 22% of the population. At the same time, Robin reviewed statistics concerning police killings of civilians in seven other American cities (Akron, Chicago, Kansas

City, Miami, Buffalo, Boston, and Milwaukee), and found black victims included among the dead more frequently that whites at ratios ranging from 6 to 1 in Akron, to 30 to 1 in Milwaukee.

Data cited by as conservative a figure as James Q. Wilson show that 5% of all blacks (over one million people) report themselves to have been unjustifiably beaten by the police (cited in Platt, 1978: 27). And Reiss, in an LEAA-financed study, found that the police used unnecessary force in fully 3% of all police-citizen encounters involving blacks, "representing hundreds of thousands of cases of brutality per year" (cited in Platt, 1978: 27).

In a most revealing article—"Violence in Detroit: A Bleaker View" (*The Progressive*, 1981)—it was pointed out that the police unit called STRESS (Stop the Robberies and Enjoy Safe Streets), which had come into existence in Detroit in 1971, in two short years had 22 killings to its credit. Similar to SWAT in Los Angeles and Atlanta, and BOSS in New York City, STRESS accounted for only 1% of the 5,500 Detroit police officers, but it soon had the highest per capita number of civilian killings by any urban police department in the country. According to the article, STRESS officers were responsible for 2.5% of Detroit's homicide rate in 1971.

Specific incidents of police homicide involving blacks as victims can be recalled ad infinitum. For example, there is the bizarre case that took place in rural Limestone County, Texas (80 miles south of Dallas), in June 1981. Three black teen-age males, who had no previous arrest records, were arrested by local white lawmen on trumped-up charges of marijuana possession. Under the most mysterious set of circumstances, they drowned while being transported across a lake in the custody of these officers. Apparently the youths had been handcuffed to each other while being taken across the water (a very extraordinary procedure for even the toughest police departments). The community believes it has solid evidence, showing a conspiracy on the part of the police officials to violate the victims' civil rights by killing them (see *Newsweek*, 1981).

In an unpublished list of incidents involving police violence against blacks, compiled by a reputable grassroots Montgomery, Alabama-based organization, the following cases—all taking place within the last two or three years—were documented:

- Birmingham, Alabama: A black woman sitting in a car was shot to death by police. Police answered a call regarding a robbery in progress. There was no connection with the woman. Police reinstated.
- Tuscaloosa, Alabama: Police turned a dog loose on a black child who was in the vicinity of a robbery.
- San Antonio, Texas: Policeman Veverka, who gave state's evidence against white police beating of (black) insurance executive (Arthur McDuffie) was acquitted by all white jury.
- Jackson, Mississippi: A disturbed pregnant black woman, Dorothy Brown, was shot down despite the attendance of a "slew of police."
- Deerfield, Florida: Black youth was in a crap game. Police broke up game,

chased youth, had him on the ground, shot him in back of head. Ruled justifiable homicide by grand jury.

- Belle Glade, Florida: Jamaican man was part of a minor traffic accident. Taken to hospital by police and left hospital. [He] broke away from police and was shot and killed. Ruled justifiable homicide.
- Miami, Florida: (events leading to the McDuffie incident): . . . Dade County narcotics detective got wrong address and beat up black school teacher. No police indicted. . . . White highway patrolman molested 11 year-old girl. Got her in his car by saying she was suspected of stealing candy. Policeman received psychiatric treatment but was not removed from duty. . . . Moonlighting Hialeah police officer shot and killed black youth. He thought youth was armed. Actually, youth was urinating.
- New Orleans, Louisiana: Five police murders of blacks occurred after white policeman killed. Algiers area of city seems to be in state of siege. Mayor had to get rid of white police chief.
- Los Angeles, California: Reportedly two police who went to quell family disruption were subsequently arrested for rape of the eight year-old daughter (Klan Watch, 1981).

Then, of course, there is the now ill-famed McDuffie incident. Arthur McDuffie, a black 33-year-old former marine and insurance salesman, was beaten to death by Miami-area policemen in December 1979. Several officers admitted that they had taken part in the savage beating, then smashed his motorcycle and falsified reports to make it look like an accident. McDuffie died of head wounds so severe that a Dade County medical examiner called them "the equivalent of falling four stories and landing between your eyes" (*Newsweek*, 1980). But after deliberating only two hours and 40 minutes, a six-man, all-white jury acquitted four white officers of all charges in connection with McDuffie's death. This startling verdict sparked three days of armed insurrection in Miami.

Finally, insult was added to injury when the white Los Angeles Police Chief (Daryl Gates) attempted to explain away the unusually high number of deaths of black suspects by police choke holds (12 since 1975) as being due to the fact that "some blacks may be more susceptible than normal people to injury when officers applied [the] choke" (*New York Times*, 1982).

From the above statistics and incidents, the case can be made that police violence directed against blacks in America represents a threat equally dangerous (if not more dangerous) to the physical survival and well-being of the black community to that of blacks killing other blacks.

Victimization at the Workplace

To further dispel the myth of so-called "black on black" or "poor on poor" crime as the single most disturbing threat to black and working class communities, let us look at some additional external threats. Reiman (1979) relates that most of us, when we think of crime, do not imagine a corporate executive sitting at his desk calculating the cost of proper safety precautions and deciding not to invest in them. The odds are, according to Reiman, that what we see in our mind's eye is one person physically attacking another or robbing him/her with the use of threat or physical force. We visualize an attacker who is not wearing a suit and tie. In fact, at the thought of crime, most of see a young, tough, "lower class" black male. But the case can be made that there are "noncriminal" actions ("crimes by any other name," as Reiman describes them) that take place every day and are far more dangerous to black and working class communities than the so-called "black on black" or "poor on poor" crimes.

Reiman (1979: 67–68) points out that work in America "may be dangerous to your health." In one year (1972), he writes, "A liberal estimate of the number of deaths caused by common crimes was 20,000." This is an alarming and considerable number, but it pales when compared to deaths on the job. Each year, according to Reiman's data, workplace injuries cause some 14,200 deaths—almost all of which are preventable by safety devices. In addition, he points out that some 100,000 people die annually of diseases that can be traced to coal tar, dust, asbestos, and other substances. All of these deaths are also preventable.

A recent *Washington Post* story relates the shocking information that federal agencies know the names of hundreds of thousands of people who have been exposed to cancer-causing chemicals on their jobs but, because of the "expense involved," have made no effort to tell them about the risk to their health. Nor has any effort been made to name or notify 21 million workers—one in every four—known to have been exposed to other hazardous materials; the government simply "waits for them to die" (*Washington Post*, 1981).

A most shocking case of corporate criminality against working class Americans was recently revealed in the CBS Television newsweekly magazine, "60 Minutes." At the Tennessee Nuclear Specialties firm (TNS)—a company which makes anti-tank penetrator shells for the United States Air Force as part of a quarter-billion dollar contract—95 workers have been on strike for well over one year because they became convinced that they were being poisoned by exposure to radioactive uranium (see CBS Television Network, 1981). Evidence was produced showing that on a "low week," workers are being exposed, on a daily basis, to an amount of radiation to the entire body that is equivalent to five chest X-rays (100–200 milligrams).

One worker, Vincent Mango, complained of constantly being tired. "I was weak. I lost a lot of weight," he said. Medical examinations showed that he had a urinary uranium level in 1980 of 1,850–1,950 micrograms. According to medical experts looking into his case, the level of uranium found in Mango's system, even by the company's criteria of 100 micrograms, was over 18 times an "acceptable" level. One black worker, Albert Patton, who had worked for TNS for six and a half years, contracted leukemia in the summer of 1980. Medical doctors treating Patton reported that, "The type of leukemia that he developed was in fact the type that is most commonly associated with radiation exposure."

In the case of TNS (as with a number of similar cases), the federal government (the supposed protector of all the people), by castrating regulatory commissions and siding with giant capitalists, has made sure to protect the interests of corporate and monopoly capitalism at the physical expense of the American working class— even to the point of murdering them. These are crimes that somehow never get counted in the FBI's "official" statistics.

A death resulting from a common or "street" crime may occur every 23 minutes (according to the FBI's 1980 statistics), but a death resulting from a preventable industrial cause occurs every four minutes. I ask: Is permitting hazards at the workplace a lesser crime than street violence?

Economic Victimization

Other forms of criminal victimization of blacks that somehow never get counted include shady business practices that are often reported in ghetto areas—a form of property theft, if you will. Taub (1970: 37–39) identifies some of these: bait-advertising of goods that are "sold out" when the customer comes in to look at specials; telling the customer that an advertised special is not of good quality and that what he really wants is some more expensive item; refusal to return deposits; misrepresentative sales contracts; used furniture sold as new; coercive pressures on buyers; attempts to collect nonexistent debts. All these practices, so frequently complained of, have their roots in the powerlessness and the lack of educational and financial resources of the urban poor.

Taub further notes:

> In today's consumer market, a specialized sales network has developed to deal with low-income blacks. The friendly smooth-talking dealer who makes the uneducated, poorly-dressed customer feel at home, gaining his confidence, offering generous credit terms impossible to obtain elsewhere—and all this right in his own neighborhood—is much easier to deal with than a hostile downtown department store salesman (1970: 38).

Prices paid for needed items, however, reflect this "special service." A Federal Trade Commission report from not so long ago concludes:

> The low-income market is a very expensive place to buy durable goods. On television sets (most of which are the popular 19-inch black and white portables), the general market retailer price is about $130. In the low-income market a customer can pay up to about $250 for similar sets. Other comparisons include a dryer selling for $149.95 from a general market retailer and for $299.95 from a low-income market retailer; and a vacuum cleaner selling for $59.95 in the general market and $79.95 in the low-income market (cited in Taub, 1970: 38).

These are property crimes committed against poor and working class blacks in their own neighborhoods. They occur, as Caplovitz (1967) points out, with the full connivance of major banks and other lending institutions, which buy up dishonestly obtained contracts. According to Caplovitz, "The finance companies know what they are doing, as do the highly respected banks who lend to the finance companies." Ghetto blacks suffer to a far greater extent from these property crimes that never get counted than they do from housebreaking, purse snatching, and auto theft. Incidentally, not considered here are deaths and maltreatment due to improper medical care in emergency wards of hospitals, where most blacks go for nearly all medical treatment. There were some 20,000 of these deaths in 1974 (see Reiman, 1979: 72–74).

Taken together, therefore, the argument can be made that the violence that black and working class Americans suffer at the hands of the police and from industrial negligence constitute a far more serious threat to their physical survival than do violent "street crimes." Also, it can be argued that the daily rip-offs that blacks and other low-income groups experience at the hands of ghetto merchants represent an even greater economic and material threat than do "street" property crimes.

Facts and Causes

Generally in discussions of "black on black" crime there is the related myth that crimes committed by blacks against other blacks require a separate analysis from the larger social reality of crime in the United States. As observed earlier, the statistics on blacks harming and ripping off other blacks are alarming and indeed frightening. They cannot be dismissed or "explained away," and no attempt will be made to do so here, because "conventional" or "street crime" is neither an admirable nor an effective means of revolutionary action, and is in some respects reactionary—it pits the poor against the poor.

But as black U.S. Congressman John Conyers (1979: 128) correctly observes, "the label 'black on black' crime gives the erroneous impression of a strange, aberrant, or exotic activity, when it is taken out of the context of the social and economic roots of crime." He continues, "The facts about Black crime have to be honestly examined and confronted. The meaning of these facts must not be misconstrued."

Let us try, therefore, to look objectively at the social and economic roots of "street crime" in the United States, because only as we look at these basic causes can we then address the incidence of crimes committed by blacks against other blacks.

First of all, given sufficient cause, there is nothing peculiar about one black criminally victimizing another black. Crime statistics from a number of U.S. jurisdictions have shown clearly that most criminal offenses, particularly of the "street" or urban variety, tend to take place within five or six city blocks of the offender's place of residence (see, e.g., Pyle, 1974), and that most homicides occur among relatives and acquaintances (see, e.g., Wolfgang, 1958). Because a significant proportion of the black population in the United States is systematically housed in overcrowded, segregated slum areas, it is therefore only logical that, given the known ecology of criminal behavior, the victims of "street crime" will more than likely be of the same race as the offender. In other words, the perpetrator of a "street crime" will generally victimize those closest at hand.

As Platt (1978) argues, there is no question that "street crime" is primarily an intra-class and intra-racial phenomenon, media stereotypes to the contrary. "White women are most likely to be raped by white men, young black men are most likely to be robbed by other young black men, and working class families are most likely to have their homes vandalized or ripped-off by strangers living only a few blocks away" (1978: 29).

What is at issue, therefore, is not the ecology of black or poor criminal victimization, but the social and economic forces that produce the victimizer. As has been argued extensively elsewhere (e.g., Platt, 1978; Gordon, 1976; Chambliss, 1976; Quinney, 1977; Krisberg, 1975), the real cause of crime in America lies *not* in the relation between victim and offender, but in the social relations engendered by the capitalist mode of production.

"Street crime," as Platt observes, "is not simply a *by-product* of the capitalist mode of production, a logistics problem to be solved by technocrats trained in 'systems analysis.' Rather, it is . . . a phenomenon *endemic* to capitalism at its highest stage of development" (1978: 29. Emphasis his). In a capitalist society such as the United States, social and economic relations are basically competitive and generate substantial inequities in the allocation of material resources.

Capitalist societies are unable to guarantee economic security to most of their individual members; thus individuals must fend for themselves, finding the best available opportunities to provide for themselves and their families. Driven by fear of economic insecurity and by competitive desire to gain some of the goods unequally distributed in the society, many individuals will eventually become "criminals." Many forms of "street crimes" thus become logical, rational responses to the structure of institutions upon which capitalist societies are based. In fact, as Chambliss (1976: 6) so succinctly put it: "some criminal behavior is no more than the 'rightful' behavior of persons exploited by the extant economic relations."

Implications for Social Policy

To dwell only on the myths relating to "black on black" crime (however important such an exercise is in and of itself) without devoting some space to the social policy implications that flow from the discussion presented here, and at least suggesting some short-term recommendations, is to run the risk of having this article dismissed as just another exercise in "radical polemics."

The social and policy implications surrounding the larger issue of blacks and crime in the United States (of which the phenomenon of "black on black" crime is simply one dimension) have been quite adequately addressed by Platt (1982). In that article (originally co-authored with Takagi and presented as a position piece for the National Association of Blacks in Criminal Justice) a number of what might be called "progressive short-term recommendations" were set forth—e.g., bringing equal justice to the bail system, abolishing mandatory sentencing, restoration of indeterminate sentencing, combating racism in criminal justice professionals, prosecution of corporate crimes and racist violence, and restoration of funding for community alternatives to imprisonment.

These are all realistic and practical objectives which, given the political will of the black and progressive leadership class, can be implemented in the short-run. However, if one were to deal specifically with the issues raised in the present discussion, a slightly modified and less comprehensive list of recommendations would emerge. The underlying theme of this article is to point out, if nothing else, the need for a new level of social awareness, a heightened consciousness in examining the problem of "black on black" crime. That is, it must be seen in perspective. At the same time however, I have argued that "black on black" crime (particularly in poor and working class neighborhoods) must also be seen in all its ugly dimensions and that it should be thoroughly repudiated by all sectors of the black community. Consequently, I shall confine myself here to two basic sets of recommendations: one dealing with the myth, the other with the reality of "black on black" crime.

A. Re-education of Minority Attitudes Toward "Black on Black" Crime

First of all, the black leadership class must actively challenge the two related myths: that "black on black" crime constitutes the most serious threat to the survival and well-being of the black community, and that this phenomenon requires a separate analysis from the larger social reality of crime in general. Black and progressive politicians, journalists, community and civic leaders, and intellectuals must be in the forefront in raising the level of the discussion of "black on black" crime, placing it in perspective with the larger and more serious crimes committed against black and poor Americans by the ruling sectors of the society. The effect of such a re-education would be an increased demand from the masses for a new level of social justice in the American society. This is not merely a call for "color blind" justice; as Platt argues: "So long as corporate and government crimes go unpunished, we cannot expect the selective punishment of working class crime to be an effective deterrent" (1982: 42).

B. Radical Community Involvement

Turning to the reality, the second recommendation calls for radical community organizing as a way of combating minority "street crime" victimization. Increasingly, local police have shown limited ability or willingness to combat predatory crime in black and working class neighborhoods. What is called for here is local leadership that recognizes and encourages neighborhood and community organizing for social defense; the type of communal and sometimes "primitive" forms of defense that rural black communities mobilized to resist the racist violence of hate groups like the Klan. Specifically, I am calling for nothing more than residents coming together and defining for themselves (free of official or academic intrusion) their own anti-crime measures and strategies for coping with crime and street criminals, then deciding how best to mobilize themselves for implementing these measures.

Under these circumstances, residents may (or may not) desire to use the local police as a resource agency—to make "official" arrests or aid resident groups in such activities as joint stake-outs. In other words, what is called for is a heightened sense of community vigilance without vigilantism. Only recently (and partly in response to a string of mysterious child killings) we witnessed the emergence of such neighborhood anti-crime groups here in the predominantly black working class neighborhoods of Atlanta, sprouting names like Atlanta Youth Against Crime, Atlanta Women Against Crime, and the Bat Patrol (the latter group, being the most aggressive in its anti-crime methods, did run into open conflict with the local police). There has emerged among these groups a collective sentiment that views the street criminal (black or white) as a parasite, a leech, a predator who should be resisted at all costs and by any means necessary.

Ultimately, however, as I have maintained throughout this discussion, the problem of street crime and street crime victimization can only be solved in the long term by a radical overhaul of the American political economy and the ideology that directs and guides the criminal justice system. An economy that generates gross levels of inequality and consequently relegates a substantial proportion of its population to permanent unemployment, joblessness, demoralization—then uses its criminal justice system to control this surplus population—cannot hope to "free" itself of the menace of predatory crime.

References

Caplovitz, David
　1967 The Poor Pay More. New York: Free Press.
CBS Television Network–"60 Minutes"
　1981 "On Strike for Their Lives." Transcript Vol. 14, No. 9 (November 29).
Chambliss, William and Mankoff, Milton (eds.)
　1976 Whose Law? What Order? New York: John Wiley.
Clark, Kenneth
　1974 Quoted in New York Times (September 18).

Conyers, Congressman John
　1979 "Main Solution Is National Plan Correcting Economic Injustice." Ebony (August).
Ebony
　1981 "Police Deadly Force: A National Menace" (September).
　1979 "Black on Black Crime" (Special Edition–August).
Gordon, David M.
　1976 "Class and the Economics of Crime." In William Chambliss and Milton Mankoff

(eds.), Whose Law? What Order? New York: John Wiley.

Klan Watch
1981 Draft on Racial Violence. Montgomery, Alabama.

Krisberg, Barry
1975 Crime and Privilege: Toward a New Criminology. Englewood Cliffs, N.J.: Prentice-Hall, Inc.

Law Enforcement Assistance Administration (LEAA)
1976 Criminal Victimization in the United States: 1973. Washington, D.C.: U.S. Government Printing Office.
1975 Criminal Victimization Surveys in the Nation's Five Largest Cities. Washington, D.C.: U.S. Government Printing Office.

New York Times
1982 "Police Chief in Los Angeles Is Accused" (May 13).

Newsweek
1981 "The McDuffie Case" (July 2).
1980 "Death on Juneteenth" (July 20).

Platt, Tony
1982 "Crime and Punishment in the United States: Immediate and Long-Term Reforms From a Marxist Perspective." Crime and Social Justice 18, pp. 38–45.
1978 " 'Street' Crime—A View From the Left." Crime and Social Justice 9 (Spring-Summer), pp. 26–34.

Progressive, The
1981 "Violence in Detroit: A Bleaker View" (September).

Pyle, Gerald F.
1974 The Spatial Dynamics of Crime. Chicago: University of Chicago Press.

Reiman, Jeffrey
1979 The Rich Get Richer and the Poor Get Prison. New York: John Wiley & Sons.

Robin, Gerald
1973 "Justifiable Homicide by Police Officers." Journal of Criminal Law, Criminology, and Police Science 54.

The Psychology of Rapists

Murray L. Cohen, Ralph Garofalo, Richard Boucher, and Theoharis Seghorn

In a series of papers by Sarafian,[16] Kozol et al.,[12] and Cohen and Kozol,[3] a Massachusetts law for "sexually dangerous persons" and a treatment center established by the law has been described. Although the specific purpose of this paper is to present some observations on the psychological factors involved in rape, the clinical data are based on experiences with this law and the treatment center, and therefore a discussion of both will be profitable.

Special legislation concerning sexual offenders is frequently enacted as the result of a social outcry to a particularly brutal or heinous crime.[9] This was the case in Massachusetts in 1957. Six weeks following his release from prison, a child molester kidnapped two boys and sexually assaulted and murdered them. In immediate response to this crime, chapter 123A of the General Laws of Massachusetts[15] was written into law as a method for preventing the premature release of a potentially dangerous person.

Even prior to 1957, Massachusetts had special laws governing sexual offenses. The first was enacted in 1947 and was entitled The Psychopathic Personality Law. This statute was applied in only one instance and was repealed 1 yr later when an alternative law was passed that removed the term "sexual psychopath" and substituted the term "sex offender." There was no provision for retaining the offender after the expiration of his sentence, whether or not he had shown any change in his proclivity for sexual aggression. In 1957, the Legislature revised the 1954 statute and provided for a commitment for an indefinite period if necessary for the protection of the public. Sections of this statute were found unconstitutional, and the entire law was replaced by the present statute, chapter 646 of the Acts of 1958. This law ordered the creation of a treatment center to achieve its purposes and fashioned a new term "sexually dangerous person."

Under this law a person found guilty of a sexual offense may be committed for one day to life under a civil commitment in lieu of a criminal sentence. Section 2 of the statute ordered the Commissioner of Mental Health to establish a treatment

Source: Murray L. Cohen, Ralph Garofalo, Richard Boucher, and Theoharis Seghorn, "The Psychology of Rapists," *Seminars in Psychiatry* 3 (August 1971), pp. 307–327. Reprinted with permission.

center for such commitments, and in 1959 a psychiatric facility was created within the Massachusetts Correctional Institution at Bridgewater. The center is staffed by psychiatrists, psychologists, social workers, and educational, occupational, and recreational therapists, who are responsible for the care, treatment, and rehabilitation of persons who come under the purview of the law.

The law provides for a truly indeterminate commitment—one day to life. Indeterminate-sentence laws usually have relatively narrow limits within a fixed minimum and maximum term. The basic legal consideration here is that the commitment is civil and not criminal. The offender is not given a fixed penalty for his crime, but rather the period of commitment is determined by his mental condition. His release occurs when the psychiatric staff judges that he will offer a minimal risk to the safety of the community.

Since enactment of this statute a number of articles have appeared containing critical comments of the law and the treatment center.[5,8,11,14,18] These criticisms discuss the legal, ethical, and scientific aspects of the legislation, but only those criticisms of interest to the mental health professional will be presented here in brief. These include problems of treatment and diagnosis and limitations of the statute to "sexually dangerous" (thus not including those who may be aggressively dangerous in nonsexual ways).

Many papers critical of the law recognize the paradox that although the indeterminate civil commitment is for the purpose of treatment, many of those offenders most subject to the application of the statute do not appear treatable by current techniques. This is a valid and worrisome observation. In a recent study of psychotherapy completed at the center, only 36% of the patients were found to be responsive to psychotherapy. This is supported by the finding that 35% of the patients committed during the first 6 yr (the first half of the total period of the existence of the center) are still committed patients. However, society has clearly taken the position that it has the right to protect its members from harm. The objections to a life commitment on the grounds of treatability are valid only when it can be demonstrated that the intent and application by society of civil commitment is not treatment and rehabilitation, but simply preventive detention.

Section 1 of the statute defines a "sexually dangerous person" as "any person whose misconduct in sexual matters indicates a general lack of power to control his sexual impulses, as evidenced by repetitive or compulsive behavior and either violence or aggression by an adult against a victim under the age of sixteen years, and who as a result is likely to attack or otherwise inflict injury on the objects of his uncontrolled or uncontrollable desires."[15] This section has been criticized for its vagueness and for its limitation to the sexually aggressive. It is pointed out that "sexually dangerous" is a social-legal concept and not a psychiatric entity. It is a term that refers not to etiology, current process, or immediate symptom, but to future behavior. Thus, the very wording of the definition lacks the clarity required for consistent reliable application. The law imposes on the psychiatrist a relatively unfamiliar demand and a responsibility that it is not certain should be given to him, and one he is frequently loathe to accept.

The problems are clearly difficult ones. If sexually dangerous is going to be determined by the part of the section that refers to past behavior ". . . as evidenced by repetitive or compulsive behavior . . . ," then it is not necessary to have the psychiatrist make the determination and there will be no way for the evaluation of change and release. If the emphasis is to be on ". . . is likely to attack . . ." there is then a behavioral prediction problem, and social scientists, other than the psychiatrist, should clearly be involved by statutory action and not only in clinical actuality.

McGarry and Cotton[14] criticize still another aspect of section 1, that aspect resulting from the exclusive features of the law ". . . if such programs for the sexually dangerous are justified, it makes no sense to exclude the repetitively aggressive dangerous offender without sexual overtones" (p. 298). Holden[11] questions this feature not only from logical, but also from legal considerations.

> [The sex offender law represents] a special way of dealing with a particular class of criminal offender and such class is exposed to greater deprivation of liberty with less procedural due process than is the case for other criminal offenders. If society's particular concern is for its own safety, it is difficult to see why sex offenders alone should be singled out for indeterminate detention. . . . (p. 29).

It is certainly a meaningful question as to why there is this peculiar separation of sexually dangerous from other forms of socially dangerous persons. It is clear that the answer resides within socio-cultural and not psychiatric data. It is a matter of social attitudes to specific criminal acts and the social response to these acts.

Despite these and other criticisms of the law, it has operated (with three amendments) since 1958. In that year the Treatment Center at the Massachusetts Correctional Institution, Bridgewater began to function, and over 2000 sexual offenders have been given preliminary examinations since that time. There was sufficient question regarding 800 of these men that they were sent to the Treatment Center for intensive study for a 60-day observation period. Of this latter group 240 men were found to be sexually dangerous as described in the law and were committed to the center.

It is quite apparent from the data gathered that the men seen under this statute are seriously sexually disturbed and represent a significant threat to society. Two of many findings demonstrate this. Unlike the general findings reported in the literature of 12–17% sexual offense recidivism, 62% of the total group screened had one or more prior convictions for a sexual offense. Of the group committed to the center, 73% had a prior record for a sexual crime. In 47% of the committed sexual offenders, force or violence was associated with the offense. This is quite different from the over-all data on sexual crimes that indicates aggression is comparatively rare.[6]

Thus the center sees a selective sample. It is precisely this selectivity that has given us the opportunity to observe characterological sexual pathology and features of character related to such pathology, without the distortions created by clinical cases showing sexual deviancy as the result of transient neurotic regressions, traumatic environmental stress, the so-called accidental sexual offense (not a deviancy), or the deviances that are better ascribed to cultural disapproval than to psychopathology. This is not the man in alcoholic stupor urinating in an alley and arrested for exhibiting himself; not the disappointed lover misunderstanding the glances of a young girl as a seductive invitation and arrested for accosting; it is not the man on a date sexually provoked and then denied whose anger triggers off a sudden uncharacteristic, explosive rape; nor is the sexual assault an expression of a subcultural double standard or masculine culture "machismo."

The patient that is seen at the center shows serious defects in social relationships and social skills, lacunae in moral and ethical attitudes, impulse-control functions that are tenuous and break down under relatively normal life stresses, ego functions (judgment, reality testing, reasoning, etc.) that seem entirely intact until he is sexually or aggressively provoked and only then do the ego distortions appear, and major disturbances in his sexual development that leave him fixated at an infantile, primitive level or make him susceptible to sudden and precipitous regressions.

The following sections of this paper will be devoted to one group of such sexual offenders, the rapist. The data were obtained from extensive clinical study involving diagnostic and psychotherapeutic interviews and psychological tests. The elaboration, correction, and refinement of these clinical observations are the result of four research studies.[2,4,13,17]

The Rapist

It is readily apparent that there is no congruence between rape and any specific diagnostic category. It is true that classic neurotic symptoms are a rarity, but all types of character neuroses, character disorders, and more severe borderline and psychotic states are represented. It is equally clear that there are some specific characteristics present in rapists that differentiate them from other criminals and from other sexual offenders. In addition, there is evidence that clear, differentiated classes of rapists can be observed, and such differentiation has significant clinical and research utility.

Guttmacher and Weihofen[10] have found discriminate classes among rapists and regard motivation as the basis for a classification.

> Forced rape . . . has several basic motivational patterns. There is the rapist whose assault is the explosive expression of a pent-up sexual impulse. Or it may occur in individuals with strong latent homosexual components. . . . These are the true sex offenders. Another type that is also sexual in origin, although not so manifestly so, is the sadistic rapist. . . . Many of these individuals have their deep-seated hatred focused particularly on women. Then there is the third type of rapist who, paradoxically is not primarily a sex offender. He is the aggressive, anti-social criminal who, like the soldier of a conquering army, is out to pillage and rob (p. 116).

The authors refer to three types. However, it appears that four groups are described, and although they do not present them in such terms, the following more dynamic statements seem to reflect their findings: (1) rape motivated by sexual impulses whose intensity has become so great that whatever defensive or controlling factors were present were overwhelmed and the sexual desire is expressed; (2) rape that is not a breakdown of defense, but is itself a defense against strong homosexual wishes; (3) rape that is the expression not only of sexuality but this impulse combined with deep-seated hatred or aggressive feelings toward women; and (4) rape that does not so much express sexual or aggressive wishes but rather a more general predatory disposition.

In a prodigious statistical study based on interviews and data retrieved from case folders, Gebhard et al.[7] describe two major categories of rapists. In their taxonomy this group is referred to as "heterosexual offenders versus adults." The two varieties of aggressive offenses include

> (1) those in which the aggression is a means to an end, and no more force is used than is necessary to achieve the end (coitus usually); (2) those in which violence is an end in itself or at least a secondary goal; in these cases the female is either subjected to more force than is necessary or she is mistreated after coitus or other direct sexual activity has ended (p. 196).

The nature of the differentiation is the motive, dealt with this time in behavioral terms. The authors do go on to discuss seven additional varieties that have little or no relationship to the two major categories quoted above, but in some instances, at least, awareness of factors other than goal behavior is indicated.

Anyone who has worked with such sexual offenders will immediately recognize the "types" referred to in the two classifications. He will also recognize the superficiality of the descriptions that results from a lack of attention to other psychological characteristics. The act of rape clearly cannot be understood unidimensionally simply in terms of motivation or, in fact, in terms of any single factor.

Williams[19] eschews classification but does show an appreciation for the complexity of rape by considering both instinctual forces and controlling forces. The latter forces involve both the developmental level of ties to the external object and the quality of the internal, incorporated, restraining figures. The instinctual forces are those of sex and aggression. The act expressed is a result of these forces and the control forces developed from object relationships. The particularities of the act represent a point on a continuum.

> Sexual crimes directed against females are thought to form part of a graduated series of actions with minor assaults at one end of the scale and lust-murder at the other (p. 563).

No effort will be made here to resolve the issue of whether rape can best be understood in terms of discrete categories or a point on a linear continuum. The multidimensional nature of the factors involved and the clinical phenomena themselves make it extremely difficult to consider the differences simply in quantitative terms. On the other hand, when considered from a multifactor point of view, the clinical data do not fit securely into categories. The compromise adopted here is to present a set of clinical classes based on descriptive and dynamic characteristics with an appropriate caveat to the reader that a typology is not intended.

Descriptively, the act of rape involves both an aggressive and a sexual component. As noted above, and in accord with the observations at the treatment center, in any particular sexual assault the part played by these impulses can be quite different. The primary aim may be hostile and destructive so that the sexual behavior is in the service of an aggressive impulse. In other instances the sexual impulse is the dominating motive, and the aggressive aspects of the assault are primarily in the service of the sexual aim. In a third pattern the two impulses are less differentiated, and the relationship between them can best be described as sexual sadism.

We have also observed a number of rapists within whom neither sexual nor aggressive impulses played a dominant role in the act itself. This is the group that Guttmacher[9] refers to as the aggressive antisocial criminal and Gebhard et al.[7] refer to as the amoral delinquent. We agree that this group should not be considered primarily as sexually deviant persons.

The remainder of this paper will be concerned with only the first three patterns of rape, since there are no new findings to contribute to the understanding of the antisocial character disorder.

The discussion of the classification will be concerned with those factors that appear to differentiate the three classes of rapists. These include the descriptive features of the act itself, the interrelationship of the sexual and aggressive impulses and the developmental level of these impulses, ego interests and attitudes, defensive structure, unconscious fantasies that appear to be directly related to the sexual assault, and the mode of object relations and the level of object ties. These factors can be conceptually considered as separate and distinct, but they do not exist as independent forces, states, or structures, and will not be treated separately.

Clinical Classification of Rape

Rape—Aggressive Aim

In this pattern the sexual assault is primarily an aggressive, destructive act. The sexual behavior is not the expression of a sexual wish but is in the service of the aggression, serving to humiliate, dirty, and defile the victim. The degree of violence varies from simple assault to brutal, vicious attacks resulting on occasion in the victim's death. The savagery of the act clearly denotes the aggressive intent. When aspects of sexuality are present, they, too, enter the service of aggression as seen in biting, cutting, or tearing of the genitals or breasts, rupture of the anus through violent insertion of some object, or in other sexually mutilating acts.

The women certainly appear to be the victims of the offender's destructive wishes, and he, in fact, describes his emotional state as anger. These women are always complete strangers. This anger that is experienced is clearly a displacement of intense rage on a substitute object. The source of this rage is most frequently the mother or her representatives in the present, the wife or girl friend.

The rape occasionally occurs in the offender's automobile where the victim is brought either by physical force or by threat with a weapon. However, the rape occurs most frequently in the victim's home with entrance gained by some ruse, the offender representing himself as a delivery man, repairman, or someone looking for a false address.

The rape often occurs in a series, and they appear as isolated instances in an otherwise relatively normal social and psychiatric history. There is, however, a long history of difficulty in heterosexual object relations in conjunction with an active sexual life. Many of these men are married and those who are not are engaged or dating with regularity. There are, however, considerable difficulties in these relationships that are marked by episodic mutual irritation and, at times, violence. They tend to experience women negatively as hostile, demanding, ungiving, and unfaithful, and frequently for good reason. The women they select are in fact assertive, active, and independent who, by their manner and attitude, ask them to accept passive components of relationships that they find intolerable. Features of the oedipal situation are re-enacted time and again in involvements with divorced or separated women who are themselves mothers or with girl friends or wives who are sexually promiscuous and not infrequently pregnant through affairs with other men.

Most of these patients have an adequate occupational history showing not only stability of work, but high level skills and achievement with qualities of inventiveness and creativity. They are competitive but are able to enter into cooperative, sharing relationships with men, although here, too, the more active features are dominant, with the passive demands of such relationships leading to conflict and anxiety. The work they do is clearly masculine as defined by this culture—machinist, truck driver, plumber, etc.

They appear generally to have mastered the various developmental tasks of childhood and latency with no gross signs of disturbance appearing until adolescence. In this period there is an impairment in intellectual attainment and excessive, exaggerated masculine activity. With regard to the latter they become involved in street brawls, become preoccupied with high speed driving, enter aggressive sports, usually outside of formal organized high-school activity, and are overzealous in physical combat. In a dramatic way there is an increase in partially controlled, socially acceptable (if not always socially approved and legally sanctioned) aggressive behavior.

In a striking number of such offenders, there is a history of prepubertal or postpubertal sexual traumata with older women, frequently the mother. These experiences appear to be directly associated not only with the generalized aggressive display, but also with the development of rape fantasies and with the rape itself. Two brief clinical cases will demonstrate this.

Bill was seen at age 14½. He was a large, well-built young boy, physically much bigger than his peers. In the summer following his tenth birthday, an attractive, married, 20-yr-old aunt took him into a picnic area, parked the car and disrobed. He recalled being in a state of panic as she took his hands and placed them on her breasts and her genitals. He remembers that the feeling of fear was accompanied by excitement and sexual curiosity. That evening he lay awake until midnight at which time he arose, dressed, and walked to her house feeling once again both apprehensive and sexually excited. Although he knew she was home, she did not answer his knocking at the door, and, disappointed and angry, he went home. Following this, he found himself preoccupied with memories of the sexual experience. He became intensely aware of older women, mentally comparing their covered bodies with the memory of the nude body of his aunt. At this time he began to have sexually sadistic fantasies involving a female teacher and his mother. In the fantasy, he would steal into a house and find the teacher or his mother fully clothed. He would assault and undress them, make love to them, and then stab or shoot them. This fantasy, with little change in content, became a nightly masturbatory ritual at puberty, and at the age of 14½ he acted out the fantasy with a neighbor. She had offered him money to help her move furniture and as he followed her up the stairs to her home which was relatively isolated, he had the thought that she was sexually provoking him. He became angry and when they entered the home he put his arm about her throat and throttled her until she lost consciousness. He undressed her and had intercourse with her during which he recalls giving vent to a steady stream of obscenities and feelings of increased anger. He wanted to stab and cut her but instead reached for a metal lamp and beat her until he thought he had killed her. Bill did not recapture the memory of the early sexual experience with his aunt until the third year of his therapy at which point there was a dream in which this aunt appears.

In the second case, the sexual traumata occurred with the patient's mother.

Following the death of his father when he was 13, his mother began to drink excessively and became increasingly promiscuous. At different times in her drunkenness she would behave in a seductive way toward him that both angered and frightened him. At the age of 19 he was making a telephone call and as he looked into the hall mirror he saw his mother, nude, walking into her bedroom, throw herself onto the bed with her legs spread in his direction. He was overwhelmed by a desire to run into the room and have intercourse with her. With this feeling there appeared the thought that at that moment any man could walk into the house and have her sexually. He became angry and wanted now to sexually assault her, specifically to kick her repeatedly in the genitals. This flooding of sexual and aggressive feelings so frightened him that he fled from the house and began a 2-wk drinking spree. This period was marked by sporadic aggressive vandalism that involved smashing store windows and breaking antennae of automobiles and ended with a rape. One evening while waiting on a corner for his girl friend, he became upset with the idea that she was out with another man. He then noticed a woman walking toward him and the thought entered his mind "if she turns right, she wants me to follow her, but if she turns left she does not." Unfortunately she turned right. He ran after her, threw her down, carried her to a deserted lot, and sexually assaulted her.

In these two cases, although different in many respects, the clinical material leaves little question that intense rage was present, that this rage was related to sexual anxiety, and that the victim was clearly a substitute object.

In nearly all of these patients there is body concern and a body narcissism. They are physically attractive and tend to be attentive to body health and hygiene. There are moderate obsessive features and clearly the explosive outbursts represent an anal-sadistic regression as a response to certain types of stress. They are capable, however, of finding socially acceptable outlets for this aggression under normal circumstances and similarly capable of aim-inhibited feelings of warmth, kindness, and love. The characteristic mode of relating, however, is in a cool, detached, overcontrolled manner. They are active, assertive, excessively counterdependent, and intolerant of the passive aspects required of true mutuality in relationships. True friendships are rare, because of their hyperalertness to narcissistic injury and, more important, because of the absence of depth and intensity in the formation of object ties. The ease with which feelings and concern for others can be withdrawn facilitates the release and expression of unneutralized aggression. What is noteworthy, is the frequent reappearance of the concern with feelings of compassion and efforts to undo, or make some kind of restitution to the victim. The full dynamic meaning of the compassion and remorse is not clear but it is evidently not understandable by a simple formula of guilt.

One observation may contribute to understanding this phenomenon and also helps to clarify the intensity of the rage and its displacement. In this type of offender there is frequently a splitting of the ambivalent feelings toward mother. Their own mothers, and women in abstract, are overidealized as the sources of fulfillment of all infantile and narcissistic needs. Real women are unfaithful, untrustworthy, and depriving. In usual circumstances these two images are fused in their relationships with women, with the splitting occurring in situations of stress.

This splitting of the mother ambivalence is only one feature of the defensive structure that includes displacement and isolation as primary mechanisms. Counterphobic attitudes prevail to assist in the defense against castration fears, but it is the ineffectiveness of this defense that gives rise to the primitive aggression when a woman is the source of the castration anxiety. Their inability to develop real devotion and loyalty makes them incapable of experiencing such traits in others, and this presents an appearance of paranoid mistrust. However, it does not have the quality of basic distrust, and the paranoid mechanisms are not seen as primary adaptive features, although they do come into play during the regressive episodes.

There is nothing noteworthy about perceptual or cognitive functioning or generally with the autonomous ego functions while such patients are in confinement. No gross impairments are present, nor is any specific pattern discernible. The average IQ of this group is somewhat higher than the other groups of rapists and is in fact higher than all other groups found to be sexually dangerous (pedophiles, incestors, etc.).

In additional comparisons with the other groups of rapists to be discussed, this group has the highest level of social and occupational adjustment, the most mature relationships with both men and women (although relations with the latter are less adequate), they are most responsive to treatment, can be released following the shortest commitment period, and the postparole adjustment is made with fewer difficulties and is most successful.

Within the center disciplinary action occasionally must be taken because of surly or unruly behavior toward security personnel or for fighting with another patient. Even when these offenders are not so involved, they frequently appear to be actively suppressing such behaviors and for the most part they are successful. They do not have an excessive disciplinary rate and among their peers they are the most socially desirable patients.

Thus, what is seen during the confinement is quite different from the behavior immediately preceding their confinement and is quite at odds with the primitive, brutal acts of sexual violence that brought about the commitment. The data seem to be best understood in terms of a decompensation approaching psychotic proportions in men who have been able to deal with their intense rage toward women in relatively successful ways. The aggression itself appears to be both the result of a splitting of the mother ambivalence and also a defense against the experience of helplessness they feel in all object relationships, but with particular intensity with women.

> Phillip was born 25 yr ago in an urban, industrial community in the Northeast. He is tall and well built and although his walk, carriage, voice, and manner is active and assertive he carries a boyish smile enhanced by a cowlick and deep blue guileless eyes. His crime belies this impression of innocence.
>
> He was committed to the center 4 yr ago following a sexual assault on a young girl. He was driving along a city road when he saw a girl, whom he did not know. He stopped his car beside her, stepped out and asked her where she was going. He didn't hear her answer and asked again in an angry manner. She turned to walk away and Phillip felt that she was trying to make a fool of him. He believed that she had first shown an interest in him and when he exposed his own interest to her, she was rejecting it. He punched her in the stomach, grabbed her under her chin, pulled her into his car, and drove away to a secluded area. After he had parked the car he told the girl to get into the back seat. When she refused, he climbed into the back and dragged her over the seat beside him. He undressed her and violently penetrated her. He states that he then withdrew, without having an orgasm and let her out of the car, threatening to kill her if she made mention of the attack. When he was arrested shortly thereafter, he immediately admitted his guilt.
>
> During the diagnostic interviews subsequent to his trial, he discussed the incident, describing himself as enraged at the time, not sexually excited. He had

gone to visit his girl friend, a "good" girl whom he had been seeing off and on since early adolescence with no sexual activity throughout the courtship. He found her necking on the porch with a black man and he drove from her house in a blind rage. He was partially aware as he drove away that he was going to look for somebody to attack sexually.

Phillip had an active sexual life, but only with girls whom he considered to be "bad." These relationships were short-lived, ending when he was directly confronted with their promiscuity. Terminating the relationship always occurred with violence either in assaults on the girls or on the boy friends that had replaced him.

His late adolescence was marked by the repetitiveness of these experiences. Over and over again he became involved with promiscuous girls who would then prove unfaithful. Although this behavior has meaning in the compulsion to repeat the oedipal situation, it must also be understood in terms of an ego split and an underlying masochism. On the one hand he could only permit himself to have intercourse with girls known by him to be sexually indiscriminate. On the other hand, he maintained the fantasy that they would be faithful to him. This latter belief he would test, not consciously, by setting up occasions for the girl to meet and enter relationships with other men. He would then feel ashamed, foolish, and hurt and would react aggressively.

Aggression characterized Phillip's behavior throughout the latter years of the latency period and through adolescence, although at no time did this behavior bring him before the authorities. Outside of the sexual offense described above, he has a negative criminal history.

Phillip began masturbating at age 13, and there appears to be nothing remarkable about the frequency or method of masturbating or the accompanying fantasies. Although there is no history of homosexual experiences, his behavior toward homosexuals indicates the presence of homosexual desires and the tenuousness of their repression. Within the center, he reacted with exaggerated, explosive anger toward homosexual invitations. Sexual intercourse began at 15 with the girls described above. His memory of his first heterosexual experience was that it was somewhat traumatic. When he was 9 or 10 yr old, he was approached by a girl who said she wanted to play ball with him and then engaged him in sexual play telling him that girls liked this kind of play. Shortly thereafter a neighborhood girl asked him to play with her and he began to fondle her believing that this was what she desired. She ran home, told her parents who in turn called the patient's father. According to the patient, the father felt so disgraced by this that they moved to a different part of the town.

This father was a strict man, the disciplinarian in the family. The mother was a somewhat passive, quiet, religious woman who rarely differed overtly with her strong, though emotionally uninvolved husband. Family life was quite stable with the father working for the same company, as a machinist, for 25 yr. There were two other children in the family, an older sister and a younger brother, both of whom appear to be living normal lives.

Phillip is a very likable young man, well thought of by the officers and his fellow patients. His anger appears to be very specific to threats to his sense of independence or challenges to his sense of his masculinity, and with projective identification, to protection of the younger or weaker patients. Under these threats, his anger explodes impulsively but not brutally. Although there is a regressive or infantile quality to what he experiences as a threat and a similar infantile quality in his inability to control the release of the aggression, the qualitative features of the aggression itself are less primitive with a relative absence of sadistic features.

Phillip was released from the Center after 2½ yr, continuing in outpatient psychotherapy. Despite the fact that his life style has remained unchanged so that he must be considered a risk to repeat his sexual assault, sufficient changes have occurred to make the risk worth taking. A brief review of his postparole life will be instructive.

His first year on parole was a traumatic one, not only for the patient but for his therapist as well. Shortly after his release, he began seeing a girl, Ann, whom he had dated prior to his commitment. She had been married, had a child, and was currently separated from her husband, although she continued to see him occasionally. Phillip became very involved with her and her son, purchasing furniture for her apartment and taking the boy on outings. He was fully aware that she was still seeing her husband and that she was having affairs with other men. In therapy he was able to discuss his sense of helpless rage and began to look more deeply into his pattern of getting involved with such women.

One evening Ann announced that she was going to invite her husband to return to live with her. A stormy scene ensued during which Phillip beat her rather severely. He then left the apartment and while driving away he saw a girl walking along the street. He stopped the car, asked her if she would join him and when she refused he jumped from the car and grabbed her about the waist. She screamed and Phillip released her, terrified at what he had done. He then returned to his car and began to drive at speeds exceeding 90 mph directly at telephone poles in an effort to kill himself. He sheered off two poles, totally wrecked the car but received only a head laceration.

He dealt at some length in therapy with this self-destructive behavior, showing some awareness of the masochistic aspects of his relationship with Ann. The pattern, however, continued. He began dating bar girls or other pick-ups and soon became intimate with a divorcee. He was seeing her for about 8 mo in a stormy relationship marked by his jealousy of her continuing contact with the parents of her former husband and with what he felt to be too close a relationship with her own brother. A serious fight erupted between Phillip and the brother, following which an argument developed with his girl friend and he lost control and struck her.

He had been living in and out of his own parental home, but shortly after this incident his father died suddenly and Phillip decided that he would move in with his mother to care for her. This takes Phillip up to the present. Whether his father's death will have the meaning of an oedipal victory and effect a change in his aggression toward self and others remains an open question.

Rape—Sexual Aim

A second pattern of characteristics that has been observed is quite different from the above. Here the act of rape is clearly motivated by sexual wishes, and the aggression is primarily in the service of this aim. The degree of aggressive behavior varies, but there is a relative absence of violence and the act lacks any of the characteristics of brutality.

The offense almost always takes place out of doors in isolated places such as darkened streets, a park, or wooded area. Most frequently the offender embraces the woman from behind touching her breasts or genitals, holding on to her with some force but not to any excessive degree. If the victim should struggle and thus require more physical effort in order to be held, the offender will release her and flee. Thus, most of the offenders are charged with assault with intent to commit rape. At other times the victim is so frightened that she passively submits, and the rape takes place without any additional force. When apprehended it is discovered that he has carried out such acts many times.

He is always very sexually aroused and fully aware of what he is doing, although at times he feels as if he were performing under a compulsion. The victim is always a stranger but not one that he comes upon by accident. She is usually someone he has seen while on a streetcar or bus and follows her off when she leaves.

It is not an impulsive act, however. This is a scene he has lived through many times in fantasy. It is a fantasy that is not only used in masturbation but one that preoccupies him throughout his waking day and is composed in a relatively fixed pattern. In the fantasy, the woman he attacks first protests and then submits, more resignedly than willingly. During the sexual act, he performs with great skill, and she receives such intense pleasure that she falls in love with him and pleads with him to return. This differs from the not unusual adolescent fantasy in that he spends a large part of the evening hours traveling about the city searching for its fulfillment and in fact acts out the fantasy over and over again.

Rape is not always a feature of his sexual fantasies. When it is, the aggressive component of the fantasied assault, although somewhat erotic, never approaches a sadistic quality and is always secondary to the sexual aim. There is no evidence from the behavior, the conscious fantasy, or what we have learned of the unconscious dynamics of the act, that the aggression is eroticized to the degree seen in the third pattern of rape to be described below.

These sexual fantasies and the frequently impotent efforts at rape are not the only indicants of a disturbed sexual life. From early in adolescence he was acting out in perverted ways. Perversions involved partial aims, part objects, and substitute objects. Although he developed erotic feelings toward both boys and girls, there was a marked inhibition to any form of interpersonal sexuality. He was voyeuristic, fetishistic, and exhibitionistic, but a real heterosexuality existed only in fantasy, and homosexuality was intensely repressed. The repressive defenses against the latter were not entirely successful, and albeit no direct acting out of the homosexual feelings occurred this was accomplished only by withdrawing and isolating himself from his male peers.

As he developed through adolescence, the guilt and shame that he felt regarding his perversions together with the need to defend by avoiding the homosexual wishes affected all peer relationships. The sense of loneliness increased, he became shy and increasingly inept and defective in social skills. The passive-feminine features of his personality became more dominant and were accompanied by intense feelings of impotency and inadequacy. Active masculinity was temporarily suspended for the passive gratifications offered by fantasy.

As such offenders approach the end of adolescence or enter young adult life the passive solution gives added strength to the underlying homosexual feelings and a breakthrough of such feelings becomes a real threat. The acts of rape occur at this time but not only as a defense against the homosexual wish. They are also efforts at renewal, an adaptive effort to escape the implications of the passive-feminine resolution. The acts also serve to protest and deny the feelings of being an impotent castrate. They are also attempts to relieve the shame related to the pregenital perversions. (These offenders are able to describe the acts of rape in great detail including their thoughts and feelings and they do this in diagnostic interviews and early in the psychotherapy. In contrast, it is frequently many years of psychotherapy before the patient brings the material on the perversions into treatment.)

This type of rapist shows little or no antisocial behavior apart from the repetitive sexual offenses. He is, in fact, socially submissive and compliant. His friends and neighbors see him as a quiet, shy, "good boy," more lonely than most, but nonetheless quite normal. There is generally an absence of even a moderate amount of aggressive and assertive behavior. His approach to the tasks of life are tentative and have a phobic quality. This lack of assertiveness combines with a very negative self-esteem and a low level of aspiration, preventing him from making significant attainments in either educational or occupational areas. There is a stable employment history, but the level of work is far below his aptitude and potential abilities. Although intelligence varies across a wide range from dull normal to bright average and above among the rapists in this group, in no instance is the potential realized. Scholastic records show poor performance and frequently withdrawal from school prior to graduation. A brief description of one young man will illustrate some of these latter observations.

Donald was first seen at age 17 following his commitment for a sexual assault. He had been walking home when he saw a young girl walking through a park. He came up from behind, placed his arms about her and threatened that he would hurt her if she resisted. She was 16 yr old. He pushed her to the ground, undressed her, and attempted intercourse, but as he penetrated her, she cried that it hurt. He withdrew and ran away. He recalls feeling sexually excited and frightened that he might be caught and that he might not have an erection or might have a premature ejaculation.

He was apprehended soon afterward and immediately confessed to an additional assault that had taken place a few weeks earlier. On this occasion, the victim had screamed despite the threats and Donald had run away.

He had always felt that he was the unwanted member of his family and described himself as "lower than a snake under a rock." He had no friends, male or female. From ages 10 to 15, he was placed in special classes as the result of being classified as retarded. The Wechsler Adult Intelligence Scale administered at the Center 5 yr following his commitment showed a verbal IQ of 93, Perform-ance IQ of 107, and Full Scale of 99, which is clearly not retardation. He de-scribes the 5 yr in special classes as "one long, unhappy nightmare."

Less than 2 yr before he committed the rape, he was convicted of being a voyeur, and since this was his first offense, the case was filed. Four months later he was again convicted of peeping and was sentenced to a training school for 1 yr. One month following his release he began his sexual assaults on girls.

The defensive structures, apart from the avoidance, repression, and inhibition described above, include introjection mechanisms, reflecting the diffusiveness in identity formation, projection of the severeness of the superego, so that he feels de-spised and anticipates rejection, and a type of denial leading to a naiveté that per-mits him to be victimized and used by others.

A very particular family pattern was noted. This pattern included a weak father, not a passive submissive man but one who found the demands of family responsi-bility too much and reneged in his role as father and husband. The mother tended to be very cold and ungiving, and an inconsistent, but harsh disciplinarian who infantilized her son by overwhelming control and suppression. These mothers ap-pear to be preoccupied with sexual morality, and the most excessive repression oc-curred in response to any expression of erotic interest or pleasure.

Despite her coldness, the young boy was completely dependent upon her. By vir-tue of her restrictive and repressive behavior he felt quite safe and protected not only from external dangers but from the threats of his own sexual wishes.

For the most part, these patients respond very well to group and individual psychotherapy and to planned programs of vocational, educational, and skill training,but the psychotherapeutic work requires a rather extended duration—of from 4 to 6 yr.

> Ted was committed to the treatment center after having been found guilty of a series of sexual offenses, legally described as "assault with intent to rape" and "assault and battery." There was a fixed and stereotyped quality to these of-fenses. He would approach a woman from behind and place one hand on her breast and the other between her legs. If the neighborhood was sufficiently se-cluded he would try to force her to the ground. If the surroundings were more public he would simply caress and fondle her until she screamed or vigorously resisted whereupon he would release her and flee. The patient admits to over 100 such assaults. There were two exceptions to the behavior described above. In one instance he threw the woman to the ground in a deserted park and choked her until she lost consciousness. When he became aware of what he had done, he fled, leaving her lying on the ground. On another occasion, in the same park, he held a knife to a woman and in her continued struggle a superficial wound was made. He became frightened and again fled.
>
> Despite his freely admitted sexual desires, and the numerous assaults that oc-curred, he did not have intercourse with any of his victims. In his treatment, a great deal of time was spent in attempting to reconstruct the thoughts and feel-

ings that preceded the assaults. For the most part, despite active effort, he was not able to recall much before the acts, although his memory was intact and surprisingly complete for the acts themselves. It was as if a veil of amnesia covered this period somewhat similar to a dissociative experience. He was able to describe a feeling of intense sexual excitement that produced a feeling that his "whole body seems to expand, and my ears would get very warm." Frequently before accosting in the evening he would be preoccupied throughout the work day with his anticipation of going out to search for a possible encounter. On other occasions, he claimed there were no such preparatory thoughts. In these instances, he would be on a bus or walking when suddenly a girl or woman would demand his attention at which point he would be overwhelmed by erotic feelings and thoughts.

These acts of rape took place over a 5-yr period, beginning when he was 17 and ending with his commitment at age 22. At the time of his arrest he was living at home with his mother, an alcoholic stepfather, and a half brother 9 yr younger than he in an industrial community, a part of a large metropolis. His mother was working to assist in the support of this lower-middle-class family. His natural father had died a few months before he was born, and his mother had remarried four years later. This marriage was never a stable one and shortly after the patient was committed, his mother separated from the second husband. Also in the family, but away from home, were an older sister and two older brothers.

He described his mother as a very cold and unloving person whose primary relationship to him was built around moral prescriptions and proscriptions. He speaks of her as one who gave him no feeling of warmth and affection but who always seemed present to confront him with his badness. He was always very dependent upon her in a manner that the mother reinforced and perpetuated. She prevented him from developing any initiative or sense of independence so that he was unable to make important occupational or other life decisions without her direct advice and suggestions. Although he loved her very much he was very afraid of her and was not able to share with her the enormous psychological discomfort he experienced throughout his life. In his earliest years there was no father present and he recalls no contact with his older siblings. His stepfather was a moody, alcoholic man, given to moments of brutality who apparently took no interest in him whatsoever.

Ted is 5′5″ tall, of slight build, and fair complexion, looking much younger than his 22 yr. His voice is somewhat high-pitched and nasal and there is a slight speech impediment. These physical characteristics contributed to rather severe problems beginning in early adolescence. Although he is of average intelligence, he left high school after his freshman year as a result of an inability to form any peer relationships and of being subjected to ridicule with which he could not cope. He was accused of being a "fairy" and on a number of occasions he was attacked by groups of boys who removed his trousers and threatened sodomy, although he always managed to ward off actual sexual contact. The following years produced no change in his social status. He had no boy friends, he dated only rarely and tentatively, and he became increasingly shy and retiring.

He saw himself as a very lonely boy, unattractive, unlikeable, socially and sexually inadequate with no self-expression outlets. He was employed on a factory assembly line in a monotonous task. Each time he would try to leave to seek out more meaningful and gratifying work, his mother would ridicule his plans and defeat his efforts before they could begin. He ultimately resigned himself to the work and established an excellent and stable work record.

As indicated, the patient never had a mature heterosexual relationship. His sexual outlet had been through fantasy and pregenital sexual behavior. He recalls that at age 8 while playing with a little girl he inserted his penis between her thighs. This type of sex play continued for some years, terminating when the girl had her first menses. When she told him of this he experienced such feelings of fear and revulsion that he avoided all heterosexual contact until his sixteenth year. At age 13 he began to develop intense voyeuristic and exhibitionistic desires so that he spent a great deal of time and effort peeping at women and exposing himself. Also at this time he found himself aroused by his mother's underclothing. The peeping, exposing, and the feel of the undergarments would excite him, and it is at this time and in these situations that he began to masturbate. The masturbation soon became compulsive and later would follow the sexual assaults that brought him to the center.

The entire pattern of his sexuality reflects the immaturity of his sexual aims and the social impotency of effecting real heterosexual relationships. The latter were reserved for his fantasies. At the age of 16 he began to go with a girl who, he stated, was quite willing to have intercourse with him but this never occurred. They did, however, engage in extensive petting, although even this was a source of great discomfort to him for he would very quickly have an orgasm and lose his erection. On numerous occasions he would masturbate or drink alcohol before going to see her in an effort to maintain his potency, but even these efforts were unsuccessful.

Rape—Sex-Aggression Defusion

The third pattern of characteristics we have observed reveals the presence of a strong sadistic component. There appears to be no ability to experience sexual excitation without some degree of violence being present. The degree of sadism is quite variable with the extreme position seen in lust murders where excessive brutality and mutilation occur before, during, and even after the murder. This is relatively rare. The most usual behavioral pattern is forcible rape where violence is used to excite the offender, and after intercourse there is no further aggression. Such an offender is frequently impotent with women until there is resistance. To become sexually excited he will provoke in a teasing, playfully aggressive sexual manner, eliciting resistant or angry behavior from his partner. Her resistance arouses in him aggressive feelings that become, as his sexual play continues, more intense and autonomous. The arousal and maintenance of the sexual desire appears to be a direct function of this initially mild arousal of aggression. It should be noted that the affect of anger is not present.

In most patients in this group the sadistic quality of their sexuality is projected onto the victim. He sees her struggle and protestation not as a refusal but as a part of her own sexual excitation. "Women like to get roughed up, they enjoy a good fight." This belief is maintained even when the victim is literally fighting for her life and the offender has to brutally injure her to force her to submit to intercourse.

Although there is some neutralization or toning down of the aggression in relationships unrelated to sexual partners or to sexual situations, even here there are qualities of untamed aggression. He is assertive, overpowering, and somewhat hostile in all situations. Warmth and affection are completely absent. The most friendly meeting is punctuated by a touching and pushing so that any encounter with such persons is a "bruising" one. In less pathological cases this is the extroverted football player type who crushes you in his narcissistic exuberance.

Such patients are usually married and in fact many have been married and divorced a number of times with, of course, never a sense of commitment to the marriage. The patient, and often his wife, are quite active in extramarital affairs. For the offender this constant search and seduction is essential for his sexual excitement, not as a defense against feelings of inadequacy but to satisfy the aggressive component of his sexual wishes. Intercourse with his wife is described as physically relieving but unsatisfactory; not infrequently, he has difficulty in obtaining or maintaining an erection. Quite often feelings of revulsion follow connubial coitus. In some instances the patient is successful in having his wife play a masochistic role and he can obtain satisfaction with the aggression modulated within the fantasy. The wife permits herself to be tied up and verbally abused as she acts out a scene of being physically assaulted and raped by a stranger.

In many ways such men are similar to the psychopathic character. There is an extensive history of nonsexual, antisocial behavior, an absence of stable object ties, a lack of concern for others, difficulty in tolerating frustration, poorly structured control functions, and a relative absence of endopsychic discomfort. Most different, and most perplexing in view of the more primitive organization of their instinctual life is the presence of industry and initiative in skill development, although this cannot be used for a socially successful occupational career. The psychopath obtains gratification in getting away with things, with getting by with active manipulation of others rather than with his own active efforts. This aspect of manipulation of others is present to a great degree in our patients, but gratification is also obtained through active mastery and personal accomplishment. These patients will manipulate, demand, and exploit in order to gratify felt needs, but there is little or no gratification simply from the act of manipulation.

Developmentally there is an absence of the latency period. Sexual and aggressive behavior toward younger children, peers, and animals is prominent throughout the prepubertal years. Other indications of impulsive behavior and general lack of control, expressed in truancy, stealing, running away, and lying, are also present.

This is a history also seen in the psychopathic character. In adolescence significant differences appear in the organization of aggression that distinguish the antisocial character from the sex-aggression rapist. In the psychopath, the aggression comes under the control of the ego and serves it in its adaptive efforts. Although there certainly is a basic hostile, angry attitude that requires little to release it in uninhibited ways, the aggression is relatively organized, controlled, and directed. In this type of rapist the aggression continues to be diffuse and unorganized; it maintains its primitive quality and cannot be pressed into the service of the ego's adaptive needs. The sexualization of the aggression (or the aggressivization of the sexuality) so overwhelms the ego when the aggression is aroused that the control and discharge mechanisms fail to function. The psychopath may commit an assault or a murder through the absence of concern for objects or to prevent detection of his pillaging. Here the behavior is organized in the service of survival, and the ego is in direct control of the aggressive discharge. In the assault or murder of the rapist the ego is completely submerged.

In comparison with the other types of rapists discussed above, patients in this group show the greatest degree of paranoid features, and under certain conditions these are of psychotic proportion. The world is perceived as a hostile place where one's survival is constantly under threat. Every human contact is made tentatively with mistrust and suspicion, experienced as a battle in which someone wins and someone loses. They cannot experience any sense of interpersonal mutuality.

Their entire life is tempestuous. Family life is marked by cruel and abusive behavior of the family members toward each other, except for the mother. Oddly enough she appears as the only member of the family with warm and compassionate feelings. Her major fault lies in her need to give that is so intense it takes on bizarre qualities. Her pathological need to give distorts her judgment of her children's behavior. She denies, rationalizes, and excuses the defective development of internal controls and actively supports a primitive oral demandingness.

The fathers of these patients were physically and psychologically cruel and sadistic not only in their own behavior, but would incite, support, and often demand physically aggressive behavior among the children.

> Frank is a 42-yr-old, white divorced man who, since age 13, has spent a total of only 5 yr out of prison. He was committed to the treatment center with a history of brutal sexual assaults on women; assaults that began shortly after his marriage at age 18, and that would occur while he was on parole from the previous offenses. In all, he has been found guilty of six separate sexual crimes.
>
> Only one of these offenses will be described, but it is quite typical. When he was 22 yr old, 5 mo after having been released from prison where he had spent 18 mo for a sexual assault, he met a girl in a dance hall. He was married at the time, but almost from the time of the ceremony he had been involved in one illicit affair after another.
>
> He spent the evening dancing with the girl and then offered to drive her and her two girl friends home. He drove one girl to her house, but when he reached the home of the second girl he learned that both she and the girl he had spent the evening with planned to leave together. He sped away, drove outside of town to a small cemetery, parked the car and told the girls he wanted to have intercourse with them. The two girls jumped from the car but Frank was able to catch each of them and knock them to the ground. One girl fell on her stomach whereupon

he leaped astride her pressing her face into the earth until she lost consciousness. Leaving her lying there for the moment, he turned to the other girl, throttled her until she too was in a semiconscious state. He then carried them back into the car, forced them to undress lighting up the interior of the car so that he might watch. He then forced each girl to fellate him under both physical force and verbal threats that they would be killed. Following this he had intercourse with one of the girls. He sat for a while with the two girls, took some money from one and then drove them home. The girls were in an hysterical condition when they arrived and a physician was immediately called. He treated each of them for multiple contusions and sedated them. The police were notified, given a description of Frank and his car and he was apprehended about 1 wk later.

When Frank was interviewed, he expressed disbelief that the police were called immediately. He stated that he may have been rough with the girls but he felt that they were quite agreeable to his advances. He had concluded that they only reported him when they saw him some nights later in a tavern. He was with his wife and therefore could not respond to their invitations to join him at their table. It was his conviction that the girls were angry out of jealousy and not because of his sexual assault.

Frank was the fourth of five children born into a very unstable and chaotic family. Only the patient's younger sister appears to be without physical or psychological stigmata. His two older brothers have criminal records that go back to early adolescence and a history of antisocial behavior in their prepubertal years. His older sister was born with a deformed hand. After some years of marriage her husband committed suicide. His father has a criminal history, and three half brothers, children of his father's from a previous marriage, all have extensive antisocial history with the oldest currently serving a life sentence for murder.

His father was an alcoholic and physically abusive to his family, especially to the patient. On one occasion he hung the patient by his tied hands in order to beat him. On still another occasion, he sat on the porch firing a rifle into the ground about Frank forcing him to ridicule himself in front of other family members. The father's criminal record included assault and rape of a young girl.

His mother was a very passive, compliant woman, who although completely unconcerned about the social or educational development of her children, was very nurturing and giving; in fact in excessive and unrealistic ways. She appeared oblivious to the social and psychological pathology in her family. Although she herself was not actively antisocial, her intense needs to mother resulted in either a denial or passive support of the psychopathy. For example during one of Frank's imprisonments she kept him supplied with contraband drugs.

The cruel and abusive treatment he received from father was only a part of the violence that surrounded Frank through his early and late childhood. His mother states that as a baby he would frequently beat his head against a wall or hit himself on the head with objects. At the age of seven he was in an automobile accident and suffered fractures of the right leg, right clavicle, right forearm, and pelvis. At age 16, he was caught in the blades of a manure spreader and received a fracture of his left leg and extensive damage to his penis and testicles.

His memory of his first sexual arousal has the same violent quality. He recalls being in a hayloft with one of his brothers and two or three of his cousins, one, a girl 2 yr older. They were jumping up and down thrashing the hay, when he noted that as she jumped her dress rose above her waist. He became sexually aroused and jumped closer and closer to her until they bounced against each other and tumbled together into the hay. This vivid memory in many ways represents the quality of his sexuality.

Frank is of medium height, extremely stocky and muscular with a short thick neck. During his commitment at the Center he was on disciplinary report repeatedly having difficulties with both security personnel and fellow patients. These patients were seriously injured in separate altercations with him and each one under similar circumstances. They had gotten him angry in some face-to-face disagreement, but he waited until he could assault them from behind or take them by surprise. In a sociometric study, Frank scored as one of the least desirable men among the patients.

His voice was loud, raucous, and demanding. His needs were peremptory and his requests were orders. Certainly a prison is a paranoid community, and Frank has spent most of his adult life in correctional institutions. Nevertheless, his suspiciousness, lack of trust, unprovoked hostility, and the projection of this hostility reflects a characterological paranoid quality that is not simply institutional.

Summary and Discussion

This paper organizes some clinical observations of sexually assaultive behavior and of the men who commit such acts. Although for purposes of exposition the data were organized into classes of rape, the heterogeneity among the patients who seem to represent types leaves no room for conviction regarding classification. However, it is obvious that character patterns exist. Paranoid features are predominant in the group Rape—Sex-Aggression, less so but still present in Rape—Aggressive Aim, and relatively absent in Rape—Sexual Aim. The primitive quality of the aggressive impulse shows the same pattern. Sexual perversions are far more common in Rape—Sexual Aim, with excessive defenses against homosexuality through exaggerated masculinity, predominant in Rape—Aggressive Aim. The level of object ties, the capacity to experience love, tenderness, and warmth, the ability to be kind and generous are clearly different among the three groups.

Their response to therapy, psychotherapy, and other rehabilitative procedures is different as is the progress of such therapy. We have had little success with the group of patients classified as Rape—Sex-Aggression. With the group Rape—Sexual Aim an alliance is established readily, but the passive, oral demanding quality of these patients makes movement slow and arduous. The primary difficulty with the Rape—Aggressive Aim group is the tendency to fall back to paranoid mechanisms wherein a negative therapeutic alliance develops and treatment is then broken. The relative absence of the capacity for warm and intimate object relationship does not permit the relationship to be sustained in the face of the regression.

We are planning a study that will evaluate the extramural adjustment of patients who have been released. On the basis of some data from an earlier study and from clinical impressions, the Rape—Sex-Aggression group represents the greatest risk of maladaptive behavior. Although the numbers are small they are still informative. Only six patients from this group have been released from the center. Two patients were released by court action with no parole or probation supervision prescribed and therefore there has been no follow-up with regard to social adjustment, but there is no evidence of any criminal acts. Of the remaining four, three have had their release revoked and the fourth is having serious difficulties in his second marriage of 6 mo.

The data for approximately 30 other rapists who have been released, although not broken down into subgroups and with no information on social adjustment, show that only one patient has committed another sexual assault. A diagnosis in terms of contemporary nosology cannot be made for the rapists we have seen; when such is attempted it is not helpful. However, there are some similarities in the three groups of rapists discussed to three diagnostic categories of Personality Disorders appearing in DSM II, which perhaps the reader has already noted.

Explosive Personality Disorder as a diagnosis is most descriptive of the group described as Rape—Aggressive Aim, but it is not adequate for it fails to reflect the pervasive hostility toward women and the feature of repetition compulsion. In our group the explosive outburst is not simply overresponsiveness to environmental pressures.

The second group, Rape—Sexual Aim, has many descriptive features in common with the category Inadequate Personality Disorder, but this diagnosis does not communicate the extensiveness of the sexual perversions against which the rape was expressed as a defensive act.

There is most clearly a similarity between the group Rape—Sex—Aggression and the diagnostic category Antisocial Personality Disorder. The clinical features of the correspondence and the dissimilarities were discussed above.

The clinical classification presented here is based almost entirely on descriptive features, and the problems attendant on such a procedure are fully recognized. It has been our experience, however, in clinical and research activity that the classification has a utility not afforded by any other currently available. It is, to state the obvious, that its usefulness or validity will be determined only by further empirical studies.

The men who have been described in this paper are clearly dangerous. Even in those instances where the aggression is minimal, each of these men has placed himself in situations with women where there is a possible threat to the life of the victim. It is also clear that we are not able to determine without extensive clinical work when, if ever, this danger is at a minimum.

We are fully aware of the objections to special sex offender statutes. These objections are not only legal and moral, but also include the diagnostic, therapeutic, and predictive inadequacies of our clinical science. Nevertheless, society has a right to be protected from such narcissistic violence. The lifelong pathological relationships with women seen in these three groups of rapists give no reason to believe that a prison sentence will make them less dangerous.

References

1. Allen, C.: A Textbook of Psychosexual Disorders. London, Oxford University Press, 1962.
2. Calmas, W.: Fantasies of the mother-son relationship of the rapist and the pedophile. Doctoral dissertation, Boston University, 1965.
3. Cohen, M., and Kozol, H.: Evaluation for parole at a sex offender treatment center. Fed. Probat. 30:50, 1966.
4. —, Seghorn, T., and Calmas, W.: Sociometric study of sex offenders. J. Abnorm. Psychol. 74:249, 1969.
5. Cotton, R.: Civil commitments from prison: Abuse of process or protection of society? Mass. Law Quart. 54, (No. 3):249, 1969.
6. Ellis, A., and Brancale, R.: The Psychology of Sex Offenders, Springfield, Ill. C. Thomas, 1956.
7. Gebhard, P., Gagnon, J., Pomeroy, W., and Christenson, C.: Sex Offenders. New York, Harper and Row, 1965.
8. Gould, D., and Hurwitz, I.: Out of tune with the times; the Massachusetts SDP statute. Boston Univ. Law Rev. 45 (No. 10):391, 1965.
9. Guttmacher, M. Sex Offenses. New York, Norton, 1951.
10. —, and Weihofen, H.: Psychiatry and the Law. New York, Norton, 1952.
11. Holden, L.: Sex psychopath laws generally: commitment of sex offenders in Massachusetts specifically. Unpublished, 1969.
12. Kozol, H., Cohen, J., and Garofalo, R.: The criminally dangerous sex offender. New Eng. J. Med. 275:79, 1966.
13. Lopez, T.: Emotional expression in the adult sex offender. Doctoral dissertation, Boston University, 1969.
14. McGarry, A. L., and Cotton, R.: A study in civil commitment: The Massachusetts sexually dangerous persons act. Harvard J. Leg. 6:263, 1969.
15. Mass. Gen. Laws. Ann. Chapter 646, Acts 1958, Chapter 123A. Amendments: Chapter 615, Acts 1969, Section 2, Chapter 123A. Chapter 347, Acts 1960, Section 9, Chapter 123A. Chapter 608, Acts 1966, Section 9, Chapter 123A.
16. Sarafian, R.: Treatment of the criminally dangerous sex offender. Fed. Probat. 27:52, 1963.
17. Seghorn, T.: Adequacy in ego functioning in rapists and pedophiles. Doctoral dissertation, Boston University, 1970.
18. Tenney, C.: Sex, sanity and stupidity in Massachusetts. Boston Univ. Law Rev. 42 (No. 1:)1, 1962.
19. Williams, A. H.: Rape-murder. In Slovenko, R. (Ed.): Sexual Behavior and the Law. Springfield, Ill., Thomas, 1965.

Rape, the Law, and Private Property

Julia R. Schwendinger and Herman Schwendinger

In the United States today, journalists and academics frequently argue that the rape laws are simply an extension of property laws that protect the interests of men.[1] Perhaps the most popular statement of this viewpoint is by Brownmiller, who argues that legal safeguards for women emanate solely from laws designed to protect man's female property.

Brownmiller provides her own interpretation of history to substantiate this standpoint. She says that because of the violence of man against man and of man against woman, women have always needed to turn to a man for protection of themselves and their children.[2] In this context, a woman's fear of being raped has been especially important. "Female fear of an open season of rape . . . was probably the single causative factor in the original subjugation of woman by man, the most important key to her historic dependence, her domestication by protective mating," writes Brownmiller.[3]

In return for male protection, women sacrificed their autonomy and ownership of their bodies. "Once the male took title to a specific female body . . . he had to assume the burden of fighting off all other potential attackers, or scare them off by the retaliatory threat of raping their women."[4] Rape was an invasion of male property rights; therefore, when the rape laws were finally developed, their focus was on property, not persons.

The notion of property is not spelled out precisely by Brownmiller, but the intimation is that women were things, like spears and flint axes, that were owned by in-

---

[1]Examples include Susan Brownmiller, *Against Our Will: Men, Women and Rape* (New York: Simon and Schuster, 1975); Lorenne Clark and Debra Lewis, *Rape: The Price of Coercive Sexuality* (Toronto, Canada: Women's Educational Press, 1977).

[2]For the theoretical models underlying Brownmiller's work, see Julia Schwendinger and Herman Schwendinger, "A Review of the Rape Literature," *Crime and Social Justice*, Fall-Winter 1976, pp. 79–85.

[3]Brownmiller, *Against Our Will*, p. 16.

[4]Ibid., pp. 16–17.

---

dividual men. Stealing or harming any of them would be an offense against the owner. Further implied is that the male whose rights were thus violated would retaliate and punish the violator in consort with other men whose interests were served by measures defending property rights. The rape law represented such a measure. A statement that sums up the notion that it continues to protect male property rights is made by Clark and Lewis in *Rape: The Price of Coercive Sexuality.* They say, "Our legal system defines and treats rape as an offense against property, and not as an offense against the person."[5]

These statements and other similar ones are provocative and their implications lead us to ask: Is rape really a property crime today?[6] Also, if rape laws in the past were actually related to property relations, were those relations based on complex social relationships, such as modes of production and social class relationships, or did the laws simply mark women as things and merely reflect the interests of individual men?

Modes of Production, Property Relations, and Control of Women

A particular socioeconomic context surrounds our discussion of laws and customs and historical changes.[7] The socioeconomic formations appearing in our references are identified by their modes of production. That is, in ancient hunting and gathering societies, production was based on *primitive communism*; it was based on *slavery* in ancient Rome, on *feudal servitude* in medieval England, and on *independent* peasantry and artisanry in a number of societies. Later, the Western European and North American nations signify the *capitalist* mode of production. We shall see that modes of production are certainly not the only factors that determine laws and customs, but they are the most important ones.

At this point, a very brief synopsis of terms will be sufficient, since the history of socioeconomic formations is not our main focus. The phrase, *mode of production*, mentioned above, is the general method of obtaining the means of life, such as food, clothing, shelter, tools, and factories, that are necessary for the survival of a people and the development of society.

One aspect of the mode of production consists of the *productive forces*, such as tools, farms, workshops, and factories, as well as the skills, energies, and division of labor among people who work. These forces reflect the relationship of people to the objects and forces of nature which must be used to create the material necessities of life. Some of these productive forces, such as tools and factories, are also

---

[5]Clark and Lewis, *Rape: Price of Coercive Sexuality*, p. 159.

[6]See also Harold C. Barnett, "The Political Economy of Rape and Prostitution," *Review of Radical Political Economics.* Women and the Economy, Spring 1976, p. 59.

[7]We do not intend in this article to present a complete history of rape law. Earlier examples of rape laws can be found in the Babylonian and Mosaic laws. For these examples, see Brownmiller, *Against Our Will*, pp. 18–19; and Cyril J. Smith, "History of Rape and Rape Laws," *Women's Law Journal*, vol. 60 (1974), pp. 188–90.

called *means of production* because they are the means by which workers produce what people need.

Another side of the mode of production, the *relations of production*, refers to certain relationships among the people themselves while they are involved in producing things. In antagonistic socioeconomic formations, these relations of production are social class relationships. Some, but not all, of these class relationships are supported by private property laws that state the basis for ownership of the means of production.

Finally, the mode of production also refers to economic and political processes, which are called *objective laws of social development*. These laws govern the development of the relations and forces of production and vary greatly from one type of socioeconomic formation to another. For instance, certain laws affect the ways in which joint-family relations in a hunting and gathering society are organized to cope with seasonal changes in food supplies. Others force capitalist firms to exploit colonial labor abroad in order to offset a falling rate of profit at home.[8]

The analysis that follows refers to changing modes of production. First, we will show some of the interesting connections between the slowly evolving rape laws and the transformations in modes of production and social institutions such as the family, church, and state, which secure these modes. The legal changes occur because the fundamental laws of a society safeguard both its dominant mode of production and the social relations based on that mode. When the dominant mode of production changes, so do the laws.

Second, we will refer to private property. The connections between the rape law and the basic structure of a society seem to be simple and taken for granted when people like Brownmiller speak about rape law and private property. However, if we are to understand these connections, we must know about the forces and relations of production that underlie a specific form of private property. Unfortunately, the plain phrase "private property" as used by Brownmiller and others does not by itself say anything about these underlying relationships.

For example, private property relations exist under the simple commodity production of small farmers and artisans whose farms and workshops may belong to them; nevertheless, these property owners earn their living by their own sweat. Such property relations (i.e., of small farmers and artisans) exist in slave, feudal, and capitalist societies; but they do not characterize the *dominant* mode of production. In each of these societies, the dominant mode of production is based on the exploitation of entire social classes and therefore involves quite different "private property" relationships. Since property relations that support a dominant mode of production often affect society as a whole, the phrase "private property" cannot be meaningfully connected with the laws that prohibit rape unless we are fa-

---

[8]For a discussion of the relation between these laws and the extended concept of mode of production, see Harold Wolpe's introduction to *The Articulation of Modes of Production: Essays from Economy and Society*, Harold Wolpe, ed. (London, England: Routledge & Kegan Paul, 1980), pp. 1–44.

miliar with how specific modes of production in a society are articulated with one another.[9]

Furthermore, even when men control women to ensure their property, this control may be legally instituted to support interests that transcend sexual distinctions. For thousands of years, for instance, the control over wives and daughters by men of property ensured the hereditary continuity of the families that owned and controlled the strategic resources of society. Such control reflected property relations based on specific types of class relationships and particular modes of production but not the interests of all men as individuals.

Finally, the control over women has functioned quite differently from the control of property. Control over women might be more fruitfully compared with social control over personal safety or socially necessary activities. The loss of women means loss of the source of life-giving activities. Anthropology shows that all societies are concerned about reproduction of the human producers who ensure the continuity of both family and tribal relationships. The biological and economic reproduction of families and tribes is protected through family or tribal control of women because women are productive in an economic and physiological sense. Women extend the lives of kinfolk and produce children whose labor will provide security in later years for the elders; and women's activities toward these ends are prescribed by custom whether family life is governed by patriarchal authority or not.

Furthermore, in numerous tribal societies, the control of women and matrimonial policies generate the social relationships that enable the circulation of economic values within and between communities. Such values are exchanged through complex forms of reciprocity, gift giving, dowry, and the simple exchange of goods and wealth. It is important to note that they are qualitatively *different* from "property values" which, in our society, are represented by "impersonal" systems of commodity prices that are equal to the value of merchandise or capital in commodity markets.[10] Furthermore, in our society, legal prescriptions for child bearing and socialization of children are quite different from those pertaining to property values. Consequently, although personal control and ownership of property are frequently equated, the application of this simple equation to the relationships between men and women is open to serious question.

Rape Laws under Roman Slavery and English Feudalism

With these observations in mind we now turn to the development of early rape laws. A history of rape law that is directly relevant to modern Western codes begins

---

[9]In the introduction to his book, Wolpe defines the concept of articulation as "the reproduction of the capitalist economy on the one hand and the reproduction of productive units organized according to pre-capitalist relations and forces of production on the other." Ibid., p. 7.

[10]Claud Meillassoux, "From Reproduction to Production: A Marxist Approach to Economic Anthropology," in ibid., p. 196.

with the class society of ancient Rome, in which both law and private property relations were highly developed. Direct ties between law, property, and rape are to be found in the law of *raptus*.[11] Raptus was a form of violent theft which could apply to both property and persons. Because it referred to abduction and not necessarily to rape, it was not a sexual crime by definition. If a woman was abducted violently and sexually molested, the crime was merely defined as theft of a woman without the consent of those who had legal power over her. Legally, the harm was committed against her father, guardian, or husband.

But this Roman conception of rape, as a property theft rather than a sexual violation, is not a historical surprise. Many women in Rome suffered the same fate as Greek women; they became possessions of propertied men to ensure the production of wealth or the hereditary continuity of a ruling class.[12] Furthermore, and most important, this designation of women's status corresponded with the Roman society's dominant mode of production. The Roman empire was not simply the most highly developed system of commodity exchange in antiquity. Its mode of production was based on the labor and sale of human commodities—slaves. The structure of this slave society directly reflected relationships organized around the concept of people as property. Great numbers of men as well as women were denied autonomy or rights over their own bodies; if slaves even ate of their free will, they were punished. They were merely private property.

The next mode of production, feudalism, was organized primarily around the aristocracy's ownership of the means of production, which was chiefly land; it also entailed various forms of servitude and personal dependence of the peasants upon their landlords, the noblemen. Nobility and serfs represented the main social classes, but, in addition, clergy, artisans, other commoners, and even slaves were incorporated into a feudal hierarchy with elaborate distinctions in social rank.

As feudal societies evolved, the changing sex laws were a barometer of the changing status of women. Feudal Anglo-Saxon laws of rape, gradual and slow as was their evolution, typify the changes. The earliest feudal laws were written in the seventh century during the reign of King Aethelbert in Kent.[13] Part of Aethelbert's law paralleled the Roman law of raptus, which made abduction illegal. Like its Roman predecessor, Aethelbert's law had no concept of transgression pertaining directly to the specific act of rape or sexual assault. If a man "carrie[d] off a maiden," compensation of fifty shillings (equivalent to a Roman ounce of silver) was to be paid "to her owner [guardian]."[14]

By the ninth century, in the reign of Alfred the Great of Wessex, a variety of terms for sexual assault finally made an appearance; however, distinctions be-

---

[11]See, e.g., James A. Brundage, "Rape and Marriage in the Medieval Canon Law," *Revue de Droit Canonique*, vol. 28 (1978), p. 63.

[12]Frederick Engels, *The Family, Private Property and the State* (New York: International Publishers, 1975).

[13]F. L. Attenborough, ed. and trans., *The Laws of the Earliest English Kings* (New York: Russell & Russell, 1963).

[14]Ibid., p. 15. All bracketed words are Attenborough's.

tween adultery and rape were not consistently made. The idea of attempted rape was introduced in the section of the law stating, "If [anyone] throws [a young woman belonging to the commons] down but does not lie with her, he shall pay [her] 10 shillings compensation." This was distinguished from actual rape, treated more explicitly in the following section: "If he lies with her he shall pay [her] 60 shillings compensation."[15] Notice a markedly significant change in the payment of restitution, that is, the award of compensation to the offended woman.

Since the social ranks (nobility, serfs, commoners) included women, there were also status distinctions specified in the feudal laws on rape. Rape victims were by no means considered fully autonomous persons, but all of them were not classified as chattel either. Instead they were ranked by their position in the feudal class structure or by their relations as wards, servants, or property of men, who were likewise identified by their feudal rankings. In this way, a freeborn woman would belong to the commons while a ward of the king would have higher rank.

Compensation for an act of violence was differentiated by the rank of the victim. King Alfred's law stated, "If anyone seizes by the breast a young woman belonging to the commons, he shall pay her 5 shillings compensation." This was a small amount because the woman was of the lower class. But what if the breast belonged to a higher-class woman? According to the law, if a "woman of higher birth" was "outraged," then "the compensation to be paid shall increase according to the wergeld." The wergeld stood for the value of a particular person's life, and it specified the amount of compensation paid by the family of a killer to the family of the person slain. Payment was made to atone for the killing and to avoid a blood feud.

Even the position of a nun was recognized by the law governing sexual assault. In the ninth century, the "lustful seizure" of a nun in Wessex required compensation twice the sum fixed for a woman belonging to the laity.

The effects of feudal ranks on law can be seen if we notice the differences in punishments for rape. King Alfred's law stipulated that if a rape victim was a female belonging to the king, the punishment was greater than if she belonged to a commoner. If the rapist was a slave, his punishment was worse than that of a freeman. "If anyone rapes the slave of a commoner," the law stated, "he shall pay 5 shillings to the commoner and a fine of 60 shillings [to the King]. If a slave rapes a slave, castration shall be required as compensation."

Thus, each victim's position in feudal society was roughly equivalent to a monetary value. Although the laws varied, this general principle had also applied under Aethelbert in the seventh century. Remember, rape itself was not stated in the law, but if a man had intercourse with a king's maiden, he was required to pay fifty shillings. The same man would pay half as much if the woman was a grinding slave. "Lying" with a nobleman's serving maid cost twelve shillings; but the amount was halved to six if the woman was a commoner's serving maid.

Just how serious rape and other sex crimes were considered during the seventh and the ninth centuries is not at all certain. We have no way of knowing exactly

---

[15]Ibid., p. 63. The remaining references from King Alfred's laws are on pp. 63–93.

what these fines meant—six shillings compensation for lying with a commoner's serving maid or fifty shillings for having sex with a king's maiden, under Aethelbert—so let us compare them with the punishments in the same period for certain crimes against men that would seem to have been quite serious. When the punishments for sex crimes are compared with punishments for crimes against men during the same reign, an educated guess becomes possible.

Under Aethelbert, anyone engaged in knife or swordplay who pierced through another man's penis paid six shillings. Causing a man to lose a foot or an eye, and thereby endangering his ability to earn a livelihood, cost the offender fifty shillings. Therefore, penetrating a commoner's serving maid's vagina was just as costly as piercing a man's penis. But sleeping with a king's maiden could have been as costly as the price of some men's lives.

All of these crimes, then, appeared to have been serious on all levels of society. As we have seen, sex crimes were also quite serious for the lowest caste. Under Alfred's law, even if it were a slave raped by another slave, the punishment was castration.

Communal Custom versus Law and the State

The frequent use of compensation as punishment for the crime during feudalism is particularly interesting. Although Anglo-Saxon law was dominated by the feudal social structure, it held to some of the traditional ways of rectifying the wrongs which were preserved by still-existent family kinship groups. The customary practice of compensating victims and their kin illustrates this relationship.

Turning the historical clock back farther we see that some of these family kinship groups had modes of production based on primitive communism. Such societies never conceived of sexual molestation as an infringement of private property because women's status in these societies was that of kin, not property.

In kinship groups certain transgressions were considered social harms rather than just individual harms, and the taboo against these forms of conduct worked accordingly. For example, a rape victim's relatives and her entire joint-family group were also harmed by her rape. If infringements of sexual taboos took place, they offended the entire group; as determined by custom, they were dealt with by the two extended families involved: the victim's family and the rapist's. To rectify the harm, some form of compensation was paid by the family of the wrongdoer to the victim and her family.[16]

---

[16]Although feudal law secured the dominant (feudal) mode of production, it recognized other modes. Consequently, these laws may have demanded mutilation (e.g., castration) or payments of fines to the state, but they also required compensation for the victim and her relatives as required under traditional authority. Further examples of the coexistence of such customary and legal punishments, which spanned traditional and feudal practice, were the blood feuding and other acts of revenge involving whole clans. Blood feuds, prefeudal in origin, were recognized by feudal courts. For further information, see Marc Bloch, *Feudal Society* (Chicago: University of Chicago Press, 1966), pp. 126–27.

Another unique factor shaping the law of rape in early English society was related to the developing power of the feudal state. Often, a fine was levied in addition to the compensation. This was new. Under King Alfred, as we have seen, a man was fined sixty shillings for raping the slave of a commoner, while the compensation to the commoner was only five shillings. The slave-owning commoner was compensated because his human property was assaulted; but what was the purpose of the fine? Furthermore, why was the fine so large—twelve times as high as the commoner's compensation? The answer lies in the transition from one mode of production to another and the cost of expanding the state. The money went to increase the King's treasury, which he used to strengthen his power to extend feudalism—an exploitive mode of production—while at the same time he undermined the earlier communal kin relations.

This cynical use of rape law to expand state resources is pointedly illustrated by Diamond, in his study of the kingdom of Dahomey.[17] Diamond found that rape was extremely rare in Dahomey's traditional joint-family groups; yet despite the rarity of rape and the effectiveness of traditional controls, the king of Dahomey invented rape as a civil crime enforceable by the state. After making the law, the king ordered women under his control to go to the local villages and seduce men into having intercourse. The entrapped men were subjected to summary trials under the new rape law and punished with conscription into the army.

Scholars traditionally claim that law is invented to preserve law and order and tranquility in society, but this was not the function of the rape law in Dahomey. "Such instances as this," Diamond observes, "only sharpen the point that in early states crimes seem to have been invented in the service and profit of the state, not the protection of persons, not the *healing* of the breach."[18] In surveying anthropological literature, Diamond found further examples of the invention of laws to serve the state rather than the population. Laws can define certain acts as crimes, but these acts may not be genuine personal and public harms.

Diamond uses these crimes to generalize about the fascinating and strange effect of a changing social structure on law in societies like Dahomey. He says, "[Laws] arise in opposition to the customary order of the antecedent kin or kin-equivalent groups; [these laws] represent a new set of social goals pursued by a new and unanticipated power in society."[19]

Thus, the Dahomean rape law did not reflect the mere whim of a capricious sovereign, nor did it contain a social problem. It was devised during a transition between the declining political control by kinship groups, and the rising power of a social class headed by king and state. The goal of the king was to undermine the customary order of the kindred organization and to consolidate and extend the ter-

---

[17]Stanley Diamond, "The Rule of Law versus the Order of Custom," *Social Research*, Spring 1971, pp. 42–72. Reprinted in *Criminal Justice in America*, Richard Quinney, ed. (Boston: Little, Brown, 1974), pp. 29–49.

[18]Ibid., p. 41.

[19]Ibid., p. 37.

ritorial boundaries of his class society by military force.[20] The parallel between the Dahomey rape law and King Alfred's rape law, which bridged the kinship and feudal orders, appears clear.

Precapitalism and Rape Law

As class societies evolved, rape laws underwent changes that heralded the modern rape law in two ways: They explicitly defined rape as a crime against the person rather than against property, and they based this crime on the forcible denial of the victim's will.

In this process, ecclesiastic law makers as well as secular legislators were involved in gradually changing legal conceptions. The medieval Catholic church, for instance, had its own juridical system which tried and punished rapists. Moreover, as early as the twelfth century, the ecclesiastic lawmakers were among the first to call for the recognition of the victim as an independent person without reference to social rank or to any guardian, owner, or employer.

The revision of the ancient laws of Rome, explicitly separating rape as a crime against the person from property crimes, occurred when a set of revised laws was compiled in the twelfth century in a collection of canon law (known as the Decretum) by Gratian, a Benedictine monk of Bologna. Gratian's legal consultants, in advising him to distinguish rape as a violent crime against the person, pointed out that raptus, according to the ancient law, referred to both property and persons. It was suggested that raptus be used solely when referring to crimes against persons and that the law of *rapina* apply to crimes against property. Gradually during the Middle Ages, "raptus," then "rape," became a crime against the person, entailing in the definition some of the same factors as appear in modern law. To be defined as rape, under the revised medieval canon law, an assault had to involve abduction, coitus, violence, and lack of free consent on the part of the woman.

Writing about the trends in rape law from the end of the medieval period, Brundage, an historian, indicated that as the law evolved, it tended to legitimate a greater personal autonomy for women in late medieval society.[21]

The new definitions of rape were also related to larger changes in legal ideas that focused on the individual as a bearer of rights without regard to social position. Eventually, the written law, for instance, no longer imposed varying punishments

---

[20]This political process as it occurred in antiquity is analyzed by Engels, *Family, Private Property and the State*, who points out, "The first attempt at forming a state consists in breaking up the gentes by dividing their members into those with privileges and those with none, and by further separating the latter into two productive classes and thus setting them one against the other" (pp. 172–73). From Engels's perspective, the new powers mentioned by Diamond extend beyond civil bureaucrats and the king's family estate. They are embodied in the class of wealthy persons who have seized political power for themselves and their families. Since the state is essential to the consolidation of class societies, most of these families control state power directly rather than operating through intermediaries.

[21]Brundage, "Rape and Marriage in Medieval Canon Law," p. 75.

when victims came from different social ranks. (Even though, as is well known, in practice some such distinctions were and are still made.)

Such ideas are taken for granted today when people speak about individual rights and responsibilities, but they required centuries of precapitalist legal development to become firmly incorporated in the criminal codes. From the twelfth to the fourteenth centuries, feudalism remained dominant; however, in the flourishing mercantile centers (e.g., in Italy before the Renaissance), individuals increasingly appeared as bearers of rights to salable things called commodities. These commodity relationships influenced laws of contract and criminal responsibility that laid the basis for modern law.

American Slavery and Racism

Modern capitalism, with its now familiar mode of production, expressed as wage labor and capital and structured by giant industries and multinational corporations, did not emerge full blown or pure. Especially in its early stages, this mode of production was articulated with other productive relationships. Articulated with the capitalist mode of production were precapitalist units of production, for example, in the feudal principalities of India and the slave plantations of North America. Therefore, besides wage labor, the primitive accumulation of capital in the United States, for instance, depended on the exploitation of convict labor, peasant labor, and slave labor.

Not surprisingly, the rape law, where there was slave labor, was restricted in scope. With reference to this, Jordan, in *White over Black: American Attitudes toward the Negro, 1550–1812*, quotes a Maryland lawyer who lived in a slave state. The lawyer stated, "Slaves are bound by our criminal laws generally, yet we do not consider them as *objects* of such laws as relate to the commerce between the sexes. A slave has never maintained an action against the violator of his bed."[22]

Other authors note that the law claimed in principle to protect women, yet did not actually include slave women.[23] Phillips, in *American Negro Slavery*, writes, ". . . although the wilful killing of slaves was generally held to be murder, the violation of their women was without criminal penalty."[24] Legally, the rape of another man's slave was "trespass" of his property, and the rape of a slave by another slave

---

[22]Winthrop Jordan, *White over Black: American Attitudes toward the Negro, 1550–1812* (Chapel Hill: University of North Carolina, 1968), p. 160. Not surprisingly, the lawyer's statement spoke of women as male property.

[23]In 1851 the Louisiana Supreme Court said, regarding the use of slave concubines, "The slave is undoubtedly subject to the power of his master; but that means a lawful power, such as is consistent with good morals. The laws do not subject the female slave to an involuntary and illicit connexion with her master, but would protect her against that misfortune." However, only naive persons can believe that courts controlled by slave owners ever protected slave women. Also, it can be argued that such judicial decisions only came about because of late developments in the history of southern slavery such as the embargo on the slave trade and the rise of the abolitionist movement.

[24]Ulrich Phillips, *Life and Labor in the Old South* (Boston: Little, Brown, 1929), pp. 273–74, 500.

had no official status, but merely produced additional exploitable children. Slave owners could do as they would with their property; and, as the records of the South show, raping slave women was common practice among owners, overseers, neighbors, and other men.[25]

Although these rapes themselves were not matters of record, the slave retaliation, and therefore the rape, was sometimes recorded. Johnston cites a number of murder trials involving black men and black women who killed masters and overseers for sexually assaulting slave women. In one instance, in 1859, a male Negro slave was tried for the murder of a white man. During the trial the slave's lawyer attempted to introduce the testimony of a slave woman, named Charlotte, who was the wife of the prisoner. The lawyer proposed to prove with this testimony that in the morning of the day on which the killing took place, Coleman, the overseer, had raped her. When her slave husband was told about the rape, he killed the overseer. However, since slaves had no access to criminal courts for redressing injuries and since they could not give evidence against whites, objections were raised and sustained against Charlotte's giving testimony in defense of her husband.[26]

Capital punishment was added to the brutality of the rape law during slavery. Edwards, in *Rape, Racism, and the White Women's Movement*, says, "Death was first made a penalty for the crime of rape as part of the Southern slave codes before the Civil War. The Mississippi slave code had a mandatory death penalty for a slave found guilty of raping a white woman."[27] While slave masters and other white men raped black women freely, black men were punished by death if convicted of raping a white woman.

The end of slavery did not mark an end to this use of capital punishment. It was maintained after slavery was abolished. The legal conditions established by the southern ruling class encouraged capital convictions of black men for rape; moreover, based on flimsy evidence, black men were frequently hanged or burned alive by white supremacist lynch mobs taking the law into their own hands.

Nor has the enlightened capitalism of the twentieth century meant an enlightened penal system. Capital punishment still epitomizes racist justice. Wolfgang and Riedel analyzed the convictions for rape in Georgia from 1945 to 1965. They conclude, "Our current analysis suggests that racial combinations of defendant and victim form the most important discriminating variable: black defendants who rape white victims are most likely to receive the death penalty."[28]

Racism and the rape laws are unquestionably inseparable. Furthermore, the rape laws of a repressive mode of production are likely to be one strand in a web of

---

[25]See, e.g., John D. Paxton, *Letters on Slavery: Addressed to the Cumberland Congregation* (Lexington, Ky.: Abraham T. Skilman, 1833), pp. 189–97.

[26]James H. Johnston, *Race Relations in Virginia and Miscegenation in the South, 1776–1860* (Amherst: University of Massachusetts Press, 1970), pp. 306–07.

[27]Allison Edwards, *Rape, Racism, and the White Women's Movement: An Answer to Susan Brownmiller* (Chicago: Sojourner Truth Organization, 1976), p. 21.

[28]Marvin E. Wolfgang and Marc Riedel, "Rape, Race, and the Death Penalty in Georgia," *American Journal of Orthopsychiatry*, July 1975, p. 667.

repressive legislation. Blacks, whether freed or enslaved, were, from the earliest colonial days, forbidden by law in southern states from having interracial sex. To protect the white race from "racial pollution," black men, black women, and white women were punished for consensual, interracial sex; but white men usually had little fear of being punished so long as they refrained from marrying black women. As recently as 1968, miscegenation laws in Virginia still paid a bounty to anyone reporting a marriage between a black and white.

Colonialism and Rape Law

More examples of rape laws where the law serves purposes of racism rather than deterring and punishing rapists are found in the history of modern colonialism. One illustration is the Papuan 1926 White Women's Protection Ordinance. Papua, previously British New Guinea, became an Australian colony in 1901.[29]

Concentrated in the town of Port Moresby, the "Europeans," as the whites were called, regarded the Papuans as black, naked, dirty, betel-chewing people who did not have the decency to use lavatories. They believed that criminal codes could be employed to civilize the natives even though the latter were stereotyped as inferior, childlike, and given to lust and immorality. These codes, however, actually supported no purpose other than repression of the Papuans, who were exploited by the Europeans as extremely low-paid wage laborers and servants.

Racist policies were gradually introduced to repress and control the native population. In 1907, gambling by natives was forbidden; in 1908 and 1925, curfews were passed in Port Moresby and in the native villages. The Papuans were prohibited from laughing at, threatening, or insulting a European. They had to use separate entrances, exits, and seating areas in places of public entertainment, and they were also served in separate sections when they shopped in the town stores.

Thus, the White Women's Protection Ordinance followed a series of racist policies introduced by the Europeans. However, the legislation itself was precipitated by a moral panic engineered by a law-and-order faction that wanted Sir Hubert Murray, the lieutenant governor, to be removed from office because they felt his policies toward the natives were not repressive enough.[30] To embarrass Murray, the faction began to publicize "a series of [native] crimes and insults" against the white population in the virulently anti-Murray newspaper. They petitioned the governor to take action and accused him of refusing to protect white women.[31]

To justify the ordinance, their petition to Murray reported three attacks against whites. In the first attack, a white woman was allegedly assaulted by a Papuan as she walked along a busy thoroughfare (her assailant was frightened off by a

---

[29]Amirah Inglis, *The White Women's Protection Ordinance, Sexual Anxiety and Politics in Papua* (London, England: Sussex University Press, 1975), p. 62.

[30]For the dynamics of "moral panics," see Stuart Hall et al., *Policing the Crisis: Mugging, the State, and Law and Order* (London, England: Macmillan Press, 1978).

[31]Inglis, *White Women's Protection Ordinance*, p. 62.

passerby). Another situation involved a child and a fourteen-year-old native houseboy who, "it was said," placed "his person" against her leg. The third case consisted of an assault on a white man, a case that had no bearing on the rape ordinance.

The clamor over the "black peril" escalated with two more attacks on white women. In one case, a merchant's wife was awakened at night by a man who was touching her, as she quaintly put it, "in the fork."[32] Peeping and touching by a black man were condemned by white men as "infamy against white womanhood and an outrage against the prestige of the white race."[33]

Eventually, to protect his position and authority among the white population, Murray issued the ordinance—a colonial version of rape law—imposing a death penalty for both rape and attempted rape of white women. After the ordinance was passed, additional policemen were hired and searches of native quarters without warrants were allowed. Finally, Murray agreed, in principle, to build a fence across the entire town to keep natives out of Port Moresby altogether unless they were shopping, working for whites, or charged by whites with a specific duty.

What is most important to note about the development of the White Women's Protection Ordinance is that the group so protected was not the group subject to attack. While black women, who were not protected by the ordinance, had been raped by white men, the record does not contain a single case of a rape of a white woman by a native. The lieutenant governor, writing to the Prime Minister in Australia in 1930, four years after passage of the ordinance, said, "It is well to remember that there has never been a case of rape of a white woman in Papua."[34]

Rape Law, Property Rights, and Married Women

As capitalism evolved, changes in the rape law initiated by the rise of class societies were spasmodic. Following the late feudal and precapitalist developments in rape law, western societies, from the seventeenth century onward, consolidated the definition of rape as a crime against an individual woman, but only so long as the rapist was not the husband.

This restriction on the married woman's rights bears special consideration because it reflected a larger code, established chiefly by the English common law, known as the doctrine of coverture, which maintained the husband's supreme authority in family life. Under this doctrine, patriarchal authority was safeguarded economically through chattel ownership codes; and the corporal punishment provisions of the codes allowed husbands to enforce their authority through violence.

English common law adopted the feudal doctrine of coverture to secure the economic base for patriarchal authority. According to this doctrine, both money and landed property, *after marriage*, ranked in law as chattel interests over which the

---

[32]Quoted in ibid., p. 58.
[33]Ibid., p. 58.
[34]Quoted in ibid., p. 117.

husband gained dominion. Upon marriage a woman turned over all her property to her husband. She lost her power to engage in contracts with either her husband or third parties. Interest and profits from the property she had owned were also transferred to her husband, and he could spend this money as he wished. Her children, too, were assigned legally to her husband, whose authority in these matters was supreme.

The ethical basis for the coverture doctrine traces back to patriarchal biblical injunctions about a husband and wife belonging to "one body." In reality, of course, this was always the body of the husband. Nevertheless, the mere survival of biblical injunctions could not have been the sole reason why the married woman's rights were restricted so severely. Single women were also severely restricted by biblical injunctions; yet, while they were denied the right to vote and serve on juries, they were not consistently discriminated against with respect to contract and property. Except for the period when the system of primogeniture prevailed,[35] propertied single women enjoyed almost equal legal status with males in certain economic exchanges. Under English common law, "If they were not under age, they could contract with other persons, sue and be sued, manage and control their lands and chattels, and appropriate for themselves earnings accruing from their property."[36]

The denial of married women's rights was grounded in a number of interrelated social conditions. During early capitalism most economic ventures were family enterprises, and therefore the legal restrictions on married women encouraged a consolidation of property that favored ever greater capital accumulation. Furthermore, by concentrating family wealth in male hands, the laws ensured the hereditary continuation of private property in a manner that dated back to the origins of social classes, private property, and sexual inequality.

Common law itself was produced largely by the rising class of bourgeois landowners and manufacturers. And because of the influence of this class on the law, similar legal standards were established for other social classes. Consequently, the legal restrictions on the wife's possession of her earnings—or her right to seek employment independent of her husband's will—were also applied to working-class families. The law required employed married women to transfer their earnings to their husbands.

This extension to the working class, however, was also favored by the economic and political forces that externalized the social costs for the reproduction of capital. These costs were shunted from business to the individual household. Elsewhere we have described how the household economy became organized chiefly around production for use and not exchange.[37] Restricting married women's productive activities to the family limited women largely to the massive production of

---

[35]Primogeniture is the right of the eldest son to inherit his father's estate.

[36]Leo Kanowitz, *Women and the Law: The Unfinished Revolution* (Albuquerque: University of New Mexico Press, 1971), pp. 35–36.

[37]For a further discussion of this issue, see Julia R. Schwendinger and Herman Schwendinger, "Rape Victims and the False Sense of Guilt," *Crime and Social Justice*, Summer 1980, pp. 11–13.

simple use values. Such values were consumed by wage earners to reproduce them-selves, to replenish their capacity to work for capital. Yet, even though housewives helped reproduce the labor force for capital, their labor was expended without monetary remuneration. The household labor of women—and married women in particular—provided services that cost capital relatively little, and it thereby sup-ported higher rates of capital accumulation.[38]

Simultaneously, the prevailing ethos of commodity-producing societies down-graded the importance of the household worker. On one hand, that ethos strongly supported the granting of moral and juridical autonomy to commodity holders, to those who were in a position to earn money. All others—who seemed to be depen-dent for their economic existence on another person's earnings—were defined as personal dependents. Consequently, the married woman was regarded as a depen-dent despite her vital contributions to her husband's welfare. Even though the hus-band was equally dependent upon her labor for his personal well-being, only he was regarded juridically as an autonomous person because of his status as a commod-ity holder, a seller of labor power or property.

The unprecedented establishment of this singular set of family relationships is masked today by political movements that eulogize the so-called traditional family and ignore that this family type became widespread only with the rise of capital-ism. The creation of the traditional family required the coercive power of the state as well as the sexist restrictions of economic life.[39] In previous centuries, for exam-ple, whether they were employed or not, whether they turned over their wages or produced use values in the home, or even if they inherited property from their fam-ilies, married women in the United States were *forced* by law to remain personally dependent on their husbands.

The Struggle for Legal Autonomy

However, during the second half of the nineteenth century, mature capitalist devel-opments rapidly generalized commodity relationships throughout the United States. At the same time, structural conditions and contradictions that could un-dermine the common-law marriage precepts regarding property ownership were established.

These social and economic developments encouraged political processes which showed that the relations between a mode of production and legal institutions are much more complicated than has been suggested previously. Usually, for instance,

---

[38]As Nancy Holstrom says, in "Women's Work and Capitalism," *Science and Society,* vol. 45, no. 2 (1981), p. 194, "Domestic labor allows a higher rate of surplus value because this socially necessary labor is either free or very cheap."

[39]Margaret George indicates that although there was some improvement initially, women's status de-clined in England as capitalism evolved from the sixteenth to the eighteenth century. Margaret George, "From 'Goodwife' to 'Mistress', the Transformation of the Woman in Bourgeois Culture," *Science and Society,* Summer 1973, pp. 152–79.

the effects of a mode can be detected in the formulations of fundamental laws. Thus, in the United States, one finds laws defining economic rights that directly reflect the primacy of private property relationships because they are supported by the Constitution. Yet, these rights were expressed in law because of the efforts of political movements, engaged in a protracted revolutionary struggle for national independence. Everywhere, in the struggle for individual rights, numerous political movements have intervened between changes in modes of production and modern legal systems.

Militant movements for sexual equality certainly played an important role in the dismantling of sexist restrictions on married women; moreover, these movements drew strength from the broad social outcry against slavery in the South and from workers' struggles for better working conditions in the North.

Leaders of the early women's movement woke to their lack of equality and the need to fight for their freedom when some of them submerged themselves in the abolitionist movement. The slave mode of production was a living contradiction within the developing capitalist mode; it was in the 1830s, during an upsurge against slavery, that early feminists, who were also abolitionists, learned to organize and tied their struggle to the antislavery movement. Attacked by the church for their public activism, they began to "answer their critics, linking the two issues of slavery and the position of women."[40]

Furthermore, with the vast accumulations of capital by landowners, the women found some ready supporters among men in their struggles for economic and property rights. Although the rich had already established a legal right to protect their daughters' property through marriage contracts and trusts, many wealthy fathers were pleased at the prospect of a less expensive and cumbersome way of assuring that their daughters' inherited money and property would not be squandered by profligate husbands. The authors of *Sexual Discrimination and the Law* point out, "This motive for reform was widely held amongst the wealthy Dutch farmers of the Hudson valley."[41]

Other forces, such as early socialist ideas about equal rights for women, came into play. In 1836, the same year that New York's revised property law for married women was introduced into the legislature, Ernestine Rose, a twenty-six-year-old Polish socialist of the Robert Owen school, emigrated to the United States. She had successfully defended her own right to her deceased mother's estate against the claims of a spurned fiance when she was younger; now, a strong supporter of women's rights, she embarked on a twelve-year campaign, soon supported by other feminists, in favor of the new property bill.[42]

Yet another historical development, the influx of women into the paid labor

[40]Eleanor Flexner, *Century of Struggle, The Woman's Rights Movement in the United States* (New York: Atheneum, 1970), p. 47.

[41]Barbara A. Babcock et al., *Sexual Discrimination and the Law* (Boston: Little, Brown, 1975), p. 599.

[42]Miriam Schneir, *Feminism, the Essential Historical Writings* (New York: Random House, 1972), pp. 125–27.

force, united women around the goal of changing the laws that discriminated against them. With the employment of women in factories and offices (there were over 4 million employed women, according to the 1890 census), women began to have self-earned incomes which under common law belonged to their husbands. The first Married Woman's Property Law gave bourgeois women the right to property they brought with them into marriage; but further struggle was necessary to achieve the later laws that gave a working-class woman the right to wages she earned.

Thus, the feudal doctrine of coverture was progressively whittled away. In the United States, a patchwork of Married Woman's Property acts, developed during the second half of the nineteenth century by all the states beginning with New York State, finally enabled married women to make contracts, sue and be sued without their husband's consent, manage and control the property they brought to the marriage, engage in wage-earning employment without their husband's permission, and keep the earnings gained by this employment.

Similar kinds of developments also dismantled the legal justifications for using corporal punishment to keep married women in their place. The state's direct enforcement of the married woman's subordination was buttressed by legal support for the customary use of corporal punishment. Old English common law, as previously mentioned, also justified the husband's use of corporal punishment to maintain his supremacy in family life. Cultural reinforcement of family violence is exemplified by a vintage American limerick:

> A woman, a dog, and a walnut tree,
> The more you beat, the better they be.

However, toward the end of the nineteenth century, the right of husbands to chastize disobedient wives forcibly was progressively narrowed and then repudiated. At least as far as legal principles are concerned, American courts finally decided "that the moral sense of the community revolts at the idea that the husband may inflict personal chastisement upon his wife, even for the most outrageous conduct."[43]

On the other hand, such decisions have not completely eliminated the legal supports for "wife beating." The "unity doctrine," the biblical injunction about a husband and wife being of one body, still has an independent effect on how domestic relations laws are written (e.g., domicile restrictions on married women) and how they are interpreted (especially as they relate to assaults on wives[44]). Also, it must be kept in mind that, with the exception of women's suffrage, legal changes affecting married women's rights have been passed individually by the different states; consequently, the rights conferred on women have been much greater in some states than in others. The lingering legal inequities due to this variation are graphi-

---

[43] *Women's Rights Law Reporter,* Spring-Summer 1977, p. 146.
[44] Ibid.

cally seen in the current state-by-state struggle for the enactment of laws similar to the Equal Rights Amendment (ERA). The passage of equal rights legislation within a number of states has eliminated some of the laws that had placed all household goods in the husband's hands. In such non-ERA states as Georgia, a couple's home belongs to the husband even if the wife paid for it; in several states, such as Louisiana, a wife can be sued for her husband's gambling debts; and in New Mexico before the state ERA was adopted, a wife could not advertise for the sale of the family dishwasher without her husband's consent.[45] In many states a housewife still cannot obtain credit apart from her husband. The legal changes removing such inequities have been uneven and have by no means guaranteed independence for women.

Nevertheless, when taken as a whole, legal changes over the last century sharply contradict any claim that the rape law or even the marriage law today is totally or predominantly organized around male property relationships.[46] The massive entrance of married women into the labor force (which is now establishing the ground for new fundamental changes in family relationships) also contradict such claims. But women in the United States need not consider these recent changes or look back at their own history to remind themselves of the nature of women's status at an earlier stage of the struggle. As recently as 1973, the condition of Irish women duplicated the status of their now-luckier sisters a century ago, even though the Irish constitution promises equality to all.

Kenny, writing in a periodical published in Brussels, says, "To begin with, the legal situation of Irishwomen must be one of the worst in Europe." A woman may not sit on a jury, and it is only since 1957 that a married woman in Ireland has been allowed to hold and dispose of property. Nevertheless, "she must have her husband's permission for almost every legal or contractual commitment: opening a charge account at the store; a bank account; a mortgage."[47]

The law also safeguards patriarchal authority over the Irishwoman's reproductive capacity and her children. She must ask her husband's permission for most gynecological operations. "*The children are his*; he is their legal and moral guardian," Kenny adds. "She may not put her children on her passport or take them out of the country without his permission—a situation which does not obtain for him."[48]

Divorces are prohibited. If she deserts her husband, she forfeits further access to the marital home or the children; yet this is not true for men. The wife is defined as chattel and the law is guided predominantly by the feudal doctrine of coverture. Yet, there is no doubt that as conditions in Ireland change—and they are being

---

[45]Carol Coe Conway's "Letter," *URPE Newsletter*, Union for Radical Political Economics, June-July 1979, p. 15.

[46]Even the exemption of rape by husbands has been stricken down in Sweden, Denmark, South Australia, the U.S.S.R., Poland, and several individual American states. See, e.g., Gilbert Geis, "Rape-In-Marriage: Law and the Law Reform in England, the United States, and Sweden," *Adelaide Law Review*, June 1978, p. 302.

[47]Mary Kenny, "Women as Chattels," *Agenor*, May-June 1973, p. 7.

[48]Ibid., p. 7.

changed rapidly by the international flow of capital from metropolitan nations—movements for sexual equality will ultimately put an end to these restrictions.

Conclusion

In conclusion, we have pointed out that the historical development of rape laws has been influenced directly or indirectly by modes of production. Consequently, rape laws are also effected by property relationships, since such relationships legally regulate particular kinds of production (e.g., commodity production) and certain relations of production (e.g., social class relations in capitalist societies).

But this article has also argued that rape laws cannot be adequately understood by reducing the relationships between men and women to "property relationships" based simply on the possession of women by men. Certainly, while this restricted use of the term *property* may have some limited meaning when referring to legal and economic relationships in certain slave societies, it is not very useful and may even be misleading when dealing with the nature of kinship societies like those in Dahomey, newly emerging feudal distinctions in ninth century England, colonial relationships in Papua, or personal dependency relations in the modern American home.

Americans who support legal reforms for greater equality for women should also recognize that, for the most part, our laws have broken decisively with the feudal doctrine of coverture and that married women are no longer legally compared with chattel. It would be an insult to the accomplishments of the women's rights advocates over the last century and one-half to overlook this qualitative change. At the same time, legal developments are taking place in a *class* society. Under these conditions, women who become wage workers can, at best, only replace personal dependency relations in the family with a double burden and a dependence on exploitation by capital. Moreover, in this mode of production, labor market exploitation continues to be sustained by sexual, racial, and economic discrimination.

Finally, some of the legal gains made in recent decades can be reversed temporarily and are now being threatened by the massive conservative backlash led by the so-called moral majority. In the name of preserving life and the family, these defenders of the "traditional family" would even go so far as to take away forcibly a woman's right to decide whether or not she will remain pregnant when she is raped. Consequently, the desire to combat violence against American women must still confront social inequities that shape the way laws are written and implemented. At the same time, women should take heart because the historical changes in law, which have been accelerating in this country, point to one conclusion: Whatever the setbacks in the struggle for legal change, they will only be temporary. They will be overcome by militant movements that recognize that the historical time for the complete recognition of women's rights has finally arrived.

The Drugs–Crime Connection

James A. Inciardi

Of the more than 3,000 people interviewed, one cohort included 573 Miami narcotics users contacted during 1978 through 1981. Although a few of them were recent admissions to local drug-treatment programs or the county stockade, the overwhelming majority—476, or 83%—were active in the street community at the time of interview. *All* were current users of narcotics. That is, they had used heroin or illegal *methadone** on one or more occasions during the 90-day period before the interview. Furthermore, like other populations of street-drug users that have been studied, most were males (68%), the median age was 26.9 years, and 52% were white, 36% were black, and 12% were Hispanic.

Without question, these narcotics users had long histories of multiple-drug use with identifiable patterns of onset and progression. Using median age as an indicator, they had begun their careers in substance abuse with alcohol at an age of 13.7 years, followed by their first other drug experimentation about a year later. Marijuana use began at a median age of 15 years, followed by the use of sedatives at 17.1 years, heroin at 18.9 years, and cocaine at 19.4 years. Any differences between the men and women in the cohort were only minor.

All these narcotics users were heavily involved with drugs, using an average of five different substances. As indicated in Table 1, *all* had used narcotics during the 90-day period prior to interview, and in excess of 90% were using narcotics either daily or several times a week. In addition, most were current users of sedatives, cocaine, alcohol, and marijuana. With regard to the high levels of multiple drug use, a 19-year-old woman who had started her drug career with alcohol at age 11 commented:

> Part of the reason [for multiple drug use] is just for the hell of it and part is because you're just so used to stickin' something in your arm or up your nose or into your mouth. In the morning I'll use a little *shit* [heroin] to get the cobwebs out of my brain and get the blood movin' around. Then when you're waitin' downtown with a few others for the *man* [the connection] maybe someone will

---

*Methadone is a synthetic narcotic drug used in the treatment of heroin addiction.

Source: From *The War on Drugs: Heroin, Cocaine, Crime, and Public Policy* by James A. Inciardi by permission of Mayfield Publishing Company. Copyright © 1986 by Mayfield Publishing Company. (pp. 123–133).

Table 1 Current Drug Use and Cumulative Frequency of Use Among 573 Narcotics Users, Miami, Florida, 1978–1981

Current Drug Use	Male, % (n = 387)	Female, % (n = 186)	Totals, % (n = 573)
Heroin/illegal methadone			
Daily	69.5	67.7	68.9
Several times a week or more	92.8	95.7	93.7
Weekly or more	96.4	98.4	97.0
Any use in last 90 days	100.0	100.0	100.0
Other sedatives			
Several times a week or more	42.6	52.7	45.9
Every two weeks or more	64.1	72.0	66.7
Any use in last 90 days	70.3	74.2	71.6
Cocaine			
Weekly or more	43.9	47.8	45.2
Any use in last 90 days	61.8	61.8	61.8
Amphetamines			
Several times a week or more	8.5	11.8	9.6
Every two weeks or more	15.8	18.8	16.8
Any use in last 90 days	21.2	22.0	21.5
Hallucinogens/solvents—inhalants			
Weekly or more	3.4	4.8	3.8
Any use in last 90 days	11.1	12.9	11.7
Marijuana			
Daily	42.1	39.8	41.4
Several times a week or more	76.0	65.1	72.4
Weekly or more	84.5	76.3	81.8
Any use in last 90 days	88.1	79.0	85.2
Alcohol			
Several times a week or more	52.7	44.6	50.1
Every two weeks or more	71.6	66.1	69.8
Any use in last 90 days	78.0	75.8	77.3

pass around a little wine and reefer. Some of us will shoot a little coke to beef up the *shit* they deal in 'round here. They try to tell ya it's "good stuff" and that's all they got. What a bunch a shit! What shit that is.

Early involvement in criminal activity was characteristic of the great majority of the narcotics users interviewed. Virtually all reported having committed crimes at some time in their lives, with the median age of the first criminal act just short of 15 years. As suggested by Table 2, a property offense—burglary, shoplifting, vehicle theft, or some other larceny—was usually the first crime committed. Interestingly, however, almost all these users differentiated between simple pilfering and more serious property crimes. A 23-year-old respondent recalled:

I used to rip off the supermarket and the 7/11 store ever since I can remember. My aunt would be goin' up and down the aisles puttin' stuff in the basket and I'd be right behind her eatin' cookies 'n candy off the shelves.... That doesn't

Table 2 Criminal Histories of 573 Heroin Users, Miami, Florida, 1978–1981

Criminal Characteristics	Male, % (n = 387)	Female, % (n = 186)	Totals, % (n = 573)
Ever committed offense	99.7	98.9	99.5
Age of first crime (median)	14.4	15.3	14.7
First crime committed			
Robbery	6.2	3.2	5.2
Assault	7.0	5.4	6.5
Burglary	27.1	6.5	20.4
Vehicle theft	7.0	1.1	5.1
Shoplifting	18.3	37.6	24.6
Other theft/larceny	16.0	10.2	14.1
Prostitution	0.0	12.9	4.2
Drug sales	3.6	2.7	3.3
Other/no data	14.5	19.4	16.1
No crime	0.3	1.1	0.5
Have arrest history	94.3	88.7	92.5
Age at first arrest (median)	16.6	17.3	16.8
Total arrests (median)	4.4	4.9	4.5
Ever incarcerated	80.9	71.5	77.8

count, it was just kid stuff and nobody cared. The first time—the first real score—I remember like it was today. I was real young—maybe 10 years old— and I was runnin' with these guys from Grand Avenue—a real tough area back in the sixties. We were in this big tool shop on the corner and this guy, I just couldn't be-fucking-lieve it. He rips open this display thing and takes out this fancy electric drill and hands it to me and puts it in my school bag and says git! I was scared shitless that we'd be caught. . . . I thought we'd really hit the big time then.

A total of 24 of the women narcotics users in the cohort had started their criminal careers with prostitution, and they too seemed to have different ways of defining whether or not their behavior was "criminal." One woman who stated that her first crime was prostitution at the age of 13, also indicated:

I had sex for the first time when I was 10, somewhere 'round there. I remember I wanted to see some Steve McQueen movie real bad. I thought I was in love with the guy [McQueen] an' I would've done anything to see that show. . . . This jerk in my class said he'd take me if I'd play around with him a little afterwards, you know. So I did. . . . But that ain't prostitution. It was just fuckin' around. We all used to do that. What about all these *fine ladies* who are taken to a *fine restaurant* and a show and after let their man put it to 'em. That's the same thing. It's just gettin' laid. It wasn't prostitution 'til I started takin' money for it and doin' it regular.

Almost all of the 573 narcotics users had been arrested at least once, usually by age 17. Most had fewer than five arrests, and the majority had been to jail or prison at least once.

The number of crimes committed by these narcotics users was extensive. As illustrated in Table 3, the 573 users reportedly committed 215,105 offenses during the 12-month period prior to interview—an average of 375 crimes per subject during the course of a year. At first glance, this figure—more than 215,000 criminal offenses—would appear astronomical, thus requiring careful analysis. For example, of the total offenses, some 38%—over 82,000—involved drug sales, and an additional 22% included other "victimless crimes" such as prostitution, procuring, gambling, and alcohol violations. As such, more than 60% of the total offenses involved crimes against the public health, order, and safety. This, however, should not be interpreted as a minimizing of their criminal patterns. On the contrary. As the data indicate, the same 573 narcotics users were also responsible for almost 6,000 robberies and assaults, almost 6,700 burglaries, almost 900 stolen vehicles, more than 25,000 instances of shoplifting, and more than 46,000 other events of larceny and fraud.

Table 3 Criminal Activity During the One-Year Period Prior to Interview of 573 Narcotics Users, Miami, Florida, 1979–1981

Crime	Total Offenses	Type as % of Total Offenses	Type as % of Sample Involved	Type as % of Offenses Resulting in Arrest
Robbery	5,300	2.5	37.7	0.8 ($n = 44$)
Assault	636	0.3	20.9	5.5 ($n = 35$)
Burglary	6,669	3.1	52.7	0.8 ($n = 52$)
Vehicle theft	841	0.4	19.4	0.8 ($n = 7$)
Theft from vehicle	3,708	1.7	28.1	0.4 ($n = 15$)
Shoplifting	25,045	11.6	62.1	0.4 ($n = 104$)
Pickpocketing	2,445	1.1	4.5	<0.1 ($n = 2$)
Prostitute theft	4,093	1.9	15.9	<0.1 ($n = 4$)
Other theft	6,668	3.1	31.1	0.6 ($n = 39$)
Forgery/counterfeiting	7,504	3.5	37.5	0.8 ($n = 59$)
Con games	3,162	1.5	23.9	<0.1 ($n = 1$)
Stolen goods	17,240	8.0	53.4	0.1 ($n = 22$)
Prostitution	26,045	12.1	22.2	0.3 ($n = 89$)
Procuring	7,107	3.3	24.1	<0.1 ($n = 3$)
Drug sales	82,449	38.3	83.9	0.1 ($n = 86$)
Arson	17	<0.1	1.7	0.0 ($n = 0$)
Vandalism	322	0.1	7.2	0.9 ($n = 3$)
Fraud	1,165	0.5	10.5	0.5 ($n = 6$)
Gambling	12,939	6.0	36.1	<0.1 ($n = 4$)
Extortion	240	0.1	7.5	0.0 ($n = 0$)
Loan-sharking	795	0.4	7.0	0.0 ($n = 0$)
Alcohol Offenses	296	0.1	6.6	7.1 ($n = 21$)
All other	419	0.2	2.3	3.1 ($n = 13$)
Totals	215,105	100.0	—	0.3 ($n = 609$)

The data in Table 3 address a number of other significant issues as well. *First,* there was great diversity in the range of the users' criminal events: 38% were robbers; 21% were assaulters; 53% were burglars; 19% stole automobiles; 38% were forgers; 24% engaged in confidence games; 53% dealt in stolen goods; 22% were prostitutes; 84% were drug sellers; and almost all were thieves. *Second,* the incidence of arrest among these narcotics users was extremely low. Of the 215,105 offenses, only 609 resulted in an arrest. Stated differently, only three-tenths of 1 percent of the crimes resulted in arrest—that is, one arrest for every 353 crimes committed. More specifically, consider the following ratios of crimes committed to ensuing arrests:

robberies and assaults	75:1
forgery and counterfeiting	127:1
burglary and other theft	219:1
drug sales	959:1
confidence games	3,162:1

Furthermore, these narcotics users reported 17 crimes of arson, 240 incidents of extortion, and 795 cases of loan-sharking. *None* of these resulted in arrest. This would certainly suggest that narcotics users, at least those studied in Miami but likely most others, are highly successful criminals that systems of urban law enforcement are unable to control. As one heroin user who specialized in residential burglary explained it:

> It is so fucking easy to take down a house, or two or three, just in one morning and there's almost no risk. At 8 o'clock in the morning mommy and daddy go off to work and the kids go off to school. By 9:30 A.M. the whole fucking neighborhood is fucking dead. Now, this is important. You go to some neighborhood like Coral Gables, South Miami, Kendall or the other places where there's lots'a bushes and trees. There's so much cover that sometimes you can practically walk right up to the back door without even lookin' around. . . . And the real funny thing is that the jerk-offs will put bars and dead bolts on the front door but'll have just a flimsy lock in the back that lets you almost dance right in. . . . There was this one place that I hit three times in the same year and they still didn't learn nothin' about locks. . . . Jerk-offs.

In addition to the 573 narcotics users, another 429 were interviewed whose current drug use did not include narcotics. In many ways they were similar to the narcotics users in terms of their patterns of onset and progression into drug use and crime. Some had experimented with heroin and other narcotics early in their careers, and a few had even used narcotics regularly for short periods. Primarily, however, their drug use focused on alcohol, sedatives, marijuana, and/or cocaine. Both their drug-using and criminal careers had begun at about age 15.

As indicated in Table 4, like the users of narcotics, these individuals were heavily involved in crime. The 429 nonnarcotic drug users reported the commission of

Table 4 Criminal Activity During the 12-Month Period Prior to Interview Among 429 Nonnarcotic Drug Users, Miami, Florida, 1978–1981

Crime	Total Offenses	Type as % of Total Offenses	Type as % of Sample Involved	Type as % of Offenses Resulting in Arrest
Robbery	1,698	1.2	29.4	2.7 (n = 46)
Assault	407	0.3	28.2	22.1 (n = 90)
Burglary	3,944	2.9	40.6	4.7 (n = 185)
Vehicle theft	618	0.5	16.3	4.4 (n = 27)
Theft from vehicle	2,536	1.9	11.9	0.4 (n = 11)
Shoplifting	21,247	15.5	33.6	0.3 (n = 66)
Pickpocketing	2,354	1.7	6.3	0.1 (n = 3)
Prostitute theft	2,245	1.6	6.1	0.1 (n = 3)
Other theft	4,548	3.3	17.2	0.5 (n = 23)
Forgery/counterfeiting	1,936	1.4	15.2	1.5 (n = 30)
Con games	2,103	1.5	9.8	0.2 (n = 4)
Stolen goods	11,960	8.7	25.9	0.2 (n = 23)
Prostitution	24,966	18.2	10.5	0.2 (n = 49)
Procuring	4,363	3.2	5.8	0.1 (n = 5)
Drug sales	38,378	28.0	30.5	0.2 (n = 66)
Arson	391	0.3	2.6	0.5 (n = 2)
Vandalism	259	0.2	5.3	0.0 (n = 0)
Fraud	1,409	1.0	7.5	0.3 (n = 4)
Gambling	8,819	6.4	17.5	0.1 (n = 10)
Extortion	50	<0.1	4.4	0.0 (n = 0)
Loan-sharking	1,506	1.1	4.4	<0.1 (n = 1)
Alcohol Offenses	1,319	0.1	7.5	3.4 (n = 45)
All other	20	<0.1	1.6	75.0 (n = 15)
Totals	137,076	100.0	—	0.5 (n = 708)

some 137,076 criminal offenses during the 12-month period prior to interview—an average of 320 crimes per respondent. Also, as was the case among the narcotics-using criminals, there were proportionately few crimes that resulted in arrest—one-half of 1% of the total.

Comparing the two groups in other ways, however, there seem to be some significant differences. The nonnarcotics users did indeed commit fewer crimes on a per capita basis. Moreover, almost two-thirds of their offenses were focused on shoplifting, prostitution, and drug sales, with the balance scattered in very small proportions throughout all the remaining crime categories. The two groups are contrasted empirically in Table 5.

Thus, it would appear that in general, the narcotics-using group were more criminally involved. They committed more crimes, engaged in a greater diversity of offenses, and significantly larger proportions committed the more serious crimes of robbery and burglary.

Table 5 Criminal Involvement of Narcotic and Nonnarcotic Drug Users, Miami, Florida, 1978–1981

	Narcotic	Nonnarcotic
Mean offenses per user	375	320
Mean violent crimes per user (robberies/assaults)	10.4	5.1
Violent crimes (% of total)	2.8	1.5
Property crimes (% of total)	36.0	39.0
Drug sales (% of total)	38.3	28.0
% robbers	37.7	29.4
% assaulters	20.9	28.2
% drug sellers	83.9	30.5
% burglars	52.7	40.6
% shoplifters	62.1	33.6

Without getting more deeply into the complexities of empirical data, how can these findings be initially interpreted with respect to the enduring questions about drug use and crime? Does drug use, and specifically heroin use, cause crime? Or are narcotics users already criminals in the first place, with drug use occurring later in their deviant careers? The answers to these questions are still not easy; the inference of causality and the age-old "enslavement theory" of addiction are issues not addressed directly . . . but some preliminary notions can be drawn from the data.

First, it would appear that although the members of both cohorts studied were already substance abusers by the time they began regular criminal activity, it cannot be said that there is an inference of causality between drug use and street crime. For the nonnarcotics users, drugs and crime seemed to emerge hand in hand. For the narcotics users, drug use did indeed occur first, but heroin use did not appear until after they were well into their criminal careers.

Second, and in a contrasting direction, it can be said that *narcotics drive crime.*[1] When comparing the two groups, the narcotics users were involved with greater frequency, intensity, diversity, and severity than the nonnarcotics users. This conclusion tends to be supported by the Baltimore studies that observed the same phenomenon when comparing heroin users during alternative periods when they were addicted and were not addicted.[2]

Third, it has been argued widely in recent years that a small number of habitual "career criminals" are responsible for a relatively great proportion of the crime in the United States. These data would tend to argue against that position. It has been estimated in recent years that there are no less than 500,000 heroin addicts in the nation. What proportion of these are "on the street" at any given time is not known, but unquestionably the number is substantial. The heroin users in this study, and the hundreds of thousands of others elsewhere in Miami, New York, Chicago, and other cities represent a rather substantial cohort of habitual offenders. As shown in the statistics presented in Table 3, some 216 heroin users were responsible for over 5,000 robberies during a one-year period, and some 302 users committed almost 7,000 burglaries during the same period of time. A number of the sampled cases were among both the robbery and burglary groups. At such rates of crime commission, it would be logical to infer that a great number of heroin users are career offenders.

In certain sectors of the political sphere it might be a great temptation to do some simple multiplication with the above figures. Given that there are an estimated 500,000 heroin users in the United States and that each user, as in Miami, commits an average of 375 crimes during a one-year period, would it not be logical to conclude that addict crime comes to 187.5 million offenses each year? Given that, would it not then be logical to incarcerate all heroin addicts and thus have an almost crime-free society? Yet reasonable people, if they were seriously to ponder such conclusions, would quickly realize the absurdity of it all. If there were indeed 187.5 million crimes being committed each year by the addict population, not to mention all the crimes perpetrated by others, American society would have long since fallen into a state of anarchy. Rather than the organized and relatively stable social system that now exists, America would appear more like the apocalyptic nightmare world of *Mad Max* and *The Road Warrior*. Going beyond simple-minded reasoning, there are some very good justifications for not venturing into such mathematical absurdities. As has been pointed out by many drug-abuse researchers and most recently by Bruce D. Johnson and his associates at the New York State Division of Substance Abuse Services, there are many different kinds of heroin users, and perhaps an even greater variety of nonheroin types. By cross classifying the type and frequency of criminal activities with the varying regularity of heroin intake, the Johnson/New York studies identified at least 27 distinct heroin-user types. At one end of the spectrum were highly predatory and dangerous armed robbers, and at the other end were innocuous low-level street drug dealers. There were also some whose only crime was the illegal possession of heroin.[3]

Fourth, it can be readily concluded that drug-related crime is out of control, with law enforcement and the administration of justice incapable of managing it. Since less than 1% of the crimes committed result in arrest, it would appear that the efficient control of drug-related crime is well beyond the scope of contemporary policing. As a Miami police officer reflected:

> I'm sure the police can do better, much better. But to bring it under complete control would be impossible. The citizen would simply not tolerate what would have to be done. If we increased the force 100-fold, and put a cop on every corner, in every doorway, on every roof, and in every house, then Miami could be crime-free. But then it would be like Soviet Russia.

Notes

1. David N. Nurco, John C. Ball, John W. Shaffer, and Thomas E. Hanlon, "The Criminality of Narcotic Addicts," *Journal of Nerv-* *ous and Mental Disease* 173 (1985), p. 100.
2. John C. Ball, Lawrence Rosen, John A. Flueck, and David N. Nurco, "The Criminal-

ity of Heroin Addicts: When Addicted and When Off Opiates," in *The Drugs-Crime Connection*, ed. James A. Inciardi (Beverly Hills: Ca.: Sage, 1981), pp. 39–75; John C. Ball, John W. Shaffer, and David N. Nurco, "The Day-to-Day Criminality of Heroin Addicts in Baltimore—A Study in the Continuity of Offense Rates," *Drug and Alcohol Dependence* 12 (1983), pp. 119–142.

3. See, for example, *U. S. News & World Report* (August 19, 1985), p. 27.

DRUGS AND CRIME 2

Myth: Drug Addiction Causes Crime

Harold E. Pepinsky and Paul Jesilow

"The use of drugs has become more extensive and pervasive, and when you have people selling drugs, you have guns, rivalries, rip-offs, and inevitably, violence."

James Sullivan
Chief of Detectives
New York City Police Department
1983

Teenagers sit huddled in a darkened school cafeteria watching a film in which the main character sticks a needle into a vein in his arm. It is difficult, however, to distinguish detail because the room he sits in is lit only by a candle that reflects off a spoon and a small plastic bag. The addict heats the white crystalline powder, with a little water, in a spoon over the flame. When the heroin is dissolved, he fills his syringe and presses the plunger. The camera zooms in on his thin unshaven face; it has sores all over it. He does not look well.

A voice from the screen says, "To be a drug addict is to be one of the walking dead. The teeth are rotted out, the appetite is lost, and the stomach and intestines don't function properly. The gall bladder becomes inflamed; eyes and skin turn a bilious yellow; in some cases the nose turns a flaming red; breathing is difficult . . . Sex organs become affected." An addict in a straightjacket stretches across the screen. The voice continues, "Imaginary and fantastic fears blight the mind and sometimes complete insanity results. Often times, too, death comes—much too early in life. Such is the torment of being a drug addict; such is the plague of being one of the walking dead." Thus, early in their lives, are most Americans educated in the "evils" of heroin.

In reality, many heroin addicts look as healthy and act as normally as most people. They can have good builds and look quite fit. Far from the stereotype of the trembling junkie, addicts often go undetected in the business world, and number among the successes. Misconceptions about heroin addiction abound.

Source: Harold E. Pepinsky and Paul Jesilow, *Myths That Cause Crime*, second edition, pp. 95–108. Published by Seven Locks Press, Cabin John, Maryland. Copyright © 1985 by Seven Locks Press. Reprinted with permission.

Demystification

Information on heroin is plentiful. Heroin is derived from opium. Morphine, the chief active ingredient of opium, is heated with acetic acid creating heroin, which is then converted back into morphine when it enters the body. When morphine reaches the brain, it is treated as if it were endorphins, a naturally occurring chemical in the body. Endorphins somehow (science does not know exactly) affect behavior and mood. Long-distance running, for example, produces endorphins which leads to a feeling of well being and creates an addiction. The runner who takes days off feels depressed. The chemical makeup of morphine and endorphins is exactly the same, so the brain treats morphine the same as endorphins.

The use of opiates (opium and its derivatives) has a long history in the United States and the world. We know opium use is at least as ancient as the Sumerians (7000 B.C.). They named the opium poppy "the plant of joy." In 1806 morphine was separated from the other components that make opium, and in 1874 the process by which morphine is converted to heroin was discovered. The main uses of opiates are medicinal, legitimately prescribed for tranquilization or sedation and relief from coughing, diarrhea, and pain.

It is doubtful that opiates have harmful effects. A 1928 study published in the American Medical Association's (AMA) Archives of Internal Medicine found that "addiction is not characterized by physical deterioration or impairment of physical fitness aside from the addiction per se. There is no evidence of change in the circulatory, hepatic, renal or endocrine functions. When it is considered that these subjects had been addicted for at least five years, some of them for as long as twenty years, these negative observations are highly significant." A search of the literature conducted in 1956 by the Canadian province, British Columbia, disclosed no studies on the proved harmful effects of addiction among the more than five hundred reports surveyed. An article in the *Bulletin of the World Health Organization* concluded that "harm to the individual is, in the main, indirect, arising from preoccupation with drug-taking; personal neglect, malnutrition and infection are frequent consequences." Edward Brecher and the editors of *Consumer Reports* were unable to find even one study of the proved harmful effects of heroin for their excellent book, *Licit and Illicit Drugs*, published in 1972. The overwhelming conclusion that one reaches from reviewing studies of the physical health of addicts is that opiates result in no measurable organic damage.

If one can believe the research, there are also no evil psychological effects of opiate addiction. It does not cause mental impairment. A study conducted in part by the Assistant Surgeon General of the United States in 1938 found that of three thousand addicts not one suffered from a psychosis caused by opiates. A 1946 study compared six hundred addicts with six hundred non-addicts and reached the same conclusion. And, in 1963, Deputy Commissioner Henry Brill of the New York State Department of Mental Hygiene and chairman of the AMA's narcotic committee, bluntly stated, "In spite of a very long tradition to the contrary, clinical experience and statistical studies clearly prove that psychosis is not one of the pains of addiction. Organic deterioration is regularly produced by alcohol in sufficient amounts but is unknown with opiates."

In truth, poor health among addicts must be attributed to the illegality of opiates. Many states require a prescription to obtain a hypodermic syringe, denying the addict access to the tools of addiction. Unfortunately, the addict must continue to take the drug. Needles are often in short supply and, therefore, are reused. Diseases spread rapidly as addicts share needles, especially since the needles are rarely sterilized.

In addition, addicts must worry about the contents of their purchases because drugs bought on the street are almost never pure. Substances added to the drug often cause illness and death.

The illegality of opiates also ensures that the street price of the drug will be high. The cost of an addiction can easily be between $20 and $100 a day, forcing addicts to devote a large share of their time and financial resources to obtaining their daily drug. Other items, such as food and medical care, come second.

The list of health problems associated with the criminalization of the addict is long. One cause of these problems seems particularly vile. Addicts known to the police are often arrested or brought in for questioning. The addict, deprived of opiates, soon begins withdrawal symptoms and, although withdrawal is rarely fatal, constant resubmission to withdrawal symptoms helps add to the addicts' health problems.

All opiates are addicting. That is, prolonged and daily use of any of the drugs creates a physical dependence. When not deprived of the drug, the addict shows no unusual behavior, and continued use in uniform amounts produces a tolerance to most of the effects. Lack of opiates, however, causes the addict to enter withdrawal—somewhat comparable to a horrible three-day case of either food poisoning, flu, or allergic reaction. All the addict desires is the drug he or she is being deprived of. Addicts hate withdrawal.

Neither physical nor mental addiction to heroin is cured by withdrawal. No study has demonstrated that more than 10 percent of those who can "kick the habit" stay off heroin. Most show far less. A California study examined 3,300 addicts committed to state facilities between 1961 and 1968. Only 300 were able to leave the programs, and it is questionable that even these 300 were no longer addicts. Another study is illustrative. In 1955, 247 addicts were admitted to Riverside Hospital in New York. Three years later, only eight were unaddicted, unhospitalized, unimprisoned, and alive. All eight, however, swore they had never been addicted, and patient records support this for seven of the eight. There has never been a rehabilitation program that could put opiate addicts back into the community unaddicted.

Early references to the use of opium indicate that addiction was not defined as a problem. No doubt, people were addicted to opium, but addicts do not behave or act noticeably different from their neighbors. Addiction only becomes noticeable when one enters withdrawal. Early opiate addicts merely consumed more opium whenever they began to feel ill. Possibly, such addicts never realized that the opium they consumed caused their illness and, at the same time, cured it.

Opiate use in this country in the early 1800s was minimal. Since the U.S. did not grow or tax opium it can be safely assumed that importation of opium was related to usage, and the evidence is that measurable opiate use in this country started about 1840. Consumption rose rapidly in the 1870s, a trend attributable to many factors, among them medical science, the Civil War, the patent medicine industry, and physicians.

Rise of Addiction Rates

Nineteenth-century scientists played a large role in the spread of opiate addiction. A major step was the isolation of morphine from opium in 1806. Morphine is easier to use than opium, which is not of a consistent potency. For this reason physicians regularly prescribed morphine, even though it is approximately ten times more powerful than opium.

With the introduction of the hypodermic syringe in 1853, the use of morphine spread rapidly. This scientific development allowed physicians to inject morphine directly into muscle, causing the drug to act more quickly. It was first used extensively during our Civil War when morphine was commonly given to relieve pain and alleviate dysentery. Many soldiers left the battle field addicted.

The patent medicine industry of the late 1800s greatly increased the number of addicts in the U.S. civilian population. These companies claimed to have products that would soothe almost any problem and, since regulation was lacking, ingredients contained in the product were not required to be listed on the package. In addition, manufacturers produced "cures" for addiction that contained opium or morphine. Patent medicines were available without prescriptions in drugstores, grocery stores, general stores, and by mail. Their names speak of another era: Ayer's Cherry Pectoral, Mrs. Winslow's Soothing Syrup, Darby's Carminative, Godfrey's Cordial, McMunn's Elixir of Opium, and Dover's Powder—to name but a few.*

Physicians in the 1800s did not enjoy the status they do today, in part because of their inability to cure disease. They practiced a brand of medicine that consisted largely of leeches and laxatives, which required the patient to have a strong constitution. Often, the patient would be killed by the cure. Opiates, in contrast, were mild and effective. A single shot of morphine would greatly decrease the patient's awareness of symptoms, make him or her feel better generally, and, not insignificantly, happy that the doctor had helped. Opiates satisfied the physicians' need to have something that worked in a world where they knew nothing. According to a

---

*The belief that one can get "high" by taking aspirin and Coca-Cola probably stems from this period. Coke, at the time, contained cocaine. Mixing one of the opiated pain killers, e.g. Godfrey's Cordial, with Coke would have created an effect far in excess of what either of the items would do separately.

study conducted shortly after 1900, physicians were responsible for one half of the addicted population.

Studies of opiate users, circa 1800 in the Midwest, reveal that women addicts outnumbered their male counterparts by at least a six to four margin. By that time, opiates had proved to be an effective pain killer for menstrual and menopausal discomfort. In addition, a woman faced much less social disapproval drinking her medicine than drinking alcohol. Quite likely, the majority of addicts were professional males and their menopausal spouses.

Before the turn of the century, an estimated 200 to 250 thousand Americans from all levels of society were addicted. It is noteworthy that then, as now, physicians were the most addicted population. An estimated 2 percent of physicians were addicts while other professional groups (lawyers and pharmacists, for example) had an estimated rate of .7 percent, compared to an estimated .2 percent for the general population.

In 1896, importation of opiates declined and, just as the rise in addiction in the late 1800s was due to many factors, its decrease following 1896 was also influenced from many sides. Among the factors that led to the decrease were public awareness of addiction and market saturation.

The general public was unaware of the addicting quality of opiates for most of the nineteenth century. Few public statements about addiction were made by either medical people or government officials. Physicians who knew that opiates were addicting might pass this information along to their patients, but most doctors lacked that knowledge. The patent medicine industry was disinclined to inform customers of the habit-forming effect of opiates because such information might lead people to discontinue use of the products and lead to lower sales. The industry strongly fought efforts that would have required disclosure on labels that their products contained opium. Thus, customers who knew that opiates were addicting might consume the drug unwittingly in unmarked medicines or under the impression that they were taking cures for addiction.

Public awareness of the addicting capacity of opiates was partly due to a general reform movement in the United States in the late 1800s. The public was angered and frightened by the ability of large companies to do as they saw fit; the ability of the patent medicine industry to market products that hid the fact that they contained opiates was a glaring example. Many writers of the period decried the situation and urged legislation to curb the abuses. The rising temperance movement helped. Most people opposed to alcohol use were also opposed to opiates.

Ironically, the introduction of heroin to consumers in 1898 was the result of growing concern with addiction. Thought to combat the withdrawal symptoms of morphine, heroin replaced morphine in many of the patent medicines. Bayer, which introduced it commercially, advertised "heroin for coughs."*

---

*In truth, heroin acts more quickly and with greater intensity than morphine and is as addicting. The fact that Bayer and other companies saw fit to use the new "nonaddicting" substance is strong evidence that the public was quite aware of the problem of addiction and wished to avoid it.

It is likely that the decrease in the use of opiates was due to market saturation as well. Following the growth of opiate use in 1870, there was a slow and steady increase until the mid 1890s. This pattern of consumption is similar to the pattern of growth one would expect for any popular consumer item whether it be hula hoops, bubble gum, or sliced bread. The product is introduced; consumer knowledge grows; people who want the product buy it; and soon most people who want the product have purchased it. Sales growth slows or stops completely.

The above factors produced an environment that was right for some type of legislation aimed at curbing the use of opiates. Addiction had been defined as a problem and reformists of the period believed that the government could change people's behavior by well-written laws and good enforcement.

Some states passed laws restricting or forbidding the use of opiates. They had little effect. A ban on the sale of opium in one state did not prevent its importation from another. Anti-opium groups therefore turned to the federal government. They pointed out that the United States had called for a world conference on opium to convene in 1909, and cited the absence of a national law on opium as a possible embarrassment to U.S. representatives at the meeting.

Three major commercial groups in our country greatly affected the first federal legislation: pharmacists, physicians, and the patent medicine industry. As David Musto describes in his book, *The American Disease*, pharmacists wished to see a ban on patent medicines containing opiates because a ban on narcotics in patent medicines would give pharmacists almost a total monopoly on the distribution of opiates. Physicians also wanted a ban on opiated patient medicines because they wanted the sole right to authorize the use of opiates. The patent medicine industry opposed the ban on opiates, realizing that the removal of narcotics from their medicines would spell the demise of the industry.

At first, it appeared that the deadlock between the two positions would mean that no federal legislation on opiates would be enacted. A ban on the importation of smoking opium was passed by Congress as a compromise before the world conference. Neither pharmacists, nor physicians, nor the patent medicine industry would be hurt by the law. The only group that smoked opium was the Chinese and they had little power in this country at that time. An official of the American Pharmaceutical Association, arguing for a ban on smoking opium, said, "If the Chinaman cannot get along without his 'dope,' we can get along without him."

The principal legislation in this country aimed at controlling the use of opiates is the Harrison Act of 1914. The intention of the law is to bring the distribution of opiates under tighter control. It requires a nominal tax, the use of special forms when transferring opiates, and a requirement that those who dispense the drugs be registered to do so. Its passage marked a major victory for medical doctors and a crushing defeat for patent medicines. The act only allowed small amounts of opiates in proprietary medicines—one quarter grain of heroin, for example, to each ounce. It permits the dispensing of stronger dosages only given by a physician, dentist, or veterinary surgeon for "legitimate medical purposes," and "prescribed in good faith." Health-care providers other than doctors were thereby effectively denied access to the major medical tool of this millennium.

In addition, addicts are denied easy access to opiates. It does not appear that the Harrison Act intended to deny opiates to addicts; neither addicts nor addiction are mentioned in the law. Early Supreme Court decisions, however, soon closed almost all legal avenues.

Supreme Court Decisions

In 1915 the United States Supreme Court ruled that possession of smuggled drugs was a crime. The decision meant that one could legally possess only opiates dispensed by a physician. By 1922 the high court had ruled that dispensing the drug to an addict "for the purpose of providing the user with morphine sufficient to keep him comfortable by maintaining his customary use" was not a legitimate medical purpose. Addiction was effectively criminalized.

Two major factors led the Supreme Court to the above decisions. First, there was a widespread belief that opiate addiction was curable. Many physicians opened clinics to cure addiction in the early 1900s and reported tremendous success in ending addictions. Some clinics were able to gain government support for the effectiveness of their treatments. It was not until the 1930s that officials realized that withdrawal of narcotics does not constitute a cure. Within about five to ten days the body will no longer exhibit the uncontrolled symptoms associated with withdrawal from opiates, but the addict soon starts using the drug again. As was noted earlier, no rehabilitation program has been successful in putting addicts back on the streets without drugs. At the time of the Supreme Court decisions, however, this was not known. It appeared to the Court that those who continued their addictions did so because of personal vice. Addicts were thought to be sick individuals who chose to remain sick.

The second major factor that contributed to the Court's decisions is related to the belief that addiction is curable. The passage of the Harrison Act gave physicians a virtual monopoly on the distribution of opiates, which allowed some physicians to make large amounts of money prescribing them. The Court acted to end this promiscuous distribution of narcotics on the belief that such physicians were keeping people addicted. Once again, the Court believed that, if the opiates were withdrawn from the patients' use, the addiction would be cured.

The Crime Cost

The cost of an addiction often requires the addict to steal or turn to prostitution, and the losses due to crimes committed by addicts are believed to be high. It is estimated, for example, that one-half of the burglaries and robberies in New York City are the work of addicts. The money that the addict takes from the public to pay for drugs often goes into the coffers of large crime organizations which allow them to expand into legitimate businesses where they continue to employ their criminal tactics.

Furthermore, we spend millions of dollars on law enforcement in a vain effort to end the illicit importation of opiates. The entire addict population of the U.S. consumes less than five tons of heroin annually; very few successful heroin shipments are necessary before the demand is met. Enforcement activities only assure the successful importer high profits by cutting out competition. Heroin costing thousands of dollars in Europe or Asia eventually sells for millions on the streets of the U.S. With the possibility of such huge profits, there will always be someone willing to undertake the business of supplying addicts with narcotics. In addition, the successful confiscation of heroin does not guarantee that it will never reach the streets. The movie, *The French Connection*, was based on a true story. The heroin that was seized in that case later disappeared from the police evidence room, most likely ending up on the streets of New York.

Conclusions

This [essay] has concentrated on opiate addiction, admittedly one of the less dangerous forms of drug addiction (alcohol use probably being the worst). The arguments for the legalization of addiction, however, are valid for the other drugs as well. Nicotine and amphetamines are harmful to the mind and body of a user and to society, but the criminalization of the addict does more harm than good. An addict is not helped by prison, and society is not helped by spending the amount of money needed to keep the addict there.

Still, maintenance of an opiate addiction should be legalized, even if we are not ready to legalize all drugs. Addicts certified by a physician should be allowed to obtain a daily amount of narcotic sufficient to prevent the onset of withdrawal. England, for example, uses a system of clinics where certified addicts are able to purchase their daily dose. The addict can easily and safely obtain the drug at an affordable price and thus has no need to turn to crime or suffer poor health to support a habit. The addict and society both benefit from such an arrangement.

The ability of an addict to obtain legally his or her drug will not suddenly end all the evils that have occurred because of the criminalization of addiction. Many individuals who steal will continue to steal. They will probably steal less, however.

A number of positive outcomes should occur from legalization. Addicts' health would improve. Most of the profit for illegal traffickers would end. The resultant decrease in pushers might reduce the number of addicts. New addicts would no longer represent a future source of income for the pusher. And finally, we would save billions of dollars on law enforcement. No longer would we pay other countries to cut their opium production. No longer would we employ people to prevent opiate smuggling. No longer would we house thousands of addicts in our prisons and jails. No longer would we treat the addict as an animal undeserving of human compassion.

ARE THERE VICTIMLESS CRIMES? **1**

Crimes Without Victims
Edwin M. Schur

The Concept

Now that several crimes without victims have been examined in some detail, it may be useful to consider more generally the meaning and significance of that phrase. It refers essentially to the willing exchange, among adults, of strongly demanded but legally proscribed goods or services. Do prohibitions of this sort, and the social problems to which they are directed (and of which they are a part), constitute a sociologically meaningful category? H. L. A. Hart has asked: "Ought immorality as such to be a crime?"[1] Crimes without victims involve attempts to legislate morality for its own sake; the two conceptions very largely relate to the same thing. From the sociological standpoint, however, reference to the victimless nature of the offense may have certain advantages. It reveals the basis for saying that certain laws are indeed designed merely to legislate morality. It also highlights an important criterion for determining which laws fall into this category—the question: "Is there, in this particular situation, any real victimization?"

Another concept closely related to the analysis in this book is *dissensus*. With respect to each of the cases examined here, there is a lack of public consensus about the law. However, consensus is similarly lacking in the enactment and execution of other criminal laws, yet not all those instances involve the peculiar characteristics of the deviance situations described here. For instance, not only is there extensive violation of existing income tax laws, but there also appears to be considerable ambivalence in public attitudes toward these statutes (at least toward their specific provisions if not their very existence). But although these laws are not easily or completely enforceable, they do not give rise to the secondary elaboration of deviance and the related problems evident in the examples discussed above. A main point of differentiation seems to be *the element of transaction, or exchange*. Crimes without victims may be limited to those situations in which one person obtains from another, in a fairly direct exchange, a commodity or personal service which is socially disapproved and legally proscribed.

This limitation is admittedly somewhat arbitrary. It can be seen that there are other offenses in which there really is no victim. And if one were solely concerned with straight description, the phrase *exchange crimes* or even *business crimes* (i.e., offenses giving rise to illegal businesses) might be almost as appropriate a label for the subject matter of this book. But, as already mentioned, the concept of victimless crime helps to pinpoint a major criterion for evaluating policies, and this, too, is of concern in this discussion. The limitation of the concept to the exchange situations keeps it from getting out of hand. In a sense, every criminal law represents a societal judgment establishing both an offender and an individual or collective victim. Where there is direct offense by one person against another person or his property, the victim and victimizer are easily identified. On the other hand, in a crime against the state or a crime against morals, the victim becomes more elusive. And when the law specifically insists that a person is a victim even if the facts contradict that contention—for instance, sexual intercourse with a girl "under the age of consent" is statutory rape, even though she consents—the victim element is blurred still further.

In the examples considered here, the "harm" seen in the proscribed transaction seems primarily to be *harm to the participating individuals themselves* (apart from any alleged harm to general morals). Does the term *self-harm*, then, adequately describe the situations being considered? Not quite. In the first place, there is much dispute as to the extent of self-harm actually involved in the various proscribed behaviors. But, beyond that, not all proscriptions of self-harm produce situations of the sort analyzed here. Thus legal attempts to ban suicide or masturbation might seem to establish victimless crime situations in the sense of prohibiting self-harm, but precisely because the offense involves only the lone individual there is little or no basis for any elaboration of the deviance. Perhaps it is *the combination of an exchange transaction and lack of apparent harm* to others that constitutes the core of the victimless crime situation as here defined. Not all "exchange crimes" would qualify, because in some there may be evident harm to others. This is seen in the case of wartime black-market operations, in which the exchange of proscribed but strongly demanded goods between willing sellers and buyers does work patently to the disadvantage of many other individuals. Perhaps it is because the buyer of such goods is attempting to get more than his fair share of commodities desired by a large proportion of the general citizenry that dispassionate observers can easily view his behavior as harmful to society.[2] Of course it must be kept in mind that even dispassionate analysts will differ in their assessments of the harm involved in particular situations, and indeed there will be some individuals who see distinct harm to others even in the nonvictim situations described in this book.

One feature which seems to characterize all crimes without victims is the unenforceability of the laws surrounding them. Such *unenforceability stems directly from the lack of a complainant* and the consequent difficulty in obtaining evidence. Also significant is the low visibility of these offenses. If for some reason the proscribed exchanges had to occur always in public, enforcement would be far more efficient. Obviously the willing nature of the interpersonal exchange and the privacy in which it can take place are related. Another apparent consequence of privacy and lack of a complainant (combined with public ambivalence about the law) is the invitation to police corruption. Outside of these points, however, there is considerable variation within the category of crimes without victims. A comparison of the three situations analyzed in this book may provide some hints as to the factors determining the expansion of deviance in the victimless crime sphere.

The Self-Image

In all three cases, the individuals involved tend to develop, in some degree, a deviant self-image. This is largely the result of the dominant social definition of their behavior as being outside the pale of respectability, and the more specific labeling of the behavior as "criminal" reinforces and heightens this process. It is, of course, very difficult if not impossible to draw a clear-cut distinction between a deviant self-image and a criminal one. In a sense perhaps only differences of degree exist. Yet the criminalization of deviance may have an especially crucial influence on the individual's view of himself. Thus, the realization that they are considered criminals and—even more significantly—the need to act like criminals causes most drug addicts in this country to develop—at the very least—a pronouncedly antisocial outlook. The doctor-addict, though also clearly a deviant, is unlikely to consider himself a criminal because he can maintain his habit with relative ease and through quasilegal means. The extent of deviant self-image seems, then, to be directly related to the degree of primacy[3] taken on by the deviant role, or the extent to which the deviant behavior comes to be elaborated into a role at all. And primacy relates closely to the *extent to which the deviant must, in order to satisfy the proscribed demand, engage himself in various instrumental and supportive activities.*

The Subculture

This raises the matter of subculture, the development of which is similarly dependent on the nature and extent of the engagement or involvement required of the particular type of deviant. There is pronounced subcultural development in the cases of homosexuality and drug addiction but none in the case of abortion. (Quite simply, in getting what she is looking for, the woman who has had an abortion has no need for frequent or continuing contact with other abortion-seekers.) Partly, it would seem, the development of a subculture has something to do with the continuing nature of the deviant behavior. Generally speaking, abortion is a discrete act, which one can easily bracket in time and space. This explanation is too simple, however, for the physician-addict is indeed continuously addicted yet he does not display subcultural involvement. It is not then merely the continuing nature of the basic deviant act that establishes the basis for a subculture but, again, the *need for continuous contact with other like individuals in order for the basic deviant acts to be carried out.* (There are, of course, psychological considerations which—as noted in the specific studies—may well exert some pressure on deviants to come together, even in the absence of practical need.) This assertion still leaves open the question of how and to what extent legal repression affects such need. Earlier chapters have suggested some instances of fairly specific and direct influence. Perhaps the best example is drug addiction, where it seems clear that the curbing of legitimate supplies tremendously increases the addict's practical need for involvement with other addicts. The role of law in stimulating the development of deviant subculture is less clear in the case of homosexuality. It is interesting to speculate, for example, that the homosexual subculture would be appreciably weaker if all confirmed homosexuals were free to embark on homosexual marriages without fear of legal interference. As noted in the introduction, it is extremely difficult, in trying to answer such questions, to analyze the effects of legal sanctions apart from the influence of the concurrently existing general social disapproval.

It should be clear from this discussion that deviant self-images and involvement in deviant subcultures are interrelated phenomena. Involvement in such a subculture, however, is not an absolute prerequisite to the development of a deviant self-concept. The physician-addict, for example, may well have a consciousness of his continuing deviance and experience great uneasiness about it, even if he has not become generally alienated and totally self-condemning. Likewise, engagement in deviant or criminal behavior may have a pronounced impact on one's self-concept even when the individual is not involved in continuous behavior patterns that imply taking on a set and deviant role. The guilt feelings of the aborted woman serve to illustrate such possibilities.

Secondary Crime

A consideration of the development of an illicit traffic reveals further variation among the three victimless crimes. In the case of abortion and drug addiction, there is a thriving illicit market, although the degree of elaboration and organization may be somewhat greater in the drug situation—owing perhaps to the continuous and particularly compulsive nature of the addict's demand. A related point may be that the addict demands a scarce commodity, whereas the abortion-seeker requires a personal service. It may be somewhat more difficult to supply the commodity, and possibly this may intensify the profit factor and thereby strengthen the black-market operation. However, it should be stressed that the *demand for services as well as that for goods can indeed provide the basis for illicit traffic.* Not only is this seen in the abortion situation, but also in the somewhat analogous cases of prostitution and gambling (which would seem to be two more major examples of victimless crime). Perhaps the most interesting point of variation regarding illicit traffic is its very slight development in connection with homosexuality. As already noted, this appears to be owing to the peculiar supply-demand situation regarding such deviance; the homosexual need not (and, in fact, may only infrequently) turn to nonhomosexuals to effect the proscribed transaction.

It may also be useful to consider why the drug addict engages in much secondary crime while the deviants in the other two situations do not. Obviously the immediate cause is the financial pressures the addict faces in attempting to support his habit. To what, in turn, may this be attributed? Again, the fact that the addict seeks a commodity might seem relevant, although this factor does not appear to be conclusive. Rather it is *the continuous need for what the illicit market has to offer, together with the fact that such offering must be paid for,* that drives the deviant into secondary crime. It is quite possible that a woman continuously seeking abortions could come under severe financial pressure and resort to crime to finance such activity. But most women do not seek abortions continuously, and so the problem does not arise (though in the lower socioeconomic strata some petty crime to finance even a single abortion may occur). Among compulsive gamblers, where there may be almost no limit to the funds the individual requires in order to engage in the desired activity, financial pressures can easily lead to secondary crime.

The Social Reaction

The analysis of abortion, homosexuality, and drug addiction also illustrates some general aspects of social reaction to deviance. In all three cases, public reaction and existing legislation are at least partly based on vital misconceptions about the nature of the deviant behavior. This is not, of course, an inevitable characteristic of public reaction to all deviance, nor is there something about the victimless crime situation that necessarily implies such misinformation. And it should be stressed that stereotyped notions certainly are not the sole support of existing reactions to these problems. Still, the prevalence of misleading notions is startling, and it is particularly interesting that in all three cases *information about relatively harmless aspects of the deviance has not received wide attention.* Thus the real effects of opiates on the addict's behavior and physical condition, the relative safety of most hospital abortions, and the nonstereotypical behavior of many homosexuals—all key facts—have been insufficiently emphasized in popular discussions of these forms of deviance. This can be attributed, in part, to mere lack of information; at the same time, it seems apparent that opponents of reform proposals have made it a point to neglect such factors—which would, after all, considerably weaken their arguments.

This suggests the importance of the group and individual functions or interests served by existing policies, which . . . may extend far beyond the obvious economic interests of illicit suppliers. Such functions vary considerably in nature and intensity. There is, for example, the rather specific and strong vested interest of a specialized law enforcement agency, such as the Federal Bureau of Narcotics. Or there may be a less direct group interest served. Thus, with regard to both addiction and abortion, present policy may in some measure reflect the medical profession's ambivalent attitude toward taking on major responsibility for management of the problem. On the individual level, punitive reactions to deviance may serve various kinds of functions. Every deviant is, in some sense, a psychological scapegoat—a social sacrifice who complements and at the same time establishes the very possibility of conformity in other group members. The special characteristics of any one form of deviance help to determine the ease or difficulty with which it can provide (at a particular time and in a particular society) a basis for such sacrifice.

In light of these considerations, it is interesting that usually the professed aim of legislation against deviance is to eliminate the offending behavior. In the case of drug addiction, for instance, the exclusive emphasis on complete cure of individual cases and on total elimination of addiction has hindered treatment experimentation and other policy reforms. In all three problem areas, the actual effect of the policies employed has been to regulate, and not to eliminate. Despite pious protestations, it seems clear that *the repressive policies discussed in this book represent societal decisions as to how the various demanded goods and services are to be allocated.* Embodied in these decisions is an insistence that social approval shall not attach to the transactions in question; but also implied is the recognition that the particular goods and services shall in one way or another be made available. The woman is to be relieved of her unwanted pregnancy, even if reputable hospitals are not to cooperate. The drug addict is to obtain his drugs, but not from legitimate medical sources. The homosexual is to pursue his sexual inclinations, but must conceal his condition and submit to a certain amount of segregation. Of course very few citizens in our society would express the collective decisions in this way. Yet one is forced to conclude that for one reason or another it has been "arranged" that these social problems shall remain insoluble. Perhaps there is much that is sociologically, as well as psychologically, suggestive in the question posed by Paul Reiwald: "Is the contention exaggerated, or does it not rather state the simple truth, that man has contrived his institutions for the combat of crime so that he may in fact maintain it?"[4]

Policy Reform

What, if any, are the over-all policy implications to be derived from this discussion of crimes without victims? I have certainly not meant to suggest that all "difficult" criminal laws ought be abolished forthwith. At the same time I have indeed tried to indicate the importance of examining the operation and impact of such laws, rather than simply accepting them as given and therefore valid. Furthermore, it must be clear that if one is to draw any policy conclusions at all in areas of this sort, ultimately a personal value judgment must be made. The discussion has, in each of the three areas examined, outlined some of the apparent consequences (or concomitants) of present policy and speculated on those which might attend alternative policies. Even such a presentation must go somewhat beyond available empirical findings. But in any case, individual evaluation of the picture presented will inevitably depend on subjective factors. In attempting to compare alternative sets of social gains and costs (which is what must be done in reaching any sound policy decision), different individuals are likely to assign different weights to particular constituent elements of the problem, and they will also differ in their assessments of the final balance of gains and costs. For this reason there is simply no way to prove scientifically the "best" policy regarding any one type of deviant behavior. What can be done—and, hopefully, what has been done—in this book is to provide a broad picture of the total problem (and of the likely alternatives), on the basis of which individuals can decide what policies to advocate and support. There are also many specific issues relating to the particular deviance situations on which further intensive research (not attempted here) will help fill in major gaps in current knowledge.

Legalization is not automatically or invariably to be preferred to criminalization. Actually the term *legalization* has been used primarily by opponents of reform, to create misleading impressions of reform proposals. For one thing, supporters of existing policies sometimes picture any one proposal for change in criminal law as part of an ominous and general trend toward the legalization of all deviance. Yet there is no general policy principle to be applied to all types of deviance. Each particular type displays its own peculiar characteristics and raises its own special problems which must be considered for policy purposes. There has also been a tendency to use the word *legalization*—with its handy connotation of *no* restriction—to exaggerate specific recommendations for reform of particular deviance policies. It has been alleged that reformers would "allow everyone free access to dope," or would permit "complete license in sexual behavior," or "let any woman wanting an abortion get one." Actual proposals for policy change are almost never so extreme. Similarly, suggestions that legalization implies moral approval or at least condonation are misleading. Liberalization of a law on deviance may imply less disapproval than currently exists, but less disapproval is not the same as positive approval. And at least from a sociological standpoint, concentration on the moral evaluation of the deviant behavior—viewed in the abstract—is hardly profitable. The more constructive sociological task is to try to understand the behavior in its relation to human needs and social values and institutions, and to help decision-makers determine which policy will best maximize social gains and minimize social costs.

An important consideration that may influence acceptance of specific policy changes has to do with the means by which the good or service might be legally provided under a nonrepressive policy.[5] In the case of abortion and addiction, the medical profession would replace the illicit operatives as suppliers of the demanded goods and services. In the case of homosexuality, no such currently legitimate source of supply would be involved. Because no "outside" group would have to be implicated in dealing with homosexuality (i.e., all that would be required would be to allow these people to conduct their own relationships without interference), in a sense reform of these laws might seem easier than in the other two examples. This difference may more likely, however, have just the opposite effect. It may be that medical provision in the abortion and addiction situations provides a basis for legitimation of the transaction not possible in the homosexuality case. (Such grounds for legitimation would be similarly lacking in the case of prostitution—where short of converting prostitution into a respectable profession there seems to be no way of altering the aura under which the services are provided.) Legitimation through medical auspices suggests the significant point that increasingly, in analyses of deviant behavior, the discussion has centered on the issue of whether the behavior in question should be considered a crime or an illness.[6] Even sociologists who would be quite unwilling to accept the proposition that all deviants in these borderline areas are sick may see a tactical need to accept the definition of illness in order to achieve humanitarian and common-sense reforms. Until the public is able to acknowledge that more subtle and sociological forms of determinism are generating and shaping deviance, this strategem will continue to be employed even in cases where it may be inappropriate.

There is, then, an urgent need for increased public education and wider appreciation of sociological perspectives on deviance. It is often maintained that public opinion will not countenance increased permissiveness toward deviant behavior. Yet, as has already been pointed out, knowledge of such opinion is actually quite limited. Furthermore, whatever opinion does exist has often been shaped by misinformation and by the very punitive policies in question. Fortunately much of this misinformation is now being brought out in the open and refuted. This is important because only as the more conforming individuals in society attempt to understand the motivations and patterns of deviance[7] can we hope to grapple effectively and sanely with what is, after all, an unavoidable aspect of social life.

Notes

1. H. L. A. Hart, *Law, Liberty and Morality* (Stanford: Stanford University Press, 1963), p. 4.
2. I am grateful to David Matza for suggesting this point and the general relevance of the black market example.
3. See Edwin Lemert, *Social Pathology* (New York: McGraw-Hill Book Company, Inc., 1951), especially Chap. 4.
4. Paul Reiwald, *Society and its Criminals*, translated by T. E. James (London: William Heinemann, Limited, 1949), p. 173.

5. I am indebted to Peter Gens for suggesting the importance of this factor.
6. See Thomas Szasz, *Law, Liberty, and Psychiatry* (New York: The Macmillan Company, 1963), especially Chaps. 2 and 3: and Erving Goffman, "The Medical Model and Mental Hospitalization," in *Asylums* (Garden City, N.Y.: Doubleday & Company, Inc., 1961), pp. 323–86.
7. See Howard S. Becker (ed.), *The Other Side: Perspectives on Deviance* (New York: The Free Press of Glencoe, Inc., 1964).

Prostitution, Addiction and the Ideology of Liberalism
Jeffrey H. Reiman

It is a sign of growing awareness of the irrationalities in our system of justice that one increasingly hears the question of whether prostitution and heroin addiction are "victimless crimes" asked, and answered in the affirmative. It is not my intention to add yet another instance of asking and answering this question. Rather I wish to explore the question and its answer with the aim of shedding light on the meaning and limits of the prevailing liberal ideology, and in particular on the "liberal conception of harm" and on the social significance of the institutions which enforce "public morality."

Let me then start where I might have been expected to end. I am thoroughly convinced that there exists no justification for laws against prostitution and heroin use in a legal system of the sort we have. And, though I should neither like to see heroin sold in supermarkets between aspirin and toothpaste nor prostitution offered as an area of specialization in business schools, I am convinced that the arguments and evidence in favor of decriminalizing both activities are overwhelming. In fact, one question upon which I will speculate is why the society chooses to maintain these acts as crimes in the face of overwhelming evidence not only of the ineffectiveness of these laws, but indeed of their effectiveness in driving prostitutes and addicts into additional and more serious crimes.

This last remark suggests something which should be obvious but often is not. That is, when we ask whether prostitution and addiction are "victimless crimes," we must distinguish the harm which comes from these activities themselves, from that which is a result of the social context in which they take place, most particularly the fact that they are crimes. Just as it would be viciously circular in considering whether homosexual behavior was harmful, to take into account the suffering of homosexuals and non-homosexuals which results from the *belief* that homosexuality is evil, it is equally circular when considering whether an act should be criminal, to take into account the harms that result from the fact that it is criminal or the fact that some people believe it should be criminal.

Source: Jeffrey H. Reiman, "Prostitution, Addiction and the Ideology of Liberalism," *Contemporary Crisis* 3 (January 1979), pp. 53–67. Copyright © 1979 by Martinus Nijhoff Publishers. Reprinted by permission of Kluwer Academic Publishers.

Once this distinction is recognized there is every reason to believe that the harms associated with prostitution and addiction flow from the social response to prostitutes and addicts rather than from prostitution or addiction *per se*. For example, it is sometimes asserted that prostitution is harmful because prostitutes are often assaulted by their patrons or because prostitutes finding their patrons, so to speak, with their pants down, capitalize on this vulnerability to engage in theft or extortion. It is readily apparent, however, that this is due to the fact that since prostitution is a crime (for both parties, that is, even though patrons are almost never prosecuted), it necessarily takes place outside of the protection of the law. Many other business relations—such as those between doctors, nurses, masseuses, and models, and their customers—take place behind closed doors with one party in a vulnerable position, and yet do not lead to any extraordinary degree of predatory behavior. Similarly, it is apparent that the harms associated with heroin-addiction, such as the pains of withdrawal or the property crimes committed by addicts in order to avoid those pains, are a function not of the use of heroin (which is a pacifying drug) but of its high price which is a direct result of the fact that it can only be obtained illegally. The British experience, and that of the U.S. prior to 1914 when literally hundreds of thousands of middle-class Americans were addicted to opium derivatives, suggests clearly that when heroin is legally and readily available, addicts can live law-abiding lives. In sum, it seems incontrovertible to me that on what I shall call the "liberal conception of harm," prostitution and addiction are harmless. Since they are harmless, they victimize no one including the prostitute or addict him/herself. And as victimless acts they have no appropriate place in the criminal law, since a "victimless crime" is the law's version of a "square circle."

Before further exploring liberal ideology and the liberal conception of harm, one additional point should be made. Even though I am persuaded that prostitution and addiction are harmless in the terms already suggested, I find myself in possession of a rather intractable conviction that they are bad. That is, even though I think that the activities of prostitutes and addicts ought not be outlawed, I feel with equal conviction that I would not want my daughter to marry one, much less be one. I shall assume without argument that this moral intuition of mine is generally shared, since much of what follows stems from exploring the tension between this moral intuition and liberal ideology.

It is important to keep in mind the distinction between liberal *theory* (which is a fully-developed theory of the proper limits of state action and which found its classical exposition in John Stuart Mill's *On Liberty*[1] and liberal *ideology* (which is the loose cluster of liberal notions that animates public discussion of criminal law). In this paper, I am primarily concerned to explore the general tendency of liberal *ideology*, and only secondarily to analyze liberal *theory* to shed light on that tendency. For these purposes it is not necessary (nor would it be possible) to identify liberal ideology by reference to some classic text generally recognized as the authoritative statement of the position. Instead I will sketch out in broad strokes the cluster of notions which I take to be at the core of liberal ideology, and which I think faithfully represents the general foundation shared by most contemporary authors (such as Packer, Schur, or Morris and Hawkins) who argue for the decriminalization of the so-called "consensual" or "victimless" crimes.

Central to liberal ideology is a specific conception of harm. It is of key importance because it spells out the *necessary* condition for any justifiable legal prohibition. No legal prohibition is justifiable unless it is aimed at preventing a harm as defined by the liberal conception. Central to the liberal conception of harm is the requirement that harm be *felt* to count as harm, that an act is harmful—and therefore legitimately prohibited—only insofar as it is likely to result in a felt harm. A felt harm in this context means either an *unwanted pain* or the *frustration of a presently or foreseeably actual desire.*

Pains which are *wanted*, directly (such as by masochists or ascetics) or indirectly (as unavoidable ingredients in the realization of a desired goal, such as the pains of surgery or dental work), do not qualify as harms. In all of this, the term "desire" is used in the ordinary sense which is not limited to organically based needs, but includes choices, preferences, wishes, longings, and the like, as well.

This conception of harm is liberal in three ways: it takes the thwarting of freedom or liberty rather than the experience of pain as its standard, it equates the prevention of harm with the maximization of liberty, and it places the burden of proof on the limiters of liberty rather than on its defenders. Let us look briefly at these three features of the liberal conception of harm.

First of all, this conception is liberal in that in defining harm in terms of the *unwanted* or the frustration of the *wanted*, it gives pride of place to free choice over suffering in determining what is harm. It is the definition of harm in terms of the "unwanted" rather than as the "painful" that generally distinguishes liberal from utilitarian conceptions of harm. Hence, the liberal conception is often linked in Anglo-American legal theory with the maxim: *Volenti non fit injuria*, to him who consents no harm is done. An illiberal conception of harm, on the other hand, might define harm as suffering *per se* irrespective of whether that suffering were the result of a free agent's choice or desire.

Secondly, it is liberal in that by defining harm as thwarting of desire, it suggests that one person's free action can only be harmful to another insofar as it thwarts that other's freedom, and therefore it provides a standard in terms of which the minimization of harm is equivalent to the maximization of liberty. Hence, it is not all surprising that the core of Mill's defense of liberty is the principle that society has no right interfering with an individual's free action except in order to prevent harm to others. In contrast to this, an illiberal conception of harm might define as harmful, acts which tend to make the actor or recipient less virtuous or less capable of serving society.

Finally, by defining harm in terms of *felt* pain or frustration, it provides a standard tied ultimately to empirical fact, i.e. an act is harmful and thus legitimately prohibited only to the extent to which it tends to actually thwart another in the exercise of his freedom. The effect of this is first of all to place the burden of proof in the lap of the one who would limit a free action to prove its actual harmfulness, and to severely restrict the types of evidence that will bear this burden. The result of this is to make it easier to defend liberty than limit it. For these reasons, the liberal conception is sometimes referred to as the "*demonstrable* harm" principle. An illiberal conception of harm might allow an individual or group to hold an action harmful because, for example, it would thwart desires that people *would* feel if they were truly "rational" or truly "human." Regardless of whether such claims could be rendered plausible, allowing them would tend to cast individual liberty loose from its secure mooring in actual desires and thus dangerously adrift in the murky waters of metaphysical speculation or inspiration.

To apply this liberal test of harmfulness to prostitution and addiction, we must, as already indicated, distinguish their consequences from those which result from the social context, particularly their criminal status. We must ask whether under the most favorable circumstances—public toleration, police protection, cheaply and readily available legal heroin clearly marked as to purity, etc.—prostitution or addiction produce *felt* harm to anyone, including the prostitute or addict. It seems to me that a convincing case can be made to prove that in both instances the answer is *no*. I will not try to make this convincing case, but I will reply to two objections that I imagine might naturally occur at this point.

It could be objected that even though a prostitute might be well protected and well paid and thus exposed to no extraordinary risk of assault or exploitation, she would surely be likely to suffer the pain of low self-esteem. But this argument seems to be the result of illicitly counting the effects of a feature of the social context whose rationality is itself to be tested, i.e. the general moral belief that prostitution is bad or unseemly. If the social definition of prostitution were brought into line with a rational estimate of its harmfulness, there is no reason to assume that prostitutes would feel low self-esteem anymore than movie actors or actresses who appear in the nude for what they take to be legitimate artistic reasons, or than urologists or proctologists who deal medically with parts of the anatomy generally regarded as unseemly.

It might also be urged that even if the addict could easily, cheaply and dependably obtain his "fix," that he would surely feel his addiction itself as a painful limitation on his freedom. But this argument as well fails to detach itself adequately from the present social context. If heroin addicts were not hounded by the police and if their drugs were in fact easily, cheaply and dependably available, then heroin addiction would represent an encroachment on an individual's life on the order of that experienced by a diabetic who must regularly inject himself with insulin. By suggesting that this actually would infringe on the individual's freedom just a few minutes a day, I do not mean to suggest that it is negligible. Surely no one who had his druthers would volunteer to become a diabetic. But then diabetes has little redeeming value, while if addicts are to be believed, heroin use can result in considerable, if temporary, pleasure—by some accounts even ecstasy. On balance then, in a world in which heroin were readily obtainable, it would appear reasonable to expect that the constraints of addiction if at all painful, would be like the pains of surgery or dental work, i.e. pains incidental to and acceptable in the light of, a desired outcome. It seems to me, that in such a world, the pains of heroin addiction at their worst would be less than the pains of nicotine addiction that would remain if cigarette smoking were found *not* to be a health hazard.

Having said all this, I find myself and assume my reader still to be, unshaken in our negative intuitions about prostitution and addiction. Must we then relegate such intuitions to the status of appendixes and other human parts that have out-lived their rational function and exist in that borrowed time during which reality catches up with reason? I think not. Indeed I think the reverse, that our intuitions about prostitution and addiction rest on a fundamental sense of what it means to be human which—even though at odds with the liberal conception sketched out and applied above—amounts to a standard for assessing human institutions with-out which we would be considerably impoverished. Indeed, though I remain con-vinced that reason demands the decriminalization of prostitution and addiction, I think that a rational foundation for our negative intuitions regarding these can be sketched out, and that once it is, it reveals the limits of the liberal conception of harm and raises disturbing questions about the larger social order.

I suspect that underlying our negative intuitions about prostitution and addic-tion, is the sense that both are forms of *degradation*. And, as I shall argue, degrada-tion is a real harm which uniquely eludes the liberal conception and thus exposes the limits of that conception.

Degradation means quite literally being demoted in grade. It refers to human activities or circumstances in which human beings fall short of their true human potential not merely by degree, but, so to speak, by a whole grade. To call prosti-tution degrading is to point to the fact that in exchanging sex for money, the prostitute is literally transforming her body into something on a lower level than a human body: something on the order of a pleasure-generating machine. There are of course many assumptions hidden here, which I shall not pretend to argue. Central is the notion that a truly human "use" of one's body is marked by the integration of desires and their physical expression. Hence a truly human sexual expression is one in which the giving of pleasure is the external shape of a sponta-neous desire to give pleasure which, in turn, is more than a desire to engender pleasing sensations on the skin of another. It is the desire to please the other per-son via his body and one's own, and thus it is the physical expression of human caring, where caring signifies a concern for the happiness and well-being of the person "inhabiting" the skin that is being stimulated. So far as we know, the ca-pacity to root sexual activity in a meaningful context of this sort, is not only unique to human beings but a unique mark of what makes human beings uniquely dignified creatures. Prostitution is degrading in that it involves wrench-ing sexual activity out of this meaningful context and thus reducing it to the level of the mechanical: The use of one's physical apparatus to produce pleasurable sensations on the skin surface of another (or for that matter, to produce the par-ticular psychological satisfactions that different customers seek), motivated nei-ther by caring about the other, nor even by an authentic desire to please the other, since this itself is merely the necessary means to satisfy to the real governing de-sire: the desire to make a living.

Addiction is degrading in that it too reflects the abdication of a characteristic which is an essential ingredient in the uniqueness and dignity of human beings: self-determination. Addiction involves the bartering away of some portion of one's self-determination, placing oneself under the control of some small chunk of the material universe: the addicting substance. I suspect that what is central here is not the extent of the loss of self-determination, but rather its relative irreversibility, and the reversing of the seeming "natural" order in which physical substances are to be controlled by human beings.

But degradation is not merely an external affair. It refers to more than human behavior *per se*. That some behavior or circumstances are degrading suggests that they rebound back on the human psyche so that it too is demoted in grade. Degraded also are the individual's sensibilities, expectations and desires. Degradation would be no more than a temporary unpleasantness if we did not also believe that its overall effect was to accustom the degraded individual to a lower level of functioning, to lower his or her capacity for experiencing at the full human potential, to cause the desires for such experience to atrophy and die. *Here is precisely the point at which degradation eludes the liberal conception of harm.* Since one's desires are themselves degraded, we lose the very standard in terms of which the liberal conception of harm is defined: the thwarting of actual desires. If degradation undermines one's desire to live to the fullest extent of human potential, then it is not likely to be perceived as a thwarting of desire, and thus not likely to show up when we apply the liberal test. What this suggests at the minimum, is that regardless of its many acknowledged virtues, the liberal conception of harm is far from value-neutral. Its underlying commitment is not merely to the value of liberty. It is biased against the discovery of those forms of harm which have the unique capacity to dull the harmed one's sense that he is being harmed. Such a harm is degradation.

The liberal will not, of course, be rendered speechless by this argument. He is likely to retort that degradation can be assimilated to the liberal conception because non-degraded activities will be preferred over degraded ones by those who have experienced both or who have knowledge of both. But this move exhibits the subtle Cartesianism which limits the liberal conception. Seeing the individual as a rational subject set over and against his alternative courses of action and choosing between them, liberalism ultimately cannot deal with the fact that the subject is also *constituted by* those alternative courses of action. To assume a rational subject who, having experienced both degradation and its reverse, remains identical through both experiences and thus able to choose between them, misses the real meaning of degradation: *the infection of the subject.* Since degradation applies not merely to acts but to desires themselves, the degraded subject is not identical with the non-graded subject. There is not—contrary to the logical requirements of the liberal conception—a stable bank of desires against which both alternatives can be tested. This is because each alternative is also an alternative structure of desires. To speak then of a judgment by one who has experienced degradation and non-degradation, is to ignore the fact that to experience degraded actions *in a degraded way* is to lack the capacity to experience undegraded acts *in an undegraded way*, and vice versa.

Philosophers like Mill have tried to show that a liberal view can distinguish between "higher" and "lower" pleasures, by asking someone who had experienced both. The assumption here is that the ability to appreciate the "lower" pleasures for what they are worth remains intact in those capable of the "higher" ones. But this strikes me as far from self-evident, since it is at least as plausible to argue that the desires which are satisfied in both these pleasures cannot co-exist in the same person, since the development of appreciation of one *is* equally the development of depreciation of the other. The fact that such arguments are generally offered by philosophers in defense of their exotic pleasures, should be enough to evoke our suspicion that the cards are stacked and to convince the voluptuaries among us that they need not worry.

Needless to add, the liberal argument holds up no better if knowledge of both is substituted for experience of both. Here too the liberal argument bangs its nose against the Cartesian wall. As soon as knowing is seen as a concrete human activity riddled by feeling and desire, then "non-partisan" knowledge of both is no more possible than "non-partisan" experience of both.

This criticism points to the ahistorical and non-dialectical nature of liberalism. Liberalism assesses a practice (by which I mean either a particular activity or an institution or a society considered as a complex of permissible activities and prevailing institutions) by the range of freedom it allows to individuals to act on their desires. But this can only be an independent test, if the individual is held to have a stable bank of desires independent of the activities, institutions, or society in which he participates, against which these practices can be assessed. Once we see that the individual's desires are neither stable nor independent, that they are shaped by the activities in which he engages and thus by the alternatives available in the social order, then the ahistorical and non-dialectical nature of liberalism threatens to render it into a question-begging ideology: Liberalism judges practices in the light of the very desires they engender. Degradation eludes it since degraded practices are ones whose harm is inseparable from the degradation of desires themselves.

We would, however, be left with little more than a caricature, if we conclude from this that liberalism is simply tied to existing desires and through them to existing institutions. Though I would like to suggest that this is the tendency of liberal *ideology* as it functions in public discussion, matters are more complex with respect to liberal *theory*. Liberal theory is not without resources for gaining a degree of independence from existing desires, nor do notions like degradation provide a route to such independence that is free of pitfalls. Since my aim is to exhibit the limits of liberal ideology, there is no need to deny that liberal theory can be extended to include even harms like degradation in its view. Indeed, the more clearly we can see this, the more clearly we will be able to see the slant built into that view and thus to understand the link between the tendency of liberal *ideology* and the structure of liberal *theory*. Let us then formulate liberal theory's best answer to the problem posed by the intuition of degradation.

This answer takes the form of posing a dilemma between liberalism and the intuition of degradation, in which liberalism may provide at least the lesser of two evils. First, the liberal theoretician points out that unless the harm of degradation is defined as the thwarting of some actual desire, it is simply somebody's intuition about how other people ought to live. Such intuitions are as much a product of existing institutions as are actual desires (and maybe more so). To prevent a morality which imposes somebody's (or some class's) intuition about the good life on others, conceptions of well-being and harm must be tied to real desires. Surely this is a kernel of good sense at the core of liberalism which we ignore only at our peril. But how can this good sense be brought together with the recognition that real desires can themselves be degraded by the very practices that satisfy them? Here the liberal theoretician reminds us that the liberal conception of harm is not limited to the thwarting of currently actual desires, but includes the thwarting of *foreseeably* actual desires as well. By stepping down hard on "foreseeably," the liberal can catapult himself over the limitation to existing desires and thus gain some independence from existing practices. He demands, not without justice, that we formulate in some empirically verifiable terms, the particular distortion of desires that degradation produces. Then he says that degradation is a harm, if and only if, individuals freed from these distortions would (foreseeably) desire non-degraded over degraded activities. Even though this smacks of the ahistorical and non-dialectical features of liberalism discussed above, it is arguably preferable to allowing ourselves to be subjected to untested intuitions about degradation. Furthermore, this way of defining degradation in liberal terms has something of the feel of a tautology. It is surely dogmatic and implausible to claim that something is superior to another unless it would be the choice of rational individuals when the impediments to rational choice were removed. Let us then grant that, thus extended, liberal theory can find a place for the harm of degradation. But this extension can only be had at a price. The price is the extension of the concept of "foreseeable desires" beyond its meaning in ordinary moral discourse.

In our ordinary thinking about moral matters, we do not limit ourselves to thinking that only the thwarting of currently actual desires constitutes harm. We customarily include consideration of foreseeable desires as well. For instance, if we think it is wrong to kill people because people want to live, we do not think it becomes right to kill them in their sleep when they are not experiencing that desire. Their desire to live upon waking is foreseeable enough to be counted as an actual desire. Similarly, if we think it is wrong to deprive someone of his belongings because he desires to have or use them, we think it is equally wrong to steal property held in trust for an infant because we foresee with certainty that he will desire to have or use it someday.

Now it should be clear that the liberal theoretician is no longer using "foreseeable" in this ordinary sense. In these ordinary cases, the foreseen desires are the standard ones felt by individuals socialized into existing practices and institutions. They are as much a part of those practices and institutions as currently actual desires are. To get independence from existing practices, the liberal theoretician must replace this ordinary notion of foreseeable desire with a theoretical construct. A foreseeable desire is then transformed into a desire which can be empirically predicted to exist when the distorting influences (also defined in empirical terms) of existing practices are eliminated. I will use the term "predictable desires" to refer to desires such as these, and reserve the term "foreseeable desires" for the ordinary reference to the standard desires in the prevailing social order.

Thus extended, liberal theory reaches a high ground independent of existing practices. Degradation is seen as a harm from this height if it is the thwarting of a desire which can be predicted to exist after the influences of existing practices are eliminated or subtracted. However, thus extended, liberal theory encounters problems of a qualitatively different nature than when it is limited to foreseeable desires. That is, the liberal theoretician can no longer find confirmation in the actual desires occurring around him in the social order. He must confirm the existence of alternative desires. But to do this he must either eliminate the influences of existing practices in *fact*, or subtract them in *theory*. In the latter case, he must piece together the findings of empirical studies (about attitudes under other conditions, etc.) and project through them theoretically to the existence of desires not conditioned by present institutions. In the former case, the liberal theoretician must actually act to eliminate the influences of existing practices by eliminating or changing those practices in fact.

If he seeks to subtract these influences in theory, he must construct a chain of predictions (a series of hypotheticals of the order of, if "a" then "b" is likely, if "b" then "c" is likely, and so on) in which each link is increasingly improbable (since each includes its own uncertainty plus that of the predictions upon which it is built). It is a chain which is weaker than its weakest link since it is the product of the weakness of each. This means that his proof of the existence of harm in existing practices by virtue of their thwarting predictable desires, will become weaker the further from existing desires he moves. But if degradation is a possibility, then the more degraded a society is, the further one will have to project theoretically to reach non-degraded desires. In short, the more degraded a society is, the less likely this will show up *convincingly* on the theoretical version of the liberal test.

On the other hand, the liberal theoretician can have factual and thus convincing evidence for predicting the desires that would exist after the influences of existing practices were eliminated, only if he first acts to eliminate them in fact. He can have this evidence *after* he has removed the very practices he sought to prove were degrading and worthy of removal. He can prove these practices are harmful only *after* acting on the belief that they are. That is, he must act on the basis of an as-yet-untested intuition like that of degradation. Since the more degraded a society is, the more will have to be changed before harm can be proven in fact, it follows that the more degraded a society is the more dependent will the liberal be on just this sort of intuition to gain an independent vantage point on existing desires and practices, and convincing evidence for predicting the existence of nondegraded desires.

The upshot of this is the following. Suitably extended, liberal theory can encompass the notion of degradation as harm. However, faced with the real possibility that prevailing practices are degraded, the liberal is himself in a kind of dilemma. If he wishes convincing evidence for the claim that practices are degrading before acting on this claim, he is not likely to find it. And if he is to find it, he must act as if the claim were already proven true. In the very degree in which a society is degraded, liberal theory will have to be guided by an as-yet-untested intuition of degradation, to preserve its independence of existing desires and practices. Hence to the extent to which liberal theory resists such intuitions and holds to actual, foreseeable or predictable desires as its standard for measuring the existence of harm, it will slant in favor of existing desires and institutions. This will be all the more true, the more degraded a society is.

Thus even though liberal theory can find a theoretical compartment for the notion of degradation, its tendency is towards existing desires and thus the institutions that produce them. When we turn from liberal theory to liberal ideology this tendency is all the more pronounced since the mark which virtually distinguishes liberal ideology from liberal theory, is that liberal ideology never goes beyond desires foreseeable in the ordinary sense. It never even seeks a vantage point beyond the standard desires built into the prevailing social order. Thus while liberal theory tends away from, liberal ideology virtually excludes, consideration of the sort of harm toward which the intuition of degradation points. With these theoretical considerations as a background, I shall confine my remarks in the remainder of this essay to liberal *ideology*.

At this point it will be fruitful to reflect on the extraordinary tenacity of the liberal conception of harm and on the equally extraordinary tenacity of our judgments about the degradation of prostitution and addiction and particularly the tenacity of institutions aimed at enforcing those judgments even though they conflict with the liberal conception. As soon as we do this, the most striking fact is that there appears no theoretically sound way to keep the notion of degradation from spilling over into large areas of human life that meet with general acceptance and approval.

It seems apparent to me that much if not most of the work that is engaged in by citizens of modern western societies, is degrading in the same way that prostitution is. A recent study done by the Department of Health Education and Welfare, found the majority of Americans to be dissatisfied with their work measured by their response to questions like: Would you do it again if you had it to do over? Would you like to see your son or daughter in the same work? In any event, it does not seem very controversial to claim that the vast majority of Americans are not engaged in work which they would still do voluntarily if their incomes were guaranteed. This is enough to suggest that like the prostitute, a very large number of Americans are engaged in using their bodies (including their brains), not as expressions of their spontaneous desire to do so, but as necessary means to the fulfillment of another desire: the desire to make a living. Indeed, Marx observes in a footnote to the *Economic and Philosophic Manuscripts of 1844*, that "Prostitution is only a *particular* expression of the *universal* prostitution of the *worker*."[2] This in turn should signal to us what may already be obvious: that what I have called *degradation*, is, after all, but another name for what Marx called *alienation*.

Marx's view is meant to be more than rhetoric. Insofar as labor is not the voluntary expression of each individual's desire to create a truly human habitat, insofar as the laborer has little real alternative but to do the job handed him by his employer and to do it according to specifications and at a pace and rhythm all of which come from outside his own desires, his labor is a prostitution of his body. It literally tears his labor out of the human context in which it would be meaningful, reducing workers to physical machines (of greater or lesser complexity) for manipulating other machines or for performing functions not yet profitably transferred to machines. To see this, one does not have to picture Charlie Chaplin engaged in stupefying repetitive work in *Modern Times*. Even the more complex tasks that make up modern industry reflect a division of a total task into details, and this in turn reflects the deeper division between conception and execution, planning and carrying out, which is modern industry's version of the alienation of body and soul that we see only too clearly in prostitution.[3]

It might be objected here that the selling of sex is qualitatively different from the selling of (other) labor, and thus that whatever else may be wrong with the condition of workers, it is merely rhetoric to assert that their labor is degrading in the same degree as the prostitute's. This argument takes as its starting point, the notion that selling sex is selling something more intimate and personal than selling labor, and thus the former is morally worse than the latter. I would certainly agree that it is an element of our beliefs that sex is more intimate than labor, and I suspect this accounts for the general feeling that the former is degrading in ways that the latter is not. But it is precisely the soundness of such beliefs that is being questioned. Is there any reason for making this distinction between the sale of sex and the sale of labor, other than to mask to the general populace the degradation that they share with the prostitute? Is the labor of the prostitute truly more intimate, closer to her soul, than the labor of a coal miner, breathing and sweating coal dust, using every muscle to carve a living out of rocks? In a world in which people tell you their job when you ask what they are, it seems to me that any work is likely to get under one's skin and become intimately bound up with who one is.

A similar point can be made regarding addiction. The vast majority of workers take orders from someone else.[4] And though they are free to change jobs, that's all they are free to do—they can change who they take orders from but not *that* they take orders. The effect of this is that in the free-est nation in the world, the majority of the laboring population has the shape and detail of its days dictated by the orders of others. So, like the addict, the general run of workers exist in a situation in which they are deprived of self-determination relatively irreversibly, and in ways which are largely dictated by the contours of the material world. Instead of being enslaved to a physical substance, their lives are structured to meet the requirements of technology and the ebb and flow of commodities. Here too, our underlying intuition about the degradation of addiction refuses to stay in bounds.

When we ask for what maintains this servitude in modern affluent societies, we find a loss of self-determination that even more strongly resembles addiction. An ever-expanding market of largely needless and self-destructing goods hawked by a massive advertising war for the hearts and minds of the people, exerts a virtually mesmerizing attraction which holds workers to the treadmill. The illusion of newness produced by advertising rhetoric, style changes, and rapid twists in fad and fashion, make the ever repeating cycle of the treadmill feel like a spiral of progress. Once it is realized that consumption is the religion of contemporary America and shopping centers its cathedrals, then Marx's often-quoted observation that religion "is the *opium* of the people,"[5] takes on new meaning. It suggests that just as Marx recognized that prostitution was only a specific instance of the prostitution of the laborer, so he might have recognized that opiate-addiction is but a specific case of the addiction of the laborer in his role as consumer.

This suggests that our negative intuitions about prostitution and addiction not only rest on a foundation from which the larger social order can be radically criticized, but that they do so in a complementary way. Prostitution is the incarnation of the degradation of the modern citizen as producer, while addiction captures his degradation as unfree producer and ultimately as consumer.

This in turn suggests that the bias we unearthed beneath the liberal conception of harm, is part of a seam running far deeper and wider than expected. If it is granted that the degradation of prostitution and addiction characterizes large segments of the society as they work and as they consume, and if it is acknowledged that this degradation not only affects their objective circumstances but infects their desires as well, then the more deeply degraded a society is, the less likely the harms it inflicts on its populace will show up when tested by the liberal conception of harm. This in turn reflects the Achilles' heel of liberal ideology. Once it is recognized that a social order is not just an apparatus for meeting existing desires, but that it insinuates itself into the hearts and minds of its people creating and shaping their desires, liberalism loses an independent vantage from which to evaluate the social order.

The freedom which is an expression of desire and the harm which is a thwarting of desire, are liberalism's positive and negative standards for assessing social and legal orders in part or in whole. Once it is seen that social orders can create some desires and let others atrophy and die, it may be that liberalism can never tell us more than how well a society is fulfilling or thwarting the desires *it* creates and nurtures. This suggests that liberalism is limited to internal critique of a social order, to evaluating it in its own terms while unable to reflect on those terms themselves. Liberalism is a tool suited to evaluating how well a society meets the needs it creates, but unable to evaluate those needs themselves. This, in turn, suggests that liberalism may be an ideology whose implicit "ideal" is a society that has perfectly shaped its citizens to need what it offers. Perhaps this explains why liberals who are enthusiastic supporters of programs for social amelioration, find themselves (much to their own puzzlement) attacked as the staunchest defenders of the status quo. Surely it explains why libertarians—who are after all just liberals whose logic is not clouded by compassion—like Ayn Rand and more recently Robert Nozick, are quite clearly the status quo's staunchest allies. In any event it suggests why liberalism as generally applied is uniquely capable of hiding from view the degradation of work and consumption in the so-called "liberal capitalist" states.

A final question brings us to the final and most speculative part of this paper. If the liberal conception's tenacity is explained in part by its role in supporting an ideology which hides the prostitution and addiction of ordinary folks, why does the society tolerate, indeed promote, institutions for enforcing our moral intuitions against prostitution and addiction? Does this not leave open the danger that the sense of degradation that shapes these intuitions may overflow its institutional containers and begin to function as a standard for evaluating work and consumption in the larger society?

My answer to this is the following. As long as human beings possess even a vague sense of the meaning of degradation, focusing this sense on a small group of people serves the goal of diverting critical attention from the degradations of the larger social order, much as projecting legendary sexual powers and appetites on blacks served to protect whites from having to face their own "sinful" natures. The fact that prostitutes and addicts are generally poor and often non-white serves the goal of distinguishing the degraded "them" from the undegraded "us." Perhaps this explains the curious fact that more than any other category of crime, we tend to think of prostitutes and addicts not merely as persons who occasionally engage in prostitution and drug use, but as types of people.

The focusing of the sense of degradation on prostitution and addiction serves the ideological function in other ways as well. It serves to tie degradation to the individual's body—inhabited by foreign substances, offered for the pleasure of strangers—and thus to deflect attention away from the degradation built into our institutions. Furthermore it serves to keep distinct what it could be most dangerous to see interconnected. The degradation of alienated production embodied in prostitution is held separate from the degradation of servitude and alienated consumption embodied in addiction, when in reality the laborer's separation from his work, his subjection to domination on the job, and his enthrallment to the gods of consumption, are but three faces of the unitary fact of his degradation. In sum, by identifying a group of people too powerless to resist total definition as *the* really degraded ones, we can convince ourselves that our lives and work are not degraded. By so intimately tying degradation to the body as distinct even from its actions in working, we hide from ourselves the less visible but more pervasive forms and forces of degradation. Finally by dividing degradation into prostitution and addiction we fail to see the interconnection between alienated work, slavish consumption, and powerlessness on and off the job.

Of course, this rather complex scapegoating process only makes sense while people still possess some sense of what human degradation means. Hence, though I am convinced of the need to decriminalize prostitution and drug-use, I am also fearful that what that reform might either herald or promote or both, is the final erosion of the sense of the meaning of human degradation, and thus the erosion of a vitally important standard for evaluating any human social order.

Notes

1. Mill's *On Liberty* was originally published in London in 1859. For a more recent presentation of liberal theory, see Hart, H. L. A. (1963). *Law, Liberty, and Morality*, Stanford, Calif.: Stanford University Press.
2. Marx, Karl (1975). *Early Writings* (ed. Lucio Colletti), New York: Vintage Books, p. 350.
3. For an extensive and well-documented discussion of this, see Braverman, Harry (1974). *Labor and Monopoly Capital: The Degradation of Work in the Twentieth Century*, New York: Monthly Review Press.
4. "In all advanced capitalist countries the proportion of self-employed has shown a marked, in some cases a dramatic, decrease, as for instance in the United States where it declined from 40.4 percent in 1870 to 13.3 percent in 1954." Miliband, Ralph (1969). *The State in Capitalist Society*, New York: Basic Books, p. 17.
5. Marx, Karl, op. cit., p. 244.

The Mafia

Ovid Demaris

It had taken him thirty-three years to arrive at this moment. Early that evening he was brought to a winery on South Figueroa Street and now he waited in a small, dimly lit room for the final act to be played out.

Jimmy Fratianno prided himself on his ability to remain calm under stress, but he could feel the excitement stirring through him. He locked the feeling inside, not wanting to share it with the other four candidates. He could hear the deep rumble of voices in the other room, the scraping of chairs, and he knew that many awaited his entrance. Standing room only, he thought, trying to lighten the feeling that was knotting his nerves.

Then the door opened and Johnny Roselli beckoned to him. "It's time," he said.

They walked down a short hallway and stopped before a closed door. Roselli squeezed his arm and smiled.

"Just a couple things, Jimmy. After you've taken the oath, go around the circle and kiss everybody and introduce yourself. Then join hands with the others. Are you ready?"

He nodded and Roselli opened the door. It was a large room and the pungent odor of fermented grapes was stronger here. There must have been fifty men in the room, many of whom he had met in the seventeen months he had been in Los Angeles. They were gathered in a circle around a long table, their faces grim, their eyes shadowed by the harsh lighting from bare overhanging bulbs.

Roselli led Jimmy to the head of the table where Jack Dragna was standing, a short, heavyset man with horn-rimmed glasses, who reminded Jimmy of a banker. Tom Dragna, as usual in sports clothes, was on Jack's left and Momo Adamo on his right.

"Jimmy, Jack Dragna's the boss of our family," Roselli said. "Momo Adamo's the underboss and Tom's the *consigliere*."

Jack Dragna raised his hand and spoke to everyone in the room. "Everybody join hands," he said.

On the table in front of where Jimmy was standing was a revolver and a dagger crossing one another. The next time Jack spoke was in a confusing mixture of Sicilian and Italian. He spoke rapidly and Jimmy tried desperately to understand what was being said to him in front of all these people.

What he was able to make out went something like this: "We are gathered here this evening to make five new members: Jimmy Fratianno, Jimmy Regace, Charley Dippolito, Louie Piscopo, and Tom's son, Louie Dragna. Now, Jimmy, you are entering into the honored society of Cosa Nostra, which welcomes only men of great courage and loyalty.

"You come in alive and you go out dead. The gun and knife are the instruments by which you live and die.

"Cosa Nostra comes first above anything else in your life. Before family, before country, before God. When you are summoned, you must come even if your mother, or wife, or your children are on their death bed.

"There are three laws you must obey without question. You must never betray any of the secrets of this Cosa Nostra. You must never violate the wife or children of another member. You must never become involved with narcotics. The violation of any of these laws means death without trial or warning."

There was more but, thirty years later, this was what Jimmy Fratianno remembered. The rest of the ritual sermon was a blur.

The next thing Jimmy heard was Jack Dragna asking him to raise the index finger of his right hand. He wondered at the request until Jack pricked his finger with a pin. A small bubble of blood burst forth.

When he looked up, Roselli winked at him. Still speaking in his Sicilian-Italian dialect, Dragna said, "This drop of blood symbolizes your birth into our family. We're one until death."

He paused a moment and then stepped forward and kissed Jimmy on both cheeks. "Jimmy, you're now a made guy, an *amico nostra*, a *soldato* in our *famiglia*. Whenever you wish to introduce a member to another member he don't know, you say, '*Amico nostra*.' In English, you say, 'This is a friend of *ours*.' But whenever you introduce a member to someone who's not a member, you say, 'This is a friend of *mine*.'"

The ceremony was over. Jimmy turned and kissed Roselli. People began talking again and Jimmy was so excited that he could feel his legs tremble as he moved from man to man, kissing and shaking hands, being slapped on the back, hearing words of congratulation. He was now a member of an ancient and extremely exclusive society. It made him a special person, an inheritor of enormous power. It was something he had wanted as long as he could remember.

In a way, it was almost as though a carefully plotted script had delivered Aladena "Jimmy" Fratianno to that room. Born on November 14, 1913, in a small town near Naples, he was brought to the United States by his mother when he was four months old. His father, Antonio, was already in this country with relatives in Cleveland. In 1915, a daughter, Louise, was born, followed by another son, Warren, three years later.

Fratianno's background was classical American Mafioso. Aladena, as Jimmy was christened, was one of thousands of Italian immigrants living in the Murray Hill–Mayfield Road district then known as Little Italy but also called the Hill.

At the age of six, he had seen three men mowed down by machine-gun fire in front of Tony Milano's speakeasy and his reaction had been an awed, "Holy mother of Jesus!"

The conditions in Cleveland's Little Italy were not all that different from those in the old country. Except, of course, that now the Italians were a minority, confined to a ghetto by their language and manners. They labored long hours in menial, back-breaking work for minimal wages, their crafts for the most part forgotten in their desperate need to provide food and shelter for their large families.

Some, however, were self-employed and could hold their heads up with pride. Among them was Antonio Fratianno, who worked as a landscape contractor and was known as a serious, sober man, a good provider, but also as the absolute autocrat of his household.

Aladena's first memory, and one he never forgot, remembering it always with a pleasurable glow, was the horse and buggy his father had bought when Aladena was three years old. They lived on East 125th Street then, and he remembered how the neighbors had admired the buggy with the fringed canvas top. He loved that horse and buggy and the way the fringe would dance happily as the horse trotted down the street. He cried the day his father sold it, harder than he did when his father used the strap on him.

His father was strict and quick to punish. Although he was strict with Louise and Warren, he spared the rod with them, a fact not lost on Aladena, who grew even more resentful. The punishment gradually became a duel of will-power between two determined enemies. The harder he was beaten, the harder he became to handle. He grew obstinate and defiant, determined to have his own way and ready to defy all who contested him.

In school he was rowdy, getting into fights with other boys and teachers, until finally he was sent to Thomas Edison, which was known as a "bad boy" school. There he formed a life-long friendship with Louis "Babe" Triscaro, who later would become an important Teamsters official and the liaison between Jimmy Hoffa and the Cleveland Mafia.

Almost from the time he could walk, Aladena had been preoccupied with the importance of money. Besides having his own paper route at the age of six, he hawked newspapers at the No. 4 gate at the Fischer Body plant, and in front of the Hayden Theater evenings and weekends. At eleven he was working with his father, putting in a six-day week during summer vacations and all day Saturdays during the school year.

During this period he gained the cognomen that would stick to him for the rest of his life. There was a policeman who used to chase him whenever he stole fruit from sidewalk stands, which was often, and one day Aladena hit the policeman in the face with a rotten tomato. The policeman gave chase. People stopped to watch, and an older man said, "Look at that weasel run!" When making out his report, the policeman wrote down the nickname and it became part of his police record, following him wherever he went.

It was just prior to this incident, that he had started calling himself Jimmy— Aladena sounded too much like a "broad's name"—and the next thing he knew he was "Jimmy the Weasel." Although at sixteen he entered amateur boxing competition as Kid Weasel, winning the Collingwood Community Center trophy in the lightweight division, his friends never used the nickname, at least not to his face.

His first experience with bootlegging was at the age of twelve. He was a waiter in a speakeasy owned by a woman called Bessie. For nearly two years he worked part time for Bessie and saw so many drunks that it turned him against liquor. He would see men come in and drink their entire paychecks, money they needed for their families. At night in bed he would think, "God, people got to be crazy to get drunk." It was the money part that bothered him the most.

His behavior in school gradually improved and he transferred to Collingwood High School for the ninth grade, but a year later he caught cold, ignored it until it turned to pneumonia, and with a fever of 106 degrees lapsed into a coma. It was two weeks before he regained consciousness and when he did he found a priest giving him the last rites. As the priest touched his tongue with the Communion wafer, Jimmy opened his eyes and said, "I'm better." Then he slipped back into his coma for another week.

By the time he opened his eyes the second time, the pneumonia had turned into pleurisy, which had created an enormous deposit of pus in his left lung and pleural cavities. It got so thick it was pushing his heart against his right lung. When all efforts to remove it with a syringe failed, Dr. Victor Tanno decided that the only way to get at it was to remove a rib. Because of his weakened condition, ether was out of the question. They would use a local anesthetic, but as Dr. Tanno warned him, it would freeze the flesh but not the bone. With Jimmy strapped to a chair, facing the back of it, and held by his mother, Dr. Tanno made the incision in his back and began cutting into the rib.

The memory of that pain would be with him all the years of his life. Fifty years later he could still remember how he had screamed and cursed that doctor, could still feel the teeth-gnashing pain of the saw cutting into bone, a pain so intense he felt blinded, his brain on fire, every nerve end begging for mercy, and he could still feel his mother's arms around him, hear her cries as if they were coming from a great distance, echoing off the walls and pounding at his ears with his own cries and curses.

When the doctor finally cut through the rib and pulled it out, the pus shot out with explosive force. Dr. Tanno laughed and said, "Look, nurse, it's like an oil well erupting."

He never returned to school. Although his grades had been below average, he was extremely quick with numbers, a talent that he had already put to practical use. At the age of fourteen, while hawking newspapers at Fischer Body, he had become acquainted with Johnny Martin, a gambler who operated games at Mike's, a Greek restaurant across the street from the No. 4 gate. Martin, who had taken a liking to the boy, spent hours in a room above the restaurant teaching him all the cheating tricks he knew. He taught him how to shuffle cards, how to deal seconds, and how to mark them during a game by using a small piece of sandpaper hidden in the palm of the hand. Jimmy got so he could mark an entire deck in less than an hour. He learned to use shaded dice, to palm the third dice, to switch, and which numbers were winners and which losers.

By the age of seventeen he had become Martin's partner at Mike's, receiving an even cut of the winnings. Later Jimmy bought a portable crap table and began holding his own games at a friend's house. Booking the game and using shaded dice, he would clear three or four hundred dollars in a matter of a few hours. This money was a far richer reward for less effort than the paltry wage he received from his father for driving a truck each day.

At eighteen he was charged with raping a twenty-five-year-old divorcee. Under cross-examination the woman confessed she had lied because she thought she could extort money from his father, and the case was dropped. But the charge of rape, like the nickname "Weasel," would become part of his police record, a blemish irrevocable for all time.

A few days before his nineteenth birthday, on a cold moonlit night, Jimmy and a friend went ice skating at Elysium Park. Jimmy could do just about anything on skates. He played hockey, was an agile figure skater, and could even dance on ice while wearing his long-bladed racers. This made him popular with the girls, which was all the incentive he needed to strut his stuff.

On this particular evening, he showed off for a girl who was with three other girls and five tough looking Polish boys. When he was leaving the Elysium, the five boys attacked him. The next thing he knew fists and feet were coming at him from all directions. He tried to fight back, but he was pounded into the ground. He was groggily crawling around on all fours when a heavy boot caught him square in the nose. Bone shattered, blood spurted out, and he flopped over on his back in time for the boot to catch the side of his nose. He rolled over on his stomach and tried to protect his face and head with his arms. He was vaguely aware of blows raining against his body but he was soon beyond pain.

He came to in a receiving hospital. The bridge of his nose was hopelessly crushed and they had to rebuild it with gristle taken from the lower part of his chest. After the operation, he was advised to return for plastic surgery when it had healed, but he never went back.

With the help of his friend, Anthony "Tony Dope" Delsanter, a husky six-footer, Jimmy went out looking for the Polish boys. He caught four of them, in the dark of night, when each was alone, and after knocking them to the ground, Jimmy had gone to work with a blackjack, breaking noses, knocking out teeth, fracturing jaws, and cracking skulls, even breaking the arm of the boy whose boot he suspected had broken his nose. All the boys required hospitalization and all needed many stitches in their heads. The fifth boy had moved away, but Jimmy continued looking for him for a whole year before he grudgingly acknowledged defeat.

For Jimmy, it was something that had to be done, a wrong that had to be righted, a vendetta in the best Italian tradition. While working the boys over with the black-jack, he had realized how easy it would be to kill. He had hit hard enough for that, he had thought at the time; it had not bothered him in the least. For Jimmy, it was an important realization.

When Jimmy was twenty, Jack Haffey, the boss of the 26th Ward, who worked as a state inspector on highway construction, confided to Jimmy that he had top po-litical connections and if they worked together they could make some money. The first opportunity was a contract calling for 25,000 yards of fill for a reservoir. Jimmy's father had two trucks, and Jimmy suggested that he lease six more. The state was paying fifty cents a yard and, with sideboards, they could load two and a half yards in their one-and-a-half-yard trucks. His father was interested until Jimmy told him it would cost $500 to get the job.

"I don't want to get in no trouble," his father said.

"You ain't going to get in trouble," Jimmy replied. "This guy's a pal of the governor."

"I don't want to do nothing crooked."

"Ah, forget it," Jimmy cried. "I can't make no fucking money with you. I'll lease some trucks and do the job myself."

The next day he became his own boss. He leased eight trucks—and gave Haffey the $500 payoff. When the first truck arrived at the reservoir, Jimmy said, "Jack, measure this truck coming in. All my trucks are the same size."

Haffey looked the truck over. "What do you think, Jimmy?"

"Three and a half yards, Jack. We're stacking them up high."

From then on, Haffey wrote down three and a half yards, which meant that Jimmy was making fifty cents extra on each load. With eight trucks making six and seven trips a day, it meant that he was earning an extra $25 to $30 a day, besides the ten cents a yard broker's fee he was making from the truck owners.

About this time, Jimmy also started booking at the local racetracks and hang-ing around the clubhouse of the Italian–American Brotherhood (IAB) on May-field Road. Run by Tony Milano (who would later become the underboss of the Cleveland family), the IAB was the hangout for all the local big shots, who sat outside in the summer, talking quietly among themselves and watching people walk by.

"Big Al" Polizzi was the boss. There was Johnny DeMarco and "Johnny King" Angersola, with his brothers, Fred and George. Jimmy also got to know the leaders of the Jewish mob, known as the Cleveland Syndicate. These men—Louis "Lou Rhody" Rothkopf, Moe Dalitz, Morris Kleinman—operated gambling joints in Cleveland, as well as in Newport and Covington, Kentucky, all with the blessings of Big Al's Mayfield Road Gang. Others in the syndicate included Ruby Kolod, Sam Tucker, and, in later years, Lou Rhody's nephew, Bernard "Bernie" Rothkopf, who would grow up to become president of the MGM Grand Hotel in Las Vegas. They also were involved in Buckeye Enterprises, which controlled various gambling concessions, and was the hidden link between the Mayfield Road Gang and the Cleveland Syndicate.

Even as a young boy, Jimmy had suspected that there was some kind of a secret

Italian organization that was more cohesive and powerful than the Jews or Irish with whom they worked, but in those days the words Mafia or Cosa Nostra were never used even on the Hill. The only reference to any crime organization ever mentioned was "The Combination." And it was The Combination which then controlled organized crime in Cleveland.

In 1934 Jimmy bought a two-year-old Marmon limousine and began chauffeuring customers from the East Side to The Combination's gambling joints around Cleveland. Lou Rhody paid him seven dollars a load. Jimmy drove the limousine himself for a while and then hired a driver.

With money rolling in from the gambling, the chauffeuring and the trucking, he bought himself a new Chevrolet coupe and began having his clothes tailor-made. He wore a broad-brimmed Capone-style hat, alligator shoes, and carried a couple thousand dollars in his pocket. Life was sweet in the midst of the nation's worst depression.

With more leisure than he knew how to handle, he turned to golf and met Bill McSweeney, a big, tough Irishman who broke heads for the Teamsters union when he was not belting golf balls out of sight. McSweeney's boss was Tommy Lenahan, a man in constant need of head breakers because the Teamsters was a small, struggling union in those days.

Jimmy's first involvement with the union was in their effort to organize the parking lots in Cleveland. With the "Neanderthal" McSweeney and others at his side, five-foot-nine Jimmy, who weighed a hundred-fifty soaking wet, would march into parking lots and throw muriatic acid on cars while his partners slashed tired and broke windshields. The pay was fifteen dollars a day, plus ten dollars a day for every man Jimmy could induce to work for five dollars a day on his crew. During the Premier Aluminum strike, Jimmy had a crew of nine, recruited from the Hill, who fought against scabs and cops, both private and public, with lead pipes, baseball bats, blackjacks, and tire chains.

Jimmy's old friend from bad boy school, Babe Triscaro, was also cracking heads on the picket lines. From the Premier it was on to the knitting mills around Seventy-ninth Street and Euclid Avenue. And from there to the transportation drivers, with special instructions from Lenahan as to whose head to break.

By the end of 1935, after an exhausting four months of hand-to-hand combat on picket lines, Jimmy came into his own. He went to Florida with the rest of the big boys on the Hill. That was the year The Combination opened The Plantation, its first gambling casino in Miami. He bought a new Oldsmobile, a flashy wardrobe, had $2,500 cash in his pocket, and some expertise in bookmaking.

Johnny Martin had long ago explained the fundamentals which had proved profitable at the local racetracks. Hialeah would be no different. "Booking at the track," Johnny had told him, "is the easiest, safest way to gamble in the world. If you know what you're doing, you'll never lose a nickel. Just balance your book and never refuse a bet. Drop all the long-shots in the box—but when you go to the window don't let the bettor know. The reason they bet with you instead of going to the window themselves is that they don't want to reduce the odds. Get yourself a runner. And at night when you go to bed, pray that your bettors get their horses from the racing form and not from some fucking hot tips. Stay away from hot horses."

On his first day at Hialeah, Johnny King introduced him to "Lucky" Luciano, who looked pretty relaxed for a man who was then the subject of the hottest investigation in New York history. Two of Luciano's boys began giving Jimmy their action, going a hundred and a hundred, win and place, on each race, each selecting a different horse from the racing form. It could not have been more perfect. The meet was fifty-five days and in that time Jimmy took them for $24,000.

When he returned home, Jimmy started booking at the World Exposition, which had moved from Chicago to Cleveland. He made his headquarters in the midgets' tent, most of whom were avid horse players. He liked their company, enjoyed their sense of humor, their ability to ignore the misfortune that had made them objects of curiosity. And they were good customers.

In the evening, Jimmy and his friends made the rounds of nightclubs, getting the best tables and hobnobbing with the owners, who showed their pleasure at meeting these rising Young Turks by introducing them to their friendly chorus girls. The friendliest girls, the ones who flattered their ego by never asking for money, were also introduced to James "Blackie" Licavoli, who was on the lam for the murder of Toledo beer baron Jackie Kennedy and his girlfriend. Blackie's cousin, Thomas "Yonnie" Licavoli, and four others were serving life terms for this crime, while five others involved in the murder had evaded justice by going into hiding. It was through Blackie Licavoli, when Licavoli went to Pittsburgh to stay with Mafia boss John LaRock (*nee* LaRocca), that Jimmy and Tony Dope met Frankie Valenti, who one day would be the Mafia boss of Rochester, New York, and would, in these early years, teach Jimmy a few tricks.

At the French Casino Jimmy first met his future wife. He walked into the place, took one look at the hatcheck girl, and immediately sent for the owner to be formally introduced. She was eighteen and her name was Jewel Switzer. She was Irish and German, with blonde hair and big blue eyes, not exactly the kind of girl Italian boys brought home to mother in those days. On August 1, 1936, they drove to Bowling Green and were married. Two months later she was pregnant.

In the summer of 1936 Jimmy and his Cleveland friends discovered that it was a lot quicker and far more profitable to rob gambling joints than to run their own crooked game. Tony Dope Delsanter, who had spent time in a reformatory, was ready for a fast score.

Their first job was a poker game. Jimmy and Tony Dope walked in without disguises, pulled out revolvers, and ordered the nine men in the room to strip down to their underwear and face the wall. They got $5,800 in cash and some jewelry.

The LaRock–Licavoli connection set up the next score. Frankie Valenti had a swanky gambling joint picked out: They went in fast, with their faces obscured by silk stockings, and Jimmy and Tony Dope, who carried sawed-off shotguns, jumped on top of crap tables and screamed, "This is a stickup, against the walls, motherfuckers," and two hundred people ran to obey their command. The take was $70,000.

It was the kind of easy score that encouraged them to try others. One was a customer of the Cleveland Trust Bank, which was just around the corner from the home of his parents on Earlwood Street. Every two weeks, this man, whom he had met at Mike's, used to draw $25,000 from his bank to cash checks at Fischer Body.

Jimmy had parked his brand new Buick, which was to be the crash car, on St. Clair Avenue, about a hundred yards away, but with an excellent view of the bank. A friend, Hipsy Cooper, in the getaway car, was about fifty yards ahead of him, and both were watching as Valenti and Tony Dope held up the man at gun point as he emerged from the bank and ran down the sidewalk toward the corner of Earlwood where Hipsy was supposed to pick them up. Except that he was not moving. Jimmy gunned the Buick, pulled up alongside Hipsy, and screamed at him to get going. But Hipsy appeared to be in a state of shock. Cursing and threatening dire retaliation, Jimmy knew that he had no alternative but to use his own car to help his friends escape. The theory of a crash car is to obstruct whatever pursuit there may be of the getaway car, regardless of the risk involved.

Jimmy skidded around the corner. He knew his friends, fleeing on foot, would head down the alley behind the bank to Blemheim, take a right, run up Blemheim about ten houses, jump a fence and dash through back yards to his house. Jimmy hit the alley, slammed on the brakes, and threw the Buick into a spinning skid, coming to a stop sideways so that it completely blocked the alley. Behind him was the man who had been robbed, standing on the running board of a car he had commandeered to give chase. And behind him was a police car, with siren blaring.

Jimmy jumped out of his car and started waving his arms in an hysterical fashion. "They've got guns," he cried. "They've got guns, I saw them, they're armed and dangerous, duck down, they've got guns and they're dangerous."

"Get the hell out of the way," the man on the running board screamed. "Let us through here."

"Oh, my God, this is terrible. They've got guns," Jimmy continued to cry, waving his arms like a man who has lost his senses.

"Get that car out of there," a policeman, hanging out the opened window of his car, shouted as he waved his hand, signaling Jimmy to move out.

Jimmy jumped into his car, spun the wheel around, threw it into reverse, and slammed on the brakes inches from the other car's front bumper. He threw up his arms in desperation, stalled the engine, turned the motor over with the ignition off, ground the gears, and finally roared out of the alley when he was sure that his friends had had ample time to reach his house.

They were sitting in the parlor, gulping steaming cups of coffee his mother had just served them, and they were livid. They wanted to kill Hipsy. "Where's the cocksucker?" Tony Dope wanted to know. "He left us there to die."

Valenti was angry but less emotional about it. "Where'd you get that *cretino*?"

"It's his first score," Jimmy said. "He panicked, froze at the wheel."

"I'm going to kill that prick," Dope promised.

"Fuck him," Jimmy said. "Let's cut it up three ways and forget him."

Jimmy's daughter Joanne was born on June 24, 1937, a beautiful, happy baby, but Jimmy had little time to spend with his family. Exactly one month later he pulled his last job for a while. The victim was Joe Deutsch, a layoff bookmaker who was too slow in paying off. When Jimmy called to ask why he had not been paid, Deutsch said, "Listen, punk, you'll get paid when I get good and ready to pay. No sooner, understand." Jimmy started screaming and Deutsch slammed the phone in his ear.

For the next few days, Jimmy was like a demented man. He told Tony Dope and McSweeney that he wanted to hurt Deutsch, and they suggested that they might as well get some money while they were at it. For a while they followed Deutsch as he made the rounds of his drops. Jimmy decided to use his Buick and Tony Dope stole some plates which they attached to the Buick's plates with clothes pins painted black.

They struck at nine-thirty on a Saturday night at the downtown intersection of Ninth and Superior, with people five rows deep along the sidewalks. McSweeney was behind the wheel of the Buick and Jimmy and Tony Dope were in the back seat, each armed with a .38 revolver. When the light turned red, they were right behind Deutsch's car. They jumped out of the Buick and came at Deutsch from both sides, with Jimmy on the driver's side. They opened the doors and Jimmy said, "Joe, move over. Don't make no dumb plays and you won't get hurt."

The moment Deutsch saw the guns, he began screaming for help. "Hit him in the fucking mouth," Jimmy told Tony Dope as he tried to shove and push Deutsch out of the way so he could squeeze in behind the steering wheel. He heard the dull thudding of Tony Dope's gun as it repeatedly smashed against Deutsch's head. Blood spurted on Jimmy's new gray gabardine suit and he screamed at Tony Dope, "Pull him away from me." The light turned green and he frantically shifted into gear. He meandered up side streets, getting away from the commercial district, until they were on a quiet residential street.

Deutsch was unconscious and Tony Dope had cleaned out his pockets. Jimmy pulled to the curb and McSweeney stopped behind them. While McSweeney removed the hot plates, Jimmy looked for a sewer to dump the plates and guns. But McSweeney had borrowed his gun from a friend and refused to throw it away. Instead he put it in the glove compartment, and with him behind the wheel, with Tony Dope at his side and Jimmy in the back seat, they decided to go to McSweeney's house for Jimmy and Tony Dope to clean up and to divide the sixteen hundred dollars found on Deutsch, which was a long way from the ten thousand they had expected.

"We nearly got in the shit," McSweeney said. "That sonovabitch screamed loud enough to wake the dead."

Jimmy laughed. "As long as he don't wake the cops."

Before he could finish the sentence they heard a siren. Seconds later a squad car pulled alongside and a policeman waved them to the curb.

They waited in the Buick as two policemen approached from both sides of the car. The officer on Tony Dope's side played a flashlight on Jimmy in the back seat.

"What happened to you, buddy?" he asked.

"I was in a little fight at the poolroom," he said, with a note of apology in his voice. "They're taking me home so I can clean up."

"Oh, yeah? Get out of the car, all of you."

What happened next was inevitable. They found McSweeney's gun and later they found Deutsch, who refused to identify his assailants, but the police lab matched the blood, and that was it.

The judge handed down ten-to-twenty-five-year prison sentences to all three. Jewel screamed when the verdict was pronounced and his mother and sister held onto each other and wept. There were tears in his brother Warren's eyes when Jimmy turned to wave to his family, refusing to walk to the railing to touch or speak to them. His father's eyes were dry as he stoically gazed at his son. He shook his head, once or twice, as if to say, "Why didn't you listen to me," but it was too late.

In 1937 the nation's second oldest penal institution was the Ohio State Penitentiary. Its forty-foot high gray stone wall covered four square blocks in downtown Columbus, an awesome, soul-chilling sight. Passing through its massive steel gates at the age of twenty-three, Jimmy knew he would have to spend some of the best years of his life behind that forbidding wall. For the first time in years, he felt weak and powerless, vulnerable in a world that could crush him like a bug.

All that he had to draw succor from was the advice an old con had given him: "Jimmy, remember one thing when you walk through that gate. Once you're in that joint, you're going to do that time. Nothing can stop that. So do good time. Learn how to relax. Forget your family, forget your friends on the outside. Pretend they don't even exist. Don't worry about nothing. Don't count the days, throw out the calendar. Sleep all you can and dream about sexy movie stars. When your pecker gets stiff in the night, think about Jean Harlow and whack it. Stay away from punks. There's nothing they can do for you that you can't do with your palm. Get involved in prison activities. Keep your nose clean but don't take no shit from nobody. Grab a club and break their fucking heads in a minute. That way nobody's ever going to fuck with you again. When you don't know what to think about, try to imagine what you're going to get for breakfast or dinner or supper. Get involved in team sports. Don't worry about cockroaches or bedbugs and rats.

"Face up to the reality of prison life. Don't talk to screws, you've got nothing to say to them. They've got nothing to do with what happens to you in there. Remember that it's the cons that run the prison. They're the clerks, they do all the paperwork, keep the files, assign the good jobs, the good cell blocks, they see that you get extra privileges. Screws don't do nothing but watch. Go to school, you won't learn nothing, but you'll get to see other cons, for that joint keeps everybody under lock and key twenty-four hours a day.

"It's a hard place and it's killed lots of good men, young and old, but it can't kill nobody that knows how to do good time. That, my boy, is the secret of surviving in that joint. Do one day at a time and let the outside world go fuck itself."

Jimmy never forgot that advice, and recites it verbatim forty years later. It served him well through the many years of time he would do.

He soon learned that it really was the cons who ruled the prison, and that the most important one at the Ohio Penitentiary was Blackie's cousin, Thomas "Yonnie" Licavoli. Yonnie got Jimmy a job in the kitchen, a prize assignment, and had him transferred from a cell block to a dormitory. For the three years that he was there, Yonnie was his protector.

In the spring of 1940, Jimmy's father brought him both good and bad news. The good news was that he had met a man who could get him transferred to the London Prison Farm for $1,500. The bad news was that Jewel, who had moved to Los Angeles with her parents, had divorced him. "She still loves you," his father said, "but they made her do it." Jimmy wanted to laugh—not that he was happy about the divorce, but because it was so unimportant at this point in his life.

There were no gray walls at the prison farm in London, Ohio. There was a cyclone fence, dormitories, freedom to talk, no marching to the dining hall, plenty of windows with no bars, and lots of fresh air and outdoor sports. From early spring to late fall, Jimmy spent most of his time playing softball. Warden William Amrine was a softball freak. He had an all-star team called Amrine's Angels which played games all over the state and the players lived in the honor dorm. Jimmy made Amrine's Angels his second year there. He was a good player, quick on the bases, slick with a glove, and the best line-drive hitter on the team. His batting average led the league for three consecutive years.

Not neglected, however, was his talent for gambling. Shooting craps on top of their bunk beds, without a backboard, Jimmy was soon an expert at a pad roll. By rolling the dice with the two sixes facing each other it was impossible to crap out on the first roll.

For a while Jimmy was the farm's fire chief and he used to sleep days. Late one afternoon he reported on sick call. Jimmy knew the doctor, who was a softball fan. He said, "Doc, this's probably going to sound awfully funny to you, but I think there's something wrong with me."

"What the problem? Getting headaches."

"Doc, I had four wet dreams this afternoon. I took four showers and scored four times for sheets. That ain't normal."

"I never heard of that," the doctor said. "What have you been eating, for Christ's sake?"

"Well, doc, when I get off work, I have a quart of half-and-half, a couple eggs, you know, and some vanilla extract, and I stir it all up like a milk shake."

"My God," the doctor said. "I've got to try that. Four? Are you sure?"

"I usually get a couple, you know, but never four before."

"My advice is stop drinking that stuff until you get out of this place."

The solution, Jimmy decided, was a three-day pass, which he arranged by having his sister send a telegram that his mother was too ill to visit him. Deputy Warden Jay Young accompanied him to Cleveland. Jimmy gave him a $250 bonus, free and clear of all expenses. When word got around the prison, officials began competing with each other for the privilege of taking him home. In all he had five three-day passes.

Jimmy was released from the prison farm on Washington's Birthday 1945. A month earlier, he had found an opportunity to visit Yonnie Licavoli at the Ohio penitentiary and had told him of his plans to remarry Jewel and move to Los Angeles.

"Jimmy, if you go to Los Angeles, get in touch with Johnny Roselli," Yonnie had advised him. "He's in the federal joint at Leavenworth right now. He got caught in that movie extortion rap with some of the top guys in the Chicago outfit, but I hear they're working out some deal to spring them. When he gets out, he'll come to L.A., and you give him my regards. Tell him I'd appreciate it if he got you straightened out with the right people." It would be two and a half years before Jimmy would finally meet Johnny Roselli.

Following his release from the prison farm, he went back to pulling jobs with Frank Valenti, trying to build up a nest egg for his California venture. To satisfy his parole officer, he managed canteens at three factories for Babe Triscaro, who was now the business agent for the trucker's local, with plush offices in the new Teamsters building.

Managing canteens looked like a legitimate job to Jimmy's parole officer, but it was a black market operation and a gold mine. He sold nylon hose, cigarettes, liquor, food and gas ration stamps—anything that was hard to get. He bought from hijackers, burglars, and hustlers, and sold at markups of two and three hundred percent. From time to time, to improve his markup, he would personally venture into the hijacking business, with the deals set up by Teamsters officials.

Jimmy and Jewel were remarried before moving to Los Angeles in June 1946. Unknown to Jewel, Jimmy had nearly ninety thousand dollars stashed in the trunk of his new Buick, the money he had been collecting to launch his California career.

His first large-scale operation in Los Angeles was as a bookmaker at the Chase Hotel in Santa Monica. He rented a three-room suite on the third floor and opened a cigar stand in the lobby. He formed a friendship with Salvatore "Dago Louie" Piscopo and gradually became friendly with the Dragnas and some of their associates. Over pizza and coffee at Mimi Tripoli's pizzeria on the Sunset Strip, and over some of the best Italian food in town at Naples, he met Giolama "Momo" Adamo, and his brother, Joe; Charles Dippolito and his son, Joe, who owned a vineyard in Cucamonga; Leo Moceri, who, like Blackie Licavoli years earlier, was on the lam from the Jackie Kennedy murder in Toledo; several Matrangas, Frank, Joe, Jasper, Leo, and Gaspare, who was not related to the other four and had once been the boss of Calumet City, Illinois, but now lived in Upland, California; Pete Milano, Tony's son; Frank "Bomp" Bompensiero, who was from San Diego and was in partnership with Jack Dragna in a couple of bars in that city, including the Gold Rail; Tony Mirabile, also from San Diego, who owned dozens of bars; James Iannone, who under the alias of Danny Wilson had acquired a reputation as a muscleman but was in fact terrified of violence; Louis Tom Dragna, who was Tom's son; Nick Licata and his son, Carlo; Frank DeSimone, who was an attorney; Sam Bruno and Biaggio Bonventre, both of whom always looked ready for action, and were; and

Simone Scozzari, who years later would be caught at the Apalachin, New York, Mafia meeting with DeSimone and deported.

It was in September 1947 that Jimmy went to Dago Louie's house to meet Roselli. He found him to be a gentleman in every sense, which pleased Jimmy because he had heard so much about this man from Yonnie and Dago Louie. Jimmy noticed that the cut of Roselli's suit was far more conservative than anything he had ever worn. Everything was subtly color-coordinated and Jimmy resolved to discard his own wardrobe which looked flashy and cheap by comparison.

Looking at Roselli only confirmed that old saying about not being able to judge a book by its cover. Some of the toughest guys he had known had often appeared more gentlemanly than the rough-looking punks who fainted at the sight of blood. Here was Roselli, looking like a man of distinction in his conservatively tailored suit, his blue eyes gently amused as he spoke in soft, modulated tones. Who would have guessed that as a kid he had been tough enough to make it with Capone at a time when tough guys were dying like flies. Later when Capone went to prison, Roselli took his orders from the new Chicago boss, Frank Nitti. Roselli was then dispatched to California, where his job was to protect Nationwide, then the only horserace wire service in the country. He also was a "labor relations expert" in the motion picture industry, keeping an eye on Willie Bioff, who Nitti had placed in charge of the International Alliance of Theatrical Stage Employees and Motion Picture Operators. Then, in 1944, on the testimony of Bioff, the top hierarchy of the Chicago mob was convicted for extorting a million dollars from the movie industry and sentenced to ten-year prison terms. Then, following his release from Leavenworth Penitentiary on August 13, 1947, Roselli had rejoined Jack Dragna in Los Angeles.

At this very moment, Roselli and his Chicago cohorts were the subject of a congressional investigation that charged they had been prematurely released from prison in a scandal that cast suspicion on the Justice Department and the White House.

But here he was, a month later, talking pleasantly in Dago Louie's parlor. The contrast and subtlety of it made a deep impression on Jimmy. Having paid his dues, Roselli could sit back and live on his reputation. The organization would take care of him. He would never want for money or power. He had it made. That was what Jimmy wanted, what was missing from his life, what made him feel like he was standing still. He needed that feeling of accomplishment, to be separated from the multitude of hustlers he worked with every day, the punks of the world. Roselli was a gentleman, a man of respect, and Jimmy Fratianno was a hustler in search of an identity.

Later in the evening, Dago Louie excused himself and Jimmy had an opportunity to relay Yonnie's message about straightening him out with "the right people." When Roselli asked if he knew what Yonnie had meant, Jimmy said, "Johnny, I've been wanting this since I was a kid. I knew the Italians on the Hill had something special going for them, but it's so fucking hard to crack."

Roselli smiled. "That's right, Jimmy, and that's the way it should be. When you get the wrong guy in there, you've got to clip him. There's no pink slip in this thing."

Following the initiation ceremony at the winery, Jimmy and Roselli went to Dago Louie's house to celebrate. Roselli lifted his glass and offered a toast to the two men he had sponsored. "*Amici nostra*," he said, "may we all live long and prosperous lives."

"I'll drink to that," Jimmy said, laughing happily. "Christ, that was really something tonight." He paused and looked at the two men. "You know, Johnny, this'll probably sound crazy, but for a while there I felt like I was in church."

Roselli nodded gravely.

"I felt like Jack was going to make me a fucking priest."

"Well, Father Fratianno," Dago Louie said, "how about a blessing?"

They laughed and both started asking Roselli questions at the same time.

"Hold it," he said. "Why don't I lay it out for you guys. You know, tell you what you should know about our thing." He paused and looked at them. "You are soldiers. In the old days they called you buttons. This is a special kind of army. It's made up of a boss, the commanding general; an under-boss, who may or may not be important, depending on the family situation, but most times he's there to back the boss's play. The *consigliere's* the adviser, the guy who's supposed to know all the ins and outs of the organization. Then there's *capiregime*, captains or skippers; and finally, *soldati* . . . See, it's really an army of captains and soldiers.

"But there's soldiers and then there's soldiers. It's like a democracy, some are more equal than others. Certain soldiers carry more respect than others. But any soldier, no matter who he is, carries the power of the organization with him wherever he goes in this country. And no other family can touch him without the approval of his boss. See, all families, no matter how big or how small, have separate but equal power. Oh, yes, going back to what Jack was saying about made guys. Whenever made guys get together to talk family business, everybody that's not made has to leave the room, no matter how much they're trusted.

"Now, the commission. It's made up of the bosses from ten families. The five New York families, Buffalo, Philadelphia, Cleveland, Detroit, and Chicago. The point is that these bosses don't have an ounce more power than any other boss. It makes no difference whether the boss is Tommy Lucchese, who's on the commission, or Jack Dragna, who's not. Their power is equal. The only purpose of the commission is to settle disputes that come up between different families. It has nothing to do with the business of individual families. If Jack wants to clip somebody in his family, or somebody else in his territory, he clips him. He don't need the commission's permission. This is his country and he runs it any damn way he sees fit. No other family can fuck with him here. If they do, then it's a problem for the commission.

"Let's say we have a problem with Colorado. Jack would go see Joe Batters (nee Anthony Accardo) in Chicago. He's the arbitrator for everything west of Chicago. He straightens it out. That's what the commission's all about. All bosses on the commission also have equal power. There's no boss of bosses, never has been.

That's all bullshit. Some bosses, maybe because they are older and wiser, command more respect than others, but that's all.

"Now you also hear a lot of bullshit about being paid for hits. Forget it. That's against the rules. You kill when you're given a contract by your skipper or sometimes it might come directly from the boss. If you're given the contract, you've got to do the hit. Most soldiers are under skippers. And it stops right there. Take Bompensiero in San Diego. He's the skipper down there and he runs the show in that town. He takes orders directly from Jack, but his soldiers take their orders from him. If Bomp says you clip somebody, you do it. You don't ask no fucking questions. You'll never make money doing work for the family. That's just part of your responsibility as a member.

"But there's another angle to this. The fact that you're a member gives you an edge. You can go into various businesses and people will deal with you because of what you represent. See, you've got all this power. Nobody fucks with you. We're nationwide. We can get things done nobody else can. And that means you can make a pretty good living if you hustle."

The Crime Network

William Chambliss

There were over a thousand people in Seattle who profited directly from the rackets, bootleg whiskey, organized theft and robbery, drug traffic, abortion rings, gambling, prostitution, land transactions, arson, phony stock sales, and usury. Everyone who successfully engages in these criminal activities must share the profits with *someone* or some group of people. The more regulated the criminal activities and the more successful the participants, the more systematized the profit sharing. The entire system is simply a collection of independent operators who cooperate and compete according to their ability, their power, and their interests.

Disparate as it is, widely distributed among people in different walks of life, and changing all the time, there is nonetheless a hierarchy. Some people are more important than others. In times of crisis some people have the power to make critical decisions while others do not. Not surprisingly, those who profit the most from the rackets and who also have the power to take action are the most likely to meet and discuss problems and prospects. In Seattle the group of power-holders who controlled and set policy for the illegal business enterprises varied. Over the years the more active participants included a King County prosecutor, a Seattle city council president, an assistant chief of police, city police captains, the King County sheriff, the King County jail chief, undersheriffs, the president of the Amusement Association of Washington (who had the only master's license for pinball machines in the county), a Seattle police major, and an official of the Teamsters Union. In addition there were persons from the business and professional community who were members of the network and who in a quiet, less conspicuous way were as influential over illegal business activities as were the more visible operatives listed above. They included a leading attorney who defended network members and joined them in investments in illegal enterprises, a realtor who arranged real-estate transactions and shared investments, an officer of one of the state's leading banks, a board member of a finance company that loaned money exclusively to businesses or individuals who were either members of or under the control of the network, and various labor union officials—mostly in the Teamsters

Source: William Chambliss, *On the Take: From Petty Crooks to Presidents* (Bloomington: Indiana University Press, 1978), pp. 61–80. Reprinted with permission.

Union, but high-level officials of other labor unions were also involved from time to time.

One of the problems with determining the real power sources in an enterprise as inherently secretive and variable as a crime cartel is of course the line between active participant (or policymaker) and compliant benefactor. For example, a prosperous retail store-owner in the city often invested in and profited from illegal enterprises ranging from real-estate frauds to drug traffic. He also financed and arranged for the transportation of stolen jewelry out of the United States to Europe, where it could be recut and sold on the European market. He never set policy, never became involved in the day-to-day decisions, never allowed himself even to be consulted about the handling of a particular problem within the ongoing enterprises. Yet he knew of most of the problems and could well have been influential had he cared to make his wishes known. He preferred to remain silent. His decision, he told me, was based on the "good old American tradition of self-preservation." He felt that the less he was involved in "administration," the more likely he was to remain unconnected publicly with the "seamy side of business." He acknowledged, however, that when a newspaper reported the death of a member of the network due to "accidental drowning," he knew it was no accident.

A further problem is to decide the point at which one has enough information to feel confident that the rumors and allegations being put forward as "facts" by informants match sufficiently with other data to be acceptable. The people mentioned so far were all well established in the minds of all my informants in a position to know. These people also exhibited life-styles which clearly showed incomes in excess of anything they could have had from their legal incomes. (The county prosecutor claimed publicly that his standard of living exceeded that which his salary could support because of monies his wife had inherited.)

But it was also alleged by some informants, who should have known, that the real power in the illegal business enterprises lay with high-ranking officials in state politics, a close associate in Seattle, and a former Seattle city council member. I was unable to establish the validity of these claims. In the end the consistency of informant reports convinced me that the governor was indeed a beneficiary of heavy political campaign contributions from network principals. He, like many others, benefited from the profits and left the management to others.

At one time (1963–65) it was fairly easy to identify seven people who constituted the backbone of the network. This group shifted, however, and some of the seven became less involved while some new people emerged as principals. Both composition and leadership are variable; success is determined by connections and profits. When drug trading becomes more precarious, the people involved may lose considerable influence; when cardrooms come under fire, those people whose profits or payoffs are principally in cardrooms lose their influence.

Whatever the composition, this coalition of shifting membership (but fairly constant leadership) persisted and had more to say about how the rackets were run than anyone else. It also met more or less regularly, but here too the pattern was not akin to a monthly board of directors' meeting but was more a series of meetings between key players from different walks of life. Politicians who were deeply involved in the network met regularly at their "businessmen's club" with members of the city council, the county board of supervisors, and several key businessmen who were profiting from the rackets. Law-enforcement officers met monthly with a pinball operator who was the head of the Amusement Association, an association of pinball operators which was the official lobby for the pinball machine owners. The head of the Amusement Association in turn met with other businessmen, at least one of whom was reputed to be the bagman for state politicians.

Some sense of the organized–disorganized nature of the rackets can be gleaned from a series of incidents in the mid 1960s which involved an attempt by Bill Bennett (P) to take over part of the pinball operation in the city. Bill's brother Frank was one of the prominent racketeers in town, a man generally believed to be involved in prostitution and the collection of payoffs for state officials (including the governor) as well as the police. Bill decided that he wanted a piece of the action in the pinball business. He tried at first to demand a territory but he met with resistance. Pinballs were at the time concentrated pretty much in the hands of several people. The only master license in the county was held by the Amusement Association. As president, Ben Cichy represented not only his own interests as the major pinball operator in the state, but also the interests of other pinball operators. Ben Cichy was well protected in his position. As president of the association that looked out for the pinball interests, he met regularly with and allegedly paid substantial sums of money to politicians, to Frank Bennett (P), and to members of the police department. In addition, the Amusement Association collected from all pinball operators a monthly fee that was used to ply state and local politicians with liquor, parties, and women for favors, not the least of which were large campaign contributions to politicians who worked in the interests of pinball owners. Thus Bill Bennett was taking on some formidable opponents when he tried to muscle into the pinball business. On the other hand, Bill and his brother Frank were well connected in political and business circles. Among others, Frank was closely allied with politicians who were the political and personal enemies of the county prosecutor and might well have been favorably disposed toward an attempt to undermine part of his political base.

When Bill's efforts to gain part of the pinball operation were turned down by Cichy and the other owners, he filed what is referred to as an "underworld antitrust suit." He and some of his men began throwing Molotov cocktails through the windows of places containing Cichy's machines. Some restaurant owners were roughed up. This caused some attention in the press, so people were getting nervous. To calm things down, the pinball operators offered to let Bill in if he would agree to pay them twenty thousand dollars for the loss of their territory plus a fee of two dollars a month for each machine over and above the fifty cents per machine that went to the Amusement Association for lobbying.

The agreement reached by the other pinball operators was, however, not satisfactory to the chief of police, who saw Bill as a "hoodlum." This was one of the few occasions when the chief put his foot down. An informant in the police department said that "in all likelihood" the chief vetoed the agreement as a result of support and instructions from the county prosecutor. Because of the trouble Bill had caused, the chief insisted that he leave the state, which he did.

Several features of this event are important. First, it underlines the competition between different persons acting primarily as individuals out to increase the size of their business and their profits. It also illustrates, however, that when the entire enterprise is threatened, it is possible for a coalition of the more powerful members of the rackets to force less powerful members to acquiesce. The incident also indicates an important element in the way any network protects itself. The two-fifty a month which Bill would have to pay for each machine was divided between protection (two dollars a month) and lobbying (fifty cents a month). The one activity is presumably criminal (by statute), the other legal.

Was This Crime Network, Then, the Local Mafia?

I talked with many people about the possibility that this network was a local branch of the Mafia. A professional thief who had also worked in the rackets (gambling, prostitution, drugs, etc.) told me, "You can forget that Mafia stuff. We are Hoosiers out here. There is no organized crime like they have back east, like in Kansas City and Cleveland. We're too independent out here."

This same feeling was expressed time and again by people at all levels. Virtually everyone in a position to know anything about the rackets in Seattle echoed these sentiments: "Every time you check the Congressional Record and you see the FBI diagramming the Mafia families in San Francisco, you can tell them to shove it up their ass, because you can't diagram this. If you do diagram it, you can't read your diagram when you're done. It's all squiggly lines: the chain of command and who's in charge of any operation and who's entitled to what cut of the graft, it's all very changeable."

Q: Is the police force more or less an independent thing, not controlled?

A: No, everybody has a part of the police department's ass. Really the police department is the biggest corporate hooker in the whole establishment. The Teamsters Union used them; Democrats at the time; the city council uses them; the license committee uses them; the prosecuting attorney also had an occasion to use the vice squad to make sure he is getting an honest count, if someone gives him trouble on pinballs. Police chief, or assistant chief, would use the department sometimes at cross-purposes to what the mayor or the prosecutor might like. The mayor or the prosecutor might not want trouble, let's say, from a bar operator, like Charlie MacDaniel. They really probably hated that, when that thing came to a head the way it did. The cops, however, went right in and hassled Charlie, because the cops were smarter. The cops know what's going on out in the street, and they knew better to make an example out of Charlie, even if it gets in the newspaper, than to lose control. The prosecutor is like any other crime boss. Something is wrong out there: he looks at a lieutenant, and he says, "Fix it." He might also add the admonition, "Don't be messy, fix it." And the henchman is a technician. Like any technician, he knows that sometimes you have to get your hands dirty when you fix the machinery. And the boss may not want any machine oil on the floor, but he may have to get some to get the machine fixed. So, beyond a certain point, if it gets messy, tough shit. Because the technician is responsible, and he doesn't want to be held responsible. And if somebody like Charlie MacDaniel gets too far out of line, you take whatever measures are necessary to cover your own ass. You worry about the boss later, see? Right now you're thinking about staying out of the newspapers, staying out of prison. So, on any given occasion, the loyalties of the policemen might be very divided; and this political structure that is controlling the rackets is very fractured. At times it is fractured along the straight Democratic against Republican lines. At times it is fractured along straight county bureaucracy against city bureaucracy. At times it was fractured along city lines, depending on who was contending for power and money. And that's why you can't chart it. It's not neat.

Q: And they're all dependent on each other.

A: And each one requires the silence of the other; no matter how ugly the fighting gets, they've got to keep it under and out of sight. This is one reason why I think there was very little killing, comparatively speaking. When people are killed, they were people within the apparatus, little people. Or people like Ben Cichy if he was, in fact, murdered, who admittedly are very visible, but for some reason somebody determined at that time that it was desperately important that he had to die.

But who exactly was it that could decide that so-and-so had to die?

I was advised by a telephone call from someone I had met in a high-stakes poker game that I should go to Vito's (P) Cafe on the second Thursday of each month and see who always ate lunch there at a table in an alcove.

For six months I went to the cafe as advised. It was indeed interesting to see, week after week, gathered at one table and talking low enough not to be heard by anyone else: the assistant chief of police, an assistant prosecuting attorney, an undersheriff, and an attorney from a firm of lawyers that specialized in criminal law.

These four people met regularly every other Thursday. Rarely, however, was the luncheon limited to just the four. A local contractor, a realtor, a businessman whose firm specialized in "investments," the head of the Far West Novelty Company and president of the Amusement Association, a hotel owner, a member of the city council, a member of the county board of supervisors, an official of the local Teamsters Union, and once a newsman from one of the city's leading newspapers.

A friend told me that one of the regulars at the Thursday luncheon would like to talk to me. A meeting was arranged, and I met Von Bennett (P) at a bar. While we were drinking beer, I taped our conversation:

Q: ___ said you would tell me about the Thursday lunch group.

A: That's the meeting of the local Mafia.

Q: What do you mean by that?

A: They're the boys that run the rackets: drugs, gambling, girls, bootleg whiskey, pinballs—all that stuff.

Q: Well, that doesn't make sense to me. I have heard that __ is the major person in the rackets—at least in some of the rackets—and he never goes there, does he? I at least haven't seen him.

A: Yeah, you're right, but that doesn't mean these guys don't run the rackets. It's like this: they work for guys with either political or police pull. They control those guys either because the big guys take a cut or because they have something on them. So this group kind of coordinates things. And they keep in touch with people in diverse fields, from bingo to booze.

Q: But how are they a Mafia?

A: Well, not like you read about a Mafia with a tightly knit organization, but these guys are as close as we come out here. They're got the most—a finger in every pie—but still, as you say, there's lots of others . . . all getting rich from the rackets. . . .

The people who are getting wealthy from the rackets are not the cafe, tavern, or cardroom owners. The people who are getting wealthy are the businessmen with capital to invest in an expanding, high-profit business, politicians and law-enforcement officers who can convert political or police power into wealth. It is an interesting, fascinating illustration of the two-faced nature of the adage that wealth is power. That is certainly true, but the other side is equally true: power makes wealth as well.

The network members who met regularly were more or less elected representatives of the business, political, and law-enforcement groups that profited most from the rackets. For a while Charlie MacDaniel was a problem for them when he was refusing to pay off and later when he tried (in vain) to publicize the existence of widespread corruption in the police department. The inner circle of the network, after consulting with their bosses and co-owners who stayed in the shadows, tried various strategies to deal with him.

The kind of publicity created by MacDaniel was extremely bad for some of the most important people in the network. Businessmen who thrived on the image of Seattle as a "clean city" and a "nice place to live" knew of the underlying life of crime, but they wanted to keep those realities from public inspection at all cost. Politicians knew of the potential careers ruined by public exposure of links to anything smacking of organized crime, so they wished to keep things quiet as well. But there were cross-pressures at work that were equally important to the smooth functioning of a crime network. A person who refused to pay his proper share (whether through the payment to the police or to the "syndicate") was a threat to the entire system. If Charlie MacDaniel didn't pay, there would be a lot more tavern, cafe, cardroom, and other business owners on the fringe of legality who would take Charlie as a model and refuse to pay as well. Thus, if someone caused trouble for the organization of vice in the city, a calculation had to be made as to how best to deal with the threat. In the case of Charlie MacDaniel the calculation that evolved out of dealing with his periodic balking at "playing the game straight" resulted in his being run out of business, out of the city, and eventually out of the state.

Notice, however, that the acts which constituted a "policy" with respect to a "problem" were the result of a *process*, not of a decision. True, someone decided what to do, but it was a matter of a series of individual decisions made by people who shared the same interests and views rather than a ruling passed down by a boss. To the extent that there was a boss, he may or may not have agreed with what finally constituted the policy. But whether he agreed or not, the policy resulted from the process of coping with a problematic situation. And, of course, some of the different people and groups involved in network activities had different interests.

One feature of criminality that is almost always overlooked is the extent to which businessmen who operate a presumably legitimate and wholly legal enterprise are involved either overtly or covertly in criminal activities. More often than is ever acknowledged by law enforcers or investigators, businessmen are the financiers behind criminal operations. In Seattle one of the city's leading jewelers served simultaneously as a financier for large drug transactions and as a fence for stolen jewelry. Often businessmen are co-opted by business and friendship ties to members of the network. A vice-president of one of the city's leading banks was a close associate of the county prosecutor, lunched with him, contributed his personal endorsement to the prosecutor's political campaigns, invested in things the prosecutor recommended, supplied links to other businessmen for the prosecutor, arranged loans, and so forth. Both the vice-president of the bank and a jeweler were key members of the network. Their money financed criminal activities and they reaped huge profits from them.

Newsmen on the city's leading newspapers were also implicated. In one case it was principally through receiving gifts from various members of the network. There were also rumors that an editor received a monthly income from the network. This seems unlikely, for the editor was not only co-opted by friendship and small favors, but the newspaper was opposed to exposing any graft or corruption lest the city reassess the value of the newspaper's property. A local politician and one-time candidate for sheriff possessed information linking an editor of one of the newspapers with a national wire service that reported racing results. The police were also aware of these links. This information was never made public, perhaps because the keepers of the news are in the end the safest possible mediums for conducting illegal business activities.

There is clearly no "godfather" in the crime network, no single man or group of men whose word is law and who control all the various levels and kinds of criminal activities. There is, nonetheless, a coalition of businessmen, politicians, law enforcers and racketeers (see diagram) who have a greater interest in the rackets than anyone else, who stand to lose the most if the operation is exposed, and who also have the power to do something when it is called for. These men do not have unlimited power, to be sure, and they must assess their power in each incident to see what is the best strategy to follow. Thus, when someone firebombed competitors, there

Seattle's Crime Network

Financiers

Jewelers	Attorneys
Realtors	Businessmen
Contractors	Industrialists
Bankers	

Organizers

Businessmen	**Politicians**	**Law-Enforcement Officers**
Restaurant Owners	City Councilmen	Chief of Police
Cardroom Owners	Mayors	Assistant Chief of Police
Pinball Machine License Holders	Governors	Sheriff
Bingo Parlor Owners	State Legislators	Undersheriff
Cabaret and Hotel Owners	Board of Supervisors Members	County Prosecutor
Club Owners	Licensing Bureau Chief	Assistant Prosecutor
Receivers of Stolen Property		Patrol Division Commanders
Pawnshop Owners		Vice Squad Commanders
		Narcotics Officers
		Patrolmen
		Police Lieutenants, Captains, and Sergeants

Racketeers

Gamblers	Pimps	Prostitutes	Drug Distributors	Usurers	Bookmakers

were some in the network who wanted to acquiesce to his demands, some who wanted to wait and see, and others who wanted to "kill that crazy son of a bitch." Killing him was a very dangerous alternative since it would surely create adverse publicity and hostility between various groups involved in the rackets. Letting him in might have the same effect. Eventually the head of the pinball operation agreed to let him in for a high price, with the tacit agreement of the other pinball operators. But the chief of police resisted and was apparently able to force Bill out of the state.

Incidentally, a leading state politician who was also involved in the rackets arranged for Bill to obtain employment with a criminal syndicate in another state. Bill apparently decided that discretion was the better part of valor.

Bill's brother Frank owned a string of taverns and cabarets, a few hotels, and the major jukebox distribution company in the state; and he allegedly controlled most of the white prostitution rings in the city. After a visit to one of his cabarets I made this record:

Frank plays with his keys constantly as he sits on the edge of his chair in his Starfire Room Cabaret. The naked women dancing on three stages simultaneously and the waitresses serving watered-down liquor stop by occasionally and ask him a question. He hands one of them the keys and gets up from time to time to do something in the back room. One of the women occasionally disappears upstairs with a customer. Frank looks totally bored by the scene. The money he's making, the naked women he's employing, the conversation about the rackets and his role in them are all old hat. What interests him is the possibility that once again, at age fifty-three, he may be going back to prison. This time it will be hard time. This time he does not have the promise of something big when he gets out. This time he will lose rather than gain.

Frank spent eighteen months in prison in 1942–43. Those months were "no picnic," but he was sustained that time by a promise given, the promise by a young politician that if Frank "took the fall" and served the sentence he would be "amply rewarded" when he was released. It was a fair deal, fair for the politician, fair for the others involved, and fair for Frank.

Frank was the son of a vegetable farmer in the county. His family was comfortable but neither notorious nor wealthy. He and some of his young friends were untouched by crime or rackets to any significant degree, but they were touched by the sin of many American men—womanizing. One of the women that Frank slept with regularly was only sixteen years old. She was also sleeping with several of Frank's friends. The young woman was arrested, and she confessed to the police that the older men had been having sex with her for some time. The police threatened all four of them with jail sentences. The four men denied the charge, and the police had only the uncorroborated testimony of the girl.

A young lawyer who was active in politics managed the business affairs of Frank's family. The four accused rapists fell to arguing among themselves as to how to get out of the predicament. They called in the family's lawyer to mediate. The lawyer contacted the police, who told him that someone had to stand trial. The police agreed, however, to drop charges on all but one of the defendants in return for a guilty plea. The lawyer took out a checklist and added up the pros and cons of having one of the four plead guilty to the charge. Some were married, some had businesses that would suffer; Frank was single and could afford the stigma. He was also only twenty-three, so the effect of having sex with a sixteen-year-old would look less awesome. The lawyer promised there would be no jail sentence, only probation or a suspended sentence. He also promised that when it was over the other men would put up the money to set Frank up in business.

The lawyer's power to negotiate a deal was less than he indicated it would be. He did get the charges dropped on everyone but Frank, but Frank had to spend eighteen months in the state reformatory. On release, however, the lawyer kept his promise and set Frank up with a liquor license, a tavern, and a going business, without Frank's having to invest any money.

While Frank was building his tavern business, the young lawyer was building a political career that led all the way to the state legislature. Frank and the lawyer-politician remained close and trusted friends. Frank, it was said, became the state politician's personal bagman. He went to the various rackets in the city and collected a monthly tithe. He collected, for example, a thousand dollars a month from the owners of bingo clubs. It was a substantial amount of money, but the profits from the bingo operation were sufficient to easily underwrite this and numerous other profit shares the owner made.

The next thirty years were good ones for Frank. He expanded his first club into the ownership of numerous other clubs, part ownership of the major jukebox distributorship in the area, partial control of some of the pinball operations, and he handled some of the organized prostitution in the city, especially the prostitution that ran out of taverns and nightclubs.

Frank also became a force to contend with. He was one of the people in the rackets who could stand up to county politicians and come away intact. On one occasion a leading politician called Frank in to put him in his place. According to someone who witnessed the encounter, when Frank entered the room, the politician said, "I understand you are the biggest pimp in the state." Frank replied, "Yeah, and I hear you like to play with little boys."

The politician had probably expected a humble racketeer to grovel at his feet. But Frank's own position in the rackets and his connections with state politicians plus some important influence in Washington, D.C., were sufficient to make it impossible for the local politico to squash him.

This did not elevate Frank to a position of omnipotence. Both he and the others would have eliminated their opponents in a moment if it could have been done without jeopardizing their own operations. But they could not. So an unappealing alliance prevailed year after year. Occasionally harsh words were spoken; threats and attempts to oust leading political supporters of each other's camps were made. But the détente persisted and indeed would persist today were it not for the fact that in time another faction emerged with the power to squash both parties to this alliance, but that gets us ahead of the story.

Two members of Seattle's leading families were also implicated through various business transactions with members of the network. The business transactions invariably came recommended by a leading local politician and brought the investors huge returns on small investments. They certainly should have realized that the enterprises were illegal, but in any case they participated and showed their appreciation by supporting the politician in the face of all sorts of opposition. When, for example, their political-business ally was threatened with exposure by a newly appointed U. S. attorney, these two businessmen flew to Washington, D.C., where they consulted with a personal friend who was an adviser to President Nixon. They asked him to have Nixon stop the inquiry. For reasons that will be taken up later their request was refused and the inquiry continued.

There were other positions (rather than individuals) that were crucial to the network's success. Two bear particular attention: the head of licensing for the county and the tax assessor. The people in these positions were never very powerful. Their careers were entirely in the hands of politicians. Nonetheless, what they did at their behest was of considerable importance to the network's continuance.

There were "considerate" assessments made on the taxable property of the two leading newspapers, the fact of which could then be used to keep them from publishing news the prosecutor did not want made public. There was also a payoff made to some politicians, a small part of which was sent down to the assessor through a firm in Portland, Oregon. This firm was hired by at least two of the state's largest industrial firms to keep the tax assessments on their corporation properties much lower than they should have been. Small wonder that the owners of these businesses always supported the cooperative politicians when they ran for office.

The head of the licensing division of the county also received a share of the profits, as well as some smaller payoffs he arranged by himself. To operate a tavern, a cabaret, a cardroom, a taxicab, or even a tow-truck company, it was necessary to have a license issued by the city's licensing division. These licenses were no less than a piece of very valuable property. They virtually guaranteed substantial profit from investment. The number of such licenses was kept to a level where anyone who had the license was certain to have his services heavily in demand. A tow-truck license cost ten thousand dollars "under the board." Depending on its location and potential, a tavern or a cabaret could cost fifty thousand dollars (plus monthly payments) to license. A cardroom might cost only one thousand dollars since there was not the certainty of profit accumulation from the cardroom. Monthly payments, however, would vary according to profits, as we have seen.

Liquor licenses were handled at the state level. The liquor board consisted of three men, all appointed by the governor for staggered nine-year terms. This board was the source of incredibly large sums for "campaign contributions" and outright graft for state politicians, especially those in positions influencing licensing and liquor policies.

At the root of the crime network's operation was the money that got shuffled from the people who operated the rackets—the bookie, the numbers man, the whorehouse operator, the drug trafficker, the cardroom manager, tavern owner, or pinball operator—to the politicians, law enforcers, and businessmen who protected the network and its enterprises. The amount of money shuffled, as we have seen, was staggering.

The day-to-day decisions might have rested in the hands of seven, nine, or ten men who consulted regularly with the other principals in the network. But for such a widespread and profitable system to persist, a set of relations far more extensive than this and beyond mere payoffs had to develop, especially since the task of maintaining control over the various enterprises and the people involved was a task of major importance to everyone.

CORPORATE CRIME 1

Illegal Corporate Behavior
Marshall B. Clinard

This research represents the first large-scale comprehensive investigation of corporate violations of law. The only previous study of a somewhat similar nature was Edwin H. Sutherland's famed *White Collar Crime*, which was the study of the violations of law by 70 of the 200 largest U.S. non-financial corporations. Corporate crime is, of course, white collar crime, but it is white collar crime of a particular type. Actually it is organizational crime that occurs in the context of extremely complex and varied sets of structured relationships and inter-relationships between boards of directors, executives, and managers on the one hand and parent corporation, corporate divisions and subsidiaries on the other.

A. Corporate Organization

A corporation is a legal entity that allows a business to use the capital provided by individuals called shareholders or stockholders. Typically, however, large corporations are management controlled by corporate executives and boards of directors; the stockholders have little influence over decisions. There are in the United States some 2 million corporations; in terms of this research and the general concern about "corporations," however, they are customarily regarded as the 500 to 1000 largest as listed in *Fortune*. The assets and sales of the largest corporate conglomerates often total billions of dollars, and their economic and political powers are enormous. Total sales of many exceed the gross national product of most countries. Some of these corporate giants control wide areas of the American economy. These large corporations have provided employment to millions of persons, and they have increased the wealth of the nation in many other ways, including payments of stock dividends to millions. By their very size they are able to organize and centralize production and distribution and to develop a high degree of concentrated specialization in specific areas. The capital resources of the large corporations enable them to develop, adopt and change technology on a massive scale. All this means that the high production and financial returns that have resulted from

Source: Marshall B. Clinard, *Illegal Corporate Behavior* (Washington, D. C.: U. S. Department of Justice, 1979), pp. xiii–xxx. Reprinted with permission.

239

modern technology and industrial expansion have removed large numbers of the population from the pressures of physical want.

Most large corporations are conglomerates; although all of them have some leading lines of business each has acquired a variety of other product lines through mergers. The movement toward mergers and subsequent mammoth size of corporations have resulted from several broad trends: a hedge against business fluctuation, the acquisition of immediate capital and assets, the acquisition of new techniques, the reduction of costs of starting a new product line, enhancement of the corporation's image of growth and extended enterprise and the presumed increases in corporate profits. About two-thirds of the manufacturing industries are highly concentrated, only a few firms controlling most of the major manufacturing sector. Over the past fifty years aggregate concentration has risen substantially.

There is considerable evidence from opinion surveys that corporate executives believe that unethical and illegal practices are common. The socio-cultural environment within which many modern American corporations operate actually encourages unethical or criminal behavior. Lawbreaking can become a normative pattern within certain corporations. The goals of a corporation and their role in it may take precedence over the personal ethics of corporate executives.

Corporations have tremendous power and influence on government; this is not true of ordinary offenders. They exert power through cabinet positions, through political influence on governmental decisions and through their ability to block legislation or weaken the ability of government regulatory agencies to enforce controls affecting them.

A complex variety of defenses are offered by corporations to explain their violations of law. These include:

(1) All measures proposed constitute government interference with the free enterprise system.
(2) The government is to blame because the additional costs of regulations and bureaucratic procedures cut heavily into profits.
(3) The government is to blame because most of their regulations are incomprehensible and too complicated.
(4) The government is to blame because the things being regulated are unimportant.
(5) There is little deliberate intent in corporation violations; most of them are simply errors of omission rather than commission, and many are mistakes.
(6) Other concerns in the same line of business are violating the law, and if government cannot prevent this situation there is no reason why other corporations cannot also benefit.
(7) Although it is true, as in price-fixing cases, for example, that some corporate violations may involve millions of dollars, the damage is so diffused among a large number of consumers that individually there is little loss.
(8) If there is no increase in corporate profits, a violation is not wrong.
(9) Violations are due to economic necessity.

(10) The corporation has changed its practices and is no longer in violation.

B. Corporations and Criminal Behavior

The very size and power concentration of such large corporations, particularly the conglomerates, raises a number of serious economic, political and even ethical questions about them. What is increasingly debatable is whether or not the goods produced by the large corporations are necessarily of the highest possible quality and safety or if they have been put on the market at the lowest possible prices. Because many are virtual monopolies, corporate pricing is often not based on competition but actually constitutes "administered pricing," that is, pricing decided by the corporation itself with limited regard to competitive factors. It has also been demonstrated that the multinational corporations have exercised undue political influence in relation both to domestic and foreign governments. Their ethical standards have been questioned in many areas, among them the misrepresentations made in their costly advertising, and there has been concern about their violations of law.

As these large corporations have grown rapidly in economic power during the past fifty years or more their activities have increasingly been regulated by a number of laws designed to control such illegal acts as restraint of trade (price-fixing and monopoly), financial manipulations, misrepresentation in advertising, the issuance of fraudulent securities, falsified income tax returns, unsafe work conditions, the manufacture of unsafe foods and drugs, illegal rebates and foreign payoffs, unfair labor practices, illegal political contributions, discriminatory employment practices, and environmental pollution.

Often businesses, particularly large corporations, complain that most government regulations are largely unnecessary. One might readily agree with this complaint if assurances could be given that the basic ingredient of strong ethical principles were guiding the conduct of corporate business. There are many types of corporate ethical violations, all of which are closely linked to corporate crime: misrepresentation in advertising, deceptive packaging, the lack of social responsibility in television programs and, particularly, commercials, the sale of harmful and unsafe products, the sale of virtually worthless products, restricting development and built-in obsolescence, polluting the environment, kickbacks and payoffs, unethical influences on government, unethical competitive practices, personal gain for management, unethical treatment of workers, and the victimization of local communities by corporations.

Many corporate practices formerly considered simply unethical have now become illegal and thus subject to punishment. They include such practices of tax evasion as false inventory values; unfair labor practices involving union rights, minimum wage regulations, specific working conditions, and overtime; violations of safety regulations related to occupational safety and health; the fixing of prices to stabilize them on the market and to eliminate competition; food and drug law violations; air and water pollution that violate government standards; violation of regulations established to conserve energy; submission of false information for the sale of securities; false advertising; and illegal rebates.

Costs of ordinary crimes are usually estimated primarily in financial terms and in the social costs of the fear they incite in the general population; far more varied are the criteria used to calculate the costs of corporate crimes. Corporate crime costs run into billions of dollars. These costs involve not only large financial losses but also injuries and health hazards to workers and consumers. They also include the incalculable costs of the damages done to the physical environment and the great social costs of the erosion of the moral base of our society. They destroy public confidence in business and our capitalist system as a whole, and they inflict serious damages on the corporations themselves and on their competitors.

The costs of specific corporate crimes are high but they fail to touch the total losses that accrue from corporate crimes. They do not cover losses due to sickness and even death that result from the environmental pollution of the air and water and the sale of unsafe food and drugs, defective autos, tires, and appliances, and of hazardous clothing and other products. They also do not cover the numerous disabilities that result from injuries to plant workers, including contamination by chemicals that could have been used with more adequate safeguards, and the potentially dangerous effects of work-related exposures that might result in malignancies, lung diseases, nutritional problems, and even addiction to legal drugs and alcohol. Nader claims that corporate crime causes injuries to persons on a larger scale than do the so-called "street crimes." Far more persons are killed through corporate criminal activities than by individual criminal homicides; even if death is an indirect result the person still died.

Corporations under the law are regarded as "persons." The bridge between the acts of individuals and an entity such as a corporation has been developed in part because many of the acts of corporations are acts that could be done by individuals such as producing injurious goods, polluting the environment, bribery or engaging in tax frauds. Corporate crime is distinguished from ordinary or lower socioeconomic crime in two respects: the nature of the violation and the fact that administrative and civil law are more likely to be used as punishment than the criminal law. Because of their more recent origin and the considerations of legislative power that both white collar and corporate bodies possess they are far less likely to be punished under the criminal law; in other cases the statute may provide for alternative sanctions such as civil and administrative actions. A corporation, moreover, cannot be imprisoned; only its executives can. Serious corporate violations of law are often handled under civil or administrative law rather than criminal law because limited government enforcement staffs often dictate that injunctions, warnings or consent agreements be used rather than prolonged civil or criminal litigation. From a research point of view, therefore, corporate crime includes any act punished by the state regardless of whether it is punished under administrative, civil or criminal law.

In the research study of corporate crime, which is the main subject of this report, however, the wide range of seriousness of corporate violations has been recognized. Consequently violations were ranked as serious, moderate and minor and much of the analyses reflect this distinction. Reporting, such as paperwork, violations and similar violations of administrative law were generally considered minor violations; other types of violations of administrative law were considered serious or moderate, depending on the nature of the violation. On the other hand, when considering enforcement actions no such distinction was generally made as to seriousness because, for example, a warning letter, an administrative consent agreement or a court-imposed consent order may actually have involved a serious or moderate violation.

C. The Regulatory Agencies

Corporate crime is controlled by a variety of federal regulatory agencies, each of which has been delegated its authority to regulate and police given areas of Congress. Such agencies have rule-making powers delegated by Congress; otherwise Congress would be faced with the enormous task of legislating thousands of additional laws. In addition, many such laws would be so controversial that any enactment would either be virtually impossible or very time-consuming. The fact that the statute creates the regulatory agency and theoretically gives it authority to do something does not mean that the instruments will actually be used effectively. Limited budget and manpower considerations, the legal and economic power of the corporations, the difficulty in securing corporate records, the relative lack of agency coordination and the consequences of too drastic of action on the economy and the public set limitations on what an agency can do in enforcement.

State agencies take only limited enforcement action against large corporations, as compared to smaller ones. The reasons for this are: (1) The responsibility for the large corporations, whose operations are generally interstate in nature, is largely left to federal agencies; (2) The intercorporate structure of the parent corporation, its divisions and subsidiaries, some wholly and some partially owned, makes state prosecution difficult; (3) Large corporations are more careful to comply with the law, and their violations are not as flagrant, in general, as those of the smaller corporations; (4) Large corporations have more and better informed attorneys than the small ones; large staffs of attorneys are available to defend the corporation both from within its own offices and through local legal counsel; and large sums of money are available for legal defense; (5) Large corporations are sensitive to public opinion and their public relations image; (6) Most states have inadequate staffs of legal and technical experts to develop and handle prosecutions, as is more likely in the case of federal agencies; (7) Large corporations have funds available to settle cases readily and easily; this is not necessarily the case with the small corporations; (8) Large corporations frequently threaten a state to close down their operations or to move outside the state if the remedial actions are thought to be too costly; and

(9) Federal preemption, which means that federal laws take precedence over similar state laws.

D. The Research Study of Corporate Violations

This study has investigated the extent and nature of corporate illegal activities, the data being examined in terms of the corporate structure and the economic setting in which the violations occur.[1] It has concentrated on an empirical investigation of the 582 largest publicly owned corporations in the United States in these areas: 477 manufacturing, 18 wholesale, 66 retail, and 21 service. The major focus has been on manufacturing enterprises, corporations in banking, insurance, transportation, communication, and utilities being excluded. The annual sales (1975) for the corporations studied ranged from $300 million to more than $45 billion, with an average sales volume of $1.7 billion for the parent firms. Data cover all enforcement actions obtainable, actions initiated or imposed by 24 federal agencies during 1975 and 1976. This reveals for the first time the wide range of the types of corporate violations, as well as actions initiated and imposed by government agencies. Predictions of violations were attempted through analyses of data in terms of corporate structure and finance that were then used to compare with firm and industry-level data. Actions against parent corporations were compared with 101 large subsidiaries, whose 1976 sales ranged from $300 million to $7.8 billion.

1. *Sources of data.* This study has used four main sources of data, although even they have not provided complete information on all corporate violations and enforcement actions. Each source has certain limitations. The findings probably represent at least a one-third undercount of actual government actions against corporations.

(1) Data obtained directly from federal agencies on enforcement actions taken against the corporations in the sample.
(2) Law Service Reports (principally those of Commerce Clearinghouse and the Bureau of National Affairs) which give decisions involving corporation cases in such areas as antitrust, consumer product safety, and environmental pollution.
(3) Annual corporation financial reports (Forms 10-K) prepared for the SEC, which include a section on legal proceedings initiated against the firms.
(4) A computer print-out of abstracts of enforcement proceedings involving corporations that have been reported in *The New York Times*, *The Wall Street Journal*, and the leading trade journals.

2. *Research problems.* Research in the area of corporate crime presents many

---

[1]The study has been supported by a grant of $247,839 from LEAA for a period of 22 months. Previously, two pilot research grants were given by the University of Wisconsin Research Committee.

difficulties not generally encountered in research on either ordinary or white collar crime that involves occupations such as various small businesses, doctors, lawyers, etc. It involves issues such as corporate organizational structure and complexity, problems of data collection and analysis, the wide diversity of sanctions, and the problems of ranking the seriousness of the violations.

Corporate crime occurs within an extremely complex organizational structure. This complexity provides methodological challenges to the quantitative researcher interested in the structural and economic correlates of corporate crime. Product diversification provides a good example of such problems. Many corporations are huge conglomerates with annual sales often totaling billions of dollars and which are derived from a variety of product lines. Although these corporations may have a "main line" of business, they derive significant portions of their income from activities remote from their central product.

Corporate subsidiaries pose special problems. Large corporations often have many subsidiaries in several product lines. In attempting to compile the violation record of corporations, ideally one would include all violations of all the subsidiaries. This is not practical in a study the size of the one undertaken here, particularly since violations of subsidiaries are often not reported with the name of the parent corporation. Consequently, in this study, it was decided to focus on those wholly owned subsidiaries with annual sales of at least $300 million. Furthermore, data are not readily available for corporate crime studies.

Research that involves the enforcement activities of numerous agencies necessitates broad knowledge of the nature of, and the differences between, an extremely wide range of possible enforcement actions. In analyzing the data about violations complicated problems are encountered in making comparisons and ranking relative seriousness. No precedents have been established, which necessitated establishing guidelines for the rankings. The coding of corporate violations and enforcement actions are immeasurably more complex than those for ordinary criminal offenses. Moreover, no precedents have been established for coding procedures, and it was necessary in this research to work out more than 450 different codes for corporate violations and sanctions.

Due to the complexity of the violations, enforcement actions, and the great amount of economic data involved, extremely complex computer programming is involved in the data analyses, and these problems are further complicated when attempts are made to predict corporate violations with economic data.

Before one considers any findings from a study of corporate violations it is essential that one recognize the significance of the small frequencies of corporate cases and why they must be evaluated differently from statistics on ordinary crimes such as assault, larceny, or burglary. A single case of corporate law violation may involve millions and even billions of dollars of losses. The injuries caused by product defects or impure or dangerous drugs can involve thousands of persons in a single case. For example, in one case, the electrical price-fixing conspiracy of the 1960s, losses amounted to over $2 billion, a sum far greater than the total losses from the 3 million burglaries in any given year. At the same time, the average loss from a larceny-theft is $165 and from a burglary $422, and the persons who commit these offenses may receive sentences of as much as five to ten years, or even longer. For the crimes committed by the large corporations the sole punishment often consists of warnings, consent orders, or comparatively small fines.

E. Enforcement Actions Initiated

The world of the giant corporations does not necessarily require illegal behavior in order to compete successfully. The fact that 40 percent of the corporations in this study did not have a legal action instituted against them during a two-year period by 24 federal agencies attests to this conclusion. On the other hand, more than 60 percent had at least one enforcement action initiated against them in the period. An average of 4.8 actions were taken against the 300 parent *manufacturing* corporations that violated the law at least once. Moreover, a single instance of illegal corporate behavior, unlike "garden variety" crime, often involves millions of dollars and can affect the lives of thousands of citizens. This study found that almost one-half of the parent manufacturing corporations had one or more serious or moderate violation; and these firms had an average of 3.1 such violations.

The study found that more than 40 percent of the manufacturing corporations engaged in repeated violations. About one-fourth had two or more serious or moderate violations. Further, 83 firms (17.4 percent) had 5 or more violations; 32 corporations (6.7 percent) had 5 or more serious or moderate violations. One parent corporation had 62 actions initiated against it.

Over three-fourths of all actions were in the manufacturing, environmental and labor areas of violation. About one-fourth of the corporations violated these regulations at least once. Illegal corporate behavior was found least often in the financial and trade areas, but even here 5 to 10 percent of the corporations did violate.

Large corporations had a greater proportion of the violations than their share in the sample would indicate. Over 70 percent of the actions were against them but they made up less than one-half of all corporations; and they had more than two-thirds of all serious or moderate violations. Each large parent manufacturing corporation averaged 5.1 violations and 3.0 serious or moderate violations. They most often violate environmental and manufacturing related regulations.

The motor vehicle, drug and oil refining industries accounted for almost one-half of all violations, and 4 out of every 10 serious or moderate violations. About 90 percent of the firms in these industries violated the law at least once, and 80 percent had one or more serious or moderate violation.

Little difference was found between parent and subsidiary corporations in the distribution of their initiated actions. Violation type and seriousness of violation were slightly related to primary industry type and size of corporation; violation type was moderately associated with seriousness. The nature of the associational measures used does not allow confident statements to be made as to prediction of violations.

F. Enforcement Actions Completed

Over 60 percent of the corporations in this study had at least one enforcement action completed against them in 1975 and 1976. The average for those with one or more was 4.2 actions. There were twice as many warnings used as compared to any other sanction type, with an average of 3.6 warnings for those corporations with at least one. Monetary penalties and orders were used many times more often than injunctions and, generally, corporations were not subjected to the full force of the legally possible sanctions when they violated the law. Corporate actions that directly harm the economy were more likely to receive the greater penalties, while those affecting consumer product quality were responded to with the least severe sanctions. Although over 85 percent of all sanctions were administrative in nature, those harming the economy were most likely to receive criminal penalties.

Large corporations received more sanctions than their proportion in the sample would indicate. They had about 70 percent of all sanctions, and tended to be assessed a monetary penalty. Small and medium firms tended to more often receive warnings and orders.

The oil refining, motor vehicle and drug industries accounted for approximately 4 out of every 10 sanctions for all cases and for serious and moderate cases. They had 3 times more actions than their size in the sample indicates, and they had 2.7 times more actions for serious and moderate cases.

Each type of violation has a typical sanction type associated with it, with level of enforcement strongly related to seriousness of violation and violation type. The court or agency nature of the enforcing institution was slightly related to sanction type, and moderately related to whether an order had a retroactive or future effect. Generally, orders by administrative agencies tend to be future in effect and court orders show no preference.

The average time to complete a case was 6.7 months. Civil cases took the longest (two and one-half years) and administrative cases took about 4 months. Serious cases took approximately 1 year and minor cases about 1 month.

Monetary penalties, although at times extremely large, tend to be in the $1000 range. Less than 1 percent were over $1 million, while over 80 percent were for $5000 or less. When those for $5000 or less were removed from consideration, there were still only about one-fifth that were over $100,000. Because of the fact that large corporations are more often assessed a monetary penalty for their minor violations, there is a general negative relationship between corporate size and amount of monetary penalty.

Corporations were most likely to consent to a future effect court order and to a retroactive administrative order. Consent agreements were more likely than unilateral orders to have a retroactive effect. Of the consent agreements, administrative agencies tended to use future effect sanctions, and courts generally did not show a preference.

In terms of repeated sanctions within a two-year period, more than one-third of the parent corporations and more than two-fifths of the parent *manufacturing* corporations had two or more enforcement actions completed against them. About one-fourth had two or more for serious or moderate violations. Moreover, one out of every six corporations had 5 or more sanctions imposed, and one out of every 13 had 5 or more sanctions in serious or moderate cases.

G. Corporate Executives

In many ways the ethical and legal problems of a corporation result from the modern corporate structure that separates ownership from management. The typical corporation is a multi-unit enterprise administered by a group of salaried and top managers with the board of directors exercising little direct power other than to dismiss management; in general, management recommendations are rubber stamped. Corporate managers have considerable autonomy, therefore, over decisions regarding production, investment, pricing and marketing as long as profits result from their decisions. For these duties executives are rewarded with salary increases, bonuses, promotions, and perks; they are penalized by demotion or dismissal. Badly performing firms are more likely to dismiss their corporate executives.

Legal difficulties are encountered in the criminal prosecution of executives. First of all, it is not easy to specify legal responsibility due to the division of tasks within a corporation and criminal liability cannot be determined without solid proof of actual knowledge of the violation. Second, corporate violations are usually far more complex than conventional crimes. Antitrust violations, for example, generally necessitate high-order economic statistical data, as well as proof of a written or unwritten conspiracy among individuals. Third, the effects of the violation are extremely diffuse in nature, such as antitrust conspiracies, pollution and substandard foods or drugs.

The government's response to corporate violations cannot be compared to its response to ordinary crime. Generally penalties imposed on top corporate management are quite lenient, particularly if one looks at them in relation to the gravity of the offenses committed, as compared to the penalties imposed on ordinary offenders. Few members of corporate management ever go to prison even if convicted; generally they are placed on probation. If they do go to prison, it is almost always for a very short period of time. In this study, for example, of the 56 federally convicted executives of all 683 corporations, 62.5 percent received probation, 21.4 percent had their sentences suspended and 28.6 percent were incarcerated. Almost all (96.4 percent) had a criminal fine imposed. Those convicted of price conspiracies and income tax violations were most frequently given more severe sentences. The average prison sentence for all those convicted, whether or not they went to prison and regardless of the offense averaged 2.8 days. There were 10 officers who had their prison sentences suspended.

A total of 16 officers of 582 corporations were sentenced to a total of 597 days imprisonment (not suspended sentences); 360 days (60.6 percent) were accounted for by two officers who received six months each in one case. Of the remaining 234 days, one officer received a 60 day sentence, another was sentenced to 45 days, and another received 30 days. The average for all imprisoned executives was 37.1 days; excluding the two six-month sentences the remaining 14 averaged 16.7 days; and excluding the 60, 45 and 30 day sentences the remaining eleven averaged 9.0 days. The 14 executives who received 60 days or less were all involved in the folding carton price-fixing conspiracy. The other case involved tax fraud. The sentences were often suspended after some parts of them were served.

Problems of modest sentence following criminal conviction of corporate executives may lie with the statutes and the judges, but there are other difficulties in securing a prison sentence. Businessmen may have sought legal advice as to how to circumvent the law even before they committed the offense, and this advice may be cited as evidence of good faith in avoiding any violation of law. Businessmen defendants in criminal cases also hire lawyers known for their skills in defending their clients, presenting arguments about the health problem of the client, his previous clear record, and the unlikely event of his becoming a recidivist, all of which should warrant a light sentence. These legal experts are able to cite many precedents where a businessman charged with similar behavior had not been punished for it. Skilled corporate counsel seek, furthermore, to restrict the evidence presented in court in an attempt to conceal other offenses; plea bargaining by a corporation in a violation may, in fact, be used to avoid naming individual members of corporate management so that they will not even be tried. Due to the problems entailed in the imposition of a prison sentence on prestigious corporate executives, some judges have resorted to imposing sentences of the performance by them of socially useful activities, a privilege rarely extended to ordinary offenders.

No pattern seems to have evolved from what happens to corporate executives after they have been charged with serious law violations or have been convicted of them. In general, however, most of them are allowed to retain lucrative retirement benefits, while others may have their salaries reduced temporarily. Some are kept in the firm for some time, or at least until the case is finally resolved, largely for public relations purposes. An ordinary criminal offender is almost never retained in his position after he has been found guilty or even charged with an offense. One year after twenty-one corporate executives were fined or sent to prison for making illegal campaign contributions in 1973–1974, for example, twelve still remained in their pre-conviction corporate positions, five had resigned or retired, two were serving as consultants, and two had been discharged.

H. Predicting Corporate Violations

The various analyses of financial and economic factors produced mixed findings in terms of the original hypotheses. While the financial results have produced some contradictions, financial strain leading to increased violations receives general—if not complete—support, especially for the measures of five-year trends in performance. The measures of firm and industry structure variously act as predicted for some violation types, contradict the hypotheses for others, and prove irrelevant to violations in many cases. Some characteristics of industries—apart from individual firm characteristics—may be related to normative patterns of behavior which are significant in the study and analysis of corporate illegalities. More intricate analyses of these data might help to explain the interrelationships between the various independent variables, and between these and offense measures.

The results indicate that, except for manufacturing violations, the measures of firm and industry characteristics were not strong predictors of corporate violations. This was not an unexpected result. Clearly something else has to be added. A more satisfactory hypothesis is that economic factors operate largely in a "corporate environment" that is conducive to unethical and illegal practices. Second, the violation measures, even when specified as to types, are still relatively broad types; in addition, the independent measures are defined at the firm and industry levels, rather than at the product line level where they may well have more predictive power.

I. Antitrust Violations

Antitrust policy and enforcement are currently experiencing a period of difficult challenges and new opportunities. Recent legislation has increased the penalties available to enforcement officials, and regulatory agencies are beginning to tackle the hard problems of increasing concentration in the economy. Historically, antitrust has failed to stem growing firm market power in many industries, with the result that prices are often relatively free from the discipline of competitive forces. Also, there have been no indications that such blatant criminal offenses as price-fixing are on the decline. The next decade will be critical for antitrust enforcement. First, the federal government's inclination and ability to successfully implement the more stringent enforcement penalties available will be determined, as will—hopefully—their deterrent effect. The results of this study indicate that as of the end of 1976, sanctions imposed against responsible corporate officials remained relatively minor. More recent Department of Justice data indicate a trend toward the issuing of harsher penalties. However, it is too early to predict what effects the more serious sanctions available will have on the attitudes of judges and juries toward their use, and toward criteria for proof. Second, the outcome of recent government concern with such structural conditions as shared monopoly is yet to be determined. New legislation may be needed to control growing concentration and problems such as parallel pricing and excessive profits. In any event, the burden on antitrust enforcement will in all probability only increase. The future structure and operation of the American economy will be heavily influenced by the direction and tenor of antitrust policy.

J. Corporate Illegal Payments

Nothing has so tarnished the image of corporations within recent years as has the public revelation of the widespread violations of law in the form of corporate illegal payments to attain certain corporate objectives. For the most part, these exposures developed from the Watergate investigations of the 1970s. The federal government's SEC disclosure drive on questionable domestic and foreign payments revealed that up until 1978 at least $1 billion had been paid illegally by many of the *Fortune* 500 largest industrial corporations. These payments have included kickbacks, foreign payoffs and illegal political contributions. Kickbacks and foreign payoffs have had a long history in a wide variety of fields; corporate contributions to political figures have been a long-established practice, but only recently have certain contributions become illegal. All of them are practiced for the purpose of influencing corporate objectives: to obtain advantages over competitors, to avoid harassment, and either to influence or support a political party in this country or abroad.

Examined together, these payments are forms of bribery, either for the purpose of selling a commodity or influencing decisions. Foreign payoffs, for example, represent another form of kickbacks; they are paid to government officials to influence certain decisions, usually by these same officials, to purchase a specific corporation's commodity rather than that of a competitor. This is similar to domestic kickbacks, but here the purchasing agents of the business concern, generally private, make decisions for the corporation. Political contributions to a specific party serve similar purposes.

The 1974 SEC investigation of foreign payoffs discovered that a large number of corporate financial records had been falsified in order to hide the source of corporate funds, along with the disbursement of "slush funds" not handled in the normal financial accountability system. These practices reflected on the honesty and reliability of corporate accounting and thus represented threats to the system of full disclosure of information which the securities laws were designed to insure in order to protect public investors. The primary interest of such disclosure is to guarantee that investors and stockholders receive accurate information on which to make informed investment decisions, to assess the effectiveness of management, and to make sure that certain corrective measures are taken by management to curb any improper practices. In the past five years much publicity has been given to the role of some accountants and auditors in the direct or indirect concealment of corporate crime particularly kickbacks, foreign payoffs and illegal political contributions.

K. Controlling Corporate Crime

This study has found that approximately two-thirds of large corporations violated the law, some of them many times. Serious and moderate violations were extensive. These violations are more likely to occur in some types of industries than in others. These conclusions are supported by data from other studies, Law Service Reports, government reports, congressional hearings, and by numerous news articles appearing in *The Wall Street Journal* and in various trade journals. The measures to deal with corporate crime, however, are quite distinct from measures used for ordinary or even white collar crime.

The control of corporate crime can follow three approaches. It can be examined in terms of changing corporate attitudes or structures, it can be viewed as requiring the strong intervention of the political state through forced changes in corporate structure and effective legal measures to deter or punish, or it can be seen as needing effective consumer and public pressures. The first approach can imply the development of stronger business ethics and corporate organization reforms. Government control of corporations, on the other hand, can mean federal corporate chartering, deconcentration and divestiture, larger and more effective enforcement staffs, more severe penalties, the wider use of publicity as a sanction, and, as a last resort, nationalization. Third, consumer pressures can be exerted through selective buying, consumer boycotts, and the establishment of large consumer cooperatives. Along with all these possible measures there is the obvious need for improved information on corporate crime.

1. *Development of stronger business ethics.* Many corporate practices formerly considered simply unethical have now become illegal and thus subject to punishment. They include such practices of tax evasion as false inventory values; unfair labor practices involving union rights, minimum wage regulations, specific working conditions, and overtime; violations of safety regulations related to occupation safety and health; the fixing of prices to stabilize them on the market and to eliminate competition; food and drug law violations; air and water pollution that violate government standards; violation of regulations established to conserve energy; submission of false information for the sale of securities; false advertising; and illegal rebates.

Many types of ethical violations exist today in business, all of them closely linked to corporate crime: misrepresentation in advertising; deceptive packaging; the lack of social responsibility in television programs and, particularly, commercials; the sale of harmful and unsafe products; the sale of virtually worthless products; restricting development and built-in obsolescence; polluting the environment; kickbacks and payoffs; unethical influences on government; unethical competitive practices; personal gain for management; unethical treatment of workers; and the victimization of local communities where plants are located for the benefit of the corporation. Businesses, and particularly large corporations, commonly complain that most government regulations are largely unnecessary. One could agree readily with this complaint if assurances could be given that the basic ingredient of strong ethical practices guided the conduct of corporate business.

In the long run reliance cannot be placed exclusively on the development of government regulations, with its concomitant legal force, to straighten out unethical practices and the lack of social responsibility among large corporations. Both management itself and the schools of business administration must show more concern with the issue of ethical standards of business conduct. The inculcation of ethical principles forms the very basis of all crime prevention and control, whether ordinary, white collar or corporate. Persons in the corporate realm, whether management or boards of directors, must recognize that the very nature of laws that regulate antitrust, pollution, unfair labor practices, product safety, occupational health and safety, taxes, and other areas represent a compelling force for compliance. The development of stronger business ethics must come first from the individual corporation and second from corporate business codes and more effective trade associations and related organizations.

2. *Corporate organizational reform.* Some experts in the area of corporate violations are skeptical of how successful legal means can be in achieving corporate compliance; the nature of the available legal means makes deterrence largely ineffective against the corporations. These experts feel that remedial actions such as monetary payments or fines do not seriously hurt a large corporation and that imprisonment, the traditional method of controlling human behavior, is impossible except for some corporation officers. The entire regulatory process is too complex to be successful.

If such a position is adopted, the major alternative appears to be some type of corporate organizational reform that would more effectively prevent violations. This includes, primarily, a more effective role for the board of directors and the appointment of public directors by government. If this is done the board of directors would be responsible not only for the corporate financial position and stockholder dividends but also for the public interest, which would include preventing illegal activities to increase profits.

3. *Corporate chartering.* A somewhat related but still different approach is the requirement that all large corporations be federally chartered and consequently subject to the control provisions of such a charter. Corporations are chartered under the laws of the various states, not under federal law. Over the years most large corporations have been incorporated in the small state of Delaware where the laws were very permissive and the state lacked strong enforcement resources as well as the will to use them. It is obvious that since the states cannot effectively accomplish this mandate against the large corporations, one alternative is for the federal government to take over the chartering. Specifically, federal chartering, it is maintained, would result in greater social responsibility, increased accountability, and wider disclosure. It would also make possible more effective regulation of corporations by various federal agencies, both in prevention and enforcement.

4. *Deconcentration and divestiture.* The extensive evidence that has been presented in this study should leave little doubt of the immensity and the corresponding power of the large corporations. Few of them operate exclusively in a single product line; rather, they have extended holdings and operations in diverse fields. In some areas so great is the concentration of a few corporations that they can virtually control prices, thus leading to frequent antitrust and other suits.

The size and the complex interrelationships of large corporations make it extremely onerous for government agencies to exercise any effective social control, or even to compete with them on an equal basis, as for example in investigations and litigation. Some government suits have involved millions of pages of testimony and documents, thousands of exhibits, and hundreds of witnesses. Conglomerates are able to maintain a high degree of corporate secrecy, since their consolidated financial statements give overall data, and the data for the subsidiaries are only occasionally given in spite of a recent court decision that requires that these data be furnished to the FTC. This thwarts the shareholders' abilities to assess the performance of individual firms and thus makes extremely arduous any enforcement efforts of the government agencies. Consequently, a partial solution would be to break up the power of the large corporations by forcing them to deconcentrate and to divest themselves of certain product lines or subsidiaries.

5. *Larger and more effective enforcement staffs.* The evidence shows that regulatory agencies, either at the federal or state level, do not have adequate resources to deal with either white collar or corporate crime. Federal regulatory agencies and the Department of Justice, as well as departments at the state level, should have greatly increased enforcement budgets with which to employ additional investigators and lawyers. Also greatly needed are adequate specialized technical personnel such as accountants, engineers, and laboratory technicians to deal with the investigation of corporate crime. It will not be easy to secure sufficient additional personnel for the enforcement of corporate regulations. Powerful opposition will come from business and conservative members of Congress.

6. *More severe penalties.* It has generally been conceded among knowledgeable persons that penalties for corporate offenses are far too lenient, as shown in this study. Administrative actions such as warnings and consent agreements are used too often. Civil and criminal actions are infrequently utilized, and monetary penalties, frequently because of statutory limitations, are often ludicrous in terms of the corporations' assets, sales and profits. Although executive responsibility and consequent criminal prosecutions are increasing, the number prosecuted is still small. In most cases of conviction the offender is put on probation.

Penalties might be increased in a number of ways:

(1) Consent decrees should be strengthened so that they call for substantial remedial actions.
(2) Where fines are fixed by statute, they would be increased to a minimum of $100,000 and a maximum of $1 million, but even these large sums can be absorbed by big corporations. Preferable would be a fine assessed in terms of the nature of the violation and in proportion to the assets or annual sales of the corporation.
(3) With few exceptions if the corporation has previously been involved in a similar offense, new cases of violation would involve administrative monetary payment or the filing of civil or criminal litigation.
(4) More adequate would be fines that are levied by the day, as in the case of the Environmental Protection Agency criminal fine of $25,000 each day a cor-

poration is in violation and $50,000 if there have been previous convictions.

(5) More extensive prosecution of corporate officials should take place. If convicted, a mandatory four months sentence, or possibly in particularly flagrant cases a minimum sentence of eighteen months, should be levied. Probation could not be given except for extreme circumstances; such factors as no prior conviction or active participation in community organizations would not be considered extreme circumstances. The use of community service instead of imprisonment would be prohibited by law except in unusual circumstances. Indemnification of convicted corporate officers by their corporations would be prevented by federal legislation which would preempt state laws permitting it. Any management official who is convicted of criminally violating his corporate responsibilities would be deprived of assuming similar management positions within his corporation or exercising such duties in any other corporation for a period of three years.

Rather than penalizing corporations the federal government might well inaugurate a program for rewarding those corporations who had not been found in violation of the law. This might be accomplished through preference in government contracts, tax breaks, or by giving such corporations some recognition, such as a symbol of compliance which could be used in their advertising. Those executives of corporations with a record of non-violation might be invited to a Washington conference where they could discuss what measures they used to achieve compliance.

7. *Publicity as a sanction.* Media publicity can be either informal or formal. Informal publicity is that ordinarily carried in the media as news items. In formal publicity the corporation is required as a part of an enforcement action to give the media an advertisement or other statement of acknowledgement of a violation and the corrective measures being taken. Studies have indicated that a relatively small number of violations, as well as enforcement actions that involve corporations, are publicized in the general media.

Publicity can also constitute a formal action, a sanction in itself. This is an effective and practical means of deterrence which is offered through the use of formal publicity methods, such as mass media advertisements (e.g., corrective advertising) setting out the details of a corporation's illegal conduct, compulsory notification to the stockholders and to others by means of an annual report, and even a temporary ban on corporate advertising. The proposed new Federal Criminal Code (Section 2005) states that a court may order a convicted corporation to "give notice and explanation of such corrections, in such form as the court may approve to the class of persons or to the section of the public affected or financially interested in the subject matter of the offense, by mail, by advertising in designated areas or through designated media or by other appropriate means."

8. *Public ownership.* Public ownership, or nationalization, is one alternative means of socially controlling certain large corporations, possibly the means of last

resort. As a viable alternative in the context of corporate crime control, public ownership should be considered only for those large industries that have become oligopolies with little or no competition and socially irresponsible both to national interests and those of the consumer.

9. *Consumer pressures.* There is an implicit assumption in the notion of social responsibility that the "good behavior" of corporations will be recognized by the consumer and rewarded in the marketplace; conversely it is implicit that irresponsibility and illegal behavior will result in decreased patronage, even consumer boycott. Were this the case consumer pressure, through the withdrawal of patronage, could be an effective tool in the control of illegal corporate behavior. Unfortunately, this relatively simple measure of social control appears not to be effective. In the first place, it assumes that persons who will withdraw patronage know that a corporation has been engaging in either irresponsible or illegal activities. Second, the relation of social irresponsibility and illegality to a corporation is complicated by the existence of multiple component firms. Third, when cognizant of the reputation of the corporation and constantly pressured by favorable corporation advertising to purchase a product, the consumer is not likely to relate the personal failure to purchase a product to the possible control of the corporation. The cooperative movement, however, offers an alternative method of controlling corporate crime; at the same time they make it possible to sell cheaper products of higher quality to the consumer. Cooperatives also offer a more active control by the consumer over management decisions than is provided the shareholders in large corporations.

CORPORATE CRIME 2

Corporate Crime: A Critique of the Clinard Report
T. R. Young

The publication of *Illegal Corporate Behavior* by the U.S. Department of Justice is a significant event in the history of American criminology.[1] For the first time, corporate crime has been separated clearly from the concept of white collar crime and studied in depth. More importantly, Clinard and his associates, Yeager, Brisselte, Petroshek, and Harries have developed analytic categories within which to analyze corporate crime as well as to gauge the patterns and relationships between corporate crime and other test variables. One may look forward to the systematic study of a form of offense which finds the entire society as its chief victim.

There have been other articles which make use of the concept of corporate crime but their major failing was the paucity of systematic study and/or the collection of adequate data.[2] The Clinard Report repairs this flaw. There have been studies which have collected nationwide samples of corporate crime but these data have been lumped in with the crimes of employees against the corporation.[3] The Clinard Report separates out the crimes of corporations themselves and does not cloud the analyses with other quite different forms of crime.

There are any number of studies of crime which use the analytic categories of the F.B.I. and report on burglary, robbery, murder, rape, and theft. However, these categories are not sensitive to the ways in which corporations may violate the law. Once in a while a chief executive officer may order a murder, a burglary, a robbery in order to advance the position of his/her organization but such crimes are, most probably, rare. A chief executive officer may steal or rape but those are private wrongs, not corporate crimes. On balance, the traditional analytic categories do not help one study corporate crime. The Clinard Report helps sharpen the intellectual tools with which to dissect corporate crime.

There is much of merit in the Clinard Report. It does much to redeem our ignorance of the illegal ways in which corporations function from day to day. However, we did not know how many crimes a given business commits per year. We still do not know. We did not know how well the American corporation is policed. We still do not know. We did not know the recidivism rate of the business corporation; we are still ignorant. We did not know whether corporate crime is increasing or de-

Source: T. R. Young, "Corporate Crime: A Critique of the Clinard Report," *Contemporary Crisis* 5 (July 1981), pp. 323–335. Copyright © 1981 by Martinus Nijhoff Publishers. Reprinted by permission of Kluwer Academic Publishers.

creasing. We are ignorant still. The Clinard Report, however, gives us a good start in learning these things and provides some base line data with which to pursue these topics. We still do not know the social and economic costs of corporate crime—we only know it is in the billions of dollars. We still do not know the way in which corporate crime distorts the allocation of resources to our social institutions. We still do not know how corporate crime affects mortality rates. We do know that unsafe drugs are marketed, unsafe foods, unsafe appliances, unsafe toys, and unsafe transportation systems are daily sold with every possible energy. Our ignorance of the form and magnitude of corporate crime bespeaks our inability to research and critique the corporation. The stratification system in the U.S. has successfully excluded such scientific study of the rich and most powerful. Clinard and his associates have found a way to penetrate such barriers. Perhaps this is the central contribution of the report.

The Clinard Report is a two-year study (1975–76) of the criminal activity of 582 of the largest corporations in the U.S. The data are based on all the criminal proceedings initiated against these companies by 24 federal agencies. The study found 60 percent of the corporations studied each had an average of 4.2 actions filed against it. The oil, auto and drug industries were the most criminal. It took about 6 months on average to complete a case: over a year for serious offenses. Large firms committed the most crimes, and paid the heaviest fines. Eighty percent of the fines were 5,000 dollars or less. Fewer than one percent of the fines were over one million dollars. Of the 56 convicted executives, 16 served a total of 597 days in prison for an average of 37.3 days. There were 1,553 findings of guilty against these 582 corporations for an average criminal rate of 2.7. The study did not include corporations in banking, insurance, transportation, communication or utilities. It did not study businesses with annual sales under 300 million dollars. Of the two million odd corporations in the U.S., data are not available for 1,999,400. Most of the crimes were committed against workers, customers and the environment.

All in all, the study shows crime to be endemic in business life. Indeed it is a way of life. While the Clinard Report has much data of value and is a pioneering venture which is long overdue, there are some conceptual, methodological and interpretative features of the study which impair its utility as an instrument by which a society can come to authentic self-knowledge and thus, control its own criminal behavior. Let us now critique the study in terms of some of its deficiencies.

The study has flaws in the omission of concepts which help one to understand the incidence and logic of criminal behavior in one of the most crime-ridden societies in the world. The concepts of capitalism, class, class struggle, community, surplus value, alienation, separation of production and distribution, profit rate, competition, and accumulation are omitted from the analysis. There is no effort to correlate corporate crime to these variables. The authors of the report do not see that corporate crime is part of class struggle. It clearly is rational to commit crime as a means to reunite production and distribution through fraudulent advertising. It is clear that profit is a sensible motive for selling unsafe products. Bribery makes sense in the competitive world of vanishing capitalists. They bribe to stay alive.

The best reason to create illegal shared monopolies is to increase the rate with which surplus value is appropriated from workers and consumers: profits have been declining since 1940, except in the monopoly sector. Without such concepts, the crime of corporate officers does not make sense yet these concepts are omitted in the analyses provided by Clinard. They are, of course, omitted in American criminology as a whole so the fault is not unique to this report.

The concept of crime itself used in the Clinard study is a major improvement over previous studies of corporate activity. The Clinard Report expands the concept of crime to embrace any act punished by the state whether that punishment derives from application of criminal law, civil law or administrative law. Ordinarily, the notion of crime would be restricted to those acts prohibited by criminal law. The inclusion of civil and administrative law is, in modern criminology, a daring act. It will be widely criticized by purists. The conceptual problem here is, of course, that to the degree corporate capital controls the legislative apparatus, it controls what is likely to be defined as illegal activity. Such a situation requires that one develop a theory of the capitalist state and test the marxist thesis that the state serves the interests of the whole bourgeoisie in the very act of making criminal law. Offe, Miliband, Poulantzas and Touraine have taken considerable interest in the role of the state in the literature.[4] Domhoff and O'Connor in the U.S. are doing good work, but nowhere is there a report on criminology which tells us exactly how biased is the law making process itself.

We can extend the work of Offe, Miliband and Poulantzas on a theory of the state in capitalist societies to criminology itself and thus advance the work of the Clinard Report. In the orthodox marxist theory of the state, the state serves the interests of the whole bourgeoisie with emphasis on whole. This means that the state keeps labor peace, regulates disputes between the capitalist class, uses its military to get and keep markets and materials abroad and eliminates foreign competition through tariff and tax. Perhaps the most important function of the state is to maintain the sanctity of the civil sphere from intrusions by the state itself. As Offe notes, all that capitalism requires is that the state enforce law that keeps all decisions out of public discourse and subject only to private (civil) agreement. If these agreements are indeed outside public (collective, whole system) consideration, then a corporation can use its strategic position of power or wealth to set whatever terms it cares to set. But as Offe, Poulantzas, Miliband and others note, the classic marxist model does not fit the data.

A new model of the state has been developed which, in broad outline, has the following character. The state, in capitalist societies, does in fact contribute to the process by which private wealth is accumulated. However, in addition to serving the interests of private capital, it must also maintain political legitimacy else itself be destroyed in its present form by palace coup or popular rebellion. The state, in an effort to secure political legitimacy invades the sanctity of the private (civil) sphere—it begins to regulate the whole bourgeoisie on behalf of labor, consumer groups, children, farmers, minorities and other sectors of the population which are able to gather together physical, economic, moral or social power. More interested in its own survival, the state sector preempts the civil sector and attempts to manage everything. Herein lies the impetus toward crime for the private corporation.

In the first instance, ordinary practices of private business come to be defined as illegal. Labor practices, marketing practices, pollution practices and fiscal practices enter into deliberations on the criminal code and become proscribed by law. In the second instance, the state sets such hard conditions for producing and selling that the corporation must violate them if it is to survive. The decline in the number of private corporations from five million to two million in the past forty years helps one understand the desperation of the private owner. Thirdly, the state acts irrationally and infuses private owners with little more than contempt for its stupidity—why obey stupid laws. The irrationality of the state is a structural irrationality which has many dimensions but centers around the practice of the state to serve special interest groups one at a time. It passes inconsistent laws. Nowhere is the general interest of over-riding import. It is important to note that the state in its preemption of economic policy does *not* thereby constitute a public sphere— the public does not make policy, the state does. The word we use for state control of policy is fascism, not socialism.

These three characteristics of the modern capitalist state erect an environment in which violation of the law by the corporation is necessary. Coupled with other political developments, capital must commit crime to survive. These conditions have been listed elsewhere.[5] What is useful to note here is that the Clinard Report does not make recourse to any theory of corporate crime. Surely the theories of crime which are everywhere found in criminology textbooks are useless to explain corporate crime. I will suggest how this theory of corporate crime might have been tested.

The Clinard Report thus does not attempt to research the harm done to the social process by acts which are perfectly legal. Among the forms of social injury not covered by the legal code is the fact of capitalist production itself. A legal system which permits the corporation to increase and reduce production/distribution in order to increase private profit is an injury against those who need food, health care and shelter and who cannot afford to pay cost plus profit. A system which permits anyone to take food from one country with low caloric intake and ship it where it can be sold for higher profits must be a criminal system.[6] Pet, Carnation and Nestles' may, with perfect legal right, take milk from countries where hunger kills thousands of children and sell it to overfed middle-class children. This must be a criminal system else the concept of crime is an empty concept. A system which, without legal penalty, permits the dumping of unsafe pesticides in third-world countries, of dangerous drugs and additives on people with no schooling with which to read the fine print—these must be crimes, but the U.S. legal system fails to call them so. A.I.D. has helped U.S. industry dump millions of unsafe contraceptive pills and deadly intrauterine devices on the women of the third-world knowing full well that these same products have killed women in the United States.[7] It requires the purest of technical reason to hold that these are not crimes in that no state apparatus cares to label them crime. On such noncrime is the thinnest, least human motive possible: to show a profit at the end of the fiscal year on an Annual Report to unknown owners of those chemical and pharmaceutical corporations.

Capitalist countries install even more deadly military systems to enforce the narrow freedom of market activity at the expense of political freedom.[8] The logics of capitalist "freedom" justify the allocation of social resources to the development and deployment of more certain forms of death. Chemical, electronic, atomic and explosive technology absorbs the genius and the wealth of American science. The spread of the means of death is, objectively, hostile to the social enterprise. Were the instruments of death spread as extensively in the human body as in the various parts of the earth, few people would have difficulty in conceptualizing that infection as pathology. The linkage of scientific activity to military purpose is a wrong on several levels of human understanding. It does not change its nature by virtue of legal definition . . . still it is crime.

The very notion of crime is safely contained within the structure of capitalist relations and, thus, defeats the critical enterprise in American criminology. No social formation should be so immunized from critique. No approach to social pathology should be so narrow and so parochial as to insulate whole social processes from study, comparison, and social transformation. The capacity to name a thing crime is constrained by the political power to control the law making apparatus. By such constraints is the quest for peace and domestic tranquility made hostage to private accumulation or to political hegemony. If one is interested in safe streets, a decent childhood for one's progeny, the preservation of trust, belief and human cooperation, one must consider the possibility that a system which promotes privatized accumulation, competition, deception, warfare and hunger is itself a criminal system whose remedy is not punishment but transformation to more social forms of production and distribution.

In this study, then, the concept of the *capitalist* firm is not employed. The omission of the word effectively divorces the crime studied from the system in which it arises. It is much like talking about child abuse apart from the concept of the authoritarian family structure. Secondly, there is no *class* analysis. The role of crime in transferring wealth from workers and customers to owners and top executives is not considered as the major dynamic undergirding this behavior. Thirdly, the authors prefer concepts such as violation, offense, illegal action, deviance, and action. In part, this wording is a matter of style. In part, it reflects a reluctance to conceptualize what corporations do as crime. Most of the tables use headings which prefer the term "violation" to "crime".[9] The corporations which commit the crimes are nowhere conceptualized as "criminals" as would easily occur where the entity in question is a specific person.

Generally, the conceptualizations are polite, tactful, objective and bland. Some passages in the "Introduction", are not so bland, but in general, the Report is an exercise in the safe science of a depoliticized sociology. It is not a scientific act to depoliticize knowledge; it is a moral act. The morality of this sort of act needs, itself, to be examined. The position of the present author is that any body of knowledge becomes the political instrument of those in power. Objective, depoliticized science can only reproduce existing stratifications in power, wealth and social honor. The facts do not speak for themselves with any power. The concepts one uses affect the likelihood a social base may be constituted. In this case, class struggle does not seem appropriate since class-based concepts are not employed.

What does seem appropriate to these authors is more liberal legislation as a solution to the problem of corporate crime. While the marxist analyst would suggest part of the solution to the problem of crime is to fashion a social revolution and to put all corporate assets and activities under collective control, a functional approach would suggest solutions which are oriented to making the corporation behave better by reform. Indeed, the bulk of the measures suggested with which to control corporate criminals are reformist in nature and well calculated to be ineffective.[10] These measures thus preserve the structure of capitalist relations. We may critique each briefly.

Development of Stronger Business Ethics

The authors do not understand that the point of forming a corporation is to avoid personal liability for criminal activity. The history of the corporation begins with the quest for an instrument by which to exploit the worker and the customer without one's private life being placed in jeopardy. To call for ethical behavior on the part of the private corporation is an exercise in economic naiveté. Ethics are only words which bind the moral and free the nonmoral to pursue whatever private goals seem compelling.

Corporation Organizational Reform

Here two options are offered. The first, more control by a board of directors, is palpable nonsense. In law, they have control. There is no empirical connection made between more board control and less crime. The second solution makes more sense on its face. The Report suggests appointment of public directors. The history of public directors is not a happy one. In the framework of capitalist relations, it usually means an opportunity for party hacks to extort and to accumulate private wealth. Just how public the directorship would be, is of central interest.

Corporate Chartering

The authors suggest federal chartering instead of state chartering. It is empirically the case that corporations charter more often in states with few laws and less policing. The primary result of this federal chartering would be to increase the rate of reported crime more than to lower the real crime rate—a point to which we shall return later. The institution of federal charter would bring the capitalist corporation under the purview of federal police. This would require the enlargement of a police capacity at the federal level. The idea that crime is cured with more policies is a fascist idea. The suggestions ignore the failures of the many federal agencies now existing. The S.E.C., the F.T.C., the I.R.S. and the D.E.A. cannot control stock fraud, criminal conspiracy to fix prices, corporate tax evasion, or dangerous pharmaceutical traffic. Would more police reduce such crime? It is an inadequate and indirect attack on a criminal system.

Deconcentration or Divestiture

If large corporations are criminal, would breaking them up into smaller corporations produce less crime or more small criminals? It is an interesting question. The federal government broke Standard Oil into smaller companies. The data do not suggest these fragments became less criminal. The same motives for crime remain. In the unlikely event that federal law broke existing corporations into fragments, one would see a desperate scramble to regain ever increasing shares of the market by whatever means came to hand. One would have five million fragments to police instead of two million.

Larger and More Effective Staffs

As noted, the fascist solution to the problem of crime is more police. A better solution is to eliminate the conditions which compel crime. Capitalist societies separate production and distribution for purpose of profit. Corporations commit crime in order to reunite production and distribution in such a way as to increase profit. Production for use instead of for profit eliminates this imperative to corporate crime.

More Severe Penalties

If penalties for corporate crime are too lenient, it does not follow that harsh penalty would reduce crime. However satisfying that may be to the victim, the empirical question is does it work? The data do not support such an argument with respect to street crime. In all probability, what would happen is that the firm would spend more money for lawyers and bribes, thus driving up the unproductive cost of business still further. More and more corporate executives would be in prison and, presumably, learn more and better ways to evade detection.

Publicity as a Sanction

The corporation with bad publicity does not stop committing crime. It merely buys the time on television and newspaper and hires more public relations persons. Again, the cost of unproductive labor is added to the price of the product. When Firestone was caught selling unsafe tires, it merely hired Jimmy Stewart to tell how nice Harvey Firestone was as a youth. When Coors beer violated the human rights of its workers with compulsory lie detector tests and with union spies, it merely added eight million dollars to its advertising budget and increased the price of its beer to cover the cost. Incidentally Coors uses ditch water to brew its beer, not crystal clear spring water.

Public Ownership

The authors suggest public ownership as a last resort. I suggest it as a first resort. They suggest it for only a few firms, I suggest it for all. A side by side comparison of corporate crime rates in socialist and capitalist societies should be made immediately to determine whether crime rates are lower and service better in each different mode of production and distribution. The data show socialist industries serve the populace better with food, health and medical care, education and opportunity.[11] The case in Cuba is interesting. All forms of crime were drastically reduced within months of the triumph of the revolution. Prostitution was almost eliminated in the prostitution capital of the Caribbean. Organized crime and its various rackets had to flee to Florida. Political crime is receding and street crime is also reduced. As far as it is possible to know, it appears that the same sort of reduction in crime took place also in China after the revolution. Without the data, it is hard to tell, but one suspects that corporate crime also fell. The case of white collar crime is unclear. This form of crime appears to have survived the revolution in the Soviet Union. What is needed is good, sound data in a good, sound theoretical framework before we can possibly know. Public ownership of the lemons of capitalist society would probably do little to abate crime. What is required is a test of public ownership within the structures of socialist relations compared to public ownership within the structure of the privatized accumulation and consumption which typifies capitalist relations.

Consumer Pressure

The suggestion that consumers pressure business is a puerile suggestion. Corporations respond to power. Writing angry letters is a petty expression of powerlessness. The suggestion to turn to cooperatives is even more feeble. Two thirds of the productive capacity of the U.S. is in the hands of these criminal corporations. Buying sugar, autos, oil, electrical, air travel, food, and other basic commodities outside the monopoly sector would be difficult indeed.

The failure to conceptualize and to analyze corporate crime from a class and conflict perspective leads to such inadequate suggestions to control crime as those above.

The Clinard Report urges the appropriation of substantial funds for research on corporate crime. The suggestion is well advised indeed. Corporate crime does far more harm to the social process than does individual crime. The sale of unsafe foods, drugs, and toys may well kill more children than are killed by their parents. The quest for profits requires systematic evasion of pollution laws. The injection of harmful chemicals into the rivers, soils, and air systems may well kill more people than overdose of dangerous drugs. The need for high-energy, high profit capital-intensive systems of production may well subvert the health of entire generations for centuries to come through radioactive poisoning. The economic power of the large corporation most probably does more to subvert the democratic process than all the ballot box stuffers, the right-wing fascists and the left-wing terrorists combined. The deception in advertising, packaging, warranties and endorsements may do harm to the human capacity for trust, for faith and for belief in ways impossible to measure. A cynical society is a society unable to engage the social process. Kickbacks, payoffs, price fixing, and political contributions may do more to create a model for private behavior than we yet understand. A single crime involving the price fixing of electrical equipment, cereal foods, or military hardware may well cost the public more than all the burglaries, robberies, and thefts committed in the U.S. in a single year combined. The profits from price fixing of electrical equipment by G.E., Westinghouse and other criminal corporations amounted to over two billion dollars. The Report notes that there are about three million burglaries a year with an average loss of about 422 dollars each.[12] This is about 1.2 billion dollars loss to the public. It is an interesting question whether three million more visible small thefts is of greater harm than one invisible theft.

All these considerations warrant a larger investment of public funds to research the magnitude and the effects of corporate crime. This field is largely ignored by the criminal justice system in the university and in the legal system itself. The collecting and reporting of corporate crime data do not interest the F.B.I. The *Wall Street Journal* and the *New York Times* report on specific cases but nowhere, other than in the Clinard Report, are there systematic efforts to make visible the parameters of corporate crime.

If American criminologists are to turn their full attention to corporate crime, there are several obstacles. First is the matter of bias. The Clinard Report places itself squarely on the side of the capitalist system when the authors protest that the costs of corporate crime "... destroy confidence in business and in *our* [italics added] capitalist system as a whole ... "[13] This bias is reflected as well in the major finding of the Clinard Report that corporate capitalism does not, necessarily, require criminal behavior in order to compete successfully.[14] This author has argued above and elsewhere that the objective conditions under which the capitalist corporation must operate require it to commit crime on a routine basis.[15] Capitalist corporations exist in a very hostile world. There are many dynamics at work to encourage corporate officers to violate the law. The Clinard Report ignores these environmental factors. Falling profits, increased labor costs, increased costs for raw materials, the formation of cartels in third-world supplier nations, increased taxes, increased concentration of wealth, increased costs for unproductive labor (advertising, lawyers, and personnel managers) all lead the corporation to crime as a way to survive.

The findings from the Clinard Report support the interpretation that crime is a natural feature of capitalism better than they support the conclusion of Clinard that capitalist firms can successfully compete without recourse to crime.[16] Consider the finding that the larger the firm the more crime it commits in proportion to size.[17] This finding lends support to the thesis that crime helps with growth and profit. It may follow that failure, stagnation, and bankruptcy is the price a business pays for honesty and truth. But that is not what the Clinard Report says. Consider the finding that two thirds of the larger corporations committed crime in the two-year period of the study.[18] Does this permit one to say there is no necessary relation between crime and capitalism as the Clinard Report insists? Or does it suggest the need for a better research design to ascertain whether the other one-third of large corporations are more successful at evading detection? One wonders if there is a single major corporation in full compliance with all labor, pollution, safety, tax and financial laws.

The preference for capitalism by the Clinard researchers leads to the omission of many research hypotheses. The preference for capitalism as a system of production and distribution informs a reluctance on the part of state agencies to force the research subject to provide the necessary data. Such preference by members of the sociology profession makes it difficult for the profession to change its code of ethics and contemplate the forcible collection of data from a research subject: in this case the corporation. This bias also informs the way in which conclusions are fashioned. As long as capitalism is held to be preferred, an objective critique of it and its relation to crime is difficult.

The Clinard study is superior to the Sutherland study on several methodological grounds laid out in the study itself.[19] As good as it is and as much as the study lends itself to great praise, still it mystifies the study of crime. The author argues elsewhere that one cannot explain corporate crime by differential association theses, by genetic theory, by anomic theory, by labelling theory, by deviant subculture theory or by culture-of-poverty theses.[20] The theories and theorists which arise in a capitalist society and which accept capitalism as a given cannot demystify the nature and variations of crime found in such a society. The Clinard Report has managed to strip corporate crime of its sociology. At no place is a *sociological* theory of corporate crime offered and tested in the Report. One cannot understand the decision of the Hooker Chemical company to deliberately pollute the ground water of Love Canal with carcinogens and other contaminates with the theories available from bourgeois criminologists. The officers of Hooker Chemical were repeatedly warned by their own staff that it was dangerous to neighbors to dump insecticide wastes in the water table.[21] Hooker Chemical does not exhibit the characteristics of criminal psychopathy, of genetic malformation, of deviant subculture, of differential association or those of a culture of poverty. Only the dynamics of capitalism—profit maximization and private accumulation—can explain this behavior. Hooker Chemical and all other capitalist corporations are engaged in class warfare against its employees, against its customers, against its neighbors and against its critics. They are winning. Concentration of wealth is proceeding apace. Growth of the international corporation proceeds rapidly while hunger and poverty in the capitalist bloc increases.[22]

A theory of crime must be posed which leads one outside the boundaries of a particular historical social order to a comparison of several different societies.[23] Crime is related to the degree to which community exists. Capitalism destroys community and all forms of crime increase as community is lost. Street crime, white collar crime, corporate crime, organized rackets and political crime increase as the dynamics of capitalism destroy the capacity to produce social relations which themselves constrain antisocial behavior.[24] What is needed is a systematic, well funded, transnational study of that thesis. The theory specified here is that the mode of production of culture determines the level of crime in a society. The more the means of producing culture is collectively controlled, the less crime. Most orthodox marxist theorists would focus on the means to produce material culture as the major independent variable. This author's thesis requires one to measure collective control over the means to produce political and ideological culture as well as food, shelter, transport, health and medical care or other material lines of production. Such sales should then be correlated to measures of crime found in that social formation.

Measures of corporate crime should be correlated with different variables embodying the social character of production and distribution for all forms of crime, measures of income inequality, caloric intake, and infant mortality rates, for example, should be correlated to the incidence of crime since they are indicators of the degree to which distribution is socialized. Street crime, organized crime, corporate crime, and political crime should vary inversely with the degree to which distribution is socialized if this author's thesis is valid. Only white collar crime— the crime of employees against their employing organization—would not be closely related to socialization of the means of production in the marxian paradigm since several generations would be necessary to eradicate the compulsion toward private accumulation as a hedge against the uncertainties of life, of social status, and of international struggle. The dynamics of social change are such that these correlations should not be linear but rather discontinuous.

If one is to study corporate crime, there is much research to be done. There are many court battles ahead to gain access to data on corporate crime. There are many professional battles ahead to force scholarly journals to publish such "radical" articles. Obtaining adequate funds from the state will not be easy. Grants from the various foundations are not likely. Developing adequate analytic categories will entail much argument and debate in the profession. Identifying relevant independent variables will entail much trial and error. Generating adequate and testable theses will occupy the genius of several generations of criminologists. Getting the cooperation of suspicious socialist countries will take many years— especially where there is reason to believe that such research is more for purposes of destabilization or disinformation than for honest critique. Just getting the research apparatus in place will require millions of dollars and thousands of professionals and technicians. All in all it is a monumental task. The genius of the Clinard Report is that these few people did as much as they have with as little as they have had to work with in the conditions in which they found themselves. One wonders what they could achieve had they the funds allocated to one F-16, Mx missile or, perhaps, the financial backing of the drug lobby in Washington. Disclosure laws of the appropriate sort would also have been useful.

Notes

1. Marshall Clinard, et al. (1979), *Illegal Corporate Behavior*, Washington, D.C.: U.S. Department of Justice.
2. See the *Yale Law Review* (1961), "Notes and comments: corporate crime 71 (December): 280–306; and M.B. Clinard and Richard Quinney (1973), "Corporate criminal behavior," Chap. 8 in Clinard and Quinney (eds.), *Criminal Behavior Systems*, New York: Holt, Rinehart and Winston, Inc.
3. E.H. Sutherland (1949), *White Collar Crime*, New York: Holt, Rinehart, and Winston, Inc.
4. Richard Weiner (1980), *The State in Capitalist Society*, Red Feather: The Red Feather Institute.
5. T.R. Young (1978), *Crime and Capitalism*, Red Feather: The Red Feather Institute.
6. J. De Castro (1976), *The Geopolitics of Hunger*, New York: Monthly Review Press.
7. *Mother Jones*, Nov., 1979, pp. 13 ff.
8. Orlando Letelier (1979), *Economic Freedom and Political Repression*, Red Feather: The Red Feather Institute.
9. M.B. Clinard, et al. (1979), op. cit., pp. 83, 85, 93, 96.
10. Ibid., p. xxv.
11. Shirley Cereseto (1979), *Critical Dimensions in Development Theory: A Test of Four Inequality Models*, Red Feather: The Red Feather Institute.
12. Clinard et al., p. xix.
13. Ibid., p. xv.
14. Ibid., p. xix.
15. Young, op. cit.
16. Clinard, et al., op. cit., p. xix.
17. Ibid., p. 171.
18. Ibid., p. 214.
19. Clinard, et al., op. cit., p. 22.
20. Young, op. cit.
21. C.B.S., 60 Minutes, 16 Dec. 1979.
22. De Castro, op.cit.
23. Such an effort is made in Young, op. cit.
24. These postulates are more closely examined in Young, Ibid.

Seeking Refuge in a Desert: The Sanctuary Movement
David Quammen

The Bedouin of the Arabian desert has a name for it: *dakhala*. A man in flight for his life can rush into the tent of another man, claim the privilege of *dakhala*, and know he will be protected by his reluctant host. The custom is sacred among nomadic Arabs. A man who provides *dakhala* lives by the rules of honor, at whatever cost to himself. He is recognized as upholding a higher law—higher than kinship, higher even than vengeance—that the desert itself has helped shape. The desert itself, yes: *dakhala* is in some measure an answer to the imperatives of landscape, a tool of wilderness survival, a hedge against heat and desolation and thirst. A fugitive in the desert can expect one of two fates: lonely death on the sands, or else *dakhala*.

In the desert of southern Arizona, today, the equivalent word is *sanctuary*. And in Arizona, today, it is a felony.

One May 1 of this year, a federal jury in Tucson convicted eight persons of violating U.S. immigration laws. Among those convicted were two Catholic priests, a granite-jawed nun, and a Presbyterian minister. Six of the defendants were found guilty of conspiring to smuggle illegal aliens into the United States; two were convicted of concealing, harboring, and transporting an illegal alien. (Three other defendants were found not guilty.) The aliens in question were Salvadorans and Guatemalans who had been displaced by the murderous chaos in their homelands, people who had come north seeking refuge. The defendants faced up to five years in prison for each of the charges against them.

The charges had resulted from an elaborate nine-month-long undercover investigation by the Justice Department called Operation Sojourner. As part of the investigation, informants working for the Immigration and Naturalization Service (INS)—which falls under the jurisdiction of the Justice Department—wore concealed tape recorders into some of the humblest church halls in the country, including a number in southern Arizona. The government eventually built its case on the more than fifty hours of tape these informants collected.

But the investigation in a sense had always been moot, for the defendants were

---

blunt about their activities. Many of them had freely admitted to journalists and anybody else who cared to listen that they were harboring Salvadorans and Guate-malans; that, yes, these Salvadorans and Guatemalans had entered the United States surreptitiously. They freely admitted that they had sought to conceal these people and protect them from deportation. The proper question, they said, was *why*. The issue, they said, was whether these particular Central Americans were "il-legal aliens" at all. Were they not in fact legitimate refugees? Did the laws of the United States forbid the harboring of such people, or mandate it?

The judge in Tucson saw things very differently, classifying all argument around these issues as inadmissible. Such words as *torture* and *death squads* were, in the courtroom, taboo. No one mentioned *dakhala*.

The trial began on October 22, 1985, and dragged on for six months; to the re-porters who covered it, to the public who followed it, it was "the Sanctuary trial." It wasn't the first such trial (two church workers in south Texas were convicted in 1985 for similar activities), and it certainly won't be the last. It was a bellwether prosecution directed against several people perceived as the founders and guiding figures of a national movement called, simply, Sanctuary. This movement began five years ago with a decision by a small Presbyterian congregation on the south side of Tucson to harbor Central American refugees. More than 300 Quaker meet-ings, Roman Catholic parishes, Protestant congregations, and synagogues are now involved—perhaps as many as 50,000 citizens. They are avowedly determined to prevent Salvadoran and Guatemalan refugees from being deported back home, where they may face imprisonment, torture, and death. The Political Asylum Proj-ect of the American Civil Liberties Union has matched the names of fifty-two refu-gees who were denied entry into the United States with the names of fifty-two people whose deaths were reported in El Salvador.

Since 1980, 500,000 Salvadorans and more than 80,000 Guatemalans have fled their countries and come to the United States. Most arrive at our southwestern border without papers and manage, by this or that maneuver, to get across. The total number of these desperate people is minuscule compared with the steady flow of undocumented Mexicans, but large enough to constitute a controversial phenomenon. Why do the Central Americans come north? According to one view (the one offered axiomatically by officials at the State Department and the INS), they are "economic migrants." In other words, they are enterprising job-seekers, no different from the Mexicans. By another view (that of Sanctuary activists), many Salvadorans and Guatemalans are "political refugees" from the war zones of Central America, and are entitled by U.S. law—not to mention the 1949 Geneva Conventions, or American tradition as inscribed on the base of the Statue of Liberty—to at least temporary protection in this country. Specifically, the Refugee Act of 1980, often cited by Sanctuary activists, defines a "refugee" as any person who is "unable or unwilling to avail himself or herself of the protection of [his or her own country] because of persecution or a well-founded fear of persecution on account of race, religion, nationality, membership in a particular social group, or political opinion. . . ." Several of those conditions do seem to fit most of the Central Americans who come north. The act also stipulates ways in which a refugee may be protected, one of which is to grant him or her political asylum.

For one reason or another, political asylum is not granted to the majority of Salvadorans and Guatemalans who apply for it. From January 1985 through August of this year, 723 Guatemalans applied for asylum; during this period, asylum was granted to seven Guatemalans. The numbers for Salvadorans are similarly gloomy: 3,586 applications made, 209 applications granted. These figures contrast sharply with those compiled for Afghans and Poles seeking asylum during this eighteen-month period (Afghans: 336 applications, 168 granted; Poles: 1,783 applications, 857 granted). The pattern within these statistics is obvious: if you flee to the United States from a Soviet-backed regime in disfavor with Washington, your chances of being officially welcomed are much greater than if you flee from one of Washington's clients. Denied almost any chance of asylum, denied exemption from deportation, Salvadorans and Guatemalans have no legal protection in the one country on earth that prides itself most stentorianly on being a haven for refugees.

So they must get over the border by stealth. Some pass through an official port of entry, bluffing fearfully with false or borrowed papers, masquerading as U.S. citizens or day-labor Mexicans. Others make the taxing and risky hike through the desert, trekking across ragged mountains and gulches and through thorn vegetation, entering the United States wherever the international fence is unwatched. Some of these hikers have been arrested, some have passed over safely, some have died gruesomely. The desert, which often seems beautiful and sometimes seems benign, can be unforgiving of inexperience and miscalculation. But it comes as a lesson of desert cultures (and not just that of the Bedouins) that where physical ecology is so harsh, so implacable, moral ecology must somehow compensate. That's what happened in southern Arizona. The Sanctuary movement, in great degree, and from the start, presented itself as an answer to the imperatives of landscape.

Of the four ecologically distinct deserts covering portions of North America—the Mohave, the Sonoran, the Great Basin, and the Chihuahuan—the Sonoran desert, in which Tucson lies, is the most deceptive. It does not appear bleak. Many sensible witnesses consider it gorgeously scenic. Despite being prodigiously dry (less than two inches of rain yearly, in some parts) and prodigiously hot (often around 120 degrees Fahrenheit), it supports more different species of plants and animals than any other North American desert. Most famously recognizable is the giant columnar cactus, the saguaro. The Sonoran desert is also home to the Gila monster, the tarantula, a profusion of black widow spiders, thirteen species of rattlesnake, almost two dozen species of scorpion, and a healthy population of vultures, which feast on fatalities. The Sonoran stretches over more than 120,000 square miles, from below Guaymas on the west coast of Mexico up to Needles, California, and from east of Tucson to the far side of the Baja peninsula, embracing a long section of the border between Mexico and the United States. With its mountains, its broad riverbeds (usually dry), and its saline basins, it is a landscape of extremity and denial: there are flash floods and drought, heat at midday that can shatter a rock, nights that can freeze a man. For most of the year, the Sonoran is a searing and inhospitable wilderness.

That's what it was when twenty-six Salvadoran refugees tried to cross, back in early July of 1980. Those who survived, themselves very near death, were rescued by the Border Patrol. In a gulch not far from a paved road, about twenty miles north of the Mexican border town of Sonoyta, members of the patrol found a trail of discarded clothing and half-naked corpses, and then thirteen delirious, heat-sick people, some of whom had smeared their faces with toothpaste or makeup as a last desperate measure against the sun. It had been a party of middle-class urban Salvadorans, women in high-heeled shoes, men carrying suitcases. They had left El Salvador in the care of two "coyotes"—mercenary smugglers—and made the long trip across Mexico by bus; just south of the U.S. border, on a bleak stretch of desert, they were told to start walking. Among their many mistakes, they had failed to bring enough water. Few canteens were found with the debris—not even empty ones. Eventually, according to reports, they had been reduced to drinking cologne, aftershave lotion, and their own urine. By one account, each of them had paid $1,200 for the privilege of being taken north. Thirteen of them died.

The survivors were brought to a Tucson hospital, and several churches were eventually asked to help them with housing and food. One of those churches was Southside Presbyterian, a small congregation in the barrio. Southside is an aberration, conforming badly to the stereotype of comfortable middle-class Presbyterianism. A little adobe building with a chain-pull bell and one saguaro out front, the church fills up on Sunday mornings with people of many complexions, people in shirtsleeves and with work-calloused hands. The Reverend John Fife, another aberration, is the minister. A tall, forty-six-year-old Anglo, gaunt and bearded and favoring denims and cowboy boots when not in his vestments, Fife came out to the desert from a mean-streets urban ministry in Ohio, never dreaming he would achieve distinction as a convicted felon. In July of 1980, he was concerned mainly with his duties as pastor of a poor congregation of Hispanics and blacks and Anglos and Indians. He could not then have placed El Salvador on a map. The deaths of those thirteen Salvadorans in the desert changed his world.

"*That* engaged my attention," he told me several years ago, the first time I spoke with him. "The fact that people were willing to risk that kind of venture, coming across our border." Fife talked to the survivors, and heard "some incredible stories about El Salvador. I had assumed that people were coming across from Central America for the same reason that people were coming across our border from Mexico. It was hard in the villages, they were poor. But these folk from Salvador were telling a *different* set of stories. They were talking about death squads, and about torture, and about the kind of terrorism and violence that we now know about."

John Fife heard the stories and was moved to act. Others in Tucson began to act too. At first their efforts were modest and quiet: providing food and shelter to refugees who managed to reach Tucson, helping them pass northward to other cities along a sort of underground railroad, raising money to bond out those who had been caught by the INS, assisting with asylum applications, conducting a weekly prayer vigil. The vigil is still held each Thursday at rush hour outside the federal building, where the INS offices are located. The federal building was chosen because it is the policies of the INS that are responsible for the wholesale rejection of asylum petitions from Salvadorans and Guatemalans, and, worse, the deportation of unsuccessful applicants. Deportation is especially terrifying to anyone who has already fled the death squads. The very act of having gone north may be counted a sign of subversive inclination, or at least of disloyalty, and any deportee who lands at the San Salvador or Guatemala City airport is marked and vulnerable.

It was the knowledge that the refugees might meet this fate that led John Fife and members of his church to decide that more drastic action was required. "We were really in despair at that point," Fife said. "We had tried the legal defense thing. We had tried the underground smuggling thing. And as far as we could see, it wasn't going to change anything. People in *Tucson* didn't even know there were refugees here, let alone [people in] the rest of the United States. The government was continuing to deport people at a rate of twenty-five or thirty a day. All of the legal defense efforts had managed to save a few people. The underground was saving a few more people. Obviously we could keep that up for the next ten years and save a few hundred people, and lose thousands. *Really*—we were trying to say—*what can we do?* And the idea of Sanctuary emerged."

Within the Judeo-Christian tradition, the concept of sanctuary dates back at least to that record of a tribe of desert-dwelling nomads, the Book of Exodus: "Then I will appoint thee a place whither he shall flee." It passed down through Roman and English law and eventually found embodiment, altered in shape but not in spirit, in the original underground railroad, which helped slaves escape northward despite the passage in 1850 of the Fugitive Slave Act, making it illegal to shield or abet runaway blacks. Many churches in the North played a crucial role in that movement.

As reincarnated in Tucson today, the spirit of sanctuary differs from its American precedent chiefly in being determinedly *public*. Fife and his congregation not only decided to harbor Central American refugees; they decided to do it openly. On March 24, 1982, John Fife announced at a press conference that Southside Presbyterian Church, joined by a handful of congregations in such cities as Los Angeles, Berkeley, and Washington, D.C., would henceforth be providing sanctuary to undocumented Central American aliens, in some cases allowing them to live on church property or in the churches themselves. Sanctuary was pledging itself to support and defend the refugees, and daring the Justice Department to make arrests.

What was the point of such provocation? "The whole function of *public* sanctuary," John Fife explained to me, "is to encourage as many churches—and people—as possible in the United States to have to deal with this moral, legal problem. To make a decision and then communicate it to the legislative bodies. And to the Administration. We need to engage the attention of as many people as we can possibly reach."

Many of the refugees who came to Tucson were brought up through the desert by a man named Jim Corbett. Corbett, who stood trial with John Fife, was acquitted thanks to an absence of evidence against him: because Corbett tended to work alone, the prosecution's star witness, Jesús Cruz—he's one of the men who infiltrated the movement in Tucson for the INS—had little to say about him. (Corbett has talked openly about smuggling refugees, but like Fife and the other defendants, he maintains that his acts are in compliance with U.S. law.)

Jim Corbett, a Quaker, is fifty-three years old. He has a degree in philosophy from Harvard, and before arthritis slowed him down he had ranched cattle in southern Arizona for twenty years. He knows the Sonoran desert well. Beginning in 1981 and until his face became too easily recognized by INS agents, Corbett guided refugees across the border. Sometimes he cadged identity papers and took people through an official port of entry, a route precarious but physically undemanding. More often, if the refugees seemed hardy, he walked the desert with them. Corbett is familiar with the terrain and capable of using it to advantage: following the natural warps of the land, dodging Border Patrol planes and eluding INS agents in four-wheel-drive vehicles and on horseback, laying up at night without a fire. By his own estimate, he has guided 1,000 refugees across the border.

Carmen Duarte of the *Arizona Daily Star* and a photographer went along with Corbett on a crossing he led in the summer of 1984. He was guiding just one refugee, a Guatemalan woman who seemed too harrowed by past ordeals to try bluffing her way past uniformed men at a port of entry. The woman's husband had been taken from their home by armed strangers (evidently because of his role in a labor union) and never seen again. She had searched for his body at a dump, among the mutilated corpses of other missing persons, but her search was inconclusive. She was warned not to report the kidnapping. And then strangers began to follow *her.* So she fled to Mexico City, there to be arrested and then raped by immigration officers, she said, before being deported by bus back to Guatemala.

She made her way to Mexico City again. This time she made contact with the Sanctuary network there, and was put in touch with Corbett. He listened to her story, understood her anguish, but warned her she would face hardships in the United States as well. Yes, he would guide her across.

He first helped her travel north to the border town of Nogales, just an hour from Tucson. Then, at a remote point along a road on the Mexican side of the border, Corbett, the woman, and the two journalists began walking. They moved slowly over sand flats and ledges of rock, taking what cover they could from the mesquite and paloverde. For the first half-hour they were precariously exposed, still within view from the road. At the sound of every passing car they scrambled for cover. Then once again they walked. And after only an hour they climbed over a fence—not a very formidable barrier, just five strands of taut barbed wire—and stepped down into U.S. territory.

That was the easy part. There was still more hiking to do. On a sunny July day in the border zone, the heat would have been fearsome and the danger of being seen by fly-over patrols would have been great; fortunately, this particular afternoon was overcast. Four miles along through the winding gulches, they stopped for the night. The woman's feet were blistered. There was a dinner of raisins and tuna and broken crackers, and then a cold night without blankets or sleeping bags. In the morning they hiked on, amid yucca and manzanita and skittering lizards, and then climbed a steep slope out of the canyon; finally they climbed down a ravine to the rendezvous point, where a car waited with water and food. By that evening, Corbett had brought the Guatemalan woman into Tucson.

Like John Fife, but in very different ways, Jim Corbett is an anomaly. Though active in a largely church-based movement, he is firmly (if politely) anti-clerical. He is an intellectual, a complex thinker and a prolific writer, who has chosen to spend much of his life looking after cattle and sheep. And the path that brought him to his work with Sanctuary is nothing if not peculiar.

Most members of the movement trace their concept of sanctuary back to Roman law, medieval canon law, English common law, or the teachings of Exodus, Numbers, and Isaiah. When Jim Corbett discusses his ideas about sanctuary, he is more apt to cite Buddhist notions of stillness, the Taoist philosopher Chuang Tzu, the anthropology of pastoral nomads in Tibet, and the practical details of goat husbandry. The nuns and priests, ministers and rabbis who play such active and conspicuous roles in the movement have come out of the church and the temple, out of missionary orders and social-action ministries. Jim Corbett has come, literally, out of the desert.

For almost two decades he has been thinking and writing about the spiritual dimensions of wilderness. The Buddhist, Hindu, and Taoist traditions all tell of the person who goes off alone into the wilderness (often a desert wilderness) for some stretch of time in order to strip away those aspects of misguided worldly concern that Corbett calls "the social busyness." The Hebrews' Sinai sojourn as described in Exodus served a similar purpose, he says, though in that case it was not a lone individual but an entire community that sought to purge itself. During the early 1970s, Corbett himself began to experiment with this kind of sojourn. He went out into the desert for long periods, taking with him only a sleeping bag and gear essential for survival; he did not take any food. Carrying food into this landscape was unnecessary, he believed. Instead, he herded along a few goats.

Corbett later completed a book-length (but still unpublished) manuscript titled *Goatwalking*. In it he distills his wealth of ranching and backcountry knowledge, knowledge flavored by his philosophic and political ideas. *Goatwalking* is an intriguing document, the quiet manifesto of a man who combines in himself some of the more appealing aspects of Thoreau, Thomas Merton, and Emiliano Zapata. It is a guidebook to revolutionary simplicity and wild-land dairying. Corbett, with his concept of goatwalking, has aligned himself with the traditional nomadic pastoralists—of ancient Sinai and twentieth-century Tibet. Like them, he has come to realize that "livestock could provide the life-support and security associated with [planted crops] while also providing the mobility necessary to escape the state."

In Corbett's usage *goatwalking* is a potent term. At the literal level it has to do with tending and traveling with half-wild grazing animals, a pastoral nomadism practiced in a wilderness landscape outside the purview of—but within the actual boundaries of—the modern industrial state. The goats are allowed to go feral; the goatwalker goes feral along with them, living on their milk and on wild plants. On a political level, Corbett recommends this goatwalking life as "the cimarron alternative." The Spanish word *cimarrón* has entered our language with two definitions, and Corbett intends them both: it means "feral animal" as well as "runaway slave."

The cimarron alternative in this sense is the act of stepping beyond societal constraints and into a state of moral freedom. The goatwalker is a runaway slave who knows how to live off the land. Naturally, therefore, he will have greater sympathy than most for his fellow cimarrons. This may all sound quixotic or woolly to you or me. But Jim Corbett happens to be the sort of stubborn Quaker moralist who turns quixotic notions into acts. *Goatwalking* was written in the 1970s, several years before Corbett met his first Salvadoran refugee. But when the need arose for a guide to lead terrified fugitives through the harsh desert and across the border, circumventing the armed minions of national policy (as distinct from law), he was ready.

The six-month-long trial of the Sanctuary defendants was an expensive prosecution, with its full share of legal technicalities and its moments of true drama and melodrama. But in the end, the proceedings were perhaps more notable for what did *not* happen than for what did. Right before the trial began, Federal District Court Judge Earl H. Carroll granted government motions to bar any testimony about human-rights abuses and death-squad killings in Guatemala and El Salvador; any testimony concerning the defendants' motivation or religious beliefs; and any testimony related to the defendants' understanding of U.S. immigration laws. Moreover, the defendants were forbidden to present arguments that those refugees they stood accused of helping were in danger of losing their lives if they were forced to return to their countries. The list of exclusions covered virtually every defense that could have been presented by the defendants' attorneys.

The trial went ahead anyway, of course, and there were other significant omissions. James Rayburn, the INS investigator who had guided the undercover operation, was never called by the prosecution to testify. The ninety-one tapes recorded during the Sanctuary investigation were edited down to ten minutes of carefully selected excerpts, and then played for the jurors. (The defense attorneys sought permission to play the tapes in their entirety, believing the defendants' activities would seem anything but criminal if understood in context. But the judge supported the prosecutor's wish to keep the jury ignorant of any such context.) Three unindicted Sanctuary workers and one refugee refused to testify for the prosecution, despite having been subpoenaed; they were held in contempt and sentenced to house arrest until the trial ended. Of the refugees who *did* testify, seemingly under duress, the prosecutor complained that their memories were selective; they more readily recollected the deaths of members of their families, the terror and violence they had fled, than whatever incriminating words had been uttered, say, by John Fife.

The defendants themselves did not testify. In the end, they presented no formal defense at all. On Friday morning, March 14, in the twenty-first week of the trial, with the prosecution having rested its case and the Sanctuary lawyers scheduled to begin calling witnesses, each of those lawyers stood up in turn and announced that the defense, too, rested its case. This might have been a strategic move: if the defendants were not permitted to mention immigration law or their religious beliefs or anything else they considered significant, what value was there in giving the prosecution a chance to cross-examine them? But it was also surely a protest, a way of asserting that the trial itself was in fact a sham.

Insofar as it was a strategy, the strategy failed. On May 1, after more than sixty hours of deliberation, the jury brought in its guilty verdict.

Late one evening near the end of the trial, John Fife sat in the living room of his Tucson home, exhausted from six months of courtroom tension, nursing a beer and telling me about the large place in his Presbyterian heart held by the spiritual traditions of the Papago Indians. It might sound as though he was digressing, but he was not.

What the Bedouins are to the Arabian desert, the Papago are to the unsparing terrain that is southwestern Arizona. They are also known, to themselves and others, as the Desert People. The area they have traditionally occupied, and within which their reservation now lies, is one of the most arid and least hospitable parts of the Sonoran—a landscape of flat valleys cobbled with windblown pebbles, sharp ridges that curl around like the walls of a labyrinth, arroyos and washes carved by torrential runoff and opening out blankly into dry basins, where nothing much grows except creosote bush. Drought is followed by flood, in Papago country, then again by drought; the desert blooms, briefly, then withers. The cycle of life for all living creatures entails unpredictable but ineluctable swings between extremes of abundance and dearth. Over the centuries, the Papago adapted themselves to this cycle.

One of their adaptations was an ethic of radical hospitality. Under the pressures of the landscape, a culture evolved in which great premium was placed on generosity, gift-giving of food and clothing, and the sharing of surplus whenever there was any surplus. Today we might see the Papagos as hopelessly improvident. But in fact they are quite provident. The limitless gift-giving is a survival strategy.

That Papago ethos informs the spirit of Southside Presbyterian Church, which was founded eighty years ago as a Papago mission, in a Tucson ghetto then known as "Papagoville." It also goes far to explain the presence in Tucson of John Fife himself.

Twenty years ago, fresh out of his first year at a seminary in Pittsburgh, Fife spent a summer on the Papago reservation; there, he fell in love with the people and the desert and the strange dynamic between the two. When the pastorship of the church in Tucson opened up six years later, he jumped for it.

"I've heard their stories," Fife told me. "We've spent a lot of time talking about traditions. I climb their sacred mountain, Baboquivari, every year. Try to get to I'itoi's cave." I'itoi is the chief Papago deity, believed to dwell at the physical center of their lands, in a cave on the steep slope of Baboquivari. "I've been on that mountain when Papago folk had visions," Fife said. "I didn't see anything—but they did." As we were talking, I noticed on the wall behind him a characteristic piece of Papago coiled basketry, shallow and circular, woven from tan and black fibers in the design of a concentric maze. At the entrance to the maze stood a small figure woven in black, recognizably human. The large silver buckle on Fife's belt bore the same pattern. The design is called I'itoi Ki, and it has a strong resonance for the Papago. Fife explained that the pattern commemorates the time when I'itoi escaped from his enemies by leading them into such a maze.

The design is also understood allegorically. "The maze represents all the complexities and dead ends of life," Fife said. In the course of a lifetime, a person must move through all those complexities, all those tribulations and misleading paths, toward the center of the maze, at which waits safety, fulfillment, Baboquivari. I was intrigued by the maze. Clearly it also represents the desert.

The sentencing of John Fife and the seven other defendants took place in Tucson on July 1 and 2. Each of them was put on probation, ranging from three to five years; one of the conditions of the probation is that they not bring in or harbor any more aliens. Even though the defendants were not sent to prison, they plan to appeal their convictions.

If it all seems a little anticlimactic, perhaps it is because the real drama has always been elsewhere—worlds away, in Central America. There, people are still being taken from their homes and killed. The Tucson defendants never forgot that, and so they were relieved at the relative leniency of their sentences, but not jubilant. There is no leniency and no suspension of sentence, after all, for those Salvadorans and Guatemalans sought by death squads, or for those who face deportation.

I did not intend this to be a rumination on the ecology and anthropology of arid lands. The moral ecology of the United States is what concerns me. Salvadorans and Guatemalans continue to be deported under the pretense that they are "economic migrants," and innocent people, America's rejects, continue to be abducted and tortured and murdered. Each of us shares responsibility with our government for those deportations. Some will try to believe that this country, with its stumbling economy, cannot afford to take in more refugees. Others will simply not want to be reminded about another group of abused, needy people. Most of us would prefer to forget the whole subject. The thing we all need to remember is the same thing that John Fife and Jim Corbett have learned: sometimes hospitality is a matter of life and death.

Reagan's Nicaraguan Policy: A Case Study of Political Deviance and Crime

Donald R. Pfost

The argument to be developed in this article is straightforward: the policies of the Reagan administration toward Nicaragua violate both international and domestic law and are, therefore, political crimes. The article will focus on documenting representative instances of these criminal acts and the laws violated. In addition, it will identify and critically analyze components of the ideology which serves to justify and mystify these crimes. Finally, it will place the criminal policies of the Reagan administration in broader context and interpret them as part of a historical pattern of interventionism in Central America which has had the aim of protecting U.S. economic and political interests in the region.

Criminologists disagree sharply over what "political crime" is. According to some analysts, such as Turk (1982: 1984) and Georges-Abeyie (1980), the concept of political crime should be restricted basically to acts by subordinate groups which violate existing laws and which are perceived by political authorities as challenging existing relationships of power. While acknowledging that political authorities do at times violate the law, as in the case of political repression, Turk suggests that these acts be treated as "political policing" or "conventional politics," rather than as "political crime" (1982: 34–35). This position has interesting ideological implications, especially when applied to international relations. To suggest, for example, that U.S. intervention in Nicaragua, Chile, and Guatemala represents "political policing" implies, among other things, that such actions are legitimate, a position which stands in contradiction to basic principles of international law.

A second approach, and the one followed in this article, takes a broader view of "political crime." Thus, according to Quinney (1975: 147–161), Roebuck and Weeber (1978), and Simon and Eitzen (1986: 199–225), political crime includes not only violations of the law which are essentially challenges to political authority by subordinate groups, but also those acts by government which violate domestic and international laws, as well as those acts by political authorities which are "deviant" in the sense of causing social injury, whether or not they are illegal as de-

Source: Donald R. Pfost, "Reagan's Nicaraguan Policy: A Case Study of Political Deviance and Crime," *Crime and Social Justice*, Nos. 27–28 (1987), pp. 66–83. Reprinted by permission from *Crime and Social Justice*, P. O. Box 40601, San Francisco, CA 94140.

fined by government. A criminology which includes, rather than excludes, such acts as objects of inquiry encourages the analysis of patterns of behavior, relationships of power and social processes which are of critical theoretical and practical importance.

Background

On July 19, 1979, a revolutionary movement led by the Sandinista National Liberation Front (FSLN), overthrew the U.S.-backed Somoza regime in Nicaragua, ending a dictatorship that had been in power for over 40 years (Black, 1981; Walker, 1982). The FSLN embarked almost immediately on a program aimed at changing the basic social structure of Nicaragua. These changes included the Literacy Crusade which, in less than a year, reduced the rate of illiteracy from over 50% to less than 15%, earning Nicaragua the UNESCO Literacy Prize in 1980 (Brandt, 1985). Basic changes in health care reduced the infant mortality rate from 121 per 1,000 births in 1979 to 75 per 1,000 births in 1984, eliminated polio by 1982, produced a sharp reduction in the rate of infant deaths from diarrhea, and significantly increased the number of health facilities, such as hospitals, health centers, and health posts. These changes earned Nicaragua the 1982 UNICEF/World Health Organization prize for the Third World Country having made the greatest improvement in health (USOCA, 1985). Agricultural reforms were instituted. Designed to increase food production, these reforms included policies that altered prerevolutionary patterns of land ownership through land redistribution and the formation of both private and state-owned cooperatives (Collins, 1985).

Even before the overthrow of Somoza, the U.S. attempted to shape the outcome of the revolution in Nicaragua. Apparently concerned about the "Marxist" leanings of some of the FSLN leaders, the Carter administration attempted to engineer an outcome that would have seen a more moderate, pro-U.S. leadership installed in post-Somoza Nicaragua, along with the retention of the hated National Guard (LeoGrande, 1982).

When the Reagan administration took office in 1981, it began almost immediately—at least as early as March, 1981 (see Oberdorfer, 1983)—to pursue policies aimed at overthrowing the Sandinista regime. While the full details may never be known, the following are well-documented examples of what these policies have entailed and what results they have produced.

The CIA began conducting a covert war against the Nicaraguan government as early as March 1981, under President Reagan's authorization (Oberdorfer, 1983). In November 1981, President Reagan authorized $19.5 million to fund CIA covert activities against Nicaragua. The administration's plan initially directed the CIA to organize a paramilitary force of 500, to be expanded later, that would be trained to destroy vital targets in Nicaragua, such as power plants and bridges, in an effort to disrupt the economy and divert the attention and resources of the government. The ostensible purpose of these covert operations was the interdiction of the flow of arms between Nicaragua and guerrillas in El Salvador (Tyler and Woodward, 1982).

Between 1981–1983, an estimated $80 million was channeled to the *contras* by the CIA (Brinkley, 1985); $24 million was authorized in 1984 (Stone, 1984: 9); on June 12, 1985, Congress approved $27 million in "humanitarian" aid to the *contras*; finally, in October 1986, Congress approved an administration request for another $100 million in aid to the *contras*.

In October 1983, the CIA set fire to oil storage tanks at Corinto, destroying 1.6 million gallons of oil; in February and March of 1984, the CIA mined the Nicaraguan ports of El Bluff and Corinto (Marcus, 1985: xvi–xvii).

On October 17, 1984, *The New York Times* reported that the CIA had published and distributed to the *contras* a manual on *Psychological Operations in Guerrilla Warfare*, which, *inter alia*, advocated political assassinations of Sandinista leaders to help overthrow the Nicaraguan government.

In May 1983, the U.S. unilaterally and without prior negotiations with Nicaragua, reduced Nicaragua's annual import quota of sugar from 58,000 to 6,000 tons (Dixon and Jonas, 1985: 52). On May 1, 1985, President Reagan declared a "national emergency" with respect to Nicaragua and imposed an embargo, which included a ban on Nicaraguan ships and air carriers from entering the U.S. (Weinraub, 1985).

During the period 1982–1984, the U.S. conducted military maneuvers in the region, including "Big Pine" I and II, "Granadero I," and "Ocean Venture '84." On October 31, 1984, U.S. SR–71 spy planes overflew Managua, causing repeated sonic booms (Marcus, 1985: xv–xviii).

Beginning in October 1986, a series of events revealed an illegal scheme by the Reagan administration to provide financial and military aid to the *contras*. On October 5, a plane carrying arms to *contra* forces was shot down inside Nicaragua by Sandinista forces. One crew member, Eugene Hasenfus, survived. Joint efforts by the CIA and private groups to aid the *contras* were uncovered (LeMoyne, 1986b, 1986c; Engelberg, 1986).

In late November, a conspiracy to aid the *contras* by diverting profits from the sale of arms to Iran began to unravel. Full details are not available at this writing, but some facts are well established. The diversion of funds, estimated to be between $10 and $30 million, involved officials of the CIA and National Security Council (Weinraub, 1986). The plan appears to have had at least the tacit support of President Reagan. Private groups with ties to the White House were involved (Apple, 1986b; LeMoyne, 1986a; Butterfield, 1986). Funds from the sale of arms may have been used during the 1986 congressional elections to finance smear campaigns against candidates opposed to U.S. aid to the *contras* (Apple, 1986a). Finally, a number of break-ins at the offices of groups opposed to U.S. intervention in Nicaragua suggested domestic spying by U.S. intelligence agencies (Glickman, 1986; Schneider, 1986).

These and other policies of the Reagan administration, some of which will be described more fully below, began to inflict heavy costs in terms of both human suffering and economic loss in Nicaragua.

Officials of the Nicaraguan government have reported that between 1982 and

1984, there were 1,877 casualties of the *contra* war. Of this total, 747 were killed, 125 wounded, and 1,015 kidnapped. Further, during this same period, the contras killed 23 primary school teachers and 135 volunteer adult education teachers, destroyed 15 rural schools, and forced the closing of 138 primary schools and 647 adult educational centers (Marcus, 1985: 296). By 1984 the *contra* war had inflicted more than 7,000 casualties, including deaths and injuries of children, mothers, youth, and the elderly, as well as military personnel (Marcus, 1985: 356). A total of 1,019 Sandinista soldiers were killed and another 1,798 wounded during 1986 (Kinzer, 1987). In relative terms, the total number of casualties is equivalent to more than three times the number of U.S. losses in the Vietnam War (Marcus, 1985: 356). Moreover, the estimated economic loss from *contra* attacks on cooperatives, health centers, daycare centers, and schools between 1981 and 1984 totaled $237 million (Marcus, 1985: 356); finally, in its case before the International Court of Justice, Nicaragua's claims against the U.S. for total damages from the war are expected to exceed $1 billion (Yerkey, 1986; Marshall, 1986).

Brody (1985) investigated reported incidents of *contra* terrorism, gathering testimony from victims and eye witnesses of attacks that had occurred throughout northern and north central Nicaragua. Sworn affidavits were obtained from the victims and witnesses to produce evidence that would be legally sufficient in a court of law. Brody concluded that the incidents investigated by this fact-finding team, while not exhaustive, revealed a distinct pattern, indicating that *contra* attacks often included:

- Attacks on purely civilian targets resulting in the killing of unarmed men, women, children, and the elderly;
- Premeditated acts of brutality including rape, beatings, mutilation, and torture;
- Individual and mass kidnappings of civilians, particularly in the northern Atlantic Coast region for the purpose of forced recruitment into the *contra* forces and the creation of a hostage refugee population in Honduras;
- Assaults on economic and social targets such as farms, cooperatives, food storage facilities, and health centers, including a particular effort to disrupt the coffee harvests through attacks on coffee cooperatives and on vehicles carrying volunteer coffee harvesters;
- Intimidation of civilians who participate or cooperate in government or community programs, such as distribution of subsidized food products, rural cooperatives, education, and the local self-defense militia; and
- Kidnapping, intimidation, and even murder of religious leaders who support the government, including priests and clergy-trained lay pastors (Brody, 1985: 21–22).

Although President Reagan attempted to discredit this report in a speech on April 15, 1985 (see *New York Times*, April 16, 1985), independent verifications conducted by Americas Watch, other human rights organizations, and *The New York Times* have confirmed the findings of the Brody report.

Health care has sustained heavy human and economic losses from the U.S.-backed *contra* war. For example, as of April 1984, at least 69 health-care providers, including doctors, nurses, technicians, and rural health volunteers had been killed by the *contras*, and 59 rural health outposts, 3 health centers, and 1 hospital had been destroyed or forced to close. The economic cost of the war in 1984 alone has been estimated at $255 million, which could have built approximately 8,000 rural health outposts, 196 health centers, or 25 hospitals of 200 bed capacity (USOCA, 1985: 3–4).

These are but a few of the facts detailing features of the policies of the Reagan administration toward Nicaragua. In what follows, an attempt will be made to demonstrate that these and other actions constitute acts of political crime and deviance.

Violations of International Law

Treaties and Customary Law

The Charter of the United Nations is the major treaty governing international relations, and its cornerstone is the principle of nonintervention (Lieverman and Schneider, 1985: 910). Article 2 requires all member nations to act in accordance with certain principles, including the following:

3. All Members shall settle their international disputes by peaceful means in such a manner that international peace and security, and justice are not endangered.
4. All Members shall refrain in their international relations from the threat or use of force against the territorial integrity or political independence of any state, or in any other manner inconsistent with the purpose of the United Nations.

Article 33 states more specifically the requirements to settle peacefully all disputes:

1. The parties to any dispute, the continuance of which is likely to endanger the maintenance of international peace and security, shall, first of all, seek a solution by negotiation, inquiry, mediation, conciliation, arbitration, judicial settlement, resort to regional agencies or arrangements, or other peaceful means of their own choice.

Further, Article 39 of the Charter authorizes the Security Council to "determine the existence of any threat to the peace, breach of the peace, or act of aggression" (Chin, 1979: 1213).

Lieverman and Schneider (1985: 10–11) note that the only exception to the principles of peaceably settling disputes is found in Article 51, which recognizes the right of individual or collective self-defense in the event of an *armed attack* against a member nation, but only *until* the Security Council has taken measures necessary to maintain international peace and security. However, the right of self-defense is limited. The use of force in self-defense is lawful in the "event of instant and overwhelming necessity," and "acts taken in self-defense must be limited to defense itself and must not be transformed into reprisals or punitive sanctions" (*Ibid.*: 11).

In addition to principles of international conduct embodied in the Charter itself, the U.S. General Assembly over the years has adopted a number of resolutions which, though nonbinding on member nations, do, nevertheless, define norms of international behavior. Several of these are relevant in the context of current U.S. policy toward Nicaragua.

In 1965, the General Assembly adopted its "Declaration of the Inadmissibility of Intervention in the Domestic Affairs of States and the Protection of Their Independence and Sovereignty." This Declaration states that "no State has the right to intervene, directly or indirectly, for any reason whatsoever, in the internal or external affairs of any other State." The resolution expressly prohibits the use of "economic, political, or any other type of measure to coerce another State in order to obtain from it the subordination of the exercise of its sovereign rights or to secure from it advantages of any kind," as well as efforts to "organize, assist, foment, finance, incite or tolerate subversive, terrorist, or armed activities directed toward the violent overthrow of the regime of another State" (*Ibid.*: 11–12).

A 1974 General Assembly resolution defined aggression as "the use of armed force by a State against the sovereignty, territorial integrity, or political independence of another State." Acts of aggression were defined as including invasion, armed attack, the blockading of the ports or coasts of one nation by the armed forces of another, and the "sending by or on behalf of a State of armed bands, groups, irregulars, or mercenaries, which carry out acts of armed force against another State" (*Ibid.*: 12).

The Charter of the Organization of American States (OAS), to which the U.S. is a signatory, establishes a number of other principles, consistent with the Charter of the U.N., which are relevant in judging U.S. policies toward Nicaragua. Article 5 of the Charter sets forth the principles that "international law is the standard of conduct of States in their reciprocal relations," that the "American States condemn war of aggression," and that "controversies of an international character arising between two or more American States shall be settled by peaceful procedures" (Chin, 1979: 327–328).

The following articles of the OAS Charter are especially relevant in the context of U.S.–Nicaraguan relations (Chin, 1979: 330):

Article 15: No State or group of states has the right to intervene directly or indirectly, for any reason whatever in the internal or external affairs of any other state. The foregoing principle prohibits not only armed force but also any other form of interference or attempted threat against the personality of the State or against its political, economic, and cultural elements.

Article 16: No state may use or encourage the use of coercive measures of any economic or political character in order to force the sovereign will of another state and obtain from it advantages of any kind.

Article 17: The territory of a state is inviolable, it may not be the object, even temporarily, of military occupation or of other measures of force taken by another State, directly or indirectly, on any grounds whatever. No territorial acquisition or special advantages obtained either by force or by other means shall be recognized.

Article 18: The American States bind themselves in their international relations not to have recourse to the use of force, except in the case of self-defense in accordance with existing treaties or in fulfillment thereof.

The OAS Charter neither contradicts nor limits the provisions of the U.N. Charter with respect to peaceful settlement of disputes; instead, it is even more explicit in prohibiting intervention into the affairs of another nation in this hemisphere (Lieverman and Schneider, 1985: 14–15).

In addition to the U.N. and OAS Charters, at least two other treaties have a significant bearing on the legality of current U.S. policy toward Nicaragua. First, the Inter-American Treaty of Reciprocal Assistance, also known as the Rio Treaty, signed in 1947, requires the parties to refrain from the threat of the use of force in any manner inconsistent with the provision of the U.N. Charter or the rest of the treaty. Second, the Treaty of Friendship, Commerce and Navigation, a bilateral U.S.–Nicaraguan agreement signed in 1956, affirms the right of each nation to engage in business within the territory of the other country on a "most favored nation" basis, declares that there shall be freedom of commerce and navigation between the countries, and requires that any disputes to the treaty shall be submitted to the International Court of Justice (*Ibid.*: 15–16).

The customary law of international affairs, especially that which has evolved during this century, clearly and consistently protects the sovereignty of nation states from outside interference (*Ibid.*: 16–20). Legal principles established at the Nuremberg Trials are particularly noteworthy. The Charter of the Tribunal defined several categories of offenses, including "war crimes," "crimes against humanity," and "crimes against peace." The latter category essentially reaffirmed the accepted international prohibition against the use of war and aggression as instruments of policy. Included among "crimes of peace" were the "planning, preparation, initiation, or waging of wars of aggression, or a war in violation of international treaties, agreements or assurances, or participation in a common plan or conspiracy for the accomplishment of any of the foregoing." The Nuremberg Tribunal took the position that aggressive war constituted a crime under international law, a principle that was subsequently affirmed unanimously by the U.N. General Assembly.

A number of hemispheric treaties and conventions also condemn the use of aggression and the threat of force as an instrument of policy and call for peaceful solutions to disputes between nations states. These include the following: the Sixth Pan-American Conference, 1928; the Seventh International Conference of American States, 1933; the Anti-War Treaty on Non-Aggression and Conciliation, 1933;

and, the Inter-American Conference for the Maintenance of Peace, 1936. All of these conventions and treaties were signed by the U.S., as well as by Nicaragua, Honduras, Guatemala, and El Salvador (*Ibid.*: 20–22).

Thus, taken together, the U.N. and OAS charters, as well as the aforementioned conventions and treaties, establish the related doctrine that war is prohibited as a means of settling international disputes, that all nations are required to use peaceful means of settling disputes, and that a nation may not intervene, directly or indirectly, into the affairs of another nation.

Economic Warfare

The General Agreement on Tariffs and Trade (GATT) prohibits discrimination in the administration of quantitative restrictions on trade with a particular nation. However, in May 1983, the U.S. unilaterally reduced Nicaragua's annual import quota of sugar from 58,000 to 6,000 short tons, without prior negotiations with Nicaragua. The Council of GATT unanimously ruled that the U.S. had violated the agreement (*Ibid.*: 36; Verhoeven, 1985: 187).

The Reagan administration has also attempted to block economic assistance to Nicaragua from international lending agencies, including the World Bank and the Inter-American Development Bank. Despite the fact that the Articles of Agreement for both of these agencies prohibit them from attempting to interfere in the political affairs of any member and from basing their decisions on the "political character" of any member, the Reagan administration has consistently opposed loans to Nicaragua, even in cases where the loan applications were judged to be economically sound by staff members and where the applications were supported by every Board member except the U.S. Thus, because the U.S. has admitted that its opposition has not been based on the merits of the projects themselves, but rather on U.S. opposition to the political character of the Nicaraguan government, these actions constitute unlawful economic warfare against Nicaragua (Lieverman and Schneider, 1985: 37–38).

Claiming authority under the International Emergency Economic Powers Act (IEEPA) of 1977, on May 1, 1985, President Reagan declared a "national emergency" with respect to Nicaragua and imposed an embargo (Weinraub, 1985). While the restrictions were not total, they prohibited the import of goods and services from Nicaragua, forbade the export to Nicaragua of most goods, and placed a ban on Nicaraguan ships and air carriers. The IEEPA states that a President may take such measures only in cases that constitute "an unusual and extraordinary threat with respect to which a national emergency has been declared . . . and may not be exercised for any other purpose" (cited in *Ibid.*: 39). In addition to the fact that it is hard to see how Nicaragua threatens the "national security" of the U.S., the embargo violates the 1956 Treaty of Friendship, Commerce and Navigation between the U.S. and Nicaragua which, according to the provisions of the treaty, can be canceled only if one year's notice is given.

The International Court of Justice

On April 9, 1984, Nicaragua initiated proceedings against the U.S. before the International Court of Justice (ICJ), alleging that the U.S. covert war violated provisions of both the U.S. and OAS Charters, as well as a number of conventions and international laws. Nicaragua also asked the Court to initiate provisional measures calling on the U.S. to immediately cease and desist its actions against Nicaragua (*Ibid.*: 32).

In apparent anticipation of this action by Nicaragua, the U.S. had submitted a letter to the ICJ on April 6, 1984, stating that, effective immediately, the U.S. would reject the Court's jurisdiction over any Central American disputes for two years. Thus, on this and other grounds, the U.S. moved to have Nicaragua's case dismissed by the Court (*Ibid.*: 33).

The U.S. declared its acceptance of the compulsory jurisdiction of the Court in 1946. This declaration, considered at the time to be tantamount to a treaty obligation, said *inter alia*, that the U.S. would accept the Court's jurisdiction in disputes over possible violations of international law in any case involving another nation which had declared its acceptance of the Court's compulsory jurisdiction. Nicaragua had done so by virtue of action it had taken in 1929, and, as recently as January 1983, the U.S. had recognized the legitimacy of this acceptance without qualification. Thus, there seems to be little question that, when Nicaragua commenced proceedings, the U.S. was compelled to accept the jurisdiction of the Court (National Emergency Civil Liberties Committee, 1985: 1–3).

On May 10, 1984, the ICJ unanimously rejected the dismissal request and unanimously voted the provisional measures calling on the U.S. to immediately cease and desist from blockading or endangering Nicaraguan ports, particularly the laying of mines (Vincour, 1984). In response to the ICJ ruling, the U.S. "expressed regret" at the Court's failure to dismiss the case, but added that it found nothing in the decision it could not accept, including the call for an end to the mining of Nicaraguan harbors. Importantly, Reagan administration officials admitted that the CIA had been involved in the mining of the harbors, but that the mining had ended in March 1984 and would not be resumed (Vincour, 1984; Taubman, 1984a). On January 19, 1985, however, the U.S. said it would no longer participate in the proceeding before the ICJ on this matter and would not consider itself bound by decisions of the Court (Lieverman and Schneider, 1985: 33).

On June 27, 1986, the ICJ rendered a number of final judgments, most of which found the U.S. in violation of international law. First, it rejected a U.S. claim that its support of the *contras* was justified on the grounds of collective self-defense. Secondly, it ruled that U.S. actions, including the support of the *contras*, attacks against the ports of Sandino and Corinto and other targets, overflights of Nicaraguan territory, and the mining of Nicaragua's harbors, violated one or more principles of customary international law, including the obligation not to use force against another state, not to intervene in its affairs, not to violate its sovereignty, and not to interrupt peaceful maritime commerce. In addition, the Court held that some acts by the U.S., such as the mining of the harbors and the May 1985 trade embargo, violated the 1956 Treaty of Friendship, Commerce and Navigation. The Court further declared that by producing and disseminating the CIA manual to the *contras*, the U.S. was responsible for encouraging inhumane acts, but found insufficient evidence to hold the U.S. directly responsible for any such acts committed by the *contras*. Finally, the Court ordered the U.S. "to cease and to refrain" from further violations of international law, ruled that the U.S. was obliged to pay reparations to Nicaragua, and called on the U.S. and Nicaragua "to seek a solution to their dispute by peaceful means in accordance with international law" (ICJ, 1986: 146–150).

In keeping with the Reagan administration's position that the ICJ lacked jurisdiction in the controversy, the U.S. was not represented at the proceedings. When the Court issued its decisions, the administration was quick to respond that it would ignore the Court's rulings and announced that U.S. policy was "entirely consistent with international law" (Marshall, 1986).

Several points about the ICJ case are relevant to the argument of this article. First, the Reagan administration openly admitted that the CIA had been directly involved in the mining of Nicaraguan harbors, a clear violation of international law. Secondly, the administration's initial claim that the ICJ lacked jurisdiction in the case, including the U.S. move to immediately reject the Court's jurisdiction over the matter, and its January 1985 pronouncement that it would no longer participate in ICJ proceedings on the matter or consider itself bound by the decisions of the Court—all constitute breaches of international law. For example, in declaring its immediate rejection of the Court's jurisdiction, the U.S. stood in violation of a provision requiring six-months' notification before such an action could become legally effective. Indeed, there is some possibility that the action taken by Secretary of State Schultz in announcing the immediate rejection of the Court's jurisdiction was itself unconstitutional in that the administration failed to seek the required congressional approval (Glennon, 1985: 682–689). Further, by declaring it would reject the jurisdiction of the Court, the U.S. breached a fundamental obligation under international law to seek the peaceful resolution of disputes. Finally, by continuing its covert war against Nicaragua, the U.S. stands in violation of the May 1984 and June 1986 orders of the ICJ to cease these actions.

Violations of Domestic Law

The Neutrality Act

Lieverman and Schneider (1985: 41–47) argue that the Neutrality Act, enacted as part of U.S. law in 1794, prohibits any U.S. citizen, *including the President*, from supporting or using private armies to attack other nations. More specifically, the Neutrality Act makes it a crime to initiate, organize, or fund a hostile expedition on U.S. territory against a foreign country with which the U.S. is at peace.

Lieverman and Schneider note that through its support of the *contras*, the

Reagan administration has undoubtedly gained a political advantage by being able to blunt domestic opposition to U.S. intervention in Nicaragua. However, these political considerations are irrelevant in assessing the legality of such a practice. The fact remains that the U.S. government's support of the *contras*, which continues as of this writing, constitutes a clear violation of the Neutrality Act, making those officials, including the President himself, criminally responsible.

Further, it would seem that other U.S. citizens, acting individually or as members of organizations, who fund or support the *contras*, also stand in violation of the Neutrality Act. Several sources have reported the existence in Florida, California, and Alabama of camps which train paramilitary forces for fighting in Nicaragua and elsewhere in Central America, and have identified private organizations which provide money, military equipment, and medical supplies to the *contras* (Adams, 1983; Dillion and Anderson, 1984; Noah, 1985; Brody, 1985: 145–151; Matthews, 1986: 28–38). To date, the Reagan administration has done nothing to limit these activities or to prosecute those involved. Of course, the revelations in November 1986 about the conspiracy to fund the *contras* with profits from the arms sale to Iran, which establish links between these groups and the White House, help to make this inaction understandable.

The Boland Amendment

The Boland Amendment, adopted by Congress on December 21, 1982, and effective to December 1983, prohibited the use of U.S. funds to overthrow the government of Nicaragua or to provoke a military exchange between Nicaragua and Honduras (Lieverman and Schneider, 1985: 47). This resolution was enacted after press reports, particularly *Newsweek*'s cover story on "America's Secret War" (November 8, 1982), made it apparent that the Reagan administration had been lying to Congress when it gave assurance that aid to the *contras* was intended to help interdict the flow of arms from Nicaragua to El Salvador, not to overthrow the Nicaraguan government. The Boland Amendment was enacted in an attempt to exercise tighter congressional control over administration policies, at least for a year.

It is evident, however, that the Reagan administration violated the Boland Amendment when it was in force. There is considerable evidence to support this conclusion. First, all seven directors of the Nicaraguan Democratic Force ((FDN), the largest of the *contra* groups, have explicitly and consistently stated that the goal of the FDN has always been and remains the overthrow of the Sandinista regime (Brinkley, 1984a), a fact of which the CIA was aware and approved both before and after the passage of the Boland Amendment. Further, in what appears to have been part of the administration's strategy of deception to win congressional and public support for *contra* aid, the CIA approached Edgar Chamorro, a FDN leader, asking him to make public statements that the goal of the rebels was to interdict the flow of arms from Nicaragua, not overthrow its government (Brinkley, 1984a, Chamorro, 1985). The point is that the *contras*, who were receiving direct support from the CIA, were attempting to overthrow the Nicaraguan government while the

Boland Amendment was in force. Finally, in the view of some in Congress, the diversion of funds to the *contras* from the sale of arms to Iran has violated the Boland Amendment (Roberts, 1986).

That the administration violated the Boland Amendment is also evident in the CIA's infamous manual on *Psychological Operations in Guerrilla Warfare*, the existence of which became public knowledge in October 1984 (Brinkley, 1984b). The manual states that following the principles of guerrilla warfare will ensure that "a comandante of ours will literally be able to shake up the Sandinista structure, and replace it," and that "the overthrow can be achieved and our revolution can become an open one . . ." (CIA, 1985: 39). These statements leave no doubt that the CIA manual advocates the overthrow of the Nicaraguan government by the *contras*. In a press release on December 5, 1984, the House Select Committee of Intelligence publicly announced that a majority of its members had concluded that the CIA manual represented a violation of the Boland Amendment (Central America Crisis Monitoring Team, 1985: 14–15).

More recently, the administration has taken the position that it is no longer prohibited by the Boland Amendment from using U.S. funds to overthrow the Nicaraguan government. President Reagan made it clear in his news conference on February 21, 1985, that the goal of U.S. policy is to "replace" the current government, and there is evidence that this has *always* been the intent of administration policy (Brinkley, 1985).

However, as Lieverman and Schneider (1985: 49) argue, the issue is not what the "real" intent of the administration has been or is. The tradition of common law holds a person liable for the "reasonable foreseeable" consequences of his or her conduct. Therefore, it is:

> legally irrelevant for the U.S. to say that it has a different purpose in mind when it gives arms and support to the *contras*. Given the information available to the government . . . , it is reasonably foreseeable that the *contras* will use U.S. aid to attempt to overthrow the present government. The U.S. is therefore a joint participant in that venture and is jointly responsible at law. The administration's attempt to distinguish between its goal and that of the *contras* has no legal distinction.

Executive Order 12333

The CIA manual violates Executive Order 12333 issued by President Reagan in December 1981 (*Ibid.*: 49–51; Neier, 1985: 104–109; Brinkley, 1984c). The Order states that:

> No person employed by or acting on behalf of the United States Government shall engage in, or conspire to engage in, assassination.

> No Agency of the Intelligence Community shall participate in or request any person to undertake activities forbidden by this order.

However, a section of the manual entitled "The Selective Use of Violence for Propagandistic Effects" states that "it is possible to neutralize carefully selected and planned targets such as court judges, *mesta* judges, police and state security officials, CDS Chiefs, etc." (CIA, 1985: 57). In another place, the manual recommends that "if possible professional criminals will be hired to carry out specific selected 'jobs'" (*Ibid.*: 84).

The Executive Order clearly prohibits activities like publishing the CIA manual. Thus, in addition to constituting unlawful intervention under international law, the CIA manual and its call for assassination violate domestic law (Lieverman and Schneider, 1985: 51).

Other Domestic Laws

In addition, a report by the Arms Control and Foreign Policy Caucus (1984, hereafter referred to as the Caucus Report) of Congress has identified four other sets of domestic laws which allegedly have been violated by administration policies toward Nicaragua. First, in April 1984, the Senate Select Committee on Intelligence charged that the CIA's failure to provide "full and current" information on its involvement in the mining of Nicaraguan harbors violated provisions of the Intelligence Oversight Act (Caucus Report, 1984: 30). Critics have also claimed that the CIA violated Section 922(a) of the U.S. Criminal Code by employing unlicensed individuals and corporations to ship weapons and ammunition to *contra* camps within the U.S. and Central America (*Ibid.*: 27).

Second, in an incident involving the downing of a U.S. Army helicopter and the killing of the pilot by Nicaraguan troops near the Honduran-Nicaraguan border in January 1984, critics have charged that the administration's failure to inform Congress of the incident violated provisions of both the War Powers Act and the Arms Export Control Act (*Ibid.*: 28–33). Third, the General Accounting Office and the House Intelligence Committee have charged the Defense Department with exceeding spending limits and illegally appropriating funds for the construction of military facilities in Honduras, the transportation of supplies and equipment to *contra* bases, and the transfer of weapons and equipment from the Defense Department to the CIA for *contra* operations. These practices, it has been charged, violated provisions of the Defense Appropriations Act of 1984, the Economy Act, and the Military Construction Codification Act (*Ibid.*: 1–7). Finally, congressional critics have charged that the failure of the Justice Department to investigate possible violations of the Neutrality Act by federal officials in planning and funding paramilitary operations against Nicaragua is itself a violation of the Ethics in Government Act (*Ibid.*: 23).

Political Crime and Ideology

The official, publicly stated policy objectives of the Reagan administration toward Nicaragua do not include reference to the aforementioned political crimes. Instead, the "official" objectives, which have been enunciated on numerous occasions and which are succinctly summarized in a State Department pamphlet entitled "Misconceptions About U.S. Policy Toward Nicaragua" (1985), reflect an underlying concern with the threat of communism and suggest that the administration intends to purge Nicaragua of its "communist" influence. This official definition of the situation functions as an ideological construct (Box, 1983), and, as such, it both justifies administration policies and mystifies the fact that they are political crimes.

According to the State Department pamphlet, the belief that U.S. policy is aimed at overthrowing the Sandinista government is a "misconception." Instead, the "facts" are that U.S. policy has four objectives:

1. An end to Nicaraguan support for guerrilla groups in neighboring countries;
2. Severance of Nicaraguan military and security ties to Cuba and the Soviet bloc;
3. Reduction of Nicaragua's military strength to levels that would restore military equilibrium to the region; and
4. Fulfillment of the original Sandinista promise to support democratic pluralism and respect for human and civil rights (U.S. Department of State, 1985: 3).

These objectives, grounded as they are in questionable evidence and specious arguments, constitute a central element in the ideological mystification used by the administration to justify its interventionist policies toward Nicaragua.

First, the Reagan administration has repeatedly claimed that the Sandinistas supply arms to the Farabundo Martí National Liberation Front (FMLN) in El Salvador. These claims appear to be almost totally groundless. David MacMichael (1984; Taubman, 1984), when working as an analyst for the CIA, prepared a report for the Agency which concluded that, with the exception of the period from late 1980 to early 1981, there was virtually no evidence of an arms flow between Nicaragua and the guerrillas in El Salvador. Despite this, the administration has continued to claim that the evidence exists.

The second goal of administration policy—forcing Nicaragua to sever its military and security ties to Cuba and the Soviet Union—embodies the central tenet in the ideological justification for U.S. intervention in Nicaragua. The other objectives flow from this key point. It reflects the general thesis, formulated by conservative groups close to the administration, such as the Heritage Foundation and the Council for Inter-American Security (1980), that Nicaragua, along with all of Central America, constitutes the most important, perhaps decisive, battleground in the struggle between the forces of democracy and totalitarianism, freedom and tyranny, capitalism and communism. It holds, in other words, that Nicaragua aligned with, perhaps controlled by, the Soviet Union and Cuba, is "exporting" revolution and spreading communism throughout Central America, a development which threatens the "national security" of the U.S. and, therefore, justifies the illegal attempts to overthrow the Sandinista regime. Among other criticisms of this view, LeoGrande (1984) and Kenworthy (1983) point out that, first, it exaggerates the strength of Cuban and Soviet influence in Nicaragua; second, it assumes that, although "indigenous" conditions of poverty, repression, and exploitation may give rise to dissatisfaction among the people of Central America, "foreign influence" is necessary for revolutionary movements to develop and sustain themselves, a belief which denies to the people the good sense to recognize their own exploitation and to organize themselves into revolutionary movements aimed at overthrowing dictatorships, as happened in Nicaragua. Finally, it ignores the effect of U.S. policy in pushing Nicaragua toward stronger ties with the Soviet Union and Cuba, perhaps forcing the abandonment of the Sandinista commitment to a policy of non-alignment, thereby making the administration policies a self-fulfilling prophecy. From the administration's perspective, this grave threat of "communism" at our doorstep justifies its attempts to overthrow the Sandinista government.

Third, the administration appears to have exaggerated, perhaps intentionally, claims about Nicaragua's military buildup which, the administration charges, threatens the security of neighboring countries and the stability of the region. Repeated allegations have been made about the "excessive" number of Nicaraguan troops, military bases, aircraft, and tanks. However, according to a study by the Central American Crisis Monitoring Team (1985: 24–27), these assertions are not supported by evidence from other sources. Further, the administration's claims appear disingenuous when placed in the context of the fact that Nicaragua is under attack, militarily and economically, by the most powerful nation in the world.

Finally, charges that the Sandinistas have failed to keep their revolutionary promise of promoting democratic pluralism and have committed human and civil rights violations are, to say the least, disingenuous. Let us consider two examples. First, Nicaragua held an election in October 1984, and despite a U.S. policy that encouraged some opposition leaders to withdraw and administration attempts to discredit the election by calling it a "sham," several international groups who observed the election concluded it was fair, open, and free (see, for example, Frappier et al., 1985; Latin American Studies Association, 1985).

Second, administration charges of widespread human rights violations are also challenged by other evidence (see National Lawyers Guild, 1986). For instance, although not denying that a small number of extrajudicial killings may have taken place, Americas Watch concluded "there is not evidence that they are encouraged or tolerated by the Nicaraguan government, nor do they represent a consistent pattern" (Brown, 1985: 163–164). Atrocities committed by the *contras*, on the other hand, are much more pervasive and reflect a policy of terrorism (Brody, 1985). Thus, the administration's claims about Sandinista human rights violations appear to be little more than a device to divert attention from the atrocities perpetrated by the U.S.-backed *contras*, acts which appear to be tacitly encouraged and condoned by the Reagan administration.

Conclusion

This article has argued that the policies of the Reagan administration toward Nicaragua violate both international and domestic laws and, therefore, constitute political crimes. That no one in the administration has been hauled off to prison, like a "common" criminal, is a tribute to the mystification efforts of the administration, a process that is aided in profound ways by the mass media, which uncritically accept and disseminate the "official" version of reality about Nicaragua (see Chomsky, 1985).

It would be a mistake, however, to view these policies as aberrations, unique to this administration. Instead, they are part of a broader historical pattern, and it is this broader view that provides a deeper and more meaningful theoretical understanding of current policies.

First, the current policies of the U.S. government are but the continuation of a long history of interventionism in Central America (see, for example, LaFeber, 1983; Bodenheimer, 1984; Black and Butler, 1982; White, 1984; Burbach and Flynn, 1984). For example, since the promulgation of the Monroe Doctrine of 1823, the U.S. has forcibly intervened in the sovereign affairs of the nations of Latin America on at least 120 different occasions; nearly 40 of these were aimed at the six Central American countries of Costa Rica, El Salvador, Guatemala, Honduras, Nicaragua and Panama, with Nicaragua itself the object of U.S. intervention no fewer than 11 times between 1853 and 1934 (ISMEC, 1984; 1–9).

Interventionism has been used to establish and protect a system of economic dependency beneficial to U.S. economic interests, particularly corporate interests. This system of dependency has been buttressed and maintained both by political means, as the installation and support of the Somoza dictatorship in Nicaragua well illustrates, and by military force, as illustrated by the direct involvement of the CIA in the 1954 overthrow of the popularly elected reformist Arbenz government in Guatemala (Schlesinger and Kinzer, 1983). As LaFeber (1984: 13–18) pointedly argues, U.S. opposition has been particularly strong against revolutionary movements in Central America because of a concern that should a progressive regime come to power and begin implementing economic and social reforms, the resulting "instability" might threaten U.S. economic and political interests.

Further, just as the Reagan administration's ongoing efforts to overthrow the Sandinista government are but part of a historical pattern of U.S. interventionism in Central America, its use of the bogey of the "communist threat" is but the echo of an ideological theme trumpeted over the past 50 years to justify that interventionism (Brenner, 1984; Miliband and Liebman, 1985). Indeed, as Brenner (1984) argues, the Reagan administration has elevated anticommunism to the level of a religious crusade. In part, this crusade embodies a worldview that explains events in terms of a conspiracy, that reduces complex issues to a simple struggle between good and evil, that prompts self-righteousness on the part of the faithful, and that rests on blind faith (*Ibid.*: 236–244). Ironically, the State Department's pamphlet, analyzed previously, ostensibly aims at correcting "misconceptions" about U.S. policy toward Nicaragua, and yet it epitomizes this nightmare fear of communism.

However, this paranoid fear of communism, real as it may be to the top policymakers, provides only a partial understanding of why the Reagan administration is so intent on destroying the Sandinistas. Obviously, the reasons are complex, but another key factor in understanding administration policies lies in what the success of the Sandinista Revolution might mean to other developing nations and the impact this might have on U.S. hegemony. In other words, the Sandinistas threaten U.S. interests by example (Black and Butler, 1982: 13–17; Berman, 1986). Simply put, if Nicaragua succeeds in creating a social order based on a mixed economy, popular democratic pluralism, and a foreign policy of nonalignment, a social order which guarantees food, decent housing, health care, and education to its people, Nicaragua will serve as a model to other Third World countries, not only in Central America but throughout the world. Such a model threatens the economic and political hegemony of the U.S., and it is because of this threat that President Reagan, acting in the interests of the capitalist ruling class, perpetrates acts of political crime and deviance against the people of Nicaragua.

References

Adams, Eddie
  1983 "How Latin Guerrillas Train on Our Soil." Peter Rossett and John Vandemeer (eds.), The Nicaragua Reader. New York: The Grove Press: 207–208.

Apple, R.W. Jr.
  1986a "North Role Cited in Bid to Unseat *Contra* Aid Foes." The New York Times (December 15).
  1986b "Supporter of *Contra* Aid Linked to White House." The New York Times (December 16).

Arms Control and Foreign Policy Caucus
  1984 U.S. Policy in Central America: Against the Law? Washington, D.C.: U.S. Congress (September 11).

Berman, Karl
  1986 "Nicaragua: The Threat Is by Example." In These Times (March 26–April 1).

Black, George
  1981 Triumph of the People: The Sandinistas Revolution in Nicaragua. London: Zed Press.

Black, George and Judy Butler
  1982 "Target Nicaragua." NACLA Report on the Americas (January/February): 2–45.

Bodenheimer, Thomas
  1984 Policing the Hemisphere: U.S. Militarism in Latin America. San Francisco: Global Options.

Box, Steven
  1983 Power, Crime and Mystification. New York: Tavistock.

Brandt, Deborah
  1985 "Popular Education." Thomas W. Walker (ed.), Nicaragua: The First Five Years. New York: Praeger Publishers: 317–345.

Brenner, Phillip
  1984 "Waging Ideological Warfare: Anti-Communism and U.S. Foreign Policy in Central America." Ralph Miliband et al. (eds.), The Socialist Register 1984. London: The Merlin Press: 230–260.

Brinkley, Joel
  1985 "Vote on Nicaraguan Rebels: Either Way, a Turning Point." The New York Times (March 17).
  1984a "A Rebel Says CIA Pledged Help in War Against Sandinistas." The New York Times (November 1).
  1984b "CIA Primer Tells Nicaraguan Rebels

How to Kill." The New York Times (October 17).

1984c "President Orders 2 Investigations on CIA Manual." The New York Times (October 19).

Brody, Reed
1985 *Contra* Terror in Nicaragua. Boston: South End Press.

Brown, Cynthia (ed.)
1985 With Friends Like These. New York: Pantheon Books.

Burbach, Roger and Patricia Flynn (eds.)
1984 The Politics of Intervention. New York: Monthly Review Press.

Butterfield, Fox
1986 "Ex-General Provided Arms Channel." The New York Times (December 6).

Central America Crisis Monitoring Team
1985 In Contempt of Congress. Washington, D.C.: Institute for Policy Studies.

Chamorro, Edgar with Jefferson Morley
1985 "Confessions of a '*Contra*.'" The New Republic (August 5): 18–23.

Chinn, Samuel Shih-Tsai
1979 Basic Documents of International Organization. Revised edition. Dubuque, IA: Kendall/Hunt.

Chomsky, Noam
1985 Turning the Tide. Boston: South End Press.

CIA
1985 Psychological Operations in Guerrilla Warfare. New York: Vintage.

Collins, Joseph
1985 Nicaragua: What Difference Could a Revolution Make? San Francisco: Institute for Food Development Policy.

Council for Inter-American Security
1980 A New Inter-America Policy for the Eighties. Washington, D.C.

Dillion, John and Jon Lee Anderson
1984 "Who's Behind the Aid to the *Contras*." The Nation (October 6): 305–319.

Dixon, Marlene and Susanne Jonas (eds.)
1985 On Trial. San Francisco: Synthesis Publications.

Engelberg, Stephen

1986 "U.S. Officials Said to Have Aided Private Suppliers of *Contra* Units." The New York Times (October 11).

Frappier, Jon, Olga Talamante, and Polly Thomas
1985 Democracy in Nicaragua. San Francisco: U.S. Out of Central America.

Georges-Abeyie, Daniel E.
1980 "Political Crime and Terrorism." Graeme R. Newman (ed.), Crime and Deviance: A Comparative Perspective. Beverly Hills, CA: Sage Publications: 313–332.

Glennon, Michael J.
1985 "*Nicaragua* v. *United States*: Constitutionality of U.S. Modification of ICJ Jurisdiction." The American Journal of International Law 79: 682–689.

Glickman, Paul
1986 "U.S.-Policy Critics See Pattern of Harassment in Burglaries." Christian Science Monitor (December 16).

Institute for the Study of Militarism and Economic Crisis (now Global Options)
1984 U.S. Militarism in Latin America. San Francisco.

International Court of Justice (ICJ)
1986 Case Concerning Military and Paramilitary Activities in and Against Nicaragua (*Nicaragua* v. *United States*). Proceedings of the ICJ (June 27): 14–150; 1023–1091.

Kenworthy, Eldon
1983 "Central America: Beyond the Credibility Trap." World Policy Journal (Fall): 181–200.

Kinzer, Stephen
1987 "1,019 Sandinista Soldiers Reported Killed During '86." The New York Times (January 1).

LaFeber, Walter
1983 Inevitable Revolutions. New York: W.W. Norton and Company.

Latin American Studies Association
1985 "A Summary Report of the Latin American Studies Association Delegation to Observe the Nicaraguan General Election of November 4, 1984." Thomas W. Walker (ed.), Nicaragua: The First Five Years. New York:

Praeger Publishers: 523–532.

LeMoyne, James
1986a "How *Contras* Got Arms: An Account from Crew." The New York Times (December 4).
1986b "U.S. Oversaw Supplies to Rebels, Officials Say." The New York Times (December 8).
1986c "U.S. Prisoner in Nicaragua Says CIA Ran *Contra* Supply Flights." The New York Times (October 12).

LeoGrande, William M.
1984 "Through the Looking Glass: The Kissinger Report on Central America." World Policy Journal (Winter): 251–284.
1982 "The United States and the Nicaraguan Revolution." Thomas W. Walker (ed.), Nicaragua in Revolution. New York: Praeger Publishers: 63–77.

Lieverman, Theodore and Peter Schneider
1985 Memorandum of Law on United States Policy Toward Nicaragua. Philadelphia, PA: Philadelphia Lawyers Committee on Central America.

MacMichael, David
1984 "Calling the Bluff." Sojourners (August): 19–22.

Marcus, Bruce (ed.)
1985 Nicaragua: The Sandinista People's Revolution. New York: Pathfinder Press.

Marshall, Tyler
1986 "World Court Rules U.S. Aid to *Contras* Illegal." Los Angeles Times (June 28).

Matthews, Robert
1986 "Sowing Dragon's Teeth: The U.S. War Against Nicaragua." NACLA Report on the Americas (July/August): 13–40.

Miliband, Ralph and Marcel Liebman
1985 "Reflections on Anti-Communism." Monthly Review (July–August): 1–29.

National Emergency Civil Liberties Committee
1985 Memorandum of the National Emergency Civil Liberties Committee on the United States, Nicaragua and the World Court. New York: NECLC.

National Lawyers Guild
1986 Freedom of Expression in Nicaragua. New York, NY.

Neier, Aryeh
1985 "The Legal Implications of the CIA's Nicaraguan Manual." CIA, Psychological Operations in Guerrilla Warfare. New York: Vintage: 101–124.

Noah, Timothy
1985 "School for Scoundrels." The New Republic (August 26): 11–14.

Oberdorfer, Don
1983 "Washington's Role Troubles Congress." The Washington Post (April 3).

Quinney, Richard
1975 Criminology: Analysis and Critique of Crime in America. Boston: Little, Brown and Company.

Roberts, Stephen
1986 "Top Legislators Promise Inquiry." The New York Times (November 26).

Roebuck, Julian and Stanley C. Weeber
1978 Political Crime in the United States. New York: Praeger Publishers.

Schlesinger, Stephen and Stephen Kinzer
1983 Bitter Fruit: The Untold Story of the American Coup in Guatemala. Garden City, NY: Doubleday.

Schneider, Keith
1986 "Pattern Is Seen in Break-ins in Latin Policy Groups." Christian Science Monitor (December 16).

Simon, David R., and D. Stanley Eitzen
1986 Elite Deviance. Boston: Allyn and Bacon.

Stone, Peter H.
1984 "The Special Forces in 'Covert Action.'" The Nation (July 7–14): 8–12.

Taubman, Philip
1984a "CIA Said to Plan Nicaraguan Strikes." The New York Times (May 3).
1984b "The C.I.A.: In from the Cold and Hot for the Truth." The New York Times (June 11).
1984c "U.S. Is Reported to Skirt Curbs in Latin Moves." The New York Times (May 18).

Turk, Austin
1984 "Political Crime." Robert F. Meier (ed.), Major Forms of Crime. Beverly Hills, CA: Sage Publications: 119–135.

1982 Political Criminality. Beverly Hills, CA: Sage Publications.

Tyler, Patrick E. and Robert Woodward
1982 "U.S. Approves Covert Plan in Nicaragua." The Washington Post (March 10).

U.S. Department of State
1985 Misconceptions About U.S. Policy Toward Nicaragua. Washington, D.C.

U.S. Out of Central America (USOCA)
1985 Health Care in Nicaragua: The Effects of U.S. Policy. San Francisco: USOCA.

Verhoeven, Joe
1985 "On the Legality of the Reagan Administration's Policies." Marlene Dixon and Susanne Jonas (eds.), On Trial. San Francisco: Synthesis: 185–200.

Vincour, John
1984 "U.S. Loses Ruling in Nicaragua Case." The New York Times (May 11).

Walker, Thomas W. (ed.)
1982 Nicaragua in Revolution. New York: Praeger Publishers.

Weinraub, Bernard
1986 "Disarray Deepens." The New York Times (November 20).
1985 "Reagan, Declaring 'Threat,' Forbids Nicaraguan Trade and Cuts Air and Sea Links." The New York Times (May 2).

White, Robert A.
1984 The Morass: United States Intervention in Central America. New York: Harper and Row.

Yerkey, Gary
1986 "U.S. Not Expected to Abide by Terms of World Court Ruling." Christian Science Monitor (June 30).

Part 3
CRIMINAL JUSTICE: LAW AND POLICING

In this section, we will shift our focus to the issue of controlling crime. We will begin with an examination of those institutions that are formally and officially charged with preventing, reducing, and eliminating crime—collectively known as the *criminal justice system*. In this section, we will look at the legal foundations of the American criminal justice system as embodied in the criminal law (assessing the role of law in human behavior and communities), and at the role that law enforcement plays both in the justice system and in the wider society.

Although we will be moving from crime to crime control here, at least two links to earlier sections, readings, and debate in this book must be highlighted. First, conservative or progressive assumptions about the nature and causes of crime are necessarily related to conservative or progressive assumptions about how crime is best controlled. Whatever is identified as the source of crime is going to influence prescriptions for reducing or eliminating it. In other words, because conservatives and progressives have strong disagreements about what crime is and where it comes from in the first place, they also have very different positions in regard to the crime control or criminal justice issues addressed in this section and the next. Second, just as most Americans rarely treat the term *crime* as problematic, they also take the nature and role of law and law enforcement in their society as self-evident. We have already seen that the conservative–progressive debate over crime challenges the popular understanding of it; so too does the debate over law and its enforcement. Conservatives and progressives make fundamentally different assumptions and provide fundamentally different answers to questions concerning the nature of criminal law, its relation to human behavior, its relation to crime, and the role of the police in American society. There is conservative and progressive conflict over what the law is, including its origin and essential function in society, and on what the police are, including their origin and essential function in society.

Presented in this section are conservative and progressive arguments surrounding five issues. First, the debate begins with a general discussion of law in society. Does the law provide the order required by any modern civilization or does it only arise to enforce order when all other sources of social harmony have disappeared? Second, we turn to the issue of gun control in American society. Are specific laws that restrict the ownership, availability, and use of firearms by private citizens a violation of constitutional rights or a necessity required by high levels of homicide and other criminal violence? Third, is another specific law, capital punishment, justified as a deterrent to criminal violence or is it morally and politically unjustifiable? Fourth, what is the role of the police in our communities? Are they enforcing the law and protecting the public or enforcing a social order that protects dominant interests? And fifth, we consider the recent expansion of private policing, policing-for-profit. Does the increased use of private security lead to a safer and more secure society, or one in which the rights and privacies of individuals and groups are more and more threatened by an expanding system of social control?

LAW: ORDER OR REPRESSION?

The conservative analysis of law as a way of governing a people or a society suggests a necessary link between law and order. Law offers and promotes a specific order for individual members of the community or society. It is expected, following the conservative approach, that the members of society, being rational, will of their own accord, comply with the law. The law requires and encourages the order that rational individuals will understand is in their interest. It is, after all, in everyone's interest to end the Hobbesian "war of all against all." Law can do this with the order it sustains in society.

Since submission to the requirements of the law are dependent on rational individuals using their free will to express their self-interest and preservation, however, the possibility of "irrational" persons choosing to violate the law always exists. Therefore, the law in its promotion of social order requires punishment. To maintain its rule, the law must punish those who violate the legal and social order. In his article, Herbert Fingarette argues that the law requires not only punishment, but *retribution*. The law and social order must be preserved in both the short- and long-term for those who rationally will it and desire it. Retributive punishment is necessary under the rule of law (as other forms of punishment may also be).

The progressive response to the conservative analysis of law and society includes an objection to the assumed relationship between law and order. From this perspective, the historical record shows that law and order rarely go together. Anthropologist Stanley Diamond, in his well-known essay "The Rule of Law Versus the Order of Custom," maintains that social order (what Pepinsky and Jesilow call "social peace") is historically associated with societies "governed" by custom and tradition, societies without law. The law only appears when inequality, injustice, unfairness, exploitation, and conflict have made social order very problematic. Division and the disorder it gives rise to destroy whatever social bond could nurture social harmony, order, and peace.

From the progressive perspective, law enters at this time. But since it usually appears with the disorder of exploitation and conflict, it has most often been a *repressive* law. It is a tool used by powerful interests in society to enforce or coerce their order on less powerful individuals, groups, or classes.

Finally, as Pepinsky and Jesilow point out in their article, the mythical belief that "law makes people behave" has had a strong hold on us. Many criminologists contend that American society is an "overcriminalized" society. If we have some social problem that persists or some part of the population that consistently behaves in a way we do not approve of, we criminalize the behavior and the person. We "make a law against it." The problem with this, from the progressive perspective, is that it does not work. In fact, more laws often mean more violations. Only conditions of relative equality, justice, and fairness can lead to the levels of social peace, harmony, and order that can reduce all forms of victimization in our communities, including criminal victimization. The law, under the opposite conditions of inequality, injustice, and unfairness, cannot be expected to "make people behave."

GUN CONTROL

"Guns don't kill people, people do." So goes the anti-gun control slogan in America. Most conservative politicians, academics, journalists, social critics, and gun owners believe that criminal violence is not controlled by legal restrictions on the importation, manufacture, sale, ownership, or use of guns, but by more restrictions and controls on criminals themselves. Many conservatives believe that their guns, or the guns of others, are indeed a constitutional right—the "right to bear arms." Don B. Kates, a liberal and civil libertarian, expresses the conservative or anti-gun control position in this section. According to Kates, prohibiting guns in the United States is both a futile and dangerous exercise: registration, restriction, and confiscation of guns would be too costly financially, too costly constitutionally, and gun control would be ineffective, or at least no more effective than the prohibition of liquor and marijuana have been. Kates points out that if liberals and progressives are really serious about the reduction of criminal violence in American society, they should shift their attention away from gun control and toward the underlying social, cultural, and institutional sources of violence.

In presenting the progressive rebuttal to this position, we have no quarrel with Kates's indication of where the "real" or "ultimate" causes of criminal violence lie in our society. We too believe that violence is structurally and institutionally, economically and politically, and socially and culturally generated. But we also believe that the availability of handguns and the lack of effective handgun control facilitate and exacerbate this violence.

In line with our article, "For Public Safety: Controlling Violence, Homicide and Handguns," we believe that the following mix of facts argue for increased regulation and even banning of handguns in the United States: the U.S. homicide rate is probably the highest in the world, much higher than those nations that have legislated and enforced very restrictive handgun regulations; in recent years roughly one-half of all murders have been committed with handguns; we probably have the most heavily armed citizenry in the history of the world; and handgun ownership appears to make armed households less safe, not more safe, since they appear to be about seven to eight times more likely to experience a handgun death as unarmed households.

In more concrete terms, we believe that the high rates of violent victimization in American society are due to structural or institutional factors. However, specific episodes of domestic violence are encouraged by the lack of effective handgun controls.

CAPITAL PUNISHMENT

In 1972 the U.S. Supreme Court struck down state death penalty laws as unconstitutional. They did not declare the death penalty per se unconstitutional, only the specific statutes. By 1987, 37 states had legally reinstituted the death penalty. More persons, nearly 1800, were sitting on death row than ever before. Upwards of 40 persons had been executed since the states had revived capital punishment. Poll after poll showed two-thirds or even as much as three-quarters of the American public supporting the death penalty. In some states, such as Florida, it has become virtually impossible to run for public office without supporting it.

Opponents of capital punishment in the U.S. have argued that the death penalty is barbaric and is not used by any other modern industrial democracy; that it constitutes state-sanctioned murder, is immoral and cheapens the value of human life; that there is evidence that innocent persons can be executed by mistake; that there is no evidence for the death penalty's deterrent effect (indeed some studies have actually shown higher rates of homicide and other criminal violence in states where there is a death penalty than in those states where there is not); and that the death penalty has always been applied in an arbitrary, capricious and discriminatory way in the U.S.—targeting primarily the poor and blacks. Is capital punishment reserved for those without capital? The report by Amnesty International expresses this thesis, as well as other oppositions to the death penalty.

Edward Koch, the mayor of New York City, presents the conservative or pro-capital punishment position here, offering a point by point rebuttal of the contentions of death penalty opponents listed above. It should be pointed out, however, that Mayor Koch does not address himself to the issue of deterrence that often surrounds the death penalty debate. One can only speculate as to why Koch leaves this untouched.

POLICING THE COMMUNITY:
PUBLIC PROTECTION OR CLASS CONTROL?

Historians of the municipal police in American society generally agree that the origins of police forces in nineteenth century cities had to do with controlling social disorder, and not crime per se. In one way or another, these historians attribute this disorder to the process of industrialization. Industrialization helped to concentrate the population in larger urban areas (at first in the Northeast and Midwest) and it was primarily in these areas that city police forces were first instituted, as a response to what was perceived to be increased levels of social disorder. Historians also generally agree that it was the "elite" in the new industrial city that felt most threatened and was responsible for the creation of the municipal police. The role of the public police force was not, as is often assumed, to protect the community from serious felony crime and victimization, but to restore and provide social order.

Nor is there any disagreement among serious students of the city police force that contemporary policing is *not* simply mechanical law enforcement. Studies of policing continue to find the police spending as much as seventy to eighty percent of their time, energy, and resources on "order maintenance"—including policing misdemeanor and "victimless" crimes, settling domestic and neighborhood disputes, working traffic, and providing security at public events.

There is widespread disagreement between conservative and progressive analysts of the police, however, over the extent to which the police should be involved in social control, rather than crime control activities, and over the fundamental nature and consequence of police work in American society.

James Q. Wilson and George Kelling, in their by now quite notorious article, "Broken Windows," make the conservative argument in this debate. Wilson and Kelling maintain that people are fearful of two things—crime and disorder. They want to be protected from both. The problem, from this perspective, is that the police have become too oriented to investigating and policing serious crime, to the detriment of policing disorder and responding to citizen fear of this disorder. In the process of becoming more oriented toward crime control, the police and their behavior have also come under more and more legal restrictions. Many of these restrictions have actually hindered the police from doing what they do best—order maintenance. According to Wilson and Kelling, these legal restrictions must be relaxed. Then police can re-establish their social control function in city neighborhoods and begin again to provide and maintain the kind of order that can allay citizen fears. Although this may involve some "kicking ass," the consequence, according to these authors, is inarguably beneficial. It is done in the interest of the public; the entire public is protected.

Sidney Harring, in his "Policing a Class Society," contends that both the historical origins and the contemporary function of the municipal police force must be understood in the context of a class society. In the context of the new and developing class structure of the nineteenth century city, the "elite" or capitalist class established and used the police institution to discipline and control the working-class and the surplus labor of the poor. Understood in this way, the social control or order-maintenance role of the early police actually constituted class control. Harring also says that although the process may be more subtle now, the order-maintenance function of the contemporary police force serves the same purpose—the control of one class by another. Harring seems to imply that following Wilson and Kelling's suggestion to expand the social control functions—as opposed to the crime control functions—of the present day city police force would not protect the public as much as it would strengthen the dominance of a ruling class over the working-class and the poor.

POLICING-FOR-PROFIT:
SECURITY OR EXPANDING SOCIAL CONTROL?

Private security—selling policing for a profit—has emerged in the past two decades as a significant and growing alternative to the perceived inefficiency, ineffectiveness, and underfunding of the public police force.

There are now probably more private than public police in the United States. Private security and policing is now a $5 to $15 billion per year industry. Historically, American industry has been the primary employer for private police, often putting them to anti-labor, anti-union uses. However, at present, as the private police make inroads into areas formerly handled by the public police, the presence of the private security force expands to apartment buildings, shops, department stores, office buildings, factories, museums, schools, universities, hospitals, theaters, stadiums, buses, and subways.

Each of the following have contributed to the rapid rise of private policing in the past two decades: perceived threats to social institutions resulting from anti-war and minority political activity; perceived increases in crimes against business; increased citizen fear of crime in neighborhoods and public institutions; the increased likelihood of theft, vandalism, and sabotage of private business during periods of economic downturn; more vulnerable corporations due to a more technological, rational, and interdependent system of economic production; and a host of more isolated occurrences like airline hijackings and executive kidnappings.

Large corporations in particular have been attracted to the "advantages" that private police have for them when compared with public police. Private policing is plentiful, flexible, inexpensive, and personalized protection, and it avoids the risks of uncovering the corporation's own irregularities and illegalities.

Pinkerton's, Inc., one of the largest private policing and private security agencies in the U.S., promotes the advantages of their services to potential consumers in their pamphlet that appears in this section.

Progressive critics of private policing would contend that Pinkerton's does not tell us the whole story. There is a dark side to private policing, according to these critics: There have been virtually no employment standards in the private police industry; the private police have tended to be untrained, unskilled, and poorly paid; there has been a high rate of turnover in the private security industry and a high rate of crime among private security employees themselves; "moonlighting" public police have made up an overworked and fatigued private police force; private and public law enforcement have often contradicted each other and worked at cross-purposes; and the private police force is less legally accountable than the public force and represents a serious threat to the civil liberties of American citizens.

But even more importantly, the rise of private policing may signal a major shift in the nature of social control in American society. In their article, Shearing and Stenning argue that as the private police force both supplements and replaces the public police, protecting corporate interests becomes more important than fighting crime, and the social control network is expanded to sanction not only traditional criminal offenders, but also those who create the "opportunities" for crimes against corporations. Beyond this, Shearing and Stenning believe that the transition from public to private policing may indicate a fundamental shift in power in capitalist societies away from the state or public sector and toward big capital or the private sector.

Law and Punishment

Herbert Fingarette

I would like to expound a retributivist view of punishment—one that shows why the law *must* punish lawbreakers, *must* make them suffer, in a way fitting to the crime, independently of any specific consequences of the punishment, even independently of any good done by the system of law as a whole. I confess, with some trepidation, that this is an extreme instance of what Professor H. L. A. Hart dubbed, in *Punishment and Responsibility*, the "fierce" version of retributivism. I would prefer to call it "strong" retributivism. He speaks of it as a "mysterious piece of moral alchemy" over which "a cloud of doubt . . . has settled." In the 1972 Supreme Court capital punishment case, *Furman* v. *Georgia*, the justices characterize the retributive use of punishment in terms of "naked vengeance," a need of our "baser selves." Retributive punishment has had a bad press among the twentieth-century enlightened. Professor A. C. Ewing undoubtedly spoke for many who have given thought to the problem when, in his *The Morality of Punishment*, he said he found retributive punishment incapable of being brought into rational connection with our other ethical beliefs. However, he did acknowledge that it is an attitude so deeply and widely held as to suggest much caution before concluding that it has no merit.

In my analysis I will show why so many have found retributive punishment to be repugnant—a view that I share—but I will also show that it is a necessity internal to law. In spite of the many roles that have been ascribed to punishment in the literature on that topic—many of them with some justice—the one role, the only role, that is strictly necessary, and that lies at the heart of punishment, has never yet been clearly disentangled and identified. I hope to do that.

Moreover, the analysis of retributive punishment that I present turns out to be easily generalizable beyond the law to any case where one person exercises power over another person's will—for example, by directing, regulating, ordering, or commanding the person how to act or how not to act. Thus the issues go far beyond those of a specialized topic in penology; the issues ultimately center on the human will, and human suffering. As far as my own discussion here goes, however, the larger issues will have to remain a matter of allusions and side remarks.

Source: Herbert Fingarette, "Law and Punishment," *The Center Magazine* 13 (January/February 1980):42–50. Reprinted with permission.

Since retributivism has had such a bad press in recent times, the question inevitably arises: How have retributivists defended their view? I have no intention of attempting here a comprehensive answer to this question. However, I do wish to begin by setting a background against which the shape of the problem as I see it, and the solution I propose, will stand out more sharply. To this end I want to review, in an admittedly brief and rather dogmatic way, some answers to the question, "Why retributive punishment?" that have already appeared in the literature, and to mention some difficulties I find with these answers.

Immanuel Kant was a "fierce" retributivist if ever there was one. In his *The Metaphysical Elements of Justice,* he held that we should punish simply out of respect for law, respect for the "categorical imperative" of retributive punishment. I think there is a truth hidden in such a thesis—I say "hidden" because Kant does not go on to answer satisfactorily the more basic question: Why would the categorical imperative of law require retribution, imposition of suffering, as the necessary response to lawbreaking?

Tradition and intuition tell us—that's what lawbreakers deserve. But reason still asks, Why? Tom steals money now; Tom is made to suffer later. Why is *that* necessary? What is supposed to be the significant relation between these two events? I have found this question deeply puzzling as soon as one strips away the often dubious assumption that the suffering will have a beneficial effect, or that it is an unavoidable side effect. In any case, the retributive intent is, specifically, to make the person suffer, not merely to tolerate this, or to use it, if appropriate, as a means to some further end.

Kant tries to justify retribution in two ways. He says, first, that justice is the condition under which the will of one person can be conjoined with the will of another in accordance with the universal law of freedom. Coercion—in this context equivalent to crime—is a hindrance to freedom; therefore the state's use of counter-coercion, in turn, to counteract the initial criminal coercion, is consistent with freedom, and is not only just but is our right.

So says Kant—but, unfortunately, all that the argument teaches, if we accept the spirit of the premises, is that anything that deters the initial coercion is in that respect conducive to justice. In spite of Kant's intent, the argument goes to the issue of deterrence, not to a formal principle of retribution. And even in regard to deterrence it fails to show that coercion is necessary; we might instead prevent criminally coercive acts by using rational persuasion, or by offering love and compassion, or financial, or psychological help. So this argument of Kant's fails to show a necessity even for coercion, much less retributive coercion.

Kant also argues that if I steal from others, I steal from myself: by making the ownership of property insecure, I render my own property insecure. If one were to take this as a dubious empirical proposition, it still would fail to show a necessity for the state to impose additional suffering. If, however, it is a matter of one's relation to the abstract principle of ownership—which is more what Kant intends—I still fail to see why additional suffering, beyond whatever is inherent in being a betrayer of principle, must be imposed by the state on the thief. Kant fails here to justify punishment for any reason—retributive or deterrent.

Ilham Dilman has proposed, in his "Socrates and Dostoevsky on Punishment" in *Philosophy and Literature*, an analogous, though more subjective, version of the second of Kant's arguments: in recognizing what we have done as a crime, we are pained by it, he says. But again I would add: even if this really is so, it does not justify the state's imposing further pain on me. So far there is no justification of punishment. Dilman then suggests that the state can punish as a way of bringing the moral significance of the affair home to the criminal. But then the imposition of such suffering is justified by reference to the aim of inducing subsequent moral reform, not to the aim of retribution for a past act. Dilman's thesis and those of philosophers from Bishop Joseph Butler to Professor J. Feinberg also fail to account for the fact that we may punish retributively even when no moral condemnation or disapprobation is in order: as J. D. Mabbott reminds us in his 1939 article, "Punishment," in *Mind*, a judge may respect the principles that motivated an act contrary to law, and yet properly punish the convicted lawbreaker. So the justified expression of moral outrage is not a necessary condition for justifying retributive punishment.

Finally, Dilman ultimately assumes what is so generally assumed, and what I find as centrally puzzling: Why should suffering be the response to wrongdoing, to lawbreaking? The idea is perfectly familiar to us. But how can we explain the connection, the connection retributivists think they intuit when they contemplate the meaning of law, lawbreaking, and suffering?

Well—isn't it a case of "tit for tat," "you get what you deserve"? Isn't it only fair that if you make someone else suffer, you should suffer? But this is not to explain or justify, only to affirm a principle of vengeance or retaliation. This does, however, suggest some important recent attempts at rationalizing the principle of retributive punishment.

Professor Herbert Morris has argued, in his book, *On Guilt and Innocence*, for retributive punishment precisely on the ground that it establishes a fair distribution of burdens and benefits: *You* accept the burden of complying with the law; however, *I* steal, and enjoy the illicit benefits; so I am punished, punished enough to cancel out the benefits I illicitly enjoyed. The balance sheet of benefits and burdens passes final audit.

Although this kind of view is intended to provide a rationale for retributive punishment, it fails to do so. On this view, provided the books are ultimately balanced, I would seem to have two equally legitimate options—paying my debts earlier in cash, or paying later in punishment. But surely that is not the intent of the law prohibiting stealing. The intent is precisely to *deny* us a legitimate alternative to paying the storekeeper for what we take. And even if I restore the balance by returning the stolen goods, and by paying back any incidental losses incurred by the storekeeper, it still remains intelligible and important—not only in principle but in the practice of the law—to ask whether I should also be punished. So Morris' kind of view—the "economic" view, one might call it—fails to account for law as prohibition, and—not surprisingly, as I will explain—this view fails to make intelligible the question of punishment as something over and above the equitable distribution of burdens and benefits.

One may emphasize the fairness aspect of the matter of distribution of benefits and burdens—that it is unfair of me to take the larcenous advantage I did, that, therefore, punishment is in order. But if we are not balancing benefits and burdens, the principle of fairness seems to pose a deterrent task, not a retributive one: Can I or others be deterred from taking unfair advantage? Imposition of suffering may or may not do that job—there is no necessary connection.

As a matter of fact, it is unclear whether and to what degree imposing suffering does have a deterrent effect. The deterrent effects of punishment are of the utmost complexity to assess; that is one reason why it is important to show—if it can be shown—that retributive punishment as the normal response to lawbreaking is necessary independently of the specific deterrent effects that may or may not be associated with a particular punishment.

There is no doubt that sometimes the ends of deterrence, rehabilitation, and promotion of the social welfare can be pursued by, among other things, inflicting suffering on lawbreakers. This is, broadly speaking, the basis on which utilitarians would justify punishing. But utilitarian approaches seem to show at most that we may have to tolerate imposing suffering as a means to these social ends. That is not the retributive insight. A rule that the guilty should be punished might be made to look plausible on rule-utilitarian grounds; but the relation between the lawbreaking and the infliction of suffering is external—it makes sense only by reason of the tacit and complex causal connections it is supposed to have with the ends approved by utilitarians. But the retributivist insight is that the sense of the principle lies *within*: There is something about the nature of law, of lawbreaking, of punishment, that makes punishment called for when the law is broken, and this fittingness is there independently of consideration of a utilitarian kind, independently of whether the suffering does happen to call the criminal back to conscience, independently of whether those who do the punishing get some expressive or vicarious gratification from it.

In short, what I have been saying up to now is that, characteristically, attempts to account for retributivist punishment of lawbreakers either turn out to be at least covertly utilitarian—i.e., aiming at deterrence of future crime or reform—or they fail to justify retributive punishment at all. And the utilitarian arguments don't appropriately justify the aim of making lawbreakers suffer; at most they justify tolerating suffering if, on the basis of complex causal hypotheses, we believe it to be a means to a desired end, or a side effect of such a means.

There have been some retributivists—e.g., M. P. Golding, A. C. Ewing, and Mabbott—who have seen that the connection between failing to comply with categorical requirements of law and being punished for such failure is not a contingent connection but is in some way an internal necessity of law. Unfortunately, these true-blue retributivists have generally remained satisfied to argue their case primarily by criticizing alternative views. Their own constructive case—if such it can be called—has rested on simple appeal to intuition. We are just supposed to "see" that if you break a law, punishment is in order. Analysis generally stops right there where it begins, and question-begging discussion is all too common in the literature.

I believe that we can go further, and that we can uncover a central and necessary connection that underlies the other reasons that may on occasion reinforce the appropriateness of punishment.

Those—e.g., Richard Wasserstrom—who have tried to show that retributive punishment of lawbreakers is justified have generally assumed that the task is one of moral justification. On the contrary, my aim here is to show how the necessity for punishment is independent of moral justification, even moral justification of law itself. In order to show that the necessity is internal to law, I will, naturally, have to comment on some features of law generally. Eventually we will come back to punishment.

Basic to my constructive analysis is a concern with law as an institution of government, an "enterprise" as Lon Fuller calls it, in his book, *The Morality of Law*, rather than as merely a set of abstract conceptions, or a system of rules or principles. I want to view law as Jerome Hall has urged us to view it in his *Foundations of Jurisprudence*, as "law-in-action." In so doing, I am not begging controversial questions about what law is in its distinctive or essential nature. I merely assume what is vague but obvious: law characteristically is an institution for government. This is one obviously legitimate perspective from which to view law, and it is the perspective from which, I believe, we get the deepest insight into punishment.

Within this larger context of law as a governing enterprise, I want to examine law more specifically, in its character as having force, as being in force, as enforceable and enforced. When I speak of the force of law I have in mind not its authority but its power—power over what people actually do, the power to make people do things, or, to use the term I will often use here, the power to require people to do things. Also closely associated with the idea of the power of law are, of course, such notions as coercion, sanction, and punishment.

That law as a governing institution does exercise power is an evident and important truth. My task here may be seen as an effort to bring out more explicitly some of what is contained in the meaning of that proposition. We do not here need to enter the persistent controversy among scholars as to whether this element of power—of coerciveness, sanctions, force—is to be viewed as the central or the distinctive feature of law, or as merely one necessary feature, or as not necessary or central at all. Associated with one or another position on this controversial question is a galaxy of names that include Kant, Jeremy Bentham, John Austin, Hans Kelsen, H. L. A. Hart, Jerome Hall, and Lon Fuller. But, whatever their differing opinions on the concept of force and the concept of law, all these people agree that if law is in practice to govern effectively, it must be able to exercise power—ultimately force.

The word I prefer to emphasize here is power, rather than force, since force seems too strongly to suggest physical force—which is what some scholars, such as

Fuller, may have taken it to mean here. But I believe we will capture what is at issue in a far more illuminating way if we think of the law exercising its power in governing even when it does not apply physical force. When we speak of a nation exercising its power, or a labor union, or the law, or even the Mafia, we do not mean to allude merely to the actual occasions of the use of physical violence or force. It is a question—not to be begged but to be elucidated—what role physical force plays in the exercise of power over people—particularly the law's distinctive kind of power to make people do things.

Of course, as others, such as Hall, Hart, and Fuller, have said, a large part of the law is designed initially to confer powers on people—the power to make bequests, or to make and enforce contracts, or to buy and own property.

But it remains the case, as Jerome Hall has pointed out, that it is the law that originally has the power, and that defines what must be done if the power of the law is to be invocable; and it is the law whose power to lay down categorical requirements must be invoked to enforce our rights and privileges. I am not trying to say that the law is really or ultimately nothing but power *over* people; I mean only to emphasize the central and necessary role played by the power to lay down categorical requirements even in those areas of law where, when looked at from another angle, law may be said to give power *to* people.

Let me enter a caveat: I am in no way meaning to deny or to minimize other dimensions of the law—its moral significance, its authority, its political significance in regard to human rights, even, perhaps, its religious or metaphysical dimensions. But my message is this—that if we want to understand the necessity for retributive punishing of lawbreakers, as distinguished from the occasional desirability or tolerability of making people suffer for other reasons connected with law and lawbreaking, we will find this necessity in the study of law as power.

I want now to call attention to a specific feature of the law's exercise of power. This feature is so characteristic, and therefore so utterly taken for granted, as to remain generally unremarked, too obvious to need mention and yet paradoxical when we attend to it directly. The paradox is that those subject to a requirement of law necessarily have—at least initially—the effective power, of their own will, to act contrariwise.

The point of laying down a requirement of law is that the person subject to law is required to *will* what complies with that law. But then it follows, as I say, that the individual also retains the power to will otherwise. This situation is characteristic of the power of law: if we did not normally retain the power of will, it would be pointless to enact laws telling us how to act.

The question to which I will return in various ways is this: What sort of requirement is this that allows noncompliance; and what is the power at issue here that leaves crucial power in the subject?

One thing I will say at once, though in itself it does not explain very much. Since we are required to will what the law says, the power of law is, specifically, power over the will, as distinguished from power merely over the body or behavior.

This distinctive power—power over the will—is also to be found, equally characteristically and essentially, in other forms of exercise of power over people: commanding, ordering, directing, requiring, regulating, forbidding—even in non-law contexts. In all these, the person subject to the requirement is required to will what conforms to the requirement, but has the power to will otherwise.

In speaking of law as an exercise of power over the will I mean to challenge doctrines to the effect that the law allows us free choice, or that it respects our choice, or respects us as a "choosing being." There is truth in this, that I will mention much later. But such doctrines have been deeply misleading. The law does not respect our choice to comply or not; its power is exercised to forbid us from freely choosing between complying or not. The law threatens us. If we do not comply, it pursues and seeks to punish us.

Even such acute commentators as Professors Hart and Morris, who have said things consistent with what I am here saying, have also and repeatedly said or implied the contrary—that we are free to disobey the law, and that in this freedom lies a fundamental merit of the law.

What truth there is in this latter view can be better expressed, I think, by saying that power over the will is a power to constrain our freedom to will something, without necessarily denying us the power so to will.

It is by reason of our not being free to disobey the law that what I am calling power over the will can be distinguished from certain other forms of influence on the will, for example, rational argument, persuasion, appeal, exhortation, request. A requirement that is disobeyed is not like a futile request. Part of the point of making a request—as distinguished from laying down a requirement—is that I am to be free to refuse the request. Not so with the requirement. The requirement has force even in relation to the noncomplying act. We have the concept of enforcing the requirement, even after the act.

But what can this mean? How is it done? In fact there are a number of ways in which this can be done. All of them have something of a retributive character, broadly speaking, though only one of these ways constitutes, strictly speaking, punishment as retributive. I will run through them, in turn, coming last to retributive punishment in the purest sense.

One such *post facto* kind of enforcement is possible when we have to do with a status defined and constituted by law. Marriage, contracts, title to property—these are statuses constituted by law, and the law can, after the fact, and retroactively, establish the nullity of such statuses. Thus, a purported contract, later shown to be based on fraud, can be rescinded, authoritatively, and retroactively annulled, declared never to have been a valid contract.

Now, annulment is not, per se, retributive punishment, since while it may result in suffering for the noncomplier, that is not the point of it. Annulment is, however, an aspect of the exercise of power over the will, since it retroactively negates putative legal statuses not in accord with the requirements of law, and regardless of the will of any noncompliant claimant. Since it is an aspect of the exercise of power over the will, I want to draw an important lesson from it immediately, before going on to consider restitution and reparation, and punishment proper (retribution).

I speak of annulment as an aspect of the exercise of power in order to bring out that the exercise of power over the will is a complex pattern in which the act of annulment is only an element, not the whole. We must see the law's exercise of power as a continuing institutional transaction, analogous, for example, to the enterprise we call a university. In such institutional enterprises there may or may not be a clear point of origin for the whole: one university may have begun under charter, but another may have emerged insensibly over the centuries; the Napoleonic Code of law originated as such at a certain time; the common law evolved; statutes and court orders have datable origins. But whether there is a clear point of origin or not, the adoption of a constitution, or the enactment of a statute, or the signing of a university charter is, at most, an initial step in a continuing, complex transaction of indefinite duration. The signing of the university charter, lacking anything more, is obviously an empty ceremony. Arrangements for buildings, faculty, students, financing must be made, and continuously remade. Degree requirements are laid down. Classes required for the degree must actually be offered; and students lacking credit for such courses must not be granted degrees. These are the sorts of things that constitute the university's exercise of its power to educate and to promote research.

In the law, the act of annulment is not an isolated exercise of power, but a phase of a larger transaction. Annulment can be seen as part of the follow-through of an exercise of power whose specific initial phase was, for example, enactment of the statute that in a later phase is now being enforced by means of the annulment. If there were no such follow-through, the enactment of the statute would amount to a *pro forma*, ceremonial act as far as the law's exercise of power is concerned. True, one might hold that the statute—viewed as an authoritative norm within the law as a system of norms—has validity. In some normative sense of the term—a sense we may here leave vague—it could be held that we are required to conform to the statute. But if there is no policy of annulling a legal status claimed under the statute— even though a normative requirement of the statute has demonstrably not been met—then in regard to the exercise of the power of the law we are not required to fulfill the condition in question. So one who is concerned with doctrine will say there is such a requirement; but one who is concerned with power, and with questions of a practical kind, will say the requirement is not serious, not enforced, is in practice not a requirement at all.

It is important to disentangle the concept of law as exercise of power from concepts of law as a system of doctrine, or rules, or principles, or norms; for, as I aim to show, the necessity for retributive punishment lies within the law as an institution exercising power.

So I conclude that annulment, then, is a phase of a larger institutional transaction whose nature as exercise of power is not determinate until it is evident whether in appropriate cases a putative requirement of law is to be enforced by annulment.

It is when the law humbles the individual's will, by reason of the earlier failure to will in accordance with law, that we have in law retributive punishment, strictly speaking. The aim here is neither to nullify nor to restore or repair the objective social conditions to meet some legal standard. It is—one may say in the Kantian spirit—a purely formal aim; it is the categorical imperative of law itself. It is of the essence of the law's power that the will be subject to law, i.e., either conform or in consequence be constrained. Without this, there simply is no power of law. My imperative—unlike the Kantian one, of course—is cast in terms of law as power. But it is a formal principle, entirely independent of the empirical consequences of the punishment. It is the principle that gives sense to the notion of a requirement upon our will, as distinguished from mere requests or appeals. It is part of what it means for the law to exercise its power over us, to require things of us, that those who do not of their own will comply are normally punished. Punishing is the humbling of the defiant—or at least the disrespectful—will.

Now I must explore, however briefly, some of the implications, and a few of the many questions, that arise from this view.

Punishment, as it emerges here, is pure suffering. To suffer, says the Oxford English Dictionary, is "to undergo," "to endure," "to have something . . . inflicted or imposed upon one," "to submit . . . ," "to be subjected to." This is the ancient sense, as old as Chaucer, and as old as the Greek *pathos*. In short, in the respect that we suffer, we experience what we do not will, or, in a stronger sense, we experience what is against our will.

It is because certain kinds of experience, such as bodily pain, the deprivation of liberty or property, separation from loved ones, the mutilation of the body, are so generally counter to our will, that they are normally associated with suffering and lend themselves to institutionalization as punishments. Punishment need not be painful, however—capital punishment need not be, nor is paying a fine. It is the humbling of the will that is of the essence. It is in this sense that, as Kant said, "If what happens to someone is willed by him, it cannot be a punishment . . . it is impossible to will to be punished." I take this to allow that we may and sometimes do cooperate in the doing of that which makes us suffer—paying a fine, surrendering to arrest and imprisonment. The respect in which this is suffering, however, is the respect in which it is something we would will not to undergo, were it not that because of our earlier noncompliance the law now imposes it. This is why I speak of humbling the will, and not of necessarily rendering it completely impotent as is done when the person punished does not cooperate at all.

I should also stress that my argument does not commit us to the Kantian form of categorical imperative that we must punish every criminal, or even more broadly, every nonconformer to law. Kant himself had finally to confess this could not rationally be accepted. My thesis requires only that there be an effective policy of punishing those who will contrary to law. Some noncompliers will escape punishment, but there may also be purposeful exceptions out of considerations of mercy and compassion, or of high state policy. But these failures and exceptions must be limited. We can express this by saying that it must be normal for people who fail to respect the law to be punished. The less persuaded we are that it is normal, the less persuaded we are that the law has genuine force.

A few words as to how to punish, and how much, are in order. "Let the punishment fit the crime." This is a good retributive slogan, and in one of its meanings it follows from what I have said. Direct imposition of suffering—frustration of the will—should fit, in the sense that it is limited in scope: it should be just what is required by the offending act, but no more, since it is against the main thrust of the law—which is to leave us our power of will.

The famous retributivist principle of *lex talionis*—the idea of retaliation in kind—takes on, in this context, a completely general meaning: The reason for punishment is an act manifesting a will that would frustrate the power of law. What is the response in kind? It is for the law, in turn, to frustrate the power of that will. I believe this formula does really capture the traditional spirit of retributive punishment as administered to a disobedient subject by a sovereign, a parent, a commanding God, or a system of law. The ever-present root of the matter, whatever the moral or religious connotations it also may have, is the clash of wills—one dominant, the other subject.

My generalized version of the *lex talionis* strips off the morally and logically impossible burden of retaliating in every case with an act of the same specific kind as the offense—the Bible's literal "eye for an eye," or the kind of specific fittingness that Kant had in mind in urging the castration of rapists.

Interpreting these principles in this way leaves room for an indefinite variety of specific forms of punishment—which we do in fact find in different times and places. What is common to all is the emphatic and direct humbling of the noncomplying will.

As for what might be called the quantitative aspect—How much suffering?—we can also derive a basic principle from my theses, and at the same time dissolve some common objections to the *lex talionis* principle. Punishment, I have said, must be limited to what is necessary; and this is determined by the gravity of the offense. There is a common—and I believe mistaken—assumption that it is the gravity of the moral wrong that determines the gravity of the offense. Of course, it is doubtful that all offenses against the law are moral wrongs. But the chief problem here is the failure to explain the supposed relationship between moral wrong and the imposition of suffering, whether as a general relationship or as a set of specific equivalences between classes of wrongs and kinds or degrees of imposed suffering.

It is my view that the gravity of the offense derives not from the putative moral wrong of it but from the gravity of the requirement it violates.

Of course moral judgments may have influenced the legislative decision to establish the requirement of law and its gravity. But other facts, too, have an important influence on the legislative decision—policy and politics, technical considerations related to the field of activity covered by the law, and considerations internal to the legal system. We do not need here to know how legislators weigh and synthesize all this in order to arrive at such decisions. They do so; and it is as an aspect of laying down a requirement that they also decide with what urgency or stringency the requirement is intended. That is, they establish, as part and parcel of the legislative act, how grave the requirement is to be, and it is this that determines, in turn, the gravity of the offense against that requirement. The graver the legislators mean their requirement to be, the graver the punishment. Or, to put it another way, the graver the requirement laid upon the subject's will, the graver must be the humbling of the defiant will.

Since the entire issue lies within one fundamental dimension—that of the will and its power—suiting the specific punishment to the specific offense poses no fundamental conceptual problem, unlike the situation when viewed in the incommensurable terms posed by the moral approach to punishment.

Up to this point, I have tried to show that the line of analysis I present generates and illuminates the pattern of elements characteristically found in the retributivist intuitions: that the offense is the sufficient ground for imposing suffering on the offender, and that the suffering imposed is to be fitting to the offense.

I add my opinion that, with a few suitable modifications, this view is also generalizable to any institutionalized transaction in which one person—whether human or divine—is taken to exercise dominion over the will of another by commanding, ordering, regulating, legislating, or otherwise laying down categorical requirements.

Now I want, finally, to turn to a few remarks on some of the moral implications of the view I have presented.

Perhaps my concern to demonstrate the necessity of punishment has obscured what I take to be self-evident: retributive punishment is in itself an evil. It is suffering which *insofar as it is retributive,* has a necessary role in law independently of particular circumstances, consequence, or moral justification. Punishment— unlike annulment or reparation—does not even constitute a kind of retroactive erasure or repair of the offending act. There *is* a reason for punishing: without this as an element in the institutional enterprise, exercising power by requiring someone to do something would be unintelligible. But, in itself, punishment has no constructive aim. If it tends to deter, or to induce moral reform, so much the better. Under ideal circumstances—i.e., entirely rational subjects and entirely reliable administration of laws that conform to the good and the right—punishment would exert a consistent deterrent and morally reformative influence. In real life, punishment may deter or reform, or it may not; indeed, it may, and too often does, have a contrary effect. And this element of contingency is one major reason why, when the general practice of punishment is justified by reference ultimately to deterrent or reformative ends, that justification is subject to serious challenge. But what is not contingent is that those who disobey requirements must be made to suffer. And yet, as I say, in that status, as something to be administered regardless of the good done, regardless of the moral context generally, punishment—the purposeful infliction of suffering on a human being—is an evil.

Of course the offender may have been the initial evildoer. But punishment adds another evil. Two evils are more evil than one, the way I do the moral addition. I have not been able to understand the moral alchemy of some retributivists who claim that when an evildoer is made to suffer, those two evils together make, in themselves, a good. Furthermore, the offender may not have done any evil at all, in which case the necessary punishment is the only evil.

It is this evil of punishment, so basic to it as retributive, that has captured the attention and evoked the abhorrence of so many critics of retribution. The view I present allows us to see this persistent and widespread criticism of retribution as valid. On the other hand, retributionists through the centuries have insisted that we must punish offenders for their offenses. On my view, in this insistence they, too, have been right.

It follows that a moral justification of punishment could only be indirect and hypothetical: if law, as a governing institution, is morally justified, then, as unfortunately necessary to law, the practice of punishing lawbreakers is in that respect indirectly morally justified as a necessary cost.

There are those who hold that law does indeed embody moral attitudes of members of the community, and that therefore punishment, as required by such law, is significant as an expression of those moral attitudes. This is essentially a historical-sociological thesis; I think there is much truth in it, though it can be misleading when social alienation is widespread. But in any case it is not necessary to my theses about punishment that the law should embody community moral attitudes.

This sociological line of thought is at times confused in the legal literature with the moral judgment that government by law (or some particular system of government by law) is morally justified. My theses presuppose no such moral judgment, however. I merely assert that if there is to be government by law—whether morally justified or not—there must be a policy of punishing lawbreakers.

It isn't even as if punishment were justified by the social aim of keeping the law effective. It is not difficult for us to imagine social situations in which the more the noncompliers are punished, the more alienated they and their sympathizers become, and the less effective the law becomes. But even so, if the law is to lay down requirements, this can only be intelligible in the institutional framework of power if there is a policy of retributive punishment—self-defeating as this policy may ultimately be. In short, deterrence is not the issue here.

Although I neither presuppose nor venture here any over-all position on the ultimate question whether law is morally justified, I do, in conclusion, have two things to say on that question. I mention them because they are so directly implied by the theses I have been developing. One line of implication tends to justify law; the other to condemn it.

I have emphasized that the exercise of the power of law over our will constitutes, as such, a denial of our freedom. But it is important to recognize the way in which this distinctive power—power over our will—does embody respect for our freedom and for our status as choosing beings. The point is that law does leave us free to do much as we will—provided that what we will also conforms to the requirements of law. In this way, a system of law, though it constrains the will in its direct import for that will, can allow an enormous residual range of freedom. There are millions of law-abiding persons in this country, and yet there are not as many as two who live exactly similar lives. This large area of residual freedom is inherently associated with power over the will. It contrasts, for example, with the exercise of power over our bodies. When the law acts to prevent some specific behavior by chaining a person's body, this also forecloses almost all other behavior as well.

Moreover, intimately associated with this residual freedom is a pragmatic benefit on so great a scale as to pertain to the evolution of the species: the law, in its exercise of power, harnesses to its aims the individual intelligences and wills of all persons subject to the power of law. For it becomes both the burden and the opportunity of all such subjects that, in carrying on the multifarious business of society, they are required to arrange, of their own initiative, how to do so in a way which, in each particular context, is law-abiding. Thus intelligence is multiplied millionfold in the service of the law, and intelligence operates on the spot rather than only in some distant government bureau.

As pragmatic, political animals, we may decide to accept as a given for our foreseeable future the fact of government under law, reassuring ourselves in part, at least, by its known moral benefits, and its clear advantages over some other ways of governing. But then, I maintain, in accepting law we necessarily accept retributive punishment.

The practical upshot of this aspect of my argument, then, is that penological reform, which is so urgently needed, is likely to meet far less popular resistance if it conforms with intuition and with reason by accepting the central retributive role of punishment as necessary. Reform should as far as reasonably possible embody measures to eliminate unnecessary suffering and degradation, to aid in deterrence, and to increase humane and constructive services, as well as taking into account whatever empirical knowledge we do attain. To reconcile all such legitimate considerations with the necessity of retribution, not to eliminate retribution, that is the practical task.

From a larger philosophical perspective, and by contrast, I would remind you that some of the great teachers of civilization have seen that punishment is dominion over the will, that it flows necessarily from law as dominion over the will, and they have for these very reasons rejected government by law in their ideal visions. Among those who saw this were Confucius, Lao-tzu, Jesus, and the inspirers of anarchist and utopian Communist thought. I now also see this as a central thesis in that amazing Old Testament text on suffering, the Book of Job. It is as important, I think, to see how law and its necessities of power corrupt human dignity at the core—by establishing dominion over the wills of human beings—as it is to see how, in other ways, the law is distinctively humane and civilizing in its mode of operation.

These, of course, are large themes, some of which I have been developing elsewhere. I mention them here only in order to emphasize that once we see punishment as an aspect of power over will, as an aspect of the clash of wills, of human subjection, we see both punishment and law in a very large context indeed, larger than is suggested by many contemporary treatments of the problem. We then see that the question of punishment cannot be encapsulated as a mere question of technical reform within the law. Discussion of the central role of punishment must rest on moral and spiritual assessments on the largest scale. This is a philosophical task that returns us to the classical contexts of man's nature and destiny. I hope I have at least helped to place the problem back into focus.

LAW: ORDER OR REPRESSION? 2

Law Doesn't Make People Behave
Harold Pepinsky and Paul Jesilow

A punishment is an evil inflicted by public authority on him who hath done or omitted that which is judged by the same authority to be a transgression of the law, to the end that the will of men may thereby the better be disposed to obedience. . . . Before the institution of Commonwealth, every man had a right to everything, and to do whatsoever he thought necessary to his own preservation—subduing, hurting, or killing any man in order thereunto. And this is the foundation of that right of punishing, which is exercised in every commonwealth. For the subjects did not give the sovereign that right, but only in laying down theirs, strengthened him to use his own, as he should think fit, for the preservation of them all; so that it was not given, but left to him, and to him only, and (excepting the limits set him by natural law) as entire, as in the condition of mere nature, and of war of every one against his neighbor.

Thomas Hobbes, 1651

Prominent as crime and punishment are in the media, Americans have come to equate law with social order. People are inclined to agree with English social philosopher Thomas Hobbes, that unless a strong sovereign uses law enforcement to beat the citizenry into line, people will carry out a war of all against all among themselves. And yet it has been shown that law enforcement systematically ignores the major portion of crime, and has little effect on the rest. Some believe that this breakdown of law and order is a recent development, that it is because law enforcement is disintegrating that disorder is rising. There is no indication, however, that law enforcement was less selective or more effectual in the past, or that Americans endanger one another's life, liberty, or property today any more than a hundred years ago.

The State as a Source of Violence

In one respect, Americans have been relatively lucky. Although they employ a remarkably large criminal-justice force, they generally have not allowed one political

Source: Harold Pepinsky and Paul Jesilow, *Myths That Cause Crime*, second edition, pp. 131–142. Published by Seven Locks Press, Cabin John, Maryland. Copyright © 1985 by Seven Locks Press. Reprinted with permission.

faction to overpower another. Hence, the kind of violence that has recently resulted in the killing of thousands of Mayan Indians by Guatemalan government forces has been avoided. The one major exception is the five-year period of the Civil War where one in six American men was killed or wounded in combat, a statistic that horribly overshadows today's police homicide reports.

By creating monopolies on force, states have the greatest capacity to do harm to people, and they do so when officials become too bent on enforcing order. The mass slaughter of Jews by Nazis in Germany represents another example of how deadly people can become in the use of state apparatus. And of course, war among states poses the greatest threat to peace and order of all, to the very existence of humanity.

It is obvious that some kind of control is necessary to restrain people from killing, raping, and pillaging one another. But it does not follow that the might of law enforcement creates this order by sending uniformed (or even plainclothes) forces to suppress the citizens.

Conditions Favoring Peace

Anthropologists have made an interesting discovery. Communities are more peaceful when ties of kinship cut across political lines. The prototype of the peaceful community is one that is matrilocal and patriarchal, that is, where men in political coalitions rule the communities, and where men move into the area occupied by their wives' families when they marry. If male political rivals start to fight in the community, it is likely that other men, who share blood ties with both disputants through marriage, will intervene to cut the fighting short. There has been a similar finding in London where family violence was lower in communities in which women stayed home and developed tight social networks with other wives. Husbands who had to answer to one another through concerted complaints from communities of wives were more restrained in their treatment of their own wives.

This does not imply that to keep the public peace women have to stay at home while men circulate. As a matter of social justice, women ought to be free to enjoy the same liberties as men. Happily, there are a number of other ways that cross-cutting ties can be established in communities.

Twenty years ago, urban planner Jane Jacobs described such communities in a much talked about book, *The Death and Life of Great American Cities*. She describes what she calls healthy urban neighborhoods as pockets in inner cities that may seem chaotic on the surface, but to the people who live, work, shop, eat, and drink there, are not only lively but safe and secure. She contrasts these neighborhoods to others that have deteriorated into filth, depression, and danger. Healthy neighborhoods are distinguished by their variety. Many activities take place there among high and low income people, old buildings are mixed with new, and short, twisting streets provide alternate paths for people to walk.

Socially, these neighborhoods are replete with cross-cutting ties. A resident going on vacation leaves a key with a small shop owner, or when a man seems to be threatening a child (who in Jacobs's illustration turns out to be a father chastising but not hurting his daughter), customers and residents who happen to be there peacefully gather around to ensure that nothing untoward happens. When a person stands at a bus stop on a Sunday, someone leans out the window to shout that the buses are not running. When inhabitants are away at work, people who work and shop in the neighborhood unselfconsciously keep watch, and at night when people are sleeping, customers in late night restaurants and bars—often "regulars" who have a stake in the welfare of the area—circulate and keep the streets secure. In the early evening, residents sit on stoops and keep the streets safe and alive. The welfare of those who live in the area depends on maintaining the goodwill of businesspeople and customers, and vice versa. Since interdependence cuts across interest groups, there are people awake and about at practically all hours of the day and night in sufficient numbers to help a spirit of accommodation and support prevail. There is no room for a gang or a clique to take possession of the neighborhood, and yet most people there belong to some identifiable group that restrains them from isolated acts of violence, predation, or destruction. It is only when one class of building or ownership or residents or entrepreneurs predominates over others that such a neighborhood begins to decline.

The impact of cross-cutting ties is corroborated by architect Patricia Brantingham and lawyer Paul Brantingham, who researched patterns of residential burglary in Tallahassee, Florida. Using any number of economic and demographic indices, they consistently find that burglary is lowest where adjoining city blocks are, on average, most alike, highest where blocks differ most. The only way to make burglary low throughout a city is to manage to have as much of the mix of people and wealth as possible contained within each and every city block. For example, the greater the spread of rents charged in each of two city blocks, the more likely that the average rent in one block will approximate the other; the more nearly each neighborhood approaches being a microcosm of the entire city, the harder it becomes to distinguish or discriminate among them. If so much variety is to be tolerated in a neighborhood, it will require that ties cut across many kinds of people who use the neighborhood, and that commonality of interest and interdependence among groups overwhelms the propensity of members of single groups to go it alone—either by taking over the neighborhood or by abandoning it.

There are obvious limits to variety that can be tolerated. Only the desperate will live or work or shop at the boundaries of a major airport, or at the gates of a smoke-producing oil refinery or steel plant. Only the wealthy can afford to live or have businesses where property taxes rise too high, or where a major department store pays high rent and is able to outsell all competitors in a neighborhood. Although there is room for some light industry, some exclusive shops, and for scattered high-rent residences, the general scale of enterprises in a heterogeneous neighborhood has to be small.

At a time when Adam Smith has gained renewed popularity among economists, it is interesting to note that his laissez-faire economy required that the average enterprise in most sectors be small. Monopolization of markets was anathema to Smith. One can easily suppose that he would have become an ally of the late economist E. F. Schumacher, who is perhaps best known for his book, *Small is Beautiful; Economics As If People Mattered.* Schumacher advocates the development of "appropriate technology" which would cost no more than five times the annual income of the lowest-paid worker who used it and would require creative input from each worker who used it. While technological ingenuity would be used to take the drudgery out of work, it would help industry remain labor intensive, requiring human labor rather than displacing it. Enterprises constructed around appropriate technology would be small, with a maximum of perhaps three hundred employees. Pay differentials in the enterprise could be tolerated, but would be restricted; workers would own the enterprise and, with representatives of community groups, sit on its board of directors. Part of the profits from the enterprise would go to the workers, part to community projects, and part to capital investment. An objective would be to have enterprises rely as heavily as possible on use of native and preferably renewable resources, and would concentrate sales as much as possible on local markets.

It is imperative that such a new economic model be followed. There is a worldwide depression because established economic bases are collapsing. World markets for finished products are nearly saturated despite the fact that a major portion of the world's work force does not actually produce. New industries, such as those in high technology, both promise to make more workers superfluous and have highly restricted markets. (The market for home computers and electronic games will only carry the sale of micro-chips so far.) Industries are borrowing more just to stay afloat while sales remain limited, and investment in plant and equipment continues to decline because there is little reason to expect expansion of consumption.

Centralized production is wasteful of finite natural resources, and heavy machinery produces intolerable pollution. As the energy demands of heavy industry become increasingly centralized, more intensive energy production is required, leading to technology such as building nuclear reactors, which is both inordinately expensive and extremely threatening to human and other life. The international interdependence of centralized production breeds such resentment and desperation during hard times that a world military holocaust looms larger. Meanwhile, the new conservative economics continues to limit investment to this losing economic cause and strangle the capacity of communities to build new economies to compensate.

The construction of new economies promises not only to contribute to peace with local communities, but to reduce the scale of and stake in international conflict. Appropriate technology does not make communities isolationist; indeed, it rests on a free exchange of information, people, and capital among communities. And as we have just seen, small-scale economies that foster cross-cutting ties actually blur community boundaries, so that it becomes less clear where one community ends and another begins. That each enterprise relies most on local resources, people, and sales scarcely implies that a business in one "locality" would compete in the exact same market as another close by. At its extreme, such an economy would entail a virtually seamless web of social, economic, and political networks around the globe. But because networks are numerous and varied, and because their members are likely to have ties cutting across many networks, the consequences of economic failure of a single network would not be nearly so severe as they are when a large plant closes in a town today, neither for the members of the network themselves nor for others near or distant.

The development of such networks would increase the odds that every member of the community would be closely tied to several more. Membership in varied networks would offer a kind of freedom of movement and opportunity to those who could shift their involvement from one network toward another. The variety of allegiances would teach each community member to tolerate differences among people.

A key to establishing social peace is to offer people constructive outlets for energies that might otherwise be expended destructively. A tragic failing of conventional thinking about crime is its preoccupation with the negative: Crime hurts, so people must *not* do it. If crime is committed, the response is also negative: Let us drive the criminality out of the offender, or at least incapacitate the offender. By its preoccupation with repressing human behavior, conventional crime control consists of cures worse than the disease they are designed to attack.

If a society wants to stop people from committing crimes, it has to invest in things they *can* do instead. Human life consists of energy that craves outlet in interaction with others; the more constructive participation of people in community life can be expanded, the more social peace will reign.

In contemporary thought, childhood is the root of all human potential and of all evil. It is fair to say that childhood experience and its connection with delinquency has been the primary focus of American criminological research. Beyond criminology, Americans are also preoccupied with how children should be taught in school and raised at home. Just as criminal justice has swung back toward punishment, so American educators and parents have swung back toward the view that rigid discipline is needed to bring up children correctly. The idea that we ought to lay down strict rules for children, and that we ought to concentrate on having them perfect the rituals we call "basic skills," is a variant on the notion that law makes people behave.

Young children are notorious for energy, the epitome of life—with all its vices and virtues—as opposed to the quietude of death. A prominent response to this energy in recent years has been to diagnose it as hyperactivity, a form of learning disability, and tranquilize it out of existence.

This view of childhood—as a basically pathological condition—has blinded us to the rich constructive and creative potential that children offer to themselves and their communities. It is not merely that children cry for attention; their energy and involvement in activity intensifies when their work gains respect and appreciation from others. If children often need to be informed that their activity is obnoxious, they respond enthusiastically when discovering alternatives that please both adults and their peers. The greatest pleasure seems to come not by simply doing as told, but by having invented or initiated or created something that others appreciate. When a child who has spontaneously picked up a cloth and started to wipe furniture earns parental approval, it is almost magical to see the child so thoroughly enjoying "work." It is some time before the child learns that work done well has to earn a material reward.

Childhood ought to dispel notions that people are naturally lazy, that all work is drudgery, and that people need a combination of coercion and bribery to be productive. Instead, apathy and laziness seem to be the learned response of those who find that creative energy invariably goes unappreciated, and concerted destructiveness shows a combination of rage and the lack of alternatives for gaining recognition and attention. It is one thing to concede adults the power to object to the intolerable and to demand what they deem necessary. It is harder to see objections and demands as the foundation of productive childraising; the child who learns to be a creative contributor to the welfare of others will do so only when adults treat objections and demands as a necessary nuisance, and appreciate creative efforts more.

What new kinds of investment are to establishing social peace among adults, appreciation of creative and constructive activity is to bringing up productive and sane children. At root, people behave best when we give them opportunities to be valued for contributions they have a hand in conceiving and initiating. When the child spontaneously wipes the furniture, it is partly our surprise at seeing unexpected initiative from others that makes it special. Law presumes that we know what we want from others. If we succeed in achieving conformity in a changing world, we are apt to be disappointed by the sterility and unhelpfulness of what we get. Children who have not yet had ingenuity and initiative disciplined out of them reveal that the best behavior we get is independent of law, not caused by it.

Human Adaptability

A century ago, Charles Darwin gave us his provocative and highly influential theory of natural selection or the survival of the fittest. His theory soon became perverted into a school of thought called "Social Darwinism." Social Darwinists hold that the people who have prospered more than others embody the traits that are genetically destined to rule and dominate the world. Whether we restrict breeding to the prosperous or try to coerce the poor into behaving like the prosperous, we are only promoting the survival of the fittest.

This flies in the face of Darwinist wisdom. Darwin noted that the characteristics that selected some species to dominate today's environment might predispose a species to extinction when the environment changes. For example, the size of dinosaurs predisposed them to dominate their environment when plant life and smaller animals that lived off of it thrived. It is now thought that the dust thrown up when one or more huge meteors crashed to earth so darkened the sky that much of the larger plant life died off, and that the dinosaurs' large appetites then proved their undoing. Darwin further held that future environmental contingencies were largely unforeseeable, as were mutations. Thus one could scarcely project which species would thrive tomorrow from knowing the condition of those of today.

Darwin went further. One could loosely predict which species were more likely than others to survive come what may, or which isolated regions were less likely to become barren than others. Species or ecological systems were more likely to survive the future if they had a large variety of characteristics. If one set of characteristics or adaptations lost the environmental gamble, a diverse gene pool would be more likely to provide a life form to fill the void. The concern is familiar to agronomists, who have aimed to diversify hybrid crops they introduce into any economy, so that if a blight were to wipe out one hybrid, the entire agricultural system would not be destroyed.

Today the world's people are learning the problem of having invested in rationalizing, systematizing, and centralizing so much of the human economy. When recession sets in in the United States, it pulls the whole world down. President Reagan has been blaming the rest of the world while the rest of the world blames America. If, on the other hand, our enterprises had generally been small, using local materials and selling locally, then (a) failure in one economy would not so easily have caused failure in others, and (b) healthier enterprises in neighboring economies could have spawned replacements for the failures. So it is with armed conflict. The more rigidly the world is arrayed around a two-power axis, the more general the threat of annihilation. The more decentralized the management of conflict and the economic and political systems on which conflict is founded, the more limited the consequences of war among any pair of communities. For the sake of human prosperity and ultimately for the sake of human survival, Darwinian theory implies that new economies ought to be built around Schumacher's appropriate technology.

Within communities, Darwinian theory provides an explanation of why crosscutting ties promote social peace. Conflict cannot be too highly organized, cannot be carried too far, because the variety of human adaptation to the environment, the variety of interest groups that intermingle, overwhelm any particular form that conflict takes. It is not law, but engineering and tolerating diversity of economic, social, and political arrangements, of organizations and enterprises in each of our communities, that makes people behave civilly toward each other.

GUN CONTROL 1

Against Civil Disarmament

Don B. Kates, Jr.

Despite almost 100 years of often bitter debate, federal policy and that of 44 states continues to allow handguns to any sane adult who is without felony convictions. Over the past twenty years, as some of our most progressive citizens have embraced the notion that handgun confiscation would reduce violent crime, the idea of closely restricting handgun possession to police and those with police permits has been stereotyped as "liberal." Yet, when the notion of sharply restricting pistol ownership first gained popularity, in the late nineteenth century, it was under distinctly conservative auspices.

In 1902, South Carolina banned all pistol purchases, the first and only state ever to do so. (This was nine years before New York began requiring what was then an easily acquired police permit.) Tennessee had already enacted the first ban on "Saturday Night Specials," disarming blacks and the laboring poor while leaving weapons for the Ku Klux Klan and company goons. In 1906, Mississippi enacted the first mandatory registration law for all firearms. In short order, permit requirements were enacted in North Carolina, Missouri, Michigan, and Hawaii. In 1922, a national campaign of conservative business interests for handgun confiscation was endorsed by the (then) archconservative American Bar Association.

Liberals at that time were not necessarily opposed in principle to a ban on handguns, but they considered such a move irrelevant and distracting from a more important issue—the prohibition of alcohol. To Jane Addams, William Jennings Bryan, and Eleanor Roosevelt (herself a pistol carrier), liquor was the cause of violent crime. (Before dismissing this out of hand, remember that homicide studies uniformly find liquor a more prevalent factor than handguns in killings.) Besides, liberals were not likely to support the argument advanced by conservatives for gun confiscation: that certain racial and immigrant groups were so congenitally criminal (and/or politically dangerous) that they could not be trusted with arms. But when liberalism finally embraced handgun confiscation, it was by applying this conservative viewpoint to the entire populace. Now it is all Americans (not just Italians, Jews, or blacks) who must be considered so innately violent and unstable that they cannot be trusted with arms. For, we are told, it is not robbers or burglars who commit most murders, but average citizens killing relatives or friends.

Source: Don B. Kates, Jr., "Against Civil Disarmament," *Harper's Magazine* 257 (September 1978): 28–33. Reprinted with permission.

It is certainly true that only a little more than 30 percent of murders are committed by robbers, rapists, or burglars, while 45 percent are committed among relatives or between lovers. (The rest are a miscellany of contract killings, drug wars, and "circumstances unknown.") But it is highly misleading to conclude from this that the murderer is, in any sense, an average gun owner. For the most part, murderers are disturbed, aberrant individuals with long records of criminal violence that often include several felony convictions. In terms of endangering his fellow citizen, the irresponsible drinker is far more representative of all drinkers than is the irresponsible handgunner of all handgunners. It is not my intention here to defend the character of the average American handgun owner against, say, that of the average Swiss whose government not only allows, but requires, him to keep a machine gun at home. Rather it is to show how unrealistic it is to think that we could radically decrease homicide by radically reducing the number of civilian firearms. Study after study has shown that even if the *average* gun owner complied with a ban, the one handgun owner out of 3,000 who murders (much less the one in 500 who steals) is not going to give up his guns. Nor would taking guns away from the murderer make much difference in murder rates, since a sociopath with a long history of murderous assault is not too squeamish to kill with a butcher knife, ice pick, razor, or bottle. As for the extraordinary murderers—assassins, terrorists, hit men—proponents of gun bans themselves concede that the law cannot disarm such people any more than it can disarm professional robbers.

The repeated appearance of these facts in studies of violent crime has eroded liberal and intellectual support for banning handguns. There is a growing consensus among even the most liberal students of criminal law and criminology that handgun confiscation is just another plausible theory that doesn't work when tried. An article written in 1968 by Mark K. Benenson, longtime American chairman of Amnesty International, concludes that the arguments for gun bans are based upon selective misleading statistics, simple-minded non sequiturs, and basic misconceptions about the nature of murder as well as of other violent crimes.

A 1971 study at England's Cambridge University confounds one of the most widely believed non sequiturs: "Banning handguns must work, because England does and look at its crime rate!" (It is difficult to see how those who believe this can resist the equally simple-minded pro-gun argument that gun possession deters crime: "Everybody ought to have a machine gun in his house because the Swiss and the Israelis do, and look how low their crime rates are!")

The Cambridge report concludes that social and cultural factors (not gun control) account for Britain's low violence rates. It points out that "the use of firearms in crime was very much less" before 1920 when Britain had "no controls of any sort." Corroborating this is the comment of a former head of Scotland Yard that in the mid-1950s there were enough illegal handguns to supply any British criminal who wanted one. But, he continued, the social milieu was such that if a criminal killed anyone, particularly a policeman, his own confederates would turn him in. When this violence-dampening social milieu began to dissipate between 1960 and 1975, the British homicide rate doubled (as did the American rate), while

British robbery rates accelerated even faster than those in America. As the report notes, the vaunted handgun ban proved completely ineffective against rising violence in Britain, although the government frantically intensified enforcement and extended controls to long guns as well. Thus, the Cambridge study—the only in-depth study ever done of English gun laws—recommends "abolishing or substantially reducing controls" because their administration involves an immense, unproductive expense and diverts police resources from programs that might reduce violent crime.

The latest American study of gun controls was conducted with federal funding at the University of Wisconsin. Advanced computerized techniques allowed a comprehensive analysis of the effect of every form of state handgun restriction, including complete prohibition, on violence in America. Published in 1975, it concludes that "gun-control laws have no individual or collective effect in reducing the rate of violent crime."

Many previous studies reaching the same conclusion had been discounted by proponents of a federal ban, who argued that existing state bans cannot be effective because handguns are illegally imported from free-sale states. The Wisconsin study compared rates of handgun ownership with rates of violence in various localities, but it could find *no correlation*. If areas where handgun ownership rates are high have no higher per capita rates of homicide and other violence than areas where such rates are low, the utility of laws designed to lower the rates of handgun ownership seems dubious. Again, the problem is not the "proliferation of handguns" among the law-abiding citizenry, it is the existence of a tiny fraction of irresponsible and criminal owners whom the law cannot possibly disarm of these or other weapons.

Far from refuting the Wisconsin study, the sheer unenforceability of handgun bans is the main reason why most experts regard them as not worth thinking about. Even in Britain, a country that, before handguns were banned, had less than 1 percent of the per capita handgun ownership we have, the Cambridge study reports that "fifty years of very strict controls has left a vast pool of illegal weapons."

It should be emphasized that liberal defectors from gun confiscation are no more urging people to arm themselves than are those who oppose banning pot or liquor necessarily urging people to indulge in them. They are only saying that national handgun confiscation would bring the federal government into a confrontation with millions of responsible citizens in order to enforce a program that would have no effect upon violence, except the negative one of diverting resources that otherwise might be utilized to some effective purpose. While many criminologists have doubts about the wisdom of citizens trying to defend themselves with handguns, the lack of evidence to justify confiscation requires that this remain a matter of individual choice rather than government fiat.

Nor can advocates of gun bans duck the evidence adverse to their position by posing such questions as: Why should people have handguns; what good do they do; why *shouldn't* we ban them? In a free country, the burden is not upon the people to show why they should have freedom of choice. It is upon those who wish to restrict that freedom to show good reason for doing so. And when the freedom is as deeply valued by as many as is handgun ownership, the evidence for infringing upon it must be very strong indeed.

If the likely benefits of handgun confiscation have been greatly exaggerated, the financial and constitutional costs have been largely ignored. Consider the various costs of any attempt to enforce confiscation upon a citizenry that believes (whether rightly or not) that they urgently need handguns for self-defense and that the right to keep them is constitutionally guaranteed. Most confiscationists have never gotten beyond the idea that banning handguns will make them magically disappear somehow. Because they loathe handguns and consider them useless, the prohibitionists assume that those who disagree will readily turn in their guns once a national confiscation law is passed. But the leaders of the national handgun prohibition movement have become more realistic. They recognize that defiance will, if anything, exceed the defiance of Prohibition and marijuana laws. After all, not even those who viewed drinking or pot smoking as a blow against tyranny thought, as many gun owners do, that violating the law is necessary to the protection of themselves and their families. Moreover, fear of detection is a lot more likely to keep citizens from constant purchases of liquor or pot than from a single purchase of a handgun, which, properly maintained, will last years.

To counter the expected defiance, the leaders of the national confiscation drive propose that handgun ownership be punished by a nonsuspendable mandatory year in prison. The mandatory feature is necessary, for otherwise prosecutors would not prosecute, and judges would not sentence, gun ownership with sufficient severity. The judge of a special Chicago court trying only gun violations recently explained why he generally levied only small fines: The overwhelming majority of the "criminals" who come before him are respectable, decent citizens who illegally carry guns because the police can't protect them and they have no other way of protecting themselves. He does not even impose probation because this would prevent the defendants, whose guns have been confiscated, from buying new ones, which, the judge believes, they need to live and work where they do.

These views are shared by judges and prosecutors nationwide; studies find that gun-carrying charges are among the most sympathetically dealt with of all felonies. To understand why, consider a typical case that would have come before this Chicago court if the D.A. had not dropped charges. An intruder raped a woman and threw her out of a fifteenth-floor window. Police arrived too late to arrest him, so they got her roommate for carrying the gun with which she scared him off when he attacked her.

Maybe it is not a good idea for this woman to keep a handgun for self-defense. But do we really want to send her to federal prison for doing so? And is a mandatory year in prison reasonable or just for an ordinary citizen who has done nothing more hurtful than keeping a gun to defend herself—when the minimum mandatory sentence for murder is only seven years and most murderers serve little more?

Moreover, the kind of nationwide resistance movement that a federal handgun ban would provoke could not be broken by imprisoning a few impecunious black women in Chicago. Only by severely punishing a large number of respectable citizens of every race and social class would resisters eventually be made to fear the law more than the prospect of living without handguns in a violent society. At a very conservative estimate, at least half of our present handgun owners would be expected to defy a federal ban.* To imprison just 1 percent of these 25 million people would require several times as many cells as the entire federal prison system now has. The combined federal, state, and local jail systems could barely manage. Of course, so massive an enforcement campaign would also require doubling expenditure for police, prosecutors, courts, and all the other sectors of criminal justice administration. The Wisconsin study closes with the pertinent query: "Are we willing to make sociological and economic investments of such a tremendous nature in a social experiment for which there is no empirical support?"

The argument against a federal handgun ban is much like the argument against marijuana bans. It is by no means clear that marijuana is the harmless substance that its proponents claim. But it would take evidence far stronger than we now have to justify the enormous financial, human, institutional, and constitutional costs of continuing to ferret out, try, and imprison even a small percentage of the otherwise law-abiding citizens who insist on having pot. Sophisticated analysis of the criminalization decision takes into account not only the harms alleged to result from public possession of things like pot or guns, but the capacity of the criminal law to reduce those harms and the costs of trying to do so. Unfortunately most of the gun-control debate never gets beyond the abstract merits of guns—a subject on which those who view them with undifferentiated loathing are no more rational than those who love them. The position of all too many gun-banning liberals is indistinguishable from Archie Bunker's views on legalizing pot and homosexuality: "I don't like it and I don't like those who do—so it ought to be illegal."

The emotionalism with which many liberals (and conservatives as well) react against the handgun reflects not its reality but its symbolism to people who are largely ignorant of that reality. A 1975 national survey found a direct correlation between support for more stringent controls and the inability to answer simple questions about present federal gun laws. In other words, the less the respondent knew about the subject, the more likely he was to support national confiscation. Liberals advocate severely punishing those who will defy confiscation only because the liberal image of a gun owner is a criminal or right-wing fanatic rather than a poor black woman in Chicago defending herself against a rapist or a mur-

---

*I reach this estimate in this fashion: Surveys uniformly find a majority of gun owners support gun registration—in theory. In practice, however, they refuse to register because they believe this will identify their guns for confiscation if and when a national handgun ban eventually passes. In 1968, Chicago police estimated that two-thirds of the city's gun owners had not complied with the new state registration law; statewide noncompliance was estimated at 75 percent. In Cleveland, police estimate that almost 90 percent of handgun owners are in violation of a 1976 registration requirement. My estimate that one out of two handgun owners would defy national confiscation is conservative indeed when between two out of three and nine out of ten of them are already defying registration laws because they believe such laws presage confiscation.

derer. Contrary to this stereotype, most "gun nuts" are peaceful hobbyists whose violence is exclusively of the Walter Mitty type. Gun owners' views are all too often expressed in right-wing terms (which does nothing for the rationality of the debate) because twenty years of liberal vilification has given them nowhere else to look for support. If only liberals knew it, handgun ownership is disproportionately high among the underprivileged for whom liberals traditionally have had most sympathy. As the most recent (1975) national demographic survey reports: "The top subgroups who own a gun *only* for self-defense include blacks (almost half own one for this reason alone), lowest income group, senior citizens." The average liberal has no understanding of why people have guns because he has no idea what it is like to live in a ghetto where police have given up on crime control. Minority and disadvantaged citizens are not about to give up their families' protection because middle-class white liberals living and working in high-security buildings and/or well-policed suburbs tell them it's safer that way.

A final cost of national gun confiscation would be the vast accretion of enforcement powers to the police at the expense of individual liberty. The Police Foundation, which ardently endorses confiscation, recently suggested that federal agencies and local police look to how drug laws are enforced as a model of how to enforce firearms laws. Coincidentally, the chief topic of conversation at the 1977 national conference of supporters of federal confiscation was enforcement through house searches of everyone whom sales records indicate may ever have owned a handgun. In fact, indiscriminate search, complemented by electronic surveillance and vast armies of snoopers and informers, is how handgun restrictions are enforced in countries like Holland and Jamaica, and in states like Missouri and Michigan.* Even in England, as the Cambridge report notes, each new Firearms Act has been accompanied by new, unheard-of powers of search and arrest for the police.

These, then, are the costs of banning handguns: even attempting an effective ban would involve enormous expenditures (roughly equal to the present cost of enforcing all our other criminal laws combined) to ferret out and jail hundreds of thousands of decent, responsible citizens who believe that they vitally need handguns to protect their families. If this does not terrorize the rest of the responsible handgun owners into compliance, the effort will have to be expanded until millions are jailed and the annual gun-banning budget closely seconds defense spending. And all of this could be accomplished only by abandoning many restraints our Constitution places upon police activity.

What would we have to show for all this in terms of crime reduction? Terrorists, hit men, and other hardened criminals who are not deterred by the penalties for murder, robbery, rape, burglary, et cetera are not about to be terrified by the penal-

---

*According to the ACLU, St. Louis police have conducted 25,000 illegal searches in the past few years under the theory that any black man driving a late-model car possesses a handgun.

Michigan court records indicate that almost 70 percent of all firearms charges presented are thrown out because the evidence was obtained through unconstitutional search.

ties for gun ownership—nor is the more ordinary murderer, the disturbed, aberrant individual who kills out of rage rather than cupidity.

What we should have learned from our experience of Prohibition, and England's with gun banning, is that violence can be radically reduced only through long-term fundamental change in the institutions and mores that produce so many violent people in our society. It is much easier to use as scapegoats a commonly vilified group (drinkers or gun owners) and convince ourselves that legislation against them is an easy short-term answer. But violence will never be contained or reduced until we give up the gimmicky programs, the scapegoating, the hypocritical hand-wringing, and frankly ask ourselves whether we are willing to make the painful, disturbing, far-reaching institutional and cultural changes that are necessary.

GUN CONTROL 2

For Public Safety:
Controlling Violence, Homicide, and Handguns
D. Stanley Eitzen and Doug A. Timmer

The Most Violent Crime

Since the Reagan administration pledged that its law enforcement, judicial, and correctional policies would focus primarily on the control of violent crime, we should take note of the data available on the most violent of crimes: murder. As we have already noted, America's reported murder rate has most definitely been on the upswing.

Table 1 gives 1980 murder rates for the 20 largest cities in the United States. But even when the murder-prone large cities are mixed in with small cities and towns and rural areas, the nation's overall homicide rate remains high. In 1974, the homicide rate in the United States reached what was then an all time high—9.8 per 100,000 population. The rate was 9.7 per 100,000 population in 1979 and even higher in 1980. . . . In every year since 1973 there have been about 20,000 murders in the United States. . . .

In an average week, about 400 Americans are murdered. Most are slain as the result of a family quarrel or neighborhood argument. Many die in gang or drug wars. Recently, as many as a third of all murders appear to be the work of strangers (to the victim). However, the most devastating statistics having to do with murder in the United States are related to handguns. Handguns have never been banned in America and only a handful of states have any meaningful and restrictive registration procedures for handgun owners. The result: more than half the people murdered in Chicago since 1970 have been the victims of handguns; more than half of all murders that result from domestic and neighborhood arguments involve handguns. . . .

The murder rate in the United States in 1979 was 9.7 per 100,000, which was probably the highest homicide rate anywhere in the world. In 1979, Japan had 1.6 murders per 100,000 population; Britain, 1.3; West Germany, 1.3—all countries, incidentally, that have legislated and enforced very restrictive handgun regulations. . . .

Source: Reprinted with permission of Macmillan Publishing Company from *Criminology: Crime and Criminal Justice* by D. Stanley Eitzen and Doug A. Timmer. (New York: Macmillan 1985). (pp. 130–132, 155, 158).

Table 1   Murder Rates

	How the 20 Largest Cities Compare		
	Population Rank	Homicides During 1980	Homicides Per 100,000 Persons
1. Cleveland	18	280	48.9
2. Detroit	6	548	46.0
3. Houston	5	644	41.4
4. Dallas	7	322	35.7
5. Los Angeles	3	1,042	35.3
6. Washington, D.C.	15	202	31.7
7. Chicago	2	863	29.1
8. Baltimore	9	216	27.5
9. Philadelphia	4	437	26.0
10. Memphis	14	166	25.7
11. New York	1	1,790	25.5
12. San Francisco	13	110	16.3
13. Boston	19	91	16.2
14. Columbus, Ohio	20	91	16.2
15. Indianapolis	12	107	15.4
16. Phoenix	11	105	13.4
17. Milwaukee	16	80	12.6
18. San Diego	8	108	12.4
19. San Jose	17	62	9.9
20. San Antonio	10	69	8.8

Source: *USN & WR* table—Basic data: Police reports, U.S. Dept. of Commerce, in *U.S. News and World Report*, "Violence in Big Cities: Behind the Surge," p. 63. Copyright © Feb. 23, 1981, U.S. News & World Report.

In spite of the Reagan administration's purported desire to control violent crime, it remained uniformly and absolutely opposed to any and all gun control legislation in the United States. The attempted assassination of Reagan himself, done with a handgun, makes this position even harder to understand. It is also true that an August 1981 Gallup Poll revealed that 91 percent of the American people favor tougher handgun controls. Even U.S. Attorney General William Smith's Reagan-mandated Task Force Report on Violent Crime concluded that "crime committed by individuals using handguns is perhaps the most serious problem of violence facing our nation today." This report also recommended outlawing the importation of handgun parts to the United States, tightening federal law to allow for easier tracing of firearms, making it more difficult for convicted felons to purchase handguns, and strengthening the 1968 federal gun-control law (a law that the National Rifle Association, an antigun control lobby that probably represents the most powerful and effective single-issue political lobby in the United States, wants to gut). All of this because "in 1978, . . . firearms were used in 307,000 murders, robberies, and aggravated assaults reported to the police; 77.8 percent of the guns used to murder were handguns. . . ." Yet, when President Reagan (September, 1981) spoke to the International Chiefs of Police in New Orleans, he verbally supported only one task force recommendation: mandatory prison terms for felons using guns, the only task force recommendation supported by the National Rifle Association.

Guns. Handguns are very much implicated in the high levels of criminal violence in the United States:

- The United States today has probably the most heavily armed citizenry in history.
- At least one half of all American households own at least one gun.
- The total number of weapons belonging to private individuals is well over 100 million . . . .

And . . .

- FBI statistics have indicated that of the 23,044 homicides committed in 1980, 50 percent, or 11,522, were handgun shootings.
- In 1980, 1426 children were killed with handguns.
- Sixty-six percent of law enforcement officers killed in 1980 were slain with handguns.
- One in nine Americans has been threatened or attacked with a handgun.
- About 2.5 million new handguns are added to the arsenal of private arms in the United States each year.
- In some areas, as many as one half of the weapons used in handgun crimes are stolen.
- Information gathered by the FBI and from foreign consulates has shown that nations with strong handgun registration and control laws have fewer per capita handgun-related deaths. In 1979, for example, 10,728 persons were murdered by handguns in the United States, but only 52 people were killed by handguns in Canada, 48 in Japan, 42 in West Germany, 21 in Sweden, and 8 in England (all of this reported by The Committee for the Study of Handgun Misuse, 1983).

Although it is no doubt true that when handguns are available, the likelihood of homicidal injury and/or death increases, this does not necessarily mean that guns cause crime. In fact, Wright et al. (1983), in an important and very recent study exploring the relationships between guns, crime, and violence, have concluded that there is little evidence to show that owning a gun is a primary cause of criminal violence. They have also argued that there is little or no evidence to either *support* or *refute* the idea that private gun ownership serves to reduce crime by deterring offenders who fear gun-wielding citizens. There is evidence, however, which suggests that households with guns present are about seven to eight times as likely to experience a handgun death as are households that do not own guns. In this sense, at least, handgun ownership appears to make households less, not more, safe.

Indeed, it may be that "crime causes guns" comes closer to the truth than "guns cause crime." Wright et al. have found a lack of pervasive evidence to support the claim that private individuals are arming themselves out of a fear of violent crime. Another recent analysis by sociologists McDowall and Lifton (1983), however, provides some of this evidence. These sociologists have found that in Detroit, for example, between 1951 and 1977, there was a direct relationship between perceptions of declining collective security and the citizen demand for legal handguns. They found that high violent crime rates, civil disorders, and negative changes in police strength led to increases in gun ownership. It is worth noting that high violent crime rates and civil disorders are both related to a complex of class inequalities. This suggests that the following "causal chain" might explain, particularly in the absence of any meaningful national gun control policy, high levels of gun ownership: high levels of class inequality lead to high levels of crime, violence, and disorder, which in turn increases perceptions of collective insecurity and then, gun ownership.

References

Committee for the Study of Handgun Misuse (1983) *Handgun Violence Fact Sheet* (June).

McDowall, D., and C. Lifton (1983) "Collective Security and the Demand for Legal Handguns," *American Journal of Sociology* 88 (May):1146–1161.

Wright, J. D., P. H. Rossi, and K. Daly (1983) *Under the Gun: Weapons, Crime and Violence in America.* Hawthorne, NY: Aldine.

Capital Punishment Affirms Life

Edward I. Koch

Last December a man named Robert Lee Willie, who had been convicted of raping and murdering an 18-year-old woman, was executed in the Louisiana state
prison. In a statement issued several minutes before his death, Mr. Willie said:
"Killing people is wrong . . . . It makes no difference whether it's citizens, countries, or governments. Killing is wrong." Two weeks later in South Carolina, an
admitted killer named Joseph Carl Shaw was put to death for murdering two
teenagers: In an appeal to the governor for clemency, Mr. Shaw wrote: "Killing is
wrong when I did it. Killing is wrong when you do it. I hope you have the courage
and moral strength to stop the killing."

It is a curiosity of modern life that we find ourselves being lectured on morality
by cold-blooded killers. Mr. Willie previously had been convicted of aggravated
rape, aggravated kidnapping, and the murders of a Louisiana deputy and a man
from Missouri. Mr. Shaw committed another murder a week before the two for
which he was executed, and admitted mutilating the body of the 14-year-old girl he
killed. I can't help wondering what prompted these murderers to speak out against
killing as they entered the death-house door. Did their newfound reverence for life
stem from the realization that they were about to lose their own?

Life is indeed precious, and I believe the death penalty helps to affirm this fact.
Had the death penalty been a real possibility in the minds of these murderers, they
might well have stayed their hand. They might have shown moral awareness before
their victims died, and not after. Consider the tragic death of Rosa Velez, who happened to be home when a man named Luis Vera burglarized her apartment in
Brooklyn. "Yeah, I shot her," Vera admitted. "She knew me, and I knew I wouldn't
go to the chair."

During my 22 years in public service, I have heard the pros and cons of capital
punishment expressed with special intensity. As a district leader, councilman, congressman, and mayor, I have represented constituencies generally thought of as liberal. Because I support the death penalty for heinous crimes of murder, I have
sometimes been the subject of emotional and outraged attacks by voters who find
my position reprehensible or worse. I have listened to their ideas. I have weighed

Source: Edward I. Koch, "Death and Justice: How Capital Punishment Affirms Life," *The New Republic* (1983). Reprinted by permission of *The New Republic*. Copyright © 1983, The New Republic,
Inc.

their objections carefully. I still support the death penalty. The reasons I maintain my position can be best understood by examining the arguments most frequently heard in opposition.

(1) *The death penalty is "barbaric."* Sometimes opponents of capital punishment horrify with tales of lingering death on the gallows, of faulty electric chairs or of agony in the gas chamber. Partly in response to such protests, several states such as North Carolina and Texas switched to execution by lethal injection. The condemned person is put to death painlessly, without ropes, voltage, bullets, or gas. Did this answer the objections of death penalty opponents? Of course not. On June 22, 1984, *The New York Times* published an editorial that sarcastically attacked the new "hygienic" method of death by injection, and stated that "execution can never be made humane through science." So it's not the method that really troubles opponents. It's the death itself they consider barbaric.

Admittedly, capital punishment is not a pleasant topic. However, one does not have to like the death penalty in order to support it any more than one must like radical surgery, radiation, or chemotherapy in order to find necessary these attempts at curing cancer. Ultimately we may learn how to cure cancer with a simple pill. Unfortunately, that day has not yet arrived. Today we are faced with the choice of letting the cancer spread or trying to cure it with the methods available, methods that one day will almost certainly be considered barbaric. But to give up and do nothing would be far more barbaric and would certainly delay the discovery of an eventual cure. The analogy between cancer and murder is imperfect, because murder is not the "disease" we are trying to cure. The disease is injustice. We may not like the death penalty, but it must be available to punish crimes of cold-blooded murder, cases in which any other form of punishment would be inadequate and, therefore, unjust. If we create a society in which injustice is not tolerated, incidents of murder— the most flagrant form of injustice—will diminish.

(2) *No other major democracy uses the death penalty.* No other major democracy—in fact, few other countries of any description—are plagued by a murder rate such as that in the United States. Fewer and fewer Americans can remember the days when unlocked doors were the norm and murder was a rare and terrible offense. In America the murder rate climbed 122 percent between 1963 and 1980. During that same period, the murder rate in New York City increased by almost 400 percent, and the statistics are even worse in many other cities. A study at M.I.T. showed that based on 1970 homicide rates a person who lived in a large American city ran a greater risk of being murdered than an American soldier in World War II ran of being killed in combat. It is not surprising that the laws of each country differ according to differing conditions and traditions. If other countries had our murder problem, the cry for capital punishment would be just as loud as it is here. And I daresay that any other major democracy where 75 percent of the people supported the death penalty would soon enact it into law.

(3) *An innocent person might be executed by mistake.* Consider the work of Adam Bedau, one of the most implacable foes of capital punishment in this country. According to Mr. Bedau, it is "false sentimentality to argue that the death

penalty should be abolished because of the abstract possibility that an innocent person might be executed." He cites a study of 7,000 executions in this country from 1893 to 1971, and concludes that the record fails to show that such cases occur. The main point, however, is this. If government functioned only when the possibility of error didn't exist, government wouldn't function at all. Human life deserves special protection, and one of the best ways to guarantee that protection is to assure that convicted murderers do not kill again. Only the death penalty can accomplish this end. In a recent case in New Jersey, a man named Richard Biegenwald was freed from prison after serving 18 years for murder; since his release he has been convicted of committing four murders. A prisoner named Lemuel Smith, who, while serving four life sentences for murder (plus two life sentences for kidnaping and robbery) in New York's Green Haven Prison, lured a woman corrections officer into the chaplain's office and strangled her. He then mutilated and dismembered her body. An additional life sentence for Smith is meaningless. Because New York has no death penalty statute, Smith has effectively been given a license to kill.

But the problem of multiple murder is not confined to the nation's penitentiaries. In 1981, 91 police officers were killed in the line of duty in this country. Seven percent of those arrested in the cases that have been solved had a previous arrest for murder. In New York City in 1976 and 1977, 85 persons arrested for homicide had a previous arrest for murder. Six of these individuals had two previous arrests for murder, and one had four previous murder arrests. During those two years the New York police were arresting for murder persons with a previous arrest for murder on the average of one every 8.5 days. This is not surprising when we learn that in 1975, for example, the median time served in Massachusetts for homicide was less than two-and-a-half years. In 1976 a study sponsored by the Twentieth Century Fund found that the average time served in the United States for first-degree murder is ten years. The median time served may be considerably lower.

(4) *Capital punishment cheapens the value of human life.* On the contrary, it can be easily demonstrated that the death penalty strengthens the value of human life. If the penalty for rape were lowered, clearly it would signal a lessened regard for the victims' suffering, humiliation, and personal integrity. It would cheapen their horrible experience, and expose them to an increased danger of recurrence. When we lower the penalty for murder, it signals a lessened regard for the value of the victim's life. Some critics of capital punishment, such as columnist Jimmy Breslin, have suggested that a life sentence is actually a harsher penalty for murder than death. This is sophistic nonsense. A few killers may decide not to appeal a death sentence, but the overwhelming majority make every effort to stay alive. It is by exacting the highest penalty for the taking of human life that we affirm the highest value of human life.

(5) *The death penalty is applied in a discriminatory manner.* This factor no longer seems to be the problem it once was. That appeals process for a condemned prisoner is lengthy and painstaking. Every effort is made to see that the verdict and sentence were fairly arrived at. However, assertions of discrimination are not an

argument for ending the death penalty but for extending it. It is not justice to exclude everyone from the penalty of the law if a few are found to be so favored. Justice requires that the law be applied equally to all.

(6) *Thou Shalt Not Kill.* The Bible is our greatest source of moral inspiration. Opponents of the death penalty frequently cite the sixth of the Ten Commandments in an attempt to prove that capital punishment is divinely proscribed. In the original Hebrew, however, the Sixth Commandment reads, "Thou Shalt Not Commit Murder," and the Torah specifies capital punishment for a variety of offenses. The biblical viewpoint has been upheld by philosophers throughout history. The greatest thinkers of the 19th century—Kant, Locke, Hobbes, Rousseau, Montesquieu, and Mill—agreed that natural law properly authorizes the sovereign to take life in order to vindicate justice. Only Jeremy Bentham was ambivalent. Washington, Jefferson, and Franklin endorsed it. Abraham Lincoln authorized executions for deserters in wartime. Alexis de Tocqueville, who expressed profound respect for American institutions, believed that the death penalty was indispensable to the support of social order. The United States Constitution, widely admired as one of the seminal achievements in the history of humanity, condemns cruel and inhuman punishment, but does not condemn capital punishment.

(7) *The death penalty is state-sanctioned murder.* This is the defense with which Messrs. Willie and Shaw hoped to soften the resolve of those who sentenced them to death. By saying in effect, "You're no better than I am," the murderer seeks to bring his accusers down to his own level. It is also a popular argument among opponents of capital punishment, but a transparently false one. Simply put, the state has rights that the private individual does not. In a democracy, those rights are given to the state by the electorate. The execution of a lawfully condemned killer is no more an act of murder than is legal imprisonment an act of kidnapping. If an individual forces a neighbor to pay him money under threat of punishment, it's called extortion. If the state does it, it's called taxation. Rights and responsibilities surrendered by the individual are what give the state its power to govern. This contract is the foundation of civilization itself.

Everyone wants his or her rights, and will defend them jealously. Not everyone, however, wants responsibilities, especially the painful responsibilities that come with law enforcement. Twenty-one years ago a woman named Kitty Genovese was assaulted and murdered on a street in New York. Dozens of neighbors heard her cries for help but did nothing to assist her. They didn't even call the police. In such a climate the criminal understandably grows bolder. In the presence of moral cowardice, he lectures us on our supposed failings and tries to equate his crimes with our quest for justice.

The death of anyone—even a convicted killer—diminishes us all. But we are diminished even more by a justice system that fails to function. It is an illusion to let ourselves believe that doing away with capital punishment removes the murderer's deed from our conscience. The rights of society are paramount. When we protect guilty lives, we give up innocent lives in exchange. When opponents of capital punishment say to the state: "I will not let you kill in my name," they are also saying to murderers: "You can kill in your *own* name as long as I have an excuse for not getting involved."

It is hard to imagine anything worse than being murdered while neighbors do nothing. But something worse exists. When those same neighbors shrink back from justly punishing the murderer, the victim dies twice.

CAPITAL PUNISHMENT 2

Against the Death Penalty

Amnesty International

Introduction

In 1972 the US Supreme Court ruled that the arbitrary manner in which the death penalty was then applied amounted to "cruel and unusual punishment", in violation of the Constitution. The ruling invalidated most existing death penalty statutes. Before this, there had already been a steady decline in the use of the death penalty in the USA, with a moratorium on executions from 1967. However, a further Supreme Court ruling in 1976 permitted individual states to reinstate the death penalty for murder according to guidelines set by the Court. The ruling upheld new laws that had already been enacted in some states after 1972 and led to a resumption of executions. Between January 1977 and May 1986, 58 prisoners were executed, with many more awaiting the outcome of legal appeals. In May 1986 a total of 1,720 prisoners were under sentence of death in 33 states, the highest figure ever recorded in the USA; 37 states had laws authorizing the death penalty at that time.

Only four prisoners were executed between 1976 and 1982, three of whom had dropped their final appeals and demanded to be executed. There has been a steady increase in the rate of executions since then, a trend which is expected to continue as prisoners exhaust their legal appeals.

Amnesty International opposes the death penalty unconditionally, believing it to be the ultimate cruel, inhuman and degrading punishment and a violation of the right to life, as proclaimed in the Universal Declaration of Human Rights and other international human rights instruments. The organization works for the abolition of the death penalty throughout the world and appeals for clemency in all cases where executions are feared to be imminent, regardless of the nature of the crime of which the prisoner has been convicted.

This report examines the death penalty in the USA from this point of view and also raises a number of concerns based on how the death penalty is applied in practice. It includes the findings of an Amnesty International mission to four states in

Source: Amnesty International, "The Death Penalty," *United States of America: The Death Penalty* (London: Amnesty International Publications, 1987):3–7, 182–191. Copyright material on pp. 343–354 reproduced with permission of Amnesty International.

1985 and information collected during the course of its general work against the death penalty since it was reinstated in the 1970s. The report was written in May 1986 but includes important subsequent Supreme Court rulings on issues related to the death penalty; it has also been possible to update some information and statistics.

In its 1972 ruling, the Supreme Court found that the unlimited discretion given to judges or juries to decide whether or not to impose the death penalty in capital trials had led to random and capricious sentencing. Several of the justices found also that the death penalty—although very rarely imposed at that time—had fallen disproportionately on the poor and on minority groups. The guidelines set by the Court in this and other rulings in the 1970s were intended to ensure that, in future, the death penalty would be fairly and consistently applied, and imposed only for the most serious and unmitigated crimes. The capital punishment laws enacted after 1972 have restricted the types of crime for which the death penalty may be imposed and provide for a separate sentencing hearing, in which juries or judges must weigh aggravating and mitigating circumstances before deciding whether to impose a life or death sentence on convicted capital offenders. Other procedural safeguards include the automatic review of death sentences by state supreme courts.

Despite these measures, there is evidence that in practice the death penalty remains both arbitrary and discriminatory. Although it is now imposed only on people convicted of murder where there are aggravating circumstances (such as an accompanying felony), only a small proportion of offenders accused of such crimes are sentenced to die. The death penalty continues to be unevenly applied, both nationally and within states, and there are wide disparities in the sentencing of similar offenders.

This report examines the circumstances which result in one offender being sentenced to death while another is not, and concludes that race, where the crime was committed, discretionary decisions taken by local prosecutors in their charging and sentencing recommendations, and the competence and resources of defence attorneys may play a greater role in determining who is sentenced to death than the nature of the crime or defendant.

It describes individual cases in which the death penalty has appeared particularly inappropriate or unfair. These include cases where executed prisoners were under 18 years old when the crime was committed, in clear violation of international standards; showed signs of mental illness or retardation or had mitigating circumstances not revealed at the sentencing stage of their trials. In several cases, disparate sentences were imposed on co-defendants against whom there was equal evidence of guilt, with one prisoner being executed while another was sentenced to life imprisonment or less. At least one execution was of a prisoner who did not commit or plan the killing but participated in a contemporaneous offence; in another, an accomplice to a murder was executed while the actual killer received a life sentence. These and other cases suggest that the death penalty has not been applied in the fair and even-handed fashion envisaged by the Supreme Court in its 1976 decision, nor has it necessarily been reserved only for the very worst crimes and the most culpable offenders.

The report looks at the appeals available to capital defendants and finds that they have not served to redress underlying deficiencies in the system. Although a relatively large number of prisoners have had their death sentences overturned on appeal, the courts are limited in their ability to assess broader issues of arbitrariness or discrimination, especially where this occurs at an early stage of the judicial process. Executive clemency, which has rarely been granted in capital cases since 1976, has also failed to safeguard against the imposition of unfair or unduly harsh sentences. Several prisoners have been executed when there appeared to be especially strong grounds for exercising clemency.

Amnesty International believes that no system of capital punishment can ensure that the death penalty is fairly and consistently applied. The US Supreme Court ruled in 1976 that mandatory death sentences, imposed regardless of any mitigating or aggravating circumstances relating to the crime or offender, were unconstitutional. However, the present system of "guided discretion" has also failed to ensure fairness or consistency in sentencing. The aggravating or mitigating circumstances that juries or judges must weigh before deciding whether to impose a life or death sentence on convicted capital offenders may be open to widely differing interpretations. The choice of sentence may depend on the skills of defence attorneys in their presentation of evidence, the vigour with which the prosecutor seeks the death penalty, the defendant's demeanour or relative status in the community, and a host of other extraneous factors. There is wide discretion, too, at other stages of the judicial process. Many crimes for which death is a possible penalty are not tried as capital crimes because prosecutors have decided to bring alternative charges. As shown in this report, factors beyond the circumstances of the crime itself may play a part in these decisions.

The report describes how the death penalty may even distort the judicial process. There is concern, for example, that a practice used by most US states of excluding opponents of the death penalty from serving as jurors in capital trials may produce juries not only more inclined to impose death sentences, but also more likely to convict, or to convict on more serious charges, than those chosen under the normal jury selection procedures. Thus, capital defendants, whose lives are at stake, may be tried before less impartial juries than those sitting in ordinary criminal trials.

Other measures, although intended to provide the maximum safeguards against error, have given rise to further contradictions. The complex and lengthy procedures and the high cost of capital trials, for example, may discourage prosecutors from seeking the death penalty in all but a few cases, increasing the disparities in sentencing among similar offenders. They have also placed heavy burdens on defence attorneys, discouraging many lawyers from taking on capital cases and making it harder for poor defendants to get adequate legal representation. These and other concerns are summarized at the end of this report.

Since 1976, the Supreme Court has continued to rule on death penalty cases;

however, its more recent decisions have tended to uphold state procedures, narrowing the ground for future appeals on broad constitutional questions. . . .

At the time of writing one of the few remaining systematic challenges to the death penalty was on the question of race. In October 1985 an appeal was lodged with the Supreme Court in which it was claimed that the Georgia death penalty statute was applied in a manner which discriminated against certain categories of offender on racial grounds. The appeal cited the findings of a detailed research study which showed that killers of whites, especially black killers, were far more likely to be sentenced to death than killers of blacks, after allowing for non-racial factors. The Court granted *certiorari* (agreed to hear the appeal) in the case in July 1986 and this decision was still pending in October 1986.

Amnesty International is aware of the serious problem of violent crime in the USA, where criminal homicides have averaged 20,000 a year from 1979 to 1985. In recent years state governments have given this, and strong public support for the death penalty, as grounds for retaining the death penalty. However, detailed research in the USA and other countries has produced no evidence that this penalty deters crime more effectively than other punishment. There is evidence, moreover, that the death penalty places a disproportionate burden on the criminal justice system and may divert resources from other, more effective, forms of law enforcement.

Although there is strong public support for the death penalty in the USA, several polls indicate that this is not unqualified. Some recent polls suggest that public support for the death penalty might decrease if other penalties were shown to be equally effective.

Certain sectors of the US population have consistently opposed the death penalty, including the leadership of most of the main religious denominations. A number of state governors have also maintained their opposition to the death penalty.

All but one of the prisoners under sentence of death in May 1986 had been convicted under state laws. The death penalty is also authorized for certain offences under federal military law—a soldier convicted of murder under the Uniform Code of Military Justice was under sentence of death at the time of writing (in addition to the 1,720 inmates reported by states to be on death row in May 1986). Several bills to reinstate the death penalty under federal civilian law have been introduced into Congress since 1972 but none has yet been enacted. A further bill was before the US Senate in May 1986.

Amnesty International hopes that this report will encourage the state and federal authorities and the public to re-examine their attitudes towards the death penalty, and to promote its abolition in all jurisdictions in which it still applies. . . .

Summary of Findings

1. The reintroduction of the death penalty in state legislation and the increase in executions in recent years are contrary to international human rights standards

which encourage governments to restrict progressively the use of the death penalty, with a view to its ultimate abolition. Proposals to reinstate the death penalty in federal law and to extend it to crimes to which it did not previously apply are also in conflict with these standards.

2. Death penalty laws in some states, or their manner of application, contravene specific international standards applying to jurisdictions which have not yet abolished the penalty. Twenty-eight states allow the imposition of death sentences on people aged under 18 at the time of the crime, in clear violation of international treaties and guidelines. Three such prisoners were executed between September 1985 and May 1986, the first executions of this kind in the USA for more than 20 years. These executions put the USA out of line with most other countries with the death penalty, which do not execute prisoners who were under 18 at the time of the crime: Amnesty International knows of only eight confirmed cases of such executions worldwide between 1980 and May 1986. As of May 1986 at least 32 other juvenile offenders were under sentence of death in 15 states.

Several prisoners have been executed who exhibited signs of mental illness, in contravention of guidelines set out by the UN Economic and Social Council in 1984 (ECOSOC Resolution 1984/50) which provide that executions shall not be carried out on "persons who have become insane" . . .

3. There are wide regional disparities in the rate at which death sentences are imposed. A Justice Department report showed that 63 per cent of those under sentence of death in 1984 were held by states in the South compared to only four per cent by states in the Northeast, a disparity which bears little relation to differences in the homicide rates between the two regions. Nearly all the executions carried out since 1976 have been in states in the South.

There are also marked disparities in the rate at which death sentences are imposed for similar crimes in different counties within those states most frequently applying the penalty. It was found, for example, that 85 per cent of death sentences in Georgia from 1973 to 1978 had been imposed in just 26 of Georgia's 159 counties, and that this was unrelated to differences in the homicide rates. Death sentences were, in fact, several times more likely to be imposed in rural areas, where homicides were less frequent, than in urban areas.

4. Although the present laws contain guidelines intended to eliminate arbitrary sentencing in capital trials, the possibility of a death sentence is largely determined by decisions taken by prosecutors at an early stage of the judicial process. Prosecutors have wide discretion in whether or not to seek the death penalty in criminal homicide cases, and, in practice, only a minority of crimes for which death is a possible penalty are tried as capital offences. Decisions to seek the death penalty may be largely determined by factors beyond the circumstances of the crime, including the financial resources available in a given district, local feeling about the death penalty and the level of publicity or community pressure in a particular case.

5. The evidence suggests that race—especially that of the victim—has an important bearing on the eventual likelihood of a death sentence. Fifty-three of the 58 prisoners executed between January 1977 and May 1986 had been convicted of

killing whites, as had the large majority of those under sentence of death during this period—even though blacks and whites are victims of homicide in roughly equal numbers. Research in Florida, Georgia, Texas and other states has shown that homicides involving white victims are far more likely to be charged as capital offences and result in death sentences than those involving black victims. This disparity may partly be explained by the fact that more whites than blacks are liable to be the victims of "capital" homicides (such as felony-related murders). However, after taking this into account, researchers have found that racial disparities remain in otherwise similar cases.

The most detailed study of racial discrimination was conducted in Georgia, where researchers examined the outcome of all homicide arrests over a six-year period, taking into account more than 230 non-racial factors. They identified a mid-range of aggravated homicides where defendants in cases with white victims were significantly more likely to receive death sentences than those with black victims, at similar levels of aggravation. These were cases in which there was most room for discretion by prosecutors or juries in seeking or imposing death sentences. In cases involving white victims, black defendants were also found far more likely to be sentenced to death than white ones.

A federal appeals court dismissed an appeal which had cited the study's findings as evidence, on the grounds that the petitioner had failed to prove intentional discrimination by the state. Although the court did not dispute the study's findings, it concluded that they could not be said to cast doubt on the fairness of the system as a whole. An appeal against this decision was lodged with the US Supreme Court in October 1985. In July 1986 the Supreme Court said that it would hear the appeal. A ruling by the Court was not expected until the end of 1986 or early 1987.

6. In most US states, opponents of the death penalty are systematically excluded from serving as jurors in capital trials (partly because their presence may prevent the return of unanimous sentencing decisions). There is concern that this practice may produce juries not only more disposed to impose death sentences but also less impartial on the question of guilt or innocence than those selected under the normal procedures for criminal trials. Concern has been expressed also at the use of peremptory challenges to exclude blacks from sitting on capital trial juries, especially if the defendant is black.

After reviewing research studies into jury attitudes and the death penalty, a federal appeals court ruled in 1985 that opponents of the death penalty may be excluded only from the penalty phase of a capital trial. However, in May 1986 the US Supreme Court reversed this decision, ruling that it was constitutionally permissible to exclude opponents of the death penalty from serving as capital-trial jurors at both the trial and the sentencing hearing. The Court questioned the value of the studies into jury attitudes but said that its decision would still stand, even if the special selection procedures in capital trials did produce jurors who were "somewhat more conviction-prone" than ordinary trial juries.

A Supreme Court ruling in April 1986 (in a non-capital case) made it easier for black defendants to challenge the striking of members of their own race from their trial juries. However, the ruling did not apply retroactively to the cases of prisoners whose convictions had already been upheld on direct appeal. After the ruling at least one black prisoner was executed in a case in which the prosecutor had struck all black members from the trial jury.[1]

7. The separate trial and sentencing phases of capital cases, each requiring the investigation and presentation of separate evidence, and the special standards involved, have placed additional burdens on defence attorneys and created possibilities for error that do not arise in non-capital cases. However, there is evidence that many indigent offenders charged with capital crimes are assigned inexperienced counsel, ill-equipped to handle such cases and working with severely limited resources. Several prisoners have been executed whose trial lawyers were reported to have spent little time preparing the case, sometimes failing to present important mitigating evidence at the sentencing hearing. Appellate lawyers in capital cases have expressed concern that such deficiencies may have contributed to the imposition of death sentences in many cases.

Most states do not provide funds for defendants to be legally represented after their death sentences have been upheld on appeal to the state supreme court. They have to rely on volunteer lawyers when pursuing *habeas corpus* appeals on constitutional issues (a point at which many death sentences have been overturned). With the growing shortage of such lawyers, there is a risk that some prisoners may not be adequately represented at this important stage. Often, a lawyer is found only after an execution date has already been set, leaving little time to prepare appeals for consideration by the courts. The shortage of volunteer lawyers has caused particular concern in some southern states, where a large number of prisoners have exhausted state appeals and where execution warrants are issued with increasing frequency.

8. A relatively large number of capital defendants have had their death sentences overturned on state or federal appeal since 1976. However, there are procedural bars to appealing on issues that should have been raised at the time of trial and some trial errors may therefore not be remedied. . . . The appeals courts are also limited in their ability to assess broader issues of arbitrariness or discrimination, especially where this occurs early in the judicial proceedings. Some state supreme courts try to ensure consistency in sentencing by comparing death sen-

---

[1] Jerome Bowden, a mentally retarded black man who was executed in Georgia on 24 June 1986. He had been sentenced to death in December 1976 after pleading guilty to a murder committed during a robbery. The prosecutor had peremptorily excluded all blacks from the trial jury and as a result Jerome Bowden was tried by an all-white jury, even though the trial took place in a region of the state with a 34 per cent black population. Although his court-appointed lawyer had failed to preserve a claim on the race question, the (now unconstitutional) jury-selection procedures used in his case would not have been grounds for a stay of execution in any event, given the US Supreme Court ruling that the new standard would not apply retroactively to past cases.

. . . the Supreme Court left open the question of whether the April 1986 ruling on peremptory challenges would apply retroactively to cases still pending on direct appeal at the time of its decision. It granted *certiorari* in two cases raising this claim in early June and its decision was still pending as of October 1986.

tences with penalties imposed in similar cases. However, many potentially capital crimes are not charged as such, because of decisions by prosecutors to accept guilty pleas to lesser charges. This limits the range of "similar" cases available to the courts for comparative review. Some state courts do not conduct any form of proportionality review of death sentences by comparing them with other cases. . . .

9. The federal courts have shown themselves increasingly unwilling to consider new constitutional questions in capital cases. Recent rulings by the US Supreme Court have tended to uphold state procedures, as is illustrated by its decision on juries (see 6 above).

Concerned about the long delays between the imposition of the death sentence and execution, the Supreme Court has also approved procedures that allow the lower federal courts to expedite their hearing of *habeas corpus* appeals in capital cases. Most capital defendants continue to spend several years awaiting the outcome of their automatic appeals to the state supreme courts; however, they may now have less time than non-capital defendants to have their final appeals on constitutional issues considered. The expedited proceedings leading up to execution in some cases have appeared contrary to the interests of justice. . . .

10. Although the executive authorities retain the power to commute death sentences to life imprisonment as an act of mercy, clemency has rarely been granted in the cases considered by them so far. State governors and pardons boards appear to take a very narrow view of the role of clemency, believing that the decisions of the courts should stand unless there are doubts about the defendant's guilt or serious legal errors. Clemency has been denied, for example, in cases where there were strong mitigating circumstances in the offender's background which the defence lawyer had failed to raise during the trial and in cases where offenders were mentally retarded or mentally ill. International standards, such as those prohibiting the execution of juveniles or the mentally ill, have also not been considered grounds for granting clemency.

11. Both the experience of being under sentence of death, and the execution itself, may cause intense suffering. Several executed prisoners have not died instantly and prolonged suffering was manifestly inflicted. This has occurred both in executions by electrocution or gas and in those by lethal injection. . . .

12. The participation by doctors in some executions appears in Amnesty International's view to have violated medical ethical standards enjoining doctors to practise for the good of their patients and never to harm them. Their actions have also contravened World Medical Association standards, which provide that a doctor's only role should be to certify death once an execution has been carried out. In Amnesty International's view, the role played by other health professionals has also been contrary to recognized ethical standards. . . .

13. Conditions on death rows in some states have improved in recent years, as a result of litigation in the federal courts. In many states, however, prisoners under sentence of death remain confined for prolonged periods to small, poorly equipped cells, with no opportunities for work, educational or rehabilitation pro-

grams and little association with other inmates. The prolonged isolation and lack of occupational facilities in such cases add to the inherent cruelty suffered by being under sentence of death. . . .

14. Considerable research in the USA has provided no evidence that the death penalty deters crime more effectively than other punishments. These findings are consistent with what is known of the relationship between crime rates and the presence or absence of the death penalty in other countries. In some US states, the homicide rate has actually increased after the resumption of executions. . . .

15. The cost and length of proceedings in capital cases have placed heavy burdens on the criminal justice system. Some judges and other law officials believe that the enormous concentration of judicial services on a relative handful of cases diverts resources from more effective areas of law enforcement. . . .

16. The death penalty does not lessen the loss to the family and friends of murder victims. Far from relieving their pain, the lengthy procedures and uncertain outcome of capital cases may prolong the anguish and suffering caused to victims' families. Indeed, executions often draw attention away from the victims and focus it on the prisoners being killed by the state, thereby increasing the feelings of rejection that the relatives of victims often experience. More effective measures of law enforcement and swifter and more certain penalties would more greatly benefit victims' relatives and potential future victims of crime. . . .

17. Many state governments justify retention of the death penalty on the grounds of strong public support for it. Although opinion polls show that a large majority of the US population favours the death penalty, this support may not be based on accurate information about the actual use of the death penalty and its effects on society. The polls also show that support for the death penalty is not unqualified. Were the public fully aware of the sound moral and practical reasons for not using the death penalty and of the alternative measures needed to protect society from violent crime, its support for the penalty would be likely to diminish.

18. The death penalty is irrevocable and can be inflicted on an innocent person despite the most stringent judicial standards. A recent study collected information on over 300 cases in the USA this century in which innocent people were wrongly convicted of offences punishable by death; some 50 of them occurred after 1970. Since 1900, 23 wrongly convicted prisoners have been executed. In many of the other cases information leading to acquittals, pardons or commutation of sentences came to light years after the original conviction. The study excluded, through lack of adequate data, many additional cases in which it was alleged that miscarriages of justice had occurred.

Conclusions and Recommendations

The death penalty denies the right to life. It is a cruel and inhuman punishment, brutalizing to all who are involved in the process. It serves no useful penal purpose and denies the widely accepted principle of rehabilitating the offender. It serves neither to protect society nor to alleviate the suffering caused to the victims of crime. It is irreversible and, even with the most stringent judicial safeguards, may be inflicted on an innocent person.

No means of limiting the death penalty can prevent its being imposed arbitrarily or unfairly. This is borne out by the experience in the USA, where the introduction of elaborate judicial safeguards has failed to ensure that the death penalty is fairly and consistently applied.

On the basis of its findings, Amnesty International respectfully submits the following recommendations to the federal and state governments of the United States:

1. Amnesty International calls on all state governments in states whose laws provide for the death penalty to abolish the death penalty for all offences in law. All measures to abolish the death penalty or restrict is use should be applied retroactively to prisoners under sentence of death, in accordance with international standards.

2. Amnesty International urges that, until the death penalty has been abolished in law, no further executions be carried out; that steps be taken to commute the death sentences of all those currently on death row, and that no further death sentences be imposed.

3. International standards cited in this report hold that the death penalty should not be extended to crimes to which it does not at present apply nor should it be re-established in states that have abolished it. Amnesty International calls upon the federal government, in keeping with these standards, not to enact the death penalty under federal law. The death penalty should be abolished under the federal Uniform Code of Military Justice.

Pending the abolition of the death penalty in law, the following recommendations should be given immediate consideration:

4. State laws and practice should conform to minimum international standards that preclude the imposition of the death penalty on juvenile offenders and the mentally ill.

5. State governors and boards of pardons and paroles should broaden their criteria for granting clemency in capital cases, so that circumstances beyond the facts of the crime and the correctness of the legal proceedings are taken into account. Mitigating circumstances in the offender's background; the presence of mental illness or mental retardation; international standards and other factors cited in . . . this report should constitute minimum grounds for commuting death sentences.

6. Amnesty International believes that the evidence of racial discrimination in the application of the death penalty is a matter for serious and urgent concern. Detailed studies, and statistics relating to the prisoners executed and those remaining on death row, suggest that disparities in death sentencing, based on racial factors, occur in states throughout the USA.

Should the findings of these studies be considered deficient, Amnesty International recommends that the executive or legislative branch of the federal government commission a serious inquiry into the question of racial discrimination and the death penalty. Amnesty International suggests that such an inquiry use impartial specialists to evaluate all relevant data concerning the arrest, charging and sentencing of criminal homicide offenders in given jurisdictions over a period of time. Information should be gathered from all those knowledgeable about the legal process, including judges, state prosecutors, defence attorneys, the police, boards of pardons and paroles, and state correctional departments.

The findings of a national inquiry into racial discrimination and the death penalty may have serious implications for the cases of many prisoners under sentence of death. In the absence of immediate measures to abolish the death penalty or commute the sentences of those on death row, a moratorium on executions should be imposed pending the outcome of the inquiry.

Any measures undertaken by the federal authorities to examine this question should not prevent individual state governments or legislatures from commissioning their own inquiries.

7. State governments should study the impact of the death penalty on the crime rate; the criminal justice system, the correctional services; the families of the victims of violent crime; and family members of condemned prisoners. They should also examine the adequacy of legal representation of poor defendants in capital proceedings, the adequacy of state clemency procedures and the fairness of jury selection in death penalty cases.

Based on this and other information, they should take steps to inform the public about the penal and criminological effects of the death penalty, including its lack of proved special deterrent effect; its high cost and limited application to criminal homicide cases; and ways in which it may distort and impede the process of justice and result in unfairness. Amnesty International believes that, should the public be fully informed about the effects of the death penalty, there would be wider acceptance of moves to abolish it.

8. Pending the introduction of measures to suspend or commute the sentences of those currently under sentence of death, the appropriate state authorities should review arrangements for the treatment and custody of such prisoners, to ensure that they do not exacerbate the already cruel, inhuman and degrading experience of being under sentence of death.

Doctors and Other Health Professionals

Amnesty International also calls on doctors and other health professionals not to participate in any way in executions or to use their professional expertise in any way which might lead to the imposition of death sentences. This would include being present at or monitoring executions while they are taking place; the treatment of insanity in order to render condemned prisoners mentally fit to be executed; and the giving of psychiatric testimony in trials which may lead to the imposition of death sentences.

Amnesty International believes that the above actions are contrary to the ethical principles relating to the role of health personnel in protecting all prisoners from torture or other cruel, inhuman or degrading treatment, adopted by the United Nations General Assembly in 1982. They are also contrary to principles adopted by the World Medical Association on doctors and the death penalty.

POLICING THE COMMUNITY: PUBLIC PROTECTION OR CLASS CONTROL? **1**

Broken Windows

James Q. Wilson and George L. Kelling

In the mid-1970s, the state of New Jersey announced a "Safe and Clean Neighborhoods Program," designed to improve the quality of community life in twenty-eight cities. As part of that program, the state provided money to help cities take police officers out of their patrol cars and assign them to walking beats. The governor and other state officials were enthusiastic about using foot patrol as a way of cutting crime, but many police chiefs were skeptical. Foot patrol, in their eyes, had been pretty much discredited. It reduced the mobility of the police, who thus had difficulty responding to citizen calls for service, and it weakened headquarters control over patrol officers.

Many police officers also disliked foot patrol, but for different reasons: it was hard work, it kept them outside on cold, rainy nights, and it reduced their chances for making a "good pinch." In some departments, assigning officers to foot patrol had been used as a form of punishment. And academic experts on policing doubted that foot patrol would have any impact on crime rates; it was, in the opinion of most, little more than a sop to public opinion. But since the state was paying for it, the local authorities were willing to go along.

Five years after the program started, the Police Foundation, in Washington, D.C., published an evaluation of the foot-patrol project. Based on its analysis of a carefully controlled experiment carried out chiefly in Newark, the foundation concluded, to the surprise of hardly anyone, that foot patrol had not reduced crime rates. But residents of the foot-patrolled neighborhoods seemed to feel more secure than persons in other areas, tended to believe that crime had been reduced, and seemed to take fewer steps to protect themselves from crime (staying at home with the doors locked, for example). Moreover, citizens in the foot-patrol areas had a more favorable opinion of the police than did those living elsewhere. And officers walking beats had higher morale, greater job satisfaction, and a more favorable attitude toward citizens in their neighborhood than did officers assigned to patrol cars.

Source: James Q. Wilson and George L. Kelling, "Broken Windows," *Atlantic Monthly* (March 1982):29–38. Reprinted with permission.

These findings may be taken as evidence that the skeptics were right—foot patrol has no effect on crime; it merely fools the citizens into thinking that they are safer. But in our view, and in the view of the authors of the Police Foundation study (of whom Kelling was one), the citizens of Newark were not fooled at all. They knew what the foot-patrol officers were doing, they knew it was different from what motorized officers do, and they knew that having officers walk beats did in fact make their neighborhoods safer.

But how can a neighborhood be "safer" when the crime rate has not gone down—in fact, may have gone up? Finding the answer requires first that we understand what most often frightens people in public places. Many citizens, of course, are primarily frightened by crime, especially crime involving a sudden, violent attack by a stranger. This risk is very real, in Newark as in many large cities. But we tend to overlook or forget another source of fear—the fear of being bothered by disorderly people. Not violent people, nor, necessarily, criminals, but disreputable or obstreperous or unpredictable people: panhandlers, drunks, addicts, rowdy teenagers, prostitutes, loiterers, the mentally disturbed.

What foot-patrol officers did was to elevate, to the extent they could, the level of public order in these neighborhoods. Though the neighborhoods were predominantly black and the foot patrolmen were mostly white, this "order-maintenance" function of the police was performed to the general satisfaction of both parties.

One of us (Kelling) spent many hours walking with Newark foot-patrol officers to see how they defined "order" and what they did to maintain it. One beat was typical: a busy but dilapidated area in the heart of Newark, with many abandoned buildings, marginal shops (several of which prominently displayed knives and straight-edged razors in their windows), one large department store, and, most important, a train station and several major bus stops. Though the area was run-down, its streets were filled with people, because it was a major transportation center. The good order of this area was important not only to those who lived and worked there but also to many others, who had to move through it on their way home, to supermarkets, or to factories.

The people on the street were primarily black; the officer who walked the street was white. The people were made up of "regulars" and "strangers." Regulars included both "decent folk" and some drunks and derelicts who were always there but who "knew their place." Strangers were, well, strangers, and viewed suspiciously, sometimes apprehensively. The officer—call him Kelly—knew who the regulars were, and they knew him. As he saw his job, he was to keep an eye on strangers, and make certain that the disreputable regulars observed some informal but widely understood rules. Drunks and addicts could sit on the stoops, but could not lie down. People could drink on side streets, but not at the main intersection. Bottles had to be in paper bags. Talking to, bothering, or begging from people waiting at the bus stop was strictly forbidden. If a dispute erupted between a businessman and a customer, the businessman was assumed to be right, especially if the customer was a stranger. If a stranger loitered, Kelly would ask him if he had any means of support and what his business was; if he gave unsatisfactory answers, he was sent on his way. Persons who broke the informal rules, especially those who bothered people waiting at bus stops, were arrested for vagrancy. Noisy teenagers were told to keep quiet.

These rules were defined and enforced in collaboration with the "regulars" on the street. Another neighborhood might have different rules, but these, everybody understood, were the rules for *this* neighborhood. If someone violated them, the regular not only turned to Kelly for help but also ridiculed the violator. Sometimes what Kelly did could be described as "enforcing the law," but just as often it involved taking informal or extralegal steps to help protect what the neighborhood had decided was the appropriate level of public order. Some of the things he did probably would not withstand a legal challenge.

A determined skeptic might acknowledge that a skilled foot-patrol officer can maintain order but still insist that this sort of "order" has little to do with the real sources of community fear—that is, with violent crime. To a degree, that is true. But two things must be borne in mind. First, outside observers should not assume that they know how much of the anxiety now endemic in many big-city neighborhoods stems from a fear of "real" crime and how much from a sense that the street is disorderly, a source of distasteful, worrisome encounters. The people of Newark, to judge from their behavior and their remarks to interviewers, apparently assign a high value to public order, and feel relieved and reassured when the police help them maintain that order.

Second, at the community level, disorder and crime are usually inextricably linked, in a kind of developmental sequence. Social psychologists and police officers tend to agree that if a window in a building is broken *and is left unrepaired*, all the rest of the windows will soon be broken. This is as true in nice neighborhoods as in run-down ones. Window-breaking does not necessarily occur on a large scale because some areas are inhabited by determined window-breakers whereas others are populated by window-lovers; rather, one unrepaired broken window is a signal that no one cares, and so breaking more windows costs nothing. (It has always been fun.)

Philip Zimbardo, a Stanford psychologist, reported in 1969 on some experiments testing the broken-window theory. He arranged to have an automobile without license plates parked with its hood up on a street in the Bronx and a comparable automobile on a street in Palo Alto, California. The car in the Bronx was attacked by "vandals" within ten minutes of its "abandonment." The first to arrive were a family—father, mother, and young son—who removed the radiator and battery. Within twenty-four hours, virtually everything of value had been removed. Then random destruction began—windows were smashed, parts torn off, upholstery ripped. Children began to use the car as a playground. Most of the adult "vandals" were well-dressed, apparently clean-cut whites. The car in Palo Alto sat untouched for more than a week. Then Zimbardo smashed part of it with a sledgehammer. Soon, passersby were joining in. Within a few hours, the car had been turned upside down and utterly destroyed. Again, the "vandals" appeared to be primarily respectable whites.

Untended property becomes fair game for people out for fun or plunder, and even for people who ordinarily would not dream of doing such things and who probably consider themselves law-abiding. Because of the nature of community life in the Bronx—its anonymity, the frequency with which cars are abandoned and things are stolen or broken, the past experience of "no one caring"— vandalism begins much more quickly than it does in staid Palo Alto, where people have come to believe that private possessions are cared for, and that mischievous behavior is costly. But vandalism can occur anywhere once communal barriers— the sense of mutual regard and the obligations of civility—are lowered by actions that seem to signal that "no one cares."

We suggest that "untended" behavior also leads to the breakdown of community controls. A stable neighborhood of families who care for their homes, mind each other's children, and confidently frown on unwanted intruders can change, in a few years or even a few months, to an inhospitable and frightening jungle. A piece of property is abandoned, weeds grow up, a window is smashed. Adults stop scolding rowdy children; the children, emboldened, become more rowdy. Families move out, unattached adults move in. Teenagers gather in front of the corner store. The merchant asks them to move; they refuse. Fights occur. Litter accumulates. People start drinking in front of the grocery; in time, an inebriate slumps to the sidewalk and is allowed to sleep it off. Pedestrians are approached by panhandlers.

At this point it is not inevitable that serious crime will flourish or violent attacks on strangers will occur. But many residents will think that crime, especially violent crime, is on the rise, and they will modify their behavior accordingly. They will use the streets less often, and when on the streets will stay apart from their fellows, moving with averted eyes, silent lips, and hurried steps. "Don't get involved." For some residents, this growing atomization will matter little, because the neighborhood is not their "home" but "the place where they live." Their interests are elsewhere; they are cosmopolitan. But it will matter greatly to other people, whose lives derive meaning and satisfaction from local attachments rather than world involvement; for them, the neighborhood will cease to exist except for a few reliable friends whom they arrange to meet.

Such an area is vulnerable to criminal invasion. Though it is not inevitable, it is more likely that here, rather than in places where people are confident they can regulate public behavior by informal controls, drugs will change hands, prostitutes will solicit, and cars will be stripped. That the drunks will be robbed by boys who do it as a lark, and the prostitutes' customers will be robbed by men who do it purposefully and perhaps violently. That muggings will occur.

Among those who often find it difficult to move away from this are the elderly. Surveys of citizens suggest that the elderly are much less likely to be the victims of crime than younger persons, and some have inferred from this that the well-known fear of crime voiced by the elderly is an exaggeration: perhaps we ought not to design special programs to protect older persons; perhaps we should even try to talk them out of their mistaken fears. This argument misses the point. The prospect of a confrontation with an obstreperous teenager or a drunken panhandler can be as fear-inducing for defenseless persons as the prospect of meeting an actual robber; indeed, to a defenseless person, the two kinds of confrontation are often indistinguishable. Moreover, the lower rate at which the elderly are victimized is a measure of the steps they have already taken—chiefly, staying behind locked doors—to minimize the risks they face. Young men are more frequently attacked than older women, not because they are easier or more lucrative targets but because they are on the streets more.

Nor is the connection between disorderliness and fear made only by the elderly. Susan Estrich, of the Harvard Law School, has recently gathered together a number of surveys on the sources of public fear. One, done in Portland, Oregon, indicated that three-fourths of the adults interviewed cross to the other side of a street when they see a gang of teenagers; another survey, in Baltimore, discovered that nearly half would cross the street to avoid even a single strange youth. When an interviewer asked people in a housing project where the most dangerous spot was, they mentioned a place where young persons gathered to drink and play music, despite the fact that not a single crime had occurred there. In Boston public housing projects, the greatest fear was expressed by persons living in the buildings where disorderliness and incivility, not crime, were the greatest. Knowing this helps one understand the significance of such otherwise harmless displays as subway graffiti. As Nathan Glazer has written, the proliferation of graffiti, even when not obscene, confronts the subway rider with the "inescapable knowledge that the environment he must endure for an hour or more a day is uncontrolled and uncontrollable, and that anyone can invade it to do whatever damage and mischief the mind suggests."

In response to fear, people avoid one another, weakening controls. Sometimes they call the police. Patrol cars arrive, an occasional arrest occurs, but crime continues and disorder is not abated. Citizens complain to the police chief, but he explains that his department is low on personnel and that the courts do not punish petty or first-time offenders. To the residents, the police who arrive in squad cars are either ineffective or uncaring; to the police, the residents are animals who deserve each other. The citizens may soon stop calling the police, because "they can't do anything."

The process we call urban decay has occurred for centuries in every city. But what is happening today is different in at least two important respects. First, in the period before, say, World War II, city dwellers—because of money costs, transportation difficulties, familial and church connections—could rarely move away from neighborhood problems. When movement did occur, it tended to be along public-transit routes. Now mobility has become exceptionally easy for all but the poorest or those who are blocked by racial prejudice. Earlier crime waves had a kind of built-in self-correcting mechanism: the determination of a neighborhood or community to reassert control over its turf. Areas in Chicago, New York, and Boston would experience crime and gang wars, and then normalcy would return, as the families for whom no alternative residences were possible reclaimed their authority over the streets.

Second, the police in this earlier period assisted in that reassertion of authority by acting, sometimes violently, on behalf of the community. Young toughs were roughed up, people were arrested "on suspicion" or for vagrancy, and prostitutes and petty thieves were routed. "Rights" were something enjoyed by decent folk, and perhaps also by the serious professional criminal, who avoided violence and could afford a lawyer.

This pattern of policing was not an aberration or the result of occasional excess. From the earliest days of the nation, the police function was seen primarily as that of a night watchman: to maintain order against the chief threats to order—fire, wild animals, and disreputable behavior. Solving crimes was viewed not as a police responsibility but as a private one. In the March, 1969, *Atlantic*, one of us (Wilson) wrote a brief account of how the police role had slowly changed from maintaining order to fighting crimes. The change began with the creation of private detectives (often ex-criminals), who worked on a contingency-fee basis for individuals who had suffered losses. In time, the detectives were absorbed into municipal police agencies and paid a regular salary; simultaneously, the responsibility for prosecuting thieves was shifted from the aggrieved private citizen to the professional prosecutor. This process was not complete in most places until the twentieth century.

In the 1960s, when urban riots were a major problem, social scientists began to explore carefully the order-maintenance function of the police, and to suggest ways of improving it—not to make streets safer (its original function) but to reduce the incidence of mass violence. Order-maintenance became, to a degree, coterminous with "community relations." But, as the crime wave that began in the early 1960s continued without abatement throughout the decade and into the 1970s, attention shifted to the role of the police as crime-fighters. Studies of police behavior ceased, by and large, to be accounts of the order-maintenance function and became, instead, efforts to propose and test ways whereby the police could solve more crimes, make more arrests, and gather better evidence. If these things could be done, social scientists assumed, citizens would be less fearful.

A great deal was accomplished during this transition, as both police chiefs and outside experts emphasized the crime-fighting function in their plans, in the allocation of resources, and in deployment of personnel. The police may well have become better crime-fighters as a result. And doubtless they remained aware of their responsibility for order. But the link between order-maintenance and crime-prevention, so obvious to earlier generations, was forgotten.

That link is similar to the process whereby one broken window becomes many. The citizen who fears the ill-smelling drunk, the rowdy teenager, or the importuning beggar is not merely expressing his distaste for unseemly behavior; he is also giving voice to a bit of folk wisdom that happens to be a correct generalization—namely, that serious street crime flourishes in areas in which disorderly behavior goes unchecked. The unchecked panhandler is, in effect, the first broken window. Muggers and robbers, whether opportunistic or professional, believe they reduce their chances of being caught or even identified if they operate on streets where potential victims are already intimidated by prevailing conditions. If the neighborhood cannot keep a bothersome panhandler from annoying passersby, the thief may reason, it is even less likely to call the police to identify a potential mugger or to interfere if the mugging actually takes place.

Some police administrators concede that this process occurs, but argue that motorized-patrol officers can deal with it as effectively as foot-patrol officers. We are not so sure. In theory, an officer in a squad car can observe as much as an officer on foot; in theory, the former can talk to as many people as the latter. But the reality of police–citizen encounters is powerfully altered by the automobile. An officer on foot cannot separate himself from the street people; if he is approached, only his uniform and his personality can help him manage whatever is about to happen. And he can never be certain what that will be—a request for directions, a plea for help, an angry denunciation, a teasing remark, a confused babble, a threatening gesture.

In a car, an officer is more likely to deal with street people by rolling down the window and looking at them. The door and the window exclude the approaching citizen; they are a barrier. Some officers take advantage of this barrier, perhaps unconsciously, by acting differently if in the car than they would on foot. We have seen this countless times. The police car pulls up to a corner where teenagers are gathered. The window is rolled down. The officer stares at the youths. They stare back. The officer says to one, "C'mere." He saunters over, conveying to his friends by his elaborately casual style the idea that he is not intimidated by authority. "What's your name?" "Chuck." "Chuck who?" "Chuck Jones." "What'ya doing, Chuck?" "Nothin'." "Got a P.O. [parole officer]?" "Nah." "Sure?" "Yeah." "Stay out of trouble, Chuckie." Meanwhile, the other boys laugh and exchange comments among themselves, probably at the officer's expense. The officer stares harder. He cannot be certain what is being said, nor can he join in and, by displaying his own skill at street banter, prove that he cannot be "put down." In the process, the officer has learned almost nothing, and the boys have decided the officer is an alien force who can safely be disregarded, even mocked.

Our experience is that most citizens like to talk to a police officer. Such exchanges give them a sense of importance, provide them with the basis for gossip, and allow them to explain to the authorities what is worrying them (whereby they gain a modest but significant sense of having "done something" about the problem). You approach a person on foot more easily, and talk to him more readily, than you do a person in a car. Moreover, you can more easily retain some anonymity if you draw an officer aside for a private chat. Suppose you want to pass on a tip about who is stealing handbags, or who offered to sell you a stolen TV. In the inner city, the culprit, in all likelihood, lives nearby. To walk up to a marked patrol car and lean in the window is to convey a visible signal that you are a "fink."

The essence of the police role in maintaining order is to reinforce the informal control mechanisms of the community itself. The police cannot, without committing extraordinary resources, provide a substitute for that informal control. On the other hand, to reinforce those natural forces the police must accommodate them. And therein lies the problem.

Should police activity on the street be shaped, in important ways, by the standards of the neighborhood rather than by the rules of the state? Over the past two decades, the shift of police from order-maintenance to law-enforcement has brought them increasingly under the influence of legal restrictions, provoked by media complaints and enforced by court decisions and departmental orders. As a consequence, the order-maintenance functions of the police are now governed by rules developed to control police relations with suspected criminals. This is, we think, an entirely new development. For centuries, the role of the police as watchmen was judged primarily not in terms of its compliance with appropriate procedures but rather in terms of its attaining a desired objective. The objective was order, an inherently ambiguous term but a condition that people in a given community recognized when they saw it. The means were the same as those the community itself would employ, if its members were sufficiently determined, courageous, and authoritative. Detecting and apprehending criminals, by contrast, was a means to an end, not an end in itself; a judicial determination of guilt or innocence was the hoped-for result of the law-enforcement mode. From the first, the police were expected to follow rules defining that process, though states differed in how stringent the rules should be. The criminal-apprehension process was always understood to involve individual rights, the violation of which was unacceptable because it meant that the violating officer would be acting as a judge and jury—and that was not his job. Guilt or innocence was to be determined by universal standards under special procedures.

Ordinarily, no judge or jury ever sees the persons caught up in a dispute over the appropriate level of neighborhood order. That is true not only because most cases are handled informally on the street but also because no universal standards are available to settle arguments over disorder, and thus a judge may not be any wiser or more effective than a police officer. Until quite recently in many states, and even today in some places, the police make arrests on such charges as "suspicious person" or "vagrancy" or "public drunkenness"—charges with scarcely any legal meaning. These charges exist not because society wants judges to punish vagrants or drunks but because it wants an officer to have the legal tools to remove undesirable persons from a neighborhood when informal efforts to preserve order in the streets have failed.

Once we begin to think of all aspects of police work as involving the application of universal rules under special procedures, we inevitably ask what constitutes an "undesirable person" and why we should "criminalize" vagrancy or drunkenness. A strong and commendable desire to see that people are treated fairly makes us worry about allowing the police to rout persons who are undesirable by some vague or parochial standard. A growing and not-so-commendable utilitarianism leads us to doubt that any behavior that does not "hurt" another person should be made illegal. And thus many of us who watch over the police are reluctant to allow them to perform, in the only way they can, a function that every neighborhood desperately wants them to perform.

This wish to "decriminalize" disreputable behavior that "harms no one"—and thus remove the ultimate sanction the police can employ to maintain neighborhood order—is, we think, a mistake. Arresting a single drunk or a single vagrant who has harmed no identifiable person seems unjust, and in a sense it is. But failing to do anything about a score of drunks or a hundred vagrants may destroy an entire community. A particular rule that seems to make sense in the individual case makes no sense when it is made a universal rule and applied to all cases. It makes no sense because it fails to take into account the connection between one broken window left untended and a thousand broken windows. Of course, agencies other than the police could attend to the problems posed by drunks or the mentally ill, but in most communities—especially where the "deinstitutionalization" movement has been strong—they do not.

The concern about equity is more serious. We might agree that certain behavior makes one person more undesirable than another, but how do we ensure that age or skin color or national origin or harmless mannerisms will not also become the basis for distinguishing the undesirable from the desirable? How do we ensure, in short, that the police do not become the agents of neighborhood bigotry?

We can offer no wholly satisfactory answer to this important question. We are not confident that there *is* a satisfactory answer, except to hope that by their selection, training, and supervision, the police will be inculcated with a clear sense of the outer limit of their discretionary authority. That limit, roughly, is this—the police exist to help regulate behavior, not to maintain the racial or ethnic purity of a neighborhood.

Consider the case of the Robert Taylor Homes in Chicago, one of the largest public-housing projects in the country. It is home for nearly 20,000 people, all black, and extends over ninety-two acres along South State Street. It was named after a distinguished black who had been, during the 1940s, chairman of the Chicago Housing Authority. Not long after it opened, in 1962, relations between project residents and the police deteriorated badly. The citizens felt that the police were insensitive or brutal; the police, in turn, complained of unprovoked attacks on them. Some Chicago officers tell of times when they were afraid to enter the Homes. Crime rates soared.

Today, the atmosphere has changed. Police–citizen relations have improved— apparently, both sides learned something from the earlier experience. Recently, a boy stole a purse and ran off. Several young persons who saw the theft voluntarily passed along to the police information on the identity and residence of the thief, and they did this publicly, with friends and neighbors looking on. But problems persist, chief among them the presence of youth gangs that terrorize residents and recruit members in the project. The people expect the police to "do something" about this, and the police are determined to do just that.

But do what? Though the police can obviously make arrests whenever a gang member breaks the law, a gang can form, recruit, and congregate without breaking the law. And only a tiny fraction of gang-related crimes can be solved by an arrest; thus, if an arrest is the only recourse for the police, the residents' fears will go unassuaged. The police will soon feel helpless, and the residents will again believe that the police "do nothing." What the police in fact do is to chase known gang members out of the project. In the words of one officer, "We kick ass." Project residents both know and approve of this. The tacit police–citizen alliance in the project is reinforced by the police view that the cops and the gangs are the two rival sources of power in the area, and that the gangs are not going to win.

None of this is easily reconciled with any conception of due process or fair treatment. Since both residents and gang members are black, race is not a factor. But it could be. Suppose a white project confronted a black gang, or vice versa. We would be apprehensive about the police taking sides. But the substantive problem remains the same: how can the police strengthen the informal social-control mechanisms of natural communities in order to minimize fear in public places? Law enforcement, per se, is no answer. A gang can weaken or destroy a community by standing about in a menacing fashion and speaking rudely to passersby without breaking the law.

We have difficulty thinking about such matters, not simply because the ethical and legal issues are so complex but because we have become accustomed to thinking of the law in essentially individualistic terms. The law defines *my* rights, punishes *his* behavior, and is applied by *that* officer because of *this* harm. We assume, in thinking this way, that what is good for the individual will be good for the community, and what doesn't matter when it happens to one person won't matter if it happens to many. Ordinarily, those are plausible assumptions. But in cases where behavior that is tolerable to one person is intolerable to many others, the reactions of the others—fear, withdrawal, flight—may ultimately make matters worse for everyone, including the individual who first professed his indifference.

It may be their greater sensitivity to communal as opposed to individual needs that helps explain why the residents of small communities are more satisfied with their police than are the residents of similar neighborhoods in big cities. Elinor Ostrom and her co-workers at Indiana University compared the perception of police services in two poor, all-black Illinois towns—Phoenix and East Chicago Heights—with those of three comparable all-black neighborhoods in Chicago. The level of criminal victimization and the quality of police-community relations appeared to be about the same in the towns and the Chicago neighborhoods. But the citizens living in their own villages were much more likely than those living in the Chicago neighborhoods to say that they do not stay at home for fear of crime, to agree that the local police have "the right to take any action necessary" to deal with problems, and to agree that the police "look out for the needs of the average citizen." It is possible that the residents and the police of the small towns saw themselves as engaged in a collaborative effort to maintain a certain standard of communal life, whereas those of the big city felt themselves to be simply requesting and supplying particular services on an individual basis.

If this is true, how should a wise police chief deploy his meager forces? The first answer is that nobody knows for certain, and the most prudent course of action would be to try further variations on the Newark experiment, to see more precisely what works in what kinds of neighborhoods. The second answer is also a hedge—many aspects of order-maintenance in neighborhoods can probably best be handled in ways that involve the police minimally, if at all. A busy, bustling shopping center and a quiet, well-tended suburb may need almost no visible police presence. In both cases, the ratio of respectable to disreputable people is ordinarily so high as to make informal social control effective.

Even in areas that are in jeopardy from disorderly elements, citizen action without substantial police involvement may be sufficient. Meetings between teenagers who like to hang out on a particular corner and adults who want to use that corner might well lead to an amicable agreement on a set of rules about how many people can be allowed to congregate, where, and when.

Where no understanding is possible—or if possible, not observed—citizen patrols may be a sufficient response. There are two traditions of communal involvement in maintaining order. One, that of the "community watchmen," is as old as the first settlement of the New World. Until well into the nineteenth century, volunteer watchmen, not policemen, patrolled their communities to keep order. They did so, by and large, without taking the law into their own hands—without, that is, punishing persons or using force. Their presence deterred disorder or alerted the community to disorder that could not be deterred. There are hundreds of such efforts today in communities all across the nation. Perhaps the best known is that of the Guardian Angels, a group of unarmed young persons in distinctive berets and T-shirts, who first came to public attention when they began patrolling the New York City subways but who claim now to have chapters in more than thirty American cities. Unfortunately, we have little information about the effect of these groups on crime. It is possible, however, that whatever their effect on crime, citizens find their presence reassuring, and that they thus contribute to maintaining a sense of order and civility.

The second tradition is that of the "vigilante." Rarely a feature of the settled communities of the East, it was primarily to be found in those frontier towns that grew up in advance of the reach of government. More than 350 vigilante groups are known to have existed; their distinctive feature was that their members did take the law into their own hands, by acting as judge, jury, and often executioner as well as policeman. Today, the vigilante movement is conspicuous by its rarity, despite the great fear expressed by citizens that the older cities are becoming "urban frontiers." But some community-watchmen groups have skirted the line, and others may cross it in the future. An ambiguous case, reported in *The Wall Street Journal*, involved a citizens' patrol in the Silver Lake area of Belleville, New Jersey. A leader told the reporter, "We look for outsiders." If a few teenagers from outside the neighborhood enter it, "we ask them their business," he said. "If they say they're going down the street to see Mrs. Jones, fine, we let them pass. But then we follow them down the block to make sure they're really going to see Mrs. Jones."

Though citizens can do a great deal, the police are plainly the key to order-maintenance. For one thing, many communities, such as the Robert Taylor Homes, cannot do the job by themselves. For another, no citizen in a neighborhood, even an organized one, is likely to feel the sense of responsibility that wearing a badge confers. Psychologists have done many studies on why people fail to go to the aid of persons being attacked or seeking help, and they have learned that the cause is not "apathy" or "selfishness" but the absence of some plausible grounds for feeling that one must personally accept responsibility. Ironically, avoiding responsibility is easier when a lot of people are standing about. On streets and in public places, where order is so important, many people are likely to be "around," a fact that reduces the chance of any one person acting as the agent of the community. The police officer's uniform singles him out as a person who must accept responsibility if asked. In addition, officers, more easily than their fellow citizens, can be expected to distinguish between what is necessary to protect the safety of the street and what merely protects its ethnic purity.

But the police forces of America are losing, not gaining, members. Some cities have suffered substantial cuts in the number of officers available for duty. These cuts are not likely to be reversed in the near future. Therefore, each department must assign its existing officers with great care. Some neighborhoods are so demoralized and crime-ridden as to make foot patrol useless; the best the police can do with limited resources is respond to the enormous number of calls for service. Other neighborhoods are so stable and serene as to make foot patrol unnecessary. The key is to identify neighborhoods at the tipping point—where the public order is deteriorating but not unreclaimable, where the streets are used frequently but by apprehensive people, where a window is likely to be broken at any time, and must quickly be fixed if all are not to be shattered.

Most police departments do not have ways of systematically identifying such areas and assigning officers to them. Officer are assigned on the basis of crime rates (meaning that marginally threatened areas are often stripped so that police can investigate crimes in areas where the situation is hopeless) or on the basis of calls for service (despite the fact that most citizens do not call the police when they are merely frightened or annoyed). To allocate patrol wisely, the department must look at the neighborhoods and decide, from first-hand evidence, where an additional officer will make the greatest difference in promoting a sense of safety.

One way to stretch limited police resources is being tried in some public-housing projects. Tenant organizations hire off-duty police officers for patrol work in their buildings. The costs are not high (at least not per resident), the officer likes the additional income, and the residents feel safer. Such arrangements are probably more successful than hiring private watchmen, and the Newark experiment helps us understand why. A private security guard may deter crime or misconduct by his presence, and he may go to the aid of persons needing help, but he may well not intervene—that is, control or drive away—someone challenging community standards. Being a sworn officer—a "real cop"—seems to give one the confidence, the sense of duty, and the aura of authority necessary to perform this difficult task.

Patrol officers might be encouraged to go to and from duty stations on public transportation and, while on the bus or subway car, enforce rules about smoking, drinking, disorderly conduct, and the like. The enforcement need involve nothing more than ejecting the offender (the offense, after all, is not one with which a booking officer or a judge wishes to be bothered). Perhaps the random but relentless maintenance of standards on buses would lead to conditions on buses that approximate the level of civility we now take for granted on airplanes.

But the most important requirement is to think that to maintain order in precarious situations is a vital job. The police know this is one of their functions, and they also believe, correctly, that it cannot be done to the exclusion of criminal investigation and responding to calls. We may have encouraged them to suppose, however, on the basis of our oft-repeated concerns about serious, violent crime, that they will be judged exclusively on their capacity as crime-fighters. To the extent that this is the case, police administrators will continue to concentrate police personnel in the highest-crime areas (though not necessarily in the areas most vulnerable to criminal invasion), emphasize their training in the law and criminal apprehension (and not their training in managing street life), and join too quickly in campaigns to decriminalize "harmless" behavior (though public drunkenness, street prostitution, and pornographic displays can destroy a community more quickly than any team of professional burglars).

Above all, we must return to our long-abandoned view that the police ought to protect communities as well as individuals. Our crime statistics and victimization surveys measure individual losses, but they do not measure communal losses. Just as physicians now recognize the importance of fostering health rather than simply treating illness, so the police—and the rest of us—ought to recognize the importance of maintaining, intact, communities without broken windows.

Policing a Class Society

Sidney L. Harring

The American police institution and its role in American society cannot be understood outside class relations and the class struggle. The fluctuating industrial economy of the late nineteenth and early twentieth centuries produced a complex set of rapidly changing class relations, and the social institutions that developed to deal with this shifting situation assumed a variety of forms. The paradox of the "friendly corner cop" who, on the one hand, directed immigrant families to local sources of welfare assistance, brought home lost kids and drunk husbands and wives, and called the ambulance when a friend fell and broke an arm, but who, on the other hand, broke strikes, locked brothers and sisters in jail, and beat friends is but one of the contradictions of the period. The police officer's role appears less contradictory, however, when viewed in terms of the necessity of legitimating state force and having relatively easy access to workers' communities. This necessity demanded a friendly, nonaggressive approach much of the time. Most workers undoubtedly learned to distinguish between the local cop and the police institution in general. Thus one could have some kind of genuine respect for, if not always complete trust in, the officer on the beat while still having no illusions about whose side the municipal police were on.

Similarly, the bourgeoisie faced its own set of contradictions concerning the police. Their completely unrealistic expectations that the municipal force could in fact effectively control urban class society led to great frustration over the failure of the police to carry out this mission. The limits of the police institution became apparent precisely as the bourgeoisie also had to respond to the first major working-class challenge to its domination of urban politics. There was confusion and disarray in the ranks of the bourgeoisie over proper courses of action in every area of urban politics, including the police issue. Massive shows of violence by both the public police under bourgeois domination and the private police of the major corporations were one response. Another was a move toward "reform" and

---

"professionalization" in order to insulate the municipal police from the rough-and-tumble of an urban politics that was becoming increasingly difficult to dominate. Although the bourgeoisie often criticized the police severely for a number of reasons, they still called on the chief and his men for help during strikes, applied for private keys to patrol boxes, demanded heavier patrols for their own residential districts, and easily induced the cop on the beat to keep rough-looking juveniles away from their shops.

The conception of a "policed society" emerged from the requirements of the ruling class of an increasingly complex urban society. The forms of policing cannot be understood as value-free and inevitable; rather, they were structured by class requirements. The police departments designed by ruling-class civic activists of the mid-nineteenth century were altered by the necessities of the actual policing of the class struggle. The earlier forces dominated (in fact, virtually run) by members of the ruling class gave way to forces dominated by political machines that only partly depended on ruling-class support and that operated, at least in part, according to legal-bureaucratic procedure. These forces were clearly more than simple adjuncts of political machines. When, beginning in the late nineteenth century, the political machines proved to be uncontrollable, "reform" movements shifted further toward legal-bureaucratic organizational forms, completing the shift to the police force we know today.

From the standpoint of the police institution itself, there is an amazing continuity over the past one hundred years. Central to this continuity is the term "professionalization"—now closely associated with the transformation of the police image in the 1960s and 1970s but actually referring to almost exactly the same changes vigorously supported by the chiefs who originally formed the National Chiefs of Police union in 1893, the direct forerunner of today's International Association of Chiefs of Police. The police chiefs of the 1890s thought that policing should be a full-time career choice, free of control by the ruling political party (meaning also independence from all forms of popular control), requiring some level of skill and training, abiding by institutionally imposed standards of professional behavior, and enjoying job tenure and promotion based on merit. The major different between the 1890s and 1970s is that the ideal of professionalization has now been thoroughly inculcated into the supposedly value-free ideology of policing. Rational-legal forms have assumed increasing dominance in all areas of the public sector as well.

Police professionalization is properly understood as simply one small part of the total process of rationalization under advanced capitalism. Consistent with the trend toward increasing domination of what sociologist Max Weber called the "rational legal" form, social expectations of the police institution have changed greatly since 1915. Much of the early criticism of the police, as we have seen, was for not doing effectively that which, we know now, could not be done. No one was fully aware of the potentialities of the police institution in the late nineteenth century, and it seems clear that much more was expected of it than it could reasonably have delivered. In the 1980s few citizens expect that the police institution alone

can restructure urban life—ironically, an urban life beset by many of the same social problems, caused by the same social forces. Some of the issues have changed;
for example, there is little police strike control activity, and standards of urban
working-class morality are only minimally determined by police action. Though
the social form known as tramping has all but disappeared, the urban unemployed
attract a large portion of police attention. Police crime control activity may well be
the least changed: virtually the same crimes are of social concern, committed by
virtually the same people, and producing the same police response as 80 years ago,
including a heavy emphasis on preventive patrol coupled with efficient response to
citizen calls for assistance. Not surprisingly, this adds up to essentially the same
police function in class society.

Perhaps the most notable change since 1890 is the high level of legitimacy that
the police institution today enjoys. Again, this is part of the tendency toward
rational-legal forms in the society at large, a tendency that has benefited many
public agencies. But it also represents a vigorous job of law-and-order salesman-
ship, with the bourgeois mass media rather successfully convincing a large proportion of the population that society is a jungle and that only the police can save our
civilization. This argument is at least 100 years old, but the social order is more
taken for granted today. This transformation in social consciousness is itself a
product of the tendency toward rational-legal forms and the intense domination of
popular ideology by the state and the bourgeoisie directly. Police success is no
longer measured in terms of the absence of conflict, as it was in the nineteenth century. Now the meager police efforts to keep violent crime in check are lauded without any expectation of success.

Marxists have long noted a central contradiction in capitalist development between the demands of the process of capital accumulation and the necessity of
maintaining some level of legitimacy for a highly stratified, inherently unjust social order—class society by definition. The process of capital accumulation—the
capitalists' continued expansion of power and wealth—historically breeds working-class struggle. Legitimation is the more complex and much less analyzed process whereby the capitalist class socializes the members of all classes to accept the
status quo, to see class society as both natural and in the best interests of all classes.

The hypothesis that the police institution is one of the important institutions of
capital accumulation stems from Marx's own observation. Stripped of its subtler
elements, it argues that the capitalist class was able to accumulate capital at the expense of the working class because, at least in part, it was backed by the coercive
power of local police institutions. Without the ability to call on local police for a
wide variety of both direct and indirect coercive services, at least some aspects of
capitalist development would have necessarily been restructured or slowed down.
Restated in the strongest terms, capitalist accumulation is an inherently violent
process that would be impossible without the backing of coercive power. This coercion need not be *state* power, although it universally came to be state power in late-
nineteenth-century Western industrial societies. The precise reasons for this could
be disputed, but will not change the course of the argument here.[1]

More complex is the whole question of the nature of the capitalist state and its municipal-level public institutions. Marxist theorists of the state have formulated numerous hypotheses to explain the complexities of this relationship, all of which deal with essentially the same problem: on one hand, the bourgeoisie clearly have been able to dominate these institutions historically; on the other hand, these institutions have seldom been *completely* dominated by the bourgeoisie and have in fact served to limit some of the powers of the bourgeoisie. This is a difficult problem, and one on which there is no general agreement. Some Marxists pose a theory of "relative autonomy," which emphasizes the partial autonomy of legal and other public institutions. But they do so at the risk of overemphasizing the quality of autonomy, forgetting that it is often an autonomy that the bourgeoisie grant under pressure at some points and then struggle to withdraw at other points. No less a historian than E.P. Thompson highlights the importance of the law to the working class as a *limiting* force on the power of the bourgeoisie.[2]

My analysis has tended toward the opposite position. Although I recognize that the capitalist class was limited by the class struggle and the democratic state form, I see the state and its municipal institutions, including the police, as instruments of the capitalist class. It is now very common for Marxist theorists to be critical of "crude" instrumentalism, but they often make the error of minimizing the extent to which the capitalist state *is* an instrument of the ruling class. I am suggesting instead that we need to focus on theoretical models that explain the limits of ruling-class domination of democratic institutions. One approach is the "class struggle" model, which regards the class struggle as the ultimate limitation on the use of the state as an instrument of the ruling class. To the extent that other classes—primarily the working class, but also the middle class—can mobilize their own power to demand concessions from the state, the ruling class must give way at certain points, sometimes much more willingly than at other times. Similarly, another approach to the limitations of the instrumentalist conception of the state is simply to recognize that there are inherent limitations on the capacity of state power. This is particularly obvious in the area of social control. Even given maximally favorable circumstances (which was never the case in America in the period under study), how much more successful could the police institution have been? Had there been larger, better-organized, professionalized, honest, well-equipped police departments from the 1880s onward, how would social control in the teeming slums of Chicago's Near West Side have differed? We have seen enough of these departments in action in the late twentieth century to know the answer.

It seems clear that, with regard to the municipal police, the relationship between the process of development and the class struggle is rather straightforward. Whatever the origins of the police (and some capitalists opposed early police forces on economic grounds), once departments were established, the importance of the police as a social control force was obvious to the capitalist class, and in city after city the police institution was reorganized and strengthened as part of a more general effort to control and stabilize potentially explosive class violence in rapidly developing cities. This police power became an important element in keeping the cities livable, orderly places for the accumulation of capital. But both the weakness of the bourgeoisie and the inherent impossibility of maintaining desired levels of control meant that contradictions developed within the police institution, including corruption and political domination as concessions to various segments of the petty bourgeoisie and a certain tolerance for prostitution, gambling, and drinking among police officers that infuriated many segments of the population (including some within the working class). This simply reflected the operational realities of controlling huge, populous areas with limited resources that were needed for "more serious" problems. Conflicts with various groups of self-styled reformers emerged from this contradiction as different segments of the population with political power came to identify distinct problem areas that differed from police concerns. Similarly, class violence was not as well controlled by the police as the bourgeoisie originally expected or hoped that it might be, and this failure can be seen as one reason for the turn toward "progressive" or "reformist" methods of controlling the class struggle, now identified with the welfare state. The police institution, in keeping with the social role to which it was assigned, moved more toward emphasis on crime control, both downplaying and obscuring the issues of overt class domination originally associated with the rise of police forces. All of these focusing points are ideal types: crime control was always associated with the police institution and always used to legitimate class repression on the part of the police; the social services performed by the police were probably proportionately as many in the 1840s as they are today, although now they are clearly less emphasized.

In this analysis of the police function it is important to note that we are not concerned with the *origins* of the police institution. The development of the early municipal police departments probably reflects all of the changing demands of rapidly expanding cities that contemporary police historians have noted: spatial complexity, growing crime rates, riotous disorder, ethnic and racial tension, expanding public services. The thesis here is simply that all these factors need to be understood in the context of the making of a class society dominated by capitalists seeking above all else conditions favorable to the expansion of capital, and that whatever the competing forces behind the *origins* of the police, the capitalist class seized the opportunity to *transform* the late-nineteenth and early-twentieth-century departments into very effective participants in the class struggle on the side of the capitalists.

We have seen that this transformation was not a simple process. Under a democratic framework, control of any public institution is not automatic but must constantly be refined and developed, with gains and losses along the way. In the last third of the nineteenth century, municipal government grew on a scale that was unprecedented in American history. Considering the lack of models, it is to be expected that there was considerable debate and confusion in all classes concerning the most efficient kinds of political action. But the central tendency was for municipal government to socialize a portion of the costs of the accumulation of capital: the training of workers; the provision of physical facilities, streets, sewers, water; fire protection; public health services (especially important in an era of disease epidemics); public welfare services; and, of course, police services. The class basis of these functions has been established in a long line of historical research. The police are properly seen as only a part of this broader process, but one fully reflecting other developments in municipal government.

Yet we also know that the police institution was different, distinguished by its unique monopoly on the domestic use of force. It is clear that force was often used and *always* potentially usable. It is this *capacity* for force that is the full measure of the violent foundation of the police institution, and in my analysis of the police I have regarded this capacity for violence as the core of the police function, not as an incidental problem area. This is not to overestimate the amount of physical coercion that the police employed, but only to emphasize that the police function is violent at its core. The arguments in the preceding chapters have aimed to show that this capacity for violence is not random; nor is it the product of unique local factors. Rather, it is systematic, performing clearly understood functions for the capitalist class. This does not mean always, but refers to dominant tendencies.

The major opposing tendency, the wide range of nonviolent social services of the police, follows from two sources. The first is simply the legitimation function. As capitalism developed, more effort was made to legitimate the various social institutions that bolstered class society. The wide range of services that police officers rendered in working-class communities served this function at a steadily increasing rate after 1900 until the current period, when many police professionals are arguing that those functions have become dominant. The second source of the social-service tendency derives from the police institution's relation to the other public institutions in class society: the range of services is so broad that the police, largely because of their capacity for violence, must serve in a catchall capacity, both protecting the operation of other social services and taking on directly some social-service functions. For example, workers have often resisted participating in public health measures, public education, welfare benefits such as public shelters and workfare schemes, but the police institution has the coercive capacity to make such schemes mandatory. Thus, even charity under capitalism must have the coercive power of the state behind it. The capacity of the police to intervene in family problems, settle informal disputes on the street, and direct those in need of help to proper institutions all turns on the capacity for violence. The police officer's recommendation that an alcoholic report to a shelter for treatment and lodging is not just another friendly suggestion: the officer has the option of arrest the next time he sees the person. This point is completely missed by those sociologists of the police institution who emphasize the social-service function of the police. Egon Bittner's "Florence Nightingale" model of the police officer confused by the institution's emphasis on pursuing "Willie Sutton" misses the point: Florence Nightingale did not need a gun, a club, mace, and handcuffs to serve her clients. The social-service role of the police requires coercion because social services in class society are unpopular and often resisted. A police officer cannot intervene in family disputes without a gun and the threat of arrest.[3]

All historians of the police agree that the police in America have a somewhat checkered history. Where differences emerge is over the question of the meaning of such phenomena as political control, brutality, corruption, inefficiency, and the like. Here I have glanced over such phenomena, seeing them as endemic in all institutions of municipal government and not particularly as "police" problems. Undeniably, such factors are a part of the American police experience, and they explain a great deal of day-to-day police activity. But all of these activities occur in a particular social context—the class society—and their full meaning can be understood solely in that context. At the outset many of these police problems can be understood as indications of the low level of legitimacy accorded the police institution, government institutions generally, and capitalist institutions themselves. It is some indication of the level of the class struggle that measures to obtain that legitimacy, such as the move toward professionalization, were reserved until well into the twentieth century. The capitalists' ability to protect their interests in spite of low levels of legitimacy necessitated high levels of class violence.

My central thesis—that it was the necessity of policing this class struggle that best accounts for the transformation of the police institution in the late nineteenth and early twentieth centuries—uses this class violence as a central organizational concept, but I am not trying to imply that no other social processes were occurring or that they did not have an impact on the police. We have seen that the transformation of the police institution can be explained in part as one aspect of the familiar process of rationalization that all social institutions went through: bureaucratization, technological innovation, Taylorization, and professionalization. But these processes as well reflect the complex array of social changes occurring in the context of intense class struggle. Rationalization is in many ways the handmaiden of legitimation. A professional police force that accomplishes class control by adhering to an apparently neutral law-and-order ideology is clearly much more efficient than a corrupt or untrained force. Rationalization alone does not offer an alternative explanation of the rise and expansion of policing; it is another aspect of the same class struggle.

The move toward the welfare state, already well under way by 1900, provides a clear and well-documented illustration of another means of social control, one that transformed a part of the police function after 1915. Intense class struggle in American society was gradually reduced by a welfare state, and this required the restructuring of some police activity. Overt violence as a tool to maintain the boundaries of class society has now been largely replaced by other social institutions, but the police will still use considerable violence to maintain those lines whenever necessary. Direct police efforts to regulate working-class activity have been largely eliminated by state and federal policy makers. "Legal" strikes have been institutionalized; companies build up huge stocks and workers set up symbolic picket lines while collective bargaining goes on. During illegal strikes, however, or strikes in areas where unionization is resisted by capitalists, the police still impede union organizing and still arrest strikers and protect company goons. Tramping and vagrancy have declined as a result of welfare state measures and are no longer serious concerns of the police.

The policing of working-class communities in the 1980s is a complex process that many observers assume is accomplished with a broad consensus. However, it is clear that young people and minorities are highly critical of police patrol practices in their communities, a criticism that has transcended the law-and-order politics of the past decade and a half. Even blacks who fear crime criticize the police activity in their communities, which is often seen as racist, unnecessarily rough and abusive, and ineffective at controlling crime. Race and class are intermingled in complex ways; complaints from blacks, who constitute a large segment of the unskilled working class, roughly parallel those of the immigrants of the 1880s. Even in the white working-class communities that approve of law-and-order political candidates, there is a tendency for parents to support children prone to frequent run-ins with local police, most often over the policing of young people's recreational activities, which now often takes the form of traffic law enforcement, since the automobile has assumed the role of the corner hang-out of 50 years ago as the scene of teen-age recreation.[4]

This is not to say that the relationship of the police institution to the class struggle is the same today as it was 80 to 100 years ago. Rather, this relationship has changed considerably because the requirements for the reproduction of capital have changed. The complex class-control requirements of the late nineteenth century that necessitated violence because of low levels of legitimacy and the relative weaknesses of other public institutions gave rise to a strong police force, willing to use violence frequently in the class struggle. The current police institution is only marginally relevant in this process; a host of other public and private institutions now have a much greater impact. Capital is today largely secure without the assistance of the police, something that was not true even as late as the 1930s, when the police had to try (futilely) to recapture General Motors plants occupied by organized and angry workers.[5] The removal of the police from overt intervention in the class struggle to full attention to more popular crime control and social-service functions has transformed the image of the police, but, I would argue, not the institution's core role. *Potentially* the police institution is still available for the same kinds of purposes that it served 100 years ago. These overt class control functions have simply been made obsolete *at this particular period of capitalist development* by the expansion of nonviolent (or, perhaps more accurately, *less* violent, since the public welfare system does much violence) control mechanisms. The importance of a relatively nonviolent police institution as a part of this entire welfare state complex cannot be underestimated: the system has a coercive *core*.

Any study of the policing of class society in America in the 1980s must focus on the area where policing intersects with the social-service sector of the welfare state. The overt class conflict of the late nineteenth and early twentieth centuries has changed and now occurs in workplaces (which are privately policed) and in the allocation of public and private services. Social class has as much to do with the allocation of social resources in the 1980s as it did in the 1880s, and cities today are equally class stratified. An official American ideology that denies the significance of this class stratification does not change this reality.

Notes

1. Lenin, *State and Revolution*. The essence of Lenin's argument is that democracy is the best "shell" for capitalism because of its capacity to obscure class exploitation and to legitimate class society.
2. Edward P. Thompson, *Whigs and Hunters: The Origin of the Black Act*, chap. 10.
3. Bittner, *The Functions of the Police*, chap. 17.
4. Here, perhaps, it is appropriate to say a few words about Sam Walker's theory that it is the public popularity of the American criminal justice system that accounts both for the best and the worst features of the system—that is, his notion of "popular justice." Besides my reluctance to label specific features as either "best" or "worst"—an ahistorical attempt to apply some 1980s value judgments to very complex social phenomena—I think the whole issue of popularity or unpopularity is not very important. Obviously, various aspects of the criminal justice system are highly popular, but they are also highly unpopular—depending on who is making the judgment and what the issue is. Walker mistakenly reads backward from the popularity that much of the criminal justice system enjoyed in the late 1960s and early 1970s. The overall record runs from bad to good, with stops virtually every place in between—hardly evidence for a theory of popular justice.
5. This example will be familiar to students of labor history as the "Battle of the Running Bulls," where General Motors workers staged an elaborate maneuver to capture several GM plants from GM police and the Flint, Michigan, municipal police in 1937. Irving Bernstein, *Turbulent Years* (Boston: Houghton Mifflin, 1969), pp. 529–530. For those unused to slang terms of the 1930s, the term "bulls" refers to the police.

POLICING-FOR-PROFIT: SECURITY OR EXPANDING SOCIAL CONTROL? 1

The Pinkerton's Inc.

Founded in 1850, Pinkerton's is the oldest private security and investigation firm in the world. We are also the largest. But, more important, the quality of our professional security services makes us the best.

As you will read in this brochure, there are many reasons why Pinkerton's excels in providing a broad spectrum of security services to businesses, corporations, institutions and other groups. One of the primary reasons is that today Pinkerton's still provides clients with the same level of professional dedication displayed by our founder, Allan Pinkerton, and his loyal team of detectives over 100 years ago as they tracked down robbers, thieves, swindlers, and criminals around the world.

Pinkerton's has a colorful past, a dynamic present and a promising future. These pages will tell you why.

Our Past

In 1850 on the second floor of a building at 89 Washington Street, corner of Dearborn, in downtown Chicago young Allan Pinkerton opened a new private detective agency. A young emigrant from Scotland, he had been the city police department's first detective the year before, but had decided to establish his own firm. The booming growth of Chicago as a major grain and cattle center in the brawling Midwest offered great promise for a firm offering security services to embryonic businesses. The initial staff included five detectives, two clerks and a secretary.

To help promote the firm's services, Pinkerton devised the familiar trademark of an open eye with the slogan—"We Never Sleep", from which the term "private eye" originated.

An early member of the staff was the first American woman detective, Mrs. Kate Warne, a young widow. She assisted Pinkerton in solving many cases during her lifetime career with the agency, including thwarting the would-be assassins of President-elect Abraham Lincoln. She and another woman, Hattie Lawton, also performed vital intelligence work during the Civil War.

Source: *Pinkerton's*, (New York: Pinkerton's Inc., 1981). Reprinted with permission.

Allan Pinkerton realized that his fast growing organization should have a basic set of guidelines to operate by and so he drew up the corporate code of ethics, "General Principles", that are still observed. Among other rules, the Principles forbade accepting rewards, working directly for political parties or vice crusaders, and investigating public officials, scandals and divorce cases.

An early client was the Illinois Central Railroad, where a vice president was George B. McClellan and legal counsel was a young lawyer from Illinois named Abraham Lincoln. In the next decade Allan Pinkerton would serve the former during the Civil War as head of the federal intelligence organization (later to become known as the U.S. Secret Service) and would save the latter from an assassination attempt as he traveled through Baltimore to his inauguration as President in Washington.

After the Civil War, America turned to the lure of the far West's vast cattle ranch, farm and mining lands. With this movement came the lawless brigands who preyed on businessmen, bankers and railroads. Often called in by owners and by states and territories without their own law enforcement agencies, Pinkerton's was the only group to cross state boundaries. Our archives are filled with reports and memorabilia of noted law breakers, including the James Boys, the Reno Brothers, the Younger Brothers, the Ford Brothers, Sam Bass, and, of course, the Wild Bunch and its famous members, Butch Cassidy and the Sundance Kid.

During the late 1800's, our people successfully battled organized crime in New Orleans and the Molly Maguires in Pennsylvania, recovered a Gainsborough painting stolen from a London art gallery, and established a rogues gallery of known jewel thieves for the Jewelers Security Alliance. They also solved the $1.5 million robbery of a Northampton, Mass. bank, and recovered all the financial assets of famed Smith College.

Allan Pinkerton died in 1884 and his two sons, William A. and Robert A., directed the company's operations. Robert's son, Allan II, eventually succeeded to the top post, to be followed by his son, Robert II, the last direct Pinkerton descendant to head the company until his death in 1967.

In the early 20th century a young British statesman, Winston Churchill, personally requested that Pinkerton's assist Scotland Yard to protect King George V during his coronation in 1911. As World War I flared up in Europe, embroiling many nations in turmoil, Pinkerton's helped to capture a German spy, who planned to blow up a French ship in New Orleans harbor, by planting an undercover agent who gained the saboteur's confidence. In World War II we provided security officers to guard the nation's war plants.

In the post-war era, services to clients began to expand and diversify extensively, especially uniformed guard operations in the industrial, institutional, public events, commercial and residential sectors.

Our Present

Today our company, staffed by over 35,000 trained employees operating from 122

offices in the United States, Canada, and England and correspondents in 60 foreign countries, offers a broad spectrum of security and investigative expertise. Clients include more than 95% of Fortune's Top 500 businesses, plus schools, hospitals, museums, airports, utilities, apartments, retail stores, banks, transportation
companies, manufacturers, distributors, commercial buildings, contractors, government agencies and professional organizations.

In Canada, Pinkerton's also operates the oldest and largest private security
and investigation organization. Two subsidiaries, Pinkerton's of Canada Limited, headquartered in Toronto, Ontario, and Pinkerton du Québec Limitée,
headquartered in Montreal, Quebec, maintain a total of 14 offices with 3,500
employees offering a full range of security and investigative services to English-
and French-speaking clients in industry, commerce, education, health care and
other fields.

In England, our subsidiary, Pinkerton's of The United Kingdom, Ltd., has full
service capability providing a full range of security and investigating services.

Our major services include:

- Industrial Plant Security
- Nuclear Plant Security
- Institutional Security
- Commercial-Residential Building Security
- Retail Security
- Construction Security
- Patrol and Inspection Service
- Community Security
- Sports and Special Events Service
- K-9 Patrol Service
- Courier Service
- Inventory Service
- Investigation Services
- Security Consultation
- Equipment Evaluation

Industrial Plants

Our uniformed officers and investigators provide protection of buildings from
vandalism and intrusion, provide traffic and perimeter control, perform fire detection rounds, guard against sabotage and theft of production equipment, raw
materials and finished goods, and report on safety hazards.

Nuclear Plants

We became involved in the special security requirements of nuclear power at one of
the very first pilot facilities placed in operation. Our role in this vital area has expanded over the years. Today, we serve many clients operating or constructing nu-

clear facilities or providing waste storage with highly trained personnel who meet the rigorous standards of these assignments. We also regularly conduct critical background investigations of contractor's and supplier's personnel that are required before access to nuclear plants is permitted.

Institutions

For hospitals, schools, colleges, nursing and retirement homes and other institutions, Pinkerton's uniformed and plainclothes officers protect students, visitors and employees, detect fire and safety hazards, patrol buildings and grounds, and control and direct traffic and guard against the sale, use or theft of drugs.

Office-Residential Buildings

With the burgeoning growth of crime in office buildings and residential apartments, our personnel secure premises, provide lobby, elevator and corridor control, direct visitors, prevent unauthorized removal of goods and provide parking lot security.

Retail Establishments

Primarily, we are called on to help reduce "shrinkage" and theft by discouraging and apprehending shoplifters and by detecting dishonest employees and suppliers, but we also secure loading docks, parking lots, and outdoor displays.

Construction Sites

Our uniformed personnel and patrol cars regularly secure contractor's equipment and supplies against theft, protect projects from vandalism and prevent trespassers, who could originate liability claims if injured, from entering the construction area.

Patrol and Inspection

Provided by trained security officers operating in clearly marked patrol cars equipped for two-way communication, this service offers an economical way for neighboring businesses to obtain security on a share-the-cost basis. Security officers move from one business to the next, inspecting premises, acting as a deterrent to thieves and vandals and warning of possible fire or water damage. In some cases, patrol units are assigned exclusively to a single client such as a school district, construction site or business community and provide intensive attention solely to facilities and property of these clients.

Residential Communities

The practice of cooperative patrol and inspection has expanded into the neighborhoods as burglary and assault rates have risen. Retained by neighborhood associations, our uniformed security officers patrol residential areas in marked vehicles, inspect homes, report any dangerous conditions and remain constantly alert to the presence of intruders and strange vehicles. Our visible presence acts as a positive deterrent to would-be thieves.

Sports and Special Events

The growing attendance at spectator sports, entertainment galas, fairs, political meetings and industrial trade shows and conventions make effective security more important than ever. Our people help control crowds, serve as parking lot attendants, ushers, ticket sellers, ticket takers, guides, and celebrity guards. Plainclothes officers also help reduce the incidence of pickpocketing and other thefts. Our people have served at world olympics, world fairs, golf tournaments, political conventions, professional-collegiate athletic contests, horse and auto races and rodeos.

K-9 Patrol

A greater margin of security can be provided when a security officer is accompanied by a trained dog. This dog, usually a German shepherd, gives earlier and more effective warning of intruders. School grounds, hospital parking lots, and industrial buildings are typical settings for K-9 patrols.

Courier Service

A special courier and escort service has been developed for financial institutions in selected geographic areas. Non-negotiable instruments, such as cancelled checks and computer printouts, are being transported from bank branch offices and central computer centers on a daily basis.

Inventory Services

Pinkerton specialists perform physical inventory of goods and materials for supermarkets, retail stores, warehouses and distribution centers. The company's investigative services are also available to determine causes of discovered shortages.

Investigations

Pinkerton's is the largest private investigative organization in the world. On any given day, our people are involved in hundreds of separate investigations for a broad range of companies in business, industry and finance; for legal, insurance and accounting firms; and for institutions and individuals. Because of our established branch office network we are able to undertake investigations anywhere in the U.S. and Canada and have in fact conducted investigations for the same client at many widely separated locations simultaneously.

We conduct undercover investigations, provide surveillance of facilities, vehicles and individuals; investigate suspected insurance and compensation fraud; perform background and applicant investigation; locate missing individuals; test employee performance; and investigate a wide variety of other matters including patent-trademark infringement. Investigations often involve the use of sophisticated electronic equipment including time lapse cameras, polygraphs (where permitted), and debugging equipment; specially equipped observation vehicles; and dogs trained to locate drugs, arms and contraband.

Increasingly, too, we provide personal protection for executives and other prominent persons, as well as their families, against threats of bodily harm, kidnapping and extortion. In cases involving travel or residence abroad, we arrange liaison with authorities fully knowledgeable about local conditions.

Security Consultation

We regularly counsel with clients on security procedures for vital facilities. Key professionals conduct thorough evaluations of security practices and provide detailed reports covering recommendations on manpower, supervision, equipment, lighting, perimeter controls and other measures necessary to provide better security.

Equipment Evaluation

We analyze and study a wide range of security devices and systems in order to make sound recommendations to clients. Since we neither manufacture nor sell security equipment, this evaluation process enables us to provide clients with completely impartial purchasing suggestions.

Quality of Service

Internal Training

Continuing education at every level is an integral, on-going part of our operations. Security officers regularly receive literature designed to enhance their ability. An unmatched series of audio-visual training cassettes is also used to upgrade the skills, appearance and performance of our people. Top officials from branch offices regularly attend an advanced training course that keeps them abreast of the latest security equipment and techniques and enables them to transmit this knowledge to local supervisory personnel. Similar training is also provided investigative personnel to upgrade skills and provide the highest degree of professionalism.

Quality Control

Every effort is made to insure that service to both security and investigative clients is maintained at the highest level possible. In addition to stringent inspections by regional offices, a continuing mail canvass of clients from our headquarters helps identify possible weakness in service so that remedial action can be taken promptly. Field inspections by headquarters officials also enables us to measure the quality of service being provided locally.

Our Future

Perhaps not surprisingly, we feel that the need for our security services will continue to grow in both the private and public sectors. The rising rate of crime, the pressing need to protect people, property and profits as well as the budget limitations increasingly faced by police authorities should all contribute to vastly improved opportunity.

We face the future with confidence, ready to build it with the same spirit of professional integrity and dedication to clients demanded by Allan Pinkerton so many years ago. It's proven successful for well over a century and a quarter and we see no reason to change.

POLICING-FOR-PROFIT: SECURITY OR EXPANDING SOCIAL CONTROL? 2

Private Security and Social Control
C. D. Shearing and P. C. Stenning

One of the most striking features of social control in North America is the pervasive presence of private security, which embraces a wide variety of services from security guards to computer fraud investigators, from home burglar alarms to sophisticated industrial and commercial surveillance systems, from anti-bugging devices to anti-terrorist "executive protection" courses. Private security offers protection for both persons and property which is often more comprehensive than that provided by public police forces. Internal security—so-called "in-house security"—has traditionally been provided by "corporate entities" (Coleman, 1974) such as profit-making corporations, and public institutions such as schools. Since the early 1960s there has been an enormous growth in "contract security," which provides police services on a fee-for-service basis to anyone willing to pay.

Private security is not a new phenomenon. Self-help and the sale of protection as a commodity have a long history (Becker, 1974; Radzinowicz, 1956). Even after the state sought to monopolize public protection through the establishment of public police forces in the 19th century, private interests continued to provide additional protection for themselves through private security (Spitzer and Scull, 1977). What is new about modern private security is its pervasiveness and the extent to which its activities have expanded into public, rather than purely private, places. In urban environments at least, private security is now ubiquitous and is likely to be encountered by city dwellers at home (especially if they live in an apartment building or on a condominium estate), at work, when shopping or banking, when using public transit, or when going to a sports stadium, university, or hospital.

In this paper we consider the extent and nature of modern private security in Canada and the United States and its implications for social control. In doing so, we draw on the findings of research which we and our colleagues have undertaken

Source: C.D. Shearing and P.C. Stenning, "Private Security: Implications For Social Control." Copyright © 1983 by the Society for the Study of Social Problems. Reprinted from *Social Problems*, Vol. 30, No. 5, June, 1983, pp. 493–506, by permission.

since the early 1970s in Canada. This has included a series of studies of the legal context within which private security operates (Freedman and Stenning, 1977; Stenning, 1981; Stenning and Cornish, 1975; Stenning and Shearing, 1979); a major survey of the contract security industry—guard and investigative agencies—in the province of Ontario during 1976, which involved interviews with security agency executives and the administration of a questionnaire to their employees (Shearing *et al.*, 1980); a similar, but less extensive, survey of "in-house" security organizations in Ontario in 1974 (Jeffries, 1977); an examination of the available national statistics on the size and growth of private security in Canada between 1961 and 1971 (Farnell and Shearing, 1977); and three related studies of police, client, and public perceptions of private security, focusing primarily on the province of Ontario, using both interviews and questionnaires during 1982.

Most studies of formal social control within sociology have focused on systems of state control. They view law, justice, and the maintenance of public order as having been virtual state monopolies since early in the 19th century. Even those studies focusing on private forms have typically examined those instances in which state functions have been contracted out to private organizations (Scull, 1977), thus implicitly reinforcing the notion of a state monopoly over such functions (Cohen, 1979).[1]

The few sociologists who have studied the modern development of private security (Becker, 1974; Bunyan, 1977; Kakalik and Wildhorn, 1977) have, with few exceptions (Spitzer and Scull, 1977), broadly followed this tradition and have treated private security as little more than a private adjunct to the public criminal justice system. They assume that private security is essentially a private form of public policing, and that it can be understood in the same way as the public police.

We argue that this approach to understanding private security is inadequate because it fails to account for some of the most important differences between private security and public police and, more importantly, between the contexts within which each operates. The context in which private security functions is not public law and the criminal justice system, but what Henry (1978:123) has called "private justice." We follow the view of legal pluralists who maintain that "in any given society there will be as many legal systems as there are functioning social units" (Pospisil, 1967:24).

We begin by examining the size and growth of private security in Canada and the United States. Then we look at changes in the urban environment which have been associated with the involvement of private security in maintaining public order. Finally we consider various features of private security: who supports it, its authority, its organizational features, and its relationship to the public police.

---

[1]An exception to this is the research on dispute resolution, especially that done by anthropologists (Nader, 1980; Pospisil, 1978; Snyder, 1981).

Table 1   Public Police and Private Security Personnel, in Thousands (Rounded)

	Police	% Increase	Security In-house	% Increase	Contract	% Increase	Total	% Increase	Ratio of Police to Security	Ratio of In-house to Contract
					UNITED STATES					
1960a	258		192		30		222		1.2:1	6.1
		51		15		103		27		
1970a	390		220		61		281		1.4:1	3.5:1
		5		18		187		55		
1975b	411		260		175		435		0.9:1	1.5:1
					CANADA					
1971c	40		25		11.5		36.5		1.1:1	2.2:1
		30		14		65		32		
1975d	51		29		19		48		1.1:1	1.5:1

Sources:
a Adapted from table 2.11 "Security Employment Trends by Type of Employer" (Kakalik and Wildhorn, 1977:43).
b Police strength figure derived from U.S. Department of Justice, Federal Bureau of Investigation (1976:26). Private security figures, which are estimates only, adapted from Predicasts, Inc. (1974:26).
c Adapted from Farnell and Shearing (1977).
d Adapted from Friendly (1980).

The Size and Growth of Private Security[2]

While private security has probably existed in one form or another in North America since the continent was first settled by Europeans, little is known about its practice prior to the mid-19th century. Older accounts contain no reliable information about the size and growth of private security (Horan, 1967; Johnson, 1976; Lipson, 1975). It was not until 1969 that the first major study of contract security was undertaken in the United States (Kakalik and Wildhorn, 1971), and not until these researchers revised their findings in 1977, in the light of 1970 census data, that a reasonably complete picture of size and growth trends became available. For Canada, the available statistical information is even less adequate.

Table 1 provides a summary of the statistics available for the United States and Canada respectively. We emphasize, however, that because of definitional difficulties and unreliable record-keeping practices, these figures are at best approximate. Table 1 shows that in the United States in 1960, private security almost equalled the public police in number. By 1970, both sectors had experienced substantial growth, with public police outdistancing private security. The early 1970s show a

---

[2]For a more detailed analysis of current statistics on the size and growth of private security see Shearing and Stenning (1981:198).

significant slowdown in the growth of public police, but a continued escalation in the growth of private security, especially in the contract security sector; by 1975, private security outnumbered public police. Between 1960 and 1975 the ratio of in-house to contract security diminished from 6:1 to 1.5:1, indicating a major restructuring of the organization of private security.[3]

Directly comparable data on the growth of private security in Canada from 1960 to 1970 are not available.[4] Census data suggest, however, that growth rates within the contract security sector may have been as high as 700 percent (Farnell and Shearing, 1977:113). By 1971, however, there were almost as many private security as public police in Canada, but in-house personnel still outnumbered contract security by more than 2 to 1. Within the next four years, both public police and private security personnel continued to increase, at approximately the same rate (30 percent). Within private security, however, contract security increased 65 percent, a rate almost five times that of the rate of growth of in-house security.

While reliable national statistics since 1975 are not available, statistics for the province of Ontario (which have in the past proved a good indicator of national trends) indicate a levelling off of contract security growth during the latter half of the 1970s. Overall, contract security in Ontario appears to have increased 90 percent from 1971 to 1980, while the growth rate of public police during the same period was 29 percent (Waldie *et al.*, 1982:8). Assuming that there has been no absolute numerical decline in in-house security, this almost certainly means that in Ontario (and probably the rest of Canada) private security now outnumbers the public police. Furthermore, contract security alone now rivals the public police numerically. In Ontario, by 1980, there were three contract security personnel for every four public police officers—15,000 contract security, and just under 20,000 public police officers (Waldie *et al.*, 1982:9).

These findings indicate that in Canada and the United States the public police have for some time shared the task of policing with private organizations, and that private security probably now outnumber public police in both countries. The major change has been the rapid growth, since the early 1960s, of policing provided on a contract basis, for profit, by private enterprise (Spitzer and Scull, 1977). This has established private security as a readily available alternative to public police for those with the means to afford it, and has made private security a much more visible contributor to policing than it has been hitherto. The result has been an unobtrusive but significant restructuring of our institutions for the maintenance of order, and a substantial erosion by the private sector of the state's assumed monopoly over policing and, by implication, justice.

---

[3]Reliable data for the United States since 1975 are not yet available.

[4]Although 1961 and 1971 census data are available they cannot be compared to establish growth rates due to changes in category definitions (Farnell and Shearing, 1977:39).

Mass Private Property

To understand the locus of private security it is necessary to examine the changes that have taken place, particularly since the early 1950s, in the organization of private property and public space. In North America many public activities now take place within huge, privately owned facilities, which we call "mass private property." Examples include shopping centers with hundreds of individual retail establishments, enormous residential estates with hundreds, if not thousands, of housing units, equally large office, recreational, industrial, and manufacturing complexes, and many university campuses. While evidence of these developments surrounds every city dweller, there is little data on how much public space in urban areas is under private control (Bourne and Harper, 1974:213; Lorimer, 1972:21). However, the available data does indicate an enormous increase in mass private property.

Spurr (1975:18) surveyed 60 major companies producing new urban residential accommodation in 24 Canadian metropolitan centers:

> Forty-seven firms hold 119,192 acres (186 square miles) of land, including 34 firms which each own more than one square mile. . . . Forty-two firms hold 95,174 apartment units including 13 firms with 123 apartment buildings. Twenty-nine firms have 223 office and other commercial buildings, while 23 firms have nearly 26,000,000 square feet of commercial space. While these commercial and apartment figures may appear large, the survey is particularly incomplete in these areas. Finally, twenty-seven firms have 185 shopping centres and sixteen firms own 38 hotels.

Gertler and Crowley (1977:289) used data collected by Punter (1974) to study four townships within 40 miles of Toronto, from 1954 to 1971. They identified

> . . . two striking changes in the ownership patterns. Absentee ownership by individuals increased from less than 5 per cent of total area to about 20 per cent; and corporate ownership of the land which was negligible in 1954 increased to more than 20 per cent in 1971, with increases occurring particularly in the investment-developer category.

Martin (1975:21), in a study of the north-east Toronto fringe, found that corporations represented 22 per cent of all buyers and 16 per cent of all sellers. He argued that these transactions represented "the nucleus of land dealer activities in the study area between 1968 and 1974" (1975:27). Gertler and Crowley (1977:290) comment on these findings:

> Land development has changed from an activity carried out by a large number of small builder/developers in the 1950s to a process in the seventies which is increasingly shaped by large public companies. These firms are vertically integrated, that is, organized to handle the entire development package from land

assembly to planning and design, construction, property management, and marketing.

The modern development of mass private property has meant that more and more public life now takes place on property which is privately owned. Yet the policing needs of such privately owned public places have not been met by the public police for two reasons. First, the routine "beat" of the public police has traditionally been confined to publicly owned property such as streets and parks (Stinchcombe, 1963). Therefore, even when they have had the resources to police privately owned public places—and typically they have not—they have been philosophically disinclined to do so. Second, those who own and control mass private property have commonly preferred to retain and exercise their traditional right to preserve order on their own property and to maintain control over the policing of it, rather than calling upon the public police to perform this function.

Because more and more public places are now located on private property, the protection of property—which lies at the heart of private security's function—has increasingly come to include the maintenance of public order, a matter which was, hitherto, regarded as the more or less exclusive prerogative of the public police. With the growth of mass private property, private security has been steadily encroaching upon the traditional beat of the public police. In so doing, it has brought areas of public life that were formerly under state control under the control of private corporations.

Legitimation of Private Security Authority

The close association between private security and private property provides its most important source of social legitimation as an alternative to systems of public justice, and helps to explain why its development has proceeded with so little opposition. Because the development of modern institutions of public justice (during the early 19th century) necessarily involved the conferring of exceptional authority, such as police powers, on public officials, it has required legislative action and all the public debate which that engenders (Baldwin and Kinsey, 1980). By contrast, the development of private security has required virtually no legislation and has generated little public interest. This is because the authority of private security derives not so much from exceptional powers as from the ordinary powers and privileges of private property owners to control access to, use of, and conduct on, their property. While modern private security guards enjoy few or no exceptional law enforcement powers, their status as agents of property allows them to exercise a degree of legal authority which in practice far exceeds that of their counterparts in the public police. They may insist that persons submit to random searches of their property or persons as a condition of entry to, or exit from, the premises. They may even require clients to surrender their property while remaining on the premises, and during this time they may lawfully keep them under more or less constant visual or electronic surveillance. Before allowing clients to use the premises (or property such as a credit card) they may insist that clients provide detailed information about themselves, and authorize them to seek personal information from others with whom they have dealings. Private security may use such information for almost any purpose, and even pass it on, or sell it, to others.

In theory, the public can avoid the exercise of such private security authority by declining to use the facilities, as either customers or employees. In practice, however, realistic alternatives are often not available; for example, airport security applies to all airlines. This is a function of both the modern trend toward mass private property, and the fact that more and more public places are now situated on private property. Between them, these trends result in a situation in which the choices available to consumers are often severely limited. Employees and customers alike must submit to the authority of property owners and their agents as a condition of use. Thus, because private security is so pervasive, and because it is found in so many services and facilities essential to modern living (employment, credit, accommodation, education, health, transportation), it is practically impossible to avoid.

The fact that private security derives so much of its legitimacy from the institution of private property involves a profound historical irony. In the United States and Canada, state power has historically been perceived as posing the greatest threat to individual liberty. The legal institutions of private property and privacy arguably evolved as a means of guaranteeing individuals a measure of security against external intrusions, especially intrusions by the state (Reich, 1964; Stinchcombe, 1963). These institutions defined an area of privacy to which the state was denied access without consent, other than in exceptional circumstances. On private property, therefore, the authority of the property owner was recognized as being paramount—a philosophy most clearly reflected in the adage, "a man's home is his castle."

The validity of this notion, however, requires a reasonable congruence between private property and private places: a man's home was his castle, not because it was private property as such, but because it was a private place. However, as more and more private property has become, in effect, public, this congruence has been eroded. The emergence of mass private property, in fact, has given to private corporations a sphere of independence and authority which in practice has been far greater than that enjoyed by individual citizens and which has rivaled that of the state. The legal authority originally conceded to private property owners has increasingly become the authority for massive and continuous intrusions upon the privacy of citizens (as customers and employees) by those who own and control the mass private property on which so much public life takes place. Nevertheless, the traditional association between the institution of private property and the protection of liberty has historically been such a powerful source of legitimacy that, despite these important changes in the nature of private property, the exercise of private security authority is rarely questioned or challenged.

What little resistance has occurred has been mainly in the workplace, and has taken one or both of two forms—one an "underground" movement, and the other a more open and organized phenomenon. The underground movement is apparent in a "hidden economy" (Henry, 1978) of systematic pilfering, unofficial "perks," "padding" of claims for sickness benefits and other forms of compensation, as means of circumventing the formal structures and procedures established to protect corporate assets and profits. While such resistance sometimes occurs on a grand scale, it is mostly informal and individualistic.

Labor unions have posed a more formal and openly organized challenge to the unrestricted exercise of private security authority. They have fought private security processes and procedures through industrial action, collective bargaining, and arbitration. For example, in our research we have encountered collective agreements containing clauses specifying in detail the occasions on which employees may be searched, the procedures to be used in such searches, and the processes to be followed in the event that employees come under suspicion (Stenning and Shearing, 1979:179). Indeed, the growing body of so-called "arbitral jurisprudence" suggests there may be a trend toward a greater degree of accountability within private justice in the industrial and commercial sectors, just as the growing body of administrative law suggests a similar trend in the public domain (Arthurs, 1979).

To regard such developments simply as resistance to the growth of private security, however, is obviously overly simplistic, since in an important way they serve to institutionalize and legitimate it. When private security has been negotiated rather than imposed, its legitimacy is enhanced, co-opting the unions in the process. Furthermore, as private security procedures become more formalized and institutionalized they are often abandoned in favour of newer, less formal, and more flexible ones. An example of this is the replacement of formal arbitration by informal on-site mediation processes. Other researchers have noted similar reactions in the fields of administrative and labor law (Arthurs, 1980; Zack, 1978).

The Nature of Private Security

Three characteristics of private security reveal its essential nature: (1) its non-specialized character; (2) its client-defined mandate; and (3) the character of the sanctions it employs. We discuss each of these in turn.

Non-Specialized Character

The criminal justice system is divided into many specialized divisions and employs people in distinct roles, such as police, prosecutors, defence counsel, judiciary, and correctional officers. In contrast, we have found that private security is often integrated with other organizational functions, as the following example illustrates.

One of the companies which we studied operated a chain of retail outlets selling fashionable clothing for teenagers and young adults. Officials of the company emphasized that security was one of their principal concerns, because the company operated in a competitive market with slender profit margins. The company tried to improve its competitive position by reducing its losses, and boasted that it had one of the lowest loss-to-sales ratios in the industry. In accounting for this, officials pointed to the success of their security measures. Yet the company employed only one specialized security officer; security was not organizationally separated into discrete occupational roles. Rather, officials attributed responsibility for security to every employee. Moreover, employees typically did not undertake security activities distinct from their other occupational activities. Security functions were regarded as most effective when they were embedded in other functions. For example, officials believed that good sales strategies made good security strategies: if sales persons were properly attentive to customers, they would not only advance sales but simultaneously limit opportunities for theft. The security function was thus seen as embedded in the sales function.

What, then, is the role of specialized persons such as security guards? Our survey of contract security guards indicated that, while they frequently engaged in such specialized security functions as controlling access to commercial facilities (26 percent), they were employed mainly to supervise the performance of security functions by non-specialized personnel (Shearing *et al.*, 1980). Thus 48 percent reported that the problem most frequently encountered was the carelessness of other employees. An important element of the security function, therefore, was to check on employees after hours, to see whether they had kept up with their security responsibilities by seeing whether doors had been left unlocked or valuable goods or confidential papers had been left in the open. When they discovered such failings, security guards would inform the employee's supervisor, using strategies such as the one described by Luzon (1978:41):

> In support of the project drive for theft reduction, Atlantic Richfield security instituted an evening patrol, still in effect. For each risk found, the patrolling officer fills out and leaves a courteous form, called a "snowflake," which gives the particular insecure condition found, such as personal value property left out, unlocked doors, and valuable portable calculators on desks. A duplicate of each snowflake is filed by floor and location, and habitual violators are interviewed. As a last resort, compliance is sought through the violator's department manager.

This feature of private security is reminiscent of the pre-industrial, feudal policing system in Britain known as "frankpledge," in which policing was the responsibility of all community members, was integrated with their other functions, and was supervised by a small number of specialized security persons—sheriffs and constables—designated to ensure that community members were exercising their security responsibilities properly (Critchley, 1978). This nonspecialized character of private security, however, creates particular difficulties in numerically comparing private security with public police and in attempting to measure the extent of the shift in policing from public to private hands.

Client-Defined Mandate

The mandate and objectives of private security, we found, were typically defined in terms of the particular interests and objectives of those who employed them. Table 2 presents results from our study of contract security in Ontario, which show that the employers of private security are most commonly private industrial and commercial corporations. Furthermore, we found that contract security agencies, in their advertising, appeared to assume that their major audience was made up of executives of private corporations, and that they typically promoted their services on the basis that they would increase profits by reducing losses (Shearing, *et al.*, 1980:163). While we do not have exactly comparable data revealing the distribution of in-house security, there is every reason to believe that here too private industrial and commercial corporations are the major users.

Private security is most typically a form of "policing for profit" (Spitzer and Scull, 1977:27)—that is, policing which is tailored to the profit-making objectives and its corporate clients. In those cases in which the principal objective of the clients is not the making of profit (e.g. where the client's principal objective is to provide health services, education, or entertainment) it will be that objective which will shape and determine the mandate and activities of private security.

This client orientation has important implications for the nature of policing undertaken by private security, and serves to distinguish it from public policing. In the criminal justice system, the state is nominally impartial and individuals are

Table 2 Classification of Five Largest Clients

	Type of Contract Security Agency					
	Guard (N = 19)		Investigator (N = 26)		G. & I. (N = 47)	
Client	%[a]	Rank	%[a]	Rank	%[a]	Rank
Industrial	42	1	31	5	70	1
Lawyers	5	c	92	1	28	c
Construction	32	2		b	55	2
Shopping Mall	21	5	35	4	36	4
Offices	32	2		b	45	3
Hospitals	10	c		b	30	5
Education	32	2		b	21	c
Insurance		b	69	2	17	c
Citizens	5	c	54	3	19	c
Government	21	5	15	c	28	c

Notes:
  [a] As a result of multiple responses, percentages do not total 100.
  [b] Client type not mentioned.
  [c] Client type mentioned but not ranked within first five.
Source: Adapted from Shearing *et al.*, (1980).

judged in terms of crimes against the public interest. By contrast, private security defines problems in purely instrumental terms; behavior is judged not according to whether it offends some externally defined moral standards, but whether it threatens the interests (whatever they may be) of the client. This establishes a definition of social order which is both more extensive and more limited than that defined by the state; more extensive because it is concerned with matters such as absenteeism or breaches of confidentiality (Gorrill, 1974:98) which may threaten the interests of the client but are not violations of the law; more limited because it is not normally concerned with violations of the law—such as some victimless crimes—which are not perceived as threatening the interests of the client.

In this sense, policing by private security is essentially victim-controlled policing. Corporate victims can maintain order without having to rely exclusively, or even primarily, on the criminal justice system. By establishing their own private security organizations directed to maintaining their own definitions of social order, corporate landlords and entrepreneurs not only ensure that their interests as potential victims are given priority in policing, but also avoid "the difficulty of proving matters in a formal system of justice arising from the extension of individual rights" (Reiss, forthcoming). With private security, conflict remains the property of victims (Christie, 1977). As one of the security managers we interviewed put it:

> See those *Criminal Codes?* I got a whole set of them, updated every year. I've never used one. I could fire the whole set in the garbage, all of them. Security is prevention; you look at the entire operation and you see the natural choke points to apply the rules and regulations. The police, they don't understand the operation of a business. They don't come on the property unless we invite them.

Just as the social order enforced by private security is defined in terms of the interests of the client, so are the resources which are allocated for enforcement and the means which are employed. Thus, a retail organization which sells clothes will usually not install surveillance systems in changing rooms; this is not because such systems are ineffective in catching thieves, but because they might deter too many honest shoppers. The inevitable result of such instrumental policing is, of course, that a certain amount of known or suspected deviance will often be tolerated because the costs or the means of controlling it would threaten the interests of the client more than the deviance itself. There is little room for retribution within this instrumental approach. Social control exists solely to reduce threats to the interests of the client and the focus of attention shifts from discovering and blaming wrongdoers to eliminating sources of such threats in the future. This shifts the emphasis of social control from a judicial to a police function, and from detection to prevention. As one steel company security director expressed it:

> . . . The name of the game is steel. We don't want to be robbed blind, but we aren't interested in hammering people. . . . I'm not responsible for enforcing the

Criminal Code; my basic responsibility is to reduce theft, minimize disruption to the orderly operation of the plant.

In our study of contract security we found that both security guards and private investigators focused attention primarily on identifying and rectifying security loopholes rather than on apprehending or punishing individuals who actually stole goods (Shearing *et al.*, 1980:178). This focus generates a new class of "offenders"—those who create opportunities for threats against the interests of the client. For example, a major Canadian bank launched an internal investigation into the loss of several thousands of dollars from one of its branches. The emphasis of the investigation was not on identifying the thief, but on discovering what breach of security had allowed the loss to occur and who was responsible for this breach, so that steps could be taken to reduce the risk of it recurring. The police were not involved in the investigation, despite the obvious suspicions of theft, and its results were the tightening up of security rules within the branch and the disciplining of the head teller who had breached them (*Freeborn* v. *Canadian Imperial Bank of Commerce*, 1981).

Even when a traditional offender is caught by private security, the client's best interest will often dictate a course of action other than invoking the criminal justice system. In 1982 in Calgary, Alberta, a bank succeeded in tracking down someone who had stolen over $14,000 from its automatic tellers. Instead of calling the police, the bank tried to persuade the offender to sign for the amount as a loan. Only when he refused to agree to this resolution of the matter was the case turned over to the police (*Globe and Mail*, 1982).

The Character of Sanctions

The fact that private security emphasizes loss prevention rather than retribution does not mean that sanctions are never employed. When they are invoked, however, they usually draw on private and corporate power, rather than state power.

The sanctions available within the criminal justice system result ultimately on the state's access to physical force, over which it has a legal monopoly (Bittner, 1970). Private security's use of force is legally limited to cases in which they act as agents of the state, using citizen powers of arrest, detention, and search (Stenning and Shearing, 1979). This does not mean that private security lacks powerful sanctions; on the contrary, as the agents of private authorities they have available a range of sanctions which are in many respects more potent than those of the criminal justice system, and which they perceive as being far more effective (Scott and McPherson, 1971:272; Shearing *et al.*, 1980:232). One of the corporate security executives whom we interviewed said:

[In a court] a different degree of proof is required; if the judge decides that there is insufficient evidence, you might be reinstated, because of some *legal* reason; in the disciplining process, I can get rid of you. If he's charged, we may have to continue him with benefits. To charge a person is a very serious thing, a very complicated process. We have to ask ourselves, do we just want to get rid of him, or do we want to throw the book at him? Maybe he's not a crook, he's just a dope.

As this example illustrates, foremost among the sanctions available to private security is the ability of corporations to restrict access to private property and to deny the resources which such access provides. Thus, private security can deny persons access to recreational and shopping facilities, housing, employment, and credit.

The essentially economic character of private security's sanctions does not mean that physical force has no bearing on what happens. When organizations want a legally imposed resolution to their problem, they can involve the police or initiate a civil suit. In drawing upon state power to support their legal rights to control access to property, organizations effectively expand the range of sanctions available to them.

Private Security and the Criminal Justice System

While many writers have suggested that private security is a mere adjunct to the criminal justice system—the so-called "junior partner" theory (Kakalik and Wildhorn, 1977)—our research suggests that many of those who control private security view the relationship quite differently. They saw the criminal justice system as an adjunct to their own private systems, and reported invoking the former only when the latter were incapable of resolving problems in a way which suited their interests.

Nevertheless, private security executives as well as senior public police officers preferred in public statements to characterize private security as the "junior partner" of the criminal justice system. For private security, this characterization minimized public fears that private security was "taking over" and that "private armies" were being created. It also carried the welcome implication that private security shared in the legitimacy and accepted status of the public police. The "junior partner" theory was attractive to the public police because it downplayed suggestions that they were losing their dominant role, while allowing them to take advantage of the interdependence of the private and public security systems.

The "junior partner" theory significantly distorts the relationship between the public police and private security in at least three ways. First, the theory implies that private security is concerned only with minor cases, thereby freeing the public police to deal with more serious matters (Harrington, 1982). Yet this proved to be *not* true for property "crime"; in fact, the reverse was probably the case. Private security routinely dealt with almost all employee theft, even those cases involving hundreds of thousands of dollars. Security directors told us that they typically reported only relatively petty cases of theft to the public police and one Canadian automotive manufacturer reported that it was their policy never to refer employee theft to the public police. Even serious assaults, such as employee fights involving personal injury, were sometimes handled internally. Furthermore, while most serious personal injuries resulting from crimes were reported to the police, most so-called "industrial accidents" were dealt with internally (Carson, 1981).

A second, unfounded implication of the "junior partner" theory is that the public police direct the operations of private security. While the public police sometimes attempt such direction by establishing crime prevention squads and acting as consultants, private security personnel often mocked what they saw as presumptuous police officials who set themselves up as "crime prevention experts." Furthermore, because private security are usually the first to encounter a problem, they effectively direct the police by determining what will and what will not be brought to their attention (Black, 1980:52; Feuerverger and Shearing, 1982). On those occasions where the public police and private security work together—for example, police fraud squads with bank security personnel—it cannot be assumed that the public police play the leading role, either in terms of investigative expertise or in terms of direction of the investigation.

Third, private security is by no means a "junior partner" to the public police in the resources it draws upon, such as mechanical hardware or information systems. Private security not only frequently has access to sophisticated weapons and electronic surveillance systems, but is well equipped with standard security hardware including patrol cars and armored vehicles (Hougan, 1978; Scott and McPherson, 1971).

What, then, is the relationship between the public police and private security? Our research left little doubt that it was a co-operative one, based principally on the exchange of information and services. This was facilitated by the movement of personnel from public police to private security (Shearing *et al.*, 1980:195). This movement was particularly prevalent at the management level. Thirty-eight percent of the contract security executives we interviewed (Shearing *et al.*, 1980:118) and 32 percent of the in-house executives (Jeffries, 1977:38) were ex-police officers. Furthermore, many organizations reported relying on ex-police officers to gain access, through the "old boy network," to confidential police information. This was particularly common within private investigation agencies (Ontario Royal Commission, 1980:166). A private investigator summed up the exchange of information between private investigators and the public police this way:

> There are approximately a hundred private investigators in Toronto who can literally get any information they want whether it is from the Police Department, Workmen's Compensation records, O.H.I.P. [Ontario Health Insurance Plan], insurance records, or whatever. In the space of a ten-minute telephone conversation I can get what it would take me perhaps three weeks to discover. With experience and contacts, a well-established investigator can provide a better quality of information and can do so at a much lower cost to his client even though his hourly rates might be twice as much as a new investigator might charge.

The extent of this cooperation with the public police was summed up by the director of security we interviewed at a large commercial shopping mall in Toronto. After noting how easy it was for him to obtain the support of the local public police, he described his relationship with them as "one big police force." Yet there was no doubt in his mind that it was *he* who effectively controlled this force, through his control over access to the private property under his jurisdiction.

Summary and Conclusions

Private organizations, and in particular large corporations, have since 1960, and probably earlier, exercised direct power over policing the public through systems of private security. The growth of mass private property has facilitated an ongoing privatization of social control characterized by non-specialized security. As a result, North America is experiencing a "new feudalism": huge tracts of property and associated public spaces are controlled—and policed—by private corporations. To undertake this responsibility, these corporations have developed an extensive security apparatus, of which uniformed security personnel are only the supervisory tip of the iceberg.

The shift from public to private systems of policing has brought with it a shift in the character of social control. First, private security defines deviance in instrumental rather than moral terms: protecting corporate interests becomes more important than fighting crime, and sanctions are applied more often against those who create opportunities for loss rather than those who capitalize on the opportunity—the traditional offenders. Thus, the reach of social control has been extended. Second, in the private realm, policing has largely disappeared from view as it has become integrated with other organizational functions and goals, at both the conceptual and behavioral levels. With private security, control is not an external force acting on individuals; now it operates from within the fabric of social interaction, and members of the communities in which it operates are simultaneously watchers and the watched. They are the bearers of their own control. Third, this integration is expressed in the sanctioning system, in which private security draws upon organizational resources to enforce compliance. Together these three features of private security create a form of social control that Foucault (1977) has termed discipline: control is at once pervasive and minute; it takes the form of small, seemingly insignificant observations and remedies that take place everywhere (Melossi, 1979:91; Shearing and Stenning, 1982).

Is private security here to stay? We think this depends less on the fiscal resources of the state, as some writers have suggested (Kakalik and Wildhorn, 1977), and more on the future structure of property ownership and the law related to it. There is little reason to believe that mass private property will not continue to develop, thereby permitting corporations to secure control over "relationships that were once exclusively in the public realm" (Spitzer and Scull, 1977:25). Thus, we believe private security will continue to develop as an increasingly significant feature of North American social life.

To the extent that control over policing is an essential component of sovereignty (Gerth and Mills, 1958:78), the development of modern private security raises the possibility of sovereignty shifting from the state directly to private corporations in both their national and, more significantly, their international guises. This in turn raises questions about the limitations of state control over private security and the validity of claims that the state is becoming more dominant in capitalistic societies (Boehringer, 1982; Cohen, 1979). Indeed, the evidence of direct control by capital over important aspects of policing points to the necessity of a thorough re-examination of conventional theoretical statements—be they instrumentalist or structural (Beirne, 1979)—about the relationship between the state and capital under modern capitalism.

References

Arthurs, Harry W.
1979 "Rethinking administrative law: A slightly dicey business." Osgoode Hall Law Journal 17(1):1–45.
1980 "Jonah and the whale: The appearance, disappearance, and reappearance of administrative law." University of Toronto Law Journal 30:225–239.

Baldwin, Robert, and Richard Kinsey
1980 "Behind the politics of police powers." British Journal of Law and Society 7(2): 242–265.

Becker, Theodore M.
1974 "The place of private police in society. An area of research for the social sciences." Social Problems 21(3):438–453.

Beirne, Piers
1979 "Empiricism and the critique of Marxism on law and crime." Social Problems 26(4): 273–385.

Bittner, Egon
1970 The Functions of the Police in Modern Society. Chevy Chase, Maryland: National Institute of Mental Health, Centre for Studies in Crime and Delinquency.

Black, Donald
1980 The Manners and Customs of the Police. New York: Academic Press.

Boehringer, Gill
1982 "The strong state and the surveillance society: Changing modes of control." Paper presented at the Australian and New Zealand Association for the Advancement of Science Congress, Macquarie University, New South Wales, Australia, May 1982.

Bourne, Larry S., and Peter D. Harper
1974 "Trends in future urban land use." Pp. 213–236 in Larry S. Bourne, Ross D. MacKinnon, Jay Siegel, and James W. Simmons (eds.), Urban Futures for Central Canada: Perspectives on Forecasting Urban Growth and Form. Toronto: University of Toronto Press.

Bunyan, Tony
1977 The History and Practice of Political Police in Britain. London: Quartet Books.

Carson, W.G.
1981 The Other Price of Britain's Oil: Safety and Control in the North Sea. Oxford: Martin Robertson.

Christie, Nils
1977 "Conflicts as property." British Journal of Criminology 17(1):1–15.

Cohen, Stanley
1979 "The punitive city: Notes on the dispersal of social control." Contemporary Crisis 3(4):339–364.

Coleman, James
1974 Power and the Structure of Society. New York: Norton.

Critchley, Thomas A.
1978 A History of Police in England and Wales: 900–1966. London: Constable.

Farnell, Margaret B., and Clifford D. Shearing
1977 Private Security: An Examination of Canadian Statistics, 1961–1971. Toronto: Centre of Criminology, University of Toronto.

Feuerverger, Andrey, and Clifford D. Shearing
1982 "An analysis of the prosecution of shoplifters." Criminology 20(2):273–289.

Foucault, Michel
1977 Discipline and Punish: The Birth of the Prison. New York: Pantheon Books.

Freedman, David J., and Philip C. Stenning
1977 Private Security, Police, and the Law in Canada. Toronto: Centre of Criminology, University of Toronto.

Friendly, John Ashley
1980 "Harbinger." Unpublished paper. Osgoode Hall Law School, Toronto.

Gerth, Hans H., and C. Wright Mills (eds.)
1958 From Max Weber: Essays in Sociology. New York: Oxford University Press.

Gertler, Leonard O., and Ronald W. Crowley
1977 Changing Canadian Cities: The Next Twenty-Five Years. Toronto: McClelland and Stewart.

Globe and Mail (Toronto)
1982 "Bank scolded over theft." October 16:11.

Gorrill, B. E.
1974 Effective Personnel Security Procedures. Homewood, Illinois: Dow Jones-Irwin.

Harrington, Christine B.
1982 "Delegalization reform movements: A historical analysis." Pp. 35–71 in Richard L. Abel (ed.), The Politics of Informal Justice, Volume 2. New York: Academic Press.

Henry, Stuart
1978 The Hidden Economy: The Context and Control of Borderline Crime. London: Martin Robertson.

Horan, James D.
1967 The Pinkertons: The Detective Dynasty that Made History. New York: Crown Publishers.

Hougan, Jim
1978 Spooks: The Haunting of America: The Private Use of Secret Agents. New York: Bantam.

Jeffries, Fern
1977 Private Policing: An Examination of In-House Security Operations. Toronto: Centre of Criminology, University of Toronto.

Johnson, Bruce C.
1976 "Taking care of labor: The police in American politics." Theory and Society 3(1):89–117.

Kakalik, James S., and Sorrel Wildhorn
1971 Private Policing in the United States. Five volumes. Santa Monica, Calif.: Rand Corporation.
1977 The Private Police: Security and Danger. New York: Crone Russak.

Lipson, Milton
1975 On Guard: The Business of Private Security. New York: Quandrangle/New York Times Book Co.

Lorimer, James
1972 A Citizen's Guide to City Politics. Toronto: James Lewis and Samuel.

Luzon, Jack
1978 "Corporate headquarters security." The Police Chief 45(6):39–42.

Martin, Larry R.G.
1975 "Structure, conduct and performance of land dealers and land developers in the land industry." Mimeographed. School of Urban and Regional Planning, University of Waterloo.

Melossi, Dario
1979 "Institutions of control and the capitalist organization of work." Pp. 90–99 in Bob Fine, Richard Kinsey, John Lea, Sol Picciotto, and Jock Young (eds.), Capitalism and the Rule of Law: From Deviance Theory to Marxism. London: Hutchinson.

Nader, Laura
1980 No Access to Law: Alternatives to the American Judicial System. New York: Academic Press.

Ontario Royal Commission of Inquiry into the Confidentiality of Health Records in Ontario
1980 Report of the Commission of Inquiry into the Confidentiality of Health Information. Volume 1. Toronto: Queen's Printer.

Pospisil, Leopold
1967 "Legal levels and the multiplicity of legal systems in human societies." Journal of Conflict Resolution 11(1):2–26.
1978 The Ethnology of Law. Menlo Park, Ca.: Cummings.

Predicasts, Inc.
1974 Private Security Systems. Cleveland, Ohio: Predicasts Inc.

Punter, John V.
1974 The Impact of Ex-Urban Development on Land and Landscapes in the Toronto Central Region, 1954–1971. Ottawa: Central Mortgage and Housing Corporation.

Radzinowicz, Leon A.
1956 A History of English Law and Its Administration from 1750: The Clash Between Private Initiatives and Public Interest in the Enforcement of the Law. Volume 2. London: Stevens and Sons, Ltd.

Reich, Charles A.
1964 "The new property." Yale Law Journal 73(5):733–787.

Reiss, Albert J.
(forthcoming) "Selecting strategies of control over organizational life." In Keith Hawkins and John Thomas (eds.), Enforcing Regulation. Boston: Kluwer-Nijhoff.

Scott, Thomas M., and Marlys McPherson
1971 "The development of the private sector of the criminal justice system." Law and Society Review 6(2):267–288.

Scull, Andrew T.
1977 Decarceration: Community Treatment and the Deviant—A Radical View. Englewood Cliffs, N.J.: Prentice Hall.

Shearing, Clifford D., and Philip C. Stenning
1981 "Private security: Its growth and implications." Pp. 193–245 in Michael Tonry and Norval Morris (eds.), Crime and Justice—An Annual Review of Research. Volume 3. Chicago: University of Chicago Press.
1982 "Snowflakes or good pinches? Private security's contribution to modern policing." Pp. 96–105 in Rita Donelan (ed.), The Maintenance of Order in Society. Ottawa: Canadian Police College.

Shearing, Clifford D., Margaret Farnell, and Philip C. Stenning
1980 Contract Security in Ontario. Toronto: Centre of Criminology, University of Toronto.

Snyder, Francis G.
1981 "Anthropology, dispute processes, and law: A critical introduction." British Journal of Law and Society 8(2):141–180.

Spitzer, Stephen, and Andrew T. Scull
1977 "Privatization and capitalist development: The case of the private police." Social Problems 25(1):18–29.

Spurr, Peter
1975 "Urban land monopoly." City Magazine (Toronto) 1:17–31.

Stenning, Philip C.
1981 Postal Security and Mail Opening: A Review of the Law. Toronto: Centre of Criminology, University of Toronto.

Stenning, Philip C., and Mary F. Cornish
1975 The Legal Regulation and Control of Private Policing in Canada. Toronto: Centre of Criminology, University of Toronto.

Stenning, Philip C., and Clifford D. Shearing
1979 "Search and seizure: Powers of private security personnel." Study paper prepared for the Law Reform Commission of Canada. Ministry of Supply and Services Canada, Ottawa.

Stinchcombe, Arthur L.
1963 "Institutions of privacy in the determination of police administrative practice." American Journal of Sociology 69:150–160.

U.S. Department of Justice, Federal Bureau of Investigation
1976 Uniform Crime Reports for the United States: 1975. Washington, D.C.: U.S. Government Printing Office.

Waldie, Brennan, and Associates
1982 "Beyond the law: The strikebreaking industry in Ontario—Report to the Director, District 6, United Steelworkers of America." Mimeographed. United Steel Workers of America, Toronto.

Zack, Arnold M.
1978 "Suggested new approaches to grievance arbitration." Pp. 105–117 in Arbitration—1977. Proceedings of the 30th annual meeting of the National Academy of Arbitrators. Washington, D.C.: Bureau of National Affairs, Inc.

Case Cited
Freeborn v. Canadian Imperial Bank of Commerce, 5(9) Arbitration Services Reporter 1 (Baum), 1981.

Part 4
CRIMINAL JUSTICE: COURTS AND CORRECTIONS

The preceding section was devoted to the fundamentals of crime control. The law establishes what behaviors are criminal. The police apprehend criminal suspects and, most critically, decide whether to make a formal arrest of suspected criminals.

This section also focuses on crime control, but it goes beyond the law and policing to issues surrounding the processing in the courts of people accused of crimes, the decision of guilt or innocence, and the confinement of criminals in correctional institutions.

After arrest and booking by the police, criminal suspects are placed in the criminal court system. The process, which ends in a decision (and if it is "guilty," a sentence), varies somewhat by the jurisdiction in which the case occurs. In general, the process occurs in several steps. First, the accused appears before the judge in a pretrial hearing. The judge examines the facts and determines if the accused should be released or confined before the trial. If the accused is released the judge determines whether the release should be based on a promise to appear in court ("release on recognizance") or whether he or she should post money ("bail") and in what amount to ensure the presence of the defendant at trial.

Second, before the trial, the prosecutor, who represents the state, gathers evidence and, if it is sufficient, presents the case to a grand jury. The grand jury hears only the prosecutor's side and if convinced, issues a formal accusation ("indictment").

Third, at any time before the trial or before the verdict in the trial, the prosecutor and the attorney for the accused may negotiate to lessen the charges and punishment for a plea of guilty. This process of plea bargaining is the rule, not the exception, in the disposition of criminal cases in the United States. The positive result of the procedure is the lessening of the burden on already overcrowded courts. The primary disadvantage is that defendants may be innocent, but plead guilty because of the various pressures on them.

If the case goes to trial, and less than 10 percent do (because the charges are dropped or because of plea bargaining), the accused is tried before a judge alone or before a judge and jury. This is a crucial decision for the accused and his or her lawyer. The decision to waive a jury trial depends on such factors as the reputation of the judge assigned to the case, and the amount of pretrial publicity (which may make an unbiased jury virtually impossible).

At the conclusion of a trial, the defendant is found guilty or not by the judge or jury. If guilty, the judge then determines the punishment of the offender.

The four issues examined in this section involve the potential for bias in sentencing, the functions of prisons, the trend toward the privatization of prisons, and what to do about crime control.

SENTENCING: JUSTICE OR BIAS?

At each of the stages in the criminal justice process, there is considerable latitude in the choices open to the authorities. Thus, there is always the possibility of bias—to be too lenient or too harsh depending on any number of factors such as the social class, race, gender, and age of the accused and the victim. This is the first issue addressed in this section—focusing on the possible bias in sentencing by judges.

PRISON: INCAPACITATION OR DISCIPLINING MARGINAL CLASSES?

The conservative rationale for imprisoning criminal offenders has usually been to deter crime or at least to gain retribution. To accomplish these things, conservatives have generally argued that the prison experience of the individual offender must necessarily be an unpleasant one. More recently, some conservative commentators have advocated "selective incapacitation" of violent offenders as a more sound justification for, and efficient use of, imprisonment. James Q. Wilson's article in this section serves as an example.

But radical criminologists Herman and Julia Schwendinger in their article, "The New Idealism and Penal Living Standards," contend that the question of who gets imprisoned and prison conditions themselves has little to do with the characteristics of individual offenders or elaborate justifications or rationales for prison. Rather, penal conditions at any given time have the wider collective and structural function of keeping the poor and working-class in line.

PRIVATE PRISONS

The prevailing mood by the public and public officials in the past fifteen years or so has favored a "get-tough" approach toward street criminals. The evidence is easily seen in the acts of legislatures, the political ideology of those selected as judges, mandatory sentencing, and the like. This greater punitiveness toward criminals has meant that more people are being sent to prison and they are staying longer, resulting in very overcrowded prisons. This crisis has placed the states in a difficult situation. There is the fiscal problem of providing thousands of new prison cells at

$50,000 to $80,000 each at a time when the states typically are underfunded. The overcrowded prisons have also created a situation where many prisoners are being released prematurely to make room for the newly sentenced; this runs counter to the prevailing get-tough, lock 'em up philosophy.

Private investors have provided one solution to this problem—prisons owned and operated privately rather than by government. This option is viewed as an attractive one by many. It appeals to political conservatives who favor privatization in hospitals, schools, and other typically government-run entities. The argument is that private enterprises are cheaper and more efficient than government operations and thus can be supplied at much less cost to society. To begin, the government does not have to pay the cost of the new prisons, saving taxpayers millions. Beyond that, the entrepreneurs argue that their expenses will be lower, thus providing another saving to the state.

Opponents of the prisons-for-profit plan argue that if profits are primary, then the concern for prisoners (e.g., civil rights, decent food, educational opportunities, medical care, and sanitary conditions) might be compromised. The prisoners may be exploited as cheap labor to enhance profits for the prison enterprise. Also, the savings to the state may be illusory, because the private prisons will be funded through tax benefits to the investors.

CRIME CONTROL: WHAT TO DO?

The final issue considered in this collection is the big one—what to do about crime? What are the policies that should be implemented to reduce crime? Conservatives and progressives have agendas for what they believe should be done. Each agenda follows from the set of assumptions that form its ideology and interpretation of social life. To represent each position, we have selected a summary statement by a leading proponent—James Q. Wilson for the conservatives and Elliott Currie for the progressives.

Sentencing and Racial Discrimination

William Wilbanks

I take the position that the perception of the criminal justice system as racist is a myth. Since this assertion can be interpreted in many ways, it is necessary to specify what it means and does not mean.

First, I believe that there is racial prejudice and discrimination *within* the criminal justice system, in that there are individuals, both white and black, who make decisions, at least in part, on the basis of race. I do not believe that *the system* is characterized by racial prejudice or discrimination against blacks; that is, prejudice and discrimination are not "systematic." Individual cases appear to reflect racial prejudice and discrimination by the offender, the victim, the police, the prosecutor, the judge, or prison and parole officials. But conceding individual cases of bias is far different from conceding pervasive racial discrimination. . . .

[I] argue that the evidence at most decision points fails to show any overall racial effect, in that the percentage outcomes for blacks and whites are not very different. There is evidence, however, that some individual decision makers (for example, police officers, judges) are more likely to give "breaks" to whites than to blacks. It appears, however, that there is an *equal* tendency for other individual decision makers to favor blacks over whites.[1] This "canceling-out effect" results in studies that find no *overall* racial effect. It is important to note that though racial discrimination has occurred in numerous individual cases against blacks and whites, there is no *systematic* bias *against* blacks.

Second, the question of whether the criminal justice system is "racist" cannot be discussed until the term *racist* is defined. . . . some appear to see any black/white disparities as prima facie evidence of racism. Thus if blacks outnumber whites in prison at a ratio of 8:1 (this is the rate ratio, controlling for the fact that blacks make up only 12 percent of the U.S. population), that disparity is viewed as racism. By that definition the criminal justice system is racist, since that 8:1 disparity does in fact exist.

If one defines racism as a conscious attitude or conscious behavior by individu-

---

Source: From *The Myth of a Racist Criminal Justice System*, by William Wilbanks. Copyright © 1987 by Wadsworth, Inc. Reprinted by permission of Brooks/Cole Publishing Company, Pacific Grove, California 93950 (pp. 5–8; 119–121).

als that discriminates against blacks, however, there is little or no evidence that most individuals in the system make decisions on the basis of race. In short, the definition of racism often predetermines the answer to the question "Is the criminal justice system racist?"

Furthermore, it should be noted that the research discussed in this volume is concerned primarily with formal *decisions* (for example, arrest, conviction, sentencing) made by those in the criminal justice system. To argue that there is no systematic bias against blacks in formal decisions does not speak to the issue of whether the police are more likely to "talk down" to black citizens or to show them less respect. The fact that a police officer may call a 40-year-old black man a "boy" does not necessarily mean that the officer will be more likely to arrest that man (or, if he does, that his decision is based primarily on the racist stereotype). As two authors state, "Harassment of minorities by system personnel, less desirable work assignments, and indifference to important cultural needs could exist, but not be systematically reflected in formal processing decisions."[2]

The focus in this book on formal decisions by the criminal justice system that affect blacks should not be construed to mean that informal decisions (as suggested above) are not important. But the charge of racism is generally directed at the formal decisions that can result in the deprivation of liberty, and thus I will focus on those decisions. Also, researching the informal decisions (harassment, talking down) is much harder and is subject to personal biases by observers.

Third, the assertion that the criminal justice system is not racist does not address the reasons why blacks appear to offend at higher rates than whites even before coming into contact with the criminal justice system.[3] It may be that racial discrimination in American society has been responsible for conditions that lead to higher rates of offending by blacks, but that possibility does not bear on the question of whether the criminal justice system discriminates against blacks.

An excellent illustration of how racial discrimination may have led to a greater likelihood of blacks' being involved in criminal activity can be found in the book *Brothers and Keepers*, an account of how two black brothers chose different directions. The author obtained a Ph.D. in English; his brother, Robby, received a life sentence for murder.[4]

> No way Ima be like the rest of them niggers scuffling and kissing ass to get by. Scuffling and licking ass till the day they die and the shame is they ain't even getting by. They crawling. They stepped on. Mize well be roaches or some goddamn waterbugs. White man got em backed up in Homewood and he's sprinkling roach powder on em. He's steady shaking and they steady dying. . . .
>
> He blew it. Not alone, of course. Society cooperated. Robby's chance for a normal life was as illusory as most citizens' chances to be elected to office or run a corporation. If "normal" implies a decent job, an opportunity to receive at least minimal pay-off for years of drudgery, delayed gratification, then for Robby and 75 percent of young black males growing up in the 1960's, "normal" was the exception rather than the rule. Robby was smart enough to see there was

no light at the end of the long tunnel of hard work (if and when you could get it) and responsibility. He was stubborn, aggressive, and prickly enough not to allow anyone to bully him into the tunnel. He chose the bright lights winking right in front of his face, just beyond his fingertips. For him and most of his buddies "normal" was poverty, drugs, street crime, Vietnam, or prison.

Thus the question of whether the criminal justice system is racist must not be confused with that of whether blacks commit crimes at a higher rate than whites because of discrimination in employment, housing, education, and so forth. It may be that racial discrimination produces a gap in offending between blacks and whites but that this gap is not increased as black and white offenders move through the criminal justice system. . . . If the gap does not increase after the point at which offenses occur, the system cannot be held responsible for the gap that results at the end of the system (prison).

Universities in the United States are sometimes accused of being racist because their student enrollment or faculty does not have the numbers of blacks one would expect given the proportion of blacks in the population. Those universities so accused often respond that they are not responsible for the failure of prospective black students or faculty members to meet admission criteria. Though one can argue that society as a whole is responsible for inferior schooling for blacks that has resulted in their being "less qualified" for admission as students or faculty, surely it would be unfair to blame the universities for this problem. In my view the university is responsible, assuming good faith and effort in student and faculty recruitment, only for the treatment of minorities once they enroll or join the faculty. Likewise, the criminal justice system is not responsible, with respect to the charge of racism, for differing levels of offending by blacks and whites. It is responsible for differential treatment once offending occurs.

Fourth, the assertion that the criminal justice system is not racist does not deny that racial prejudice and discrimination have existed in or even been the dominant force in the design and operation of the criminal justice system in the past. There is evidence suggesting that racism did permeate the criminal justice system in earlier periods of American history, especially in the South.[5] The evidence regarding northern cities, however, does not support the discrimination thesis. Roger Lane, perhaps the most prominent historian of U.S. criminal justice, found no evidence of systemic racial discrimination in the criminal courts of nineteenth-century Philadelphia "or indeed for those in any northern city in the same period."[6] But the question today concerns whether the operation of the system *at this time* is characterized by racial prejudice and discrimination. I believe that there is insufficient evidence to support the charge that the system is racist today.

Fifth, I am not suggesting that the nondiscrimination thesis has been proven by the existing literature. But surely the burden of proof rests on those who hold that the system is racist. Though I do believe that the weight of the existing evidence supports the nondiscrimination thesis (NDT) rather than the discrimination thesis (DT), I do not believe that the case for the NDT has been proven. The belief that the criminal justice system is racist is a myth in the sense that there is insufficient evidence to support this position.

What Is Known about Race and Sentencing: A Summary

This [essay] has attempted to point out the difficulties in proving or disproving the existence of racial discrimination at the point of sentencing by illustrating how different research methods and interpretations lead to different conclusions about a race effect. You should not be left with the impression, however, that these difficulties prevent us from really knowing anything about race and sentencing. Several findings appear to be generally valid across the literature.

1. *Racial discrimination in sentencing has declined over time.* Two reviews of the literature suggest that a race effect was more likely to have been found (and if found more likely to have been greater in magnitude) in studies from the 1960s and earlier.[7] One study that examined burglary and robbery cases in Milwaukee courts for an eleven-year period found that a race effect found for 1967–1968 had disappeared by 1971–1972 and 1976–1977.[8] The authors of that study attributed the "racial neutrality" in later years to changes in the composition of the judiciary, a greater bureaucratization of the prosecutorial and defense bar, and the rise of decision rules that reduced the effect of judicial ideology on outcomes.

2. *Race of defendant does not have a consistent impact across crimes and jurisdictions.* In other words, some studies have found that in some jurisdictions blacks receive harsher sentences for some crimes but more lenient sentences for others.[9] Likewise, although blacks may be more likely than whites to be sent to prison in one state, they may be less likely in another. California and Pennsylvania illustrate this change in the "direction" of the relationship between race and sentence. . . . Also even within a state the extent of a race effect may vary sharply between rural and urban courts.[10]

3. *Race of victim may be a better predictor of sentence than race of defendant.* This is certainly true for death penalty cases, but the research in noncapital cases has seldom included race of victim as a variable, and thus the pattern is less clear.[11] However, studies finding that cases involving white victims received harsher treatment than cases involving black victims also find that white defendants were treated more harshly than black defendants (since much crime is intraracial). Thus if one argues that racial discrimination exists because of favoritism to white victims (that is, by harsher sentences to offenders against white victims), one should also argue that reverse racial discrimination exists against white defendants because of their tendency to victimize other whites. It is curious that harsher treatment of white defendants is seen as racial discrimination against blacks.[12]

4. *Extralegal variables (for example, race, sex, age, socioeconomic status of defendant) are not as predictive of sentence as legal variables (for example, type of crime, strength of evidence).*[13]

5. *The black/white variation in sentences is generally reduced to near zero when*

several legal variables are introduced as controls.[14]

6. *The race effect, even before controls, is not "substantially" significant, in that the predictive power of race is quite low.*[15] Given this result it is difficult to maintain the position that race has a "pervasive" effect on sentences. In other terms, it is difficult to argue from the available evidence that black defendants "always" or even "often" receive harsher sentences (either with respect to the in/out decision or in length of prison term) than whites.

7. *There is no evidence that black judges are less likely than white judges to send blacks to prison or to give them lengthy terms.* The only study comparing sentencing by black and white judges found that all sixteen black judges gave harsher sentences to black defendants than to whites and that the black judges sentenced black defendants more harshly than white judges did.[16] If one argues that racial disparity in sentencing is indicative of racial discrimination, it is clear that black judges are more racist than white judges. The most likely interpretation is that blacks were sentenced more harshly by both white and black judges because of factors other than race that were deemed appropriate to consider. The fact that there is no evidence that black judges "make a difference" suggests that racial discrimination is not an important factor in criminal sentencing.

8. *Most sentencing studies have a large residual variation, suggesting that the models used did not fit the actual decision-making process of judges.*[17] The large residuals suggest that we know very little about sentencing as a result of the statistical studies that have been conducted.

9. *Since most sentencing studies have not examined the sentences of individual judges, the possibility remains that racial discrimination (both for and against blacks) exists on a rather large scale for individual cases but that the harsher and more lenient sentences by individual judges cancel each other out, thus producing no overall race effect for the court as a whole.*

Notes

1. J. L. Gibson, "Race as a Determinant of Criminal Sentences," *Law and Society Review* 12 (1978), 455–478.

2. S. Zimmerman and B. C. Frederick, "Discrimination and the Decision to Incarcerate," in D. Georges-Abeyie (ed.), *The Criminal Justice System and Blacks.* New York: Clark Boardman, 1984, 277.

3. M. E. Wolfgang, "Race and Crime," in H. J. Klare (ed.), *Changing Concepts of Crime and Its Treatment.* Oxford: Pergamon Press, 1977.

4. J. E. Wideman, *Brothers and Keepers.* New York: Holt, Rinehart, and Winston, 1984.

5. See, C. R. Adamson, "Punishment after Slavery: Southern State Penal Systems, 1865–1890," *Social Problems* 30 (1983), 554–569.

6. R. Lane, *Roots of Violence in Black Philadelphia, 1860–1900.* Cambridge, MA: Harvard University Press, 1986.

7. M. J. Hindelang, "Equality under the Law," *Journal of Criminal Law, Criminology and Police Science* 60 (1969, 306–313; and G. Kleck, "Racial Discrimination in Criminal Sentencing," *American Sociological Review* 46 (1981), 783–805.

8. C. R. Pruitt and J. Q. Wilson, "A Longitudi-

nal Study of the Effect of Race on Sentencing," *Law and Society Review* 17 (1983), 613–635.

9. See, for example, H. A. Bullock, "Significance of the Racial Factor in the Length of Prison Sentences," *Journal of Criminal Law, Criminology and Police Science* 52 (1961), 411–417.

10. C. E. Pope, "The Influence of Social and Legal Factors on Sentence Disposition," *Journal of Criminal Justice* 4 (1976), 203–221.

11. Kleck, op. cit.; R. Berk, "Racial Discrimination in Capital Sentencing," paper presented at the American Society of Criminology, Cincinnati (November 1984).

12. S. R. Gross and R. Mauro, "Patterns of Death: An Analysis of Racial Disparities in Capital Sentencing and Homicide Victimization," *Stanford Law Review* 37 (1984), 27–120.

13. Kleck, op. cit.; P. Burke and A. Turk, "Factors Affecting Post Arrest Dispositions," *Social Problems* 22 (1975), 313–332.

14. J. Hagan, "Extra-Legal Attributes and Criminal Sentencing," *Law and Society Review* 8 (1974), 357–383.

15. Ibid.

16. T. M. Uhlman, *Racial Justice.* Lexington, MA: D. C. Heath, 1979, pp. 70,71.

17. Hagan, op. cit.; Kleck, op. cit.

The Class Bias in Sentencing

Jeffrey H. Reiman

> He had a businessman's suit . . . but Jack L. Clark no longer had a business. His nursing home construction company had collapsed in a gigantic stock fraud, leaving shareholders out $200 million . . . Ten million of the swindled dollars had allegedly gone for Clark's personal use, and prosecutors accused him of stashing away 4 million unrecovered dollars in a retirement nest egg. Out of an original indictment of 65 counts, Clark had pleaded guilty to one charge. He faced a maximum penalty of a $10,000 fine and five years in prison. But the judge, before passing sentence, remembered the "marked improvement" in care for the elderly that Clark's nursing homes had provided . . . He considered that Clark was a 46-year-old family man who coached little kids in baseball and football. Then he passed sentence. No fine. One year in prison. Eligible for parole after four months.
>
> In another federal courtroom stood Matthew Corelli (not his real name), a 45-year-old, $125-a-week laborer who lived with his wife and kids in a $126-a-month apartment. Along with three other men, Corelli had been convicted of possessing $5,000 of stolen drugstore goods that government prosecutors identified as part of a $63,000 shipment. The judge considered Corelli's impoverished circumstances, his number of dependents, the nature of his crime, and then passed sentence: four years in prison. Or in other words, four times the punishment Clark received for a fraction of the crime.[1]
>
> Jack Greenberg took $15 from a post office; last May in Federal Court in Manhattan he drew six months in jail. Howard Lazell "misapplied" $150,000 from a bank; in the same month in the same courthouse he drew probation.[2]

The first quotation is the opening passage of a magazine article on white-collar crime, aptly titled "America's Most Coddled Criminals." The second quotation is the opening paragraph of a *New York Times* article, more prosaically titled "Wide Disparities Mark Sentences Here." Both, however, are testimony to the fact that the criminal justice system reserves its harshest penalties for its lower-class clients and puts on kid gloves when confronted with a better class of crook.

The system is doubly biased against the poor. First, there is the class bias *be-*

Source: Reprinted with permission from Macmillan Publishing Company from *The Rich Get Richer and the Poor Get Prison* by Jeffrey H. Reiman. (New York: Macmillan 1984). (pp. 94–101).

tween crimes that we have just seen. The crimes that poor people are likely to commit carry harsher sentences than the "crimes in the suites" committed by well-to-do people. Second, for *all* crimes, the poor receive less probation and more years of confinement than well-off defendants *convicted of the same offense*, assuring us once again that the vast majority of those who are put behind bars are from the lowest social and economic classes in the nation.

The *New York Times* article referred to above reports the results of a study done by the *New York Times* on sentencing in state and federal courts. The *Times* states that "crimes that tend to be committed by the poor get tougher sentences than those committed by the well-to-do," that federal "defendants who could not afford private counsel were sentenced nearly twice as severely as defendants with private or no counsel," and that a "study by the Vera Institute of Justice of courts in the Bronx indicates a similar pattern in the state courts."[3]

Looking at federal and state courts, Stuart Nagel concludes that

> not only are the indigent found guilty more often, but they are much less likely to be recommended for probation by the probation officer, or to be granted probation or suspended sentences by the judge.

And, further, that

> the federal data show that this is true also of those with no prior record: 27 percent of the indigent with no prior record were not recommended for probation against 16 percent of the non-indigent; 23 percent indigent did *not* receive suspended sentences or probation against 15 percent non-indigent. Among those of both groups with "some" prior record the spread is even greater.[4]

Eugene Doleschal and Nora Klapmuts report as "typical of American studies," Thornberry's analysis of "3,475 Philadelphia delinquents that found that blacks and members of lower socioeconomic groups were likely to receive more severe dispositions than whites and the more affluent even when the appropriate legal variables [i.e., offense, prior record, etc.] were held constant.[5] More recently, applying more sophisticated statistical techniques to the data upon which his Philadelphia study was based, Thornberry concludes, "When seriousness, prior record and SES [socioeconomic strata] were held constant, blacks were significantly more likely than whites to receive more severe dispositions." Although he finds the effect of socioeconomic status weaker than in the earlier study, Thornberry writes, "When the variable of race was suppressed . . . , SES was found to be significantly related to dispositions such that lower SES subjects were treated more severely than their high SES counterparts."[6]

Studying the experiences of 798 burglary and larceny defendants in North Carolina, Clarke and Koch find that "other things being equal, the low-income defendant had a greater chance than the higher-income defendant of emerging from the criminal court with an active prison sentence. . . . Our tentative conclusion is that most of the influence of income on the likelihood of imprisonment among the defendants studied is explained by the poorer opportunity of the low-income defendant for [release on] bail and his greater likelihood of having a court-assigned rather than a privately retained, attorney."[7] Analyzing data from Chicago trial courts, Lizotte finds that, other things being equal, "laborers and non-whites are . . . twice as likely as proprietors to stay incarcerated between arrest and final disposition [i.e., not be released on bail]. Further, other factors being equal, laborers and non-whites are given longer prison sentences than higher SES groups."[8]

As usual, data on racial discrimination in sentencing exist in much greater abundance than data on class discrimination, but they tell the same story of the treatment of those who cannot afford the going price of justice. Most striking perhaps is the fact that over 44 percent of the inmates of all correctional facilities in the United States—state and federal prisons as well as local jails—are black, while blacks account for a little under one-quarter of all arrests in the nation. Even when we compare the percentage of blacks arrested for serious (i.e., FBI Index) crimes with the percentage of blacks in federal and state prisons (where presumably those convicted of such offenses would be sent), blacks still make up over 46 percent of the inmates but only about 33 percent of the arrestees, which is still a considerable disparity. Furthermore, when we look at federal prisons, where there is reason to believe racial and economic discrimination is less prevalent than in state institutions, we find that the average sentence for a white inmate in 1979 was 98.9 months, as compared to 130.2 months (over 2½ years more!) for nonwhite inmates. The nonwhite inmate serves, on the average, 20 more months for a drug law violation than the white inmate, and almost twice as long for income tax evasion.[9]

Studies have confirmed that black burglars receive longer sentences than do white burglars. And blacks who plead guilty receive harsher sentences than whites who do, although by an act of dubious mercy of which Americans ought hardly be proud, blacks often receive lighter sentences for murder and rape than whites as long as the victim was black as well.[10] According to a recent four-state study of capital sentencing, this dubious mercy extends to the death penalty. In Florida, for example, blacks "who kill whites are nearly forty times more likely to be sentenced to death than those who kill blacks." Moreover, among "killers of whites, blacks are five times more likely than whites to be sentenced to death." This pattern of double discrimination was also evidenced, though less pronouncedly, in Texas, Ohio, and Georgia, the other states surveyed. Together, these four states "accounted for approximately 70 percent of the nation's death sentences" between 1972 and 1977.[11] Note that these discriminatory sentences were rendered under statutes that had passed constitutional muster and were therefore presumed free of the biases that led the Supreme Court to invalidate death penalty statutes in *Furman* v. *Georgia* in 1972.

Mary Owen Cameron studied the sentencing practices of judges in the Chicago Women's Court during a three-year period. Her findings were as follows:

Judges found sixteen percent of the white women brought before them on charges of shoplifting to be "not guilty," but only four percent of the black women were found innocent. In addition, twenty-two percent of the black women as compared to four percent of the white women were sent to jail. Finally, of the twenty-one white women sentenced to jail, only two (ten percent) were to be jailed for thirty days or more; of the seventy-six black women sentenced to jail twenty (twenty-six percent) were to be jailed for thirty days or more.[12]

An extensive study by the *Boston Globe* of 4500 cases of armed robbery, aggravated assault, and rape, found that "blacks convicted in the superior courts of Massachusetts receive harsher penalties than whites for the same crimes. . . . The median time served by blacks is nine weeks longer than that served by whites for armed robbery, 13½ months longer for rape and about equal for aggravated assault. . . . The typical minimum sentence for blacks . . . on all three crimes combined is more than a year longer than for whites."[13] The authors of a study of almost 1200 males sentenced to prison for armed robbery in a southeastern state found that "in 1977 whites incarcerated for armed robbery had a greater than average chance of receiving the least severe sentence, while nonwhites had a greater than average chance of receiving a moderately severe sentence."[14] A study of 229 adjudicated cases in a Florida judicial district yielded the finding that "whites have an 18 percent greater chance in the predicted probability of receiving probation than blacks when all other things are equal."[15]

Another study has shown that among blacks and whites on death row, whites are more likely to have their sentences commuted. And blacks or whites who have private counsel are more likely to have their execution commuted than condemned persons defended by court-appointed attorneys.[16]

As I have already pointed out, justice is increasingly tempered with mercy as we deal with a better class of crime. The Sherman Antitrust Act is a criminal law. It was passed in recognition of the fact that one virtue of a free enterprise economy is that competition tends to drive consumer prices down, so agreements by competing firms to refrain from price competition is the equivalent of stealing money from the consumer's pocket. Nevertheless, although such conspiracies cost consumers far more than lower-class theft, price-fixing was a misdemeanor until 1974.[17] In practice, few conspirators end up in prison, and when they do, the sentence is a mere token, well below the maximum provided in the law. Thus, based on the government's track record, there is little reason to expect things to change significantly now that price-fixing is a felony.

In the historic *Electrical Equipment* cases in the early 1960s, executives of several major firms secretly met to fix prices on electrical equipment to a degree that is estimated to have cost the buying public well over a billion dollars. The executives involved knew they were violating the law. They used plain envelopes for their communications, called their meetings "choir practice," and referred to the list of executives in attendance as the "Christmas card list." This case is rare and famous because it was one in which the criminal sanction was actually imposed. Seven executives received and served jail sentences. But in light of the amount of money they had stolen from the American public, their sentences were more an indictment of the government than of themselves: *30 days in jail!*

Speaking about the record of federal antitrust prosecution, Clinard and Yeager write that "even in the most widespread and flagrant price conspiracy cases, few corporate executives are ever imprisoned; of the total 231 cases with individual defendants from 1955 to 1975, prison sentences were given in only 19 cases. Of a total of 1027 individual defendants, only 49 were sentenced to prison."[18] There is some (slight) indication of a toughening in the sentences since antitrust violations were made a felony in 1974, and penalties were increased. "In felony cases prosecuted under the new penalties through March 1978, 15 of 21 sentenced individuals (71 percent) were given terms averaging 192 days each."[19] Nevertheless, when the cost to society is reckoned, even such penalties as these are hardly severe.

Indeed, Clinard and Yeager maintain that "There is even more leniency for corporate than for other white-collar offenders. Few members of corporate management ever go to prison, even if convicted; generally they are placed on probation."[20] In their study of 56 corporate executives who were convicted of criminal offenses, 40 either received probation or a suspended sentence. Only 16 were actually sent to prison. These 16 "were sentenced to a total of 594 days of actual imprisonment (an average of 37.1 days each). Of the total days of imprisonment, 360 (60.6 percent) were accounted for by two officers, who received six months each in the same case."[21] The remaining 14 served an average of 16.7 days each.

In general the crimes of the poor receive stiffer sentences than the crimes of the well-to-do. For instance, Marvin Frankel points out, in his book *Criminal Sentences: Law Without Order*, that "of 502 defendants convicted for income tax fraud 95, or 19 percent, received prison terms, the average being three months. Of 3,791 defendants sentenced for auto theft, 2,373, or 63 percent, went to prison, the average term being 7.6 months."[22] More recent figures fit this pattern. A statistical report of the Federal Bureau of Prisons yields information about the average sentences received by inmates of federal institutions and the average time served until parole (see Table 1). Keep in mind while looking at these figures that *each* of the "crimes of the affluent" costs the public more than *all* of the "crimes of the poor" put together.

A study of sentencing practices in the Southern District of New York, optimistically entitled *Justice in Sentencing*, found

> plain indications that white collar defendants, predominantly white, receive more lenient treatment as a general rule, while defendants charged with common crimes, largely committed by the unemployed and undereducated, a group which embraces large numbers of blacks in today's society, are more likely to be sent to prison. If these indications are correct, then one may conclude that poor persons receive harsher treatment in the Federal Courts than do well-to-do defendants charged with more sophisticated crimes.

Table 1 Sentences for Different Classes of Crime

	Average Sentence (in months)	Average Time Served Until First Release (in months)
Crimes of the poor		
Robbery	131.3	44.4
Burglary	63.4	31.6
Larceny/theft	31.0	17.1
Crimes of the affluent		
Embezzlement	18.8	10.3
Fraud	22.0	11.0
Income tax evasion	15.5	7.9

Source: Federal Bureau of Prisons—Statistical Report, Fiscal Year 1976.

Specifically, the study reports that "during the six-month period covered by the Southern District of New York sentencing study, *defendants convicted of white collar crimes stood a 36% chance of going to prison; defendants convicted of nonviolent common crimes stood a 53% chance of going to prison*; and defendants convicted of violent crimes stood an 80% chance of going to prison."[23] Several things are worthy of note here. First, the study carries forth the distorted conventional wisdom about crime by distinguishing between "white-collar" and "common" crime, when, as we have found, there is every reason to believe that white-collar crime is just as common as the so-called common crimes of the poor. Second, the disparities reported refer only to likelihood of imprisonment *for any length of time*, and so they really understate the disparities in treatment, since the so-called common crimes also receive *longer* prison sentences than the white-collar crimes. But third, and most importantly, the disparities cannot be explained by the greater danger of lower-class criminals because even the perpetrators of *nonviolent "common" crimes* stand a 50 percent greater chance of going to prison than do white-collar crooks.

A graphic illustration of the way the criminal justice system treats the wealthy is provided by Fleetwood and Lubow in their article "America's Most Coddled Criminals." They put together their pick of ten convicted white-collar criminals, comparing their sentences with the crimes they committed.

Equally eloquent testimony to the merciful face that the criminal justice system turns toward upper-class crooks is found in a *New York Times* report on the fate of 21 business executives found guilty of making illegal campaign contributions during the Watergate scandal:

> Most of the 21 business executives who admitted their guilt to the Watergate Special Prosecutor in 1973 and 1974—especially those from large corporations—are still presiding over their companies. . . .
> Only two went to jail. They served a few months and were freed. . . .
> Furthermore, the fines of $1,000 or $2,000 that most of the contributors of illegal funds had to pay have not made much of a dent in their style of living. . . .

An investigation into the whereabouts and financial status of the 21 executives involved in illegal contributions leads to a conclusion that the higher the position the more cushioned the fall—if indeed there was a fall.[24]

The *Times* report also includes a chart illustrating the fate of these upper-class criminals, who were found guilty of nothing less than participating in schemes that undermine the independence of the electoral process—guilty, that is, of contaminating the very lifeblood of democratic government. . . . As for the government officials themselves (and their hirelings) who were directly responsible for the Watergate crimes, their treatment has also been relatively gentle.

On either side of the law, the rich get richer . . .

References

1. Blake Fleetwood and Arthur Lubow, "America's Most Coddled Criminals," *New Times* (September 19, 1975), pp. 26–29. *New Times Magazine,* copyright © 1975. Reprinted by permission of *New Times Magazine.*
2. Lesley Oelsner, "Wide Disparities Mark Sentences Here." *The New York Times,* September 27, 1972, p. 1. Stuart Nagel writes, "The reasons for the economic class sentencing disparities, holding crime and prior record constant, are due possibly to the quality of legal representation that the indigent receive and probably to the appearance that an indigent defendant presents before a middle-class judge or probation officer." "Disparities in Sentencing Procedure," *UCLA Law Review,* 14 (August, 1967), p. 1283.
3. Oelsner, p. 1.
4. Stuart Nagel, "The Tipped Scales of American Justice," in *Law and Order,* Abraham S. Blumberg (ed.), (Aldine-Trans-action, 1970), p. 39.
5. Eugene Doleschal and Nora Klapmuts, "Toward a New Criminology," *Crime and Delinquency Literature* 5 (December 1973), p. 613.
6. Terence P. Thornberry, "Sentencing Disparities in the Juvenile Justice System," *Journal of Criminal Law and Criminology* 70, No. 2 (Summer 1979), pp. 164–171, esp. p. 170.
7. Steven H. Clarke and Gary G. Koch, "The Influence of Income and Other Factors on Whether Criminal Defendants Go to Prison," *Law and Society Review* (Fall 1976), pp. 57–92, esp. pp. 81, 83–84.
8. Alan J. Lizotte, "Testing the Conflict Model of Criminal Justice," *Social Problems* 25, No. 5 (1978), pp. 564–580, esp. p. 564.
9. *Sourcebook-1981,* pp. 463, 477, 490.
10. Henry Allen Bullock, "Significance of the Racial Factor in the Length of Prison Sentences," in *Crime and Justice in Society,* ed., R. Quinney (Boston: Little, Brown, 1969), p. 425; also, Marvin E. Wolfgang and Marc Riedel, "Race, Judicial Discretion and the Death Penalty," in *Criminal Law in Action,* ed., Chambliss, p. 375.
11. William J. Bowers and Glenn L. Pierce, "Racial Discrimination and Criminal Homicide Under Post-Furman Capital Statuses," in H. A. Bedau, ed., *The Death Penalty in America* (New York: Oxford University Press, 1982), pp. 206–224.
12. William J. Chambliss and Robert B. Seidman, "Sentencing and Sentences," in *Criminal Law in Action,* ed., Chambliss, p. 339; reporting the findings of Mary Owen Cameron, *The Booster and the Snitch: Department Store Shoplifting* (New York: Free Press, 1964).

13. "Blacks Receive Stiffer Sentences," *The Boston Globe*, April 4, 1979, pp. 1 and 50f.

14. Randall Thomson and Matthew Zingraff, "Detecting Sentencing Disparity: Some Problems and Evidence," *American Journal of Sociology* 86, No. 4 (1981), pp. 869–880, esp. p. 875.

15. J. Unnever, C. Frazier, J. Henretta, "Race Differences in Criminal Sentencing," *The Sociological Quarterly* 21 (Spring 1980), pp. 197–205, esp. p. 204.

16. Marvin E. Wolfgang, Arlene Kelly, and Hans C. Nolde, "Comparison of the Executed and the Commuted Among Admissions to Death Row," in *Crime and Justice in Society*, ed., Quinney, pp. 508, 513.

17. "Antitrust: Kauper's Last Stand," *Newsweek*, June 21, 1976, p. 70. On December 21, 1974, the "Antitrust Procedures and Penalty Act" was passed, striking out the language of the Sherman Antitrust Act, which made price-fixing a misdemeanor punishable by a maximum sentence of one year in prison. According to the new law, price-fixing is a felony punishable by up to three years in prison. Since prison sentences were a rarity under the old law and usually involved only 30 days in jail when actually imposed, there is little reason to believe that the new law will strike fear in the hearts of corporate crooks.

18. Clinard and Yeager, *Corporate Crime*, pp. 291–292.

19. Ibid., p. 153.

20. Ibid., p. 287.

21. Ibid., p. 291.

22. Marvin E. Frankel, *Criminal Sentences: Law Without Order* (New York: Hill and Wang, 1972), p. 24, footnote.

23. *Justice in Sentencing: Papers and Proceedings of the Sentencing Institute for the First and Second U.S. Judicial Circuits*, eds., Leonard Orland and Harold R. Tyler, Jr. (Mineola, N.Y.: Foundation Press, 1974), pp. 159–160. (Emphasis added.)

24. Michael C. Jensen, "Watergate Donors Still Riding High," *The New York Times* August 24, 1975, sec. 3, pp. 1, 7. Copyright © 1975 by The New York Times Company. Reprinted by permission.

PRISON: INCAPACITATION OR DISCIPLINING MARGINAL CLASSES? 1

Incapacitation

James Q. Wilson

When criminals are deprived of their liberty, as by imprisonment (or banishment, or very tight control in the community), their ability to commit offenses against citizens is ended. We say these persons have been "incapacitated," and we try to estimate the amount by which crime is reduced by this incapacitation.

Incapacitation cannot be the sole purpose of the criminal justice system; if it were, we would put everybody who has committed one or two offenses in prison until they were too old to commit another. And if we thought prison too costly, we would simply cut off their hands or their heads. Justice, humanity, and proportionality, among other goals, must also be served by the courts.

But there is one great advantage to incapacitation as a crime control strategy—namely, it does not require us to make any assumptions about human nature. By contrast, deterrence works only if people take into account the costs and benefits of alternative courses of action and choose that which confers the largest net benefit (or the smallest net cost). Though people almost surely do take such matters into account, it is difficult to be certain by how much such considerations affect their behavior and what change, if any, in crime rates will result from a given, feasible change in either the costs of crime or the benefits of not committing a crime. Rehabilitation works only if the values, preferences, or time-horizon of criminals can be altered by plan. There is not much evidence that we can make these alterations for large numbers of persons, though there is some evidence that it can be done for a few under certain circumstances.

Incapacitation, on the other hand, works by definition: its effects result from the physical restraint placed upon the offender and not from his subjective state. More accurately, it works provided at least three conditions are met: some offenders must be repeaters, offenders taken off the streets must not be immediately and completely replaced by new recruits, and prison must not increase the post-release criminal activity of those who have been incarcerated sufficiently to offset the crimes prevented by their stay in prison.

Source: James Q. Wilson, *Thinking About Crime*, second edition (New York: Random House, 1983), pp. 145–161. Reprinted with permission.

The first condition is surely true. Every study of prison inmates shows that a large fraction (recently, about two-thirds) of them had prior criminal records before their current incarceration; every study of ex-convicts shows that a significant fraction (estimates vary from a quarter to a half) are rearrested for new offenses within a relatively brief period.[1] In short, the great majority of persons in prison are repeat offenders, and thus prison, whatever else it may do, protects society from the offenses these persons would commit if they were free.

The second condition—that incarcerating one robber does not lead automatically to the recruitment of a new robber to replace him—seems plausible. Although some persons, such as Ernest van den Haag, have argued that new offenders will step forward to take the place vacated by the imprisoned offenders, they have presented no evidence that this is the case, except, perhaps, for certain crimes (such as narcotics trafficking or prostitution), which are organized along business lines.[2] For the kinds of predatory street crimes with which we are concerned— robbery, burglary, auto theft, larceny—there are no barriers to entry and no scarcity of criminal opportunities. No one need wait for a "vacancy" to appear before he can find an opportunity to become a criminal. The supply of robbers is not affected by the number of robbers practicing, because existing robbers have no way of excluding new robbers and because the opportunity for robbing (if you wish, the "demand" for robbery) is much larger than the existing number of robberies. In general, the earnings of street criminals are not affected by how many "competitors" they have.

The third condition that must be met if incapacitation is to work is that prisons must not be such successful "schools for crime" that the crimes prevented by incarceration are outnumbered by the increased crimes committed after release attributable to what was learned in prison. It is doubtless the case that for some offenders prison is a school; it is also doubtless that for other offenders prison is a deterrent. The former group will commit more, or more skillful, crimes after release; the latter will commit fewer crimes after release. The question, therefore, is whether the net effect of these two offsetting tendencies is positive or negative. The evidence presented . . . bears directly on this issue. All studies of the extent to which prisons reform offenders are also, in effect, studies of whether they *de* form them. In other words, when we compare the post-release crime rates of persons who have gone to prison with the crime rates of similar persons who have not, we can ask whether prison has made them better off (that is, rehabilitated them) or made them worse off (that is, served as a "school for crime"). In general, there is no evidence that the prison experience makes offenders as a whole more criminal, and there is some evidence that certain kinds of offenders (especially certain younger ones) may be deterred by a prison experience. Moreover, interviews with prisoners reveal no relationship between the number of crimes committed and whether the offenders had served a prior prison term.[3] Though there are many qualifications that should be made to this bald summary, there is no evidence that the net effect of prison is to increase the crime rates of ex-convicts sufficiently to cancel out the gains to society resulting from incapacitation.

In short, the three conditions that must be met for incapacitation to reduce crime are in fact met. What remains is to find out how much crime is reduced by sending offenders to prison and then to ask whether those gains in crime reduction are worth the cost in prison space and (possibly) in justice.

In Search of Individual Offense Rates

To determine the amount of crime that is prevented by incarcerating a given number of offenders for a given length of time, the key estimate we must make is the number of offenses a criminal commits per year free on the street.[*] If a community experiences one thousand robberies a year, it obviously makes a great deal of difference whether these robberies are the work of ten robbers, each of whom commits one hundred robberies per year, or the work of one thousand robbers, each of whom commits only one robbery per year. In the first case, locking up only five robbers will cut the number of robberies in half; in the second case, locking up one hundred robbers will only reduce the number of robberies by 10 percent.

In the first edition of this book, I reported, in the concluding chapter, on the work that had just been completed by Shlomo and Reuel Shinnar in which they produced an elegant mathematical formula for estimating the crime-reduction potential of incapacitation under various assumptions. Their key assumption was that the average rate of offending—that is, the number of crimes committed by the average criminal per year free—was ten. On the basis of this assumption and others, they estimated that the street robbery rate in New York State would be only one-fifth what it was in 1970 if every person convicted of such a crime spent five years in prison.[4]

About the time the Shinnars published this argument, other scholars were appearing in print with estimates of the individual offense rate that were much lower than ten. David Greenberg, using various methods, estimated that the average offender commits something on the order of two serious[†] offenses per year.[5] Based on this estimate, Greenberg concluded that if society were to increase the length of the average prison sentence by one year (it is now two years), we would cut the rate of serious crime by only about 4 percent.[6] Stevens Clarke undertook to calculate the incapacitative effect of prison on juvenile offenders (Greenberg had been concerned with adults) and decided that, at least in Philadelphia, the proportion of all serious crimes averted by the present sentences given to young offenders was no more than 4 percent.[7] Stephan Van Dine and his colleagues at the Academy for Contemporary Problems made an estimate of the crime-reduction effects of imposing a five-year prison term on all persons convicted of a felony in one county in Ohio, and concluded that this stringent policy would reduce violent crime by only

---

[*]Scholars who study incapacitation call the number of crimes committed per offender per year free "lambda," or λ. To avoid technical terminology, I will refer to it as the "individual offense rate."

[†]By "serious," Greenberg meant one of the seven "index" crimes as classified by the FBI—murder, aggravated assault, forcible rape, robbery, burglary, larceny, and auto theft.

4 percent.[8] Since so many different critics were arriving at similar low estimates of what incapacitation might produce, many persons began questioning the large crime-reduction effects claimed by the Shinnars.

At this point, the matter was taken up by a panel of experts appointed by the National Research Council (a part of the National Academy of Sciences) ... Jacqueline Cohen of Carnegie-Mellon University prepared, at the invitation of the panel, a careful analysis of the competing claims of various scholars. She concluded that Greenberg and Clarke both "underestimate the individual crime rate."[9] Reexamining Clarke's data under more reasonable assumptions, Cohen decided that the proportion of serious crimes averted by present imprisonment rates for juveniles was two to three times larger than that estimated by Clarke and, by implication, the number of crimes that could be prevented by increasing the use of prison would also be much higher.[10] Similarly, Greenberg made some questionable assumptions, as well as an error in his calculations, that rendered his estimates of dubious value, but there was no easy way to revise his calculations to provide a better estimate.[11]

Though the panel did not deal with the Van Dine estimates, other scholars did. Three separate articles were published pointing to a fundamental error in the Van Dine calculations.[12] In their rejoinder, the Van Dine group, in effect, conceded the correctness of the criticism and in subsequent published work revised their estimate of the incapacitation effect upward.[13] What they had originally done was to assume that the persons arrested in Ohio had committed only the crimes for which they were charged and that the only additional crimes that would be averted by sending them away to prison for long terms would have been those other crimes for which they had previously been arrested. They assumed, in short, that these offenders never committed any crimes that did not lead to an arrest. Since this was obviously untrue, their original, very low estimate of the crime-reduction effect of incapacitation had to be in error.

Cohen and the panel concluded in 1978 that the most important research task confronting persons interested in incapacitation was to obtain better estimates of individual offense rates.[14] A major step in that direction was taken the following year with the publication of a new estimate, the most sophisticated to date, of those rates. Working with individual adult criminal records of all those persons arrested in Washington, D.C., during 1973 for any one of six major crimes (over five thousand persons in all), Alfred Blumstein and Jacqueline Cohen suggested that the individual offense rate varied significantly for different kinds of offenders. For example, it was highest for larceny and lowest for aggravated assault. But they also found, as had other scholars before them, that there was not a great deal of specialization among criminals—a person arrested today for robbery might be arrested next time for burglary. The major contribution of their study was the ingenious method they developed for converting the number of times persons were arrested into an estimate of the number of crimes they actually committed, a method that took into account the fact that many crimes are not reported to the police, that most crimes known to the police do not result in an arrest, and that some crimes are likely to be committed by groups of persons rather than by single offenders. Combining all the individual crime rates, the offenders in this study (a group of adults who had been arrested at least twice in Washington, D.C.) committed between nine and seventeen serious offenses per year free.[15]

This number was strikingly similar to the original estimates used by the Shinnars that had provoked so much criticism. And confidence in the Blumstein-Cohen estimates was increased when the results of a major study at the Rand Corporation became known. Researchers there had been interviewing prisoners (first in California, then in other states) to find out directly from known offenders how much crime they were committing while free. No one can be certain, of course, that the reports of the convicts constitute an accurate record of their crimes, undetected as well as detected, but the Rand researchers cross-checked the information against arrest records and looked for evidence of internal consistency in the self-reports. Moreover, the inmates volunteered information about crimes they had committed but for which they had not been arrested. Still, it is quite possible that the self-reports were somewhat inaccurate. However, it is reasonable to assume that inmates would be more likely to conceal crimes they did commit rather than admit to crimes they did not commit. Thus, any errors in these self-reports probably lead to an underestimate of the true rate of criminality of these persons.

The Rand group found that the average California prisoner had committed about fourteen serious crimes per year during each of the three years he was free.[16] This number falls squarely within the range estimated, using very different methods, by Blumstein and Cohen and, again, is comparable to the original estimate of the Shinnars. To state the California findings in slightly different terms, if no one was confined in state prison, the number of armed robberies in California would be about 22 percent higher than it now is.[17]

After their initial survey of 624 incarcerated male felons in California, the Rand group enlarged their study to include about 2,200 inmates in the states of California, Michigan, and Texas. Again, they gathered self-reports on crimes committed while free. This larger survey produced even higher estimates of individual offense rates. A person serving time in California for robbery, for example, would on the average admit to committing fifty-three robberies per year free; in Michigan, the number was seventy-seven. Those who were active burglars reported committing ninety burglaries per year in California. Interestingly, the offense rates of Texas inmates were much lower—on the average, robbers committed nine robberies a year and burglars committed twenty-four burglaries.[18] This apparently was because Texas sent to prison so much larger a fraction of its convicted robbers and burglars that many inmates were low-rate offenders; in California and Michigan, where sentencing policies seem more lenient, a smaller proportion of low-rate offenders wind up in prison.

But the Rand group learned something else which would turn out to be even more important. The "average" individual offense rate was virtually a meaningless term because the inmates they interviewed differed so sharply in how many crimes they committed. A large number of offenders committed a small number of offenses while free and a small number of offenders committed a very large number of offenses. In statistical language, the distribution of offenses was highly skewed. For example, the median number of burglaries committed by the inmates in the three states was about 5 a year, but the 10 percent of the inmates who were the highest-rate offenders committed an average of 232 burglaries a year. The median number of robberies was also about 5 a year, but the top 10 percent of offenders committed an average of 87 a year. As Peter W. Greenwood, one of the members of the Rand group, put it, incarcerating one robber who was among the top 10 percent in offense rates would prevent more robberies than incarcerating eighteen offenders who were at or below the median.[19]

Not long after the Rand group began publishing its findings, Brian Forst and his colleagues at the Institute for Law and Social Research (INSLAW) in Washington, D.C., began to release data from their survey of 1,700 federal offenders whose criminal careers they had followed from 1970 through 1976. These persons also had high individual offense rates, nearly eight nondrug crimes per year free. And they also had a highly skewed distribution of offenses—over half were not known to have committed even one crime after being released from prison, but the other half committed at least nineteen per person per year.[20] Once again, more evidence that incapacitation makes a difference to society, at least if it is directed at the right offenders.

"Selective" Versus "Collective" Incapacitation

The initial response to the view of the Shinnars was not only that they exaggerated the number of crimes being committed by active, serious offenders, but that they neglected the great cost of reducing the crime rate by locking up a larger fraction of these offenders or by keeping those already inside locked up for longer periods of time. The argument that the Shinnars had greatly exaggerated individual crime rates was eventually disproved, as we have seen. But the argument about cost remained. Even the Shinnars admitted that if New York State were to follow their recommendations and send every convicted mugger and robber to prison for five years, the state would have to find prison space for an estimated forty to sixty thousand persons convicted of these "safety" crimes.[21] But as of 1970, only five years before the Shinnars published their study, New York State was incarcerating only nine thousand persons for having committed a violent crime or burglary and was holding in prison only a little over twelve thousand persons for all felonies combined.[22] Thus, to accommodate the Shinnars' plan, the space available for persons convicted of violent crimes and burglary would have to be increased (at a minimum) four-fold.

Joan Petersilia and Peter Greenwood, both members of the Rand group, also came to the conclusion that reducing crime by a significant amount through longer prison terms would be very costly. They analyzed the arrest records of 625 persons convicted in Denver, Colorado, of serious crimes between 1968 and 1970. Instead of estimating the effect of differing sentencing policies on a large group of offenders whose individual behavior was unknown, they looked at the actual arrest record of each person individually and asked whether a particular sentencing policy (say, a three-year mandatory minimum) would have led to the imprisonment of the offender for his last offense and thereby have prevented the offense from being committed. Knowing this, they could then calculate how many additional persons would have to be sent to prison. Their analysis suggested that incapacitation works, but at a price. If every person convicted of a felony received a five-year prison term, the number of felonies committed would drop by 45 percent but the size of the prison population would increase by 450 percent. If the mandatory five-year term were reserved for repeat offenders, such as convicted felons who had previously been convicted of a felony, then the crime rate would drop by 18 percent and the prison population would increase by 190 percent.[23]

These conclusions about the cost of achieving large crime reductions through incapacitation were sobering, but one finding was also puzzling. The Petersilia-Greenwood data clearly indicated that reserving the mandatory minimum sentence for repeat offenders would be no more advantageous—in terms of crimes prevented for a given increase in prison population—than if it were imposed on all convicted persons, including first-time offenders. At first blush, this seemed contrary to common sense. If recidivists commit a disproportionately large share of all serious crime, how can it be that locking them up for five years would cut the crime rate by a smaller fraction than would be achieved by locking up first-time offenders?

One explanation for the puzzle, suggested by Petersilia and Greenwood, was that most repeat offenders are already given prison terms by judges and so there is not much more to be gained by insuring that every repeat offender gets a long term.[24] But another possible explanation became clear to the Rand group as they studied the self-reports of prison inmates in three states. They learned from their survey that a small number of offenders have very high offense rates. Suppose that judges, in sentencing criminals, *do not know who the high rate offenders are* and thus give the longest sentences to persons who may not be the most serious criminals. Judges, we know, give the longest sentences to persons who are convicted for the most serious crimes and who have a long prior record.[25] That seems reasonable until one asks whether a person convicted of, say, robbery who has a prior conviction for a felony is any more likely to be a high-rate offender (that is, a frequent recidivist) than a person convicted of robbery who does not have a prior record.

It would seem plausible to assume that high-rate offenders have longer rap sheets than low-rate offenders. After all, a person who has committed a dozen robberies is more likely to get arrested and prosecuted than one who has committed his first stick-up. Judges make this assumption when they give longer sentences to a robber who has a prior conviction than to one who has been convicted for the first time. But we cannot be certain this assumption is correct, and researchers at Rand have found evidence that should make us question it.[26] In their study of California prison inmates, they learned that judges are more likely to send low-rate burglars to jail than to prison. Since jail terms ordinarily cannot exceed one year, this means that the low-rate burglars who wind up in jail will usually be serving shorter sentences than the high-rate ones who wind up in prison. So far, so good. But the match between rate of offending and the choice between jail or prison is not very close. For example, of the high-rate burglars, over half went to jail rather than to prison. Not only do most low-rate burglars get a break, so also do most high-rate ones. And if we look just at those offenders who are in prison, we find that the time they serve there bears little relationship to the rate at which they are offending while free on the street. In California, imprisoned low-rate robbers and imprisoned high-rate robbers serve almost identical sentences—about fifty months. Indeed, imprisoned low-rate burglars actually serve longer sentences (thirty months) than do imprisoned high-rate burglars (twenty months).[27]

The California study is one of the few of its kind, and we cannot be certain that the poor match it discovers between rate of offending and length of prison term would be true if the study looked at all robbers and burglars (and not just at those in prison) or looked more closely at the exact nature of the robberies and burglaries these persons committed (and not just at the number). But at the very least, the Rand data should force us to take a hard look at the relationship between official records (such as rap sheets) and actual offense rates.

Whatever the exact nature of that relationship, all the evidence we have implies that, for crime-reduction purposes, the most rational way to use the incapacitative powers of our prisons would be to do so selectively. Instead of longer sentences for everyone, or for persons who have prior records, or for persons whose present crime is especially grave, longer sentences would be given primarily to those who, when free, commit the most crimes. Exactly the same conclusion was reached by Brian Forst and his colleagues who studied the careers of criminals in the federal system.[28]

But how do we know who these high-rate, repeat criminals are? Knowing the nature of the present offense is not a good clue. The reason for this is quite simple— most street criminals do not specialize. Today's robber can be tomorrow's burglar and the next day's car thief.[29] When the police happen to arrest him, the crime for which he is arrested is determined by a kind of lottery—he happened to be caught red-handed, or as the result of a tip, committing a particular crime that may or may not be the same as either his previous crime or his next one. If judges give sentences based entirely on the gravity of the present offense, then a high-rate offender may get off lightly because on this occasion he happened to be caught snatching a purse. The low-rate offender may get a long sentence because he was unlucky enough to be caught robbing a liquor store with a gun.

Prosecutors have an understandable tendency to throw the book at persons caught committing a serious crime, especially if they have been caught before. To a certain extent, we want to encourage that tendency. After all, we not only want to reduce crime, we want to see criminals get their just deserts. Society would not, and should not, tolerate a system in which a prosecutor throws the book at purse snatchers and lets armed robbers off with a suspended sentence. But while society's legitimate desire for retribution must set the outer bounds of any sentencing policy, there is still room for flexibility within those bounds. We can, for example, act so that all robbers are punished with prison terms, but give, within certain relatively narrow ranges, longer sentences to those robbers who commit the most crimes.

If knowing the nature of the present offense and even knowing the prior record of the offender are not accurate guides to identifying high-rate offenders, what is? Obviously, we cannot ask the offenders. They may cooperate with researchers once in jail, but they have little incentive to cooperate with prosecutors before they go to jail, especially if the price of cooperation is to get a tougher sentence. But we can see what legally admissible, objective attributes, of the offenders best predict who is and who is not a high-rate offender. In the Rand study, Greenwood and his colleagues discovered, by trial and error, that the following seven factors, taken together, were highly predictive of a convicted person being a high-rate offender: he (1) was convicted of a crime while a juvenile (that is, before age sixteen), (2) used illegal drugs as a juvenile, (3) used illegal drugs during the previous two years, (4) was employed less than 50 percent of the time during the previous two years, (5) served time in a juvenile facility, (6) was incarcerated in prison more than 50 percent of the previous two years, and (7) was previously convicted for the present offense.

Using this scale, Greenwood found that 82 percent of those predicted to be low-rate offenders in fact were, and 82 percent of those predicted to be medium- or high-rate offenders also were. To understand how big these differences are, the median California prison inmate who is predicted to be a low-rate offender will in fact commit slightly more than one burglary and slightly less than one robbery per year free. By contrast, the median California inmate who is predicted to be a high-rate offender will commit ninety-three burglaries and thirteen robberies per year free. In other states, this prediction scale may be more or less accurate.

A similar, though not identical, scale was developed by Brian Forst and William Rhodes at INSLAW and was based on their study of federal offenders. High-rate offenders (what they call "career criminals") are likely to be those who are young, who use heroin sometimes and who use alcohol heavily, who have a long criminal career (and thus who started in crime at an early age), who have served a long prison term, and whose present offense involves violence. Applying this scale to federal offenders whom they followed for five years, Forst and his associates found that 85 percent of those predicted to be career criminals were in fact rearrested, most of them within twelve months; only 36 percent of those not predicted to be high-rate offenders were rearrested.[30]

Opinions differ as to the effect on the crime rate and prison population of making sentences for high-rate offenders longer than those for low-rate ones. Greenwood applied his scale to California and found that if all low-rate robbers received two-year prison terms (most now receive longer ones) and all high-rate robbers received seven-year terms (most now receive shorter ones), the number of robberies committed in the state would drop by an estimated 20 percent with no increase in the prison population.[31] In a state such as Texas, which already has a tough sentencing policy, the gain from shifting to this more selective approach would be less.

Even at Rand, colleagues of Greenwood disagree about the policy implications of the fact, which they do not dispute, that a handful of high-rate offenders is responsible for much crime. Jan and Marcia Chaiken argue that while the factors Greenwood uses enable him to identify that *group* of offenders who are especially dangerous, they will lead to substantial errors when they are used to identify any *individual* as a high-rate offender, especially if the identification must rely only on that information currently available in official records.[32] In a forthcoming review of this and related issues, a group at Harvard headed by Susan Estrich, Mark H. Moore, and Daniel McGillis argues that it would be better to improve the ability of police and prosecutors to identify and arrest high-rate offenders than to improve the ability of judges to sentence convicted offenders; indeed, if we solved more crimes, the judges would have more reliable official information about who the dangerous offenders really are and therefore could more effectively apply their existing rules of thumb in choosing sentences. I am skeptical that we can much improve our ability to solve crimes and so I doubt that this strategy will make sentencing decisions any easier. Judges now incarcerate selectively and always will; the central question is whether we can improve on the basis for that selectivity. Further research may well overcome some of the problems in the Greenwood scale. And in the meantime, Greenwood and the Chaikens agree that we can now identify the low-rate offenders with substantial accuracy. At a minimum, we can do a better job of keeping sentences for these persons short so as not to consume scarce prison space needed for those persons whose behavior is morally more repugnant or statistically more risky.

Some Policy Issues

Obviously, a policy of reducing crime by selective incapacitation (that is, by adjusting prison terms to reflect predicted individual offense rates) raises a number of issues. Though these issues are important, one must bear in mind that they cannot be resolved by comparing selective incapacitation to some ideal system of criminal justice in which everyone receives exactly his just deserts. No such system exists or ever will. One must compare instead the proposed policy with what exists now, with all its imperfections, and ask whether the gains in crime reduction are worth the risks entailed when we try to make predictions about human behavior.

The first issue is whether it is permissible to allow crime-control to be an objective of sentencing policy. Some persons, such as Andrew von Hirsch, claim that only retribution—what he calls "just deserts"—can be a legitimate basis for sentencing.[33] To some extent, he is undoubtedly correct. Even if we were absolutely certain that a convicted murderer would never murder again, we would still feel obliged to impose a relatively severe sentence in order to vindicate the principle that life is dear and may not be unlawfully taken without paying a price. Moreover, the sentences given low-rate offenders must reflect society's judgment as to the moral blame such behavior deserves, and the sentences given high-rate offenders ought not exceed what society feels is the highest sentence appropriate to the crime for which the offenders were convicted. And low-rate offenders should get a sufficiently severe sentence to help persuade them, and others like them, not to become high-rate offenders. Still, after allowing for all of these considerations, there will inevitably remain a range of possible sentences within which the goal of incapacitation can be served. The range will exist in part because there is no objective way to convert a desire for retribution into a precise sentence for a given offense and in part because legislatures will almost invariably act so as to preserve some judicial discretion so that the circumstances of a case which cannot be anticipated in advance may affect the sentence. Among those circumstances is a concern for protecting society from the threat that a given offender represents.

The second issue is whether our prediction methods are good enough to allow them to influence sentence length. The answer to that question depends on what one will accept as "good enough." Absolute certainty will never be attainable. Moreover, criminal justice *now*, at almost every stage, operates by trying to predict future behavior. When a prosecutor decides how much plea bargaining he will allow, he is trying to predict how a judge or jury will react to his evidence, and he is often trying to guess how dangerous an offender he has in his grasp. When a judge sets bail, he is always making a prediction about the likelihood of a person out on bail showing up for his trial and is frequently trying to predict whether the person, if out on bail, will commit another crime while free. When a defense attorney argues in favor of his client being released on his own recognizance, without bail, he is trying to persuade the judge to accept his prediction that the accused will not skip town. When the judge passes a sentence, he is trying, at least in part, to predict whether the convicted person represents a future threat to society. When a parole board considers a convict's application for early release, it tries to predict—often on the basis of a quantitative system, called a "base expectancy table"—whether the person will become a recidivist if released. Virtually every member of the criminal justice system is routinely engaged in predicting behavior, often on the basis of very scant knowledge and quite dubious rules of thumb. The question, therefore, is this: are the kinds of predictions that scholars such as Greenwood and Forst make about future criminality better (more accurate) and thus fairer than the predictions prosecutors and judges now make?

A third issue is tougher. Is it fair for a low-rate offender who is caught committing a serious crime to serve a shorter sentence (because he is not much of a threat to society) than a high-rate offender who gets caught committing a relatively minor offense? Probably not. Sentences would have to have legal boundaries set so that the use of selective incapacitation could not lead to perverse sentences—armed robbers getting one year, purse-snatchers getting five. Since, to the best of my knowledge, selective incapacitation has never been made the explicit basis of a state sentencing policy, we cannot be certain how manageable this problem of reconciling justice and crime control will be.

Finally, there is bound to be a debate about the legal and even ethical propriety of using certain facts as the basis for making predictions. Everyone would agree that race should not be a factor; everyone would probably agree that prior record should be a factor. I certainly believe that it is proper to take into account an offender's juvenile as well as his adult record, but I am aware that some people disagree. But can one take into account alcohol or drug use? Suppose the person claims to be cured of his drinking or his drug problem; do we believe him? And if we do, do we wipe the slate clean of information about these matters? And should we penalize more heavily persons who are chronically unemployed, even if unemployment is a good predictor of recidivism? Some people will argue that this is tantamount to making unemployment a crime, though I think that overstates the matter. After all, advocates of pretrial release of arrested persons, lenient bail policies, and diverting offenders away from jail do not hesitate to claim that having a good employment record should be counted in the accused's favor. If employment counts in favor of some, then obviously unemployment may be counted against others. Since advocates of "bail reform" are also frequent opponents of incapacitation, selective or collective, it is incumbent on them to straighten out their own thinking on how we make use of employment records. Nonetheless, this important issue deserves thoughtful attention.

On one matter, critics of prison may take heart. If Greenwood and the others are correct, then an advantage of selective incapacitation is that it can be accomplished without great increases (or perhaps any increases) in the use of prisons. It is a way of allocating more rationally the existing stock of prison cells to produce, within the constraints of just deserts, greater crime-control benefits. Many offenders—indeed most offenders—would probably have their sentences shortened, and the space thereby freed would be allocated to the small number of high-rate offenders whom even the most determined opponents of prison would probably concede should be behind bars.

They ought to take heart, but not too much heart. The estimates of the crime-reduction effect of selective incapacitation are based on a static world—a fixed number of criminals committing a predictable number of crimes. But crimes rates have been increasing since the early 1960s and no sharp, lasting downward trend is yet in evidence. Moreover, states such as California, though they have experienced greatly increased prison populations, still make much less use of prison than does, say, Texas, so that in California a significant number of offenders, perhaps serious ones, are not confined at all.

Even if the recent modest decline in crime rates were to continue, the number of persons in prison would probably increase for the next several years. This is because a decline in crime rates would likely reflect, at least in part, a decline in the number of young males in the population. But young males are less likely to go to prison than older males, in large measure because of the tendency of judges to defer a sentence to prison until the offender has acquired a lengthy criminal record—which means until he has become older. This tendency is especially marked in those places where judges in adult courts do not see, or are not influenced by, the juvenile record of adult offenders. Thus, the peak in commitments to prison will occur some years after the peak in crime rates. Moreover, the size of prison populations is determined not only by the number of new commitments, but by the length of the sentence of persons in prison. Those sentences have not been getting shorter of late. (Ironically, they have not got much longer, either, despite the fact that a growing fraction of the persons in prison have committed violent or other serious offenses.[34]) Combining all these factors, Alfred Blumstein and his colleagues at Carnegie-Mellon University, using Pennsylvania data, predict that prison populations in that state will not reach their peak until 1990, and perhaps later.[35]

If one adds to all this the extreme level of overcrowding now characteristic of many state prisons, the case for prison construction becomes very strong. One can moderate this need to a degree by shortening some of the very longest sentences, but no one has yet calculated how large a gain in prison space such sentence shortening would produce. And if one believes that deterrence works . . . then one may wish to see a larger fraction of convicted offenders get some prison term, even if just a short one. None of this is to deny that real opportunities exist for exploiting nonprison methods of handling the nonviolent, less serious offender—restitution, community service, intensive probation, halfway houses, and the like. But even after making the largest possible allowance for such commendable methods, it is hard to escape the realization that, however selectively we set the sentences for robbers and burglars, the need to accommodate a rising level of new commitments and to relieve present overcrowding and the bestiality that so often accompanies it, new facilities will be needed.

Some persons find prison construction undesirable because they think prisons are deplorable. Such sentiments are sometimes organized into movements designed to place a moratorium on prison construction. It is never clear what alternative such persons would suggest. As of November, 1979, well over half (58 percent) of all state inmates were imprisoned for a violent offense, 14 percent for murder alone. Only 7 percent were in prison because of drug offenses. Of the one-third who were serving time for nonviolent property crimes, over half were burglars.[36] Who among these prisoners should be released to relieve overcrowding and accommodate new commitments? And the number who would have to be released to eliminate overcrowding is very large, as can be inferred from the fact that, if one uses 60 square feet per prisoner as the standard, then 58 percent of all one-person cells and 90 percent of all two-person cells are overcrowded.[37] Vague talk about "alternatives to incarceration" is no substitute for a clear, quantitative estimate of how many persons can be diverted, safely, from prison and where these diverted persons are to go.

Indeed, much of the debate about incapacitation is not about its crime-reduction potential or the relationship between imprisonment and a social concern for appropriate retribution; it is rather about a set of diversionary arguments designed to make American penal policy look as bad as possible while sidestepping any serious confrontation with the hard policy choices.

One such argument is: "The United States already imprisons a larger proportion of its population than any other civilized nation, or at least any civilized nation outside the Soviet bloc." This is like disproving the need for hospitals by saying that the United States already hospitalizes a larger fraction of its population than any other nation. It implies that we are sending people to prison without any regard to the number of crimes committed (or sending them to hospitals without regard to whether they are sick). The proper question is whether we imprison a higher fraction of those arrested, prosecuted, and convicted than do other nations. No comprehensive international data exist on this subject, but such comparisons as do exist suggest that the argument that this country overimprisons is, to say the least, questionable. Kenneth I. Wolpin at Yale compared the probability of being convicted and imprisoned for various offenses in England and the United States. In the period 1961–1967, persons who were prosecuted for robbery in England were much more likely to be convicted than those prosecuted for that crime in the United States (about 79 percent were convicted in England, only 42 percent in this country). Of those convicted of robbery, a higher percentage (48 percent) were imprisoned in England than in the United States (31 percent). On the other hand, sentences for robbery tended to be longer in the United States.[38]

A second argument is: "Sending a person to prison costs more than sending a person to Harvard." God knows, Harvard is expensive enough. I am relieved to hear that something else costs more. But I assume that most parents send their children to college rather than to prison for reasons other than its being cheaper. Similarly, society sends criminals to prison rather than college, despite the fact that it costs more, because society believes it is getting something for its money from prison that it could not get from college: greater safety (temporarily), some prospect of deterrence, and the satisfaction of its desire for lawful retribution. I wish persons who point to the costs of prison as if that were a conclusive argument would apply that view consistently. For example: "It costs more to send children to Harvard than it would cost to send them to work in the coal mines." Or, "We cannot afford to send sick people to hospitals because it costs $50,000 (or whatever) per bed to build a hospital."

A third argument: "If we build more prisons, we will fill them up whether we need to or not."[39] Or put in other words, the size of our prison population is determined, not by the crime rate, but by the capacity of our prisons. A much-heralded study by Abt Associates in 1981 seemed to provide evidence to confirm this view. On the average, it claimed, new additions to prison capacity are filled to overflowing within two years after completion and filled past the level of overcrowding within five years.[40] The Panel on Sentencing Research of the National Research Council took a close look at the Abt findings and concluded that they were seriously in error. To use the council's words, the Abt study "provides no valid support for the capacity model."[41] Among the errors it discovered were computational mistakes, implausible assumptions, and a failure to look at the very different experiences of individual states (fifteen of which actually experienced decreases in their prison populations between 1971 and 1975).[42]

The problem of how best to manage our prison populations cannot, obviously, be left to such sloganeering. Neither can it be left to the whims of state legislators who find it politically irresistible to vote for tougher penalties for certain crimes but politically awkward to vote for the money to pay for the necessary additions to prisons or to allow new prisons to be built in their districts. It is possible to think sensibly about the uses of prison by asking what kinds of offenders should be sent to what kinds of facilities and for how long, by estimating carefully both the prison-capacity and crime-reduction implications of any proposed sentencing policy, and by avoiding the tendency to think that the best way to handle crime is always to impose the longest possible sentences.

Notes

1. "Prisons and Prisoners," Bureau of Justice Statistics *Bulletin*, January, 1982.
2. Ernest van den Haag, *Punishing Criminals* (New York: Basic Books, 1975), pp. 52–60.
3. Mark A. Peterson and Harriet B. Braiker, *Doing Crime: A Survey of California Prison Inmates* (Santa Monica, Calif.: Rand, 1980), pp. x, 50.
4. James Q. Wilson, *Thinking About Crime* (New York: Basic Books, 1975), p. 201; Shlomo and Reuel Shinnar, "The Effects of the Criminal Justice System on the Control of Crime: A Quantitative Approach," *Law and Society Review* 9 (1975): 581–611; Benjamin Avi-Itzhak and Reuel Shinnar, "Quantitative Models in Crime Control," *Journal of Criminal Justice* 1 (1973): 196–197.
5. David F. Greenberg, "The Incapacitative Effect of Imprisonment: Some Estimates," *Law and Society Review* 9 (1975): 566, 570.
6. Ibid., p. 572.
7. Stevens Clarke, "Getting 'Em Out of Circulation: Does Incarceration of Juvenile Offenders Reduce Crime?" *Journal of Criminal Law and Criminology* 67 (1974): 528–535.
8. Stephan Van Dine et al., "The Incapacitation of the Dangerous Offender: A Statistical Experiment," *Journal of Research in Crime and Delinquency* 14 (1977): 22–34.

9. Jacqueline Cohen, "The Incapacitative Effect of Imprisonment: A Critical Review of the Literature," in *Deterrence and Incapacitation: Estimating the Effects of Criminal Sanctions on Crime Rates*, ed. Alfred Blumstein et al. (Washington, D.C.: National Academy of Sciences, 1978), p. 201.
10. Ibid., p. 203.
11. Ibid., p. 206.
12. Barbara Boland, "Incapacitation of the Dangerous Offender: The Arithmetic is Not So Simple," *Journal of Research in Crime and Delinquency* 15 (1978): 126–129; Jan Palmer and John Salimbene, "The Incapacitation of the Dangerous Offender: A Second Look," *Journal of Research in Crime and Delinquency* 15 (1978): 130–134; P.M. Johnson, "The Role of Penal Quarantine in Reducing Violent Crime," *Crime and Delinquency* 24 (1978): 465–485.
13. S. Van Dine et al., "Response to Our Critics," *Journal of Research in Crime and Delinquency* 15 (1978): 135–139; Stephan Van Dine et al., *Restraining the Wicked: The Dangerous Offender Project* (Lexington, Mass.: Lexington/D.C. Heath, 1979).
14. Cohen, "The Incapacitative Effect of Imprisonment," p. 206.
15. Alfred Blumstein and Jacqueline Cohen, "Estimation of Individual Crime Rates From Arrest Records," *Journal of Criminal*

Law and Criminology 70 (1979): 585.

16. Peterson and Braiker, *Doing Crime*, pp. vii, 32.

17. Ibid., p. 35.

18. Peter W. Greenwood, *Selective Incapacitation* (Santa Monica, Calif.: Rand, 1982), pp. 43–44.

19. Ibid., p. 46.

20. Brian Forst et al., "Targeting Federal Resources on Recidivists," Final Report of the Federal Career Criminal Research Project (Washington, D.C.: INSLAW, 1982), pp. 18–19.

21. Shinnar and Shinnar, "The Effects of the Criminal Justice System," pp. 605–606.

22. Cohen, "The Incapacitative Effect of Imprisonment," p. 218.

23. Joan Petersilia and Peter W. Greenwood, "Mandatory Prison Sentences: Their Projected Effects on Crime and Prison Populations," *Journal of Criminal Law and Criminology* 69 (1978): 604–615.

24. Ibid., p. 615.

25. For a survey of such findings, see *Research on Sentencing: The Search for Reform*, a report of the Panel on Sentencing Research of the National Research Council (Washington, D.C.: National Academy Press, 1983), chap. 2.

26. Greenwood, *Selective Incapacitation*, pp. 52–53.

27. Ibid., p. 99.

28. Forst et al., "Targeting Federal Resources."

29. Blumstein and Cohen, "Estimation of Individual Crime Rates," p. 581; Peterson and Braiker, *Doing Crime*, p. 40; Marvin Wolfgang et al., *Delinquency in a Birth Cohort* (Chicago: University of Chicago Press, 1972), p. 206.

30. Forst, "Targeting Federal Resources."

31. Greenwood, *Selective Incapacitation*, Figure 5-2.

32. Jan M. Chaiken and Marcia R. Chaiken, *Varieties of Criminal Behavior* (Santa Monica, Calif.: Rand, 1982).

33. Andrew von Hirsch, *Doing Justice: The Choice of Punishments*, a report of the Committee for the Study of Incarceration (New York: Hill and Wang, 1976).

34. James Q. Wilson, "Who Is in Prison?" *Commentary* (November, 1976), p. 57.

35. Alfred Blumstein, Jacqueline Cohen, and Harold D. Miller, "Demographically Disaggregated Projections of Prison Populations," *Journal of Criminal Justice* 8 (1980): 22.

36. Bureau of Justice Statistics, "Prisons and Prisoners," in *Bulletin*.

37. Ibid.

38. Kenneth I. Wolpin, "An Economic Analysis of Crime and Punishment in England and Wales, 1894–1967," *Journal of Political Economy* 86 (1978): 819–820. See also James Q. Wilson, "Crime and Punishment in England," *The Public Interest* (Spring 1976): 18–19.

39. This argument, along with other, equally dubious ones, was put forward in William G. Nagel, *The New Red Barn: A Critical Look at the Modern Prison* (New York: Walker and Co., 1973).

40. Kenneth Carlson, *Population Trends and Projections*, vol. 2 of *American Prisons and Jails* (Washington, D.C.: National Institute of Justice, 1980), pp. 53–56, 173–186.

41. National Research Council, *Research on Sentencing: The Search for Reform*, chap. 5.

42. Alfred Blumstein, Jacqueline Cohen, and W. Gooding, "The Influence of Capacity on Prison Population: A Critical Review of Some Recent Evidence," *Crime and Delinquency*, forthcoming.

The New Idealism and Penal Living Standards

Herman Schwendinger and Julia Schwendinger

As the economic crisis deepens, the advocacy of punitive sanctions has become academically fashionable. Dusting off moth-eaten fables about the role of punishment in society, academic pundits have joined the law-and-order processions, chanting faithfully that only pain deters crime. "Without fear of punishment man would be a wolf to man!" they cry out to the public at large. Punishment brings order, peace and harmony; therefore, it is the only just method for dealing with crime—so it is proclaimed.

Cogent objections are hurled from the dissenting scholars watching these processions. Some protest the fixation on punishment because it undermines policies aimed at rehabilitating offenders and eliminating the causes of crime. Others are indignant because the rationalizations for greater punishment encourage overcrowded prisons and unbearable increases in prison budgets.

But the rationalizations for punishment are especially objectionable in light of prevailing standards of prison life. Imprisonment, after all, transcends the mere denial of individual liberty. It represents the deprivation of living standards or even the extinction of life itself. Further, as we have indicated in another article, "Standards of Living in Penal Institutions," prisons are class institutions whose social orders are constrained by commodity relationships and bourgeois norms. Because of these constraints, penal practices converge on marginal members of the labor force and standards of living in prison are generally set below the average levels for free marginals. In this context, a classical approach to punishment based on the principle of *least eligibility* prevails, and social, political, cultural and economic deprivations are ideologically equated with "fundamentally fair" punishments.[1]

Recent statements by the defenders of the Texas Correctional Department provide an ironic illustration of the principle of least eligibility. In a civil suit against the Department, prisoners detailed the agony, violence and overcrowding in the

Source: Herman Schwendinger and Julia Schwendinger, "The New Idealism and Penal Living Standards," *Crime and Social Justice*, No. 13 (Summer 1980), pp. 45–51. Reprinted by permission from *Crime and Social Justice*, P.O. Box 40601, San Francisco, CA 94140.

prisons. They spoke endlessly about slave conditions in the prison workshops and farms, the unclean hospitals and unqualified medical personnel, and the brutal assaults by guards. Nevertheless, in defense of the Department, the Assistant State Attorney General reportedly said that not only are the living conditions in the state's prisons better than in some impoverished areas of southern Texas, but inmates are safer inside than they might be outside in the barrios of Houston and San Antonio.[2] By implication, Texas prisons are beneficent institutions. They accommodate offenders whose standards of life outside do not even make them eligible for the conditions of life inside.

The logical force of the Assistant State Attorney General's remarks takes the classical principle of least eligibility for granted. So, too, is this principle taken for granted by criminologists who favor the new "realism"[3] in crime control but who conveniently ignore the reasons why *"just deserts,"* however it may be defined, becomes "cruel and inhuman punishment" in practice.

The conditions in American prisons cry out against this principle, and its taken-for-granted universe of discourse. These *lawless* prison conditions also mock the advocates of more Draconian penal practices and their claim that such "just measures of pain" are necessary for an *orderly* society. Social justice at a minimum calls for policies that will *not* increase crime and that will *not* encourage further deterioration of the standards of life for marginal members of the labor force in prison or in society at large.

An inquiry into humanist crime control strategies as well as those of the neo-conservatives is the topic of this essay.

New Ideologists for an Old Punishment

Thanks to Clarence Schrag (1977), it is now recognized that the representatives of the neo-conservative trend differ in detail among themselves and that their fundamental assumptions are veiled by rhetoric and disclaimers. Nevertheless, their basic axioms can be expressed in three sentences: Punishment is necessary because it alone will *deter* crime. Punishment is the only *just* method, because it is absolutely deserved by offenders. To deter crime fairly, the administration of punishment must become the *paramount function* of the criminal justice system.

This punitive function is used as the overriding measure of efficiency. Courts, for instance, are deemed inefficient when they concentrate on matters that do not make punishment certain. Courts are said to be overly concerned with civil liberties and the determination of guilt; therefore, they do not focus on sentencing offenders and too many criminals escape punishment.

Furthermore, penal practices that do not punish offenders are severely criticized. In this view, rehabilitation programs waste state funds. They are usually not punitive and they reportedly do not reduce recidivism. Social reforms are also considered worthless because they allegedly do not deter crime. And the social theorizing that justifies such reforms is discredited for the same reasons. Thus, representatives of the punitive trend, such as James Q. Wilson (1976), call for the virtual abandonment of social theories of crime, since theorizing about root causes cannot supply an adequate basis for social policy. In place of these theories he offers the worldly wisdom of utilitarianism. Wilson writes, "The radical individualism of Bentham and Beccaria may be scientifically questionable but prudently necessary."

The empirical claims and policy conclusions, indicated above, are composed of half-truths, stereotypes and reactionary principles. Apparently, the contradictions between the classical bourgeois conception of punishment and the empirical study of penal practices have moved the field beyond the point where any genuine scientific justification for more punitive policies can be developed. Moreover, though the representatives of this punitive trend may be influential in government, they are truly Kafkaesque in their crackpot realism. They insist that their social policies are realistic and prudent even though their theories are wrong and their policies bound to fail.

Pursuit of the neo-conservative recommendations will have little or no effect on crime but it may reinforce police-state tendencies. Indeed, given the continued crisis conditions, the implementation of their punitive policies will contribute to the higher incidence of violence in certain economic crimes. Given the socioeconomic laws that determine the real conditions of existence in most American prisons, their doctrines and policies will reinforce the class pressures that maintain substandard conditions, brutality and crime inside the prisons.

On the other hand, the weighty conclusions above cannot be applied with equal force to every ideological representative of the punitive trend in crime control. Among these representatives there are adherents of a "justice model" who, in addition to a similar view of punishment, advocate fairness in prison management through prisoner self-government, legal aid, ombudsman services for conflict resolution, and "flat time" rather than indeterminate sentences. The justice modelers also call for the demolition of the fortress prison, frequently blamed for the inequities of the American prison system. Exponents of this trend recommend construction of smaller prisons that segregate prisoners with similar classifications. Furthermore, although another "justice" feature proposes that prisons merely execute sentences and not attempt to rehabilitate offenders, the sentence itself should involve deprivation of liberty and not the denial of other rights accorded free citizens (Fogel, 1975:202).

This genuine concern for the rights accorded free citizens echoes demands of the prisoners' movements and their supporters outside prisons. But, since no adequate theory about the nature of penal practices is advanced by the developers of the justice model, it hardly surpasses the demands of the movements themselves. The recommendations of the justice model merely take their place in the long list of denied prisoner rights. Even the principles for determining the relative priority of each right are nowhere explicitly addressed. Consequently, as is frequently the case with such lists, the dominant instrumentalities, such as legislatures and administrative authorities, are left to determine what kinds of rights under prevailing circumstances are to be implemented and what kinds are to be ignored.

Although criminologists have adopted the rhetoric of prisoners' rights originating in the prisoners' movements and their supporters outside, they do not necessarily perceive the movements as crucial for the development of these rights. To the contrary, they explicitly regard prisoners as somewhat passive "consumers," who have needs for personal dignity, medical care, etc., which can be met by "state services" advised by planning experts.

Inevitably, in this formulation, legislative mandates and administrative rules are considered the main mechanisms for implementing the standards of equity suggested as rational grounds for prison policies. For instance, the exponents of the justice model contend that "the lawless life" among prisoners can be subjected to the "rule of law" and that the "wanton" and "discriminatory" "anomie of sentencing and paroling" can be eliminated by legislation. Hence, courts should function with the aid of tighter rules and more uniform procedures; plea bargaining and parole boards should be replaced by a strict adherence to written laws and mandatory sentences. "In the quest for fairness," one representative of this legalistic trend states, "we seek justifications in the law for the decisions of those who exercise wide discretion" (Fogel, 1975:189).

Several fundamental flaws underlie this legalistic point of view. Despite the rhetoric of prisoners' rights and the imagery of the planning expert, the justice model plays into the hands of conservative intellectuals who also believe that, in addition to curbing abuses of power, procedural rules will create a harmonious and well-integrated justice system. To accomplish this agreeable aim, the justice model shuns any fundamental change in structural and administrative relations; it fixates, instead, on the control over discretionary behavior of lesser state functionaries and workers. In the past, this discretionary behavior often escalated rather than ameliorated prison protests and uprisings. Consequently, the justice model provides administrative guidelines for higher political functionaries who focus on the control of the same discretionary behavior rather than basic change to prevent repetition of the massive prison protests in the 1960's and early 1970's.

Such political realities emphasize the technocratic utopianism that underlies the class-neutral planning image of the justice model and its rhetoric of prisoners' rights. The model incorrectly assumes that legality alone, in the absence of class struggle, will establish a noncontradictory correspondence between an integrated system of administrative rules and an ethical system of penal practices. It is assumed that such rules can actually create a just society behind bars. Inmates will neither be rehabilitated nor deterred but removed from society and punished in a manner that is harmonious with democratic norms.

Neo-Idealism and the Contemporary Crisis

The justice model subscribes to an idealistic metaphysics about the nature and function of punishment in law—a metaphysics which is shared by all the academic representatives of the punitive trend. As indicated, these academics repeatedly refer to the fundamental fairness of punishment and its utility for deterrence. The principle of fairness (or "just deserts") calls for graded punishments whose severity conforms with the crimes committed; consequently, "fairness" implies the legitimacy of retribution where punishment fits the crime.

The common legal and philosophical antecedents of the punitive trend can be noted and a classification can be suggested. Underlying these justifications for punishment is the idealism of the classical liberal perspective toward law. Based on a mixture of utilitarianism (e.g., Beccaria) and German idealism (e.g., Kant), this form of idealism emerged toward the end of the mercantile period and in the transition to industrial capitalism. Reflecting the main demand of the bourgeoisie with regard to criminal law, bourgeois intellectuals at that time proposed the formulation of "precise calculable standards of conduct" based on "legality at all costs on one side, [and] retribution and nothing but retribution on the other" (Rusche and Kirchheimer, 1968: 102). Although eclecticism prevails today, some academic representatives of the punitive trend favor utilitarianism while others are more inclined to German idealism. Fairness, for example, often bows to Kant's logic of punishment and not to Beccaria's utilitarianism. Van den Haag (1975:183) says, "Even if nobody needs to be deterred . . . punishment must be inflicted for the sake of justice because it is deserved." Nevertheless, the punishment advocates as a group more or less update the idealist program implicit in the classical approaches to law, and therefore it is fitting to see them all as *neo-idealists*. As indicated earlier, they are also called "realists"—a term hinting at genuine accomplishment; but, in our opinion, "neo-idealist" is a more historically correct classification.

The programmatic aims associated with this neo-idealism rest ostensibly on an objective calculus of punishments concentrating on the act and not the person of the wrongdoer. Moreover, supposedly, an accurate determination of punishment in proportion to the damage inflicted can be applied, in principle, to everyone. Thus, since they are based on the classical theory of law, the neo-idealist policies (e.g., "flat time," mandatory sentences and "swift and certain punishments") presumably transcend "particularistic," "arbitrary" and "subjective" judgments that are influenced by class, racial, sexual, bureaucratic and other factors.

However, while classical liberals legitimated significant reforms in criminal law, they never created a system of justice based on abstract principles independent of class factors. In fact, in light of the dialectic of legal repression discussed in our previous article, their theories simply legitimated as "retribution" and "deterrence" the use of prison sentences and prison labor (as opposed to torture and mutilation, for example) under *developing capitalist* conditions. They thereby tacitly legitimated qualitatively distinct sets of rules being applied to different social classes and used by officials to govern the varying forms of class conduct. Thus, since their theories veiled the class differentiations in and the structural determination of penal practices, they reinforced the bourgeois hypocrisy that continues to permeate the justice system. Today, the same shortcomings apply to programmatic statements by neo-idealists. Consequently, their principles for devising an *equitable* calculus of punishments (e.g., "flat time," etc.) cannot be taken at face value.

Furthermore, the motives expressed by neo-idealists cannot accurately inform us about the outcomes of their policies. Original proponents of the justice model, for instance, felt that rehabilitation programs, rather than being eliminated altogether, should be restricted and made voluntary and thus not imposed on prisoners. Nevertheless, whatever the expressed qualifications, the justice model now also justifies objectively retrogressive outcomes because of its insistence that social policies give priority to punishment rather than rehabilitation. Punishment, as we have seen, is classically associated with deprivation of living standards. Rehabilitation, on the other hand, has served as the master symbol in bourgeois ideology that legitimated innumerable reformist struggles against this deprivation. By discrediting rehabilitation as a basic principle of penal practice, the justice modelers have undermined their own support for better standards of living in penal institutions.

In addition, this undermining effect is taking place at a time when prison standards are being directly threatened nationally by political developments during a period of sustained economic crisis. Throughout our country, there is intensified competition for state funds. Agriculture, multinational, small business and regional interests are demanding state subsidies, investments, tax credits, etc., to spur capital accumulation and/or prevent deterioration of their market positions. Such demands—in the relative absence of pressure from politically developed working class movements—are forcing general readjustments in state policies that align state expenditures more closely with capital and, in particular, with monopoly capital.

This alignment does not necessarily lower state expenditures even though it encourages "cost-cutting" where the growth of capital is not affected. Thus, it stimulates social policies that warehouse prisoners as cheaply as possible. But it also supports expenditures for the expansion of the criminal justice system, up to and including the construction of new prison facilities. Such expenditures, among other things, are aimed at safeguarding capital and the state from the social and political instabilities caused by crisis conditions. Under these conditions, reformist strategies for ameliorating substandard living conditions in prison are given even less priority in favor of strategies that contribute to the growth of capital.

On the other hand, using the notion of rehabilitation has severe limitations, because it explicitly justifies better living standards only when they contribute to lower recidivism. Within bourgeois ideology, therefore, both rehabilitation and punishment, among other things, symbolize practices that aim at deterring crimes by manipulating living standards of individuals. Generally, in this context, rehabilitation is associated with better standards. However, as operant conditioning programs sometimes testify, rehabilitation programs based on the calculated manipulation of living standards downward[4] as well as upward are still favored today. The supportive relations between rehabilitation and human rights are therefore ambiguous and by no means assured. This ambiguity underscores the importance of articulating the struggle for better standards in different terms.

For this reason it is vital to distinguish the principle of individual and collective rights of prisoners apart from the principle of rehabilitation which has been developed by bourgeois professionals and reformers. Programs that implement the right to education and the right to work at decent wages may be rehabilitative but such programs should be justified primarily on the basis of elemental rights for prisoners. Thus, ideological struggles for prison reform should adopt the vocabulary of citizens' rights and human rights rather than that of the rehabilitative ideal.

Structural Reforms

Since prisoners' rights can be supported by law, it cannot be inferred from our criticism of neo-idealism that we are totally negating the positive role of legal avenues in prison reform. Certainly legal means of ameliorating the brutal standards of life in prison are available. Current court decisions, however, demonstrate that legality has limits unless it is propelled by popular struggles. Consequently, the most important strategic reforms in penal practices, at the very least, call for significant shifts in power relations in particular directions within prisons. These shifts require the combined efforts of prisoners' unions, prisoners' political organizations, working class movements and other groups outside.

Discussion of such shifts at this particular period in time may seem utopian because of the conservative climate in our society. Also, to discuss strategies for change in a speculative fashion undoubtedly reinforces such an impression. However, whether they can work is an empirical question that cannot be swept aside legitimately. This is especially true in light of the fact that no other social policies offered by criminologists will significantly alter prison life for the better.

The forces that propel prison standards upwards are not simply composed of social movements and prison reformers. As indicated, prison standards are generally tied to standards of living in the political economy and when these standards rise, one can expect social pressure to improve prison conditions. Yet it must also be kept in mind that standards of life for marginals outside diminish during economic crises and consequently prison standards too can move downward. Generally, the post-World War II years witnessed upward movements in standards of life, an expanding job market that made rehabilitative programs in prisons attractive, and probation and parole became viable alternatives to prisons. Today, socioeconomic patterns have changed for the worse and even though probation and parole are strongly maintained, this is so partly because they are less expensive than imprisonization.

Prisoners are now being herded into prisons in larger numbers and the correlation between unemployment and imprisonization alone suggests why this is happening. Also, as times grow hard, many people, viewing crime from a classical bourgeois standpoint, become mean-spirited. They emphasize punishment as the quick fix for the crime problem. The academic advocates of punitive policies are among this group and their antiquated justifications for punishment simply represent ideological reflexes of the same changing economic and political scene.

During these times, higher living standards generally cannot be achieved or maintained without struggle by working class organizations. Within the prisons, moreover, no general proposal for the expansion of prisoners' legal rights can be adequate without prisoners' unions and political organizations as the central working class agencies for implementing these rights. Legitimating the unions, for instance, will go further toward the realization of these rights than any technocratic fantasy about rules of equity and procedure instituted by legislative agencies and prison authorities alone.

But prisoners' unions and especially their more militant members face problems that are even more severe than the worst forms of repression against labor leaders prior to the passage of the National Labor Relations Act. Every legal and illegal means possible, including the use of informers, provocateurs, solitary confinement, "mail censorship, lockups, beatings, transfers, false disciplinary charges and prosecution, exclusion of press and visitors from the prisons" (Martin, 1976:53), become part of the repertoire of administrators and guards to destroy militant prisoner organizations. The same repressive measures are applied to prison political organizations. Here, the repressive measures already mentioned are extended to include assassination (e.g., George Jackson). Such measures are aimed particularly at the suppression of revolutionaries who threaten the preconditions for bourgeois-imposed prison order.

Since the early 1970's revolutionary movements have subsided; moreover, the systematic suppression of these movements has inevitably been accompanied by an increase in control over "inmate cultures" by lumpen-proletarian elements. This increase has been expressed by the vigorous renewal of gang violence based on racial hatreds and irregular economic activities. In a California prison, for instance, John Irwin (1977:34) reports, "The emergence of the [Chicano prisoner] Mafia and then La Familia was occurring when the attention of the administration was focused on political activities. This is not to say that they did nothing about the violence related to gang fights, but they remained more concerned about 'revolutionaries' and took more action against persons suspected of political activities. This had the consequence . . . of removing those persons who might have maintained alternative social structures and prevented the total dominance of gang violence."[5] Due to the same causal relationships, fairly similar developments occurred outside of prisons among the marginals in ghettos and slums. Here, official repression of radicals was also accompanied by the support of such organizations as the Blackstone Rangers, whose extortion and other crimes are a matter of record.

To curb criminal violence and support left-wing political movements in prison, some of the aforementioned proletarian rights, such as the right to organize and affiliate with prisoners' unions, to freely engage in political activities and join political parties, to strike and to bargain collectively, are strategically important. These can be secured by public pressure and legislative enactment. Not only are these rights important for their own sake, but they are also vital pre-conditions for a whole ensemble of human rights related to standards of living in prisons. It goes without saying that these rights cannot be safeguarded without firm administrative policies that punish any criminal conduct aimed against their implementation.

Also strategically important for prison reform are policies that safeguard interchanges between prisoners and working class movements and their allies. At present, interchanges with groups interested in social justice and willing to work with prisoner organizations, for example, are prevented by administrative policies that censor mail and visiting privileges. When interaction between prisoners and outside groups is allowed, it is usually based on relations with middle class liberal reform groups that support the bourgeois imposed-order in prison. In fact, the band-aid reforms recommended by such groups are, at times, a major source of legitimation for the maintenance of this kind of social order.

Prisoners' rights and organizations do not have to be justified by their effects on recidivism. They have their own justifications. On the other hand, prisoners' unions could counter recidivism by bargaining to alter present rehabilitation programs which primarily slot ex-offenders into unstable, low-paid, low status, secondary labor market jobs. Agitating with working class groups outside the prison for full employment would also indirectly reduce crime. Furthermore, some of the present rehabilitation programs might acquire greater effectiveness regarding recidivism if they were interfaced with working class movements as well as economic firms outside the prison. From the 1960's onward, ghetto working class movements such as the Black Panthers and the Young Lords emerged and inevitably opposed street crime, because these crimes victimized members of the great popular classes (marginal workers and their families, other working class factions, small shopkeepers, etc.). Just as crime control policies would more likely succeed if they were dynamically connected with progressive working class movements, certain rehabilitation programs (e.g., halfway houses, work furlough programs, etc.) would more likely succeed if they were linked to such movements. At present the integration is virtually impossible because of the implacable hostility against progressive groups by local, state and federal agencies and alternatively because of the distrust progressive groups hold toward the agencies. But the possibilities should be kept in mind because socialist experiences show that similar reforms work if they are carried out in a different framework.

Given the organizational preconditions in prisons for human rights and the supportive activity of working class movements and their allies, it would then be possible to introduce the participatory forms of prison government that might alleviate prison brutality and crime. For a partial documentation of the antecedents of such forms of government, see Thomas Murton (1976:189–225). Antecedents of such participatory governments also contradict the myths about the necessity of conventional custodial policies required for making prisoners and prisons secure.

Consider, for example, the role of the National Prisoners Reform Association (NPRA) in the Massachusetts maximum security prison at Walpole. Prior to 1973 the NPRA chapter at Walpole had demanded recognition as a labor union and bargaining agent for the prisoners. Rather than just meeting with legislators to plead for small reforms, the NPRA also sought to gain power over running the prison. "The NPRA backed up its demands with a strike so effective that the state was forced to have its license plates made by a commercial firm outside Massachusetts for two years."

Then, in 1973, the Walpole guards' union staged a two month strike of its own to counter the reforms won by the NPRA. At that time, Martin (1976:53) reports, ". . . Commissioner Boone, in his first real concession to prisoners, [had allowed] the NPRA and its outside supporters to run the prison and to conduct a citizen observer program. The observer program was an unprecedented example of community involvement in the prison: for nearly four months, hundreds of citizens working three shifts a day freely entered the prison to assist the NPRA. The observer program and the NPRA both came to an abrupt end when Governor Sargent yielded to public pressure from the guards' union, ordered the State Police to restore 'order' to the prison, and fired Commissioner Boone."

While community people and prisoners governed the prison, prison brutality and crime were reduced. After the state police restored "normal order" in prison, these characteristics resurged. In addition, the militants who had helped stabilize an alternative social order were put into 24-hour lockup under the most degrading and inhuman conditions. In 1976, after three years passed, they were still locked up.

The Massachusetts Department of Corrections then introduced complementary strategies for controlling those inmates whose consciousnesses had been heightened. The department prevented contact between prisoners and left-wing organizations. This repression was combined with increased relaxation of contacts with conservative business groups, churches, apolitical social service agencies and moderate liberal organizations that voluntarily remained within administrative norms. Such groups, Martin (1976:54) notes, might work for liberal legislation but they "would not consider organizing for brothers and sisters unjustifiably transferred or thrown into segregation."

While prison administrators suppressed militants, the development of moderate liberal prisoner organizations in Concord and Norfolk prisons was encouraged by bourgeois reform groups. Militants who emerged within these prisons were first isolated and then transferred to Walpole or Bridgewater prisons. Implicit in this latter control strategy were the practical consequences of liberal reforms based on recommendations for smaller prisons where populations are housed on the basis of similar types of offenders and offenses. One might also expect such prisons to be segmented by socioeconomic, racial and ideological gradients. Certainly if militant prisoners are grouped with the most violent prisoners, one can expect them to be exposed to the most exploitative and brutal modes of prison life—unless, of course, political events dictate otherwise.

Footnotes

1. The principle of "least eligibility" modifies and expands the concept of "less eligibility" which is advanced in relation to prisons by Rusche and Kirchheimer (1968). We prefer the phrase "least eligibility" because it distinguishes the prison population from people on welfare and it denotes a more comprehensive deprivation of social, cultural and political as well as economic standards of life.
2. See "Inmates Tell of Texas Brutality," *New York Times*, (November 11, 1978, Section A:8).
3. To understand the new "realists," see Tony Platt and Paul Takagi's (1977) excellent analysis.
4. Some of the rightful criticism of the "medical model" by prisoners' unions, radical criminologists and justice modelers refers to repression of individual rights at state prisons like Marion (Indiana) and elsewhere. Medical models developed especially by behavioral modification experts focus heavily on deprivation of living standards as punishment.
5. Joan Moore's (1978) new book, *Homeboys*, also provides very important insights on the development of Chicano gangs in California prisons.

References

Fogel, David
1968 We Are the Living Proof. Cincinnati: W.H. Anderson Co.
Irwin, John
1977 "The Social Structure of Corrections and Punishment."
Martin, Bob
1976 "The Massachusetts Correctional System: Treatment as Ideological Control." Crime and Social Justice 6 (Fall-Winter): 49–57.
Moore, Joan
1978 Homeboys. Philadelphia: Temple University Press.
Murton, Thomas
1976 The Dilemma of Prison Reform. New York: Holt, Rinehart and Winston.
New York Times
1978 "Inmates Tell of Texas Prison Brutality." November 11, Section A:8.
Platt, Tony and Paul Takagi
1977 "Intellectuals for Law and Order: A Critique of the New 'Realists'." Crime and Social Justice 8 (Fall-Winter):1–6.
Rusche, Georg and Otto Kirchheimer
1968 Punishment and Social Structure. New York: Russel and Russel.
Schrag, Clarence
1977 "Rediscovering Punitive Justice." Criminology 14 (February):569–73.
Schwendinger, Herman and Julia R. Schwendinger
1980 "Standards of Living in Penal Institutions." In David Greenberg (ed.), Crime and Capitalism. Palo Alto: Mayfield Press.
van den Haag, Ernest
1975 Punishing Criminals: Concerning a Very Old and Painful Question. New York: Basic Books.
Wilson, James Q.
1976 Thinking About Crime. New York: Basic Books.

PRIVATE PRISONS: PUNISHING-FOR-PROFIT **1**

Punishment for Profit

Kevin Krajick

Since some of Pennsylvania's worst delinquents are kept at the state training school at Weaversville, what you see upon first arriving on the grounds are mostly things you'd expect: the 12-foot-high, razor-ribbon-topped fences, the heavy mesh over the windows, the high-intensity lights outside. If you drive around the big two-story brick building that is the Weaversville Intensive Treatment Unit and park in the small asphalt lot out back, however, you can push through a propped-open door and walk up a flight of stairs before you come to the first locked steel door. There, at the top of the stairs, a small painting hangs on the wall that pictures a fox terrier sitting on his hind legs, one ear tilted attentively toward the bell of an old-fashioned phonograph horn. Sound familiar? It's the traditional logo of the RCA Company, of course. So, what's RCA got to do with Weaversville? Answer: RCA *runs* Weaversville. The state commits delinquents there, and the company makes a modest profit on the operation.

This little-known institution, which has been around for eight years, makes RCA a pioneer in a growing industry that could begin to take off this year: private prisons. Faced with record increases in the prisoner population, state and Federal administrators have become so beleaguered by overcrowding, bureaucratic delays, politics, lawsuits, and money shortages that they have begun turning to private enterprise to help them fill some of the ballooning demand for institutions. At the same time, a few pioneering corporations are trying to convince skeptics—and there are many—that they can do the job efficiently and humanely.

"The question is whether business is just going to run an outmoded and inhuman system more efficiently, or is going to bring some real improvements and new ideas," says Jerome Miller, a former corrections administrator and leading spokesman for institutional reform who runs the National Center on Institutions and Alternatives, a Virginia company that offers alternatives to prisons.

There are as yet only a few scattered private institutions. Their customers include the U.S. Bureau of Prisons, the Immigration and Naturalization Service, and the state of Florida. But negotiations are going on between companies and per-

Source: Kevin Krajick, "Punishment for Profit," *Across the Board* 21 (March 1984), pp. 20–27. Reprinted with permission from The Conference Board and the author.

haps a dozen state and local governments, and some companies hope to get into the business in a big way in the near future. Among them are Control Data, RCA, and some of the nation's largest industrial-security concerns.

"We're on the cutting edge of a whole new industry," says Travis Snellings, chief financial officer of the Corrections Corporation of America, a Nashville-based company that started business last June and recently landed its first contract.

There have been few private prisons since the 19th century, when some states shipped convicts to entrepreneurs, who used them as slaves on plantations and in factories. The terrible treatment that these prisoners received came to light during a wave of prison reform in the 1870s, and the states took back control of the institutions.

In the 1970s, the private sector entered the scene in a more beneficent role, providing a range of newly popular alternatives to prisons under contracts with governments. Companies set up thousands of halfway houses, drug-treatment programs, and group homes, most of them on a nonprofit basis. In some states, these companies have become permanent parts of the corrections system, and provide the majority of community programs. Lately, private enterprise, along with a few nonprofit organizations, has been taking an increasing role in the institutions, providing contract-medical, educational, and food services.

Necessity is the force behind the corporate prison movement. The total state and Federal prison population, now close to 450,000, has been growing at a record rate of 20 percent in the past 18 months. Local jails, with more than 200,000 inmates, have faced a similar deluge. Because of complex bureaucratic procedures and the unwillingness of politicians to spend enough money on new prisons, few agencies have been able to keep up with the increases. The result has been crowding, increasing institutional violence, deteriorating services, and countless lawsuits brought by inmates seeking to improve conditions. Many states and localities have recently come under court orders to unclog their institutions, and some have been forced to release inmates early to do it.

Enter the new corporate wardens, who say that with modern management techniques and private capital they can build institutions faster and run them more cheaply than can government. Unlike most of the 1,000-plus private halfway-house vendors, they are talking about punishment for profit. Considering that governments may spend as much as $10 billion this year on corrections, there seems to be great potential for profits.

RCA's Weaversville Unit, probably the first modern private detention institution, was opened in 1975. RCA took over the school soon after the Pennsylvania Attorney General informed corrections officials that they could no longer keep hard-core delinquents in state prisons. Unable to come up with a new facility right away, the officials turned for help to RCA, which was then contracting with the state to provide educational programs for delinquents. RCA set up Weaversville in a state-owned building in just 10 days and was rewarded with a contract to run it.

What does RCA get out of the deal? Probably the company makes no more than about $40,000 a year under its government contract. Thus the venture is as much a philanthropic and public-relations gesture as it is a business investment. Of course, the deal could backfire and the company could be hurt if some widely publicized act or scandal erupts at the school. So far, however, the school has brought only good press; it has remained uncontroversial and, according to juvenile-delinquency experts, is very well run.

In 1982, the state of Florida turned over the Okeechobee School for Boys, one of its three juvenile training schools, to the Jack and Ruth Eckerd Foundation. The foundation, financed by the fortunes of the Eckerd drugstore chain, had been running "wilderness-experience" programs for troubled children for several years but had never been involved with hard-core delinquents. Jack Eckerd, a powerful figure in Florida politics, first proposed the idea of the foundation running Okeechobee to Gov. Bob Graham. State officials, burdened with a large delinquent population and lacking money for programs, approved, hoping that Eckerd could do a better job than they were able to do. The Eckerd Foundation is a nonprofit enterprise, and officials of the organization say they took on the project as a public service. With about 400 residents, the Okeechobee School is the biggest privately run institution.

The Federal Government has recently signed contracts that will soon make it the biggest customer for private lockups. The largest demand comes from the Immigration and Naturalization Service (INS), which has captured a growing number of illegal aliens in recent years and locked them up pending deportation hearings. An average of 2,000 are now in detention on any given day; the majority are kept in INS-operated detention centers, or in local public jails that receive perdiem allowances from INS for each alien. A year ago, the agency also began contracting with Southwest Behavioral Systems, a California-based, for-profit halfway-house company, which now holds about 350 INS prisoners in converted motels surrounded with fences in San Diego and Pasadena, California, and in Denver, Colorado. The INS has also contracted with the Corrections Corporation of America to operate a detention center in Houston—the company's first contract. The firm is building its own $4 million, 300-bed facility, which was scheduled to open in February, at a charge to the INS of about $24 a day per prisoner.

The Federal Bureau of Prisons is about to award a contract for the largest private prison so far—a 575-bed medium-security prison, also for illegal aliens, to be situated somewhere in the Southwest. There are about 1,500 illegal aliens serving terms in the overcrowded Federal prisons for immigration offenses. William Garrison, a spokesman for the Bureau, explained the decision to contract for a private institution: "Rather than build our own institution for something that might be a temporary phenomenon, we decided not to take the risk. Besides, it takes two or three years for us to site and build a place. This is an immediate need, which the private sector has offered to fill. If at some point we don't need the place anymore, we can just terminate the contract." The contract proposal allows contractors to charge up to $45 a day per prisoner, which Garrison says will save the Bureau about 25 percent of what its own costs would be.

The Corrections Corporation of America (CCA) is one of the front-running bidders for the contract. The company was founded by Thomas Beasley, a 41-year-old entrepreneur and Tennessee Republican politician whose other businesses include real-estate and insurance ventures. CCA is backed with money from Nashville's Massey Burch Investment Group, the same firm that started the now giant Hospital Corporation of America. Beasley, who has no prison-management experience, has hired several well-connected former corrections officials, including T. Don Hutto, a former commissioner of corrections in both Arkansas and Virginia, and Maurice Sigler, retired chairman of the U.S. Parole Commission.

Beasley plans to run the Corrections Corporation's prisons much like the Hospital Corporation runs its hospitals—with large purchase orders and centralized accounting and management, and by hiring experienced professionals from public agencies to run the day-to-day affairs of the institutions.

Hutto says he can do the job more efficiently as a CCA vice president than as a public official. "Government is inherently wasteful," he said. "It has agencies on top of agencies overseeing everything, and complex political processes. You can spend two or three years and millions of dollars and still not have a prison. CCA, on the other hand, can build in a matter of months," he said. "We can also get better prices from contractors. Contractors always charge the government more money." Hutto points out that CCA is free to rapidly expand or reduce the number of its employees without being restricted by Civil Service rules, and that it can pay less than government agencies do by hiring nonunion help—practices that characterize the existing private institutions.

CCA officials say they are negotiating with about a dozen state, Federal, and local agencies for possible contracts, but Hutto would identify only a few of them, saying that the rest are "still in the more sensitive stages"—meaning that he doesn't want the competition to know where the action is.

He is probably right not to show his cards, for he has a number of energetic competitors who probably would like very much to see them. The Bureau of Prisons' request for bids on its alien prison has drawn a tremendous response, according to one high official, and some of the companies that have bid have little or no experience in working with offenders. Bids have come in from manufacturing firms, industrial-security companies, halfway-house companies and architectural concerns that have designed jails and prisons.

RCA has bid on the contract. "We plan to actively pursue this type of business using Weaversville as a model," said Al Androlewicz, an RCA vice president in charge of education and human services. "Weaversville was once viewed as a one-shot deal, but we see now that times are changing."

Control Data Corporation, a conglomerate that deals mainly in computers, also has been pursuing the prison business. In 1982, the company was one of a half-dozen bidders on a contract to run a women's prison for the state of Minnesota. Control Data raised $15 million to build and staff the institution, but state officials eventually backed down on the idea and decided to run the prison themselves. Company spokesmen say that Control Data is actively involved in proposals to run private prisons, but they will not discuss specific negotiations. Control Data now holds a large interest in City Ventures, a company that sells vocational-training programs to prison systems.

Efficient as these profit-making concerns may be, the institutions they run are bound to reflect to some extent the aims, the limitations, and perhaps the abuses of the government systems of which they become a part. Nothing demonstrates this more clearly than the contrasts between RCA's Weaversville School and the Eckerd Foundation's school in Okeechobee.

Weaversville is part of a relatively progressive juvenile system; Pennsylvania has made a commitment to running small, well-funded institutions, and to finding alternatives to institutions for as many youngsters as possible. There are about 180 delinquents in four secure facilities, the smallest of which is Weaversville, which houses an average of 20 inmates at a time. The state runs separate programs for retarded and severely disturbed juvenile offenders.

Because of its intimate scale, Weaversville hardly seems like an institution. Inside, it resembles a college dormitory. Unlike many juvenile institutions, it is clean, quiet, and relaxed.

In the lower story of the building, the residents have their own carpeted rooms, to which they have their own keys. Many of the rooms are plastered with rock-music posters, and some residents have their own stereos from home (there is only one television, in the dayroom, and use of that is limited).

The classrooms and conference rooms, where residents spend much of their time, are upstairs. Weaversville has more staff than residents—usually about 30, including teachers, psychologists, and caseworkers. Most of the residents are years behind in school, so there is a heavy emphasis on remedial education, especially reading, which is taught by specially trained teachers. Another big feature of the program is daily group-therapy sessions, in which staff members encourage the residents to explore the problems that brought them to Weaversville. The caseworkers arrange for families of many of the inmates to visit regularly for counseling sessions.

On a recent visit to the school, this reporter found residents spending time with staff members in groups of three or four, or engaged in individual tutoring sessions. The atmosphere was considerably more casual than in most public schools, with teachers and students joking easily with each other at times. Yet everyone had something to do—no one was just "hanging out."

"This place really does a lot for you," said one 17-year-old inmate who had done time in four other settings, including other training schools. "It's so small, you can't get away with anything. . . . You have to face your problems."

"Weaversville is better staffed, organized, and equipped than any program of its size that I know," said James Finckenauer, a Rutgers University professor of criminal justice who has studied delinquency programs nationwide. He thinks the fact that the facility is privately run helps: "In a lot of public institutions, you find that the staff has the attitude that it's just there to do a job and then leave at the end of the day. At Weaversville, you've got people who see their job as more expansive."

Henry Gursky, a psychologist who is the manager of Weaversville, said, "We're able to do what we do because somebody up there in the state really cares about these kids. They give us whatever we need." The state budgets more than $40,000 a year for each resident at Weaversville. About 5 percent of that is RCA's profit.

Gursky, who worked for the state mental-health system before coming to Weaversville eight years ago, said that RCA headquarters' involvement in the school's day-to-day affairs is minimal. "I feel pretty good about working for RCA, but I don't know a lot about them," he said. The company's main functions seem to be reviewing financial decisions and issuing paychecks from its distant headquarters in New Jersey. "My commitment is to the kids, not RCA," said Gursky.

The Florida School for Boys at Okeechobee is a far cry from Weaversville. The American Civil Liberties Union and a coalition of other public-interest groups are suing it and two other Florida training schools run by the state for what the court complaint calls "cruel and abusive conditions of confinement." The class-action lawsuit, filed in Federal District Court in January 1983, includes a long list of allegations: overcrowding, unsanitary conditions, inadequate feeding and clothing of the residents, poor security, which has resulted in frequent beatings and sexual assaults among residents, grossly inadequate medical care, lack of psychological counseling, and a general "atmosphere of fear and violence."

The Eckerd Foundation is not named in the suit, nor do most of the school's critics blame the foundation for the alleged conditions there. Critics say that Eckerd has inherited the fruits of the state's antiquated and harsh policies toward delinquents—policies that make it difficult for anyone to run a decent facility.

Florida gives Eckerd less than one-half the money per resident at Okeechobee that Pennsylvania gives to RCA for Weaversville. Juvenile-justice experts say that Florida imprisons too many delinquents in training schools to begin with, and that all the schools are too big for their own good. Okeechobee alone is more than twice the size of the Pennsylvania institutional system, which virtually guarantees that few inmates will receive individual attention. Because of a shortage of qualified staff, some educational programs have waiting lists; the lawsuit charges that the programs are inadequate and poorly organized in any case.

One major factor contributing to the problems at all three schools is the disparate mix of residents who are sent there. The state does have a variety of alternative, nonresidential programs for young offenders, but there are not enough slots to go around, so the runoff is sent to places like Okeechobee. For many who are sent, the setting is completely inappropriate; the Eckerd Foundation reported to the state in October that it was receiving a "large and increasing number" of retarded and severely disturbed offenders, for which the school has no programs, and who are disrupting the institution. In addition, an astounding 32 percent of those sent to the training schools last year were up on their first commitment to the state—no other, less drastic alternative had been tried. These first-timers are mixed in with the tougher, more experienced offenders.

"Okeechobee is just a dumping ground," said state senator Don Childers, whose district includes the school. "I don't think there's anything Eckerd can do that will have a meaningful effect if they don't control the budget and they don't control who gets sent to them. . . . I think they thought they could turn that place around overnight, but they've found they can't."

Eckerd officials agree with most of the critics. William Ross, the foundation's director of administration, says the worst problems are the overcrowding and the uncontrolled mix of psychotics, hard-core delinquents, and first-time offenders, which he says creates "havoc." He agrees the school's sheer size and remoteness (it is in the swampy, rural interior of central Florida) are also problems, and that many of the residents don't belong in a training school. "The ACLU suit has helped bring attention to the problems," he said. "We hope that now the legislature will become more aware of the needs."

Visitors familiar with the school say that Eckerd has tried to make improvements within its limited budget. Buildings that had been neglected by the state have been patched up and painted, and the staff has made an effort to make the interiors of the barrackslike structures more cheery, and the food has been improved. Broken toilets and screens have been repaired and dilapidated equipment replaced. The foundation is donating $280,000 this year to raise salaries in hopes of attracting more qualified staff. Last year, Eckerd officials persuaded a grocery-store chain to donate some equipment for a bakery where residents receive training, and it has bought sneakers and computer terminals. "There is a definite commitment to making the place work," said John Conway, the public defender in West Palm Beach, the nearest city to Okeechobee. "But it's going to take more than a few sneakers."

Al Hadeed, one of the attorneys suing the school, thinks that private enterprise should get involved with running institutions only if it is ready to be more aggressive about changing the system than he thinks Eckerd has been. "If the private sector wants to make a case for relevancy in this business, then it will have to make a break with the past," he said.

Some business people think that the private sector is ideally suited to this purpose. "I think that business is the shining hope for corrections," said Richard Mulcrone, former head of the Minnesota corrections system and past chairman of the state's parole board. Mulcrone now works for Control Data. "It's hard for the government to change its own stagnant institutions, but business has the advantage of coming in from the outside," he said. "If anyone can do it, they can."

But the idea of private prisons is a touchy subject for many corrections professionals. For one thing, they are worried that companies will begin meddling in state and local politics in order to secure contracts. Last September, the Texas Legislature passed a law sponsored by the Texas Sheriffs' Association, authorizing counties to contract for private jails. No jails have yet been opened under the law, but Robert Viterna, director of the state Jail Standards Commission, termed the legislation "strictly a private-interest bill," put through by former lawmen interested in getting into business.

This spring, the New Mexico State Legislature will consider a similar bill. The power behind that legislation is Colorado oilman and cattle magnate O. Wesley Box. Box has the support of authorities in seven rural counties who want to have him build and run two regional jails for them. The county officials are lobbying for the bill because they believe that Box, with his business experience, can run the jails better than they can. Box forthrightly admits that he is lobbying because he foresees a growth in the counties' jail population, which will mean profits for him.

This aspect touches a deeper reservation that some have about private prisons. "Should justice be a profit-making enterprise?" asks Mark Cunniff, director of the National Association of Criminal Justice Planners. "Should it be an industry that's manufacturing a consumer product? We're talking about taking away people's liberty, and I have questions about the propriety of anyone but the state doing that."

Observers like Cunniff worry that business will make good on their promises to imprison more cheaply by cutting back on services, which would worsen the already dreadful quality of life in many institutions. The comparison that skeptics most often make is with the private for-profit nursing-home industry. "I once had to care for an elderly relative in a private nursing home," remembers Perry Johnson, Michigan's director of corrections. "They were terrible people ... leeches. Everything was for money, and the clients suffered. If the companies do prisons like they do those places, we'll be set back 100 years."

The Federal Bureau of Prisons does have standards for the operation of its own institutions, which are uniformly better run and less unpleasant than most state prisons. Their proposal for the illegal-alien prison calls for the contractor to adhere to those standards. The bureau intends to have full-time employees monitoring the institution, as the INS already has in its contract-detention centers.

When Florida state legislators agreed to have the Eckerd Foundation take over the Okeechobee school, they made the deal contingent upon Eckerd admitting out-of-state observers to assess the operation. A team from the American Correctional Association (ACA), the country's most prominent organization of prison professionals, is to do a study of the school this year.

However, the nursing-home industry also is regulated by a variety of inspectors, and that regulation has not necessarily produced well-run institutions.

Most observers acknowledge the possible dangers but are willing to give business a chance. "Complex problems require complex solutions," said Anthony Travisono, director of ACA. "It is true that the profit motive could cause a conflict of interest, but for that very reason, people are going to watch private industry very closely, probably more closely than they watch the public sector."

T. Don Hutto emphasized the delicacy of his company's business: "If the private sector is going to do this, then we have to do it carefully and right. We have to show that we have something to contribute to the field."

PRIVATE PRISONS: PUNISHING-FOR-PROFIT 2

The Downside of Private Prisons

Craig Becker and Amy Dru Stanley

"Punishment for Profit," "The Corporate Warden," "Incarceration Unlimited." With these headlines, business journals have proclaimed a new opportunity for venture capital: criminal punishment. From prison financing to prison management, business has entered the corrections field. "There's a whole new industry developing," says *Barron's*, "from the unlikely meeting of pinstripes and prison stripes."

More than business interests are at stake in the increasing resort to the private sector to finance, service and even run state and Federal correctional institutions. Senator Arlen Specter calls this trend "the major unexamined new social policy of the 1980s," and held hearings on the subject before a subcommittee of the Senate Appropriations Committee last month. It is also high on the agendas of politicians on the far right. In his current bid for the Republican nomination for lieutenant governor of Virginia, political fund-raiser Richard Viguerie has endorsed the transfer of the state's entire penal system to private control.

Prisons are big business. Last year, Federal, state and local governments spent a total of $10 billion on corrections; Federal and state prisons house nearly 450,000 inmates; local jails hold over 200,000. The prison population has doubled in the past decade. Penal institutions are more than 10 percent above capacity, and more than two-thirds of them are under court orders to ease overcrowding.

Despite the states' growing desire to place people behind bars and popular demand for tougher sentences, taxpayers have been unwilling to pay for the prisons they want to fill. That contradiction has created an opening for private capital. With state governments expected to spend $5 billion on construction of new prisons over the next four to five years, brokers have devised lease-purchase agreements, a new form of financing prisons that is attractive to investors and public officials. Capital to pay the construction costs is raised by private offerings, and the facility is leased to the government, which acquires title when the term is up. The interest on these "certificates of participation" is tax-exempt, and the investment

---

is secured by the inmates themselves, since default would lead to their eviction. As a Miami businessman boasted to *Financial World*, "It is the only real estate investment where you're guaranteed 100 percent occupancy—at least." Finally, lease-purchase deals offer a way of bypassing taxpayer opposition. After voters in New York State rejected a $500 million bond issue for a prison in a 1981 referendum, the Legislature authorized the Urban Development Corporation to float bonds and begin construction. Citizens' groups sued the state, arguing that the measure deprived the public of its constitutional right to vote on the creation of state debt. The State Supreme Court, however, dismissed the suit, holding that taxpayers lack standing to contest the matter.

New York Senator Alfonse D'Amato has sponsored legislation to enhance the attractiveness of lease-purchase deals. His Prison Construction Privatization Act of 1984, currently in committee, would permit prison financiers to claim investment tax credits and accelerated depreciation. D'Amato contends that the bill would "unleash private capital" to build $1.5 billion worth of prison space for 50,000 inmates. "The private jail market is ripe," *Barron's* claims. "And it's the brokers, architects, builders and banks—not the taxpayers—who will make out like bandits."

Financing prison construction is only one facet of private interest in the corrections field. In thirty-nine states and the District of Columbia, private firms provide services ranging from job training to meal preparation within publicly managed prisons. Several of these companies are now preparing to own and operate penal institutions. Hundreds of halfway houses for prisoners are already managed by private groups. According to the Justice Department, six states have contracted with private firms to operate juvenile detention facilities. The Federal government spends $21 million a year to house 3,200 inmates, largely illegal immigrants, in 300 private institutions. An analyst at the accounting firm Touche Ross expects a flurry of public offerings for jail management companies within the next two years.

Major corporations whose public images are hardly those of private jailers are doing business in incarceration, though some are involved only indirectly. E.F. Hutton, Merrill Lynch, Lehman Brothers Kuhn Loeb and Shearson Lehman/American Express have all orchestrated lease-purchase deals. Shearson Lehman claims to have arranged over $350 million in corrections financing in the past three years. Other corporations, however, are intimately involved in penal management. One of the firms, Control Data, owns a large interest in City Venture, which until recently sold vocational training programs to prisons. In 1982, Control Data bid on a contract to run a women's prison in Minnesota and raised $15 million to build and staff the institution. The deal fell through, however, when state officials decided to run it themselves. In January 1982, the corporation formed a corrections systems division, managed by Richard Mulcrone, former chairman of the Minnesota State Corrections Authority.

Another firm, RCA Service Corporation, operates Weaversville Intensive Treatment Unit in Pennsylvania, a facility for juvenile delinquents. "We plan to pursue actively this type of business using Weaversville as a model," says Al Androlewicz, RCA vice president for education and human services. "Weaversville was once viewed as a one-shot deal, but we see now that times are changing."

The largest of the private operators, Corrections Corporation of America, was formed in 1983 by Thomas Beasley, a Tennessee entrepreneur involved in real estate, insurance and Republican politics. The venture was funded with $10 million raised largely by a Nashville venture-capital firm, Massey Burch Investment Group, which also launched a thriving private hospital corporation. Two former state corrections officials are vice presidents of the company, T. Don Hutto, former Commissioner of Corrections in Arkansas and Virginia, and Travis Snellings, former budget director of Virginia's Department of Corrections. Maurice Sigler, former chair of the Federal Parole Commission, serves on its board of directors. They operate two detention facilities for the Immigration and Naturalization Service and a treatment center for the Federal Bureau of Prisons.

Hutto's record with the Arkansas prison system demonstrates his approach to prison management. In 1978, while he was Commissioner of Corrections, the U.S. Supreme Court ruled that the state's entire penal system constituted cruel and unusual punishment. In an unwitting but remarkable forecast of Hutto's career, the Court found that he and his assistants "evidently tried to operate their prisons at a profit." Inmates were required to work on the prison farms ten hours a day, six days a week, often without suitable clothing or shoes, using mule-drawn plows and tending crops by hand. Sometimes they were forced to run to and from the fields. Punishment for minor misconduct included lashing with a wooden-handled leather strap five feet long and four inches wide and administering electric shocks to "various sensitive parts of the inmate's body." The trial court characterized the prisons as "a dark and evil world completely alien to the free world."

Numerous smaller firms are also competing for private corrections contracts. Behavioral Systems Southwest, founded by Ted Nissen, a former official of the California corrections system, runs small detention facilities in Arizona, Colorado and California and has annual earnings of $6 million; Palo Duro Private Detention Services, run by T.L. Baker, former sheriff of Amarillo, Texas, has contracted with the Bureau of Prisons to house illegal aliens. Buckingham Security of Lewisburg, Pennsylvania, is negotiating the most ambitious deal, a contract with eight states to house inmates in a maximum security prison to be built near Pittsburgh. Buckingham is run by Charles Fenton, who served as chief warden at three major Federal prisons, and his brother Joseph, a Pennsylvania businessman. In 1980, a Federal jury found that as warden of the Lewisburg penitentiary, Charles Fenton had inflicted cruel and unusual punishment on two inmates, beating them with ax handles while they were handcuffed and shackled. The jury refused to award the prisoners damages, on the ground that Fenton acted in self-defense.

While entrepreneurs seek profits in private prisons, public officials claim they are more economical and efficient. Corrections Corporation charges the I.N.S. $23.84 per prisoner per day to operate a facility in Houston, compared with the $30.26 it costs Federal facilities. Palo Duro has offered to house Federal prisoners for $22 to $27 each per day; the Bureau of Prisons spends $35 a day. One way to hold down costs is not to build new facilities. Behavioral Systems houses prisoners in four converted motels surrounded by barbed wire. Other economies are less visible. Major savings come from reduced labor costs. Private prisons need not abide by Civil Service hiring and promotion regulations or provide pensions and other benefits. The firms provide minimal job training, and not one is unionized. As Hutto told *State Legislatures* magazine, "Government is inherently wasteful. . . . Every time you want something, you have to go through a complex political process."

The trend toward contracting out detention coincides with the growing support for turning a profit on prison labor. For two centuries penal theorists have noted the systematic relationship between criminal punishment and factory discipline; now the aim is to unite punishment and production into one institution. Since 1981, Chief Justice Warren Burger has campaigned to convert prisons into "factories with fences." Burger advocates the repeal of Federal and state laws that restrict the sale of prison-made goods—"walls of economic protectionism," as he put it in a speech last summer at George Washington University. The Federal statute barring the interstate sale of such goods has already been amended to allow seven "pilot projects." Florida plans to transfer all fifty-six of its prison industries, which had total sales of $22 million in 1981, to private hands. In 1982, Prison Rehabilitation Industries and Diversified Enterprises (PRIDE) assumed control of the first such business, the printing operations in Zephyrhills Correctional Institution. Jack Eckerd, a millionaire businessman and head of PRIDE, explained, "The purpose of PRIDE is to make prison industries and their products more profitable." John King, former Secretary of the Louisiana Corrections Department, says Burger's proposal would transform prisoners from "a liability into an asset." As Secretary, King oversaw the Angola Penitentiary where 4,747 prisoners pick cotton, harvest corn and cultivate soybeans and other crops. According to King, "The principles of management are the same whether you're making chocolate-chip cookies or incarcerating people."

Private prisons intersect with the collapse of public welfare services and the trend of "privatization," the performance of public functions by private business. It also coincides with the move toward "deinstitutionalizing" state facilities that supervise the aged, retarded and mentally ill. Private corrections originated in institutions where the line between dependence and deviance, between care and punishment, is blurred: halfway houses, juvenile facilities and detention centers for illegal aliens. Now, however, private institutions incarcerate adult offenders serving long-term criminal sentences. That threatens the civil rights of prisoners as well as the power of citizens to influence penal power.

It is a principle central to liberal thought and democratic government that only the state possesses the authority to deprive people of their liberty. The right to punish, wrote Locke, is the essence of political power. In November 1981, the American Civil Liberties Union sued the I.N.S. and a private company that ran a small detention center for illegal aliens, charging that the conditions violated the Fifth

Amendment's due process clause. Counsel for the Houston A.C.L.U., Stefan Presser argued that the Constitution does not allow government "to retail out the detention of human beings." Chief Judge John Singleton of the U.S. District Court for the Southern District of Texas held that "detention . . . is the exclusive prerogative of the state." Yet he left unchallenged the delegation of this function to private jailers, finding only that they are subject to constitutional restrictions.

Private operators deny that they wield state powers. Responding to a series of questions put to Buckingham Security by the Pennsylvania Bureau of Corrections in 1984, the corporation's attorney stressed that "the authority exercised by Buckingham's personnel . . . will be purely ministerial." Their only function is to "house and feed inmates convicted under the laws of the States and the Federal Government."

But these private jailers will not simply dispense punishment ordered by the courts; the coercive power of the state will rest in their hands. They will make decisions every day that touch the most intimate concerns and the most basic needs of their charges. Prison managers will distribute "good-time credits" affecting prisoners' chances of earning parole. Yet their main concern will be maximizing profits and minimizing costs.

The contrast between public and private prisons should not be overstated, however. The current system of incarceration cannot be defended as ideal. Although the Supreme Court has said there is "no iron curtain drawn between the Constitution and the prisons of this country," it has been reluctant to intervene in protecting prisoners' rights or enforcing penal accountability, favoring a "broad hands-off attitude toward problems of prison administration."

For the state to abdicate its power of punishment to the lowest corporate bidder will seal off prisons more completely from constitutional and popular controls. It will also sever any connection between justice and punishment, transforming the terms of the debate over the social objectives of incarceration from retribution, deterrence and rehabilitation to productivity and profit. In a letter three years ago to *The Philadelphia Inquirer*, Norman Nusser, who has served seventeen years of a twenty- to forty-year prison term, wrote:

> Corrections is already too much of a business and needs to become less so. Too many people already are making a living from our misery. It is now subsidized sadism. Is our society to put sadism on a profit-making basis? . . .
>
> Look in the financial section of your daily newspaper to see how many points Prison Industries went up today. If there has been a prison riot and $50 million worth of machinery and plant are destroyed, the stockholders will sell out in droves.

Until citizens and public officials recognize that unrestrained expansion of the marketplace will aggravate rather than resolve the crisis in corrections, ingenious entrepreneurs will continue to capitalize on crime. Meanwhile, the debate in the courts and legislatures may soon spill violently into the cell block.

CRIME CONTROL: WHAT TO DO? 1

Crime and Public Policy
James Q. Wilson

If we are to make the best and sanest use of our laws and liberties, we must first adopt a sober view of man and his institutions that would permit reasonable things to be accomplished, foolish things abandoned, and utopian things forgotten. A sober view of man requires a modest definition of progress. A 20 percent reduction in the number of robberies would still leave us with the highest robbery rate of almost any Western nation but would prevent over one hundred thousand robberies. A small gain for society, a large one for the would-be victims. But even this gain is unlikely if we do not think clearly about crime and public policy.

The quest for the causes of crime is an intellectually stimulating, though, thus far, rather confusing, endeavor. To the extent we have learned anything at all, we have learned that the factors in our lives and history that most powerfully influence the crime rate—our commitment to liberty, our general prosperity, our childrearing methods, our popular values—are precisely the factors that are hardest or riskiest to change. Those things that can more easily and safely be changed—the behavior of the police, the organization of neighborhoods, the management of the criminal justice system, the sentences imposed by courts—are the things that have only limited influence on the crime rate.

If the things we can measure and manipulate had a large effect on the crime rate, then those effects would by now be evident in our statistical studies and police experiments. If crime were easily deterred by changes in the certainty or severity of sanctions, then our equations would probably have detected such effects in ways that overcome the criticisms now made of such studies. If giving jobs to ex-offenders and school dropouts readily prevented crime, the results of the Manpower Demonstration Research Corporation experiments would not have been so disappointing. If new police patrol techniques made a large and demonstrable difference, those techniques would have been identified.

In a sense, the radical critics of American society are correct: if you wish to make a big difference in crime, you must make fundamental changes in society. But they are right only in that sense, for what they propose to put in place of existing institu-

Source: James Q. Wilson, *Thinking About Crime*, revised edition (New York: Random House, 1983), pp. 250–260. Reprinted with permission.

tions, to the extent they propose anything at all except angry rhetoric, would probably make us yearn for the good old days when our crime rate was higher but our freedoms were intact. Indeed, some versions of the radical doctrine would leave us yearning for the good old days when not only were our freedoms intact, but our crime rate was lower.

I realize that some people, not at all radical, find it difficult to accept the notion that if we are to think seriously about crime, we ought to think about crime and not about poverty, unemployment, or racism. Such persons should bear two things in mind. The first is that there is no contradiction between taking crime seriously and taking poverty (or other social disadvantages) seriously. There is no need to choose. Quite the contrary; to the extent our efforts to measure the relationships among crime, wealth, and sanctions can be said to teach any lessons at all, it is that raising the costs of crime while leaving the benefits of noncrime untouched may be as shortsighted as raising the benefits of noncrime while leaving the costs of crime unchanged. Anticrime policies are less likely to succeed if there are no reasonable alternatives to crime; by the same token, employment programs may be less likely to succeed if there are attractive criminal alternatives to working. If legitimate opportunities for work are unavailable, some people may turn to crime, but if criminal opportunities are profitable, some persons will not take the legitimate jobs that exist.

Some persons may believe that if legitimate jobs are made absolutely more attractive than stealing, stealing will decline even without any increase in penalties for it. That may be true provided there is no practical limit on the amount that can be paid in wages. Since the average "take" from a burglary or mugging is quite small, it would seem easy to make the income from a job exceed the income from crime. But this neglects the advantages of a criminal income: one works at crime at one's convenience, enjoys the esteem of colleagues who think a "straight" job is stupid and skill at stealing is commendable, looks forward to the occasional "big score" that may make further work unnecessary for weeks, and relishes the risk and adventure associated with theft. The money value of all these benefits (that is, what one who is not shocked by crime would want in cash to forego crime) is hard to estimate but is almost certainly far larger than either public or private employers could offer to unskilled or semiskilled young workers. The only alternative for society is to so increase the risks of theft that its value is depreciated below what society can afford to pay in legal wages, and then take whatever steps are necessary to insure that those legal wages are available.

The desire to reduce crime is the worst possible reason for reducing poverty. Most poor persons are not criminals; many either are retired or have regular jobs and lead conventional family lives. The elderly, the working poor, and the willing-to-work poor could benefit greatly from economic conditions and government programs that enhance their incomes without there being the slightest reduction in crime (indeed, if the experience of the 1960s is any guide, there might well be, through no fault of most beneficiaries, an increase in crime). Reducing poverty and breaking up the ghettoes are desirable policies in their own right, whatever their effects on crime. It is the duty of government to devise other measures to cope with crime, not only to permit antipoverty programs to succeed without unfair competition from criminal opportunities, but also to insure that such programs do not inadvertently shift the costs of progress, in terms of higher crime rates, onto innocent parties, not the least of whom are the poor themselves.

One cannot press this economic reasoning too far. Some persons will commit crimes whatever the risks; indeed, for some, the greater the risk the greater the thrill, while others (the alcoholic wife beater, for example) are only dimly aware that there are any risks. But more important than the insensitivity of certain criminals to changes in risks and benefits is the impropriety of casting the crime problem wholly in terms of a utilitarian calculus. The most serious offenses are crimes not simply because society finds them inconvenient, but because it regards them with moral horror. To steal, to rape, to rob, to assault—these acts are destructive of the very possibility of society and affronts to the humanity of their victims. Parents do not instruct their children to be law abiding merely by pointing to the risks of being caught, but by explaining that these acts are wrong whether or not one is caught. I conjecture that those parents who simply warn their offspring about the risks of crime produce a disproportionate number of young persons willing to take those risks.

Even the deterrent capacity of the criminal justice system depends in no small part on its ability to evoke sentiments of shame in the accused. If all it evoked were a sense of being unlucky, crime rates would be even higher. James Fitzjames Stephens makes the point by analogy. To what extent, he asks, would a man be deterred from theft by the knowledge that by committing it he was exposing himself to one chance in fifty of catching a serious but not fatal illness—say, a bad fever? Rather little, we would imagine—indeed, all of us regularly take risks as great or greater than that: when we drive after drinking, when we smoke cigarettes, when we go hunting in the woods. The criminal sanction, Stephens concludes, "operates not only on the fears of criminals. [A] great part of the general detestation of crime . . . arises from the fact that the commission of offenses is associated . . . with the solemn and deliberate infliction of punishment wherever crime is proved."[1]

Much is made today of the fact that the criminal justice system "stigmatizes" those caught up in it, and thus unfairly marks such persons and perhaps even furthers their criminal careers by "labeling" them as criminals. Whether the labeling process operates in this way is as yet unproved, but it would indeed be unfortunate if society treated a convicted offender in such a way that he had no reasonable alternative but to make crime a career. To prevent this, society should insure that one can "pay one's debt" without suffering permanent loss of civil rights, the continuing and pointless indignity of parole supervision, and the frustration of being unable to find a job. But doing these things is very different from eliminating the "stigma" from crime. To destigmatize crime would be to lift from it the weight of moral judgment and to make crime simply a particular occupation or avocation which society has chosen to reward less (or perhaps more!) than other pursuits. If there is no stigma attached to an activity, then society has no business making it a crime. Indeed, before the invention of the prison in the late eighteenth and early nineteenth centuries, the stigma attached to criminals was the major deterrent to and principal form of protection from criminal activity. The purpose of the criminal justice system is not to expose would-be criminals to a lottery in which they either win or lose, but to expose them in addition and more importantly to the solemn condemnation of the community should they yield to temptation.

If we grant that it is proper to try to improve the criminal justice system without apologizing for the fact that those efforts do not attack the "root causes" of crime, the next thing to remember is that we are seeking, at best, marginal improvements that can only be discovered through patient trial-and-error accompanied by hardheaded and objective evaluations.

There are, we now know, certain things we can change in accordance with our intentions, and certain ones we cannot. We cannot alter the number of juveniles who first experiment with minor crimes. We apparently cannot lower the overall recidivism rate, though within reason we should keep trying. We are not yet certain whether we can increase significantly the police apprehension rate. We may be able to change the teenage unemployment rate, though we have learned by painful trial-and-error that doing this is much more difficult than once supposed. We can probably reduce the time it takes to bring an arrested person to trial, even though we have as yet made few serious efforts to do so. We can certainly reduce any arbitrary exercise of prosecutorial discretion over whom to charge and whom to release, and we can most definitely stop pretending that judges know, any better than the rest of us, how to provide "individualized justice." We can confine a larger proportion of the serious and repeat offenders and fewer of the common drunks and truant children. We know that confining criminals prevents them from harming society, and we have grounds for suspecting that some would-be criminals can be deterred by the confinement of others.

Above all, we can try to learn more about what works and, in the process, abandon our ideological preconceptions about what ought to work. This is advice, not simply or even primarily to government—for governments are run by men and women who are under irresistible pressures to pretend they know more than they do—but to my colleagues: academics, theoreticians, writers, advisers. We may feel ourselves under pressure to pretend we know things, but we are also under a positive obligation to admit what we do not know and to avoid cant and sloganizing.

In the last decade or so, we have learned a great deal, perhaps more than we sometimes admit. But we have learned very little to a moral certainty. Any effort to reduce crime is an effort to alter human behavior at moments when it is least well observed and by methods (deterrence, incapacitation, rehabilitation) whose effect is delayed and uncertain. Under these circumstances, we may never know "what works" to a moral certainty. Why, then, gamble on what we (or at least I) think we know? I offer Pascal's wager. If altering the rewards and penalties of crime affects the rate of crime, and I act on that belief, I reduce crime. If such strategies do not work, and I act on the false belief that they do, I have merely made swifter, more certain, or more severe the penalties that befall a person guilty in any event and to that extent have served justice, though not utility. But if I do not believe in them, and they do in fact work, then I have condemned innocent persons to suffer needlessly and have served neither justice nor utility.

But what, precisely, ought we to do if we act on the belief that we know, though with some uncertainty, how to reduce crime marginally? The purpose of this [essay] is not to offer a detailed set of anticrime policies, it is only to teach people how to think about crime (and especially how to think about the kind of research that is done about crime control). But it would be unfair to the reader to leave him or her to guess what the author believes ought to be done after learning to think this way.

The policy implications of what I have learned are in many ways so obvious that many readers will wonder why it is necessary to struggle through all these facts, regression equations, and experiments to accept them. There are many reasons why it is necessary to find evidence for the obvious, not the least of which is that many people still do not find them obvious, or even reasonable. If you doubt this, attend a city council meeting on the police budget, a legislative debate on the criminal laws, a convention of judges discussing sentencing, or a conference of criminologists.

A reasonable set of policies would, to me, include the following. Neighborhoods threatened with crime or disorder would be encouraged to create self-help organizations of citizens who, working in collaboration with the police, patrol their own communities to detect, though not to apprehend, suspicious persons. Densely settled neighborhoods would make extensive use of foot patrol officers and would hire off-duty police and, perhaps, private security guards to help maintain order and to prevent disreputable behavior in public places from frightening decent persons off the sidewalks or from encouraging predatory offenders to use the anarchy and anonymity of the streets as an opportunity for serious crime. Drug dealers would be driven off the streets.

The police would organize their patrol units to help maintain order and to identify and, where possible, arrest high-rate offenders. Detectives and patrol officers would make thorough, on-the-spot investigations of recent, serious offenses. As much information as possible would be gathered about the records and habits of high-rate offenders and officers would be given strong incentives to find and arrest them. Even when they are caught committing a relatively minor crime, these career criminals would be the object of intensive follow-up investigations so as to make the strongest possible case against them.

All persons arrested for a serious offense and all high-rate offenders arrested for any offense would be screened by prosecutors who would have immediately accessible the juvenile and adult criminal records of such persons so that a complete picture of their criminal history could be readily assessed. Those who commit very serious offenses and high-rate offenders who have committed any offense would be given priority treatment in terms of prompt follow-up investigations, immediate arraignment, bail recommendations to insure appearance at trial, and an early trial date so that those who cannot post bail will have their cases disposed of swiftly. One prosecutor would handle each priority case from intake to final disposition. Victims and witnesses would be given special assistance, including counseling on procedures, money aid (where appropriate) to compensate them for their time away from work, and the early return of any stolen property that has been recovered.

Well-staffed prosecutorial and public defender's offices would be prepared for an early trial (or plea-bargain) in these priority cases; judges would be loath to grant continuances for convenience of counsel. Sentencing would be shaped, though not rigidly determined, by sentencing guidelines that take into account not only the gravity of the offense and the prior conviction record of the accused, but also the full criminal history, including the juvenile record and the involvement, if any, of the accused with drug abuse. The outer bounds of judicial discretion would be shaped by society's judgment as to what constitutes a just and fair penalty for a given offense; within those bounds, sentencing would be designed to reduce crime by giving longer sentences to high-rate offenders (even when convicted of a less serious offense) and shorter sentences to low-rate offenders (even if the offense in question is somewhat more serious).

Persons convicted of committing minor offenses who have little or no prior record would be dealt with by community-based corrections: in particular, by supervised community service and victim restitution. Probation officers would insure that these obligations are in fact met; individuals failing to meet them would promptly be given short jail sentences.

Offenders sentenced to some period of incarceration would be carefully screened so that young and old, violent and nonviolent, neurotic and psychotic offenders would be assigned to separate facilities and, within those facilities, to educational and treatment programs appropriate to their personalities and needs. Progress in such programs would have nothing to do, however, with the date on which the offenders are released. Time served would be set by the judge, perhaps with stated discounts for good behavior; rehabilitation, to the extent that it occurs at all, would be a benefit of the programs but not a circumstance determining the length of the sentence. Parole boards might make recommendations to the sentencing judge or to the governor about sentences that ought to be commuted or shortened in the manifest interests of justice, but they would not determine release dates. Parole officers would continue to assist ex-offenders in returning to the community, especially with jobs and limited financial assistance, but there would be no assumption that these services would reduce the recidivism rate or that the parole officer would oversee the behavior of the offender in the community.

Prisons would be of small to moderate size and in no facility housing violent or high-rate offenders would double-bunking occur. Contraband flowing into or out of the prisons would be strictly controlled. The first objective of the guards would be to protect society by maintaining secure custody; their second (and perhaps equally important) objective would be to protect the inmates from one another. Guards would be sufficiently numerous so that they were not forced to choose between controlling the prison by terror or abdicating control of it to organized groups of inmates.

People will disagree with one or more elements of this sketchy set of proposals; I myself may change my mind about the details as I learn more about what works and think harder about what justice requires. But in broad outline, it strikes me neither as an unreasonable set of ideas nor one likely to be rejected by most citizens. There is no idea on this list that is not now being implemented in at least one jurisdiction, and large numbers of these ideas are being practiced in a few jurisdictions. But in general, and in most places, this package of ideas is resisted in practice just as it may be applauded in theory. The blunt fact is that the criminal justice system in this country does not, for the most part, operate as I have suggested.

Neighborhood and citizen patrols are often resisted by the police who fear a loss of their monopoly of power, by individual officers who fear a loss of their jobs, and by citizens who are quickly bored with volunteer work. Community-involved foot patrol is resisted by many police supervisors who fear loss of control of the beat officers. Assigning officers to neighborhoods on the basis of levels of public disorder and concentrating police investigations on high-rate offenders are resisted by citizens who judge the police entirely on the basis of how swiftly they dispatch a patrol car in response to a telephone call reporting a burglary that might have occurred many hours or even many days earlier.

Supporters of the family court system resist making juvenile criminal records routinely available in adult courts and many prosecutors who, in fact, could obtain such records often do not because of the expense and bother. Prosecutors have come to embrace the idea of "career criminal" programs, but most of these are limited to adult offenders and even to those adult offenders who have committed very serious crimes, regardless of whether they are in fact high-rate offenders. The offices of prosecutors and public defenders are often so thinly staffed that asking for court continuances is absolutely essential. And even where it is not essential, it is usually convenient. Postponing cases is for prosecutors a way of evening out the workload and for defenders a way of making the evidence turn cold and the witnesses lose interest.

Many probation departments have created victim restitution and community service programs, but they often discover that persons ordered to participate in them ignore the order with impunity, because judges are not inclined (or are too busy) to enforce the order with appropriate sanctions. If a large fraction of all fines levied by judges are not paid in full, is it any wonder that community-based corrections so often result in offenders walking away from them?

Judges are by and large opposed to any substantial restriction on their right to sentence as they see fit, whatever the cost in crime control or fairness. They favor "guidelines," but only those they themselves have developed and that they are free to ignore. Some thoughtful legislators support more restrictive guidelines, but these are often based merely on the gravity of the instant offense and take little account of the crime-control possibilities of selectively incapacitating high-rate offenders. And less thoughtful legislators find it much more appealing to call for massively severe sentences without regard to whether they will ever be imposed.

Taxpayers overwhelmingly want the system to crack down on serious and repeat offenders, but they regularly vote down bond issues designed to build the necessary additional prisons and they oppose having new facilities located in their neighborhoods. These taxpayer revolts are aided and abetted by pressure groups that are hostile to incarceration, retaining in the face of all evidence to the contrary a faith in rehabilitation and reserving their feelings of vengeance for "white-collar" criminals (especially those who might have served in conservative administrations).

In short, the entire criminal justice system, from citizen to judge, is governed by perverse incentives. Though many of its members agree on what they wish to achieve, the incentives faced by each member acting individually directs him or her to act in ways inconsistent with what is implied by that agreement.

In evidence of this, consider the following. Police officers want to arrest serious offenders—they are "good collars"—but making such arrests in ways that lead to conviction is difficult. Those convictions that are obtained are usually the result of the efforts of a small minority of all officers. Arrests that stand up in court tend to involve stranger-to-stranger crimes, to occur soon after the crime, and to be accompanied by physical evidence or eyewitness testimony. The officers who look hard for the perpetrators of stranger-to-stranger crimes, who gather physical evidence, and who carefully interview victims and potential witnesses are a small minority of all officers. . . . Brian Forst . . . found, in six police jurisdictions, that about one-half of all convictions resulted from arrests made by only one-eighth of all officers. Indeed, one-quarter of the officers who made arrests produced zero convictions. Though these differences were in part the result of differences in duty assignments, they persisted after controlling for assignments.[2] For many officers, it is much easier to take reports of crimes, mediate disputes, and turn big cases over to detectives who often take up the trail when it is cold. Despite these differences in behavior, Forst found that the most productive officers tend to get about the same number of commendations and awards as the least productive ones.

Prosecutors also behave in many cases in ways inconsistent with a crime-control objective. In the 1960s, many of them took cases to court more or less in the order in which the arrests had been made. Then they began to assign higher priority to grave offenses. While an improvement, this still resulted in resources being concentrated on persons who had committed serious offenses, rather than on high-rate offenders. . . . these are not necessarily the same persons. By the late 1970s, many career criminal programs had become quite sophisticated: they gave highest priority to grave offenses and to offenders with long or serious records. But even now, many jurisdictions limit the selection of cases to persons with serious adult records, ignoring the high predictive value of the juvenile record and the drug-abuse history. Some prosecutors will concentrate their follow-up investigations on persons who have committed serious crimes and neglect the crime-control value of investigating suspected high-rate offenders who may have been caught for a non-serious offense.

Judges must manage a crowded docket, dispose of cases quickly, and make decisions under uncertainty. Some are also eager to minimize their chances of being reversed on appeal. These managerial concerns, while quite understandable, often get in the way of trying to use the court hearing as a means of establishing who is and who is not a high-rate offender and of allowing such distinctions, as well as the facts about the gravity of the case, to shape the sentence.

To the extent the incentives operating in the criminal justice system have perverse and largely unintended effects, it is not clear what can be done about it. The "system" is not, as so many have remarked, in fact a system—that is, a set of consciously coordinated activities. And given the importance we properly attach to having an independent judiciary and to guaranteeing, even at some cost in crime control, the rights of accused by means of the adversarial process, there is no way the various institutions can be made into a true system. The improvements that can be made are all at the margin and require patient effort and an attention to detail. Sometimes a modest leap forward is possible, as when prosecutors began using computers to keep track of their cases and to learn about the characteristics of the defendants, or when legislators began experimenting with various kinds of sentencing guidelines. But mostly, progress requires dull, unrewarding work in the trenches. There is no magic bullet.

Throughout all this, our society has been, with but few exceptions, remarkably forebearing. We have preserved and even extended the most comprehensive array of civil liberties found in any nation on earth despite rising crime rates and (in the 1960s) massive civil disorder. Though proposals are now afoot to modify some of these procedural guarantees—especially those having to do with the exclusionary rule, the opportunity for unlimited appeals, and the right to bail—they constitute, at most, rather modest changes. If adopted, they would still leave our criminal justice system with a stronger set of guarantees than one could find in most other nations, including those, such as Great Britain and Canada, that we acknowledge to be bastions of freedom. We have chosen, as I think we should, to have a wide-ranging bill of rights, but we must be willing to pay the price of that choice. That price includes a willingness both to accept a somewhat higher level of crime and disorder than we might otherwise have and to invest a greater amount of resources in those institutions (the police, the prosecutors, the courts, the prisons) needed to cope with those who violate our law while claiming its protections.

For most of us, the criminal justice system is intended for the other fellow, and since the other fellow is thought to be wicked, we can easily justify to ourselves a pinch-penny attitude toward the system. It is, after all, not designed to help us but to hurt him. If it is unpleasant, congested, and cumbersome, it is probably only what those who are caught up in its toils deserve. What we forget is that the more unpleasant the prisons, the less likely judges will be to send people to them; the more congested the prosecutor's office, the less likely that office will be to sort out, carefully, the serious and high-rate offender from the run-of-the-mill and low-rate offender; the more cumbersome the procedures, the less likely we and our neighbors will be to take the trouble of reporting crimes, making statements, and testifying in court.

Wicked people exist. Nothing avails except to set them apart from innocent people. And many people, neither wicked nor innocent, but watchful, dissembling, and calculating of their chances, ponder our reaction to wickedness as a clue to what they might profitably do. Our actions speak louder than our words. When we profess to believe in deterrence and to value justice, but refuse to spend the energy and money required to produce either, we are sending a clear signal that we think that safe streets, unlike all other great public goods, can be had on the cheap. We thereby trifle with the wicked, make sport of the innocent, and encourage the calculators. Justice suffers, and so do we all.

Notes

1. James Fitzjames Stephens, *A History of the Criminal Law of England* (New York: Burt Franklin, 1973), vol. 2, pp. 80–81 (first published in 1883).

2. Brian Forst et al., *Arrest Convictability as a Measure of Police Performance* (Washington, D.C.: INSLAW, 1981).

Fighting Crime

Elliott Currie

In the 1970s the supposed paradox of rising crime in the midst of rising "affluence" and a multitude of social programs helped speed the demise of the liberal perspective on crime and punishment. In the 1980s conservatives face a similar dilemma: the paradox of high and generally increasing crime in the face of an array of "hard" crime-control strategies that have been in place for some years. To be fair, the catastrophic levels of criminal violence we still face don't entirely refute the right's program, such as it is. But the paradox does put the burden of proof on a strategy that systematically downplays crime's causes while laying most of the responsibility for crime control on an already beleaguered criminal justice system.

At the same time, a simple reaffirmation of the conventional liberalism of the 1960s won't do either. That liberalism has been considerably overmaligned in the recent past; it had its enduring truths as well as its damaging misperceptions. One of the enduring truths was that the criminal justice system alone cannot prevent crime and that, indeed, it tends to break down when called on to do so. Where some variants of criminological liberalism fell down most heavily was in their nonintervention—their tendency to deny the seriousness of crime and, relatedly, to view almost every kind of intervention into the lives of offenders (not to mention high-risk communities or families) as an invasive and coercive application of social control.

Again, it's important to give credit where it's due. Liberal criminology's abhorrence for coercion and its keen sense of the threats lurking behind "benevolent" state intervention remain usefully cautionary, especially given the sometimes unsavory history of the rehabilitative ethic in American justice. But the result, often, was to disparage the potential of interventions that could be supportive, guiding, or nurturing as well as those that were clearly repressive.

Is there a third position beyond both of these? I think there is. It has three main themes. First, we need to shed any lingering embarrassment about wholeheartedly supporting criminal justice agencies trying to do their job. It's crucially important to insure sufficient police resources to protect communities as well as possible.

Source: Elliott Currie, "Fighting Crime," *Working Papers for a New Society* 9 (July–August 1982), pp. 17–25. Reprinted with permission.

Giving prosecutors enough resources to do their job well and fairly is all to the good, and so is insuring safe—and decent—conditions of confinement for truly violent people. All of these things are necessary supports to communities now torn by intolerable levels of violence, and we need to say so unequivocally—and to be willing to fight for them, if necessary, in the face of official indifference or hostility.

But this doesn't add up, by itself, to a strategy against crime. Such a strategy requires two more broad elements. On the one hand, we need to affirm that there's such a thing as social pathology. The personal and familial ills that violent crime often reflects are deep ones. They won't be adequately addressed without intervention programs that are rooted in appreciation of the level of damage we may often need to undo. On the other hand, we need to be toughminded enough to insist that even the best efforts at prevention and rehabilitation will be crippled without a renewed commitment to attacking the larger social and economic forces that are generally understood—even by most serious conservatives—to generate crime. In short, we need to develop a range of strategies at ascending levels of intervention, from nuts and bolts programs to a larger, more encompassing vision of what it would take to build a society less driven by violence.

And, in fact, we know more about what needs doing than is commonly supposed. This isn't to say that we know *enough*, or that we could launch a full-blown, credible anticrime program this week. Nobody, least of all the right, has a program that will stop crime tomorrow, or even next year. The beginning of seriousness is to acknowledge that. Failing to do so, in the name of an imagined political pragmatism, is a classic example of what C. Wright Mills called "crackpot realism."

But there *are* programs that we know enough about to be able to say with some certainty that they would help reduce crime in the near term. They should be implemented now, on a large scale. There are others about which we know less, but which seem sufficiently promising to warrant wide experimentation and evaluation. Finally, we know a good deal about some of the kinds of larger social interventions necessary to bring down the crime rate for good. The obstacles to them are mainly political.

The suggestions that follow aren't meant to be exhaustive, but to begin to reframe the debate about what might work to prevent serious crime. By design, some interesting areas of experimentation are left out—victim compensation, offender restitution, bail reform—not because they're unimportant, but because they're not necessarily aimed at crime reduction itself. Nor shall I address such issues as the relation between drugs and crime, which are sufficiently complex to require separate treatment.

Most of the things we can do to reduce crime involve going beyond the traditional boundaries of the criminal justice system. One theme that recurs with maddening frequency in the evaluations of rehabilitation programs is that even good, relatively successful programs are stymied by the dismal life chances faced by enrollees when they leave. It does only minimal good to put a youth in a job-training program, backed by, say, peer counseling and family therapy—and then drop him off into a community with 50 to 60 percent youth unemployment, where jobs and a sense of community purpose have long since fled. The point is obvious—but needs constant repeating, if only because it helps us put the celebrated "failure" of social programs for offenders into perspective. Recent evidence points to three key areas of intervention likely to have the biggest payoff in crime prevention. They are the labor market, the family, and—somewhat less tangibly—the network of community supports.

There simply isn't compelling evidence that American justice in general (whatever might be the case in some particularly disorganized or inefficient jurisdictions) is massively derelict in its handling of violent criminals, in ways that are discernibly resolvable through identifiable changes in police or court practices. There are exceptions, however, and they need to be remedied. The most important one is family violence—an issue that's rarely discussed by most people who adopt an otherwise "hard" attitude toward the police and courts, largely because of the pervasive gender bias that remains built into American criminal justice in most places.

Much of the rhetoric about violent crime—especially from the right—is about "stranger-to-stranger" crime; its imagery is the shadowy mugger who robs and maims in the street. But it's a criminological truism that much violent crime—particularly murder and assault—takes place among people who know each other, and often within families. (Half of all murders in 1980 were among relatives or acquaintances, 16 percent among immediate family members.) And it's also widely understood that police, prosecutors, and judges tend to downplay family violence or to treat it as a civil rather than criminal matter. One result of this uncharacteristic leniency is that, not infrequently, someone winds up getting killed.

Data from the Police Foundation and the National Crime Survey show that domestic violence often takes the pattern of repeated smaller incidents leading up to really serious, sometimes life-threatening violence. Police often do little in the early stages of the process, partly because they feel the courts won't back them up anyway. James Q. Wilson, who often writes more perceptively about police work than other matters, has plausibly argued that more use of arrests at the early stages would bring substantial gains.

If nothing else, it would serve as one way of affirming the community's condemnation of routine brutality in the home. Similarly, this is where a "crackdown" in the courts might do some real good, at least in bringing repeat offenders to some kind of justice. A careful study of an LEAA-funded family violence program in the District Attorney's office in Santa Barbara, California, by Richard Berk and his colleagues, doesn't tell us whether the program actually reduced family violence, but it does show that the program greatly increased the number of offenders brought to account in the courts. Not too surprisingly, though, programs to lower the boom on men who routinely attack their wives don't often appear in the conservative panoply of schemes to increase the "costs" of crime. (The same point applies to lax treatment of rape—though here, largely due to successful efforts by the women's movement, there's evidence of improvement.)

The point here can't be repeated too often: progressives should most certainly support "getting tough" with brutal people in cases where they now escape serious treatment. That's fine as far as it goes. The difficulty is that it doesn't go very far. And the problem with the conservative version of that stance is its steadfast refusal to entertain seriously the potential of *other* kinds of intervention.

One casualty of that mentality has been programs to reintegrate offenders into the community—what, before the term acquired a bad name, used to be called "rehabilitation." There's some evidence that the 1970s pessimism over the "failure" of all rehabilitative programs was somewhat exaggerated even at the time. In the past several years, backed by increasingly sophisticated methods of testing and evaluation, a more complex and encouraging picture has emerged. Several kinds of programs have demonstrated effects ranging from the promising to the clearly workable. Among the latter are at least two programs—supported work and economic cushions for ex-offenders—one of which, supported work, has strong potential for prevention as well as rehabilitation.

Initiated in Europe, and first tested in this country by the Vera Foundation, supported work puts people who have special difficulty in the normal labor market into an intensive, carefully supervised work program designed to encourage self-support by gradually increasing rewards and responsibilities. Vera's early experiments with supported work for ex-addicts were successful enough to spur an elaborate field test with four different populations, sponsored by several federal agencies and directed by the Manpower Demonstration Research Corporation (MDRC). The results aren't unequivocal, but they are very promising. The program strongly reduced crime among a sample of ex-addicts, and also strongly boosted the work stability and earnings of a sample of welfare mothers.

The program has less clear-cut impact on another sample of ex-offenders and on a sample of disadvantaged youth. The reasons aren't entirely clear, but one undeniable reality is that the program actually involved fairly minimal changes in the social and economic situation of its enrollees. It generally placed them in low-level jobs, with wages that began around the minimum and ended, by design, below prevailing wage levels. And after the program, participants were dropped back into the unstable, low-wage labor markets from which they'd come. What might happen in a program capable of providing better jobs and higher wages, coupled with a commitment from private or public employers for post-program jobs, is an exciting question, and one we'd be foolish not to investigate.

It's important to understand that substantial results were achieved with very difficult populations that have traditionally responded poorly, if at all, to more traditional programs. Ninety percent of the addicts in the MDRC experiment had been arrested at least once; half hadn't worked at all in the year before entering the program. The crime most strongly suppressed by the program was robbery, one of the most frightening—and persistently increasing—of violent crimes. The ex-addict program's benefits to the taxpayer, moreover, exceeded its costs by over $4,000 per enrollee, according to MDRC's cost-benefit calculations.

Even if it were to turn out that supported work is most effective mainly with offenders who also happen to be addicts, it could make a substantial difference in urban crime rates. (Over 40 percent of the repeat offenders in the RAND sample of

California felons were hard-drug abusers.) But supported work's promise in the long run is clearly greater than this—particularly given its successes with welfare mothers, a point we'll come back to in a moment.

Most people released from prison are thrown back into the community without jobs or financial resources, and with the added disadvantage of being tagged as ex-offenders. The pressure to go back to crime for sheer economic reasons alone (not to mention anger and frustration) is obvious and often compelling under those circumstances. In the 1970s the Department of Labor sponsored studies of the impact of giving stipends—at about the level of unemployment insurance—to enable ex-offenders to manage while readjusting to the community and the job market. Despite the meager levels of support, the programs significantly lowered re-arrests, not only for property crimes but violent crimes as well, by up to about 30 percent.

Again, as with supported work, what's striking about this is that clear-cut results were accomplished with so little. This suggests that higher levels of support, and more consistent linkage of prison release with jobs, could well be an important attack on one of the most obvious and most preventable sources of recidivism.

One of the most interesting possibilities of both programs is that, used on a large scale, they would allow us to keep a lot of property offenders out of the prisons—thus freeing space for more dangerous offenders without the costs (economic and otherwise) of new construction. While the "more prisons" approach to crime appears to address a real and pressing problem (with the prisons already bursting, how can we cope with violent offenders if we don't build new ones?), it fails to mention that, increasingly, the prisons are swollen because of an influx of property criminals, not violent ones. The proportion of inmates sentenced for violent crimes dropped about 10 percent nationally from 1973 to 1978, about 25 percent in the northeastern states, according to the National Institute of Justice's study of prison crowding. A few states now have a high proportion of violent versus property inmates: most do not.

The evidence strongly suggests that many property offenders would be better served outside the prisons in programs like supported work. In most states, that would make it possible, at no greater cost, to reserve the existing correctional system for people too dangerous to operate safely outside it. By itself, that would be an important reform toward rendering the processing of *violent* offenders less capricious. The over-use of prison is one of the most persistent sources of inefficiency in criminal justice today; as a main source of prison overcrowding, it's heavily responsible for court backlogs and excessive plea-bargaining.

Beyond these two programs, there are others directed at offender rehabilitation whose potential is less certain, but well worth further experiment and evaluation.

One of the most thoroughly self-defeating aspects of the right's usual approach to crime is that it offers few, if any, means of intervening with high-risk people between the extremes of doing nothing and putting them in prison. That, in part, is a function of a world-view that can't envision a role for society as a whole other than the last-resort power to coerce and punish. But this attitude cripples thinking about mechanisms of positive intervention into the lives of young people before they've committed the two, three, or six crimes that will reliably bring apprehension and eventually imprisonment. And, as a National Academy of Sciences study of rehabilitation programs pointed out in 1979, in the absence of credible alternatives short of the most drastic ones, judges will often do nothing with young offenders, or send them to probation, which often amounts to the same thing.

There is considerable, if scattered, evidence that good effects can be expected from a variety of interventions lying between probation and incarceration—ranging from family counseling through community advocacy to intensive residential care. Some studies suggest that for even the hard-core, repeat violent offenders, community-based, intensive service programs can reduce youth crime.

The key term here seems to be "intensive." One frequent, somewhat subterranean, finding in many otherwise depressing accounts of the failure of social programs for delinquents is that, almost regardless of the particular focus, more intensive, higher quality programs seem to work better.

One example of this is a Chicago program called Unified Delinquency Intervention Service (UDIS). UDIS was designed to offer alternatives to imprisonment for serious young, repeat offenders. It provided a central agency to direct youth to a wide range of services, mostly ones that already existed, and to follow them through "intensive case management"—close supervision and concern by a staff devoted solely to that purpose. The levels of intervention ranged from placing the youth at home and linking them with job, education, and advocacy programs in the community, through group homes and out-of-town placement in residential work programs, to intensive residential psychiatric care.

The outcome of the UDIS program has been controversial. Somewhat ironically, neoconservatives have managed to seize on the program as proof that the best approach to youth crime is increased use of prisons.

One evaluation of UDIS—the author was Charles A. Murray, who recently argued in the *Wall Street Journal* that social welfare expenditures cause poverty—found that although the UDIS program indeed reduced re-arrests strikingly, a control group of young offenders sent to traditional youth prisons were re-arrested even less. Murray's conclusions have been challenged on methodological grounds, but even if they are correct they hardly prove that the best approach to youth crime is more imprisonment.

What the program actually seems to show is what it in fact was designed to test—that even for the *very* toughest of young offenders, *alternatives* to imprisonment can work well if they are more carefully coordinated and more seriously and intensively managed than is usually the case.

That can cost money; but as the NAS panel on rehabilitation points out, it's sometimes very fruitful to spend well-targeted money to find out what *could* work, and worry later about how to make it cost less. From the evidence we have, the programs worth exploring ought to include at least some of these elements: they should be community-based, involving considerable participation from families and other adults; they should involve aggressive advocacy with local institutions; and they should emphasize real changes in the options available to youth, especially in the labor market, rather than abstract efforts to change their "attitudes" or other aspects of their "human capital."

Some of these programs would certainly help reduce crime—and in ways that are consistent with deeper social values; making people better able to support themselves, integrating them more closely into community life, avoiding the alienation and routine violence of prison life. And some of them also promise to be extraordinarily cost-effective, even in the short run. But it is, unfortunately, Utopian in the worst sense of the term to expect that they will go very *far* toward reducing crime, short of some larger intervention into the context in which the programs must necessarily operate—especially the conditions surrounding early childhood development and the local labor market.

It's here that the traditional progressive emphasis on the need to attack the "roots" of crime is most compelling. If the main limitation on a strategy of "incapacitating" criminals is that a much larger pool of potential offenders lies ready to fill the shoes of those we lock up, then it's obvious that a serious approach to controlling crime must make a substantial investment in prevention. In the past, though, "prevention" has often been a vague and easily abused notion, encompassing everything from better street lighting to the elimination of poverty, disease, and poor housing. But we can be more precise.

The MDRC supported-work evaluation, for example, makes the point repeatedly in analyzing the relative failure of the program to transform behavior that intervention in the job market and family and community supports are a crucial part of prevention. It turned out to be difficult to keep youth motivated to stay in the program, in part because of their "realization that the program will at best prepare them for an uncertain opportunity for an entry level job."

It's hardly accidental that every advanced society with a lower level of violent crime than ours has also historically had a much more effective and humane employment policy, providing better cushions against the disintegrative and degrading effects of "market" forces. Sometimes this is accomplished through public employment and extensive retraining and benefit systems, as in Scandinavia; sometimes mainly through private planning, as in Japan (now undergoing something of a national sense of crisis because its unemployment rate has reached a whopping 2.2 percent of the labor force). But it's difficult to deny the close connection between those policies and lower rates of crime.

The central importance of a full employment policy in reducing crime is sometimes obscured because the connection between jobs and crime turns out to be more complicated than we may have thought. A number of classic studies—notably those of M. Harvey Brenner at John Hopkins University—have turned up precise correlations between changes in the national jobless rate and rates of serious crime and other pathologies. Yet as the economist Ann D. Witte has pointed out, on the basis of an extensive review of studies of employment and criminality, those connections don't always show up strongly in many other empirical studies. There are several reasons why. Some kinds of crime, like employee theft, decline when unemployment rises. More importantly, the stronger connection is between crime and the absence of what Witte calls "economic viability"—good jobs with decent wages. The economic context of crime is not just the rate of unemployment itself but the more general conditions of the secondary labor market. The strength of this connection is sharply apparent in the RAND study of California "repeaters." Only about one-third of the adults even reached the RAND researchers' rather generous category of the "better employed," defined as having worked at least three-fourths of their "street" time and earning all of $100 a week. Even at this level, being "better employed" made a big difference, and not just for property crime rates. Even for crimes of violence, the "better employed" committed crimes, while on the street, at a rate just over *one-fourth* that of the other inmates; and not only committed fewer crimes, but less serious ones as well.

This suggests that job quality and stability are the real issues. Simply forcing the urban unemployed into new variants of low-wage, menial labor as much current administration urban policy proposes, won't begin to come to grips with urban crime. Nor can we expect much help from a strategy of general economic expansion if it doesn't include well-targeted employment and training programs for the kinds of people typically left behind.

It's on the question of the role of the labor market in crime that a progressive vision of crime control must most emphatically stick to its guns. If there is a way to cope with violent inner-city youth crime while the official jobless rate for black youth hovers around 40 percent, we have yet to hear what it is. Insisting on a jobs policy as a first-order response to youth crime is sometimes scorned as politically unrealistic in the current climate, whatever its intellectual or moral merits.

A recent Field Institute poll in California sponsored by the National Council on Crime and Delinquency, however, suggests that this pessimism misreads the public perception of crime and its remedies. When asked, "What will reduce crime in California," half of the respondents agreed that more prisons would; slightly more than half that more police would; but three-fourths agreed that more jobs would. Likewise, the *San Francisco Chronicle*, not generally noted for its radicalism on domestic issues, recently editorialized that "prisons never really address the roots of the juvenile crime problem," and agreed with the former director of the California Youth Authority that "jobs are the number one factor to combat juvenile crime." These sentiments turn up in many places; they're straws in the wind, suggesting that the climate of opinion may be shifting.

Part of the timidity about insisting on the jobs connection is the tendency to think of employment policy as a "long term" solution, as opposed to harder headed, more immediate steps to prevent crime—like building prisons. But that's simply wrong, and it's time to say so. It now takes a couple of years to plan a prison and several more to build it (six, all told, in the case of a high security facility recently completed in Minnesota). A public employment program can be put in place in a few months.

Again, few conservatives have denied the crucial role of employment in crime. Instead, they prefer to argue that the state of the labor market is beyond the reach of public policy. Wilson, acknowledging that high youth unemployment doubtless works to decrease the benefits of lawful behavior, argues that "we have learned through painful trial and error" that it's much more difficult than "we" thought to do anything much about the youth unemployment rate. That, of course, isn't what "we" have learned at all. What "we" have learned is that it's hard to do much about youth unemployment as long as youth's chances for serious work are determined almost wholly by the private market.

The same holds for the role of family problems in youth crime. The important truth in the neoconservative emphasis on family life is that by the time some youth arrive at the portals of the juvenile justice system, they may well be damaged beyond the point of being helped by any "rehabilitative" program we know how to devise. Where the right is terribly wrong is in its pretense that the family as a context for development is an impossible or inappropriate arena for public policy. The result, in effect, is to pin much of the blame for the crime rate on poor women—while ignoring, or tacitly encouraging, the larger social and economic assaults on the quality of family life.

Neoconservatives make much of the rapid growth of families maintained by women as a cause of crime, especially among blacks. And the connection is a real one, often found in empirical studies and brought home, less scientifically, by a look at who winds up in youth prisons (only 29 percent of male and 19 percent of female wards in the California Youth Authority, in 1980, came from "unbroken" families). What's ignored is that the research shows that these families produce a disproportionate amount of aggression and violence in children not because they have one parent or because that parent is a woman, but because they typically lack enough outside resources, human and material, to insure an adequate developmental environment. In such families, as the psychologist E.M. Hetherington and her co-authors put it, the "developmental disturbances" that often result, among other things, in higher rates of delinquency "do not seem to be attributable mainly to father absence but to stresses and a lack of support systems that result in changed family functioning for the single mother and her children." The same developmental damage is equally likely to take place in two-parent families plagued by severe internal conflict or abuse. Hetherington's conclusion follows from that observation. "It is critical" she says, "to develop social policies and intervention procedures that will reduce stresses and develop new support systems for single-parent families."

Some of those policies and procedures, at least, are far from mysterious (and they apply equally to high-risk, two-parent families as well). Some are relatively long term ones—like changing the terms and conditions of women's work and beginning to control the forces that now so wantonly separate families from kin and friendship networks. But some family support interventions can be short range. There are no serious *technical* problems that prevent us now from providing adequate income support for family heads who are unable to work, or from developing, on a large scale, the already tested supported work strategy for welfare mothers (as distinguished from Reagan-style "workfare"). Changing the pinched and deeply stressful state of dependent poor families can have an impact on youth crime in fairly short order. As a RAND survey has shown, many felony offenders were already "doing crime" well before they were thirteen years old.

Another promising avenue is the development of comprehensive multi-service programs for high-risk families. One notable example is the HEW-sponsored Child and Family Resource Programs, initiated in the 1970s to link a variety of child development programs into a single coherent support service. The CFRP's combined services include crisis intervention, education against child abuse, family counseling, Head Start and tutoring programs, meals for children, and pre- and post-natal health counseling. They were designed too, to encourage substantial parent involvement in policy-making. The General Accounting Office, not normally prone to superlatives in its usually tight-fisted analyses of social programs, waxed enthusiastic about CFRPs in a 1979 report, concluding that the programs significantly improved the quality of life in poor families and could substantially reduce expenditures for later health care, welfare assistance, and youth and adult corrections—all at a cost of about $3,000 per family in 1977 dollars.

The GAO argued that these early childhood intervention programs would reduce delinquency mainly through improving early parent-child relations and school performance, and both possibilities fit well with what a growing body of research has to say about family and developmental influences on youth and adult crime. We don't know how much crime we could prevent by developing a better range of supports for early child development. We do know that there are very good reasons for expecting the effects to be substantial.

That many other countries at our level of development do much better at providing family supports tells us, once again, that the conditions of family life—correctly pinpointed by conservatives as deeply implicated in crime rates—aren't beyond the reach of public policy. The same may be said regarding the role of the "community" in crime prevention. By now, "community" has become a predictable buzzword at all points on the political spectrum, and nowhere more so than in debates about crime. Just about everyone agrees that "community" is important in preventing crime, but nearly everyone has a different conception of what "community" means and what might be done to create or restore it.

The variety of "community crime prevention" programs initiated in the 1970s (often under the auspices of LEAA) included everything from police programs to engrave valuables or install better locks, through "Neighborhood Watch" programs, to civilian anticrime patrols, to more comprehensive efforts combining local block organization, public education about crime, and closer involvement between citizens and police. But—like the experiments in innovative police strategies during the same period—the results have been ambiguous, if the criterion is reduction of serious crime. Citizen crime prevention programs have often given community residents a potentially valuable sense of participation in a common effort, and sometimes reduce the fear of criminal victimization. But there is little solid evidence that they have substantially reduced crime, even in their target communities—not to mention in neighboring areas to which some local crime may simply be displaced. Much the same uncertainty seems to apply to citizen patrols. A RAND analysis of dozens of different community patrol efforts wouldn't venture to assess their crime-preventing role, but was generally supportive of their ability to generate a sense of citizen involvement at a low cost.

There seems little wrong with these programs in principle; early fears that they might turn out to be trojan horses allowing a coercive state to dominate poor and minority communities were clearly overblown. The tradition of crime prevention through neighborhood organization is a long one and hasn't lacked good ideas and excellent innovations. But it has often foundered on one persistently thorny problem. By itself, local volunteerism is likely to have limited impact as long as the larger forces ripping apart the community's infrastructure are left intact. Good community crime prevention programs can at the very least help pull a neighborhood together and improve its sense of security. But it's important to keep the attraction of community involvement from masking the lack of hard evidence, so far, that these programs actually prevent much serious violent crime. Some community activists are enthusiastic about the more recent breed of community prevention efforts across the country. We should certainly continue to support and explore those programs—but also to sort out more carefully what's effective in them and to think through ways of linking them to other strategies, especially job creation.

The same strictures apply to another much-promoted crime prevention approach of the past decade—the idea of crime prevention through "environmental design." Much effort was put into schemes to redesign public areas—in particular, public housing projects—to create more "defensible" space, by redesigning entryways and access patterns or making projects more open to routine scrutiny by residents. Again, though, the results, while not entirely discouraging, aren't impressive. A recent study of a *well*-designed public housing project that still suffered very high crime rates suggests why. As Sally Merry argues, even if such places are architecturally designed to be "defensible," they won't be well defended if the *social* organization of the community is itself fragmented, anonymous, and lacking in networks of social support and concern.

This suggests that what's most important in community crime prevention are the broader forces that make for community stability and sustain local social networks.

Here is where conservative thought *ought* to have something to offer. One of the most damaging flaws in liberal thinking about social policy has been its tendency to downplay the importance of social bonds and communal supports in preventing or mitigating social pathology. Yet what passes for a discussion of these issues in much recent neoconservative writing verges on the banal. An example is a recent article in the *Atlantic* magazine on the police and neighborhoods by James Q. Wilson with George Kelling of the Police Foundation. Wilson and Kelling take off from the fact that most recent experiments in new police strategies seem to have little impact on the crime rate. Acknowledging that unhappy conclusion, Wilson and Kelling argue that the police can, nevertheless, play an important role in insuring public "order" in neighborhoods where "order" is defined as protecting the "community" against infractions against "civility" by insolent youth, drunks, or other sundry undesirables. To achieve this, they argue, the police ought to be freed to do what they probably do best—establish control over the streets by rousting drunks and suspicious strangers and "kicking ass" with gang youth. All of this, Wilson and Kelling conclude, may mean playing somewhat fast and loose with hard-won legal restraints on police conduct—but that's probably a small price to pay for the return of civility to the community. Nothing is said about why there are so many drunks or beggars or unruly youth in these communities in the first place, nor about where they might go once sternly sent on their way by the sturdy guardians of the local sensibility. There's a lot to be said, certainly, for integrating the police more closely into community and street life, and nothing to prevent us from exploring ways to do that more effectively. But—as Wilson and Kelling generally acknowledge—the relevance of this for actually preventing serious *crime* is not immediately apparent.

A much more compelling approach to crime prevention on the community level has come, somewhat surprisingly, from a set of investigations sponsored by the American Enterprise Institute on the role of "mediating structures" in preventing various kinds of social pathology. By "mediating structures," the AEI writers mean intermediate institutions, like neighborhoods, kinship structures, and ethnic organizations, lying between individuals and the larger bureaucratic structures that loom over much of their lives. In an analysis of the importance of "mediating structures" in crime prevention, Robert Woodson (formerly of the National Urban League) makes a strong case for the effectiveness of nonprofessional, community-based agencies sharing a common culture with violence-prone youth.

For Woodson, the best example is Philadelphia's House of Umoja, a community-based residential program for black youth gang members. As Woodson describes it, Umoja's approach involves creating a familial atmosphere with conscious efforts to instill a sense of ethnic pride and purpose and a strong emphasis on youth participation in decision-making. Some observers credit Umoja with dramatically reducing deaths from gang violence in Philadelphia. Others are more skeptical.

What makes the "mediating structures" model interesting is that it happily, if somewhat uneasily, merges some of the traditional themes of both the right and the left. The right's enthusiasm, however, is sometimes based on a calculated misperception of what these programs are really about. Ronald Reagan himself boosted the House of Umoja as a fine example of how private action and volunteerism could replace the bumbling and expensive public sector. But as the *New York Times* pointed out, the House of Umoja had already been heavily funded with federal money, and now stood to lose some of its most interesting projects because of administration cutbacks in social programs.

Shorn of the inflated boosting of the virtues of volunteerism and the related attack on the public sector, the crime-preventing role of "mediating structures" fits well with evidence from a variety of other sources. Here the data generally become less "hard," but are more than suggestive. A large and growing body of research has demonstrated the importance of communal networks of support in mitigating the impact of social and economic stress, with very significant consequences not only for crime but for physical and mental health as well.

Cross-national studies, too, strongly suggest the importance of communal supports in crime prevention. One of the clearest sources of the low crime rates in two of the countries most extensively studied—Japan and Switzerland—is the extent to which economic development seems to have taken place within the bounds of pre-existing ties of kinship and local community. This is in addition to their relatively narrower spread of income inequality and miniscule rates of unemployment.

Swiss economic development, as Marshall Clinard has argued in his *Cities with Little Crime,* was far more decentralized throughout the countryside, and took place in the context of a political system strongly committed to local self-government and broad community participation. The result, in Clinard's view, was that the Swiss rise to industrial "affluence" wasn't accompanied by the level of disruption and fragmentation that wracked most other advanced societies—and that, we need to add, has historically been most severe in the United States, unique among developed countries in the extent to which we have routinely allowed whole communities to be shredded through rapid, uncontrolled capital mobility.

One clear implication of this is that much could be gained, over the long term, through integrating community programs specifically designed for crime prevention with broader strategies of locally based economic development. That kind of strategy would importantly mesh several different themes that emerge from what we've learned from recent research and program development. On the one hand, it could come to grips with the main problem bedeviling programs like supported work: the gap between the supportive program and some means of stable employment over the longer term. On the other hand, a strategy of community-based economic development has the promise of directly attacking the forces that now split and undermine family and community supports. We can't know the precise results, because we've not tried it. But as a broad framework for a longer term strategy against crime, it has the great virtue of fitting squarely with what we know about the uses and limits of the preventive and rehabilitative programs we *have* tried.

Like the evidence on family, that on the role of community support also tells us much about what *not* to do if we're serious about crime. In the process, it again reveals the fallacy of the right's fashionable insistence that "government" is powerless to do anything about the causes of crime.

In fact, of course, the opposite is true. "Government" in the United States is already deeply implicated in policies that cause families and communities to disintegrate, and in deflecting policies that might help hold them together. "Government," indeed, can fairly be said to have followed a pro-crime policy for years. Government tax and subsidy policies supported the vast uprooting of population through a "modernization" of agriculture closely entwined with the disintegration of the social fabric of the cities. Government spurred the out-migration of industry and jobs that aggravated it further. Government regularly induced unemployment, community decline, and geographic uprooting in the service of the putative fight against inflation. Government helps subsidize the multinationals' cataclysmic reordering of social life in the "developing" world, some of which spills back across the borders as high crime rates in migrant communities.

Under the auspices of the right, "government" will certainly do so even more, by aligning itself ever more closely with the most disintegrative forces of the private market. This is the ultimate paradox of the neoconservative position on crime. They have successfully posed as the guardians of domestic tranquility for decades, but everything we know about crime tells us that it's precisely the kind of policies they typically promote that bear a large part of the responsibility for the level of crime and violence we suffer today.

If we wanted to construct a hypothetical model of what a particularly crime-prone society might look like, it would clearly contain these elements: It would separate large numbers of people, especially the young, from the kind of work that could integrate them securely into community life. It would promote development and distribution policies that sharply increased inequalities between sectors of the population. It would shift vast amounts of capital and technology around rapidly without regard for the impact on communities, causing massive movements of population away from family, neighborhood, and community supports in search of livelihood. It would resolutely avoid providing new forms of support and care for those uprooted (in the name of preserving incentives to work and paring government spending). It would promote an ethos of intense interpersonal competition and a level of material consumption which many citizens could not lawfully sustain.

Are there approximations of that model in the real world? Yes, indeed; it looks a lot like some developing countries—Brazil, Mexico, Puerto Rico, the Philippines— that are undergoing the harsher variants of an "economic miracle." And sure enough, those countries have among the highest levels of violent crime in the world. But we don't have to look that far; it also looks uncannily like Reagan country.

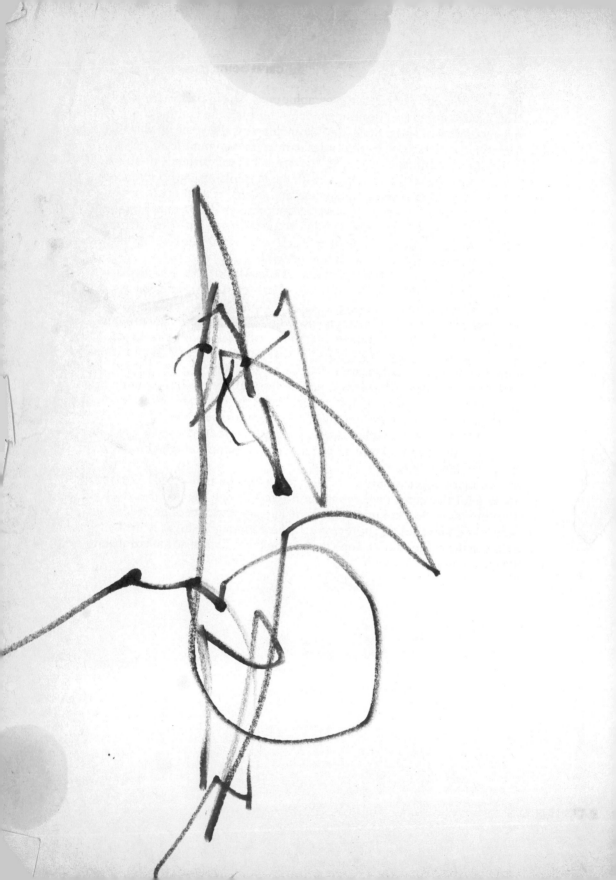